Praise for *Judgment in Moscow*

"Russian interference in American politics didn't start in 2016, but stretches back decades. Vladimir Bukovsky uses the Kremlin's own documents to show this and much more: how the Soviet Union provided a false face to the world and how Soviet leaders used Western leaders as dupes or willing actors. *Judgment in Moscow* provides the written Nuremberg trial the Soviets never got when the USSR fell."
—**Anne Applebaum**, author of *Gulag: A History* (Pulitzer Prize), *Washington Post* columnist, and visiting Professor of Practice at the London School of Economics

"Russian interference in Western politics has been in the news of late, but Bukovsky's deep dive into Soviet-era documents demonstrates that for much of the 20th century it was not paranoid fantasy, but cold, hard fact."
—**Glenn Harlan Reynolds**, Beauchamp Brogan Distinguished Professor of Law, University of Tennessee and author of *An Army of Davids*

"The most important work to appear for decades on the Soviet empire and its aftermath."
—**Edward Lucas**, former senior editor of *The Economist*, from the Introduction

"Offering crucial archival documentation of the crimes of the Soviet era, Vladimir Bukovsky demonstrates how the failure to address its past has doomed Russia to repeat it. This book is essential for understanding why Russia did not make the transition to democracy after 1991 and why the men who now rule the Kremlin operate just like the communist apparatchiks and KGB bureaucrats who preceded them."
—**Amy Knight**, author of *Orders to Kill: The Putin Regime and Political Murder*

"A fascinating work which demolishes a few more myths prevalent in the West about the Soviet Union and the Cold War. . . stunning revelations."
—**Richard Pipes**, former director of Harvard's Russian Research Center and member of the National Security Council

"A massive and major contribution. . . highly valuable material."
—**Robert Conquest**, author of *The Great Terror* and *Harvest of Sorrow*

"At last, a book in the West that describes the Red Empire as seen by we who had to live under it."
—**Mart Laar**, former Prime Minister of Estonia and recipient of the Truman-Reagan Medal of Freedom

"*Judgment in Moscow* is an essential warning of the dangers of collaborating with authoritarian regimes. It's also a timeless reminder that evil doesn't die, but must be battled back constantly. The crimes of the Soviet Union were enabled by appeasement and rationalization by politicians in the free world who ignored that the lesser evil is still evil. Today we are witnessing a similar plunge into the depths of moral equivalence and convenient deals with dictatorships. As Bukovsky writes in *Judgment in Moscow*, using a word much in vogue today, 'any sane person knows full well when he has entered into collusion with evil.'

"Vladimir Bukovsky's moral compass has never failed, always pointing at the truth regardless of the circumstances or consequences. No one has written with greater clarity on why engagement between the free world and despots spreads corruption, not freedom. He writes, 'The voice of conscience whispers that our fall began from the moment we agreed to "peaceful coexistence" with evil.' We have fallen far indeed, and *Judgment in Moscow* holds the mirror of history up to politicians today proclaiming the need to find common ground with a dictator like Vladimir Putin."
—**Garry Kasparov**, former world chess champion and author of *Winter is Coming*

"*Judgment in Moscow* combines a devastating archival documentation of key points in Soviet history with a passionate polemic directed at those in the West who averted their eyes, minimized, or justified Communist totalitarian oppression and Soviet aggression. Students of Soviet history as well as historians of the Western reaction to Soviet communism must grapple with his Soviet archival documents and listen to Bukovsky's fervent indictment of Western apologists."
—**John Earl Haynes**, author of *In Denial: Historians, Communism, and Espionage*

"After 23 years of underhand censorship, Vladimir Bukovsky's *Judgment in Moscow* has finally appeared in English. In 1995, thanks to his access to the secret documents of the Soviet Communist Party and the KGB, he was the first to reveal in detail how the totalitarian USSR misled and manipulated Western public opinion and, by corrupting its politicians and supporting guerrilla groups and terrorists, sought to subvert and destroy democracy. This is a fundamental historical study and major testimony by one of the great dissidents."
—**Stéphane Courtois**, editor of *The Black Book of Communism*

"A glimpse into what should have happened if Russia's leaders had had the courage to fully account for the Soviet past."
—**Vladimir Kara-Murza**, Russian opposition politician and contributing writer to the *Washington Post*

Reviews

"If you seek to understand why we now face a renewed Cold War, one even more dangerous than the first, this is the first book you must read. If you seek to understand Russia's interference in electoral democracies throughout the free world, this too is the first book you must read. But above all, if you seek to understand why you never even heard about this book—published in nine languages, an international bestseller—this is the book you must read."
—**Claire Berlinski**, contributing editor of *City Journal* and author of *Menace in Europe: Why the Continent's Crisis Is America's, Too*

"Steve Ditko introduced me to the writings of Vladimir Bukovsky, a heroic figure we both had come to admire and respect. We were eager to read *Judgment in Moscow*, but no publisher was brave enough to publish it. Now, at last, it is available, and every bit as worthy as we anticipated. A giant of the 20th century now makes his mark on the 21st."
—**Robin Snyder**, writing and editing partner of Steve Ditko, original artist of Spider-Man

"Everyone who cares about liberty should read this book."
—**Evgeny Kissin**, award-winning classical pianist

"'The inhuman Utopia fell, but neither spiritual freedom nor honorable thought has risen from the ruins.' So writes the incomparable Vladimir Bukovsky in *Judgment in Moscow*, his long-awaited epic examining the ghastly intertwining of Communist East and Free West, and how it could possibly be that judgment of the crimes of communism still eludes a world sick with socialism. With disarming intimacy (you can almost see the conversational curls of cigarette smoke), Bukovsky tells a dark new history of deception, corruption and betrayal on both sides of the Iron Curtain as gleaned from masses of never-before-seen secret Kremlin documents; these historical contributions can hardly be overstated. However, what makes the book unique and even transformative lies in Bukovsky's eyewitness and personal experience of the dark history he relates.

"Soviet dissident, KGB prisoner, then celebrated former dissident and exprisoner, Bukovsky has lived his entire life on these same battlefields, East and West, now ruins. If *Judgment in Moscow* can't infuse the survivors with conscience, nothing can."
—**Diana West**, author of *American Betrayal*

"The heroic Soviet dissident, Vladimir Bukovsky, makes use of extensive first hand documents that he personally stole from Russia's Central Committee (C.C.) archives, which have never before been accessible to Americans.... Up until now, the depth and extent of the Kremlin's subversion of America has been understood by just a limited number of subject matter experts. But that could all change now."
—*American Thinker*

"This book will be a hard pill to swallow for many in the United States and the West. It raises uncomfortable moral dilemmas and exposes Western weaknesses... this book may shed some light on the nature of the current Russian regime and why, after our apparent victory in the Cold War, we face a Russia seeking once again to expand its influence in Eastern and Central Europe and which denies freedom and liberty to its people."
—*New York Journal of Books*

"*Judgment in Moscow* remains an extremely powerful and important source for anyone who wants to understand the true nature of our deadly adversary. Bukovsky recounts such secrets as the Kremlin's clandestine payments to foreign Communist parties and leaders, covert paramilitary training in places like Czechoslovakia for their foreign comrades, and extensive disinformation campaigns throughout the West. He also details the cooperation between the Kremlin and our own political class.

"Time for you to catch up on the corruption of our elite, on the basic facts of the Cold War, and on one of the most remarkable men I know."
—**Michael Ledeen**, Freedom Scholar at the Foundation for the Defense of Democracies

Praise for Vladimir Bukovsky

"A hero of almost legendary proportion among the Soviet dissident movement."
—*The New York Times*

"Bukovsky's heroic speech to the court in defense of freedom, and his five years of martyrdom in a despicable psychiatric jail, will be remembered long after the torturers he defied have rotted away."
—**Vladimir Nabokov**

"A human rights champion undeterred by fear."
—Pussy Riot's **Nadezhda Tolokonnikova**

"Bukovsky did what any decent man should have done, but what only a hero is capable of doing."
—**Leonard Ternovsky**, Soviet dissident

JUDGMENT IN MOSCOW

Also by Vladimir Bukovsky

To Build a Castle: My Life as a Dissenter
To Choose Freedom
USSR: From Utopia to Disaster
EUSSR: The Soviet Roots of European Integration (with Pavel Stroilov)

VLADIMIR BUKOVSKY

JUDGMENT IN MOSCOW

SOVIET CRIMES AND WESTERN COMPLICITY

Translated by Alyona Kojevnikov
English edition prepared by Paul Boutin

Ninth of November Press

Judgment in Moscow is a publication of Ninth of November Press.

Contact:
Elizabeth Childs, Bukovsky Center
info@vladimirbukovsky.com
https://vladimirbukovsky.com/

The right of Vladimir Bukovsky to be identified as the author of this work has been asserted in accordance with the Copyright, Designs and Patents Act 1988.

Originally published in Russian under the title *Московский Процесс*
Copyright © МИК 1996.

Electronic edition ISBN 978-0-9980416-0-5
Paperback edition ISBN 978-0-9980416-1-2
Hardcover edition ISBN 978-0-9980416-2-9

English edition prepared by Paul Boutin.

Cover design by Ana Grigoriu-Voicu, https://books-design.com/.

Author photo on hardback cover by photographer Wojtek Duszenko/Agencja Gazeta, http://agencjagazeta.pl/.

Typeset by Joel C. Salomon.

Copy edited by Ben Zwycky, https://benzwycky.com/.

Contents

Author's Preface

This book was written more than twenty years ago and published in many languages, but not English. The reason for this is amply explained in the book, and I don't think I need to repeat it here. Rather, I have to explain how it was resurrected contrary to my expectations.

"We cannot guess ahead/What echo our words shall have," said a Russian poet some 150 years ago. Indeed, when I was introduced to the famous pianist Evgeny Kissin, the last thing I expected was to talk about this book. Yet that is what he wanted to do, insisting that it must be published in English. Thanks to his persistent efforts, it finally is.

Twenty years is a long time, particularly in view of the many things that happened in the meantime. At first I thought I would have to update it significantly. But after rereading it for the first time since I wrote it, I discovered (to my dismay) that it needs no updating at all. Alas, my worst forecasts have come true: failure to finish off the Soviet system conclusively has led to its revival. Clearly Putin and his KGB cohorts would have never climbed to power if Russian society had the courage to launch what we advocated twenty-three years ago: a Nuremberg-style trial and lustrations. Without it, the country went full circle and reverted back to the USSR.

So this book is as topical today as it was two decades ago. The only changes made in this edition are in chapter 6, and even those were not corrections, but additions. At the time of writing, I did not have all the necessary documents at my disposal, and made some assumptions on the basis of circumstantial evidence. Since then quite a lot of those documents have surfaced and confirmed my guesses, enabling the expansion of chapter 6.

However, the credit for this achievement must go to Pavel Stroilov, not to me. After I published this book in 1995–1996, the Russian authorities would no longer permit me to visit Russia, and I needed a capable assistant on the spot. It happened that such an assistant emerged all by himself; back in 1991, upon returning from my first trip to Moscow, I received an unexpected letter. Its wording suggested the writer was more accustomed to speaking Russian than English:

"Good day, Vladimir Konstantinovich! My name is Pavel and I am 7 years old. I have read in a newspaper that you don't like communists. I dislike them, too. Let's keep a company."

Naturally I responded that of course we, the anticommunists, must stick together. But as I live in Britain, he must improve his

English, and I sent him a lot of books for that purpose. By the age of twelve Pavel was fluent in English, and a few years later became a student in one of Moscow's universities.

Around 1999–2000, when he was seventeen or eighteen years old and still living in Moscow, we discussed the idea of his trying to continue my work in the Russian archives and copy more secret documents. As Pavel likes to say, he became my "man on the inside" in Russia.

In particular, we discovered that a large body of top-secret Communist Party documents had been semi-officially copied from the Kremlin archives in the "revolutionary" chaos of 1991, and could now be accessed in the Gorbachev Foundation Archive more easily than their originals in the official Kremlin files. However, there were restrictions on which documents you were allowed to see, and a ban was imposed on removing or copying any of the material. Yet ultimately he was able to gain access to many prohibited documents, also to secretly electronically smuggle out a huge number of them —somewhere between fifty thousand and one hundred thousand pages. This was quite sufficient for Pavel to complete chapter 6 (for which we all are indebted to him).

We are also grateful to Alyona Kojevnikov, who translated this book into English brilliantly and incredibly quickly. It must surely be a world record!

Special thanks to John Crowfoot for his invaluable work with my archive, Originally placed on the internet by Yulia Zaks and Leonid Chernikhov in 1999, it consists of documents I copied in Moscow in 1992 that serve as the foundation of this book. However, the archive required a major effort to be put in order, a task accomplished ably by John. He also deserves credit for the meticulous translation of dozens of documents into English.

Finally, we must applaud the publisher, Ninth of November Press, for daring to publish a book no other English-language publisher in the world had the courage to touch for twenty years. A special thanks also goes to the dedicated volunteers who donated their time to prepare this book.

Vladimir Bukovsky
Cambridge, November 2018

Introduction

By Edward Lucas,
former senior editor of *The Economist*
and author of *The New Cold War*

This book is on one level an archival achievement: the distillation of thousands of top-secret Kremlin documents, brought to light by the author's ingenuity and determination in the brief window that opened after the collapse of communism.

But it is far more than that. It is the story of a terrible crime and three great scandals.

The crime is the decades-long despoliation of the countries and peoples held captive in the Soviet empire, at the cost of millions of deaths and hundreds of millions of blighted lives. The communist regime was not only responsible for misery and mass murder at home. It was also a grave threat to the freedom and prosperity of the rest of the world, a danger that we survived more by luck than by judgment.

Human history is studded with other great real and possible horrors. But it has never witnessed misdeeds accompanied by such deceit and willful ignorance. As Vladimir Bukovsky makes clear, the outside world never fully understood the Soviet system. This is the first scandal depicted in the book: the West's deluded belief that the Soviet empire could be managed, dealt with, and even reformed. Bukovsky repeatedly juxtaposes accounts of Western leaders' timidity, naivety, and worse, with documents detailing the internal deliberations of the regime. He shows what was really going on during the invasion of Afghanistan, the Moscow Olympics of 1980, the imposition of martial law in Poland, and much more besides.

The second scandal is that in the years following 1991, the perpetrators of this great evil were not held to account; there were no Nuremberg Trials of the kinds faced by the Nazis, no South African–style truth and reconciliation commission. Instead, sections of the old KGB and Communist Party elite rebuilt their power, in sinister alliance with the petty crooks and con men who flourished in the "wild capitalist" conditions of the 1990s. Vladimir Putin's Kremlin exemplifies this hybrid creature, which fuses political, economic, and gangland power.

The third scandal concerns the book itself. Researched and written by a moral giant, it is the most important work to appear for decades on the Soviet empire and its aftermath. But it is only now, nearly three decades late, available to the English-speaking world. Elizabeth Childs and her small publishing house deserve plaudits for having stepped in where the big beasts of the literary world have quailed and failed.

It is easy to see grounds for hesitation. Bukovsky is sweeping and unsparing in his condemnation of Western cupidity and culpability. Some will find his judgments on individuals too harsh. Some of those named in the book may feel tempted to turn to their lawyers to rebut the allegations. Some of the author's critique of Western Utopianism may irk readers, such as his distaste for feminism and environmentalism. His view of the European Union as Soviet-inspired is controversial.

But the book is worth reading for other reasons. At its heart is a still-unacknowledged gap in perceptions. The wily gerontocrats of the Kremlin saw the world about them, with its threats and opportunities, with surprising clarity. So too, despite censorship, propaganda, and intense official secrecy, did many of those imprisoned inside the Soviet empire (though not, the author notes, the cosseted and self-regarding intelligentsia). It was only in the free and supposedly well-informed West that the fog was thick, even when refugees from communism such as Bukovsky tried to enlighten their Western hosts about the real nature of the Soviet regime.

In one of the book's many enjoyable aperçus, Bukovsky quotes another émigré, the late Andrei Amalrik, who noted that Western experts on the Soviet Union reacted to firsthand witnesses of Soviet reality rather like ichthyologists confronted with a talking fish. They were intrigued by the phenomenon, but they dismissed any thought that this strange creature might be saying something useful about fish.

That arrogance is still the West's besetting sin. In the years when the Soviet threat was real, we refused to learn from those who tried to explain its true nature. Now we regard the lessons of the past as irrelevant. The Soviet experiment collapsed in failure, at horrendous cost. What does that have to do with us, thirty years later? Surely the aim now should be to put the past behind us, to normalize relations with Russia, to find common ground and to broker deals?

Clearly Putin's Russia is not the Soviet Union. It is much smaller and weaker. It is (at least since the Chechen bloodbath ended), less repressive at home. It has not, so far, resorted to the systematic use of coercive psychiatry that the KGB inflicted on Bukovsky and others.

But the similarities outweigh the differences. Russia is still an empire. It has "soft power"—a cocktail of Orthodox religiosity, half-baked history, social conservatism, and anti-Western bile — that wins friends and influences people. Through "hybrid warfare," the Kremlin deploys weapons against the West of far greater sophistication than those available to the Soviet-era Kremlin. The internet has given wings—anonymity, immediacy, and ubiquity—to what we once called *dezinformatsiya*. The modern financial system allows the Kremlin's dirty money to slosh through our politics and public life. We are vulnerable to bluff and physical intimidation, skeptical of confrontation, and eager for compromise. Our security cultures have decayed, our spy catchers are out of practice, our Kremlinologists out of date. As a result, Russia plays *divide et impera*, stoking polarization and mistrust between countries and within them, with increasingly potent effect.

Though our response to the Soviet threat was, as Bukovsky depicts, often too accommodating, we are even weaker and more muddled now. Vladimir Putin has a weak hand, but he is playing it well. He could win. We could lose. Few have reflected on what life would be like if our alliances splinter and hostile autocracies gain the upper hand.

It is not too late to learn the lessons of the past. For anyone who cares about the freedom, security, and self-respect of the West, *Judgment in Moscow* is alarming, painful, essential reading.

Edward Lucas

16 May 2018

This Book and its Sources

On Archival Sources and Footnotes

The archival documents referred to in this book were photocopied in Russia in the early 1990s. Many of them are available in the Bukovsky Archives online, a resource that may be searched by date or by theme—https://bukovsky-archive.com.

The dates and original reference numbers of documents cited in the text have been included throughout this book. When an English translation is available the date is followed by an asterisk, e.g. 29 December 1980*, Pb 230/34. (If the document is one of the few not in the online archive it is included in the footnotes and its status is denoted with a circumflex, e.g. 5 January 1981, St 244/50^. Of the 334 citations of archival documents in the book, only two dozen are from documents not currently online.)

The original departmental numbering of most of these documents is prefixed either by the letters "St," indicating their origin in the CPSU Secretariat, or "Pb," denoting a document of the most powerful body in the Soviet Union, the Politburo of the CPSU Central Committee. A common suffix is -A, indicating a document submitted to the Politburo by or on behalf of KGB chairman Yuri Andropov.

Marked Secret or Top Secret, these memoranda and decisions were often further classified as "Special File," "Of Particular Importance," and the highest level of all, "For Your Eyes Only," thereby imposing additional limits on their accessibility within the highest echelons of the Party (see 23 April 1974*, 1071-A/ov, a communication between Andropov and Soviet leader Leonid Brezhnev).

• • •

The book has been translated from the 1996 Russian edition (*Moskovskii protsess*), in a version edited and prepared by the late Natalya Gorbanevskaya. Its publication in Russian was funded by the Solzhenitsyn Foundation and Ilya Roitman.

Chapter Six, "The Revolution that Never Was," has been updated for the present edition by the author, drawing on materials from the Gorbachev Foundation archives in Moscow: they were brought to England by Pavel Stroilov (the Stroilov Archive—SA).

Almost all the footnotes were derived and adapted from the 1995 French edition of *Judgment in Moscow* (copyright Éditions Robert Laffont, Paris). I added a handful myself.

John Crowfoot
August 2018

Part I

In the East

But Judea clamoured all around,
Of the dead declined to be reminded

ALEXANDER GALICH

Chapter One

Phony War

1.1 Who cares?

There is a huge pile of papers before me on my desk, some three thousand pages marked "Top Secret," "Special File," "Exceptional Importance," and "For Your Eyes Only." At first glance, they all look the same: In the top right-hand corner, the slogan "Workers of the world, unite!" is almost a taunt. On the left is a severe warning: "To be returned to the CC CPSU [Central Committee of the Communist Party of the Soviet Union] (General Department, 1st section) within 24 hours." On some the terms are more generous—the document may be retained for three or seven days, or, less frequently, for two months. Lower down, in large letters right across the page, are the words: "THE COMMUNIST PARTY OF THE SOVIET UNION. CENTRAL COMMITTEE." Further down are codes, reference numbers, date, a list of those who reached the decision in question, voted in a round robin, and initialed the document, and the names of those charged with implementing the said decision. But even the latter were not entitled to see the entire document. They received an abstract from the minutes, the content of which they could not publicize in spoken or written form. A reminder of this runs in fine print in the left margins of the pages (5 October 1979*, St 179/32, p. 2):

Rules concerning abstracts from minutes of the Secretariat of the CC CPSU

1. Photocopying or making notes from minutes of the Secretariat of the CC CPSU, also making any reference to them in oral or written form, in the open press or other publicly accessible documents is categorically forbidden. Retyping the resolutions of the Secretariat of the CC is also proscribed, as is any reference to them in official orders, instructions, directives and any official publications whatsoever.

2. Access to secret and top secret directives (abstracts from minutes) of the Secretariat of the CC CPSU, sent to party committees, ministries, departments or other organizations, is granted only to persons directly involved with the implementation of the relevant directive.

Comrades who have read abstracts from the minutes of the Secretariat of the CC may not publicize their content.

3

(Affirmed by CC CPSU resolution of 17 June 1976, St 12/4)

The rules governing the use of Politburo documents are even stricter (cf. 28 January 1980*, Pb 181/34, p. 1):

ATTENTION

A comrade in receipt of top secret documents of the CC CPSU may not pass them into other hands nor acquaint anyone with their content without special permission from the CC.

Photocopying or making extracts from the documents in question is categorically forbidden.

The comrade to whom the document is addressed must sign and date it after he has studied the content.

This was how the CPSU ruled: secretly, leaving no traces, and at times even no witnesses, confident that it would last for centuries, just like the Third Reich. And their aims were not too dissimilar, either. Moreover, unlike the Reich, it might have succeeded, had not something occurred that had not been foreseen by Karl Marx, Vladimir Lenin, or the majority of people on earth. The documents spread across my desk were not addressed to me, I had no part —at least no direct part—in their implementation, and I have no intention of returning them to the first section of the General Department. Shamelessly usurping other people's privileges, I study the signatures of Leonid Brezhnev, Konstantin Chernenko, Yuri Andropov, Mikhail Gorbachev, Dmitry Ustinov, Andrei Gromyko, and Boris Ponomarev. I read their handwritten comments in the margins, their profound decisions concerning everything in the world, from arrests and exile of those they considered undesirable to the financing of international terrorism, from disinformation campaigns to the preparation of aggression against neighboring countries. These papers contain the beginnings and the ends of all the tragedies of our bloodstained century, or, to be more precise, of its past thirty years. Obtaining them cost me a great deal of effort over a period of more than a year. Moreover, had I not succeeded, it is highly likely that they would have lain secret for many more years, if not forever. Yet the restrictions laid upon them by the CC CPSU resolution of 17 June 1976 continues to exercise a mystical power, because nobody dares to publicize these secrets.

Some three or four years ago, every one of these papers would have fetched hundreds of thousands of dollars. Today I offer them free of charge to the most influential newspapers and journals in the world, but nobody wants to print them. Editors shrug indifferently: *So what? Who cares?*

Like the poor unfortunate in a Soviet joke who went around looking for an eye and ear doctor because he kept hearing one thing and
seeing something totally different, I begin to doubt my eyes, my ears,
and my memory. At night I have nightmares. Businesslike young
men with dedicated faces pursue me all over the world, demanding the immediate return of documents to the first section of the
General Department. And indeed, more than three days, even two
months, have passed since the documents came into my hands,
but I still haven't found a use for them. So how does one differ-
entiate between nightmare and reality in such a situation? Only a
few years ago, all that is set out in these papers was hotly denied,
rated at best as anticommunist paranoia, at worst as slander. Any
one of us who dared, in those not-so-distant times, to mention "the
hand of Moscow" was immediately castigated in the press and accused of "McCarthyism" and became a pariah. Even those disposed
to believe us would raise deprecating hands: all this is guesswork,
assumptions, there is no proof. Well, here is the proof, signed and
numbered, available now for analysis, study, discussion. Take it,
check it, print it!

And the answer I get is: *So what? Who cares?*

Naturally, there are already numerous theories to explain this
puzzle. "People are tired of the Cold War's tensions," I am told.
"They don't want to hear any more about this. They simply want
to get on with their lives, work, rest. . . and forget this whole nightmare." "Too many communist secrets have appeared on the market
at one time," I hear from others. And from yet another school of
thought, "The thing to do is wait until all this becomes history. At
the moment it's still politics." But somehow, I find none of these explanations convincing. One may say that by 1945 people were tired
of the Second World War, and of Nazism to the same degree, but
this did not serve to impede a cascade of books, articles, and films
on the subject. Indeed, an entire industry of antifascist productions came into being, and understandably so: the need to fathom
that which has just occurred is much more acute than the need to
gain insight into events further removed historically. People need to
comprehend the meaning of events in which they have had to play
a part, to evaluate their sacrifices and efforts, to draw conclusions
for the edification of posterity. This is an attempt to prevent the
repetition of past errors and, at the same time, a kind of collective
therapy to heal the wounds of the past. Undoubtedly, admitting the
truth about recent events is always a painful process, at times even
scandalous, because the participants in yesterday's drama are usually still alive, and in some cases even continue to play a prominent
public role in the lives of their countries. But when have consider-

ations like these ever restrained the press? On the contrary, a juicy
political scandal, which may be deadly to someone, is only fodder
for the press, like a snake to a mongoose. So why has our mongoose
suddenly grown so timid?

Right in front of me lies a document concerning a person I have
never met, about whom I never knew anything, but who, it emerges,
is well known both in his own country and in international political circles. Moreover, it appears that he could have become the
president of Finland. The title of the document is not exciting: "On
measures connected with the 50th birthday of the chairman of the
Social Democratic Party of Finland, K. Sorsa." Nor was the text of
the resolution adopted by the Secretariat of the Central Committee (16 December 1980*, St 241/108) particularly interesting: it
instructed the Soviet ambassador in Helsinki to pay Kalevi Sorsa
a visit with birthday greetings, and to present him with a gift on
behalf of the CC CPSU. Possibly the seeming innocence of this particular paper explains why I got it so easily, without any fuss or
bother, from the Central Committee archive. The puzzling thing
was that it was marked "Top Secret." This aroused my curiosity:
why should a decision to convey birthday greetings to the leader of
the largest political party in a neighboring neutral country, a former
prime minister, be shrouded in such secrecy?

So I started digging deeper in order to obtain supplementary
documents to this resolution of the CC—after all, it made its resolutions on the basis of various reports and recommendations. Nothing was ever done just like that. And finally, after many attempts
and stratagems that I won't detail, I got hold of the materials I was
after, or rather, a report by the International Department of the
Central Committee (11 December 1980, 18-S-2161).[1] I reproduce
it here in full.

Secret

CC CPSU

On measures connected with the 50th birthday of the
chairman of the Social Democratic Party of Finland K. Sorsa.

On 21 December 1980, the chairman of the Social Democratic
Party of Finland (SDPF), K. Sorsa, celebrates his 50th birthday. In his party and governmental activities (as Prime Minister,
Minister of Foreign Affairs and chairman of the parliamentary
committee on foreign affairs), Sorsa consistently maintains positions friendly to the USSR and the CPSU, promotes the development of Soviet-Finnish relations and fosters stable contacts

---

[1] 16 December 1980* St 241/108, p. 3

between the SDPF and our party. On the international scene, first and foremost in the Socialist International, Sorsa, in confidential collaboration with us, works for détente, for the limitation of the arms race and for disarmament.

In view of the above, and the circumstance of Sorsa's election as one of the vice-chairmen of the Socialist International at its last congress, where Sorsa will continue to coordinate the activities of this organization on matters of détente and disarmament, and bearing in mind his contacts with other political forces, we deem it worth instructing the Soviet ambassador in Finland to congratulate Sorsa on his 50th birthday and to present a gift.

Draft CC CPSU resolution appended.

Deputy head of the International Department of the CC CPSU (A. Chernyaev)

11 December 1980

Clearly, the above information is not unimportant, and for Finland it is sensational. It shows that a man who declared his candidacy for the post of president of Finland in 1992 engaged in "confidential collaboration" with an enemy power while holding the posts of prime minister, minister of foreign affairs, and leader of the largest political party. It is not unlikely, moreover, that he was Moscow's man in the Socialist International, where, as vice-president, he would have exercised enormous influence. Let us recall that period, the last contortions of the Cold War: European streets teeming with Moscow-inspired peace demonstrations, protesting against NATO plans to site medium-range nuclear missiles in Europe. At the center of the campaign, European socialists and social democrats, many of them in the governments of their own countries, or at least leaders of the main opposition forces. And in the center of that center, Sorsa, who coordinated the Socialist International's activities on matters of détente and disarmament while "confidentially collaborating" with the CPSU on these very issues. Not bad, is it?

One would think that a piece of information such as this would be a treasure trove for the Finnish press in the run-up to the presidential election. But no. *More than six months passed after this document was offered to the largest newspapers in Finland—with no result.* So what? Who cares? It was only half a year later, thanks to the efforts of some of my friends, that the document finally made the papers in Finland,[2] and Mr. Sorsa, after a public scandal, withdrew his candidacy.

---

[2]"Archives show that Sorsa had Moscow's special favour," *Ilta-Sanomat*, 10 July 1993.

I can find no explanation for such a state of affairs. I am told that "people are tired of the Cold War," that they do not want to know about that very recent past. But is it the task of the press to decide what the public should or should not know about their future president? Surely the press has a duty to inform the public, and then let the public decide what it needs or does not need to know. There's no doubt that if the information had concerned a putative president's love affair or some petty corruption, it would have made front-page headlines in every Finnish newspaper.

It is interesting to recall how several years earlier, a grandiose scandal erupted in another neutral European country, Austria: it became known that presidential candidate Kurt Waldheim had, some fifty years ago, "collaborated confidentially" with the Nazis as a mere junior officer. And, although the electorate chose to ignore this fact, the Austrian press was full of the matter down to the smallest detail. Indeed, the whole world raised a storm of protest, and the world press covered it as an event of primary importance. The strange thing is, however, that in this instance, nobody thought to say:

"So what? Who cares?"

• • •

It could be argued, of course, that Finland is a special case, and that the term Finlandization is no accident—that, in actual fact, the whole country could be said to have "collaborated confidentially" with Moscow. For Finland, this is no crime and no sensation. And what else could be expected from a small, neutral country that has to live side by side with the Big Gray Brother? But Norway is also a neighbor, and it did not Finlandize. Geography is not the crucial factor. The term Finlandization was not coined in Finland, but in West Germany, by no means a neutral country, and one that, unlike Finland, the West felt obligated to defend. But it was in West Germany that this process took root and flourished.

Yet even Germany, despite a readiness to open the Stasi archives, stopped short of putting Erich Honecker on trial, no doubt because it was feared that he would make good on his threat to reveal a whole host of interesting stories. Nobody is particularly keen to dig deeper into the origins of "Ostpolitik," to reevaluate it, or to take a new look at the past activities of such public figures as Willy Brandt and Egon Bahr—even though there is much that deserves closer scrutiny. Take, for example, this document (9 September 1969*, No. 2273-A):

Top secret
Special File

USSR Committee for State Security
of the USSR Council of Ministers
9 September 1969
Moscow

To the CC CPSU

The Committee for State Security reporting on a meeting between a KGB source and "Krupp" corporation director, Count ARNIM von ZEDTWITZ, which took place at the request of the latter in May this year in the Netherlands.

ZEDTWITZ is a confidant of BAHR, a prominent member of the Social Democratic Party of Germany, who handles the planning, coordination and study of key issues of West German foreign policy. ZEDTWITZ stated that he had approached the source at Bahr's direct request in the hope that the entire content of the discussion would be relayed to the Soviet leadership. Citing Bahr, ZEDTWITZ said the following:

"The more sensible" leaders of the SPD have reached the conclusion that it is essential to seek new approaches to the conduct of "Ostpolitik" and wish to establish direct and reliable channels of contact with Moscow.

According to some opinions in West Germany, recent official contacts have yielded negligible results, because each side, due to its official position, has done little other than to make "purely propagandistic" declarations. Contacts with embassy officials in Bonn are also undesirable: it is difficult to maintain them unofficially, and information about any meetings provides immediate ammunition for the political opposition.

In view of this, Bahr feels it would be desirable to conduct a series of unofficial negotiations with representatives of the USSR, which would place neither side under any obligations should the talks yield no positive results.

ZEDTWITZ states that there are forces within West German industrial circles who are prepared to assist the normalization of relations with the USSR, but their opportunities are limited in that the economic ties between West Germany and the USSR are still "embryonic."

In ZEDTWITZ's opinion, the Soviet Union does not make sufficient use of the levers of foreign trade in reaching its political goals, though even now it would be possible to employ measures to exclude the participation of German specialists in the Chinese missile and nuclear programs, and also to counteract West German politicians' tendency to flirt with Mao.

According to available data, the leadership of another party in power in West Germany—the CDU [Christian Democratic Union of Germany]—is also taking steps to establish unofficial con-

tacts with Soviet representatives and has expressed a willingness to conduct "a broad dialogue to clarify many issues" for
both sides.

Analysis of available information gives evidence that two leading, competing West German parties fear that their political opponents will seize the initiative in the matter of regulating relations with the Soviet Union, and are prepared to conduct unofficial negotiations, unmentioned in the press, which could later
serve to strengthen their situation and prestige.[3]

Consequently, the KGB feels that it would be appropriate to continue unofficial contacts with the leadership of both parties. In
the course of the development of such contacts it would be advantageous, using our foreign trade possibilities, to try to exert
a profitable influence on West German foreign policy, and also
to ensure a flow of information about the positions and plans
of the Bonn leadership.

We request authorization.

CHAIRMAN OF THE COMMITTEE FOR STATE SECURITY
ANDROPOV

This is not just an interesting document, it is a historical one.
This was the foundation of Ostpolitik, subsequently the policy of
détente, the most shameful chapter in the history of the Cold War.
Germany was under no threat, it gained nothing substantial from
this policy, yet East-West relations became infected with the virus
of capitulation for a very long time. As a result of this turnabout
the Western world, instead of the united opposition to communism
of the late 1940s and early 1950s, was forced, at best, to waste its
energies on a fruitless struggle with this tendency to capitulate—at
worst to retreat—in order to preserve its unity.

In fact, this document determined the course of international
politics over the past twenty-five years, *yet no major German periodical was willing to publish it.* Three years later, the journal *Der
Spiegel*[4] pulled some quotes from it (without my consent and with
no mention of the source). The reaction was nil, total indifference.

Could it really be true that nobody is interested? Could it be
that now, with the collapse of communism, we feel no desire or
even duty to examine the circumstances that resulted in this policy
being forced upon the world, to determine the motives of its creators
(the German social democrats), to evaluate the damage to NATO's
collective defense—or, in the final analysis, to assess the damage

---

[3]The SPD and CDU were then coalition partners in government.
[4]"Pact with the Devil: Egon Bahr's back-channel to the Kremlin," *Der Spiegel*,
13 February 1995.

this policy caused to the peoples of the USSR and Eastern Europe, by prolonging the lives of their communist regimes by at least ten years?

And the social democrats themselves—do they feel no need to make an honest assessment of their policy concerning the East? Ironically, the architects of Ostpolitik are being touted as heroes and are claiming that the downfall of communism in the East was a product of their "delicate" games with Moscow. This is shameless beyond belief. According to such criteria, Neville Chamberlain could have declared himself the victor in 1945, as peace with Germany was finally reached.

Take another example from another country, Japan, which was also protected by the American nuclear umbrella since the end of the Second World War. This did not prevent Japanese socialists from receiving illegal financial aid from Moscow through the companies and cooperatives they controlled (31 October 1967, St 37/46),[5] organizations tactfully described in Central Committee documents as "firms of friends." One would assume that the largest opposition party, with many members of parliament and with a broad social base, could have ensured its own financial independence. Yet it became enmeshed in debts in 1967 (to the tune of some 800 million yen), ran for help to its ideological neighbor, pulled off some shady deals with timber and textiles, and became hooked. By the 1970s the Japanese socialists were even receiving funds from Moscow for their election campaigns (3 March 1972, St 33/8). It is not too difficult to guess what would have happened to Japan had they won the elections. Perhaps a new term, Japanization, would have been born.

The amazing thing is that although the actions described above are a crime according to Japanese law, the proof, for some reason, did not arouse the interest of the Japanese press or law enforcement agencies. Well, if it had been a matter of illegal kickbacks from Japanese businessmen. . . .

Furthermore, in the fall of 1994, the *New York Times* treated its readers to a sensational scoop:[6] it reported that in the 1950s, the Central Intelligence Agency gave financial support to the Liberal Party of Japan in order to support it in its struggle against the growth of communist influence. Now there's a sensation! Something for the American reader to deplore. But the same *New York Times* showed no interest when I offered them documentation con-

---

[5]See also 28 February 1968 (St 45/4)^ (no online version available).

[6]Tim Weiner, "CIA Spent Millions to Support Japanese Right in 50s and 60s," *New York Times*, 9 October 1994, p. 14. https://www.nytimes.com/1994/10/09/world/cia-spent-millions-to-support-japanese-right-in-50-s-and-60-s.html

cerning Soviet aid to Japanese socialists. From the *New York Times*'s viewpoint, this was nothing to shout about.

And so it goes, from country to country, from document to document. Some do not want to know because this is the past; others because for them it is not yet the past. Before, many feared to know, because communism was so powerful; now it is supposed to be so weak that it is not worth knowing. There is either too much or not enough information. A thousand and one reasons, each more feeble than the last, with the same results. Seemingly serious, honest people, overcome by embarrassment and winking at me in a conspiratorial manner, tell me that "unfortunately, this isn't enough. Now, if you could get hold of this or that further document...." As if, for some odd reason, I am supposed to be the only interested party in the entire world, and therefore the onus is on me to find or furnish evidence. Or, as if I am trying to talk them into something indecent, something that is just not done, and they have seized a convenient reason to decline. Surely, if the events in question had occurred fifty years ago, there would be no need to try to persuade anyone or to prove anything. Why indeed? To bring to justice those who took part in Nazi atrocities is a sacred task, the duty of one and all. But God forbid that you should so much as point a finger at a communist (let alone his fellow traveler); that is improper, a witch hunt. Such astounding duplicity! When and how did we let ourselves become bound by this flawed morality? How has humanity managed to survive decades of moral schizophrenia? After all, untroubled by any humanitarian waverings, we continue to hunt down senile eighty-year-olds in the jungles of Latin America for the evils they perpetrated half a century ago. They are murderers, they cannot be forgiven. Proudly, we declare: This must not be repeated. Never again! And a noble tear moistens our eye. But when it comes to putting Honecker in the dock, a man on whose orders people were being killed as little as a few years ago—why, every heart was outraged! It would be inhuman, he's old and sick.... And we release him into the jungles of Latin America.

This is what I call worldwide Finlandization.

1.2   Cold cash

Due to our thoughtless practice of double standards, Western communists have long ago become a privileged herd of sacred cows. They can do whatever they like, they receive advance forgiveness for any wrongdoing or crime for which an ordinary person would spend years in jail. For instance, they simply lived on Soviet money, although even this was hotly denied three to four years ago, and it was "just not done" to talk about this publicly. Now there is documentation, receipts and descriptions of how this money was passed through the KGB, depicted in detail in the Russian press, but the tacit veto on this subject in the Western press remains in force.

Puzzling, isn't it? I'm not talking about the times of Lenin and Stalin, which have been well and thoroughly documented, and, perhaps, are no longer of great interest to the general public; I'm talking about our times. Those who took part in such activities are still alive and should be called upon to answer for their deeds. After all, even in countries where receiving funds from abroad for political activity is not considered a crime, the receipt of such money tax-free cannot be overlooked by the authorities. After all, tax evasion landed Al Capone in jail, nor was the vice president of the USA, Spiro Agnew, shown any mercy.

Nevertheless, not a single country in the world is so much as looking into the financial operations of local communists, although there are clearly astounding levels of systematic chicanery involved.

Thus in 1969, in an effort to bring some order into the distribution of such assistance, Moscow created a special "International Fund to Aid Left-Wing Workers' Organizations" with a general sum of $16,550,000 in annual assignations. Naturally, Moscow was the largest donor—its contribution was $14 million—but the Eastern European brothers also chipped in (8 January 1969*, Pb 111/162): the Czechs, Romanians, Poles, and Hungarians put in half a million each, Bulgaria $350,000, and the East Germans $200,000. Out of the thirty-four recipients for that year, the biggest were the Italian Communist Party or PCI ($3.7 million just for the first six months!), the French Communist Party or PCF ($2 million) and the Communist Party of the USA ($1 million).[7] And the smallest recipients were the Mozambique Liberation Front at $10,000, and the chairman of the Communist Party of Sri Lanka, Comrade [Sugiswara Abeywardena] Vikremasinghe, at $6,000.

And so it continued until 1991, with the difference that the number of recipients by 1981 had grown to fifty-eight, and the payment to the US Communist Party had grown to $2 million (29 December 1980*, Pb 230/34).

By 1990, the last year of its existence,[8] the fund had swelled to 22 million dollars, and the beneficiaries to seventy-three "commu-

---

[7]The Communist Party of Great Britain reportedly received £100,000 a year from Moscow between 1957 and the mid-1970s. See Kevin Davey, *Moscow Gold? The Soviet Union and the British Left*. [S.I.]: Aaaargh! Press, 2017, p. 102, fn.

[8]11 December 1989 (St 175/3), p. 1 in 5 December 1989* (no number).

nist, workers' and revolutionary-democratic parties and organizations."

The Soviet contribution to the International Fund increased correspondingly. By the 1980s the Soviet share was $15.5 million, in 1986 it was $17 million, in 1987 it was $17.5 million, and in 1990 it was the entire $22 million. It so happened that with the deepening crisis of communism, the Eastern European comrades defaulted on their contributions one after the other, leaving it to Big Brother to pick up the revolutionary bill. There was certainly cause for concern.

Valentin Falin, the head of the International Department, said in a report[9] to the Central Committee on 5 December 1989 that:

> The International Fund to Aid Left-Wing Workers' Organizations has consisted, for many years, of voluntary contributions from the CPSU and other communist parties in socialist countries. However, by the end of the 1970s, Polish and Romanian, and, from 1987, Hungarian comrades ceased to participate in the fund, citing currency-financial problems. In 1988 and 1989, the Socialist United Party of Germany and the communist parties of Czechoslovakia and Bulgaria declined to contribute to the fund with no explanation, and the fund existed solely on moneys apportioned by the CPSU. The share paid by the above three parties constituted $2.3 million in 1987, i.e. around 13 percent of the total sum of the fund. [...]
>
> Parties that have regularly received specific sums of money from the fund over many years rate this form of international solidarity very highly, and feel that it would be impossible to replace by any other form of assistance. The majority of these parties have already submitted motivated applications for aid in 1990, and some requested that the amount be increased substantially.

An equally anxiety-provoking problem was the continuing fall of the dollar, which depreciated this form of international solidarity —those damned capitalists just couldn't get their inflation under control! Hence the dilemma: on one hand, the aim was to bring capitalism to its knees, but on the other hand, a weakening of capitalism made the communists themselves suffer. So what was to be done? However, a way out was found: the head of the International Department of the CC at that time, Anatoly Dobrynin (the very same Dobrynin who, in his tenure of the Soviet ambassadorship to the USA, was lauded in liberal American circles as a pro-Western, enlightened person with whom one could do business), simply sug-

---

[9]5 December 1989* (no number)

gested[10] that all payments should be calculated in a more reliable currency—the hard currency of the ruble. This suggestion was approved (30 November 1987*, Pb 95/21), and the Soviet contribution was designated as 13.5 million "hard" rubles for that and the following year,[11] when the no less "pro-Western" Falin replaced his enlightened colleague as head of the International Department. Toward the end, however, worries about the dollar retreated into the background, the Eastern European brothers scattered in all directions, and for the final year, 1990, the State Bank of the USSR (Gosbank) assigned the entire 22 million greenbacks.[12]

Obviously, long years spent in Western capitals did not quench revolutionary fervor, and the imminent collapse of the empire did not undermine feelings of international solidarity. This is all the more curious in view of the circumstance that the decisions were made by a Politburo headed at that time by supposedly the most pro-Western, liberal, and pragmatic General Secretary of the CC CPSU with whom the West "did business." The only thing these "liberals" tried to achieve was to sweep all traces of their activity under the carpet, so that their illegal export of foreign currency into neighboring countries would not surface and undermine the West's faith in glasnost and perestroika. By that time, the receipt of Western credits had become the overriding concern of the Kremlin "reformers," and too much talk as to where these funds were channeled could not contribute to the success of that business.

In other words, they tried to replace direct hard currency smuggling with more refined methods of financing through "firms of friends." The suggestion was debated by the Politburo (4 February 1987), studied by the International Department of the CC,[13] discussed with the clients, but finally rejected (21 November 1987).[14] As Anatoly Dobrynin reported to the CC:[15]

> The possibilities of transferring aid through trade relations with firms controlled by fraternal parties is currently limited to a very small number of parties.
>
> Many firms controlled by communist parties are economically weak, with limited contacts and trade possibilities, some of them are even in deficit. The firms of only a certain number of fraternal parties—the French, Greek, Cypriot, and Portuguese

---

[10]30 November 1987* (Pb 95/21), p. 6.
[11]28 December 1988* (Pb 144/129), p. 1.
[12]11 December 1989 (St 175/3), p. 1 in 5 December 1989* (no number).
[13]See 30 November 1987* (Pb 95/21), pp. 3–6.
[14]30 November 1987* (Pb 95/21), p. 1.
[15]30 November 1987* (Pb 95/21), pp. 3–5.

—are in a situation to develop cooperation with Soviet foreign trade organizations in a way which would bring them tangible profit. The percentage of profits paid by firms into party budgets is, as a rule, insignificant—from 1 to 5 percent from gains or concluded contracts.

The financial activities of firms or businesses controlled or owned by communist parties are subject to hard scrutiny by taxation and fiscal bodies in their countries. More or less significant payments by these firms into their party coffers could become a cause for continual speculation by the bourgeois mass media. While not rejecting the principle of the possible receipt of aid through trade organizations, the comrades from fraternal parties consider this method to be 'the hardest to conceal and potentially dangerous' (Gaston Plissonnier, French CP).

Parties that have, for a lengthy period, received regular aid from the International Fund for Aid to Left-Wing Workers' Organizations, are counting on the preservation of this form of expressing solidarity with them. For some of them—first and foremost the underground ones—income from the fund is the only means of financing their activities; for others aid from the fund is a major part of their resources for financing organizational, political, and ideological work (including the publication and distribution of newspapers and other printed matter).

The cessation of financial assistance from the International Fund would, for most of the recipient parties, be an irreparable loss, which would inevitably have an extremely negative effect on their activity. Even parties that own businesses and trade or intermediary firms would have to cut back at least some important undertakings without income from the fund, which would, in turn, lead to a decrease in their political weight and influence, and lessen their ability to have an effect on the development of social and political processes in their countries.

At the present time, neither the fraternal parties nor the Soviet foreign trade organizations are prepared for the transfer of financial assistance through foreign trade channels. For most parties, this is simply unacceptable because they own no enterprises or trading firms. But they need financial aid more than ever.

Clearly, the clients dug in their heels and refused to replace their revolutionary romanticism with the prosaic concerns of the tradesman. Moscow, however, remained restless: the following year, the whole circus was repeated—the discussions, the reports to the Central Committee (this time by Falin), and the decision (28 December 1988).[16] The same arguments were aired, only this time we learn

---

[16]28 December 1988* (Pb 144/129), p. 1.

in greater detail to what use the aid was put (28 December 1988*):

> The money received from the fund is used by the parties, at their own discretion, for fundamental aspects of party-political activity (the work of the CC, payments to retired party activists, publications, the hire of halls, election campaigns etc.).
>
> The leaders of fraternal parties rate this form of solidarity very highly, and feel that it cannot be replaced by aid in any other form. This was reiterated recently by Plissonnier, who stressed that the receipt of aid from the fund in no way limits the independence of individual communist parties in determining their stance on any political issue. At the same time, the cessation or decrease of this aid would deal a great blow to the political activities of the parties, especially in matters concerning events of national significance (elections, congresses, conferences), all of which call for substantial expenditure.

So Moscow never did manage to wean these communist sucklings from her maternal breast and persuade them to switch to the principle of "socialist self-financing" as a means of sustenance, even though attempts were made practically every year. As late as 1991, some six months before the crash, meetings continued with the abovementioned Plissonnier from the French CP, as did discussions concerning "the development of business ties with the CPSU and suggestions concerning trade-economic relations via firms of friends" (17 January 1991, 6-S-44).

It is not hard to calculate that only counting the period since 1969, and only in this particular form of "international solidarity," the French CP, for example, received no less than $44 million, the Communist Party of the USA some $35 million, and the Italians even more. All in all, beginning with 1969, Moscow gifted its brothers something to the tune of $400 million, and that does not include other forms of financing. These are substantial sums. So how is it that they are of no interest to Western taxation, fiscal, and banking bodies? After all, this is mostly Western money, aimed at rescuing the latest Kremlin "dove" from the clutches of surrounding Kremlin "hawks," (or "reformers" from "conservatives," depending on the time), that is now being demanded, plus interest, from the destitute peoples of the former USSR. In other words, money thrown out by the West for the salvation of world communism. So let every country claim payment of these debts from its domestic communists. Would this not be easier and more just? Especially as penniless Russia will never be able to pay.

But this idea evokes no enthusiasm, because under closer scrutiny, it would not be just the communists in the dock.

1.3   "Firms of Friends"

Despite all the recipient parties' pleas of poverty, aid from Moscow via "firms of friends" was a far from negligible contribution to their budgets. Unfortunately, I lack sufficient documentation to paint the full picture of this sphere of activity, but even those materials I have at my disposal are sufficient to make an assessment of its magnitude.

By the looks of it, one of the first Western communist parties to adopt the "socialist principle of self-repayment" was the Italian CP, at that time the largest and most influential in Europe. Looking through the lists of the International Fund's clients (29 December 1980*, Pb 230/34), I was surprised to note that the Italian comrades ceased to figure in them from the end of the 1970s, although in the beginning they were at the head of these lists, having received a hefty $3.7 million for just six months in 1969. *Poor souls,* I thought. *They must have suffered for their honesty and principles, refused to abandon their faith in 'communism with a human face,' and Moscow turned off the tap of fraternal aid to punish them.*

And it is true that at that time the Italian comrades were displaying real heroism: they had divorced themselves from Moscow on the issue of human rights, condemned the Soviet invasion of Afghanistan, and come out in support of Poland's workers' union Solidarity, while we cynics thought this was nothing but window dressing. I must confess that for a moment there, I felt ashamed of my cynicism. Alas, I could have spared my blushes—the Italian CP had no intention whatsoever of perishing from a surfeit of honesty. On the contrary, its contacts with Moscow deepened perceptibly —the Politburo even adopted a special resolution, "On Increasing Work with the Italian Communist Party" (10 June 1980, Pb 203/1), and a short time earlier, in October 1979, they appear to have settled their financial relations. At least they were settling them, as detailed in the following document (5 October 1979*, St 179/32):

Top secret
Special File

To the CC CPSU

On the reception of comrade D. Cervetti, member
of the leadership of the Italian CP by the CC CPSU

A member of the leadership of the Italian CP, the secretary of the CC PCI on coordination, comrade A. Natta, has been instructed by comrade [Enrico] Berlinguer to report that PCI leadership member comrade D. Cervetti, who arrives in Moscow on 7 October this year for a short rest, been instructed to discuss a number of special questions, including financial ones, with the CC CPSU (coded telegram from Rome, spec. #1474 of 3 October 1979). We feel it would be feasible to fulfill this request of the PCI leadership and receive comrade D. Cervetti in the CC CPSU to discuss the matters that interest him. Draft CC CPSU resolution appended.

> Deputy head of the International Department of the CC CPSU ([Vadim] Zagladin)

4 October 1979

Naturally, one can only guess what financial questions were discussed by comrade D. Cervetti and comrades Ponomarev and Zagladin in the Central Committee, but the following Politburo document (18 January 1983*, Pb 94/52) characterizes the nature of the financial relations of the CPSU with the PCI as follows:

> "Workers of the world, unite!"

To be returned within 3 days to the CPSU
(General Department, 1st section)

> THE COMMUNIST PARTY OF THE SOVIET UNION.
> CENTRAL COMMITTEE.

> Top secret
> Special File

> FOR YOUR EYES ONLY

> To comrades Ponomarev, Patolichev, Smirtyukov

Abstract from minutes #94 of the meeting of the Politburo of the CC CPSU of 18 January 1983

> Concerning the request of our Italian friends.

Instruct the Ministry of Foreign Trade (comrade Patolichev) to sell the firm "Interexpo" (president—comrade L. Remiggio) 600,000 metric tons of oil and 150,000 metric tons of diesel fuel on a normal commercial basis, but with favorable terms and at a discount of around 1 percent, and to extend the payment period by three to four months, so that our friends will stand to gain approximately 4 million dollars from this commercial operation.

> SECRETARY OF THE CC

Here we encounter an exception to the rule, a significant exception, and moreover one that had enormous consequences: these and a number of other documents concerning the unsavory past of the PCI filtered through into the Italian press sometime around the end of 1991 and beginning of 1992. There was even some talk of an investigation of possible violations of tax legislation. The reaction was instantaneous: the very people who suggested an investigation found themselves under investigation. The Italian magistrature (which had been actively infiltrated by the PCI in recent years) came awake abruptly from a seemingly deep and dreamless sleep, and discovered an astounding degree of corruption in the financing of virtually all the major Italian political parties, except, naturally, the PCI. The scenario that followed can be likened to Stalin's Great Terror of 1937–1938, if not in magnitude, then certainly in style: literally a third of the members of the Italian cabinet found themselves in prison or under investigation. The terror, which went under the proud title of the "Clean Hands Operation" (so reminiscent of the *chekists'* motto: "Clean hands, cool heads, fiery hearts") cut a swath through the entire Italian establishment, sparing neither politicians nor businessmen nor government officials. Thousands of people were imprisoned; arrests were carried out almost invariably on information given by those behind bars in order to secure their own release. There were a number of suicides. Admittedly there was as yet no torture, no executions by firing squad—the Italian communists were, after all, "communists with a human face." At the same time Italy, which had been flourishing nicely, began to fall apart: the economy tottered on the brink of collapse, the rate of the lira plunged drastically, the machinery of government ground to a standstill, unemployment soared. So who is to come to the rescue of the country, who is worthy to rule it other than those who have clean hands?

"But there really was corruption!" protesting voices will cry. Yes, there was—and this is the crux of the matter—throughout the entire postwar period. Moreover, it was as widespread a violation as exceeding the speed limit. Everyone in Italy knew about it, including today's magistrates with their clean hands. Yet for some reason, nobody bothered to fight it until the PCI came under threat of exposure and on the verge of ruin without financial aid from Moscow. The Italian communists really had nothing to lose except their chains, and the prize would be the whole of Italy in their grasp.

But just like their clean-handed Soviet predecessors fifty-five years earlier, they had no comprehension that terror is an ungovernable force, which can easily turn on its perpetrators. Then they would be reminded of their trade with Moscow "on a normal commercial basis," their mercenary control of virtually all trade between the USSR and Italy, thanks to which the largest communist party in Europe existed for decades.

Needless to say, other communist parties traded with the CC CPSU on the same "normal commercial basis" for years, but the example of what happened in Italy does not facilitate public discussion of the problem. The French were probably ahead of their Italian colleagues. At least one document points to the likelihood of this: the resolution of the secretariat concerning a ten-year extension of the repayment of a loan of 2.8 million by the West German firm Magra GmbH, controlled by "French friends" (16 December 1980, St 241/99). In recommending this resolution, the International Department of the CC reports[17] the following:

> The firm 'Magra GmbH' is owned by the French CP, and for 15 years has been purchasing ball bearings from the foreign trade organization 'Stankoimport' for sale in West Germany. A debt of 2.8 million arose as a result of the firm's investment of this sum into expansion and because of a decline in demand for ball bearings in West Germany.

From 1965, this firm and its French offshoot, Magra-France, dealt successfully in Soviet goods for the benefit of communism. In Germany alone, ball bearings were sold to the tune of 10 million hard currency rubles. Yet another document (26 August 1980, St 225/84) charges that "in connection with ideas expressed by [Jean] Jerome," a member of the Central Committee of the French CP, the Ministry of Foreign Trade and the State Planning Committee (Gosplan) are to "devise and implement means for the further growth of trade and economic ties with firms of our French friends," such as Comex and Interagra. And the number of such firms equaled the number of "ideas" nursed by J. Jerome. Clearly comrade Plissonnier could have had little cause for complaint.

Nor were others left behind. Even in far-off Australia, the local socialist party sought "that debts incurred by the Australian firm 'Palanga Travel' to the sum of 2,574,932 rubles for the charter of the cruise ships 'Fedor Shaliapin' and 'Khabarovsk' in 1974–1975 be written off" (23 December 1980, St 242/76). It is not clear whether this is their firm[18] or would become theirs in exchange for the debts' being written off.

The Greek publisher and industrialist George Bobolas even earned inclusion in the title of a CC CPSU resolution (11 April 1980, St 206/58), "On Cooperation with G. Bobolas," in which the Ministry of Foreign Trade and the State Committee of the USSR on Foreign Economic Relations are instructed "in the presence of other equal opportunities to give preference to G. Bobolas, in view

---

[17] 16 December 1980 (St 241/99), pp. 3–4.

[18] The Socialist Party of Australia was set up in 1971 by members of the Australian Communist Party who did not approve of the leadership's "Eurocommunist" tendencies and criticism of the USSR.

of the positive part he has played in the development of Soviet-Greek links."

At first glance this does not seem too heinous—a small reward for the comrade for his tireless efforts in the cause of good neighborly relations. However, from appended documents and especially from the report submitted to the Central Committee by deputy chairman of the KGB, Semyon Tsvigun,[19] it emerges that these tireless efforts were made in the field of KGB "special measures." The *chekists* had their own understanding of good neighborly relations: G. Bobolas's publishing house Akadimos was used by them as a "publishing base for ideological influence in Greece and in Greek communities in a number of countries." Bobolas's devotion to promoting good neighborly relations with the Soviet Union resulted in certain material loss (including losses incurred with the publication of a Greek translation of Brezhnev's book *Peace: Mankind's Best Reward* with a foreword by the author), therefore "in order to achieve a degree of compensation, G. Bobolas seeks to establish business contacts with the Ministry of Foreign Trade and the State Committee on Foreign Relations by the conclusion of rather large, mutually beneficial deals."

Subsequently there were a number of scandals involving Bobolas. Naturally, having received such strong preferential status in the conclusion of "mutually beneficial" business deals, he did not sit idly by, nor did he disappoint his Soviet partners, and a couple of years later began publishing the newspaper *Ethnos*, the main mouthpiece for Soviet disinformation in Greece. Attempts were made to expose him, but he fought back, even suing *The Economist* for libel and nearly winning the case!

Time passed, and Bobolas grew from a building contractor into a media tycoon: he became co-owner of Greece's largest television channel, Mega, and acquired interests in the cinema and audio industries, and governments—both socialist and conservative—continued to give him huge construction contracts. In other words, he was seen as a solid citizen, a pillar of society and Greek democracy.

But after the passage of many years, the good neighborly regime in Moscow collapsed, and the newspaper *Pravda* trembled on the brink of bankruptcy and closure. For some time it disappeared from the newspaper stands; then it suddenly sprang into life again and began to flourish, allegedly, on funds provided by Greek communists. Officially, *Pravda*'s fairy godmother was named as one Yannis Yanikos, a partner in Bobolas's past publishing feats.

---

[19]11 April 1980 (St 206/58), pp. 5–6.

It is anybody's guess how many such Bobolases Moscow spawned over the past seventy-five years. It is unlikely that anyone will seek to investigate this matter after the catastrophe in Italy, and without a thorough investigation it is not possible to gain a full understanding of all the complexities of relations between Moscow and the firms it dealt with in those times. Where did business end and politics begin? Who were Armand Hammer and Robert Maxwell: businessmen who became agents, or agents who became businessmen? I am firmly convinced that no businessman at that time could have had purely business relations with the USSR. One cannot deal with the devil without becoming his servant. Even leaving aside the dubious morality of selling one's class hangman the rope of which Lenin spoke, it was hardly possible to fraternize with the Soviet demons without becoming corrupt.

Moreover, the people who sought such relations in those days were a particular breed with particular views. Here, at first glance, is a perfectly simple and clear document, devoid of any secrets: "On the Opening of Representations of a Number of Foreign Firms in Moscow" (5 January 1981, St 244/50). There would seem to be no reason to suspect anything shady: these were established firms with solid turnovers trading on the basis of mutual benefit. Yet for some reason this document is also stamped "top secret." A closer look at the résumés in the document shows that one of the firms has a prominent Western politician on its board of directors, another helps to influence the policies of its country's government "in directions favorable to our interests." The third—a Spanish firm, Prodag, S.A.—is an absolute paragon: it pays its bills on time, has been trading with the USSR since 1959, and is a reliable partner—"statistics for 1979 show that some 50 percent of the entire trade between Spain and the Soviet Union went to the firm 'Prodag'." Only the last line sheds a glimmer of light: "At the present time, the firm's president, R. Mendoza, is preparing the publication of L.I. Brezhnev's work 'Peace, Disarmament and Soviet-American Relations.'"

By 1981 the offices of 123 such firms were open in Moscow. Who can say what they did when they weren't engaged in matters of trade? Why did they need, in those times, to open offices in Moscow? What are they doing now? And how many were there that didn't bother with official representation? Nobody is even trying to find out. What's the difference? Who cares? All this is in the past, people tell me.

"The Cold War is over, haven't you heard?"

How can anyone not hear, when it's being shouted from the rooftops by precisely those for whom it never existed, who, at best, closed their eyes to it? The Gulf War is over, too, yet the investigation of firms that dealt with Iraq is only just beginning to unfold. No war is over until the minefields and unexploded bombs are cleared away, until gangs of marauders and surviving foes are disarmed. Otherwise, peaceful existence could turn into a horror worse than the war itself.

At the same time, the issue of firms that traded with the Soviet Union becomes increasingly urgent as time goes by. It is no secret that in his last couple of years in power, and especially in 1990–1991, Gorbachev privatized, as it were, the activities of the CPSU, encouraging the apparatus and in particular the KGB to set up "joint ventures" (JVs) with Western businesses. Their growth in those years was astronomical, involving, presumably, "firms of friends" and other "businessmen" allied to the KGB. Such a scenario suggests itself quite logically, bearing in mind Gorbachev's determination to place "international aid" on a commercial basis. And who better for the KGB to deal with than those whom it already knew and could control? Starting with laundering party funds and transferring the resources within their grasp (gold, oil, precious metals), these malevolent, mafia-like structures grew like a cancer, absorbing practically all "private" enterprise in the countries of the former USSR. Now, with the emergence of these countries into the world market, it behooves us to deal with yet another international mafia, a much more frightening and powerful one than any Colombian drug cartel or the Cosa Nostra.

1.4   Intellectual Shenanigans

Not surprisingly, Moscow's aid to its clients was not limited to what is described above. As reported by Falin to the Central Committee (28 December 1988*), apart from direct financing and financing via commercial channels, there was also the "supply of paper for newspaper printing, invitations of party activists for study, rest and medical treatment, purchase of the parties' publications, payment of some party representatives' travel from one country to another, etc."

The "etc." included, for instance, the support of a whole network of bookshops owned by "friends" in many countries. This program, which was instituted in the 1960s via the foreign trading agency Mezhdunarodnaya kniga, was not cheap. Firstly, all these shops were opened with Soviet funds, loaned and, needless to say, never fully repaid. Secondly, they all traded at a loss that would be later written off "at the request of our friends' leadership." Expenses varied, depending on the place, time, and circumstances. For instance, the opening of Collet's bookshop in London cost Moscow £80,000 (or 124,000 hard currency rubles), and the contract with the firm directly envisaged "the covering of a possible deficit from the sale of Soviet publications in the first years of the shop's existence."[20] The opening of a similar shop in Montreal a few years earlier had cost only $10,000 Canadian. The sum of the debts written off varied from 12,300 hard rubles for the Israeli Communist Party's Popular Bookshop in 1969, to 56,500 hard rubles for the Belgian Communist Party's bookshop Du Monde Entier, to $300,000 to the Communist Party of the USA's firms Four Continents Book Corporation, Cross World Books & Periodicals, and the Victor Kamkin Bookstore.[21] Not even Australia was forgotten; its Socialist Party's New Era Books & Records owed Moscow 80,000 hard currency rubles.

In the absence of complete information, it is hard to determine the overall loss from this brisk commercial activity. The report submitted by Mezhdunarodnaya kniga to the Central Committee in 1967 shows that the total volume of the firm's "export to capitalist countries" was worth 3.9 million hard rubles for that year and that the overall sum of deferred debts equaled 2.46 million, and bad debts 642 thousand. For that time, these were considerable sums. Nonetheless, the export continued, and by 1982 there was a new series of debts to be written off, including $460,000 to the US Communist Party's firms Imported Publications and International Publishers (5 January 1982**, St 44/7).

Then there was paper for fraternal publications, supplied gratis in enormous quantities. The decision to establish a special fund for this purpose was taken in 1974,[22] but the actual cost to the Soviet Union is impossible to estimate, because at that time the production and transportation of anything at all in the USSR had no real assessment, and was conditionally expressed in "cashless transfers." To put it plainly, this was a bottomless well. For example, in 1980 alone, this special fund supplied brothers abroad with thirteen thousand tons of paper.[23] I have no idea what the Western price for this would have been, but a very approximate assessment on the basis of very conditional calculations yields a figure of 3.5 million rubles per annum.

Eventually, as of 1 January 1989, the fund ceased to exist, and

---

[20] 3 February 1976 (St 203/10)^. From the mid-1930s onwards, the wealthy British Communist Eva Collet Rickett financed left-wing bookshops in London, Hull, Cardiff and Glasgow. Following her death, the new agreement secured the future of Collet's, a bookshop on the Tottenham Court Road.

[21] 15 April 1968 (St 50-148), p. 16.

[22] 28 May 1974 (St 126/7)^.

[23] 15 October 1980 (St 233/8), p. 5.

the then Premier Nikolai Ryzhkov ordered that "expenses connected with the production and supply of paper for newspapers out of the special fund set up to cover the needs of fraternal parties is to be transferred to USSR state assignations for free aid to foreign countries" (24 December 1988, No. 578). We will probably never learn exactly how much all this cost a country in which the shortage of paper was so acute that in order to purchase a new book, one was required to submit twenty kilos of paper for pulping.

But that's not all. There was yet another form of aid for fraternal publishing: the direct purchase of these publications by the Soviet Union, allegedly for sale to foreign students and tourists. I have no systematic, year-by-year information about this, but with the escalation of the crisis in the Soviet Union, the authorities were forced to review all their revolutionary expenses, including this one. Thus we learn that by 1989 the purchase and transportation of ninety titles from forty-two countries consumed 4.5 million hard rubles per annum—around $6 million at the exchange rate of the time!

One must also remember the "material maintenance" of the Moscow-accredited correspondents of these fraternal publications: from the end of the 1950s, probably for camouflage purposes, the bill for this was footed by... the Soviet Red Cross. But as the crisis escalated, the unthinkable happened: the Red Cross rose up in arms and refused to pay, citing government cuts of its own budget as the reason (6 February 1990, St 10/1). When the expenses were totted up, the result was astounding:

> At present, there are 33 foreign correspondents in Moscow, who occupy 33 apartments, including 7 correspondents' points. Apart from financial maintenance, they enjoy free post, telegraph and telephone services, gratis renovation of apartments and correspondents' points, free travel within the Soviet Union and abroad, medical treatment and resort facilities, also at the expense of the Soviet side. Practically every correspondent has a secretarial assistant, whose salary is paid by the Executive Council of the Soviet Red Cross and Red Crescent Society. The expenses arising from the presence of this category of foreign correspondents exceeded one million rubles in 1989 alone.

It became necessary for the Central Committee to review this form of international solidarity, too.

The above only relates to "foreign correspondents," but there was also the cost of maintaining visiting communist leaders, who were received in much grander style. It should not be forgotten that in those days medical treatment, housing, and education were all officially free in the Soviet Union, and were thus not included in the arithmetic. Nonetheless, in 1971 alone, the hospitable Central Committee assigned 3.2 million hard rubles for these purposes, in the expectation of receiving 2,900 highly valued guests, of whom at least one hundred were expecting medical treatment (28 July 1971*, St 123/30). There were also services that cannot be assigned a value in either dollars or hard rubles. Here, for instance, is a handwritten request from the General Secretary of the Communist Party of the USA, Gus Hall, on behalf of comrade James Jackson, a leading Marxist thinker and main theoretician of the party, who was very keen to be awarded an honorary doctorate in history. Surely this should not be too hard to arrange with, say, Moscow State University? Why, of course not, comrades! No problem whatsoever!

As is noted in the accompanying memo from the International Department of the Central Committee,[24] not only would this serve "to raise his authority in democratic negro circles," but it would also "make it possible for him to secure a teaching post at New York University, where the party has lately been working actively." So it pays to have friends in the right places. Even the president of the United States cannot make you a professor at New York University, but the Politburo can.

It must be noted that some of these more innocent communist shenanigans did receive some coverage in the Western press. Not the documents themselves, but passing reference to them in some newspapers, and mainly in humorous form, as in look at those silly Russians, fancy throwing money away on such nonsense. Moscow's assistance to the Communist Party of the USA was perceived as the funniest thing of all: why on earth was it necessary? After all, there are only about forty thousand communists in the whole of the USA. But the newspapers' jokes were wide of the mark. Moscow needed the Communist Party of the USA not for elections to Congress, but for a totally different reason. After all, this was not a party in the traditional sense of the word but rather a paid Soviet *agentura*. And having forty thousand agents in your enemy's midst is no mean achievement. One should not forget that back in 1917, Lenin also started out with only forty thousand comrades.

As for the books, newspapers, and journals—there is not much to laugh about there, either. Following in Lenin's footsteps, they all began with the printed word and ended with terror. Here is one example of what the Communist Party of the USA was up to in 1970 (28 April 1970*, 1128-A):

---

[24] 1 October 1969 (25-S-1765), p. 1.

USSR COMMITTEE of State security of the
Council of Ministers of the USSR

28 April 1970
Moscow

To the CC CPSU

In recent times the radical negro organization "Black Panthers" has been subjected to harsh repression by the US authorities headed by the FBI, who consider the "Black Panthers" to pose a serious threat to national security. Police provocations and trials of "Black Panthers", the broad coverage of the terrorist actions of the authorities against the activists of this organization, have resulted in a significant growth of the "Black Panthers'" prestige in progressive circles in the US. In view of the circumstance that the "Black Panthers" are a dynamic negro organization which poses a serious threat to America's ruling classes, the Communist party of the USA is attempting to influence the organization in the necessary direction. This policy of the CP is already yielding positive results. There is a discernible tendency among the "Black Panthers" to increase cooperation with progressive organizations which are opposed to the existing system in the USA.

Because the rise of negro protest in the USA will bring definite difficulties to the ruling classes of the USA and will distract the attention of the Nixon administration from pursuing an active foreign policy, we would consider it feasible to implement a number of measures to support this movement and assist its growth.

Therefore it is recommended to utilize the possibilities of the KGB in African countries to inspire political and public figures, youth, trade union and nationalist organizations to issue petitions, requests and statements to the UN, US embassies in their countries and the US government in defense of the rights of American negroes. To publish articles and letters accusing the US government of genocide in the press of various African countries. Employing the possibilities of the KGB in New York and Washington, to influence the "Black Panthers" to address appeals to the UN and other international bodies for assistance in bringing the US government's policy of genocide toward American negroes to an end.

It is likely that by carrying out the abovementioned measures it will be possible to mobilize public opinion in the US and in other countries in support of the rights of American negroes and thereby stimulate the "Black Panthers" into further activation of their struggle.

We request authorization.

CHAIRMAN OF THE COMMITTEE FOR STATE SECURITY
ANDROPOV

... Like a murky dream, I recall my cell in Vladimir Prison, and *Pravda* headlines screaming: "Free Angela Davis!" Reading this is comical, when you have been sentenced to seven or ten years' imprisonment for reading a proscribed book or for a word of criticism. To those of us who had been schooled by prison, the scenario was clear as crystal: a straightforward case of being an accomplice to murder. She gave her Black Panther boyfriend's brother the arms with which he killed court officials and policemen in order to escape. What could be simpler? But the world was going mad: "a courageous woman" and "activist of the negro movement." At this time Californian lawmakers abolished the death sentence, so the jury was able to clear her completely to the utter delight of all progressive mankind. Vera Zasulich,[25] no more, no less! It was only much later, after the court cleared her, that *Pravda* published the proud admission: "Member of the Central Committee of the Communist Party of the USA, Angela Davis."

They were allowed to get away with anything, even murder.

1.5 "Special Aid"

There was yet another form of "international solidarity" that cannot be measured in dollars or rubles, and that is not as harmless as scrounging an honorary degree. This kind of aid was so veiled in secrecy that any documentation pertaining to it carried the "special file" designation. Yet even with this degree of secrecy, the Central Committee chose to cloak the gist of the matter with descriptions such as "special training," "special equipment," and "special materials, and more specific details were written in by hand—even the CC's vetted typists were not sufficiently trusted. And woe betide the country that became the recipient of this sort of "aid," for it would shortly become one of the world's "hot spots," even if until then it had been peaceful and prosperous. This is how it looked (italics indicate handwritten insertions) (27 December 1976*, St 37/37):

Workers of the world, unite!

TO BE RETURNED WITHIN 3 days to
the CC CPSU (General Department, section II)

---

[25]A revolutionary known to every Soviet schoolchild, Vera Zasulich (1849–1919) seriously wounded the governor of St. Petersburg when she attempted to assassinate him in 1887. She was put on trial but acquitted.

COMMUNIST PARTY OF THE SO-
VIET UNION, CENTRAL COMMITTEE

Top Secret
(Special file) of 27.XII.1976

Abstract from minutes #37 par. 37gs Secretariat of the CC
Request by International Department of CC CPSU

Satisfy the request made by the leadership of the Argentinean
CP, the People's Party of Panama, the Communist Party of El
Salvador and the Communist Party of Uruguay and receive *10*
communists from Argentina, *3* from Panama, *3* from El Salvador and *3* from Uruguay in the USSR for up to 6 months in
1977 for *training in matters of party security, intelligence and
counterintelligence.* Organization of the training is to be handled by the Committee for State Security of the Council of Ministers of the USSR, reception, services and maintenance by the
International Department and by the Administrative Department of the CC CPSU. The round-trip travel expenses for *10*
Argentinean comrades between Buenos Aires and Moscow, *3*
comrades from El Salvador between San Salvador and Moscow
and *3* Uruguayan comrades between Montevideo and Moscow
should be charged to the Party budget.

SECRETARY OF THE CC

Sent to: comrades Andropov, Ponomarev, Pavlov

Such "special training" in the KGB was usually the first step of
the process. Just in the decade 1979–1989, it was received by more
than five hundred activists from forty communist and "workers'"
parties from various countries, including members of their Polit-
buros and central committees.[26]

Then came the next step (18 August 1980*, St 224/71):

18 VIII 1980
TOP SECRET
SPECIAL FILE

RESOLUTION

SECRETARIAT OF THE CC OF THE COM-
MUNIST PARTY OF THE SOVIET UNION

Request by International Department of the CC CPSU

Satisfy the request of the leadership of the Communist party
of El Salvador to give *military training instruction lasting up to
6 months* in 1980 to *30* Salvadoran communists who are currently in the USSR.

---

[26] 10 April 1989* (St 99/248), p. 5.

Reception, service and maintenance, *the organization of training* for *30* Salvadoran communists, and also their travel expenses from Moscow to El Salvador to be charged to the *Ministry of Defense.*

(signed: A. Chernyaev)

Results of vote (signatures):

[Andrei] Kirilenko   [Mikhail] Zimyanin   [Mikhail] Gorbachev
[Ivan] Kapitonov   [Vladimir] Dolgikh

———

Excerpts to comrades: Ustinov, Ponomarev
Sent out: 18 VIII 1980

Normally, in order to get to the heart of the matter, one must look at the appendices to the resolution, or at the comrades' request itself. And here it is:

Top Secret
Translated from the Spanish

To the CC CPSU

Dear comrades!

I should like to ask your consent to undertake the *military training* of *30* of our young communists, who are currently in Moscow, for a period of 4–5 months in the following fields:

6 comrades for *army intelligence,*

8 comrades to be trained as *commanders of guerrilla units,*

5 comrades to be trained as *commanders of artillery,*

5 comrades for training as *commanders of sabotage units,*

6 comrades for training in *communications*

Thanking you for the assistance which the CPSU gives to our party.

SCHAFIK HANDAL
General Secretary of the CC of the
Communist Party of El Salvador

23 July 1980
Moscow

Translated by: (V. Tikhmenev)

Then comes the final stage of the process (20 August 1980*, St 225/5), after which the world press is filled with reports about a "sudden crisis" in that poor country, the suffering of its people and the evil doings of—no, not Moscow-trained communist bands, but the beleaguered government, which is stigmatized by the press as a "bloody junta." And why not? After all, the government is a visible entity, its members can be shown on television, they can be bombarded with wrathful protests with complete impunity. Now, the comrades in Moscow are a different kettle of fish altogether. It's better not to tangle with them.

VIII   1980   TOP SECRET

SPECIAL FILE

RESOLUTION

SECRETARIAT OF THE CC OF THE COM-

MUNIST PARTY OF THE SOVIET UNION

At the request of the leadership of the Communist Party of El Salvador

1. Satisfy the request of the leadership of the Communist Party of El Salvador and instruct the Ministry of Civil Aviation to arrange, in September–October, the delivery of a consignment of *60–80 tons of Western-manufactured firearms and ammunition* from Hanoi to Havana, to be passed on to our Salvadoran friends via Cuban comrades.

   Expenses connected with the delivery of *the firearms* from Hanoi to Havana should be charged to the state budget as gratis aid to foreign countries.

2. Approve the texts of telegrams to Soviet ambassadors in Cuba and Vietnam (appended)

(signed: A. Chernyaev)

———

Results of vote (signatures of CC Secretaries):   Kirilenko Rusakov   Gorbachev   Dolgikh   Zimyanin   Kapitonov

———

Excerpts to comrades: Gromyko, Ponomarev
comrades: Bugayev, Garbuzov (without appendices)
Sent out: 20 VIII 1980.

Top Secret

Special File

Appendix 1

Urgent

To HAVANA

SOVIET AMBASSADOR

662. Inform the General Secretary of the CC of the Communist Party of El Salvador, comrade Schafik Handal, or, in his absence, a representative of the Communist Party of El Salvador, that the request for a consignment of *Western-manufactured*

firearms from Vietnam via Cuba was studied and endorsed at the relevant level. Also, inform the leadership of our Cuban friends about the above, stressing that the decision was taken bearing in mind that there is already agreement on this matter between comrades F. Castro and S. Handal.

For your information: delivery of *the firearms* will be by Aeroflot aircraft. Give all necessary assistance in organizing the transfer of this cargo via Cuban comrades to our Salvadoran friends. Report upon completion.

(signatures: Chernyaev, Rusakov)

I took this example at random from hundreds of similar ones, and also because of the noise kicked up at the time in the left-liberal press concerning events in El Salvador. And all because— oh, the shame of it!—the government of El Salvador fought back instead of bowing to the historically inevitable advance of progressive forces and dying quietly in some Salvadoran gulag. The greatest outburst of righteous indignation was directed, of course, at Ronald Reagan, who decided to help Salvador instead of sitting back and waiting for his turn. Heavens above, what a to-do there was! What screams about violations of human rights by the Salvadoran army, as though one can talk of human rights in the middle of a plague epidemic. One would think there had been at least one precedent of a civil war in history (including in the USA) in which the warring sides conducted themselves in strict accordance with the UN Declaration of Human Rights! One might ask, did at least one of these loud-mouthed champions of the left condemn the atrocities perpetrated by the Bolsheviks during the civil war in Russia? Of course not; these were invariably justified as historical inevitability. I recollect how the left intelligentsia wrote that "the birth of a child is always accompanied by pain, suffering and blood." So it behooves one to know what kind of child to have: if the baby is a "progressive" one, then the blood is justified. Incidentally, the left-liberal intelligentsia went into similar hysterical convulsions over neighboring Nicaragua. No effort was considered too great to help ensure victory for the Sandinistas and to wipe out all opposition. The US Congress dreamed up the most unbelievable stratagems in order to tie President Reagan's hands, to the accompaniment of a worldwide campaign of "solidarity" with little, defenseless Nicaragua, which had become "a victim of American aggression." In 1985, a group of friends and I addressed a petition to Congress[27] in which we ex-

---

[27]See *New York Times* (18 April 1985), *Frankfurter Allgemeine Zeitung* (30 March 1985), *Le Monde* (21 March 1985), *De Telegraaf* (27 March 1985), *Le Soir* (27 March 1985).

pressed our support for Reagan's policy in Nicaragua and pointed out, among other things, that the Sandinistas' aim was to establish a totalitarian, communist regime with the help of the USSR, and therefore Western democracies should support the opposition of the Nicaraguan people to this imposition. The outcry that this caused was hard to believe. What accusations were flung at us! At best, we were depicted as victims of paranoia, seeing Reds under every bed. Yet now, in black and white, I read:[28]

Secret

To CC CPSU

On the signing of a plan of ties between the CPSU and the Sandinista National Liberation Front (FSLN) of Nicaragua

At a meeting with the temporary Soviet charge-d'-affaires in Nicaragua (c/telegram from Managua, spec. #47 of 26.2.1980), member of the leadership of the FSLN, Henri Ruiz, suggested that CPSU and FSLN ties, to which the Nicaraguan side attributes great significance, should be discussed during the Nicaraguan Republic's party-government delegation's visit to the USSR.

The FSLN is the ruling political organization. The leadership of the FSLN considers it essential to establish a Marxist-Leninist party on the basis of the front, with the aim of building socialism in Nicaragua. At present, for tactical reasons and in view of the existing political situation in the Central American region, the leadership of the FSLN prefers to make no public statements about this ultimate goal.

We believe it would be possible to accept the offer made by the leadership of the FSLN, and suggest signing a plan of contacts between the CPSU and the FSLN for 1980–1981 during the delegation's visit to Moscow.

Expenses for undertakings arising from the bilateral ties plan could be covered by the party budget. The matter has been approved by comrade E.M. Tyazhelnikov.

Draft resolution of the CC CPSU appended.

Deputy Head of International Department
Deputy Head of the CC CPSU (K. Brutents)
Organizational & Party Work
of the CC CPSU (P. Smolsky)

14 March 1980
#25-S-458

So the revolution in Nicaragua occurred on 17 July 1979, and on

---

[28] 18 April 1980 (St 204/57)^.

19 March 1980 an agreement was signed in Moscow by Ponomarev on behalf of the CC CPSU, and the abovementioned Henri Ruiz for the FSLN. By December, the FSLN newspaper *Barricada* was already being printed on Soviet paper (15 October 1980, St 233/8), and up to one hundred Sandinista activists per annum were receiving "special training" in Moscow. At the time of our petition in 1985, this "small, defenseless country" was simply a Soviet puppet. Plain and simple. And yet the shouting. . . .

Actually, there is no reason to be writing about this in the past tense, for all these vocal champions of liberty are still thriving and trying to form public opinion. It has not entered their heads to repent, or at least apologize for the past. By no means! Investigations into the financing of the Contras continued in the USA till very recently. Even as I write these lines, a special commission of the UN, with the Orwellian name "The Truth Commission" has completed a review of events in El Salvador and censured the government for violations of human rights. The retirement of a number of officers has been recommended, but there has not been a single word about any "commanders of guerrilla units" or "commanders of sabotage units." Naturally, the conclusions of the commission make no mention of Soviet aggression, of the "special training" received in Moscow by communist thugs, of the delivery of "Western-manufactured" firearms—all this, mark you, a long time before Ronald Reagan became president of the USA—yet his administration is subjected to severe censure. And learning of the conclusions reached at such a high level, I could not help but wonder: has the Cold War ended, or not? And if it has—who won?

• • •

This is just one example of a small, jungle-covered country that nobody really needs. The thing is, there are hundreds of such examples. My table is covered with thousands of "resolutions" and "decisions" concerning dozens of countries, the whole blood-soaked history of our time. Only on rare occasions, by the whim of Fate, did the putative tragedy become a farce, which only served to stress the criminal nature of communist business (5 May 1974*, Pb 136/53).

Workers of the world, unite!

To be returned within 24 hours to the CC CPSU
(General Department, 1st section)

THE COMMUNIST PARTY OF THE SOVIET UNION.
CENTRAL COMMITTEE

TOP SECRET
Special File

To comrades Andropov, Ponomarev – all items
G. Pavlov – item 2.

Abstract from minutes #136 of the meeting of the Politburo of
5 May 1974

On aid to the Communist Party of Italy.

1. Satisfy the request of the leadership of the Italian Commu-
    nist Party and provide special training in the USSR to *19*
    Italian communists, including *6* for training in radio com-
    munications, work in *BR-3U* radio stations, training in ci-
    phering (up to 3 months), *2* instructors for the preparation
    of radio telegraphists and cipher officers (up to 3 months),
    9 in methods of party organization (up to 2 months) and *2*
    for a course in *disguise techniques* (up to two weeks), also
    the training of *1* specialist as a consultant on special types
    of internal broadcasting (up to one week).

2. Reception and maintenance of the trainees is to be the re-
    sponsibility of the International Department and the Ad-
    ministrative sector of the CC CPSU. The Committee for
    State Security of the Council of Ministers of the USSR will
    be responsible for training in radio and ciphering work and
    for providing interpreters for all special training programs.
    Training in matters of party organization and in *disguise*
    techniques will be the responsibility of the International
    Department of the CC CPSU and the Committee for State
    Security of the Council of Ministers of the USSR. Expenses
    connected with the stay [of the Italians] in the USSR and
    their travel to Moscow and back is to be charged to the
    budget for reception of foreign party workers.

3. The Committee for State Security of the Council of Min-
    isters of the USSR is charged with developing a commu-
    nications program and ciphered documents for one-way
    radio transmissions of circular ciphered telegrams to *13–
    16* regional centers of the Communist Party of Italy, and
    also ciphered documents for reciphering within the two-
    way radio network.

4. Satisfy the request of the leadership of the PCI and prepare
    500 blank and *50* named (for senior PCI workers) forms of
    Italian foreign and internal documents, *50* spare sets of
    the same documents modeled on Swiss and French sam-
    ples, also wigs and *disguise necessities*. Preparation of the
    forms and *disguise necessities* will be the responsibility
    of the International Department of the CC CPSU and the
    Committee for State Security of the Council of Ministers of
    the USSR.

5. Approve text of telegram to the KGB resident in Italy.

SECRETARY OF THE CC

The story goes that, back in 1974, the Italian communists raised such a hullabaloo about a possible right-wing coup, that they finally came to believe in it themselves. And, having done so, they sent tearful pleas to Moscow to help them prepare to go underground. One can imagine how the comrades in the Kremlin laughed at the mental picture of fifty Italian comrades sneaking across France in wigs and false beards, for all the world like the villains in a comic opera, clutching French passports forged by the KGB! One can only speculate on whether the training by the International Department included lessons on how to gesticulate in the French manner.

But this is just a rare amusing exception to the overall grim rule. Usually there is nothing to smile about in such documents. On the contrary, their dry, official clichés only hint at pictures of death and destruction, so familiar to everyone from nightly television news broadcasts over the past thirty years. Almost every such tragedy had its beginnings in a neatly typed CC resolution, voted on in the customary round-robin manner, with the invariable clarion call "Workers of the world, unite!" in the right-hand corner. Even I was amazed by the scope of this murderous activity across five continents. Even Hitler could not have dreamed up something like this. The tempest they unleashed swept away millions of lives in Ethiopia, Vietnam, and Central America; it will rage on in Angola, Sudan, Somalia, and Afghanistan long after the last communist regime vanishes from the face of the earth.

The Middle East is a part of the globe where blood and violence have become so commonplace that nobody recalls now what started it all. Only recently, as a consequence of the Gulf War, has there been renewed consideration of the role played in that region for decades by the Soviet Union, and its support of the regime of Saddam Hussein. Yet this is only one aspect of its long-term strategy, and not the worst at that. Lebanon, for instance, was almost annihilated as a state with the Soviet Union's participation. "Special assistance" for Lebanese "friends" began at the end of the 1960s and continued, in grandiose proportions, right up to our times. The supply of arms, usually channeled through Syria, goes back to at least 1970, and by 1975 had grown so immense that one delivery consisted of six hundred Kalashnikov submachine guns, fifty machine guns, thirty antitank RPG-7s, three thousand hand grenades, two thousand mines and two tons of explosives (10 October 1975, Pb 192/6). By the mid-1980s, the Soviet Union was training at least two hundred Lebanese thugs per annum, of whom 170 were activists of the Lebanese communist party and thirty of the Progressive Socialist Party (9 February 1987**, St 39/65).[29]

Another example is Cyprus, where the same "special assistance" was rendered to the Progressive Workers' Party from 1971 at least,[30] and the delivery of arms began right before the outbreak of civil war, in July 1974 (8 June 1974, 1853-A).

Finally, Palestinian terrorism, for which there were vehement denials of any connection by the Soviet leadership and its Western apologists. A number of eloquent documents can be found below (23 April 1974*, 1071-A/ov):

Top Secret
SPECIAL IMPORTANCE
Special File

USSR Committee for state security of the
Council of ministers of the USSR

23 April 1974
MOSCOW

TO Comrade L.I. BREZHNEV

Since 1968, the KGB has maintained a secret working contact with *Wadie Haddad, Politburo member* of the Popular Front for the Liberation of Palestine (PFLP), *head of the PFLP's external operations section.*

In a confidential conversation at a meeting with the KGB resident in *Lebanon* in April of this year, *Wadie Haddad* outlined a prospective program of sabotage and terrorism by the PFLP, which can be defined as follows.

The main aim of special actions by the PFLP is to increase the effectiveness of the struggle of the Palestinian movement against Israel, Zionism and American imperialism. Arising from this, the main thrusts of the planned sabotage and terrorist operations are:

- employing special means to prolong the "oil war" of Arab countries against the imperialist forces supporting Israel,

- carrying out operations against American and Israeli personnel in other countries with the aim of securing reliable information about the plans and intentions of the USA and Israel,

- carrying out acts of sabotage and terrorism on the territory of Israel,

- organizing acts of sabotage against the diamond center, whose basic capital derives from Israeli, British, Belgian and West German companies.

---

[29]See also 20 April 1985 (318/5/0219).
[30]19 July 1971 (St 10/53)^.

In order to implement the above measures, the PFLP is currently preparing a number of special operations, including strikes against large oil storage installations in various countries (Saudi Arabia, the Persian Gulf, Hong Kong et al), the destruction of oil tankers and supertankers, actions against American and Israeli representatives in Iran, Greece, Ethiopia, Kenya, an attack on the Diamond Center in Tel Aviv, etc.

W. Haddad asks that we help his organization with the procurement of several kinds of special technology necessary for carrying out certain sabotage operations.

Cooperating with us and appealing for our help, *W. Haddad* is fully aware of our opposition to terrorism in principle, and does not pose us any questions connected with this sphere of the PFLP's activity.

The nature of our relations with *W. Haddad* allows us a degree of control over the activities of the PFLP's *external operations section*, to exercise an influence favorable to the USSR, and also to reach some of our own aims, through the activities of the PFLP while observing the necessary secrecy.

In view of the above, we feel it would be feasible, at the next meeting, to give a generally favorable response to *Wadie Haddad's* request for special assistance to the PFLP. As for concrete questions of supplying aid, it is envisaged that every instance will be decided on an individual basis, bearing in mind the interests of the Soviet Union and preventing any detriment to the security of our country.

We request authorization.

CHAIRMAN OF THE COMMITTEE FOR STATE SECURITY
ANDROPOV

Across the top of the first page, Brezhnev wrote in by hand:

Report to Comrades Suslov, M.A.   Podgorny N.V.   Kosygin A.N.
Grechko A.A.   Gromyko A.A.   (circulate)

The signatures of the named comrades, in the above order, follow Brezhnev's in the left-hand margin. At the end of the last page, there is a handwritten addition: "Consent reported to the KGB of the USSR (comrade Laptev P.P.) 26.IV.74."

Obviously, they did not feel that the interests of the Soviet Union were under any threat, because the romance with Haddad continued. In September of that year the Politburo even sanctioned his secret visit to Moscow and gave its blessing to further cooperation (16 May 1975*, 1218-A/ov):

Special Importance

Special File

USSR COMMITTEE for State Security
of the Council of Ministers of the USSR

16 May 1975
MOSCOW

To Comrade BREZHNEV, L.I.

In accordance with the decision of the CC CPSU, on 14 May the Committee for State Security gave trusted KGB intelligence agent, *W. Haddad*, head of the external operations section of the Popular Front for the Liberation of *Palestine*, a consignment of foreign-produced arms and ammunition (submachine guns— 53, hand guns—50 including 10 fitted with silencers, ammunition—34,000 rounds).

The covert delivery of arms was carried out in the neutral waters of the Gulf of Aden at night, with no direct contact, and with full observance of secrecy by an intelligence-gathering vessel of the navy of the USSR.

W. Haddad is the only foreigner who knows that the arms were supplied by us.

CHAIRMAN OF THE COMMITTEE FOR STATE SECURITY
ANDROPOV

Naturally, the Politburo had dealings not only with the PFLP but with other terrorist organizations, including the Palestine Liberation Organization, to which, at Yasser Arafat's request, it even supplied "special equipment" in Tunisia in 1983 (21 June 1983**, Pb 113/110). Apparently they were not even squeamish about buying stolen goods from the Palestinians, or rather exchanging them for weapons (27 November 1984*, Pb 185/49):

Workers of the world, unite!

To be returned within 3 days to the CC CPSU
(General Department, 1st section)

COMMUNIST PARTY OF THE SOVIET UNION.
CENTRAL COMMITTEE.

TOP SECRET
SPECIAL FILE
Special Importance

FOR YOUR EYES ONLY

To comrades Ustinov, [Viktor] Chebrikov—all
[Pyotr] Demichev—p.p. 2v,4,
Sergeychik—p.3,
Garbuzov—p.4 (condensed)

Abstract from minutes #185 of a meeting of the Politburo of the CC CPSU of 27 November 1984

Request by the Ministry of Defense and the Committee for State Security of the USSR.

1. To endorse the suggestions of the Ministry of Defense and the Committee for State Security of the USSR, set out in a memorandum of 26 November 1984.

2. Instruct the KGB of the USSR to:

   a) inform the leadership of the Democratic Front for the Liberation of Palestine (DFLP) of the Soviet side's agreement in principle to supply the DFLP with special equipment to the sum of 15 million rubles in exchange for a collection of art objects of the Ancient World,

   b) accept DFLP requests for delivery of special equipment within the limits of the above-named sum,

   c) join forces with the Ministry of Culture of the USSR in taking the necessary steps concerning the legal side of acquiring the collection of artifacts.

3. Charge the State Committee for Economic Relations and the Ministry of Defense with studying the request of the Democratic Front for the Liberation of Palestine for special equipment to the sum of 15 million rubles (within the scope of the nomenclature permitted for supplies to national liberation movements), forwarded via the KGB of the USSR, and record suggestions for their fulfillment, approved by the KGB of the USSR, in the standard fashion.

4. Instruct the Ministry of Culture of the USSR to:

   a) receive a collection of art objects of the Ancient World, detailed in a special list, from the KGB of the USSR.

   b) in consultation with the KGB of the USSR, determine the place and special conditions for housing the collection ("golden store"), its secret expert study and future exhibition. In consultation with the Ministry of Finance of the USSR, submit an estimate according to standard procedure for the necessary financial assignations,

   c) confer with the KGB of the USSR about the individual or group displays of the collection.

SECRETARY OF THE CC

On a recent visit to Moscow I tried to find some traces of this collection. Apparently most of it is housed, still sealed, in a safe in the Kremlin Armory. Nobody got around to opening it, and at present nobody dares to touch it, even though the Politburo and the KGB no longer exist. So it is still a mystery what is in this collection and where it was stolen from. It would also be interesting to learn how many people were killed with the "special equipment" it paid for.

1.6   Sympathizers and Fellow Travelers

It's highly unlikely that we will ever learn the answers to these questions. The movers and shakers of today have little interest in digging for the truth. Who knows what one may come up with? You may start out with the communists and end up with yourself. As the English wisely say, people who live in glass houses shouldn't throw stones. This saying is well remembered. Yes, of course, it is not a good thing that the communists received handouts from Moscow. But were they the only ones? Here, for example, is a resolution of the CC CPSU concerning "Fulfilment of a request by American public figure and financier Cyrus Eaton to be presented with a new troika of horses by the Soviet government."[31] One might expect that such a well-to-do gentleman would be in a position to buy the horses he fancied without going bankrupt.[32] But think of the honor and glory: a present from the Soviet government! So he managed to wangle this "present" in order to raise his prestige. And this was in September 1968, just as Soviet troops were invading Czechoslovakia, so most likely he was able to drive his troika grandly across American soil at the same time that Soviet tanks were rolling around Prague. Any more questions to the communists about handouts?

Yes, the communists were undoubtedly agents of evil, and spread communist lies throughout the free world for money. But were they alone? I have a whole stack of documents which show how this was also practiced by most of the world's leading television companies, who even paid the USSR hard currency for the privilege (27 August 1966*)!

Secret
Copy #1

To the CC CPSU

The Novosti Press Agency [APN] has received a request from representatives of the American television company ABC concerning the creation of a joint special television report on the life of

---

[31] 20 September 1968 (1712, St 13/9)^.

[32] The Pugwash Conference took its name from the small fishing community in Nova Scotia (Canada) where Eaton grew up. He hosted the first conference there in July 1957.

a worker's family from the "Rostselmash" factory in Rostov-on-Don. The film will show various aspects of the life of a working-class family, and the family will be used to illustrate the achievements of the Soviet government over the past 50 years.

The film will be shown to APN for approval before it appears on television. The Radio and Television Committee (comrade Mesyatsev) has no objections to the project.

We believe it would be feasible to accept the company's offer.

Request authorization.

V. Zaychikov
First deputy chairman of the
Press Agency Novost Administration
23 August 1966

Or the following (6 March 1967*):

Secret
Copy 1
Ex. #170c
6.3.67

To the CC CPSU

The senior APN correspondent in the USA, comrade G.A. Borovik, has carried out a preliminary sounding about the possibility of broadcasting a program about Vietnam by one of the largest American television corporations. The program is based on Soviet documentary films with a commentary by G.A. Borovik. The company will pay 9–27 thousand dollars for the program.

The US section of the Foreign Ministry of the USSR (comrade G.M. Kornienko) supports comrade Borovik's suggestion and considers it essential that the commentary to the program should be approved by the Foreign Ministry.

"Sovexportfilm" (comrade A.B. Makhov) has consented to the inclusion of Soviet documentary footage on Vietnam into the program.

The administration of APN considers that it would be feasible to:

1. Endorse comrade G.A. Borovik's offer concerning the preparation of a television program on Vietnam for American television, bearing in mind that the commentary to the program shall be vetted by the Foreign Ministry of the USSR.

2. Authorize comrade G.A. Borovik to negotiate with American television companies concerning broadcasting of the

program on propagandist and economic terms favorable to
us.

We request authorization.

B. Burkov

Chairman of the Administration
of the Novosti Press Agency

4 March 1967.

Imagine the situation: American soldiers are fighting against Soviet "friends" in Vietnam, and in the meantime, a leading American
network is buying a Soviet propaganda film about that country. And
so it went, from year to year, and not only in the USA. It happened
in Japan, in Britain, in Finland, in France. The subjects were as
varied as the sums in hard currency, with only one basic condition
remaining unchanged: "note that according to the terms of the contract, the film may be shown on American [British, Japanese, etc.]
television only after it has been approved by APN." There is such an
amount of material on this that I finally gave up noting it down.

Here is a brief résumé of what I did record:

- 6 January 1969. On APN negotiations with the *New
  York Times* on the joint preparation of materials about the
  USSR in 1969–70.

- 30 July 1970. On the joint television program "In the Land
  of the Soviets" by APN and American producer J. Fleming."

- 20 May 1971. Joint APN and Granada (England) television
  program "Soviet Woman".

- 26 May 1971. Joint APN and BBC television program "The
  Culture and Art of Georgia."

- 28 December 1971. On TASS [major Russian news agency]
  negotiations with Reuters.

- 22 August 1972. On joint APN and Granada filming on
  "The Education System in the USSR."

- 13 March 1973. Joint APN and BBC film about Novgorod.

- 28 June 1973. On the joint APN and BBC production of
  the film "Kiev: city, events, people."

- 10 July 1973. On the joint APN and Thames Television
  production of a 4-part series about the role of the USSR
  in World War Two.

- 24 October 1973. On the joint production by APN and the
  BBC of a documentary film about Shostakovich.

- 27 May 1974. On the shooting of a BBC television program on matters of European security under the control of the State Committee for Radio and Television.

- 18 June 1974. On the joint APN and BBC filming of the television program "Lake Baikal."

- 14 February 1975. On production assistance and consultation to the BBC in the making of a feature film about the Soviet conductor [Boris] Aleksandrov.

- 9 April 1976.[33] On the joint APN and Weekend Television production of the program "The Soviet Union After the 25th Congress of the CPSU."

- 26 May 1976.[34] On the joint production by APN and Yorkshire Television of a film about "A Soviet Family."

- 10 July 1979 (St-166/12). On production and consultation assistance to the American television company PTV Productions Inc. in filming a multi-series documentary film about the museums, architecture and historical monuments of the USSR.

- 3 April 1980 (St-205/31). On production and consultation assistance to the American company Foreign Transactions Corporation in creating a series of documentary films devoted to the cultural program of the 1980 Olympic Games in Moscow.

- 1 July 1980. On production and consultation assistance to the English television company Granada in filming a documentary on the history of Soviet cinema (1 July 1980, St 17/10).

You may ask: What's wrong with that? It's a perfectly innocent subject. But you would be wrong, for the Soviet embassy was of the opinion that "a series of films about Soviet cinema could have a desirable propaganda effect, especially in view of the current situation in England."

It is sad but true that Western television companies, who are always so proud of their independence, systematically carried out productions under the ideological control of the CC CPSU, and even paid hard cash for it. To put it plainly, they served as channels for Soviet propaganda. So it is hardly likely that they will censure communists who did exactly the same thing, only in the line of duty to their party.

Beyond any doubt, the activities of the communists undermined and threatened the security of the West. But in this dangerous

---

[33]9 April 1976 (St 5/6)^.
[34]26 May 1976 (St 10/23)^.

game, they were not the only ones to dance to Moscow's piping. Let us recall at least the mass marches of the "peace movement," and even those for unilateral disarmament. Millions of people were infected by this madness, including a significant part of the intelligentsia. They will hardly wish to dig out the archives that contain the indisputable proof of their folly. I wrote a book[35] at the time about Moscow's cynical manipulation of this movement, which became a virtual instrument of Soviet foreign policy. It is amusing to recall how the liberal intelligentsia castigated me for this book. Now we have the documents that justify every word I wrote, but nobody wants to publish them.

There are some documents I never expected to see. For instance, documents concerning the foundation and work of the Independent Commission on Disarmament and Security Issues, the so-called Palme Commission. Created on the initiative of Olof Palme, in between his two terms as the prime minister of Sweden, this organization rapidly became the most authoritative Western forum on matters of disarmament and security. One of the most important reasons for this was the committee's reputation of being an objective non-government body, independent of any blocs, and also the high profile of its members. Apart from Palme himself, it included such prominent politicians of differing political views as former US secretary of state Cyrus Vance, former British foreign secretary David Owen, former German minister of special affairs Egon Bahr, General Obasanjo of Nigeria, former prime minister of the Netherlands Joop den Uyl, etc. In other words, it was a veritable political Olympus of that time, whose opinions could not be ignored by all Western governments. Alas, this Olympus also proved to be a Soviet instrument "to promote, in influential political circles of the non-socialist part of the world, Soviet proposals for the end of the arms race and to expose the militaristic policies of the US leadership and NATO" (10 November 1980, 18-S-1989).[36] The instrument was so successful, that it seems to have tried too hard — it began to be accused of prejudice: "Many of the proposals and recommendations approved and adopted by the Committee for inclusion in the final document reflect the Soviet position on the key issues of disarmament and security in direct or indirect form," stated the Soviet delegate, Georgy Arbatov, in his report to the Central Committee (28 December 1981, No. 0147). "However, despite agreeing gener-

---

[35]Vladimir Bukovsky, "The Peace Movement & the Soviet Union", *Commentary*, 1 May 1982 (published as a separate booklet by The Orwell Press, London, 1982). https://commentarymagazine.com/article/the-peace-movement-the-soviet-union/

[36]14 November 1980 (St 237/54), p. 4.

ally with the Soviet point of view on many issues, such members of the Committee as C. Vance, D. Owen, E. Bahr and a number of others tried to avoid wording which would be an exact repetition of Soviet terminology, and explained in private conversations that they had to beware of accusations that they are following 'Moscow policies'" (indicating, in this connection, that a number of articles had appeared in the Western press, particularly in the USA, which accused the Palme Commission of just that).

As God is my witness, "paranoid" though I may be, I never would have expected such cynicism, especially from Dr. David Owen. However, he is not the only prominent personality whom I had respected and who proved to be a bitter disappointment. Much as I would like to spare them, and not mention their names, I do not think I have the right to do so. Here is a document which I found extremely upsetting (17 July 1979*, St 167/18):

Secret

To the CC CPSU

During the Soviet Goskino [State Committee for Cinematography] delegation's stay in Cannes (France) at the 32nd International Film Festival in May this year, there was a meeting with the prominent American producer and director Francis Ford Coppola.

F. Coppola told the chairman of Goskino of the USSR that he had a discussion with the President of the United Sates, J. Carter, who expressed an interest in the making of a joint Soviet-American film on disarmament. According to F. Coppola, the president linked this project with the forthcoming summit meeting in Vienna and the signature and ratification of the second treaty on the limitation of strategic arms (SALT II). The American side feels that such a film would promote the growth of mutual trust between the Soviet and the American peoples, the formation of a positive international appraisal of this treaty, and serve the further development of Soviet-American cultural cooperation.

Speaking for his own firm, Zoetrope Studios [Omni Zoetrope], F. Coppola offered to undertake the financial and organizational requirements for the American side. As F. Coppola is acknowledged as one of the most influential American cinematographers in both business and creative circles, his participation could serve as a certain guarantee of high artistic merit and widespread distribution of the film.

If agreement is reached, the Soviet side will reserve the right to exercise control over the ideological and artistic content of the film at all stages of its production. The most outstanding cinema workers could be assigned to write the scenario and carry out the filming. On such terms, it would be feasible to agree to a joint Soviet-American production of such a film.

With a view to its practical realization, it is imperative at this stage to enter into negotiations with F. Coppola and sign a preliminary agreement, which could be done when he comes to the 9th International Cinema Festival in Moscow in August this year.

I request a study of this proposal.

Chairman of Goskino of the USSR
F.T. Yermash.

I was unable to find out whether Francis Ford Coppola made this film, but can only hope that he did not, that something happened to prevent it. It is too distressing to think of this wonderful director making a film on disarmament under the ideological and artistic control of the Kremlin "godfathers." But one thing is crystal clear: neither the press, nor the business world, nor public celebrities, nor the cultural heroes of the West managed to preserve their chastity. And although communism has collapsed, they have remained pillars of society, the establishment. They are the most vociferous now in claiming that the Cold War is over, but they refuse to specify who the losers were. Even as I sit at my desk, the BBC World Service broadcasts an episode from a series about the Cold War, and I am astounded by their cynicism: the same names, the same tired clichés about "anti-communist paranoia," about "McCarthyism," about the poor intelligentsia (Western, of course) that suffered such persecution.... Not a shadow of regret, not the smallest effort to reassess its past, not a grain of truth. Unbidden, lines from one of Alexander Galich's poems come to mind:

And marauders stood around the grave
As guards of honor. . . .

• • •

No matter how cynical one may be, it is extremely naive to think that we can step over mountains of corpses, wade through rivers of blood and keep going, without looking back, as though nothing has happened. The past will inevitably come to haunt us, poisoning public life for generations. Yet our "marauders" do not care about the future; all they want is to preserve their position right now, by suppressing the truth at any cost, albeit for just a few more years. And, so far, they have been remarkably successful, all the vaunted freedom of the press notwithstanding.

The best illustration I can offer is the fate of this book in the United States. It was bought by Random House in 1995 for a considerable amount of money, but the contract was not finalized or signed by the publisher right away. Instead its senior editor, one Jason Epstein, tried — for the next five months! — to force me to rewrite the whole book from the political perspective of the liberal left.[37] Oh no, he did not say in so many words that he simply disagrees with me politically — on the contrary, in almost every fax I received he emphasized his sympathy for my views — he just wanted to "improve" the book by correcting "several misstatements of fact and overstatements." You see, "American readers will be surprised to read" this or that, they "would not understand"....

"You have written an important book, whose message should not be weakened by... overstatements and unproven assertions. ... The contribution that you make in your book toward an understanding of the Cold War will be much strengthened if you will consider the editorial suggestions I have made here...."

The trouble was that his "suggestions" concerned the very basic concepts of the book:

"Is there really any doubt about who lost the Cold War? Your suggestion that there is will puzzle American readers, since everyone here assumes that we won and the Russians lost. ... Nor did the Soviets come close to winning the Cold War, so your remarks to the contrary will be puzzling."

"One of our readers alerted me to the fact that you seriously misrepresent the meaning and significance of the Helsinki [Accords]... [which was] a win-win document for the West."

"It will also surprise American readers to learn that such 'liberal' foundations as Ford, Rockefeller, etc. gave 'billions' to the peace movement. This simply isn't true and will lead Americans to mistrust your argument in general. Similarly, your criticism of Helsinki Watch that it worried more about problems in the US than in the USSR is untrue and will offend American readers."

In vain I tried to explain that my "misrepresentation" of the Helsinki agreement is in fact a prevalent opinion among Russian dissidents, publicly expressed by us on numerous occasions; that the source of my information on the "liberal" foundations' policy in the 1980s is a *New York Times* article (which, in turn, quoted the pres-

---

[37] In the late 1960s Epstein reacted indignantly to revelations about covert funding of the American Committee for Cultural Freedom. See Jason Epstein, "The CIA and the Intellectuals," *New York Review of Books*, 20 April 1967. https://www.nybooks.com/articles/1967/04/20/the-cia-and-the-intellectuals/

ident of the Rockefeller Brothers Fund),[38] while the source on the
Helsinki Watch is one of Random House's own publications. As for
"surprising" the American public, I firmly responded that I would
not mind that:[39]

"I suspect they ought to be surprised quite a lot if they are to
learn the truth about the Cold War. In fact, I will be delighted if
they are surprised: I could never understand the motivation of an
author who writes unsurprising books."

All to no avail. Mr. Epstein objected to almost everything else in
the book: my "supercilious tone," my "rhetoric," my "treatment of
documents," and, ultimately, the documents themselves. Some of
those objections verged on the absurd:

"... I think you are making more of the Sorsa memorandum
than the language justifies. Was Sorsa really "Moscow's Man," or
merely someone who maintained positions congenial to the USSR
but was otherwise his 'own man'?"

"As for the memorandum concerning ABC..., the real issue here
is that... ABC may have agreed to submit the film for approval to
Soviet censors. Did ABC actually do this? ... If the film was made,
was it Soviet propaganda? ... It is of course perfectly normal that
in a joint production both sides should have the right to approve the
final product, and if either side insists on language unacceptable to
the other, the project is terminated. There is nothing sinister here
in principle, but there would be if the resulting product amounted
to Soviet propaganda."

"I don't understand what you mean... when you say that the
press, the business world, etc. failed to preserve their chastity. If
you mean to imply that the press, etc. were in the service of the
USSR, nobody here will take you seriously."

But his particularly vehement objections were provoked by some
documents concerning Western public figures, such as:

"... the memorandum about Francis Ford Coppola. ... It
should be easy for you to learn whether Coppola made such a film
and agreed to accept Soviet censorship. Mr. Coppola is an important figure in the US, as you know, and a letter or phone call from
you to him would settle the matter."

In short, I was required, in no uncertain terms, to drop some
documents while reinterpreting others in order to show that "...
the Soviets failed and their attempts at manipulation seem now, in
retrospect, to have been pathetic or even comical. What strikes me

---

[38]Kathleen Teltsch, "Philanthropies Focus Concern on Arms Race," *New York
Times*, 25 March 1984, A.1.

[39]Faxed letter from Vladimir Bukovsky to Jason Epstein, 5 October 1995.

in the documents you reproduce—and will strike other American readers as well—is how clumsy, self-deceiving and stupid these Russians were."

That was clearly beyond my level of tolerance. So, politely but firmly, I explained to Mr. Epstein[40] that "due to certain peculiarities of my biography, I am allergic to political censorship."

"Surely, Mr. Epstein, we do not need to prove that a documentary on the life of a 'worker's family' in Rostov-on-Don, or the one on the 'Soviet Woman,' made under Soviet supervision and with their approval, couldn't be anything but Soviet propaganda (not to mention the one on Vietnam, with the text approved by the Soviet Foreign Ministry). How would you feel, Mr. Epstein, about a film on 'German Woman' made with the approval of Dr. Goebbels in 1938? Would you need specific proof that it is, indeed, Nazi propaganda? Would you demand such proof from a survivor of Auschwitz?

"Surely, you do not expect me to falsify history in order to please your liberal readers? For if you do, you are going to be disappointed. And if you don't, why do you insist on your own interpretation of the Soviet efforts as 'pathetic,' 'comical' or 'clumsy'? Since I am the author of this book, I will be the judge of whether the 'Russians' were self-deceiving and stupid, or clever and cunning. And, somehow, I do not recall anyone laughing at them at the time (including your liberal readers)."

Furthermore, I explained that only he and his friends seem to be puzzled by my concept of the Cold War.

"I can think of a few more (most of them could be found among the so-called 'liberal Left'), who have strived all these years to present the Cold War as some obscure quarrel between the 'Russians' and 'Americans.' The rest of the world perceived it as an ideological confrontation between communist dogma and democracy, between the communists and their sympathizers on the one hand, and the democrats on the other. Only if you accept this concept will you understand why, despite the collapse of the Soviet Union, the communists are still in power in Russia, in almost all former Soviet republics, in Poland, Hungary, Rumania, Bulgaria, while their accomplices in the West are still very much a part of the establishment."

As for his suggestion to call Coppola and ask him about the documentary on disarmament, I advised him in return to call Arbatov and find out how much his memo on the Palme Commission proceedings was "self-serving."

---

[40]Faxed letter from Vladimir Bukovsky to Jason Epstein, 27 December 1995.

This was our last exchange; Mr. Epstein dropped the contract. In his short parting message he wrote:

"I don't want to involve myself in a quarrelsome editorial relationship. From your letter it seems certain that were we to proceed, such a relationship would be inevitable. ... The last thing I want to do is challenge your politics, with which in any case I don't disagree, but I simply can't publish a book that accuses Americans like Cyrus Vance and Francis Ford Coppola of unpatriotic—or even treacherous—behavior."

Do I need to add that Random House is one of the biggest and most influential publishers in America, whose rejection of a book is bound to affect any other attempts to publish it? In fact, it was nearly two years before I could find anyone interested either in the USA or in Britain, while the book had already been successfully published in France and Germany.

But the most disturbing aspect of the story is that this blatant attempt at political censorship in a country so proud of its freedom did not provoke public indignation there. I talked to many journalists and public figures, offering them my correspondence with Mr. Epstein as proof; they shrugged it off. So what? Who cares?

As someone has recently said so aptly:

"This is worse than a conspiracy—this is consensus."

1.7   So who won?

Thus ended this war, probably the strangest war of all in our times. It began with no declaration and ended without celebratory firework displays. It is not even possible to put a precise date and time to its start and finish, and even though it probably swallowed more lives than World War Two, we do not want to total up its victims. No monuments will be erected to mark this war, no eternal flame will burn on the grave of its unknown soldier. Even though this war was decisive to the fate of all humanity, its soldiers didn't march off to the sounds of a band, nor were they greeted with flowers upon their return. It was probably the most unpopular war of all those we know. At least, from the point of view of the side that seems to have won it. But there is no rejoicing now it is over. The losers signed no instruments of capitulation, the victors received no rewards. On the contrary, it is the very ones who, for all intents and purposes, were the losers, who are now dictating terms for peace, writing history, while those who supposedly won maintain an embarrassed silence. And do we really know who the victors are? Who are the vanquished?

Any event in our lives, even if it is of small significance, comes under the scrutiny of some commission or other. Especially if people have been killed. A plane crash, a railroad disaster, an industrial accident—and experts argue, conduct analyses, seek to determine the degree of guilt of contractors, builders, service personnel, conductors, inspectors, or even governments if they had the slightest connection with what occurred. As for any armed conflict between countries—that will certainly not escape examination. Yet here we have a conflict that lasted at least forty-five years (possibly even seventy-five), that affected practically every country in the world, cost scores of millions in lives and hundreds of billions in dollars, and—as has so often been claimed—almost brought about global destruction, which is not being examined by a single country or international organization.

Even a petty crime is subject to investigation, judgment, and punishment. War crimes are no exception. I am not talking about the Nuremberg Trials and subsequent hearings which, to this day, are obliged to investigate crimes committed fifty years ago. There is a current example: the war in Bosnia is not over yet, but there is already an international tribunal to investigate the crimes committed in it. Again, our strange war is an exception to the rule—is it over or not? Did we win, or did we lose?

Actually, in many cases it is not even necessary to convene a special court: for example, the murder of captive Polish officers in Katyn Forest was already acknowledged as a crime against humanity at the Nuremberg Trials. Yet the man in charge of the execution —the former head of one of the directorates of the People's Commissariat for Internal Affairs (NKVD), Pyotr Soprunenko—is still alive and well in Moscow on a good pension. Everyone knows this, Muscovites willingly point out the windows of his apartment in a house on the Garden Ring. MGB investigator Daniil Kopelyansky, who interrogated Raoul Wallenberg, is also thriving, as is the organizer of Trotsky's assassination, Lieutenant General Pavel Sudoplatov, but neither Poland nor Sweden nor Mexico are seeking the extradition of these criminals. A recent example is former KGB general Oleg Kalugin, who, on his own admission, organized the murder of Bulgarian dissident Georgi Markov in London in 1978—the famous case of the poisoned umbrella. Kalugin even wrote about this not so long ago in the popular British tabloid *Mail on Sunday* under the challenging headline "I Organized Markov's Execution." Kalugin furnishes some fascinating details: it appears that the grateful Bulgarian "brothers" rewarded him with a hunting rifle. He frequently travels abroad, promotes his book, gives interviews to the press—and it never enters anyone's head to arrest or question him, even though the Markov case is still open.

In any case, thousands of thugs who received KGB "special train-ing" are still at large and live next door to us, just like those who received illegal funds, like the "commercial" friends, like millions of sympathizers and accomplices, apologists and concealers, millions who set the intellectual fashion that dictates that while everyone is equal, the communists are more equal than others. All of these would not be too hard to locate, given the desire to do so. At least, they would be much easier to find than former Nazis in Paraguay. But nobody will tackle this task for one simple reason:

There has to be a victory before the setting up of a Nuremberg-style international tribunal.

Rudolf Hess died in Spandau Prison but Boris Ponomarev, for instance, is a pensioner at liberty in Moscow, all because National Socialism was defeated, but International Socialism was not.

It was easier with Nazism. It was more straightforward in its reliance on brute force and made less effort to masquerade as hu-manism. It forced its neighbors to resist, and they, although un-willing at first, took up the challenge. Yet imagine if the "phony war," which began in 1939, had stretched out over the next forty to fifty years with no further military action. Life would have gone on as usual, despite a certain coldness in relations with Germany. In time, the regime would have "mellowed": there would have been no-body left to put in concentration camps or destroy in gas chambers. Eventually domestic reformers would be launched (especially af-ter Hitler's death), then proponents of "peaceful coexistence" would appear (especially after Germany had developed nuclear weapons). Trade would grow, as would common interests. In other words, the Nazi regime would become quite respectable without changing its nature by one iota, acquire contacts and well-wishers, fellow travel-ers and apologists. And then collapse some fifty years later, having exhausted its economic resources and the patience of its people. I would wager that with such a scenario, there would have been no Nuremberg Trials.

But it all happened otherwise. Having found the courage to resist evil, humanity also found enough decency to take a hard look into its own soul and, no matter how painful the process, to condemn all manifestations of collaboration. Yes, it was easier for them, they won, they had something to be proud of, they had a moral right to judge those who capitulated. The Nuremberg Trials are not beyond criticism, but their accomplishment was immense—they restored the absolute moral norms for human behavior, they reminded a shattered world of the basic principle of our Christian civilization: that we have freedom of choice and, consequently, bear personal responsibility for how we exercise it. At a time of mass madness and total terror, they affirmed a simple truth, known from Biblical times and lost in the scarlet tribulations of the twentieth century: neither the opinion of the surrounding majority nor an order from a superior nor even a threat to one's own life releases one from personal responsibility.

But what is happening today is in direct contrast to Nuremberg. Today's world has nothing of which to be proud, it found neither the courage to withstand evil nor the honesty to admit it. Our misfortune lies in that we did not win: communism fell by itself, despite universal efforts to rescue it. And this, if you like, is the greatest secret of the Central Committee documents lying on my desk. So is it really surprising that nobody wants to publish them?

Is it so surprising that alongside our willingness to examine every accident, we refuse to investigate the greatest catastrophe of our time? For in our heart of hearts we already know the conclusions such an investigation would yield, as any sane person knows full well when he has entered into collusion with evil. Even if the intellect provides specious logical and outwardly acceptable excuses, the voice of conscience whispers that our fall began from the moment we agreed to "peaceful coexistence" with evil.

This manifested itself even before Nuremberg, when Stalin was acclaimed as a great champion of democracy, and at Nuremberg, where the Soviet Union ranked as a member of the prosecution and not of the accused, and in the late 1950s and early 1960s, when Nikita Khrushchev's term "peaceful coexistence" entered the political lexicon. And every time, the price was paid with the blood of the innocent—the accepted currency in deals with the devil: the blood of the Cossacks handed over to Stalin for reprisals, the blood of the nations of Eastern Europe betrayed by the Yalta Agreement, the blood of the Hungarians, Cubans, Cambodians. . . .

But the final deal with the powers of evil was struck in our own time, when Brezhnev was in power. It is useless to plead innocence and seek justification by claiming ignorance of the means to combat that evil; everything was patently obvious. In circumstances where we refused to maintain "good neighborly relations" with evil, where it was rejected as unacceptable, we knew perfectly well what to do. And if racism, for example, was such an evil, nobody sought to combat it by increasing trade or cultural cooperation with South Africa. On the contrary, a boycott was deemed the only adequate response, and it was enforced so strictly that not a single sportsman could go there without destroying his career. Yet it was considered acceptable to attend the Olympic Games in Moscow at the height of mass arrests and aggression in Afghanistan. I should like to see what would have happened to anyone who had dared to suggest holding the Olympic Games in Johannesburg or Pretoria at that time!

Moreover, as racism was proclaimed an evil, not a single newspaper would publish anything written by supporters of apartheid, all proud proclamations about freedom of the press notwithstanding. Racist groups were subject to open police repression, and anyone suspected of harboring racist sympathies would be unable to make a career in any sphere whatsoever. Yet in this instance, there were no protesting outcries about "witch hunts." Racism was surrounded by a *cordon sanitaire* of intolerance, and was thus unable to spread further or become an accepted fact of life. Communism, however, was made respectable, acceptable. It was considered improper to fight against it; "broadening contacts" with it was the recommended recipe. So it grew and flourished, engulfing half the world. Is this not painfully obvious? Is there a single person alive who does not understand this?

Did not those politicians who encouraged the growth of economic relations with the Soviet bloc realize that they were breeding Hammers, Maxwells, and Bobolases? Did they not know, when they welcomed delegations of Soviet leaders and "deputies," that these were not statesmen and parliamentarians, but cutthroats and their puppets? Did they not see, when they signed agreements on "cultural exchanges," "scientific cooperation," and "human contacts," that they were thereby buttressing the power of the KGB over society, for it would be the KGB choosing the right candidates for such contacts?

The great majority understood everything, knew or guessed it, but remained silent, because they did not seek to oppose communism, only to survive. To survive at any cost, sacrificing conscience, reason, innocent people, and whole countries in the process. And in the final instance, sacrificing their own future, because the logic of survival has its roots in the concentration camp principle: you die today, and I will die tomorrow.

The world was immeasurably lucky; that tomorrow did not come. The monster died before it reached the world's jugular. Now that communism has collapsed, the Iron Curtain has fallen and exposed a vista of poverty and devastation, and its crimes cannot be swept under the rug, that much-touted "coexistence" can be seen for what it really is. Just as criminal, for the myth has dispersed and fear has flown, "coexistence" stands exposed as nothing more than moral capitulation before evil, a criminal complicity. What can we say in justification to future generations? That we had to survive? But the Germans needed to survive, too, after the First World War, so they followed Hitler. Why, then, were they judged at Nuremberg? They sacrificed Jews, gypsies, and Slavs, just as we sacrificed dozens of other nations—in order to secure our own survival.

But just like the Germans in 1945, we are reluctant to scrutinize ourselves, to dig into the past in order to avoid scandal. Like them, we close our eyes and reiterate that we "knew nothing," that "we took no interest in politics"—and even had we known, "What could we have done?"

And was it, really, just a German phenomenon? I can well remember the perplexity of my parents' generation some thirty-five years ago, when the so-called "crimes of the personality cult" were aired for the first time. Oh, they knew nothing about it, of course. And even if they knew a tiny bit, they believed that it had all been for the good of mankind. And confronted with indisputable facts (it was hardly possible, after all, not to notice the slaughter of sixty million people), they would submit as an ultimate justification of their behavior, that they were scared. Scared when they marched under red banners and sang revolutionary songs, scared when they raised their hands at the mass meetings in support of the party's policy, scared when they were rewarded, decorated, and promoted for doing good work. Just like the three lucky monkeys who see no evil, hear no evil, and speak no evil, they "believed" in communism because they "didn't know" about its crimes, and they didn't know because they were afraid to open their eyes. One must survive somehow, after all. . . .

. . . And I also remember a film I saw as an adolescent in post-Stalin Moscow, in which every frame, every word was like a breath of fresh air. The film was about a wise old judge who had come to Germany from small-town America, and who was trying to understand how seemingly normal, honest, and hard-working people with an ancient culture could have arrived at the horrors of Auschwitz. I remember the closing scenes as if I saw them only yesterday, and the words of the sentence:

"The real complaining party at the bar in this courtroom is civilization. But the tribunal does say that the men at the dock are responsible for their actions. The principle of criminal law in every civilized society has this in common: any person who sways another to commit murder, any person who furnishes the lethal weapon for the purpose of the crime, any person who is an accessory to the crime is guilty."

Then, as now, it was not easy to say those simple words—political interests, the very same need to survive, the moral blindness of Man, which prevents him from seeing his own part in a crime against humanity. What could he, a lone individual, do? He ignored the voice of his conscience, like everyone else, but he could not possibly know that the end would be mountains of corpses and torrents of blood, could he?

And why bother? I bet that in five years time, those you have sentenced will be released, says the smart defense lawyer sarcastically. Well, responds the wise judge, "what you suggest may very well happen. It is logical in view of the times in which we live. But to be logical is not to be right. And nothing on God's earth could make it right."

More than thirty-five years have passed, but this film has remained in my mind despite long years of imprisonment and exile, cruelty and bitter disappointments. Sometimes I think that I would not have endured otherwise, for logic was always against us. But I remembered:

Nothing on God's earth can make it right.

That film was called *Judgment in Nuremberg*.[41]

---

[41] Spencer Tracy played the judge and Maximilian Schell the young German lawyer. Schell and Abby Mann, scriptwriter for the 1961 film, won Academy Awards for their contribution. (The movie was directed by Stanley Kramer.)

Chapter Two

The Night After the Battle Belongs to the Marauders

2.1 Back to the Lubyanka

As fate would have it, this whole treasure came into my hands quite unexpectedly when I, after many months of fruitless endeavor, had given up hope of ever seeing anything. The euphoria of 1991 had evaporated and hopes of rapid changes had faded, not only for the rebirth of the country, but even for something moderately reasonable or merely decent. The restoration of the *nomenklatura*'s power was in full swing, and I had almost made up my mind not to come to Moscow again—not to agonize needlessly over its hopeless squalor.

But there was no peace for me back home in Cambridge, either. The old, familiar world was changing with every moment. As though shaken by the mighty forces of entropy engendered by the collapse of immense structures in the East, it, too, began to disintegrate for no obvious reason. It was as though a mighty hand had plucked out some invisible pivot of our lives, robbing them of meaning and support: an idea which had ruled the world for two centuries was in its death throes. Instinctively, everyone knew that its death was as inevitable as it was desirable, but it is hard to let go for fear of the unknown, so we continue to mill around in one spot at a total loss. Only the "intellectual elite," with limpet-like determination, continued to cling to the shards of a utopia that had long since degenerated into an absurdity. Like a centipede with a broken back, it continued to wriggle and jerk, but with no coordination. On the one hand some mythical "new world order," "global village," and "federal Europe": on the other ecologists, feminists, defenders of animal and plant rights. And, inevitably, shameless justification of their behavior during the Cold War. Total chaos. And what I feared most came to pass: the former cowardly refusal to fight had turned into an inability to recover. The inhuman utopia fell, but neither spiritual freedom nor honorable thought rose from the ruins. There was nothing but an absurd, pathetic farce. The unnumbered millions of victims died in vain; humanity did not become better, wiser, more mature. . . .

For Russia, the result was a shoddy tragicomedy in which former second-rate party bosses and KGB generals played the part of leading democrats and saviors of the country from communism. All that was most ugly, rotten, and base, which had lurked in the darkest corners of the communist dungeon and survived due to a total absence of conscience, now strutted in the center of the stage. They were those whom prison jargon calls "jackals": for as long as there are real gangsters in the cell, they are neither seen nor heard, huddling on the floor under the lowest bunk. But when the ranking thieves are marched off to the camps, the jackals emerge and begin to throw their weight around until another real gangster appears, and they dive back to the floor. Looking at this "jackals' democracy," one cannot help recalling Vladimir Vysotsky's prophetic words:[42]

> I live. But I'm surrounded
> By beasts, to whom the wolf's cry is unknown.
> They're dogs—our distant kindred,
> Whom we regarded as our prey.

Generally speaking, I continued going to Russia by force of an old, ingrained habit of never giving up, sound reason notwithstanding. After all, had we not devoted our whole lives to a totally hopeless cause?

And in any case, what else could I do? It is incredibly hard to come to terms with the thought that your whole life was lived in vain, and that all the efforts and sacrifices were meaningless. So that is why, clenching my teeth and overcoming revulsion, I continued to shuttle to Moscow, meeting the new "democratic" leaders and trying to persuade them to open up the party archives. And the longer this went on, the harder it became to abandon my idea, although its chances of success lessened with every visit.

The so-called putsch of August 1991 was hardly over when I was already in Moscow, trying to prove to the new masters of Russia's fate that opening up the archives was in their own interests. A wounded animal should be killed before it gets its second wind. The main thing was not to allow the party a respite for recovery. It is imperative, I said again and again, to create a commission to investigate all the crimes of communism, preferably an international commission, so there could be no accusations of political bias and cover-ups. The case against the putschists could be expanded into a trial of the CPSU. And it should be investigated openly, i.e. *now*, without delay, in the full glare of publicity and television cameras, just like the congressional hearings in the USA. . . .

---

[42]Vladimir Vysotsky (1938–1980), a hugely popular actor and songwriter, was an inimitable performer of his own songs, which circulated widely in unofficial recordings (*magnitizdat*). Vladimir Vysotsky, "Where are you, Wolves?! (Hunting by Helicopter)," *Pesni i stichi* (Songs and Verse), New York: Izd. Literaturnoe zarubezh'e, 1981, (in Russian), pp. 309–310.

It was a unique moment; everything seemed possible. The *nomenklatura*[43] was in disarray and agreeable to anything, fearing only kangaroo courts and public lynchings. Seeing the statue of "Iron Felix" hanging in a noose above its pedestal made their blood run cold.[44] In such circumstances, it would have been quite possible to convene, if not a Nuremberg tribunal, then at least something similar, and, by force of its moral influence on our confused world, even more significant.

The most surprising thing is that this almost happened. Intoxicated by its unexpected victory, the Russian leadership did not look too far ahead, and knew nothing of the external world. But the prospect of finishing off its closest rival seemed both logical and attractive.

"You know," I was told, "that's not a bad idea at all. The only thing is, it shouldn't proceed from us, the government. You should set the ball rolling."

Agreed. The chairman of the All-Soviet Television Company (VGTRK), Yegor Yakovlev,[45] was summoned hastily and even thought up how to get things off the ground as sensationally as possible: a televised dialogue with the newly appointed head of the KGB, Vadim Bakatin.

It was the beginning of September, Moscow had not yet rallied after the putsch, there were still barricades around the "White House" and flowers on the Garden Ring marking the spot where three young men had been killed, when we—a television crew, Yakovlev, and I—drove to the notorious building on the Lubyanka. Everything was just as it had been in my youth: the Detsky Mir (Children's World) shop on the corner and the grim KGB building in the center, opposite the Dzerzhinsky Square metro station; only Iron Felix's empty pedestal bore witness to recent events. It was unbelievably strange to see that pedestal daubed with graffiti such as "Down with the CPSU!" or the communist hammer and sickle with an equal sign joining it to a Nazi swastika. These were removed every night by someone's caring hands, but reappeared inevitably the next day.

---

[43]The administrative and managerial elite of the Soviet Union, appointed by the party and usually party members themselves. With family members, a privileged caste three million strong in Brezhnev's day.

[44]In 1991, after the failure of the August putsch, statues of Soviet leaders in the center of Moscow (Felix Dzerzhinsky, Yakov Sverdlov, and Mikhail Kalinin) were taken from their pedestals and placed in a park by the Moskva River. In Russia and many other former Soviet republics—though not in the Baltic states or Ukraine—the ubiquitous statues of Lenin remain untouched to this day.

[45]In the mid-1980s Yegor Yakovlev was appointed chief editor of the new Russian-language version of *Moscow News*, which was chosen to be a flagship publication of perestroika (see Chapter 3.12).

So it went on for several weeks, until people tired of the game. And then carefully inscribed words in white paint appeared on the clean pedestal: "Forgive us Felix for failing to save you". The *chekists* got the last word after all.

The guards at the entrance presented arms, either because we were accompanied by Bakatin's assistant or because this was the standard greeting for VIPs. I could not help recalling how I was brought here twenty-eight years before, without honors and via the back entrance, where the sergeant on duty was interested only in the contents of my pockets. A whole lifetime had passed between these two visits, if not a whole epoch. However, I felt neither triumph nor pleasure at this memory. On the contrary, a feeling of impotence and the comprehension of a life sacrificed for nothing took on a concrete form: "I spent my whole life fighting this organization," I thought, "and yet it still stands. And who can say who shall outlive whom?"

Naturally, Bakatin's choice as interlocutor for me was not a random one. It was known that he was very decisive, and even though his career under Gorbachev had been an unremarkable passage from the post of a regional party secretary to minister of internal affairs, he loathed the department whose head he was now. When Gorbachev offered him the post of KGB head immediately after the putsch, at the Presidential Council of the USSR, he first refused, saying that "this organization should be dissolved."

"Well, we are charging you to do just that," said Boris Yeltsin.[46]

At the time of our meeting, Bakatin had been in his new position for just over a week, but had already removed a whole number of services from the KGB and allocated them to other ministries. As for the nefarious Directorate "Z", the successor of the Fifth Chief Directorate, which dealt in political repression, this he had closed altogether. He had not had time to become accustomed to his huge new office, and seemed somewhat ill at ease. In any case, when I asked him who had occupied this office before him, he spent a long time, with the air of a schoolboy figuring out a new electronic toy, looking for the right button on his intercom to summon his assistant.

As becomes a real *chekist*, the assistant appeared noiselessly, like a mushroom from the ground after the rain.

"Tell us the history of this office."

No, it had never been occupied by Yuri Andropov. His office was in another building. This office had housed Viktor Chebrikov, then

---

[46]See Vadim Bakatin, *Getting Rid of the KGB*. Moscow: Novosti, 1992, p. 22 (in Russian).

Vladimir Kryuchkov. . . .

Bakatin was clearly somewhat embarrassed by his new position, by my visit, and especially by our forthcoming discussion. Obviously he knew the theme in advance and had no need to fear that I would resort to any dirty tricks. But the television camera, now— what would get into the picture?

"What, full view? Even my socks?"

For some reason, the prospect of showing his socks on television was what confused him most.

Preparing for the discussion, I had mentally divided it into three parts, three subjects, which would make it possible to advance the idea of an international commission, moreover in a way that would reduce its likely opponents to a minimum. I already knew that at an earlier press conference Bakatin had spoken against the public exposure of former "stoolies"—that is, the KGB's secret informers. I had no real objections to this, because in a country where if not every tenth person was an informer, as in the GDR [German Democratic Republic], then every twentieth assuredly was, it would be impossible and senseless to begin with their exposure. Just as senseless, incidentally, as putting each and every member of the CPSU on trial. First because there was no clearly defined demarcation between members and non-members of the party, an informer and an ordinary Soviet conformist. With the exception of a handful of "renegades" like us, this was a demoralized country. So what was one supposed to do now? Institute a new gulag?

Bearing in mind the purely legal difficulties, the scope of the problem, and the resistance of those very informers and their bosses, now ensconced at all levels of the present government, it would have been simply impossible to start the process with them. Even in the Czech Republic, the only former communist country to have the courage to begin the process of lustration, the public reaction was sharply negative, and the process had become bogged down hopelessly because of the question of informers.

In any case, this would have been useless, if not downright harmful. The aim was not to winnow the more guilty from the less guilty and punish the latter, but to attain a moral cleansing of society. Not mass hysteria, reprisals, denunciations, and suicides, which such an investigation would invariably provoke, but repentance. And in order to achieve this, the entire system and the crimes it perpetrated should have been put on trial, while it would have been quite sufficient to pronounce judgment on its leaders, who were already in prison for organizing the putsch.

On this matter Bakatin and I were in complete agreement, and I deliberately started the discussion with this, in order to demonstrate my total support for his position and set the right tone for the rest of the encounter. I considered it vital to show the millions of people who would see the program that we, former political prisoners and dissidents, had no desire to seek revenge, that the foundation for my proposals was not vengeance but interests much more far-reaching and not at all personal. Moreover, in doing so, I was not being two-faced; I honestly do not live in hatred and have no wish to be avenged, because I was never anybody's victim. All that happened to me happened by my own free choice and with a full realization of the consequences.

As for seeking vengeance by prosecuting informers, that would be total nonsense; unlike most of my fellow citizens (including Bakatin), I knew these people well. From those who were deliberately planted into our prison cells to the infiltrators sent to penetrate our circles, I was fully aware that the majority of them were people who had been broken, or who were blackmailed or threatened into becoming agents for the KGB. Nobody can really know how he will act under extreme pressure, so nobody who has not experienced this for himself has the right to judge others. And those who have passed through such an ordeal themselves are usually loath to sit in judgment.

However, if I was prepared to be as lenient as necessary in this matter, two other issues called for total implacability. First and foremost, our duty before history to reveal all the secrets hidden in the archives, and for this purpose it was proposed to convene an international commission consisting of prominent domestic and foreign historians. In discussing this subject I deliberately lumped together the killing of Sergey Kirov, the assassination of John F. Kennedy and the attempt on the life of Pope John Paul II in order to make a bridge to the last, main theme—the international crimes of the CPSU and the KGB. This subject was still taboo in the USSR. The average Soviet citizen was still supposed to believe that even though the communists were guilty of crimes against their own people, of repressions and destruction of the economy, in external matters they were just like everyone else, neither better nor worse. *À la guerre comme à la guerre.* The Americans were no angels either. As for intelligence—well, doesn't every state, even the most democratic one, have an intelligence service?

This dangerous delusion, assiduously cultivated at the time by the press and the powers that be, had to be exploded, together with the mythical image of a valorous Soviet intelligence officer, a hero and a patriot. It had to be made perfectly clear that the Soviet Union had no "normal" foreign policy, and what it called foreign policy was nothing less than decades of criminal activity against humanity. For this reason I kept this subject for the end, when our discussion already sounded like a meeting between two old buddies in perfect harmony. Then I began to talk about things not known to the average viewer: about Soviet sponsorship of international terrorism, involvement in the narcotics business, the bribing and blackmailing of foreign politicians, businessmen, cultural figures, about the colossal system of disinformation built up by the KGB abroad.

"After all," I insisted, "we have an intelligence service apart from the KGB—the GRU, military intelligence, which really does deal with military matters. This is a separate case altogether. But the KGB is a political body. It enmeshed an enormous number of foreigners, whom the KGB either bought or blackmailed. This is not a question that can be ignored. I quite understand all the complexities of dismantling such a system, but it cannot be allowed to stand. If we do not get rid of it, our country cannot win trust. . . . We can hardly have a normal state if this body continues to exist. . . .

"Furthermore, we have a certain obligation before the international community, and other countries, to help them rid themselves of the evil which this system engendered.

"Of course," I cautioned in closing, "there is also the issue of the security of our own state. For instance, Western experts estimate that the KGB, through its activities abroad, managed to amass such resources, having their own banks, front organizations and enterprises, that it can easily continue to exist and function for at least another decade even if it is closed down in Moscow. Such views exist in the West, and, of course, you cannot simply let the matter slide, for it could turn around and threaten you."

To give Bakatin his due, he did not argue or remonstrate, and when he did answer, he mainly pleaded ignorance. And he could hardly do otherwise, being so new to the job.

"Espionage is the most difficult matter for me at the moment," he mumbled. He has a rather strange manner of speech, a sort of uninflected muttering, with no clear beginning or end. "In this instance, even in my plans of action, in my calendar, my personal calendar, I have transferred intelligence matters to a rather different level.

"I do not think they have any documentation concerning the criminal activities of which you speak. Even if there are some facts about which I know absolutely nothing, that some of them, I don't know, it could be that some of them did engage in this concretely. . . . If this is so, then everything needs to be examined, dismantled. . . . And this is very serious. We don't know much at all about what they do abroad. . . ."

It seemed that if he was not frightened, then he was at least perturbed, especially by what I said about KGB resources abroad. He kept repeating that he could not let this pass unnoticed, that all this must be investigated and—most importantly—that he was prepared to support my idea fully:

"Generally speaking, I agree with you in principle that the truth must be reestablished. It must at least be determined. But right now, at this moment, I cannot set out the terms for the convocation of an international commission. I cannot do so," said he at the end of our discussion. "There are also some legal aspects which must be taken into account. ... It was in our department's interests to keep all this secret, so many did not know. So such a proposal must be accepted in principle. In principle. We must consider how to go about it."[47]

"Well, Vadim Viktorovich," I said, extending my hand, "I would like to wish you success, express my sympathy, and to shake the hand of the first head of the KGB I have ever met. ..."

And—*mea culpa*—for a moment I actually believed that this could happen: that we would meet again, without any television cameras, discuss the legal aspects of the situation, work out our aims and get down to business. ... And why not? Yeltsin would sign a decree, I would call up my historian friends from the Hoover Institution, people like Robert Conquest, specialists from the "Memorial" organization in Russia, whistle up some students from the Historical Archival Institute, and dig into the documentary cellars. In those days everything seemed possible, days when the hand of the people equated the hammer and sickle with the swastika on the empty pedestal in the middle of Dzerzhinsky Square.

For a fleeting moment I imagined how this simple equation would become what it always should have been—a self-evident truth, like Orwell's "2+2=4."[48] Such a small, simple thing, yet how much cleaner and more honest our life would become. ...

But the next moment the vision fled, to be replaced by reality.

How can this nice mumbler, who is so touchingly embarrassed by the prospect of showing his socks on television, deal with this monster? He will not even have an inkling of what is going on behind his back.

---

[47]Quoted by the Radio Free Europe/Radio Liberty (RFE/RL) Research Institute, "An unexpected interview," the *Soviet Media News Digest*, No 796, pp. 21–25, 9 September 1991

[48]The alternative equation (2+2=5) in Orwell's *Nineteen Eighty-Four* alludes to Stalin's slogan of completing the first Five Year Plan (1927–1932) a year ahead of time.

The friend who was waiting for me outside dealt the final blow, hammered the last nail into the coffin with a laconic observation: "It's people like you who are needed here, not people like him."

2.2 The Immortal KGB

Our discussion with Bakatin was shown on television on 9 September, immediately after the news at 9:00 p.m., and almost in its entirety, with just a few minor, unexceptional editorial cuts. The program lasted some twenty minutes but provoked a turbulent reaction. The response of the press was, overall, favorable, the stress being placed on the "extraordinary" fact of such a dialogue: how the times have changed, how the country has changed! The most popular publications of that time—the newspaper *Izvestia*[49] and the magazine *Ogonyok*[50]—published articles about our meeting with my commentary, in which I tried to develop the subject further. Naturally there were those who reproached me for being too soft on informers, and especially for shaking hands with the head of the KGB. I was neither surprised nor upset; in times like these, loudmouths and fools are always hyperactive, and earning political capital with cheap demagogy is their favorite pastime.

It was much more important that my amiable purring did not lull those whom it concerned most closely—the "professionals." They understood all too well what I was driving at, and my calm and friendly tone probably alarmed them much more than threatening tirades or furious demands for retribution would have done. Only a few days later, the head of the First Chief Directorate of the KGB at that time, Lieutenant General Shebarshin, appeared on television and, without mentioning my discussion with Bakatin, assured the viewers—in passing, as it were—that there could be no sensational exposures about the activities of the KGB abroad. Clearly, this was a signal to their people and their numerous partners that there was no cause for concern.[51]

Then came a flood of articles by former intelligence officers with "democratic" reputations, aimed at showing that my impression of the scope of their activities was vastly exaggerated. Retired intelligence officer Mikhail Lyubimov wrote in *Ogonyok*:[52]

---

[49] Albert Plutnik, "Interview between a Famous Dissident and the KGB Chairman," *Izvestia*, No. 216, 10 September 1991, p. 3.

[50] Ilya Milstein, "Vladimir Bukovsky: 'Creating a Team for a Pogrom,'" *Ogonyok*, No 39, 21–28 September 1991, pp. 28–29.

[51] *Vzglyad* (TV program), Ostankino (Central Television), 27 September 1991.

[52] Mikhail Lyubimov, "*Drang nach Westen*: A KGB Distraction Maneuver That Fooled No One in the West," *Ogonyok*, No. 43 (19–26 October), 1991, p. 29.

> Even veteran dissident Vladimir Bukovsky, whose knowledge of
> the KGB is not merely theoretical, mentioned in passing in his
> epochal interview with Bakatin that it would be better for our
> country to limit itself to military intelligence, and put an end
> to the political one. "This is a wise and progressive sugges-
> tion, but one wonders how much support it would gain from
> Western governments, which, apart from military intelligence
> organizations, have the Central Intelligence Agency, MI6, BND
> and Mossad. Bukovsky also advanced a thesis that the external
> intelligence of the KGB engages in the massive dissemination of
> disinformation abroad.

This was followed by a detailed denial claiming that there was
no enormous disinformation system, just a few pathetic efforts, a
handful of forged documents that had fooled nobody but only "provoked anger with their creators."

> I have had enough experience in the sphere of 'active measures'
> to assert that forgeries are a tiny fraction of intelligence work,
> the lion's share is devoted to reworking our propaganda in or-
> der to give it a "Western" gloss. ... Most of this so-called
> work consists of mere pinpricks that go unnoticed in the enor-
> mous stream of Western information, they contributed nothing
> to the Soviet foreign policy interests of the time—those vapid
> and murky policies were headed toward their doom, and could
> not be saved by either the propaganda or the agitation issuing
> from "Western sources."

In short, there were no such things as a system of disinformation, agents of influence, or forces of peace, progress and socialism. And, like an illustration to this thesis, the *Los Angeles
Times* published an article by a prominent American political scientist (reprinted immediately in the Russian newspaper *Kultura*[53]
that was full of the standard KGB disinformation about dissidents:
that they are all crazy extremists, and Bukovsky, to compound the
felony, "enters into discourse with the new head of the KGB, as
though someone authorized him to do so, and proposes the destruction of the KGB archives so that the names of informers will
never become known."

It was hard to say immediately whether this highly respected
American gentleman was an agent of influence, or whether he was
briefed by one, but *Kultura* is not likely to be a subscriber to the
Los Angeles Times. Much later, when I tried to find the original

---

[53]"Press Testimony. A Maelstrom of Dissidents Lost in the Wild," *(Sovetskaya)
Kultura*, 30 November 1991, p. 12. See RFE/RL Research Institute, *USSR Today:
Soviet Media News and Features Digest*, 4 December 1991.

publication, it transpired that the *LA Times* has never published such an article. It is still a puzzle where it did come from.

Finally, the First Chief Directorate of intelligence was speedily transferred out of the KGB into the newly formed Foreign Intelligence Service, answerable directly to Gorbachev and headed by his friend Yevgeny Primakov. Naturally there were much more serious reasons for this than our discussion with Bakatin, primarily the danger of the breakdown of all union structures in the process of the Soviet Union's disintegration. But it is clear that there was another reason—specifically to protect intelligence from any investigations and reforms, or, to use the words of the cloak-and-dagger brigade who strove to this end, to "get rid of the KGB tail." So they dived for shelter behind the broad back of the president, taking their secrets with them.

Bakatin, who, as mentioned earlier, kept deferring this problem to the back of his "personal calendar," was probably only too glad to be rid of the KGB. Admittedly, he made honest efforts later to follow up the crimes committed by his organization that I had spoken about. But—wonder of wonders!—he was unable to come up with anything substantial. Even with very old matters, offering only historical interest, such as the Kennedy assassination and the attempt on the Pope, it somehow turned out that the poor, maligned KGB had nothing to do with them at all. It even proved impossible to find anything new about the persecution of Alexander Solzhenitsyn and Andrei Sakharov—only after lengthy wrangling and denials of the existence of any documents was it suddenly "discovered" that hundreds of files concerning KGB operations had been allegedly burned in 1990.

Bakatin was unable to remove the seal of secrecy from even that small amount that came to light. For instance, the quite innocuous file on the surveillance of Lee Harvey Oswald during his stay in the USSR thirty-five years earlier first got stuck in the hands of innumerable committees, then suddenly surfaced in Belorussia, within the fief of the KGB of the now-independent Republic of Belarus. And there it stayed until Bakatin was removed from his post. The KGB apparatus openly acted the fool, not caring whether anyone believed it or not.

I do not know whether Bakatin realized that he was being played for a sucker, but his memoirs, *Getting Rid of the KGB*, sound rather naive. They certainly got rid of him fast enough, but the KGB remained. Splitting up the KGB into separate directorates and services, which is what Bakatin tried to do during his hundred days as head of the KGB, was as pointless as chopping off a lizard's tail or dividing an amoeba. The result was that every unit regenerated itself and even expanded, just as in the fairy tale in which every dragon tooth grows into a new dragon. Those archives were the essence of the KGB, the heart of the dragon, hidden behind seven seals. The only way to vanquish the beast was to pierce its heart, but the hero of the story, who was supposed to accomplish this magnificent feat, went on a drunken spree instead. Yeltsin, who straight after the putsch had signed a decree transferring the KGB archives to the Russian Archives Administration, seemed to lose all interest in this matter (as in all other matters of importance to the country). An interdepartmental committee was appointed to handle the transfer of the archives, in which KGB personnel gravely discussed "problems of transfer" and, not surprisingly, could find no solutions to them. It's a complex matter, isn't it? Another Supreme Soviet committee was formed, headed by a Stalinist general, the "historian" Dmitri Volkogonov—there must be a legal basis when all is said and done, how can anything be done lawlessly? It was no trifling matter to decide whether to set the seal of secrecy at thirty or seventy years in the past. So the merry-go-round began to spin, and is spinning still. As for the documents—not a single one has been transferred to this day. Meanwhile, mysterious "commercial structures" began to appear around the archives, and a brisk trade in documents ensued, but only those deals that profit the KGB, and only through the reliable hands of those who suit the KGB. And again, double-dyed disinformation was turned loose upon the world, this time under the guise of historical truth. . . .

2.3   In the Belly of the Beast

I was neither discouraged nor caught at a disadvantage. Even before the meeting with Bakatin, I had placed no great hopes in the KGB archives, but concentrated my attention on the archives of the Central Committee of the Communist Party of the Soviet Union, which immediately after the putsch had been sealed, together with the Central Committee building on the Old Square (Staraya Ploschad). First, they were already in the hands of the Russian leadership, with which I had at least some contact. Second, I knew that these archives would contain everything, including reports by the KGB which, as they always maintained, was merely the cutting edge of the party, its armed brigade. In the post-Stalin era, at least, the KGB was under the iron control of the Central Committee, and could undertake nothing significant without Central Committee approval.

So a few days after arriving in Moscow in August 1991, thanks to contacts within the Russian leadership, I met the head of the government's Federal Archive Agency, Rudolf Germanovich Pikhoya, to establish the principles of the work of the future international commission. And a few days later, with a certain degree of elation and trepidation, I entered the huge complex of buildings of the Central Committee on 12 Kuybyshev Street (nowadays Ilyinka Street), where both the archives and the archive administration were housed. The buildings, which are linked by endless corridors and elevated walkways, seemed dead. The archive administration occupied only one floor of Number 12; the rest was like the labyrinth of the Minotaur, the entrance and exit of which could not be found without Ariadne's thread. The superb parquet flooring of the corridors seemed to stretch into infinity past sealed office doors that still bore the nameplates of their former occupants, erstwhile omnipotent apparatchiks. Here and there, mounds of files and papers marked "top secret" lay right on the floor. I picked up one at random and glanced at the contents: it was a report by some regional party committee about youth work. For a second I felt a pinch of apprehension: what if there was nothing here other than such endless accounts of fulfilled plans and propagandist activity? Moscow had been full of rumors about the mass destruction of documents, about mysterious trucks that had removed bales of papers several nights in a row after the putsch....

Pikhoya reassured me. Yes, some papers really were destroyed, but they were, seemingly, operative documents concerning the putsch. The archives themselves, as far as it was possible to judge, had not suffered. The decree ordering the seizure of the party archives had been signed by Yeltsin on 24 August, and the commission with the new guards had entered the Central Committee buildings that same night. At first the electricity supply was cut off to prevent any use of shredding machines, but then it had to be turned on again, because it was impossible to find anything in the dark. The shredding machines were already jammed with hurriedly destroyed documents and not in working order.

"The first step was to seal the doors to all the offices," said Pikhoya, "and now we are bringing all the papers from the offices into one large room, where we sort and number them. Nobody can remove anything from here, and, in fact, it is impossible for the old personnel to enter the building, even to collect personal belongings. The guards were all replaced by cadets from the militia academy in either Vologda or Volgograd."

It was a fact that all the entrances and exits were manned by sturdy young men with submachine guns. We literally stumbled into one of them, a strapping young fellow with a childish, bewildered face, as we turned a corner:

"Can you tell me where the canteen is?" he asked pleadingly. "I've been wandering around for half an hour, and still can't find it. . . ."

As it turned out, the former CC buffet in the basement had survived, but it was empty of any tempting, hard-to-come-by delicacies. Whatever else the staff of the CC might have overlooked at the last moment, it wasn't a stick or two of smoked sausage.

Experience showed that it was well-nigh impossible to destroy any archive material selectively, or, for that matter, to forge it. In the first place because it had been established that there were at least 162 archives, totally unconnected to each other by cross-referencing in card indexes or by computer; the communist regime trusted nobody, even its own apparatus. It would take months of searching just to establish whether there were any copies of a document from one archive in another, or a reference to a document whose original was housed elsewhere. And even if it was established that a copy existed, it would be extremely difficult to change anything; every archive had its own inventory, and the documents were numbered consecutively, had reference numbers and a register of all incoming and outgoing papers. The bureaucratic state did not stint on paper; probably that was why it was always in short supply. Just the archive containing a listing of all party members, the so-called united party ticket, consisted of 40 million items. As for party archives throughout the whole country—they numbered billions of documents.

I went into one of these archives—consisting of the personal dossiers on CC *nomenklatura*—out of sheer curiosity, together with a group of journalists invited by Pikhoya. An immense room with high, figured ceilings—before the revolution this had been either a bank or an insurance company—was filled with metal stacks on sliding rails. The central control panel, located on a dais at the entrance to the room, had dozens of buttons, pressing one of which would cause the needed stack to shift slowly, exposing shelves covered with personal dossiers. There were up to a million files concerning the living and the dead, Politburo members and ordinary CC staff.

This particular archive soon became a showpiece: it was here that foreigners, journalists, and high-ranking visitors were brought to demonstrate the daring and democracy of the new custodians of party secrets. Journalists were usually shown the files on Kliment Voroshilov, Anastas Mikoyan, and, occasionally, Mikhail Sholokhov, drawn as if at random from the shelves. This was effective and safe. In reality, the administrators of the archive were in no hurry to lay bare its mysteries, let alone to fight for their publication. They were no fighters, just typical Soviet bureaucrats who had built their careers under the old regime, cowardly and cunning, like all slaves. Their attitude toward the authorities, their overlords, was a slave's mixture of fear and hatred, and the more they hated, the more they wanted to cheat their masters in some way. So they regarded the unexpected bounty that fell into their hands as their personal windfall, to be guarded jealously from all outsiders.

Even the standard bureaucratic types were represented in their midst, just as in any Soviet department. One acted out the part of the honest party faithful, waging relentless war against corruption, but was finally caught selling documents to journalists. Another appeared to be a man of the intelligentsia—civilized, fond of discussing abstract values, talking about our duty to history, even though it was common knowledge that he was not above allowing foreign colleagues access to certain secret papers in return for invitations to speak at international conferences, thereby earning himself a reputation as "a prominent historian". It never entered any of their heads that all of this was dishonest, shameful, or reprehensible. What can be done if Soviet people have no conscience? There's not a fiber in their brain that retains any traces of moral norms.

It stands to reason that from their point of view, I was an outsider, a thief eyeing their riches from whom they tacitly agreed to protect their "personal property." Moreover, they simply could not understand my motives—what was it I was after, anyway? Was I trying to get a cut for myself? The mere thought of handing over all this bounty to humanity with no profit seemed to them a madness comparable to that of a banker handing out money to all and sundry in the streets. As I had come to them under the aegis of their new masters, their initial attitude to me was predictable: nobody dared direct refusal—who knows who's backing him, after all? —so they agreed with me in everything just in case, but managed to invent new excuses for delay every day. First they claimed it was necessary to await the promulgation of new legislation concerning state secrets; then that the proposal to convene an international commission required approval by the legislature, and so on. Their main concern was to have the matter placed into the hands of innumerable Supreme Soviet committees, where it would sink without a trace in endless debates conducted by yesterday's party bosses, who had undergone a metamorphosis and emerged as today's "elected representatives of the people."

Finally I became totally fed up, time was pressing, and I could wait no longer, so I was forced to have a harsh and candid talk with Pikhoya, to explain to him that he and his underlings held no copyright to history, and never would. He defended himself rather limply, mainly by reiterating the need for a relevant law, talking of the generally accepted thirty-year moratorium on state secrets in other countries, England for example. The trouble is that the Soviet people know everything about the West, especially that which they shouldn't know. However, he had no choice but to sign—albeit with a marked lack of enthusiasm—our agreement:

On the International Commission to study the activities
of Party structures and state security bodies of the USSR.

1. Archive materials concerning the activities of the CPSU and state security bodies have been made available pursuant to Decrees #82 and 83, signed by the Russian President on 24.08.91. It is acknowledged that the activities of these organizations were of an international nature and concerned the interests of many countries. In view of this circumstance, the engagement of only domestic experts would be insufficient to deal with this complex of problems. Moreover, foreign archives contain materials which would be valuable in increasing the scope of the study of the history of the abovementioned organizations. The inclusion of foreign scholars in the examination would also lend credibility to the findings of the Commission. As a result of the above, *on the initiative of the Committee for Archival Affairs under the Council of Ministers of the Russian Federation*, the following have agreed to form an international commission for a full and detailed study of the archive materials which have become available:

   • The International Council on Archives (Paris)
   • The Hoover Institution of War, Revolution and Peace (Stanford, California)
   • American Enterprise Institute (Washington)
   • Research Department of Radio Liberty (Munich)
   • Russian University of Humanities
   • The scientific informational and educational center Memorial

   The Commission will involve foreign and domestic experts in its work on both a temporary and full-length basis.

   The Commission will not concern itself with current defense matters, with persecution of any individuals because of their former activities or causing damage to any country whatsoever.

   The aim of the Commission is to carry out a comprehensive and objective study of all the abovementioned materials and let history be the judge.

In pursuit of this aim, the Commission reserves the right to draw necessary materials from other document storages (archives).

2. Organizational Principles

The Commission *per se* is composed of representatives of the founder-organizations listed above, which decides all administrative and financial questions.

Working groups organized on the principle of specific activities (thematic, chronological, etc.) with input from invited experts.

3. Activities

The founder-organizations undertake the financing of the program and will take all necessary steps to ensure the safety of the materials issued for its work.

The Commission undertakes to use any possible income from publication of any of the materials to finance its work and to support archive activity.

As a result of its studies, the Commission proposes to computerize the archive materials and publish them as collections of documents or monographs.

R.G. Pikhoya   V.K. Bukovsky
11/09/91

The italicized phrase in the document was written in by hand by Pikhoya, just in case: the commission may or may not come into being, but the initiative must be credited to his committee, as if to stress: everything belongs to me, anyway, and I'm the boss around here!

So after a month of rushing around Moscow, I flew home with a faint hope that my idea would bear fruit. There was no definite decision, no certainty that the people I had met were reliable, no supporters. Just one sheet of paper with Pikhoya's signature—what was it really worth?

But I was unable to achieve anything else. In that phantom kingdom, nothing was certain, nothing was final. Everything could change at any moment. Even promises made publicly were no longer considered binding. Nobody could say for sure who was in power today, and what they would decide, let alone predict, tomorrow. The feeling was that a person exists while you clutch him by the sleeve, and the minute you let go, he disappears, dissolves: one moment he's there, the next moment he's gone. The only person who seemed stable in that situation was Yeltsin.

"Now it's all up to President Yeltsin," I told journalists before my departure. "As soon as he gives the go-ahead, we'll start work."[54]

2.4   A Drunken Wedding

Time passed, but there was no improvement. The Russian leadership was fully paralyzed, as though it had expended all of its energy during the three days of the putsch. It is a unique historical fact that Yeltsin did absolutely nothing during his first hundred days in power. For a while he dropped out of sight completely; some said that he was drinking, others that he had gone off somewhere to rest. But even when he reappeared, he was neither able to devise a program of action nor set concrete goals. First he started reshuffling the old bureaucratic pack of cards, which only made it expand, and then he rushed off with his whole entourage to the Caucasus with the intention of reconciling the Armenians and the Azerbaijanis; he would proclaim a state of emergency in Chechnya one day, and then rescind it the next. The whole country, like a rudderless ship in a storm, raced along at the mercy of the winds and waves. Or, rather, like a drunken wedding party doing a round of all the taverns in the town with music and gypsies. At least, this is a fair picture of the way Yeltsin's entourage lived at that time, in a constant round of all sorts of feasts and celebrations. It was impossible to get hold of anybody, either at home or in their offices. I spent weeks of wearing fingers to the bone dialing Moscow numbers until I stumbled onto the rhythm of this *dolce vita* more or less by chance. Apparently all of Moscow was engaged in "presentations," a word borrowed from the English, but meaning just about any kind of social eat and drink gathering in the Moscow context, be it to mark the opening of some new center or firm or some anniversary or other. And milling about in a crowd with a glass in one hand and a smoked salmon sandwich in the other is not conducive to reaching agreements on serious matters.

In the meantime, events were developing in a manner highly unfavorable to my plans. The *nomenklatura* was reviving visibly and filling the vacuum at the top. This was done quite openly, to the accompaniment of assertions in the press that the governing of the country should be left in the hands of the "professionals." The tone was even rather demanding, to the effect that the old regime had not allowed the professionals free rein, and now the new au-

---

[54]Marina Moulina, "Give the Documents to the Historians and Bin the Denunciations," *Sobesednik* [*Interlocutor*], September 1991, No 39, p. 5.
http://xn--80aagr1bl7a.net/index.php?md=books&to=art&id=1451

thorities were heading in the same direction. And it was somehow overlooked that there were never any professionals involved in the government of the Soviet Union apart from professional builders of communism, i.e. the *nomenklatura*. It was they who wrecked the country, bankrupted its economy, and finally could not even organize an effective putsch.

As a result the investigation of these comrades—the putschists—fizzled out. Before leaving at the end of September, I managed to make a television program for Russian television under the title *Two Questions to the President* in order to promote the idea of opening an investigation on "the case of the CPSU." We suggested organizing it on the Watergate model, in which there were two key questions: What did the president (in our case Gorbachev) know, and when did he know it? These were not idle questions, as there were growing indications that Gorbachev had known of everything in advance, and that the so-called putsch was his attempt to declare a state of emergency while hiding behind the backs of his comrades. Our program, conducted along the same lines, suggested the necessity of a Watergate-type public hearing.

Yet even this seemingly self-evident idea sank in the overall Russian chaos. On one hand, Yeltsin did not get around to making a decision; on the other, the newly buoyant *nomenklatura*, including elements of Yeltsin's entourage, swept everything under the rug of innumerable investigation committees that consisted, naturally, of "professionals." As a result, the leaders of the August 1991 putsch are at liberty, and will probably never be brought to trial. Instead of a court hearing, there was a rather feeble Supreme Soviet hearing in October 1991, at which some of the delegates did call for a more comprehensive investigation of the circumstances of the putsch and even of the entire activity of the CPSU, but their communist colleagues, naturally, objected. A three-ring circus, no less! Since when has it been obligatory to seek a criminal's consent before putting him in the dock?

It is curious that the prospect of an examination of the criminal activities of the CPSU did not arouse any enthusiasm even among the "moderate" public. For some reason, people were particularly concerned about the international aspect. Some facts had come to light during various investigations, mainly about the communist parties, and not very significant ones, at that—for instance, about the pumping of millions of dollars from the state coffers into "firms of friends."[55] Yet this was already enough to cause an outcry:

---

[55]Evgeny Sorokin, "Putting the CPSU on Trial", *Pravda*, 23 October 1991.

"Judging by all, the investigation will yield a great many documents of this nature," wrote *Izvestia*,[56] "and it is impossible to estimate the consequences of this work, for the scandal seems likely to spill over into the international arena, have a serious effect on the careers of many politicians, affect the activity of foreign communist parties and many commercial structures, raised on the financial leaven of the CPSU."

Alas, *Homo sovieticus* cannot hear such words as *foreign* and *abroad* without wetting his pants. Yeltsin proved to be no exception: on 14 January 1992 he signed a decree "On the protection of state secrets of the Russian Federation," which reinstated practically all the norms of secrecy of the former USSR. When I returned to Moscow in March of 1992, I encountered a typical example of Soviet window dressing. On one hand there was the triumphant opening of the Center of Contemporary Documentation in the Russian State Archive of Recent History, which allegedly contained the party archives and made them available for public scrutiny. As a result of Pikhoya's efforts, this had been trumpeted in the domestic and foreign press as the latest milestone on the road to a new democracy. And it is true that after getting a pass, one could go up to the second floor of the former Central Committee building, into the reading room, and even have a look at the inventory lists of the documents. On the other hand, this was where the democracy of the new Russian authorities came to an abrupt end, because no actual documents of any interest could be drawn and studied. Actually, even before you were allowed to look at the inventory lists, you were instructed in the rules of the Center, which meant that in accordance with Yeltsin's decree, the following documents were inaccessible:

1. All documents from after 1981;

2. All materials concerning decisions made by the Secretariat of the Central Committee from after 1961;

3. All materials with "special file" classification;

4. All materials from after 1961 concerning the International Department, The Foreign Cadres Department, the International Information Department, The Administrative Organs Department, the Central Committee's Defense Industry Department, the KGB, or the GRU.

[56]I. Yelistratov, "The Inquiry into the CPSU Reaches far Beyond Russia's Borders," *Izvestia*, No. 253, 23 October 1991, p.1.

If you really wanted to, you could acquaint yourself with plenums on agriculture or the fulfilling of five-year plans. If not, then not. I was even denied access to those documents that concerned me personally, my fate, my life, and that were listed in the inventory among the decisions of the secretariat. As for some international commission—forget it! In vain I waved our agreement under Pikhoya's nose, pointing out his signature: he merely glinted at me with his spectacles and reiterated:

"That's no longer valid."

His signature on an agreement forwarded to me shortly after I left Moscow and signed in October with our founding organizations proved equally invalid. Presumably the same applies to all other agreements he signed with other organizations, to whom he intended to sell the same goods over and over behind our backs. There were about a dozen of them, each one of which had proudly announced to the press that it had obtained exclusive access to party secrets. A month or so later, the same claim would be made by yet another equally triumphant body. There is nothing surprising in this, because Pikhoya's dream was as simple as it was unattainable: to make lots and lots of money without letting a single document out of his hands and, God willing, without bringing down his bosses' wrath on his head. He dreamed of millions of dollars to be made in exchange for accounts of youth work conducted by the party, sold to crowds of eager buyers with the air of a benefactor to mankind. As was to be expected, he ended up with nothing, and took umbrage at the West as a whole.

"Those sons of bitches," he complained bitterly (to me, of all people!). "They all want exclusive rights. Well, now I won't give anything to anyone!"

Undoubtedly, the thirty-year moratorium ("just like in England") so favored by him was enshrined in Yeltsin's decree not without Pikhoya's assistance. After all, only that which is forbidden has a market value, and only that would become his personal property to do with as he wished. The permitted materials aroused no interest, because they would have to be issued free of charge.

So my idea of a Nuremberg-style trial perished stillborn, and with it the possibility of a fitting conclusion to the biggest war waged by mankind. Nobody in our immense country, devastated by that war, was moved by a sense of duty—to history, to truth, to the memory of its victims. Nobody evinced any interest apart from the carrion-crows which appeared from nowhere to tear at the fresh corpse. Bureaucratic nonentities, who suddenly found themselves occupying seats of power, pandered to their own feelings of self-importance by exercising a free hand with something to which they had no moral right: our heritage. Insignificant nobodies who had worn through the seats of their pants by sitting in party committees denied us, who had borne the brunt of the great struggle, the possibility to learn the whole truth about our lives. Was I to endure this, too?

Leaving Moscow again at the end of March, I gave a number of biting interviews, pulling no punches. So that, I said, is the real nature of your "democracy," which has risen in defense of communist secrets.[57]

"Can you imagine a thirty-year moratorium being placed on all Nazi documentation after the fall of Germany? The new Germany did not hide the old Germany's secrets. When one makes a serious break with the past, there is no need to conceal that past."

Even *Izvestia* did not pluck up enough courage to publish this interview for a couple of weeks.[58] I thought that they would never get around to it. To hell with them all! An effective slap in the face can only be administered to someone who has some sense of honor, so my words would have been wasted anyway.

In all honesty, I had no intention of going to Russia again.

2.5   Dialectics Not According to Hegel

As the Russian saying goes, one wouldn't have luck if not for a disaster: by the spring of 1992 the communists had become brazen enough to lodge an appeal in the Constitutional Court of Russia against Yeltsin's decree outlawing the CPSU.

To an impartial observer, this must have looked like a bad joke— one group of communists litigating with another group of communists about the constitutionality of the ban on their former party, in a court whose entire membership were also former communists. And this, mark you, in a country without a current constitution, only the old constitution of the former USSR, for which the lawmakers could not agree on a replacement and that they had therefore amended several hundred times. A situation like this beggars the inadequate imagination of Franz Kafka and reduces Georg Wilhelm Friedrich Hegel's conception of dialectics to childish babble.

However, for Yeltsin and his entourage, this was no joke. The possibility of the court accepting the appeal was a real one—at least seven of the twelve judges were openly sympathetic to the CPSU—

---

[57]Tatyana Potyanikhina, "'No One Here Needs Us,' says Vladimir Bukovsky," *Vechernyaya Moskva*, 7 April 1992, p. 2.

[58]Albert Plutnik interview, "Vladimir Bukovsky: To Keep to the Right, a Strong Left Opposition Is Needed," *Izvestia*, 3 April 1992, No. 80, p. 3.

and the consequences could be positively horrifying. Apart from political complications, it would mean the return of the recently appropriated party property (including the Central Committee complex on the Staraya Ploschad, which was now newly occupied by the Russian leadership), to say nothing of the party archives. So it stood to reason that in his address to the US Congress in the summer of 1992, Yeltsin cited this court case as one of the most urgent problems facing the country.

Alarm, even panic seized all the president's men. And this led to what I had spent almost a year trying to achieve: the CPSU archives were opened, at least in part, and I, who had been hurriedly summoned to Moscow as an expert witness to the proceedings, received access to them. That was the categorical condition I made—payment, if you like, for my participation in the pending farce.

As was to be expected, our aims were somewhat different: the commission selecting documentation from the archives was seeking only illustrations of the unconstitutional activities of the former party leadership, and the materials they chose were insufficient for a systematic study. It was a miscellaneous collection of documents relating to different periods and grouped pretty much at random into forty-eight volumes under general headings such as "Violations of human rights," "Terrorism," "Corruption," and so on.

Moreover, the general feeling of uncertainty and ambiguity in the country was reflected in the composition of the commission and its methods of work. Since neither the president nor the government could come up with a clear definition of Russia's interests, decisions concerning what was still a state secret and what was not were made *ad hoc* by these functionaries with party pasts, whose reasons were at times positively surreal. For instance, I learned by chance that it had been decided not to lift the seal of secrecy from a list of Western journalists who were on the KGB payroll.[59] Obviously I wanted to find out why.

"How on earth could we reveal this?" was the response. "After all, these people are still alive. . . ."

But the most striking thing about these people was their staggering ignorance and provincial mentality. These people, who represented the new political elite, the brain trust of Yeltsin's team, his closest and most trusted advisers, simply knew nothing about the outside world. I happened to see the minutes of one of their meetings, where it was recorded that it was decided not to declassify a document concerning the KGB's financial assistance to Rajiv

---

[59]A document did appear concerning KGB payments to the "legendary" Australian war reporter Wilfred Burchett, see 25 October 1957* (St 52/128).

Gandhi. It later emerged that the members of the commission did not know that Rajiv Gandhi was long dead, and they feared that if the document were to become public, it could provoke unrest in India!

In any case, strictly speaking, this commission only saw what it was allowed to see. In other words, matters that could no longer be concealed. In the shifting world of the communist twilight, nothing was really what it seemed. Among other things, the staff of the archive, without whom no commission would be able to find anything, were often former CC technical personnel, and would have gotten their jobs, in most cases, through high party connections, sometimes even relatives. It was hard for people like that to overcome the instinctive habits arising from years of working in the most secret repository of the most secretive state on earth. As a result, any searches for documents came up against the silent but stubborn reluctance—almost sabotage, in some cases—of archive staff to issue any of the materials entrusted to them, a reluctance that can be encountered in the archives of normal countries too. In this case, the reluctance of some was fortified by fear, of others by the typical Soviet aim of extracting the most profitable personal benefit from anything within one's jurisdiction, of others still by political sympathies; in some it was a classic manifestation of the desire of a petty bureaucrat to exercise his powers to the full and humiliate anybody seeking his services. All this, in sum, constituted an insurmountable obstacle. Those staffers who behaved like normal people and were willing to cooperate with researchers could be counted on the fingers of one hand.

It is not hard to imagine what the commission's members had to go through to scrape together those forty-eight volumes. They began work in April, straight after the matter was taken up by the Constitutional Court, yet when I arrived at the end of June, things had barely begun to move. Documents dribbled in all summer and autumn; some of them were found toward the end of the process, and only because of Yeltsin's personal intervention. Yet some remained forever unlocated. I was able to appreciate the difficulty of extracting any information when, dissatisfied with what the commission was finding, I began to demand supplementary documentation. Nobody refused me directly, but documents and culprits alike remained elusive. And what can one say to a bland assertion that this or that document cannot be found? It is true that locating documents in the CC archives is not a simple matter, as the holdings consist of several billion bits of paper.

The matter was complicated further by the circumstance that the archive had been split up, and its most important part—the archive of the Politburo, with all its decisions and minutes of meetings from 1919—had been transferred to the Kremlin in 1990 and amalgamated with Gorbachev's presidential archive. It was physically impossible to get in there without special permission from Yeltsin, who had inherited it along with the Kremlin at the end of 1991. In the main CC archive it was at least possible to check the inventory lists (a kind of catalog or register giving the date, reference number, and title of each CC decision) before trying to secure a document, but the Politburo archive was totally inaccessible. Obviously one cannot request the issue of a document if one does not know of its existence. The staff of the presidential archive were openly mocking in their reply to my detailed queries: "No document found. Can you give us the date and reference number?", knowing full well that I could not possibly do so.

The Central Committee archive was not much better: the inventory gave only an approximate idea of the content of a document —in most cases just its official title, along the lines of "Query from the International Department" or "Memo from the KGB" of such and such a date. So you have to sit there and ask yourself, do you need this document or not? Is it worth weeks and months of determined effort to secure it? And more often than not, after you have jumped through innumerable hoops, the document turns out to be useless. Just like the fisherman in the Russian fairy tale, you cast your net into the sea, and it comes up full of nothing but seaweed....

I had to employ all my prison experience of methodical struggle with the bureaucratic machine. Every time, I had to reach the top and organize pressure from there on the lower ranks, invent countless reasons why I needed this or that particular document for my appearance in the court. I think there wasn't a trick I didn't try. From the arsenal of our prison stratagems, there was only one I consciously never employed: bribery. Maybe I was wrong, but it seemed to me that it would be too demeaning to descend to this level, as it would have been offensive to, say, a former inmate of a Nazi concentration camp to try to buy documents indicting the Nazis from the SS. The thought that the scum who had built their former well-being on our bones would derive profit now from their erstwhile activities was too repugnant to contemplate. Regretfully, I must confess that there were times when, infuriated by the sabotage practiced by these dregs of humanity, I would think longingly about how, had I the power, I would take them out into the yard in small groups, put them up against the wall, and shoot them. Then go back inside and ask in a quiet, even voice, "Now, how about that document? Has it turned up yet? No?"—and take the next group out to the yard.

I do not know whether I had simply forgotten the servility of the Soviet people, their dishonesty and willingness to bow only to force, or whether their final demoralization occurred during the fifteen years that I was out of the country. But whatever the reason, I found that I could not deal with them without a constant feeling of revulsion. They seemed to be some sort of hybrid—Nikolai Gogol's heroes with the psychology of Fyodor Dostoyevsky's personages, aggravated by seventy-five years of Soviet life. I am amazed by the thoughtlessness of Western businessmen who scurry to enter eastern markets at a time when even I find it hard to distinguish the motives of my former countrymen. These motives, even in a casual, superficial encounter, are incredibly numerous and, more often than not, completely irrational. Take, for example, the nondescript, nervously sweating man who came up to me in a corridor in the archive complex, motioned me into his office, and surreptitiously showed me a bundle of documents. *What does he want?* I thought. *Why is he doing this?*

"Can I copy these?" I asked.

"Heavens, no, under no circumstances. . . ." Hands raised in horror, desperation in his eyes.

"Can I read them?"

"Give them a glance. . . maybe you'll need something. . . ."

The documents were nothing special; I had seen much more interesting ones. These I can do without, they do not tell me anything really new, but it seems awkward to just stand up and leave— *What does he want?* I feel sorry for him, too—he tried, even now he's in a lather—from his own daring? From nervousness? From the stuffiness in the room?

"And if I do need them?"

He remained silent.

I feel somehow dirty, any moment now I'll probably start sweating, too. Does he want money? Praise? Love? I don't know. I'm almost prepared to divert from my usual practice and give him some money, just to put an end to the situation. But what if he takes offense? What if he's acting from the heart, and not out of mercenary considerations?

"So I can't copy them?"

"No, no, impossible. . . ."

A long, painful pause.

"You need some help?" He purses his lips and sweats even more profusely. Sure enough, I've offended him. Devil take it, what was I supposed to do? What did I misunderstand in that mysterious Slavic soul? Maybe he genuinely wanted to help me, and this was the only thing he could think of? Or maybe, having lived all his

life in unswerving obedience to the regime, he has suddenly re-
belled, and accomplished an enormous feat of courage by showing
me those papers? Only the courage was insufficient to let me copy
them?

Actually, those who actively hated me or secretly sympathized
with my aims were, in both cases, a minority. Most of the staff,
that ever-present silent majority, were completely indifferent to my
work in the archive. Even the curious matter of my presence in the
former building of the Central Committee (where the archives were
housed after the August 1991 putsch), whose walls were still hung
with portraits of Marx and Lenin and whose doors bore nameplates
like "Deputy sector head, Perepelkin G.V." did not affect them in any
way. In fact, all the changes taking place in the country were perceived by them as nothing more than yet another change of bosses.
I realized quite soon that their attitudes to me—sycophantic willingness to please one day, polite indifference the next, and cold
formality on the day after that—did not signify anything personal,
but were a precise reflection of which way the wind was blowing in
the higher echelons of power. In time I became so accustomed to
this that I used it to gauge the political climate in the country at a
given time and could reach an unerring conclusion as to which side
in the permanent Russian struggle for power had the upper hand
that day. Moreover, having determined the latest moves at the top,
I could predict unfailingly whether I would or would not be given
some document.

Sad as it is, it looks as though the silent majority in the whole
country is the same, accustomed as it is to being merely the *corps de
ballet* of the performers at the center of the stage. How could these
people possibly be transformed by some "democratic innovations"
or "market relations"? In this kingdom of functionaries, where a
bureaucrat became a poet and a poet a bureaucrat, the interpretation of "democratic ideas" was very idiosyncratic: it was understood
as the right of a functionary to disobey his direct superior, having
proclaimed the "sovereignty" of his region, city, enterprise. But no
common interest came to replace blind obedience; the idea of "the
common good" had been exploited too long and too brazenly by the
communists. As a result the country, the society, falls apart without the support of vertical connections. Yet every separate shard
retains the Soviet mentality, with all its servile system of relationships.

It is no better with those who came to believe in "market relations." It is hard to imagine human material more unsuited to
business. First and foremost, Soviet man believes that any business is founded on the cheating of one side by another. Otherwise,

how does one make a profit? At whose expense? If this had been considered prejudicial, even criminal, in earlier times, it has now, at the whim of Russian history, become the norm. This is perceived as the capitalism that was proscribed by the communists for so long because they wanted to keep its benefits for themselves, as they did with black caviar and quality smoked sausage: they withheld it from the people in order to eat it themselves.

This is no joke, it is a sad reality. It is simply impossible to explain to a Soviet man that business can only function properly when it benefits *everybody*. Talk of honesty, of the principle that a businessman's reputation is his most important asset, elicits the same sardonic grimace that Soviet propaganda in earlier times did; yes, all this must be said for the sake of appearances, it's ideology, but in practice. . . .

Born in falsehood, raised on deceit, Soviet man is firmly convinced that the world is created on the principle of a *matrioshka* doll: what is on the outside is just an illusion for fools, whereas what is inside, real, is completely different. As he is afraid of appearing a fool more than anything else in the world, the prospect of reaching an agreement with him, let alone doing business together, is mind-boggling. After all, he must first determine what is *really* behind your offer, who is standing behind you, who is standing behind them, and so on, right down to the last *matrioshka.*

Therefore, even before you've opened your mouth, he is already firmly convinced that you intend to cheat him, while his aim is to cheat you. What kind of a basis is this for any business? At best, like Gogol's Korobochka, he will go off to find out "the going price for dead souls," and will do his utmost to sell the same consignment of goods to several persons at once. At worst he will try to sell something he does not have, or buy something without paying a kopeck. The latter option is his idea of business virtuosity, an achievement of which only the smartest can boast: if the aim of business is to buy at a lower price and sell for a higher one, then the ideal is straight-out theft. And when he finally ends up with nothing, he takes umbrage at the whole world.

If this description does not fit the majority of people in today's Russia, it nevertheless applies to a very great number. Unfortunately, their superiors are no better, all those Pikhoyas with their naive get-rich-quick schemes. What did he gain from all his efforts, intrigues, worthless agreements with Western institutions? All to end up like the proverbial dog in the manger. Now, in view of the Constitutional Court hearing, the "biggest boss" forgot about his decree, and the vaunted thirty-year moratorium, and demanded the opening of the storehouse, forcing Pikhoya, the very picture of a dekulakized peasant, to give up "his" property. Because, despite all his ambitions, he was (and remains) only a steward, charged with looking after goods belonging to someone else.

He was a pathetic sight. I thought he would have a seizure at any moment. In fact, he did take to his bed with a heart attack—or maybe he feigned one in a last desperate effort to weasel out, who can say? But his heartless superiors dragged him out of bed and to the archive—open up and search! When did the Russian leadership care about anyone's heart attacks? So Pikhoya, clutching his chest and swallowing pills, searched. And I, acting through his bosses —a deal is a deal; if you want my help, you open the archives— extracted document after document from him.

Only four months earlier he had refused to show me something that concerned me personally: the Central Committee decisions as a result of which I was thrown into prisons and expelled from the country. Now, timidly and almost without protest, he opened even special files, KGB reports, International Department documents. The holy of holies of the Central Committee.

"You see, Rudolf Germanovich," I could not resist saying to him once when it was just the two of us in the conference room of the Constitutional Court, "remember how you used to declare—'nobody,' 'never'. . . . Was it worthwhile resisting so much in order to have to give up everything now?"

"Never mind," he muttered glumly, "this madness with the court will end sooner or later, and everything will return to normal."

He was right. The court ended, and by spring 1993 my golden rain ceased as unexpectedly as it had begun. The archives were shut tight, the thirty-year moratorium was restored, and even what I had managed to salvage in the frenzied time of the court hearing, all the volumes of documents amassed by the commission, were once again classified as secret. Maybe forever.

Being no less perspicacious than Pikhoya and feeling certain that I would not be able to make any copies—either for lack of a photocopier, or because of the necessity of obtaining special permission for every scrap of paper, or for God knows what other reasons—I took the precaution of acquiring a miracle of Japanese technology: a portable computer with a handheld scanner. At that time this piece of technology had only just appeared in the West, and it was completely unknown to our Russian savages. Because of this I was able to sit right under their noses and scan piles of documents, page after page, with no worries about the curious, who kept coming up to admire my machine.

"Look at that!" would exclaim the leaders of democratic Russia, peering admiringly over my shoulder. "Now that must have cost a few bucks!"

Nobody realized what I was doing until the court hearing was almost over, until December 1992, when one of them suddenly saw the light and yelled loudly enough to be heard a block away:

"He's copying everything!!!"

There was a deathly hush. I kept scanning, as though I had not heard.

"He'll publish everything *over there!!!*"

I finished working, packed up my computer, and headed calmly for the door, looking neither left nor right. From the corner of my eye I could see the horrified faces of Yeltsin's elite, frozen in unbelief, and Pikhoya's childishly hurt features, which seemed to say:

So let him! Serves you all right!

Nobody said a word as I made my way to the door. They were probably busy calculating what untold millions I would make in the West.

... And that is how the pile of papers marked "secret," "top secret," "special importance," and "special file" came into my hands. Thousands of priceless pages of our history.

2.6   All rise, the court is in session!

The hearings of the Constitutional Court on "the case of the CPSU" opened with a great deal of pomp on 7 July 1992. The judges in their specially sewn black gowns were all former members of the party. The plaintiffs were the former secretaries of the Central Committee and Politburo members, the defendant the presidential team, vice-premiers, ministers—also former party functionaries, but junior in rank to their opponents. Even the "experts" had all been professors of party institutes. To complete the picture, it must be mentioned that this entire show was acted out in the building of the now defunct Party Control Committee of the CC CPSU. It was all highly reminiscent of an interparty investigation into nonpayment of membership dues.

Presiding over the court was Valery Zorkin,[60] also togged out in a black gown, but with a gold chain of office around his neck. He was intently studying a small brass gong on the table before him, obviously trying to estimate how hard he could strike it without sending it flying.

---

[60]Reduced to a simple judge of the Constitutional Court after the October 1993 events, Zorkin was again appointed chairman in February 2003 with the approval of Vladimir Putin. In January 2018, aged seventy-five, he was appointed to a sixth term as the court's chairman.

"Is he, at least, an honest and decent person?" I asked disconsolately of my neighbor, a representative of the presidential side.

"Oh, yes," he answered cheerfully. "He's one of ours. Marvelous man — used to be a professor at the Academy of the Ministry of Internal Affairs."

I bit my tongue. Served me right for asking silly questions. Our understanding of "ours" and "theirs," "decent" and "not decent," were clearly quite different.

This court case, which boiled down to the overlapping claims made by two factions of the divided CPSU to the property of their former party, was a pale travesty of the Nuremberg-style trial I had envisaged, and my participation in it must have looked incongruous. For one thing, the whole idea of the investigation of such a case by the Constitutional Court instead of a criminal court was a fundamental compromise, which effectively tied the hands of those who took part in the process. Everyone, including the president of Russia, understood that it was essential to proscribe the CPSU because it was a criminal organization, and not because its activities had, allegedly, breached the Constitution it had created itself. To prove the latter would be as impossible as making a definitive ruling on what came first, the chicken or the egg. Moreover, several hundred amendments had been introduced into this Constitution for the very reason that it had been adopted for the convenience of the communists. So it would be legitimate to ask, in breach of which Constitution had the CPSU acted? The original, unamended one, or the current, amended one, which rendered their activity unconstitutional? Nonsensical ravings, no more, no less.

As was to be expected, the press and the public saw through this cunning move—the Russian people may be passive, and careless, and God knows what else besides, but they have never been stupid. The newspapers had a field day wondering, with seeming incomprehension, why the court was not applying international legislation, which was quite adequate. For example, *Rossiyskaya gazeta* discussed this on 30 June 1992. On 15 June 1992, *Vechernyaya Moskva* published an article by A. Melechnikov entitled "No Statute of Limitations":

> There is the London Agreement of 8 August 1945 concerning the prosecution and punishment of the main military criminals of the Axis countries, the judgment of the international Nuremberg military tribunal of 1 October 1946, the 11 December 1946 resolution of the General Assembly of the UN adopting the principles contained in the charter and the judgment of the Nuremberg tribunal as acting norms of international law. There

is the international pact on "the unacceptability of a statute of limitations on war crimes and crimes against humanity"

The norms contained in the abovementioned sources were first applied to German National Socialism. But it would be wrong to assume that the situation which has arisen on the territory of the former USSR differs in principle from that, which was assessed in the judgment of the International Military Tribunal of 1946. It has emerged that both states—Germany and the USSR—cooperated in the attack on Poland in 1939. Then, in accord with secret agreements with Germany's political leaders, Soviet communal socialism attacked Finland, annexed Lithuania, Latvia, and Estonia and part of the territory of Rumania. As for the killing of thousands of Polish prisoners seized in the aggression against Poland—is this not a uniquely cynical and inhuman war crime?

The criminal organization that exercised power in the USSR drew no conclusions from the Nuremberg process, at which, by force of historical realities, the dock was occupied solely by the National Socialist German Workers' Party.

Let us remember: 1950—participation in the outbreak of civil war on the Korean peninsula.... 1956—armed intervention in the internal affairs of Hungary.... 1968—identical intervention in the internal affairs of Czechoslovakia. And 1979—the invasion of Afghanistan.

It would seem that nothing could be simpler, more convincing, more logical. But no, the former communists did not summon sufficient resolution, could not take such a step. Neither Yeltsin nor his entourage wanted to be identified as accomplices in crimes against humanity. Instead they had to think up an awkward and convoluted caveat—prove that the CPSU had "substituted itself for the state" and was thereby unconstitutional. But not criminal—God forbid! The court forbade the use of this term—it was, after all, the Constitutional Court, which was not empowered to deal with crimes.

The representatives of the CPSU were quick to exploit this weakness. On the opening day of the hearing, *Pravda* devoted its whole front page to the case, quoting members of the president's team when they were party officials next to their more recent pronouncements, under a huge headline: "Gentlemen! When Were You Telling the Truth? Yesterday or Today?"

The same could be said of most of the witnesses for the presidential side—all former party members, if not leading party figures. So the defenders of the CPSU chose what they thought was a very cunning strategy of putting the same question to every witness: "Do you consider that all party members are responsible for the party's activities?" What could these former party members answer? Nobody wanted to assume equal responsibility with their former party.

"Aha!" crowed the CPSU side. "But the party is, after all, the 18 million members who comprised it, not a mere handful of leaders."

Then, triumphantly, they produced their witnesses—provincial party members who, under oath (and quite sincerely) assured the court that they had never taken part in any unconstitutional activities. And it is hardly likely that CPSU members in the Vologda region engaged in international terrorism, invaded neighboring countries, or even persecuted dissidents. They were preoccupied with bringing in the harvest and fulfilling five-year plans.

Moreover, the CPSU representatives (who are experts in dialectics, after all) insisted that the party had changed completely after some congress/plenum/resolution that denounced past actions, and by virtue of this could not be brought to book. All right, several tens of millions of people were killed under Stalin, nobody is denying that, but, after all, this was roundly condemned by the Twentieth Congress of the CPSU. Yes, Khrushchev and Brezhnev had committed their share of offences, but they were denounced later, were they not? The last time "undesirable practices" were denounced was in 1991, which allegedly signaled a total rebirth of the party, so right now they could live and flourish as never before. But, alas, for no reason whatsoever, they were banned. . . .

Unfortunately, the presidential side could not come up with a convincing rebuttal of such specious reasoning. For they, who had also been brought up on dialectic materialism, considered that since *they* had left the party and condemned it a year or two ago, *they* bore no responsibility for the past. Furthermore, they believed that they had a perfect right to sit in judgment on their former colleagues, who had been less quick on their feet. It was patently obvious why they were so eager to have me, and two or three other dissidents, appear as witnesses: we were not bound by party dialectics, and, in our responses to questions, we could say what none of them could.

There was also the fact that our very presence endowed the proceedings with some kind of meaning. This was certainly felt, if not understood, by all present, and that is why the judges and the CPSU members were unfailingly respectful in their dealings with us. This clearly annoyed some of the people on the presidential team, even though they were probably unaware of the true reason for their discomfiture. One of them informed me, quite out of the blue, that he had demonstratively quit the party on 19 August, the first day of the putsch; presumably I was supposed to be amazed by such daring. Another one described to me at tedious length how cruelly and unjustly he had suffered for his freedom of thought: instead of being promoted to the post of a Central Committee secretary, he had been "exiled" as an ambassador to a Western country. These were not even the birth pangs of conscience, rather something like the yearning in the eyes of a monkey surveying his tailless lineal relative.

Oddly enough, the participants and the spectators of this farce treated it with equal seriousness. Not a shade of irony, not a hint of any understanding of the absurdity of the situation. A cordon of militiamen restrained the crowds that gathered every morning outside the building, those clutching red rags on one side, those with white-blue-red banners on the other. The courtroom was packed with press and interested onlookers: CPSU supporters sat to the right of the aisle, the president's supporters to the left. And God forbid you sit on the wrong side! Former Central Committee secretaries, Politburo members—people who, until recently, held the fate of the world in their hands—and those in whose hands their own fates now rested, sat in that stuffy room for hours, trying not to miss a word. What were they hoping to hear, what truths did they think to discover? Summoned as witnesses, they got tangled up in stupid and petty denials, lost their tempers and cursed, just like inexperienced thieves caught with their hands in the till. The once-all-powerful Yegor Ligachev spent all the long weeks of the process sitting on the edge of his chair, straining forward with a hand to his ear, a pose someone much younger than he would have found difficult to sustain. What could this old buffoon possibly not know about his own party? Former Politburo member Alexander Dzasokhov, like a guilty schoolboy, denied his own signature under some document. Surely he could have thought up something more convincing? Falin, who had been summoned from Germany, wriggled around like a handful of worms. These were powerful figures, I had seen their signatures under truly frightening documents and resolutions that had cost many people their lives. I had imagined them to be perfidious, omnipotent fiends, but seen up close, they turned out to be fools. Poorly educated, inarticulate, and only capable of the stereotyped thinking of *Pravda* editorials.

Those on the presidential side were not much better. They were a touch more intelligent and better educated, but only superficially. Looking at this lineup of the Soviet elite, I recalled an old joke that went around in the 1960s, that there are three qualities that cannot coexist biologically in one person: intellect, honesty, and party membership. One of the three was invariably excluded, so the result could be either a smart son of a bitch or a stupid party hack.

When the crisis of the regime came, that is exactly how they divided up: while the minority of clinical idiots continued to march, waving red banners, the cynical majority was quickly metamorphosing into "reformers", "democrats", "nationalists" and "free marketeers." As far as they were concerned, the events in Russia did not constitute a revolution, nor liberation from totalitarianism, and certainly no sacrifice of their ideals, but simply an opportunity to advance their careers, jumping a couple of the old hierarchical steps in one go. How could CC secretary for propaganda from the Ukrainian satrapy, Leonid Kravchuk, pass up the chance to become president of a sovereign, nuclear state? Or economics editor of *Pravda*, Yegor Gaidar, the post of prime minister of Russia? And who cares whether this is now called democracy or socialism? For people like these, who were devoted only to their own privileges, "democracy" meant merely new opportunities for deceit, and the "market economy" meant only one thing: corruption. For that reason they would stifle any independent initiative under the guise of stamping out corruption, while justifying their own corruption with "market forces." Having seized power with a Lenin-like grasp, they would never allow anything new to develop, apart from one thing: a new mafia in place of the old.

No more than a month after the August putsch, the new "democratic" rulers had moved into the Kremlin, taken over the buildings of the Central Committee on the Staraya Ploschad, appropriated government cars, occupied special dachas and special apartments, registered in special clinics, and gained access to special supplies of goods and foodstuffs. They stole on a scale unimaginable even in Brezhnev's time. There was no way they would let all this slip through their fingers into the hands of the less wily members of the former party.

This was the foundation of the process in the Constitutional Court, its hidden essence. I spent half an hour in the courtroom on the first day and did not enter it again until I was called to give my testimony. Instead of that, I sat in the rest room, where one could watch the proceedings on a monitor if necessary, and scanned documents. Or went across the road to the Central Committee archive. When I got tired of sitting over my computer, I would go out and stroll along streets I knew from childhood, but there was little left from those days; it was like being in a completely unknown city. Moscow resembled a monstrous ruin, as though it had been subjected to intense bombardment by American warplanes. Whole streets had disappeared, replaced by ditches—were they antitank defenses, or was someone laying new sewage pipes? Who could say? Row upon row of empty houses with sagging facades and blind windows huddled on each side. Grass and small bushes sprouted through mounds of fallen plaster. It was obvious that this desolation was not new, that this had happened over many long years, probably since the time when, due to some mysterious cataclysm, all life here came to a standstill. I could not even find the house in which I had lived: it had been demolished with all the other houses on our block, and a huge apartment block for the military, built in the "late evil empire" style, now occupied the site. It was only here and there that a sudden glimpse of a miraculously intact piece of bas-relief on some half-ruined house or the rusty railings of an old fence would stir up memories of a different image of the city. It was here, by the time I was some fifteen years old, that I realized just what a country it was that I had been born into, and where I lived in hostile surroundings, like an advance party of a universal liberation army, operating behind enemy lines. I had dreamed of these streets in my prison cell, these alleys and courtyards had helped me to escape from the KGB on countless occasions, these houses were the only friends I could trust completely.

Had this all been just a dream? The houses and courtyards that could have substantiated my memories were no longer there. The army did not come to the rescue of its scouts—it emerged, much later, that there was no such army. Everything in my life proved to be a host of phantoms, nothing more. All that remained was an enormous cemetery, in which, as everyone knows, victory belongs to the worms.

There was also dismay, bitterness, a feeling of helplessness and of a wasted life:

Why the hell could we not have brought this chapter of our history to a worthier conclusion? What did we overlook? Where did we go wrong? Or were all our efforts hopeless and senseless right from the start?

Chapter Three

Back to the Future!

3.1 So where did we go wrong?

Strangely enough, I did not see the possibility of such an outcome for Russia for quite some time, right up to the emergence of Gorbachev and his glasnost. Prior to that I had always assumed that the fall of the communist system would occur about ten years later, toward the end of the century, and would be much more radical than it turned out to be. It stands to reason that the inevitability of its fall was beyond doubt, but when and how? Some ten or fifteen years ago the question seemed mainly academic. Our discussions in the 1970s were begun by Andrei Amalrik in his "Will the Soviet Union Survive Until 1984?," in which, as we see now, he predicted the scenario of the disintegration of the USSR into separate republics quite logically and accurately. It is immaterial that he postulated that the first impetus precipitating the disintegration would be war with China, which never occurred; this is overshadowed by his much more important basic thesis that the ageing of the regime and the growth of opposition (including the rise of nationalism) would render the USSR *incapable of surviving a serious crisis.* The same issue was postulated in many other books of that period, from Solzhenitsyn's *The Oak and the Calf* to my *To Build a Castle.*

This question of when and how was much more urgent than it seemed at the time, something I realized only upon my arrival in the West. What appeared obvious to us by virtue of our experience was regarded here not as just a subject for discourse, but rather an absurd and even dangerous émigré delusion, similar to the belief of Cuban anticommunists in an easy victory after the Bay of Pigs invasion. The West did not want to take us seriously. At best, Westerners regarded us as a curiosity—just as an ichthyologist, as was keenly noted by Amalrik, would listen to a fish that had suddenly started to talk, but remain convinced that in any event he knew far more about that fish than it was capable of telling him.

Meanwhile the entire policy of the West regarding the Soviet bloc revolved around this question, and if we were right to speak of the ageing of the regime that made it unable to withstand a serious trial, then the West needed to create a deliberate tension, forcing the regime to expend its last strengths. In fact, this did happen to some extent at the beginning of the 1980s, when the hard-line policy of Reagan and Thatcher (coinciding, moreover, with the crises in Poland and Afghanistan) did force the regime to overextend itself to a degree it could not endure.

But the ten or fifteen crucial years were lost. If the West had accepted our advice and taken the path of sharpening relations instead of "defusing" them—and, most importantly, proved capable of mastering the tactics of ideological warfare, the Soviet regime would have collapsed ten years earlier, and the outcome would have been completely different. At least there would be no confusion regarding who was the conqueror and who was the conquered, in which case the process of recovery in Russia would be now as successful as that in the Czech Republic.

In the 1970s, however, this was only the stuff of dreams. The reality called for the need to fear the direct opposite—the full capitulation of the West before the Soviet juggernaut. Yet if we were more or less united and did our best to counter the West's lack of moral fiber, the issue of how the regime would crash remained hotly disputed even in our midst.

Solzhenitsyn's sensational "Letter to the Leaders of the Soviet Union," which was not uninfluenced by Amalrik's book, raised the question of the transitional period from totalitarianism to democracy for the first time, and incited a veritable storm of protests. It seems amusing now to recall that Solzhenitsyn was attacked primarily for daring to presume the inevitability of such a period, to doubt the feasibility of hopes for the immediate triumph of democracy after so many decades of total bondage. My God, the accusations flung at him by demagogues of all colors, both Western and émigré—that he was a monarchist, a Khomeini-ite, and was practically launching an attempt to seize power. In fact, Solzhenitsyn was deeply immersed in researching the 1917 revolution, and simply wanted to warn about the possibility of a repetition of the same scenario in Russia—and as we see now, he was much closer to the truth than his opponents.

My participation in this debate was partly fortuitous, and partly dictated by circumstances. By the time of my release and expulsion, the debate had degenerated into open persecution of Solzhenitsyn, the absurdity of which I found infuriating. At that time I disliked speculations concerning the future, considering them to be not only futile but harmful, only good for fragmenting our already insignificant forces. What is the sense of arguing about what could replace the communists, who have no intention of surrendering their positions and continue to torment our friends in prisons, while the whole world is prepared to bow to them and assume what biologists call the submissive posture?

Launching into a discussion, they will invariably descend into mutual accusations of pernicious intentions, for each one of them goes beyond the limits of arguing about the matter in substance and dons a toga of righteousness, crushing his opponent with the moral superiority of his aims. Furthermore, give the intelligentsia the chance of an unfettered discussion about the future, and it will invariably reach the level of the "higher wisdom" voiced by all the blabbermouths of all times and nations, claiming that nothing should be done at present because it will only make things worse in the future. That is exactly what occurred this time around too, even though it is simply impossible to think of anything worse than a communist dictatorship. But that is what the intelligentsia is for, to exercise an unbridled imagination capable of inventing itinerant phantoms. So having argued *ad nauseam* and also accused Solzhenitsyn of all the deadly sins, the intelligentsia arrived at the conclusion that God forbid anyone do anything, or the communists might metamorphose into a more terrible monster—such as national bolshevism, which they saw as the goal of that traitor Solzhenitsyn.

The highly respected professor of logic Alexander Zinoviev stated directly, with all the implacability of his chosen discipline, that "if tomorrow I were offered the choice between the Soviet type of rule and Solzhenitsyn's type of rule, I would choose the former."

In a word, much as I tried to avoid entering into these senseless disputes, purely practical considerations demanded involvement if only to put an end to a squabble so ruinous to us all. It was something like the regrettable wartime necessity of pulling back troops from the front in order to quell a rebellion in the rear. Now, looking back over these pages ("Why are Russians Quarrelling?",[61] I find it intriguing to recall what I thought about the "transitional period" at that time, back in 1979:

> "Undoubtedly, all predictions concerning an imminent revolution in the USSR are ludicrous, and their propagation criminal, just like the preaching of terror. Only sentimental writers can assert that revolutions are born of poverty and popular lack of freedom, in a time when people are at the end of their tether. Nobody knows fully why revolutions occur, but in circumstances of need and hunger people are more inclined to theft, to individual rebellion, or to dull submission. A person deprived of liberty knows nothing of his rights and is, in any case, too debased to demand any rights at all. An able government has no trouble suborning the more gifted and energetic individuals among a mass of disunited, embittered people. In other words, all this

---

[61] *Kontinent*, quarterly (Paris), No 23, 1980.

leads to the stagnation and decay that we see in the USSR. In this condition, even if some magical external force were to remove the existing structure of state rule, it would unleash an all-out catastrophe, anarchy, and mutual destruction.

Revolutions usually occur when real poverty and deprivation of rights are long gone, but accumulated hatred and distrust of the authorities render every reform unacceptable and insufficient. In such circumstances an indecisive or inept government is a sure guarantee of revolution.

Expecting justice or freedom from a revolution is incredibly naive. Every social upheaval brings the worst dregs of society to the fore, and "those who were nothing, will become everything." A revolution promotes the most cruel, ignoble, bloodthirsty people with strong and despotic personalities. Predatory chieftains. After a fierce civil strife the most ruthless and cunning of them concentrates all power in his hands. That is, revolutions always end in tyranny, not freedom and justice.

Can all this happen in the USSR? Sadly it can, but probably not soon. For the time being, the existing powers are sufficiently strong to avoid any reforms. Even the curtailed Alexei Kosygin reforms were not passed in their original form. This is not devoid of its own logic. The authorities are fully aware that the existing unwieldy bureaucratic apparatus could not cope with the elemental pressure generated by significant reforms. The brash Mauser-toting young men who played the game of the revolutionary hurricane are long dead. The communist regime of today's Soviet Union is probably the most conservative in the world. Even Khrushchev turned out to be too daring. To date, no forces independent of the government that could force the state to institute reforms have emerged in our country.

The period of formation of such forces may last as long as it takes, depending on the behavior of the government, the international situation, and so forth. Current economic difficulties will not motivate the powers that be to enact significant reforms. Thus, regrettable though it may be, no rapid improvements can be expected, let alone radical changes. One may only hope for a gradual growth of independent social forces against a background of stagnation and decay. At present, all that can be seen are the mere contours of these emerging social forces: nationalist movements, religious movements, civil liberties movements (composed mainly of the intelligentsia), and the first green shoots of a workers' movement."

In my perception at the time, this transitional or preparatory period meant "the struggle of the country's social forces for their independence, a struggle in which there would be increasingly less totalitarianism and more democracy, until such time as revolution became unnecessary. That is to say that in my view, this period of transition has already begun."

Our task, *ipso facto*, was to promote the growth and strengthening of this movement and its nonviolent traditions, gaining its acknowledgement and support by the West, so that in the moment of the regime's final crisis there would be a force capable of ensuring a maximally painless, bloodless transition. All our efforts both within the USSR and in exile were directed toward this end.

Clearly, at the time nobody could foresee all the twists and variations to come, but even now, knowing the subsequent turn of events, I see no serious error in my reasoning. Apart from a peaceful revolution, there is no civilized solution to the problem that would prevent, on one hand, a monstrous bloodbath, and on the other, gradual decay and demise of the country alongside the regime. Yet in order for such a scenario to work, the Soviet citizen must cease to be a Soviet citizen for at least a moment. He must reject the temptation of being a time-server, step over the fear of repressions, i.e., make an effort, *his own choice*, in order to become a normal human being.

In all probability this would have happened despite all the repressions, were it not for Gorbachev's "cunningstroika," which, one can assume, was the brainchild of the sagacious Central Committee, in part as a means of averting just such an outcome. But in hoping for the salvation of the system by way of long overdue and half-hearted reforms, the CC blundered into that very scenario of loss of control over the process of which I wrote. This was the end of the communist regime, just as ignoble as its beginning, entangled in conspiracies, sinking in putsches, and condemning the country to disintegration and unrest. For Gorbachev's "reforms" were aimed at preventing, at all costs, the formation of those *independent social forces* that could ensure stability in the transitional period.

The regime was doomed, but before breathing its last it still had time for a final villainy: it turned the country into a whore through the false promise of easy recovery, without effort or sacrifice. The success of this deception, especially among the intelligentsia (the man in the street was deeply suspicious of Gorbachev's stratagems), was much more depressing to behold than all the reconstructed trickery of Soviet leaders. Communists are communists, with all their typical assurance that with a degree of deceit it is possible to outsmart the economy and fool the people, cheat history, and sail into paradise as if in all innocence, remaining unnoticed until someone blows the whistle. Yet when I saw how easily and willingly the intelligentsia accepted the possibility of salvation "from the top," it was a body blow.

Could it be that there was not one person in Russia who did not understand that this party, mired as it was in corruption, lies, and crimes, was guilty of leading the country into a dead end? Could it be unclear to anyone that the depths of this party, which had spent half a century in deliberate recruitment of careerists and scoundrels into its ranks, could never be a source of renewal? Was it not obvious that salvation from the catastrophe they had perpe- trated required, first and foremost, guarding the country *from* them, and not acting *with* them?

Of course not; the intelligentsia understood everything well enough. All these questions were the subject of endless debates raging across Moscow kitchen tables back in the 1960s. The sim- ple truth is that of all the social groups in the USSR, the intelli- gentsia was the most acquiescent, the best fed, and, like Professor Zinoviev, "preferred" the Soviet regime (while cursing it at the same time). And now—what good fortune!—the Master finally allowed *self-expression* in the press. How could one not rejoice? How could one not praise the Master?

Giving credit to the adroitness of the Soviet leaders, who man- aged to knock together a "bloc of communists and non-party mem- bers" even on the edge of doom (moreover, on the basis of anticom- munist feelings!), it was impossible to ignore the fact that the Rus- sian intelligentsia, contrary to Anton Chekhov's precepts, was still unable to rid itself of the internal slave, not by drop or by trickle. In any event, the cronyism of permitted glasnost bound it just as eas- ily as Lenin bound the Russian rabble by encouraging it to "steal what was stolen." The imaginary threat of a return of the former masters made them all obedient instruments in the hands of com- munist manipulators. The original sin of Gorbachev's "freedoms" lay in that they had been *gifted*. What has been gifted and not earned makes it akin to something stolen: it can be taken back, accompanied by a slap on the head. What use is there in thinking about alternatives? God grant that the Master does not return and send you out to the barn for a good thrashing.

To use the slang appropriate to this instance, Gorbachev's glas- nost made the intelligentsia a painted whore to a much greater degree than Brezhnev's censorship. No matter how bad things were before, society still retained certain criteria regarding com- mon decency, certain rules of moral hygiene observed by morally healthy people, while one who was infected knew of his affliction and was visible to others. This signaled the start of particularly disgusting times, when it became impossible to tell the difference between the ailing and the healthy, and all criteria were sacrificed to the noble cause of "saving perestroika" from conservative dreamers. This led to the total "Yevtushenkovization" of the intelligentsia and the "Medvedevization"[62] of the entire country. All of a sudden, everyone became great politicians, and decent people were relegated to obscurity while compromises with conscience were approvingly dubbed "political expediency." Having restructured themselves in one go, they stepped forward in unison under the slogan "Living without lies at all costs!" And lo! here is yesterday's strangler overwhelmed by his own liberalism, while yesterday's liberal is not averse to doing a little strangling himself.

Naturally, this was strongly assisted by the unquestioning support of Gorbachev by the West, as a result of which the situation in the country, which was already sufficiently complex, became tangled into a state of utter hopelessness. At this point in the crisis, for the enormous number of people in the communist world who were not used to independent thought, the "opinion of the West"—which was actually the opinion of the Western establishment—was just as inarguable as Holy Writ to a religious believer. So since the West had proclaimed Gorbachev a hero, and his perestroika to be democracy, who in Russia would dare to raise a dissenting voice?

The West had its own share of those keen to believe Gorbachev's fables. Or, at the very least, it was deemed wise to encourage the "rebuilders" as a reward for their diligence. And it is true that people tried: they brought down the Berlin Wall, repealed article 6 of the Constitution, published *The Gulag Archipelago*, and did not even imprison anyone for the last couple of years. What more can you ask for?

Oh, I was told, you suffered too much at their hands. You can't be objective. There must be a point beyond which the Soviet regime ceases to be the Soviet regime, and the communists to be communists, so our hostility must be replaced by good will.

What could I answer? How is it possible to explain to people who have never lived under this regime that communism is not a political system and not even so much a crime as a sort of mass illness, like an epidemic of the plague? It is impossible to take offence at the plague, one can neither quarrel nor make amends with it, one can only become infected or not. Consequently there is no chance of "reconstructing" or "reforming" the plague: one must strive to recover from it, straining every sinew of the will to live. As a rule, the ones who do not try to fight and who sink into apathy do not survive.

This thoughtless euphoria in the West undermined the last chance of victory over communism, and alongside that the small-

---

[62]Roy and Zhores Medvedev. See Biographical Notes.

est hope for Russia's recovery. It was as if the Allies at the end of the Second World War had not demanded the unconditional capitulation of Nazi Germany, but contented themselves with its perestroika, namely a certain liberalization of the regime. Had that been so, what would Europe be like today? Certainly there would be no democracy but, as is elegantly phrased nowadays regarding former communist countries, no post-Stalin period. Marshal Petain would have been a hero who "saved" France, and the participants of the Resistance would be regarded as irresponsible adventurers who only impeded the wise Vichy reformers with their extremism.

The result was catastrophic. Among other things, it contributed to the already pending schism in our movement, pushing part of it under Andrei Sakharov's leadership into a suicidal alliance with the acolytes of perestroika. So lo and behold, former political prisoner and priest Gleb Yakunin urged people to vote for ex-KGB general Kalugin, who had been an organizer of killings of dissidents in the past. In view of all this, how was it possible to determine who was a real democrat and who was one of Gorbachev's adherents? I shall never forget how, opening his puppet parliament in the spring of 1989, Gorbachev made the grand gesture of inviting Sakharov to step up to the podium, thereby covering up all the lies, all the manipulations and falsifications of the dying regime.

"Andrei Dmitrievich, may I invite you. . . ."

I can still see this scene before my eyes—the scene of the inglorious end of everything I had lived for. Almost thirty years of stubborn striving aimed at the creation of independent social forces turned to ashes. And even though Sakharov, to give him his due, realized his error shortly before his death, tried to form a party of opposition, and even called for a campaign of civil disobedience toward Gorbachev's regime, it was too late.

Now, when history has pronounced its verdict, there is no need for me to prove who was right. The communist regime collapsed despite the efforts of the entire world to save it, thereby confirming what the fish tried to tell the ichthyologist: about his ageing, and that he could not be reformed, but that it is possible (and necessary) to liquidate him, that the threat of nuclear war shall disappear only with his liquidation. The West-acclaimed communist reformers and their Nobel Peace Prizes have disappeared from the stage without managing to produce a "socialist market model." Who remembers them now? But the ruined country remains, with no future, no hope of salvation, the remnants of whose former life are now home to bands of marauders, while millions of impoverished, downcast people tramp glumly past the rubble of their dwellings.

3.2 Secretive times

As it happened, I did not bother to copy many documents about Stalin's repressions, just a few to illustrate that time and that amazed me with their sheer cynicism. It was, in fact, a conveyor belt of death, working nonstop and according to plan, just like Soviet industry in its entirety. Although we know most of these stories from books and accounts, some of the documents impressed even me by their seemingly commonplace inhumanity. It is one thing to know about something, quite another to see a careless note from Stalin sentencing 6,600 people to death with a casual stroke of the pen (31 December 1938*).

The scope of socialist transformation of the country was such that the leaders were uninterested in individuals. The count embraced thousands, tens of thousands, divided into categories. Upon fulfilment of the plan ("quota") regarding enemies of the people (just like reports on the harvest or the yield of milk), republics, regions, areas, and districts reported to Moscow about work accomplished and, as is done under socialism, requested permission to exceed the plan as a demonstration of zeal (4 February 1938*, No. 95/III).

> Moscow, CC CPSU(b) to comrade STALIN
>
> The troika has completed its work, within the quotas of the region 9,600 persons comprising kulak, SR, rebel and other anti-Soviet elements have been tried. Additionally, kulak-White Army elements conducting subversive activity have been uncovered, in total for the region—up to 9 thousand kulak anti-Soviet elements.
>
> The regional committee requests the introduction of an additional quota of 3 thousand for the first category, 2 thousand for the second category, and for an extension of the deadline until 20 March.
>
> Regional committee secretary of
> the CPSU(b) Yu. Kaganovich.[63]

Having conferred, the leaders kindly granted permission for the cull to be continued and then, it may be assumed, set off for a cultural evening at the Bolshoi Theatre to enjoy a performance of *Swan Lake*.

> Extract from the Minutes N58 of the meeting of the Politburo of the CC CPSU(b). (17 February 1938*, Pb 58/57).
>
> Decision dated 17.2.1938.

---

[63]This is not the Lazar Kaganovich mentioned elsewhere, but his brother.

57. Question regarding the NKVD.

To permit the NKVD of Ukraine to conduct arrests of kulak and similar anti-Soviet elements and to examine their cases by troikas, raising the quota for the NKVD UkSSR [Ukrainian Soviet Socialist Republic] by thirty thousand.

Special troikas usually consisted of the first secretary of the regional committee (a district or the CC of a republic), the head of the relevant department of the NKVD, and the regional public prosecutor (for the district or republic). It stands to reason that they simply could not cope with work on such a scale. Over 1938 alone, quotas increased, terms were extended, and the whole meat grinder threatened to become uncontrollable. Finally, in November, Stalin ordered the termination of the work of the troikas and the transfer of new cases to the courts (15 November 1938, P64/22).

It is hard to imagine how people who experienced those times — both executioners and victims — could remain psychologically sound. And is it really possible to distinguish one lot from the other? For instance, this is a report from an NKVD officer to Nikolai Yezhov in October 1937 about "glitches" in the functioning of the machine (31 October 1937*):

> Several days ago the inhabitants of one of the collective farms in the Kuznetsky District complained to the regional committee instructor that not far from them, a mass killing had taken place during the night. A check discovered that 8 enemies of the people had been shot in the woods during the night pursuant to sentencing by a special troika. The head of the regional commissariat for internal affairs (RONKVD), who had been expelled from the party on the previous day for connections with exposed enemies of the people, sanctioned a provocative act, having failed to ensure that the executed persons were buried.
>
> The indicated head was arrested. The executed enemies of the people were interred.
>
> Due to poor security, there were two incidents in investigators' rooms of the Kuybyshev NKVD in which 2 enemies of the people under interrogation jumped out of the window and fell to their deaths.

I would not care to hazard a guess as to how many people they killed—I found no figures concerning the numbers shot—but judging by a report to Stalin from Lavrentiy Beria and Andrey Vyshinsky in February 1939, it emerges that from 1927 the troikas and special tribunals of the secret police (OGPU and NKVD) sentenced *two million one hundred thousand people* to imprisonment and internal exile alone (5 February 1939, 530/B). This does not include the courts and tribunals that also labored without respite, or the mass deportations of "kulaks" in the period of collectivization.

The years 1937 and 1938 gained particular notoriety only because the repressions at that time affected the communist leaders themselves. For simpler people, other years were no better. Even the war did not ease their lot: it suffices to recall that entire peoples were deported, and millions of prisoners of war passed from German concentration camps to Soviet ones. It is not so well known that the fighting spirit of the troops was also underpinned by repressions.

"From the beginning of the war to 10 October of this year, the Special Departments of the NKVD charged with protection of the rear detained 657,364 soldiers who had abandoned their units and fled the front," reported the deputy head of the Department of the Special Operations Executive of the NKVD, Commissar for State Security Solomon Milshtein, to his boss Beria (31 October 1941*).

> Among those arrested by Special Departments were:
> spies 1,505
> saboteurs 308
> cowards and panic-mongers 2,643
> deserters 8,772
> spreaders of provocative rumors 3,987
> individuals inflicting self-harm 1,671
> [...]
> TOTAL: 25,878
>
> Pursuant to the resolutions of Special Departments and sentences handed down by military tribunals, 10,321 individuals were shot, of which 3321 were executed publicly in front of soldiers' ranks.

All this relates only to the first three months of the war at the actual front line. As far as the *chekists* were concerned, their writ ran the entire length and breadth of the enormous country, with the front being everywhere, and the sophistication of their methods could be reduced to the point of absurdity. Many of their "operations" came to light only in 1956, during the so-called "thaw," when the party control committee reviewed the cases of innocent repressed party members. Here is a case in point (4 October 1956*, St 1061):

> Investigation established that in 1941, acting with the sanction of the leadership of the NKVD USSR, the Khabarovsk regional NKVD set up a bogus Soviet border post 50 km from the city

of Khabarovsk, near the village of Kazakevichi, close to the border with Manchuria and a "District Japanese Military Mission" to which state security officials referred as "the mill" in correspondence. The NKVD plan was that such a fake Soviet border post and Japanese border and intelligence bodies was a test for Soviet citizens who were suspected of hostile activity by state security organs.

In practice, however, this undertaking was crudely perverted and employed against innocent Soviet citizens, not genuine enemies of the Soviet state.

The former head of the Khabarovsk NKVD department [Sergei] Gogolidze and the former head of the second department of the NKVD USSR [Pyotr] Fedotov used "the mill" for the purpose of fabricating accusatory materials against Soviet citizens.

A "check" at the notorious "mill" began with a person suspected of espionage or other anti-Soviet activity being approached to carry out an NKVD mission across the border. After receiving the consent of the "suspect" to go on the mission, his crossing into Manchurian territory would be staged from the fake Soviet border post, where he would be detained by supposed Japanese security officials. Subsequently the "detainee" would be taken to the premises of the "Japanese Military Mission" and interrogated by NKVD personnel posing as Japanese intelligence officers and White Russian émigrés. The aim of the interrogation was to get the "subject under questioning" to admit his ties with "Soviet intelligence" to the "Japanese authorities," with the employment of intense pressure, threats and torture in order to break the "detainee" morally. Many persons deliberately placed in such an unexpected and difficult situation, believing that they had really fallen into enemy hands and could be killed at any moment, told the NKVD officials masquerading as Japanese of their connection with the NKVD and the instructions they had been given as to what they were supposed to do in Manchuria. A number of these people, terrified of the mortal danger in which they found themselves, would furnish some information about the USSR under threat of torture and death.

Once the interrogation, which could last days or weeks, was over, the "detainee" would be recruited by the alleged "Japanese intelligence" officers and returned to the territory of the USSR, charged with an espionage mission. The grand finale of this provocative game would be the arrest of the "suspect" by the NKVD to be arraigned for high treason, followed by sentencing by a Special Session to lengthy terms of imprisonment or execution.

By such means, 150 people "went through the mill" from 1941 to 1949 and, although they were subsequently exonerated (the majority postmortem) and this whole *chekist* enterprise condemned as "antistate" in Khrushchev's time, none of the *chekists* involved were ever brought to book. Most of them were simply pensioned off, and even the inventor of that reprehensible "mill" and its permanent curator, Fedotov, got off lightly with a rebuke for overstepping party responsibility. This is hardly surprising in view of the fact that practically the entire leadership of the country was involved, to one degree or another, in "Stalin's" repressions, starting with the head of the KGB of the time, General Ivan Serov, who was directly linked with the Khabarovsk mill (12 September 1956*)[64] and ending with Khrushchev himself.

Brezhnev, who made his career relatively late in the final years of Stalin's rule, also had time to participate in this countrywide meat grinder. Upon becoming the first secretary of the CC of Moldavia in 1950, he hurried to ask for additional quotas to cull hostile elements (6 October 1952, No. 10931). By that time the "class struggle" had subsided somewhat, so there were no big pickings left. A few pitiful survivors were all that remained from previous purges: around 735 kulak families (2,382 persons), 735 kulak "loners," and sectarians—850 families of Jehovah's Witnesses and 400 families of Innokentivites, Archangelists, Sabbatarians,[65] Pentecostals and Seventh-day Adventists, totaling about 6,000 souls. Not much of a catch, but vigilance had to be maintained.

The cadres were Stalinist, and could not be expected to be too strict in their condemnation of "isolated breaches of Soviet legality in the period of the Cult of Personality." Moreover, they had no intention of stopping political repressions as such. Contrary to popular opinion, the "thaw" was very relative: only its scope and style changed, but not the essence. It is curious to note that many years later, in 1975, the head of the KGB, Yuri Andropov, vexed by our campaign in defense of human rights, justified himself before the Central Committee by pointing out that many more people were imprisoned under the "liberal" Khrushchev than on his watch (29 December 1975*, 3213-A):

> As to measures of criminal prosecution concerning the so-called "dissidents," by which the West usually means persons whose actions come under articles 70[66] and 190-1[67] of the

---

[64] 4 October 1956* (St 1061), p. 8.

[65] A variety of indigenous, loosely Christian sects.

[66] Article 70 — Anti-Soviet Agitation and Propaganda (https://chronicleofcurrentevents.net/article-70/), "shall be punished by deprivation of freedom for a term of 6 months to 7 years, with or without additional exile for a term of 2 to 5 years, or by exile for a term of 2 to 5 years."

[67] Article 190-1 — Dissemination of fabrications known to be false (https:

Criminal Code of the RSFSR, the figures are as follows: In the
period from 1967... to 1975, 1583 persons were sentenced
under the indicated articles. In the preceding nine-year period (1958–1966), the number of persons sentenced for anti-
Soviet agitation and propaganda amounted to 3448 persons.
Incidentally, in 1958, precisely the period that is frequently referred to in the West as "the period of liberalization," when N.S.
Khrushchev declared on 27 January 1959 that there were "no
facts of bringing persons to book for political crimes," 1416 persons had been sentenced, which is almost as many as in the last
nine years.

The West has always preferred to think in stereotypes, and see
a liberal in each new Soviet leader. Nobody was denied this acco-
lade: not Stalin, not Khrushchev, not Brezhnev, not Andropov, to
say nothing of Gorbachev. Maybe this arose from the persistent
Western dream that the communist threat would somehow simply
disappear, without struggle and risks. In the words of a popular
ditty:

Got up early one fine day—
Soviet power's gone away!

This was the dream of those who were not the worst by far—the
worst suggested killing the Soviet anaconda "with kindness" by suc-
cumbing to it body and soul. I remember well how I was castigated
by the English intelligentsia in 1978 after the publication of my
book *To Build a Castle*, simply because I was insufficiently respectful toward Khrushchev and his "thaw." How dare I commit such
sacrilege! Indignation knew no bounds, especially in the *Guardian*,
which always thought it knew everything about our life better than
we did. Actually, if there was something to distinguish Khrushchev
from all the other leaders after Lenin, it was his rather naive belief
in the imminent triumph of communism. He prepared for this with
enormous energy, at the very time when the West was weaving him
the garland of a liberal (3 September 1953**).

RESOLUTION

On the organization of the 12th (special) department under the
Second Chief (intelligence) Administration of the MVD USSR
[Ministry of Internal Affairs of the USSR] dated 9 September
1953, Moscow

//chronicleofcurrentevents.net/the-rsfsr-criminal-code/article-190-1/) which defame the Soviet political and social system, "shall be punished by deprivation of
freedom for a term not exceeding 3 years, or by corrective labor for a term not exceeding one year, or by a fine not exceeding 100 rubles."

1. To charge the MVD USSR (Comrade Kruglov) with organizing the twelfth (special) department under the Second Chief (Intelligence) Administration of the MVD USSR for the purpose of conducting sabotage at important military-strategic objects and communications on the territories of the main aggressive states—USA and England, and also on the territories of other capitalist countries used by the aggressors against the USSR.

   To acknowledge the feasibility of conducting terrorist acts [crossed out and overwritten by hand, "active measures"] toward the more active and hostile enemies of the Soviet Union among prominent figures in capitalist countries, particularly dangerous foreign spies, leaders of anti-Soviet émigré organizations and traitors to the Motherland.

2. To establish that all activities of the MVD USSR regarding the 12th (special) department are subject to preliminary scrutiny and sanction by the Presidium of the CC USSR.

3. To confirm the status, structure and personnel of the 12th (special) department under the Second Chief (intelligence) Administration of the MVD USSR.

Secretary of the CC CPSU N.S. KHRUSCHEV

Some liberal, wasn't he? As for those of us who were incarcerated during his "thaw," the above document comes as no surprise. The killings, the kidnapping of leaders of émigré organizations, were well known at the time, just like Khrushchev's invention—psychiatric repression.

Furthermore, as we see now in documents,[68] the course toward partial de-Stalinization after the leader's death was inevitable, and the first to suggest it was not Khrushchev but... Beria. Naturally, he was not prompted by the goodness of his heart or any striving toward the purity of Lenin's ideas, but a vicious power struggle. Being the head of the MVD USSR and state security at the time of Stalin's death, he had access to the archives of these organizations, which, obviously enough, he used against his opponents. Starting rehabilitation on cases in which they, and not he, had been involved by force of circumstances, Beria set the rules of the game for all post-Stalin battles for power. Khrushchev and company had no choice but to remove him physically and, having done so, resort to his methods. But the genie was out of the bottle, and putting it back was impossible.

---

[68]Yakov Etinger, "The Beria Affair Forty Years On," *Russkaya mysl*, 18–24 November 1993 (in Russian), p. 17.

Strangely enough, Beria, who entered into history as no more than Stalin's executioner and pathological murderer, emerges as a politician with imagination. His campaign for selective rehabilitation was not limited to a fight for power, he saw it as a new party line for de-Stalinization. Among other things, in the realm of foreign policy, he suggested reaching agreement with the West for the reunification of both Germanys into a neutral state for the price of 10 billion dollars, which is exactly what, thirty-five years later and much less successfully, was accomplished by Nobel Peace Prize winner Gorbachev. It is easy to imagine how the West would have glorified Beria if had he won the power struggle. The entire post-Stalin period would be known as "Beria's thaw," and nobody would spare a thought for Khrushchev.

In any case, the Khrushchev rehabilitation as such was much less honest than was thought by many at the time. For instance, as was recorded in a note to the CC from Vladimir Semichastny, the head of the KGB at the time (25 December 1962*, 3265-S), practically until the end of Khrushchev's reign the families of those who had been shot on rulings of the troikas were simply being lied to about the fate of relatives who had disappeared without a trace:

> In 1955 the organs of the KGB, acting with the knowledge and consent of the relevant bodies and by agreement with the Procuracy of the USSR, the Committee for State Security issued directive N108cc, which determined the procedure for examinations of applications by citizens interested in the fate of persons shot on rulings of extrajudicial bodies (former College of the OGPU, troikas of the DP OGPU-NKVD-UNKVD USSR and the Procuracy of the USSR). In accordance with this directive, state security organs were to advise families of convicted persons that their relatives had been sentenced to 10 years in corrective labor camps where they died later, and in mandatory cases involving the settlement of property or other legal matters, to register the deaths of the executed in registry offices with the issue of death certificates to the interested parties, in which the date of death would be indicated within the limits of 10 years from the date of arrest, while the cause of death would be purely fictitious.
>
> The establishment of the indicated procedure in 1955 was motivated by the circumstance that in the period of mass repressions great numbers of people were unjustly sentenced, therefore admitting the truth about the real fate of those repressed could have a negative effect on the situation of their families. It was further assumed that advising the bereaved families of the truth concerning the execution of their relatives could be exploited at the time by individual hostile elements to the detriment of the Soviet state.

> The existing procedure for the reporting of fictitious data relates mainly to innocent Soviet citizens who were unjustly executed on rulings of extrajudicial bodies in the period of mass repressions.
>
> Resulting from the reviewing of criminal cases from 1954 to 1961, around half of those shot on the orders of extrajudicial bodies were rehabilitated. In most cases, relatives were falsely informed that deaths had occurred in places where the relatives served their sentences.

It stands to reason that Semichastny does not suggest that the KGB should admit to lying and tell people the whole truth, he simply recommends "giving verbal information regarding the true circumstances of the death" to repeated applicants especially, as he writes that there are fewer such enquiries every year, "and the registration of the deaths in question in registry offices should note the date of execution, without indicating the cause of death, as is done by the Military College of the Supreme Court of the USSR and military tribunals with regard to persons shot upon court rulings."

So to this day we do not know the whole truth about that terrible period. All we have are scraps, fragments, events, and stories that are occasionally hard to distinguish from apocrypha circulated so widely "in secretive times, now almost legendary" (as was keenly observed by Vysotsky). There have been relatively recent exhumations of formerly secret mass graves, but it is impossible to determine the truth from these pitiful scattered bones.

And do we really want to know that truth? I fear that those days of raging insanity shall always remain a black, terrifying block in the minds of people, no matter how many new documents we may find.

3.3 Our "thaw"

It is probably for this reason that I believe more in the legends, songs, images, and sounds of my childhood: to me they are a more faithful reflection of those times. If the images in my memories are invariably murky gray, coarse-grained pictures, similar to old photographs or cinema newsreels of those years, then the sound predominating my childhood was the even, intense roar of motors somewhere over the horizon, unnerving and provoking. It was as though a child's ear could hear something that adults, always immersed in their cares, could not—the incessant working of the infernal machine of the regime.

This was a time of some kind of strain, almost hysteria. On one hand pompous Stalinist parades, salutes, and First of May demonstrations with the participation of practically half the city's population; on the other hand the miserable, poverty-stricken life in barracks and communal housing, with continuous brawls and drunken curses, with ubiquitous cripples around bars and groups of hoodlums in the yards. And the uglier that everyday life was, the more official heroic bravado sounded from loudspeakers. It was everyone's duty to be a hero, as was proclaimed in the well-known song:

> *If the land demands you be a hero,*
> *We shall all respond to that great call.*

The liberated man in a socialist society was obligated to become a supreme being, conquer natural forces, reverse the flow of rivers and transform deserts into flowering gardens. This had its own inexorable logic: creating a heaven on earth required daily miracles.

So these were made-to-order heroes. Always half-starved, always in sweatshirts or military uniform (I do not recall any other types of apparel in my childhood); but pilots stormed the skies, polar explorers conquered the North. Almost with their bare hands, heroes dug canals, built dams, and constructed the largest industrial complexes in the world. The triumphant proletariat swept from victory to victory, demonstrating the invincible force of collective labor.

Of course, all this state-generated romanticism had nothing in common with real life. Despite his burning desire to laud the achievements of the builders of the "garden city" in the midst of impassable taiga, the greatly talented poet Vladimir Mayakovsky unintentionally exposes the sheer absurdity of the situation:

> *Workers squat in the mud,*
> *Chewing sodden bread.*

You see this picture, it is real, so it is totally impossible to accept the pathetic, not to say hysterical, conclusion:

> *I know the city shall be,*
> *I know its gardens will bloom,*
> *When people such as these*
> *Exist in the Soviet land!*

No way shall "people such as these" build any kind of "garden city" if they can't even build themselves a clean canteen and keep bread out of the rain, but prefer to sit meekly in the mud. These are no legendary heroes of yesteryear, conquerors of great natural forces, but prisoners, if not *de jure* then *de facto*.

Heroism is an extremely cruel phenomenon in itself, for it is rooted in self-sacrifice, but when raised to the level of state ideology it also becomes absurd. Nature is not kind to heroes; there cannot be many of them in any nation at any time. What, then, is the "mass heroism" so persistently preached by the system, other than a mass and far-from-voluntary sacrifice? Simply speaking, it is mass murder—just as "conquering Nature" merely denotes its barbaric destruction. Only much later did the people of that time realize, with hindsight, that the superhuman and the inhuman are but two sides of the same coin. While some few burned with genuine fervor, others shook with fear, and in the meantime cynical demagogues continued their climb to power and perished in subsequent purges. This generation was reduced to ashes, destroyed itself in backbreaking labor, perished in camps, laid down its life on the front of "class struggle," and always to no avail. Their sacrifice was senseless: the mighty canals and dams turned rivers into evil-smelling bogs, and the gigantic industrial complexes turned once-fertile lands into deserts, as if Nature, that eternal "enemy of the people", retaliated by wiping out their grandiose schemes.

The absurdity also lay in that heroic impulses, just like any emotional outbursts, are easily inspired but impossible to control and, moreover, to direct exclusively to the benefit of the state. The "Soviet man" the system intended to create was impossible by definition, just as there can be no such thing as an obedient rebel, a conformist revolutionary, or a cowardly hero. Hence the popular outbursts, brawls, and criminality on one hand, and the endless make-believe lies on the other. The country cannot order anyone to become a hero at certain hours of the day and in certain circumstances. If you were raised from childhood to revere the example of someone who throws himself in front of an enemy machine gun or a young girl who dies in one of Hitler's torture chambers without betraying her comrades, it is almost impossible to equate these examples with the atmosphere of lies and malicious denunciations in which you have to live.

In any event, romantic propaganda must have posed serious problems to the work of the *chekist*s. For example, it is amazing to learn that some people actually managed to endure the abovementioned Khabarovsk "mill" without breaking before either the "Soviet" or the "Japanese" side despite weeks under torture, so the *chekist*s ended up shooting them without trial in order to sweep the situation under the carpet. Such a stupendously heroic act at the infernal "mill" sends shivers up one's spine (4 October 1956*, St 1061, p. 5):

> On 21 November 1947, [ethnic Chinese] Soviet citizen Yan-Lin-Puo, who worked as a cook at the "FB" [false border post, the official title of the fictitious "Japanese Military Mission] became so incensed by the lawlessness in that place that he smashed all the dishes and destroyed all kitchen implements of Japanese manufacture. Department head Popov and unofficial collaborator Chu-Tsin-Lin, fearing that Yan-Lin-Puo might flee across the border, shot the latter.

Even those two unfortunate people mentioned in Frenkel's report, who jumped to their deaths from the investigation rooms in Kuybyshev, also committed an act of heroism, exposing *chekist* lawlessness at the cost of their own lives. And how many of them were there, those who did not surrender, did not break, died biting and scratching with no hope of even the grateful memory of their descendants? History has not preserved their names, all we have are the legends, but it was purely due to them that such evil, which had become a generally accepted norm, did not engulf the whole world.

Strange as it may sound, the war brought a certain degree of normality into the paranoid ravings of the 1930s. At least there was now a real enemy, a real threat to the lives of loved ones, and thus a fully understandable need to risk one's life to save them. Yet the same concern was the reason for the success of Stalin's patriotic propaganda, which infected the wartime and postwar generations with the virus of heroism. We grew up knowing nothing but war, ruination, and death, knowing from babyhood how to sell our life more dearly:

> *And in basements and semibasements*
> *Children dreamed of fending off tanks*[69]

Yes, it was probably not just the propaganda. Sometimes I think that we must have been born with some secret aim embedded in our genes. It seems as if the nation made a desperate last-ditch effort to survive, and brought forth a generation of kamikazes which, should Hitler have reached Siberia at least, would have torn his hordes to shreds. Europe was endlessly lucky that the war was over by the time we grew up. But it ended, and the snotty-nosed kamikazes lived on, bitterly disappointed that they had not fired a single shot and incapable of anything else.

The consequences were catastrophic for the regime. On one hand, the country was swamped in criminal romanticism, which, despite all attempts to stem it, remained the prevalent "ideology"

---

[69]Vladimir Vysotsky, "Ballad of Childhood," *Pesni i stichi* (Songs and verse). New York: Literaturnoe zarubezh'e, 1981, pp. 16–18.

of young people, and in the end overcame communist teachings. Making all allowances for postwar confusion, fatherlessness, and so on, the antistate direction of this impulse is clear: all the "romantics" left "the yards and alleyways as thieves" and not Komsomol volunteers on communist construction objects. Those who ended up in the camps were subjected to the fiercest of reprisals. "Juveniles," comprising almost 40 percent of prisoners in 1956, were completely uncontrollable, according to the findings of all the commissions sent by a frightened CC to sort out this phenomenon (22 August 1956, St 21/4).

> On the other hand, wartime heroism awoke a spirit of rebellion among the people. Riots broke out in the camps and outside them, shaking the very foundations of the system. Change would have been inevitable even if Stalin had lived longer, although his death was certainly a turning point. Among other things, the wave of uprisings in Eastern Europe, and especially the Hungarian Revolution of 1956, was definitely connected with this occurrence and electrified the atmosphere in the Soviet Union itself. It fell to our contemporaries in Budapest, not us, to fling themselves under tanks, which earned them our sympathies. I think that of all the 1,416 sentenced in 1958 under article 70 mentioned by Andropov,[70] the majority went to prison "for Hungary," as it was called in those days. Leafleting, arson, and simple refusal to take part in elections became widespread occurrences (5 March 1957, 465-S).

The intelligentsia livened up, too, especially the scientific circles —in physicists, the microbe of free thought had not been completely eradicated, even under Stalin. The then head of the KGB, Serov, reported to the Central Committee in 1957 (19 December 1957*):

> "Landau[71] has gathered a group of theoretical physicists from a number of anti-Soviet and nationalistically inclined Jewish academics."

It is interesting to read this report now, thirty-five years later; it is comprised mainly of Lev Landau's statements, overheard by the *chekists* and quite typical in the circles of the intelligentsia at the time:

> Identifying rebels with the Hungarian people and the working class, he characterizes events in Hungary as the "Hungarian

---

[70] 29 December 1975*, 3231-A.

[71] Lev Landau (1908–1968) became a member of the USSR Academy of Sciences in 1946. He received the Nobel Prize for Physics in 1962.

revolution," as "a very positive, admirable event" in which "stalwart people" are fighting for freedom.

"... The Hungarian revolution—this means practically the entire Hungarian nation that has risen up against its subjugators, i.e., against a small Hungarian clique, and mainly against ours.

"... The real descendants of great revolutionaries of all times.... What they have just shown is deserving of emulation. I am prepared to bend the knee to Hungary."

Commenting on the policies of the Soviet government regarding this matter, he declares:

"... Our lot have decided to spatter themselves with blood.

"... We have criminals ruling the country."

On 12 November 1956, during a discussion in his apartment regarding our actions in Hungary, he answered his interlocutor's remark that "if Lenin were to rise from his grave, his hair would stand on end." Landau replied:

"On the other hand, Lenin also had his hand in the till. Think of the Kronstadt uprising. A dirty business. The working class of Petrograd and the seamen in Kronstadt rose up. They had the most democratic of demands, and all they got was bullets... it's a fascist system.

"... The first thing to happen back in October 1917 was a transfer of power over several months. It was given over fully into the hands of the party apparatus. The party issued an immediate dispensation: steal what was stolen and keep it for yourself. They did everything very methodically.

"... It was not an error, it contained an idea. This was the basis of the revolution."

In answer to the question: "So that means the idea is depraved?"—Landau responded: "Of course."

"... I believe that while this system exists, there is no sense in fostering hopes that it will lead to something decent, there never was such a hope, in a way it's even laughable. I'm not counting on it.

"... There is now an opportunity I had never imagined, the possibility of a revolution in the country. Just a year ago it seemed nonsensical to think of a revolution here, but it is not so far-fetched now. It will happen, it's not an absurdity."

Yes, this is exactly what we thought at the time, that was how we felt, from adolescents to academicians. It was this belief, and not the "liberalism" of the leadership that nurtured the "thaw." This was the foundation of our movement, our struggle against the sudden onset of winter, the sense of which is incomprehensible to those who have not lived under constant strain, did not hear the roar of the state's infernal machine with their own ears, did not have childhood dreams of jumping under tanks.

As for the leaders, all of them from Khrushchev to Gorbachev strove only to smother this spark of hope, justifiably seeing it as a threat to their power. To them, Stalin's time was always a "golden age," a time they did not wish to remember outside the boundaries of official legends. Even thirty years down the road their only regret was that Khrushchev rocked the boat too much in the heat of the struggle for power (12 July 1984*, Pb). How they yearned to rewrite history, to strike out any mention of zigzagging "thaws," how they missed the former clarity of the Leader and Teacher, his firm hand and his eagle eye gazing into the future!

> MEETING OF THE POLITBURO CC CPSU 12 July 1984
>
> [Konstantin] CHERNENKO. In addition to the agenda I would like to inform you of certain letters I have received.
>
> As you know, we have reached a decision concerning one letter. This was V.M. Molotov's[72] request concerning his reinstatement in the ranks of the CPSU. I have received Molotov and talked with him. He greeted our decision with great joy and almost shed a tear. Molotov said that this decision was like his rebirth. Molotov is 93 years old now, but he looks sufficiently spry and speaks clearly. He said that the Politburo of the Central Committee maintains and continues the work that the party conducted so diligently. The only bad thing is that you, like us before you, work until all hours. Molotov stated that he is interested in the press and reads periodical publications. His words were: you are doing everything right, and for this you have the support of the people.
>
> [Dmitry] USTINOV. Coming from him, this is a valuable assessment.
>
> CHERNENKO. Molotov said that he does not understand people who join the opposition due to some personal grievance. He said that he had reached an understanding of his own errors and drawn the relevant conclusions. After our discussion Viktor Vasilyevich Grishin returned his party ticket to Molotov at the city committee headquarters.
>
> [NIKOLAI] TIKHONOV. On the whole, we did right to reinstate him in the party.

---

[72]Vyacheslav Molotov was Stalin's prime minister (1930–1941) and foreign minister (1939–1949). He was removed together with Lazar Kaganovich and Georgy Malenkov from the Central Committee and Politburo in 1957, and all three were expelled from the party in 1961.

CHERNENKO. But on the heels of this, the CC CPSU received similar letters from Georgy Malenkov and Lazar Kaganovich, also a letter from [Alexander] Shelepin in which he claims that he was a consistent opponent of Khrushchev and sets out a number of requests. Allow me to read Kaganovich's letter. [Reads letter.] A letter of analogous content was received from Malenkov, with an admission of his errors.

TIKHONOV. Maybe we should do nothing with these letters for the time being?

CHERNENKO. We can put these letters aside for the time being, but agree to consider them after the XXVII Party Congress.

USTINOV. In my opinion, we should reinstate Malenkov and Kaganovich in the party. After all, they were prominent figures, leaders. I say straight out that if it were not for Khrushchev, they would not have been expelled from the party. Furthermore, there would not have been such scandalous outrages that Khrushchev allowed regarding Stalin. Whatever anyone may say—Stalin is our history. Not a single enemy brought us so much trouble as Khrushchev with his policies concerning the past of our party and state, and with regard to Stalin too.

[Andrei] GROMYKO. I think that these two should be reinstated in the party. They were part of our leadership and the government, were responsible for various sectors of work for many years. I doubt that they were unworthy. Khrushchev's main concern was to decide questions concerning cadres, and not expose errors committed by individual persons.

TIKHONOV. Perhaps we should return to this matter at the end of the year or the beginning of next year?

[VIKTOR] CHEBRIKOV. I would like to report that for some time now Western radio stations have been talking about Molotov's reinstatement in the party. Moreover, they claim that up to the present time, the workers of our country and party know nothing about it. Maybe we should place a notice about Molotov's reinstatement in the party in the Information Bulletin of the CC CPSU?

As for the matter of reinstating Malenkov and Kaganovich in the party, I would ask that we take some time to prepare a report on the resolutions written by these people on lists of the repressed. In the event of their reinstatement, we can expect a significant stream of letters from those rehabilitated in the 1950s who, naturally, will be opposed to their reinstatement in the party, especially Kaganovich. We must be prepared for this. I am sure that such a report should be taken into account by the Politburo CC upon reaching a final decision.

TIKHONOV. Yes, if it were not for Khrushchev, they would not have been expelled from the party. He smeared us and our policies in the eyes of the whole world.

CHEBRIKOV. Furthermore, under Khrushchev a number of persons were unlawfully rehabilitated. The truth is that they had been punished quite deservedly.

MIKHAIL GORBACHEV. I think there is no need to publish anything in the Information Bulletin of the CC CPSU regarding Molotov's reinstatement in the party. The department organizing party work can send operational advice about this to regional party committees.

As for Malenkov and Kaganovich, I am also in favor of their reinstatement in the party. There is probably no need to tie this in with the date of the forthcoming party congress.

[Grigory] ROMANOV. Yes, they are very old, they could easily die soon.

USTINOV. In the matter of assessing Khrushchev's activities I stand fast, as they say, to the death. He did us a great deal of harm. Just think of what he did to our history, to Stalin.

GROMYKO. In the eyes of the external world, he inflicted an irreparable blow on the positive image of the Soviet Union.

USTINOV. It is no secret that the Westerners have never liked us. But Khrushchev furnished them with arguments and materials that have besmirched us for many years to come.

GROMYKO. In fact, it is thanks to this that the so-called "Eurocommunism" was born.

TIKHONOV. And what did he do with our economy? [. . .]

GORBACHEV. What about the party, which he split into industrial and rural party organizations!

USTINOV. [. . .]

In connection with the 40th anniversary of the victory over fascism, I would suggest addressing another question, as to whether we should rename Volgograd back to Stalingrad. Millions of people would welcome this. However, this is a matter for consideration, as they say.

GORBACHEV. This suggestion has both positive and negative aspects.

TIKHONOV. In a recent good documentary film, *Marshal Zhukov*, Stalin is portrayed quite fully and well.

CHERNENKO. I saw it. It is a good film.

USTINOV. I must make a note to see it.

CHERNENKO. As for Shelepin, his request centers on receiving benefits equal to those of former Politburo members.

USTINOV. In my opinion, he is quite adequately provided for

with what he was granted upon retirement. He should not be making such requests.

CHERNENKO. I think that at the moment we can limit ourselves to an exchange of views. But you realize that we shall have to get back to these matters.

TIKHONOV. We hope you have an enjoyable vacation, Konstantin Ustinovich.

CHERNENKO. Thank you.

3.4   We are too few

We were always told: "There are far too few of you. What influence can you have?" And we always agreed: yes, we are few. In answering questions about the possible number of participants of the movement or the number of political prisoners, we preferred to decrease rather than increase the figures. Sorry—that's how many there are. Such is our society, such is our country, that no more willing figures came forward. Nowadays, when I am asked, this is what I reply, especially to my contemporaries, with the added comment, "If you had joined us, that would have been one more."

But they always find a host of weighty reasons, explaining convincingly why they simply could not do so.

We also answered that the issue was not one of numbers or even practical results, but the principle of the inner freedom and moral responsibility of man. It should be a normal need, just like the need to breathe, eat, move.[73] But this was something nobody wanted to hear. There had already been too much philosophy in our lives, and too few practical results. It was far too intricate: For your own benefit, you have to reject normal life, forgo a career, go to prison? So where is the benefit?

It is amazing, nonetheless, that in the face of such hopelessness, after so many decades of terror that seemed to have driven all the humanity out of people, it emerged that there were more of us than we could have dreamed, and our effect on the regime was much greater than we'd thought. It was enough to take just a cursory glance through the documents of the Central Committee to see this. Their sheer volume was incredible. The KGB informed the CC of everything, even the most trivial things about our movement, and the CC, or even the Politburo, had to reach decisions concerning every minute detail. Not just our arrests, court hearings, exiles,

---

[73]See Andrei Amalrik's "Open Letter to Anatoly Kuznetsov" (https://chronicleofcurrentevents.net/2013/10/11/11-14-samizdat-update/), *Chronicle of Current Events*, 31 December 1969 ("Samizdat Update").

house searches, but even the pettiest operational information had the attention of these fifteen very elderly and extremely busy people, as this report by KGB head Andropov to his CC colleagues shows (31 July 1967*, 1931-A):

> Information has been received that candidate of biological sciences Zhores MEDVEDEV, residing in the city of Obninsk in the Kaluga region and employed by the Institute of Radiology, acting together with his close friend Valery PAVLINCHUK, has begun to make typewritten copies of A. SOLZHENITSYN'S unpublished novel *The First Circle* for purposes of disseminating it among academics in Obninsk. For this reason, scientific employee of the Institute of History of the Academy of Sciences of the USSR Pyotr Ionovich YAKIR, known to be a participant in a number of antisocial manifestations and author of politically detrimental pronouncements, plans to travel to Obninsk. In view of the fact that SOLZHENITSYN'S novel *The First Circle* is a politically pernicious work, receipt of its copies by P.I. YAKIR warrants his detention and confiscation of such copies and instructing the Obninsk city committee of the CPSU to take measures to put an end to Zh. Medvedev's antisocial activity. I request consideration of this matter.

And they did look into it. The word *Agreed* is written by hand in the margins, followed by the signatures of Mikhail Suslov, Boris Ponomarev, Andrey Kirilenko... incredible! Even all of our samizdat was forwarded to them by Andropov (11 June 1968*, 1372-A):

> Operational measures have established that [Pavel] LITVINOV, [Natalya] GORBANEVSKAYA, YAKIR and certain like-minded persons have produced and are circulating a document entitled "Human Rights Year in the Soviet Union" (copy attached) containing slanderous accounts of court cases in Moscow and Leningrad and brief contents of letters and appeals discrediting the Soviet bodies of power and government. Submitted for your information.

Just try, in those times, to have your complaint read by a member of the Politburo! Hopeless. Everything got stuck within the apparatus, and was forwarded to the people you were complaining about. And now the complaint not only had to be read but required a decision. A miracle indeed! The most effective method of making the authorities think. And this was only samizdat and operational measures. Our arrests, trials, and sentences made them argue occasionally, reserve decisions for additional review of the problem, return to it several times. These people worked, thought, decided. They did not sign anything automatically. I was almost touched to see that the entire Politburo met to consider whether to publish a small piece in *Evening Moscow* [*Vechernaya Moskva*] after my trial in 1967 (4 September 1967*, Pb 1393). As Andropov reported to the CC:

> In addressing the court the accused Bukovsky, whose crime lay primarily in the organization of an antisocial demonstration, attempted to cast a political light on the trial, declaring the actions of the authorities and the court to be unconstitutional, and conducted himself throughout with the clear intention of gaining mention in the foreign press as a victim of political persecution rather than an antisocial criminal. [...] Due to the circumstance that Western reports concerning this trial have distorted its essence, it would appear feasible to publish a short piece on the matter in the *Evening News* (attached).

The attached fourteen-line draft of the piece was headed "In the Moscow City Court." The intention was to state that I had pleaded guilty and, consequently, all rumors of any kind regarding my address to the court amounted to nothing more than false bourgeois propaganda. Nothing more, nothing less than another small lie in the cause of socialism. Yet they did meet, they did discuss the matter, they voted on it. The results of the vote are appended: Brezhnev for, Kirilenko for, Kosygin on vacation, Kirill Mazurov no comment, Arvids Pelse for, Suslov on vacation.

It emerges that there were some unpleasant disagreements among them. For example, there were documents concerning trials of demonstrators protesting the Soviet invasion of Czechoslovakia in 1968. Pack them off to the camps and throw away the key. Yet even in this instance, things were far from simple: Pavel Litvinov's grandmother, widow of Maxim Litvinov, the erstwhile people's commissar for international relations, who was a longtime acquaintance of Mikoyan, appealed to the latter (4 September 1968*) to keep her grandson out of prison. Mikoyan forwarded her letter to Brezhnev, with a handwritten annotation: "Leonid Ilyich! May I request your attention. To conduct a court case that, as they say, 'is in the pipeline,' against Litvinov's grandson and others would simply supply our enemies with ammunition. They have already served their time. In this instance, it would be wiser to merely issue a warning. A. Mikoyan. 13/IX."

Below this Brezhnev wrote, "Advise the members of the Politburo," which is followed by the signatures of the members. Not bad going. Even though the trial did take place eventually, Litvinov and two more of the accused were not sent to the camps, but into internal exile, although this penalty was not envisaged under the article in question.

There are many thousands of such documents—thousands of hours of work. Even if we had achieved no more, we had sapped some strength from the governing machine, distracted its attention from global revolution. Such intense interest by the authorities in our activities was not a manifestation of paranoia. They were perfectly aware of the danger posed to them by our very existence, because they were under no illusion regarding the people's love of their rulers. In a totalitarian system, even one dissident is dangerous, especially if that system has proclaimed itself to be perfect. Nobody can be dissatisfied in the socialist paradise: according to Marxist ideology they could not exist, especially fifty years down the road after the revolution.

Therein lay the fundamental dilemma of the communist authorities: on the one hand, the number of dissatisfied people—dissidents, to say nothing of open enemies of the regime—should have continued to decrease over the course of the "building of socialism," and repressing them would have been counterproductive; on the other hand, allowing political opponents—in view of widespread public dissatisfaction—was downright dangerous. This accounts for the tactic of lowering the numbers of political prisoners while simultaneously increasing pressure on dissidents: the aim was to break the dissidents' spirit, to "disarm them ideologically," and in later times even throwing them out of the country in order to avoid imprisoning them. They referred to this practice under the tortuous label of "prophylactic work on averting crimes."

By such means, the number of political prisoners did not reflect the prevailing mood in the country but was merely a confirmation of human endurance; as a rule, those who broke were not imprisoned. Allowing for this, we were not so few after all. Ensuing from the abovementioned report by Andropov to the CC in December 1975 (29 December 1975*, 3213-A), the number of those sentenced solely for anti-Soviet agitation and propaganda between 1958 and 1967 amounted to 3,448 persons, and from 1967 to 1975, 1,583 persons. From subsequent reports by the KGB to the CC, it emerges that all efforts and "prophylactic measures" aimed at achieving a substantial decrease were to no avail: in the period from 1977 to 1987, 905 persons were sentenced.[74] (Figures for 1976 were not found.) Moreover, these only concerned the people the regime was forced to identify openly as its political opponents, not including those relegated to psychiatric institutions, exiled abroad, sentenced

---

[74] 11 May 1987 (6/2140), see p. 7 in 1 February 1987* (183-Ch).

for attempts at illegal crossing of borders or treason, or sentenced on "religious" and fabricated criminal grounds. Of these we simply know nothing.

It appears that in the entire post-Stalin period, they failed to break at least six thousand people. Even in the wave of Gorbachev's "releases," when prisoners were freed in exchange for a promise to desist from any further "antisocial" activity, there were still 233 people held in prisons and camps, 55 in various exiles, 10 being held under "religious" articles, 96 in psychiatric incarceration, 31 released from imprisonment, and 51 not finally prosecuted—in all, 476 individuals.

The numbers were not the main issue. The very fact of the existence of people who had openly challenged totalitarian enslavement and stood fast before the fury of the state had enormous moral significance for the country. This is probably akin to the significance for a religious believer caught up in worldly squalor of knowing that in some monastery there are mortals like him who "live by truth." And this knowledge may enable him to resist occasional temptations. In any event, that something like that was the case was evident in the attitudes of both our jailers and genuine criminal prisoners toward us. I shall never forget how the local criminal godfather of the camp in which I was the only political prisoner gathered all the thieves prior to his transfer elsewhere and issued his final orders. At the end he poked me with a finger and said severely: "Look after this one. We're all here for something each one of us did, but he's here for the good of everyone."

It is amazing that decades of communism had not managed to destroy such ideas in people. As for the guards, they regarded us with almost superstitious awe. Invariably, even in Vladimir Prison, there would be at least one who would agree to post an illegal letter or pass a note into another cell. Considering the volume and detail of information that Western radio stations were able to air at that time, one can only guess how our incarceration in, say, that same Vladimir Prison affected the population of that city. Especially during our hunger strikes and other strikes. It was probably for this reason that no regional party committee would agree to have us on their territory, inventing all sorts of reasons to get rid of us, while the CC had no idea how to relocate us (17 March 1978*, 492-Ch). Debates on this matter dragged on for years. The following was written to the CC by both Chebrikov and Schelokov:

> The Ministry of Internal Affairs [MVD] of the USSR and the KGB under the Council of Ministers of the USSR support the proposal of the Vladimir regional party committee of the CPSU re-

garding the transfer of particularly dangerous state criminals from prison No. 2 of the Administration of the Vladimir regional executive authority to another corrective labor institution of the Ministry of Internal Affairs.

The question of relocating particularly dangerous state criminals was considered by our departments in 1977. At that time, with allowance for the reasons advanced in the note of the regional party committee of the CPSU in Vladimir, it was deemed feasible to relocate the indicated prisoners (their numbers vary between 40 to 60) to prison No. 4 of the MVD of the Tatar ASSR (Autonomous Soviet Socialist Republic). It was also borne in mind that there are no military or other important objects in the city of Chistopol, where prison No. 4 is located. Chistopol is 144 km from the city of Kazan, is far removed from any of the country's large industrial or cultural centers and has no sufficiently developed means of transport to other districts. Prison No. 4 was built back in the XVIII century and is unconnected with the past imprisonment of revolutionaries and other progressive figures. . . .

• • •

It stands to reason that from a numerical point of view, this was merely the tip of the iceberg. An idea of the actual situation can be gleaned from the data of the *chekists*' "prophylactic work" (16 November 1972*, Pb 67/XVIII):

Pursuant to the instructions of the CC CPSU, agencies of the KGB are conducting wide-scale prophylactic work for the prevention of crimes, countering efforts aimed at attempts to organize subversive activities by nationalistic, revisionist and other anti-Soviet elements, and also pinpointing groups of a politically detrimental nature in various locations. Over the past 5 years, 3096 such groups have been exposed, 13602 of their participants have undergone prophylaxis, including: 2196 participants of 502 groups in 1967, 2870 participants of 625 groups in 1968, 3130 participants of 733 groups in 1969, 3102 participants of 709 groups in 1970 and 2304 participants of 527 groups in 1971.

Similar groups were uncovered in Moscow, Sverdlovsk, Tula, Vladimir, Omsk, Kazan, Tyumen, in Ukraine, Latvia, Estonia, Belorussia, Moldavia, Kazakhstan and other places.

The measures undertaken have resulted in a significant decrease in the number of annual arrests for anti-Soviet agitation and propaganda.

Most of those who have undergone prophylaxis reached the correct conclusions, returned to constructive participation in social life and work, and engaged conscientiously in assigned industrial and employment activity. However, some of them con-

tinue to perform actions that under certain conditions may become criminal and inflict considerable damage on the interests
of our state.

In order to increase the preventive influence on persons attempting to enter the path of committing particularly dangerous
crimes, and also enable the more decisive prevention of undesirable manifestations by antisocial elements, it is deemed feasible, in case of necessity, to permit the agencies of the KGB to
issue official written warnings in the name of the authorities,
demanding the cessation of such dangerous political activity
and clarification of the possible consequences for the continuation of such activity.

In our opinion this would raise the moral responsibility of persons undergoing prophylaxis, and in the event of their committing criminal activity and facing criminal charges, would be important for assessing the criminal's personality by bodies conducting the preliminary investigation and the courts.

Naturally, their request was granted. And the relevant Order of
the Presidium of the Supreme Soviet of the USSR appeared on 25
December 1972. Yet despite all the efforts of the *chekists*, domestic
opposition continued to grow. Thus, three years after the promulgation of this order, Andropov reported (29 December 1975*, 3213-A),
"For the period of 1971–1974, 63,108 persons went through prophylaxis. For the same period, the activities of 1839 anti-Soviet
groups were exposed at the formation stage through prophylaxis."

It emerges that the average annual number of the latter did not
decrease at all, while the number of those subjected to "prophylaxis"
increased tenfold. But this was still not all, because the KGB did
not subject all active enemies to "prophylaxis." Andropov continues
in the same report:

Alongside prophylactic measures, operative and other measures unconnected with criminal prosecution were and are employed. We have been able to break up a number of nationalistic, revisionist and other anti-Soviet groups while they were
still forming. Compromising these bodies inspiring antisocial
behavior enabled the prevention of undesirable consequences
in a number of places in the country. Such measures as depriving certain individuals of Soviet citizenship and expulsion
abroad also proved worthwhile. ... Furthermore, the operational situation was improved by the issue of exit permits for
numerous extremists to emigrate from the Soviet Union to Israel.

So were we many, or few? Andropov considered that among the
adult population that had gone through the war alone, "the num-

ber of such people amounts to hundreds of thousands." I believe he underestimated their numbers greatly. For example, his reports hardly mention those peoples "punished" (exiled under Stalin) nor religious movements, especially in terms of proscribed denominations and confessions. Yet these amounted to millions of people, for whom the Soviet Union was a prison, and our contacts with them developed from the 1960s. Andropov reported to the CC (10 June 1968*, 1342-A):

> The KGB has received operative information that in discussion with one of his friends, [Pyotr] GRIGORENKO stated that he was aware of the alleged intention of representatives of Crimean 'autonomists' to send an appeal to the UN signed by 250,000 Tatars, requesting support for their demands. Approving of this action, GRIGORENKO predicts that it will elicit 'an enormous response.' The Committee for State Security is implementing all necessary measures to prevent possible hostile actions by nationalistically inclined Crimean Tatars and other antisocial elements.

Or here is another example of the time:

> The Committee for State Security has received information regarding the intention of individual German extremists residing in Kazakhstan and Moldavia (12 June 1975*, 1482-A) to inspire Soviet citizens of ethnic German origin to stage group refusals to participate in elections to the republican Supreme Soviets on 15 June 1975 and local elections to the Councils of workers' deputies, if their demands for emigration to the Federal Republic of Germany are not met. ... At the same time, on the days preceding the elections, "activists" of the so-called "movement for the emigration of Germans to the [Federal Republic of Germany]" in Moldavia organized a collective visit to the republican MVD USSR and the KGB (70 persons), demanding approval of their applications to leave the USSR, and extremists in Kazakhstan produced a number of slanderous appeals to international organizations with collective signatures, and attempted to send their representative to Moscow for the purpose of handing this material to foreign journalists or dispatch to the West via A. SAKHAROV. ... Measures taken at the Dzhambul station on 7 June 1975 resulted in the confiscation of "appeals" to the UN, the Geneva Conference, the chancellor of the FRG and other addressees from one TERMER, in the name of 900 families of ethnic Germans (more than 6,000 persons), which contained tendentious information regarding the situation of Germans in the USSR and requests for assistance in emigrating to the FRG.

So life in the USSR may have only seemed serene and carefree to Western politicians; their Soviet counterparts were perfectly aware of the volcanic crater on whose edge they perched. The empire was straining at the seams long before the appearance of Gorbachev, as Andropov reported (30 December 1980*, St 243/8):

> "Negative processes have been noted in a specific part of the indigenous population of the Karachay-Cherkess autonomous region, characterized by nationalistic, anti-Russian feelings. This has caused antisocial manifestations and criminal acts. Measures are being taken for their prevention and termination."

The issues here were killings and mass unrest.

Tatars and Germans, Jews and Baltic peoples, Ukrainians and Moldavians fought for their national identities by all available means. But all the threads from the far-flung parts of that vast country led to Moscow, where all our channels of contact with the external world were, our *glasnost.* To them we served as an inspiration, an exemplary and organizing factor. So Andropov had good reason for concern. How could the Politburo not monitor every breath we took?

In the end, those engaged in the most "passive" forms of resistance—proscribed religious communities, disseminators of samizdat, authors of anonymous protests—were the most numerous. How could we possibly determine how many people were involved in this activity? Even the KGB couldn't come up with a final figure. Let's say that it is possible to quantify persecution on religious grounds; on average, probably some two or three hundred people a year were imprisoned and another ten thousand underwent "prophylaxis,"[75] but it is impossible to establish the total number of religious believers, just as it is impossible to establish how many read, copied, and shared samizdat with their friends. It would have been millions at least. Therefore the Politburo also had to read these materials; it was necessary to know what millions of people were reading in the country they subjugated, in which not a single comma could be typed on a label without censorship.

The question of samizdat was of serious concern to the leadership; in 1971 alone, the matter was discussed three times by the Central Committee, and the CC was to return to this issue in every subsequent year. In December 1970 (15 January 1971*, St 119/11) Andropov reported the following:

---

[75]Peter Reddaway, "Reassessing the Past: Sovietology and Dissidence; New Sources on Protest," *RFE/RL Research Report*, Vol 6, No 5, 29 January 1993, pp. 12–16.

An analysis of the so-called "samizdat" literature circulating among the intelligentsia and students shows that in recent years "samizdat" has undergone qualitative changes. Five years ago the materials going from hand to hand were mainly ideologically slanderous works of fiction, but now the greatest turnover relates to documents of a schematic political nature. In the period from 1965 more than 400 various investigative studies and articles have appeared on economic, political and philosophical themes, in which the historical experience of socialist construction in the Soviet Union is criticized from all angles, which revise the internal and external policies of the CPSU and offer all kinds of programs for opposition activity....

... There is a certain consolidation of fellow thinkers on the basis of the production and dissemination of "samizdat" literature, and noticeable attempts at the creation of something akin to an opposition.

Around the end of 1968 to the beginning of 1969, opposition-minded elements came together in a political core named the "democratic movement," which, by their estimation, is endowed with the three signs of an opposition: "it has leaders, activists, and depends on a significant number of sympathizers; without taking on the clear form of an organization, it sets itself definite aims and selects specific tactics; strives for the achievement of legality." ...

... The centers of distribution of uncensored materials remain Moscow, Leningrad, Kiev, Gorky, Novosibirsk and Kharkov. In these and other cities, some 300 persons have been identified as calling themselves "anti-Stalinists," "fighters for democratic rights" and "members of the democratic movement" and engaging in the production of individual documents and miscellanies — the *Chronicle of Current Events*,[76] *Ukrainian Herald, Social Problems* and others. In 1970 a group of Zionist-minded elements in Moscow, Leningrad and Riga began issuing a journal entitled *Exodus*....

... The Committee for State Security is taking all necessary steps to put an end to the attempts of individual persons to use "samizdat" as a vehicle for slandering the Soviet state and social system. They are brought to book on criminal charges in accordance with current legislation, and persons who fall under their influence undergo prophylactic measures.

At the same time, bearing in mind the ideological transformation of "samizdat" into a form of expression of opposing moods and views, and the aim of imperialistic reactionaries to employ

---

[76]A typescript journal produced every two to four months in Moscow between 1968 and 1983 by an "anonymous and changing group of human rights activists" (Reddaway).

"samizdat" for purposes hostile to the Soviet Union, it would appear feasible to charge the ideological apparatus with the task of studying the problem and evolving the requisite ideological and political measures for neutralizing and exposing the antisocial leanings contained in "samizdat," as well as proposals for identifying the factors that facilitate the appearance and dissemination of "samizdat materials."

So in actual fact, the government already acknowledged us to be a political opposition and, irrespective of its seeming inviolability, was ready to adjust its line accordingly. It is quite another matter that by virtue of its senescence and ossification the regime was already incapable of political flexibility, and after *half a year* of work, the Central Committee finally passed the resolution "On Measures for Countering Illegal Dissemination of Anti-Soviet and Other Politically Harmful Materials," an extremely senseless document that brought together all possible combinations of repressive and corrective-propagandist actions. The only concession was made in the last, ninth clause (28 June 1971, St 8/37):[77]

The Department of Culture of the CC CPSU, the Press Committee under the Council of Ministers of the USSR and the Union of Writers of the USSR are instructed to study the matter and submit suggestions regarding the feasibility of publishing certain works by authors who arouse the interest of some creative workers and students and whose works have not been republished in the USSR after the 1920s.

The result was, I believe, a publication of Nikolay Gumilyov's poems, and that in a limited edition. For obvious reasons, this had no effect whatsoever on the growth of samizdat: it continued to expand, creating an alternative to the official press and giving Andropov headaches. New forms came into being—cinema samizdat, record samizdat, etc.—an alternative culture that weakened the control of the party over creative intelligentsia and particularly young people. Once again, Andropov sounded the alarm (19 May 1975, 1241-A):[78]

In the course of implementing measures aimed at the termination of hostile enemy actions, facts have emerged indicating that in circles of creatively gifted or ambitious young people wanting to prove themselves in this sphere there is a tendency to group on an unofficial basis, manifested in literary readings, exhibitions of art and graphics, staging of plays in private dwellings

---

[77]See 21 April 1971 (St 2/2), p. 6.
[78]19 June 1975 (St 173/4), p. 3.

and randomly selected premises. There is a noticeable tendency toward the issue and circulation of typewritten journals, composed of unpublished works.

A study of the situation in such groupings in Moscow has shown that left to its own devices, part of the creative youth finds no socially useful application of its abilities and can take the path of undesirable developments which, as a rule, are inspired by persons engaged in antisocial activity, or by foreigners. . . .

. . . Therefore, at present there is the danger of the emergence of ungovernable groupings of creative young people, existing alongside official creative associations.

It is a fact that this period saw such notorious events as the exhibition of nonconformist artists in Izmaylovsky Park,[79] the attempt to establish a section of the International PEN (now PEN International) in Moscow,[80] the institution of a Moscow chapter of Amnesty International (12 April 1975, 878-A), and, a little later, the appearance of the uncensored miscellany "MetrOpol" and the founding of the Helsinki Groups (social groups for monitoring observance of the Helsinki Accords) with all their commissions, committees, and working groups. Even the first independent trade union appeared at the end of 1977 (see 6 April 1978, 655-A). This was the beginning of the process of structural formation of the opposition, which probably coincided with the loss of control over young people, something that posed a particular threat to the regime.

• • •

In essence I do not recall that this control was ever effective, existing mainly on paper—in the reports of Komsomol and party committees concerning "blanket coverage" and propagandistic enterprises. However, toward the end of the 1960s and the beginning of the 1970s, young people became noticeably politicized. This was manifested mostly in anonymous protests—leaflets, graffiti on walls, displays of national flags in the republics, and anonymous letters addressed to the authorities. Any provocative event, such as a jubilee, a general holiday, the elections, was usually accompanied by such "outbursts of hooliganism" by young people. Andropov reported a case in point in April 1970 (27 April 1970*, 1118-A):

The jubilee celebrations marking the 100th anniversary of the birth of the founder of the Soviet State, V.I. Lenin, proceeded in an organized manner throughout the country, in an atmosphere of heightened activity, industrial and political enthusi-

---

[79] 20 May 1975 (No 97), p. 9 in 19 June 1975 (St 173/4).
[80] 5 April 1975 (784-A).

asm of the Soviet people, demonstrating once again unshake-
able popular unity and solidarity around the Central Committee of the Communist Party of the Soviet Union. Nevertheless,
155 politically harmful acts of hooliganism in connection with
the jubilee were recorded in certain areas of the country in the
period of preparation and conduct of the celebrations. This includes 55 in 1969 and 100 in 1970.

Manifestations of this kind were also noted in Ukraine, Kazakhstan, Lithuania, Belorussia, Estonia, Moldavia, the Turk-
men Soviet Socialist Republic, the Maritime and Khabarovsk
districts, and the Moscow, Leningrad, Kuybyshev, Rostov and
other regions. Actions of this kind by hooligan elements destroyed or damaged some statues, busts and bas-reliefs of the
leader, a significant number of panels, stands and banners, as
well as portraits, slogans, posters, reproductions, wall newspapers and other festive tributes.

[...]

70 persons were charged with committing crimes, 65 were ordered to undergo prophylaxis and 7 were detained for investigation for politically pernicious acts and hooliganism.

In 18 cases, these manifestations were particularly audacious
and were aimed at casting a shadow over the Soviet people's
celebration of the 100th anniversary of the birth of V.I. Lenin.

And here is a typical report to the CC regarding the celebration
of the First of May 1975 (4 May 1975*, 1103-A):

The First of May celebrations passed in a normal atmosphere
and with great political enthusiasm throughout the country.

Nevertheless, certain negative manifestations were noted in
some parts of the country.

Leaflets with hostile content were distributed in Moscow,
Odessa, Kishinev and the Rostov region.

In the district center, Pustomyty, of the Lvov region, 13 flags of
the union republics were burned near the monument to the
soldier-liberators. Flags were also destroyed in Moscow and
Kharkov. In the city of Grodno, a portrait of the founder of the
Soviet State was defaced.

[...]

The relevant measures were taken with respect to the indicated
acts.

Most of the persons perpetrating these hostile acts have been
identified.

In fact, far from all perpetrators were usually identified—some 50
or 60 percent, of whom half would face "prophylaxis"; the rest would

be imprisoned, customarily on criminal charges (such as hooligan-ism). With the inclusion of anonymous letters, such occurrences would amount to between ten and twenty thousand per annum throughout the country.[81] More often than not, the "criminals" turned out to be young people, often adolescents and schoolchil-dren, who at times had already managed to create illegal organiza-tions. Of course, we had no idea of the scope of such occurrences, nor did we ever hear anything about them. Still, without them the picture of the situation in the country and of its prevalent mood would be incomplete, just as the nervousness of the authorities could not be comprehended fully without this background.

Imagine how the CC must have felt receiving several reports such as this every day (19 March 1970*, 699-A):

> The Administration of the KGB for the Krasnodar district uncov-ered an illegal "Club for the Struggle for Democracy" in Tuapse, comprised of 14 students in classes 8–9 of secondary school No. 3. Of these, 7 are members of the Komsomol.
>
> [...] The members of this "Club" drew up a program and a charter, issued handwritten journals entitled "The Democrat" and "The Russian Contemporary," containing poems and arti-cles written by members of the "Club" based on the reports of Western radio stations. Each member swore an oath, had a pseudonym, a membership ticket and paid membership fees.
>
> The program of the "Club" envisages the establishment of a party of "democrats" in the country and seizure of power once the members reach adulthood. Their immediate aim was the production and dissemination of documents with anti-Soviet content and the recruitment of new members. In carrying out this program, [...] they chalked anti-Soviet graffiti on asphalt roads and fences in various places in Tuapse in December 1969 upon the 90th anniversary of the birth of Stalin. In February 1970 they produced more than 40 leaflets in the name of the "All-Russia Union of Democrats" containing a call for the over-throw of Soviet power and the formation of illegal political par-ties. These leaflets were distributed throughout the city.
>
> All the members of the "Club for the Struggle for Democracy" are minors. In view of this, it was decided not to institute crim-inal charges, but limit the matter to enacting prophylactic mea-sures.

(12 June 1970*, 1610-A):

---

[81] Peter Reddaway, "Reassessing the Past: Sovietology and Dissidence; New Sources on Protest," *RFE/RL Research Report*, Vol 6, No 5, 29 January 1993, p. 15.

The KGB Administration of the Sverdlovsk region uncovered an illegal youth group calling itself "The Free Russia Party" or "The Revolutionary Workers' Party." [...]

Using a typewriter, the members of this group produced around 700 anti-Soviet leaflets in two shifts. ... On 7 November 1969, a significant proportion of these leaflets were released from the viaduct over the Cosmonauts' Prospect in Sverdlovsk onto the heads of the festive column from the electric trains repair works and a group of demonstrators from the Polytechnic and Law institutes.

(26 August 1970*, 2353-A):

In February 1970, seven handwritten leaflets were disseminated in the city of Ryazan , signed by the "Black Angels," the authors of which slandered the Soviet government and called for the organization of strikes and demonstrations. It was established by the usual methods that the leaflets were produced and distributed by 9th grade pupils in Ryazan school No. 42. ... They all repented, and in the presence of their parents promised the KGB that they would never again commit any antisocial acts.

The presence of such moods among the youth on one hand, and the growth of organized opposition on the other, created a situation in the country that was highly dangerous for the regime. The authors of a comprehensive study conducted by the KGB in 1976 (28 December 1976, St 37/14, p. 4), while trying to lay the blame for everything on the influence of bourgeois propaganda and Western "subversive centers," records some extremely interesting data[82] nonetheless. Out of 3,324 "antisocial manifestations" over a period of three years, there were 4,406 young people involved; 60.3 percent of these acts were committed by students and 22.4 percent by school pupils.

Seventy-two percent of these young people (3,174 individuals) acted alone, the remaining 1,232 individuals within the composition of 384 groups.[83]

---

[82]28 December 1976 (St 37/14), p. 10.
[83]12 December 1976 (2798-A), p. 11 in 28 December 1976 (St 37/14).

Forms of manifestation	Number of manifes-tations	Persons involved
Expressing slanderous and other politically damaging assertions	1509 45.4%	1598 36.3%
Participation in group actions violating public order	99 3.0%	495 11.2%
Participation in antisocial actions based on imitation of "hippies"	152 5.5%	382 8.7%
Production and dissemination of slanderous and ideologically pernicious documents (excluding leaflets)	252 7.6%	323 7.3%
Production and dissemination of leaflets, slogans, posters	167 5.0%	277 6.3%
Desecration of the state crest, flag, monuments, portraits	90 2.7%	115 2.6%
Verbal and written threats directed at the Soviet party apparatus	50 1.6%	53 1.2%
Transfer (attempts at transfer) of slanderous and ideologically pernicious materials abroad	26 0.8%	33 0.8%
Production and dissemination of anonymous letters with slanderous and ideologically pernicious content	33 1.0%	32 0.7%
Attempts to establish contact with foreign anti-Soviet centers	16 0.4%	17 0.4%
Production and display of nationalistic flags	6 0.2%	15 0.3%
Other manifestations	894 26.8%	1066 24.2%

Manifestations committed from capitalist positions, hostile to socialism, comprise 32.4% of the total number of manifestations.[84] They were committed by 1,269 persons (29%).

Various forms of hostile ideology	Number of manifes-tations	Persons involved
Ideology of bourgeois nationalism (except Zionism)	364 33.7%	674 43%
Zionist ideology and pro-Israeli sympathies	188 17.5%	242 15%
Ideology of revisionism and reformation	377 35%	445 28%
Religious ideology	88 8.2%	128 8%
Fascist and neo-Nazi ideology (views)	60 5.6%	80 6%

Here we are talking about those who could (or dared to) formulate their ideological platform clearly. But those "without ideas" were no better.

---

[84] 28 December 1976 (St 37/14), p. 13.

The participants of groups of so-called hippie emulators in Moscow, Leningrad, Kiev, Vilnius, Tallinn, Rostov-on-Don, Odessa, and a number of other cities called for a review of the moral and ethical norms of socialist community life, questioned the revolutionary traditions of the past and the spiritual heritage of conservative forebears, and advocated overcoming inertia and struggling for the freedom and democratization of society on the basis of hippie ideas.

Around 40 percent of all those subjected to prophylaxis in the country in the years 1970 to 1974 were young people up to the age of 25.[85] The same applied to criminality in general; for instance, more than half of those sentenced in 1971 through 1973 who were charged with the manufacture and sale of drugs were under the age of 29, while the numbers of those subjected to administrative measures for the consumption of alcohol and public intoxication were 2,533,443 young people in 1973 and 2,616,708 in 1974.[86] On average, minors (those up to 18 years of age) committed around one hundred thousand crimes per year, of which 47 percent were committed by groups.

Similarly interesting information was contained in other studies cited in this report. Data from a study of "the audience of Western radio stations in Moscow," conducted by the Department of Applied Social Studies of the Institute for the Study of Science of the Academy of Sciences of the USSR, indicate that:

> To a greater or lesser degree of regularity, these radio stations are listened to by 80% of students and around 90% of senior secondary school pupils, state vocational schools and technical colleges. For the majority of these individuals, listening to foreign radio has become a habit (32% of students and 59.2% of senior school pupils listen to foreign broadcasts no less than once or twice a week.)[87]

This was also our audience, monitoring our activity through broadcasts from London, Munich and Washington, the very generation of thirty to forty-year-olds that took to the streets 15 years later.[88]

> Many of the students that had undergone prophylaxis indicated in their replies that they taped radio broadcasts of ideologically hostile works, after which these recordings were disseminated on audio tapes or as typed texts. Among other things,

---

[85] 28 December 1976 (St 37/14), p. 17.
[86] See 28 March 1974 (No 34), pp. 3–11 in 16 April 1974 (St 121/23).
[87] 12 December 1976 (2798-A), p. 18 in 28 December 1976 (St 37/14).
[88] 28 December 1976 (St 37/14), p. 21.

this was the channel that provided them with information regarding a number of SOLZHENITSYN's anti-Soviet declarations and libels, SAKHAROV's treatise "Thoughts on peace, progress and intellectual freedom," and various "studies," "appeals" and other documents containing defamatory concoctions, slandering Soviet reality. [...]

As for the degree of influence, the greatest is from materials produced illegally within the country.

At the same time, the authors note that there is a marked decline in interest in studying Marxist-Leninist theory in institutions of higher education as well as a decline in "passive participation of a certain part of the student body in the social and political life of collectives." In a nutshell, there is every reason to affirm that by the 1970s the regime had practically lost the young people, and our influence on them grew by leaps and bounds. How could an ageing, bureaucracy-ridden party counter such a threatening turn of events? It had nothing to offer but repressions, "prophylaxis,"—that is, threats of further repressions—and a massive increase in its already despised propaganda. Reporting on work accomplished over several years prior to the collapse of the communist regime (26 December 1986*, 2521-Ch), KGB head Chebrikov, Procurator General Alexander Rekunkov, Minister of Justice Boris Kravtsov and the Chairman of the Supreme Court of the USSR Vladimir Terebilov proudly told the CC the following:

For purposes of exposing the subversive activity of imperialist special services and their allied hostile elements among Soviet citizens, much work has been accomplished with the aid of the media. Over the past ten years, 150 cinema and television films have been released with the use of materials provided by the security services (mainly short documentaries and newsreels); over four years, 262 books and brochures have been published, as well as 178 articles in journals and 250 in newspapers. Propaganda in the form of lectures is continuously devised by KGB personnel, the Procuracy and court and judicial bodies. Educational work with prisoners is conducted systematically and with social involvement, which yields its own positive results.

They were especially proud to report that over four years, from 1982 to 1986, they had managed to break more than a hundred people. This process was also overseen by the CC, which did not begrudge its valuable time. And when the time came to save their skins from inevitable doom, they were forced to introduce a controlled "glasnost," beginning it with attempting to break the remaining *zeks* [prisoners], thus destroying the core of the opposition. This procedure was directed by Gorbachev personally.

3.5   The law and feasibility

"Honorable judges! Today is a very special day for me: for the first time in my life I appear in court not as an accused, but as a witness...."

The comical aspect of the situation was augmented by the fact that appearing in court for the first time in 1967 as the accused, I had spoken about the same things—about lawlessness, about the unconstitutional nature of the CPSU itself, and about the political repressions it perpetrated. It was all so similar, except that now, exactly twenty-five years later, I could have repeated my address word for word in the Constitutional Court of Russia, and nobody would have noticed any difference. I cannot help recalling how I prepared for that first "final word" to the court (prior to that I had been classed as insane twice, and was tried in absentia), how I managed to get hold of the legal codes from the administrators of Lefortovo Prison by threatening a hunger strike, and how I even forced them to buy a Constitution of the USSR, of which there was not a single copy in the investigative prison of the KGB. Then there was the official dreariness of the trial and the tense expectation of the end, when I was entitled to that "final word"—the only form of uncensored speech in the land at that time. (Yet who knew? They could simply interrupt, without letting me finish speaking. This was not unprecedented.) And finally—the culmination of the entire drama, when, waving the KGB copy of the Constitution, I was able to speak for almost one and a half hours, expecting to be pulled up short by the judge at any moment. So on the question of the unconstitutional nature of the CPSU I was a genuine expert. But if at that time this was considered slander against the state and social system of the USSR, it was now deemed state wisdom in the highest degree, supported by the authority of the president of Russia himself. So what was I to do—rejoice or grieve? Take pride in that I had preceded my contemporaries by a quarter of a century, or be perplexed that such a simple truth had not entered their heads two and a half decades earlier?

The emphatic nature of our movement in defense of rights always brought forth a mass of bewilderment and even censure. It was not that the fact of violation of their own laws by the communist authorities was a secret to anyone, but the idea of their observance was too complicated. On the contrary, it would have been hard to find someone in those years who was unaware of all the facts, who did not see them. But what for? What would be the point?

So what, you want to perfect the Soviet regime? sneered Soviet people, generally from the ranks of those who thought that we were "too few" to join.

Tell us, when will your movement finally stop citing Soviet laws and move to open action? asked those in the West, who had never lived under the heel of the regime.

There was never a way to explain to certain kinds of people that the movement for defense of rights is not mimicry, not a tactical ploy, but that just like the refusal to engage in violence or underground activity, it was the principle on which our position rested. Yet it was not the complexity of our position that was the problem. What complexity could there be when we had the painful example of the results of the former Russian revolution before our eyes every day?

How could anybody not realize, even in the 1960s, that violence does not lead to a lawful state, or the underground to a free society? Even from a more practical point of view, is it not obvious that if there is an insufficient number of people in the country capable of simply demanding what is their due under the law, you won't be able to find an enormous number of valiant men ready to shoot the entire KGB, the party apparatus, and a goodly portion of the Soviet army? But if one fine day there is a sufficient number of people demanding their rights, there will be no need for firing squads.

In the end these were all excuses, self-justifications. A Soviet citizen was unable to force himself to demand something from a nuclear superpower. He could steal, but making demands stuck in his throat. Not all were even able to bring themselves to refuse to cooperate with the authorities. Someone had to do all this before their eyes, quite openly, even demonstratively, in order to dispel the mystical, irrational fear of the Soviet authorities, the halo of their omnipotence. In this sense nothing could be more destructive than a demonstration of the authorities' lack of effectiveness on one hand, and their lawlessness on the other.

After all, what more could be done? Scattering leaflets or creating underground "parties" with a couple of friends was the province of schoolchildren, but even they understood that this was futile. What was needed was *legal* opposition that would be able to unite and foster independent social forces in the country. And legal means that respect the law and operate within its framework.

In the meantime, the regime had its own problems with the law, which it was unable to solve from the time of the revolution, and never solved. In the first place, because ideology in general and the Marxist-Leninist version in particular are incompatible with the concept of law. Ideology is a legend, a myth, and thus unavoidably inconsistent, while the entire sense of the law lies in its internal consistency. Communist practice was all the more inconsistent, being a compromise between ideology and reality. And what was "done" and what was not on any given day was known only at the top of the pyramid of power. It was necessary to know how to construe even secret instructions.

Let us move on. The task of ideology is to explain everything on earth in veiled concepts, not amenable to precise definition; the task of the law is to determine everything with maximum precision, leaving no loopholes. And how can these two things be reconciled? For instance, how can dialectical materialism be codified? The result would be something akin to the efforts of medieval scholars to calculate exactly how many angels can fit on the head of a pin.

But the main reason for the incompatibility of the law with ideology in a totalitarian state lies in that here ideology, not the law, must dominate by definition, and if ideology cannot rule *through the law*, then it becomes *above the law, ruling from behind its back*, as it were. Just as the party—the standard-bearer of the ideology—rules from behind the backs of other state structures and is a suprastate formation. Bearing in mind the global aims of this ideology (and with it, those of the party), the law simply transforms into a fiction, an offshoot of propaganda calculated to create an attractive image of "the world's most democratic" socialist state. This was glaringly obvious in the example of the Stalinist constitution, written expressly for propagandistic purposes and therefore very convenient for us.

In practice, the law existed only on paper; the country was governed in accordance with an endless stream of departmental, state, and party instructions and resolutions, which were frequently contradictory and mainly confidential. To reduce all this to a single noncontradictory state was beyond even the party's ability. "Telephone law" flourished; a call from a party boss would be the latest legislative act.

In all fairness it must be said that the ideology was just as incompatible with other areas of life such as economics and science, for the very same reasons. Initially the law was our weapon, simply because it was a weapon the authorities turned against us. And we, truth be told, honed it to perfection, to the state in which any trial of any one of us ended in the defeat of the authorities. So much so that unlike Stalin's show trials, our trials were conducted in maximum secrecy, were concealed from the public as much as was physically possible, and mentioned in the press—if they were mentioned at all —merely in response to "the slurs of bourgeois propaganda."

Undoubtedly it was not easy to achieve such a state of affairs;

it required great stamina and precise conduct that demanded not simple incarceration, but incarceration "on one's own terms," with maximum detriment to the authorities, i.e., with maximum violation of the law on their part. For example, in 1967 I did not simply organize a demonstration and receive a sentence of three years— no, I solved the "theorem" of the unconstitutional nature of article 190-3 of the Criminal Code of the RSFSR.[89] This is exactly how the demonstration was calculated, as well as our future arguments under investigation and in the courts, so that the authorities could sentence us only in breach of the law, abandoning any semblance of legality. In the indicated case in breach of the Constitution, which guarantees freedom of demonstration.

I must say that in this instance, I managed really well. Even the head of Lefortovo Prison acknowledged openly that we had been imprisoned illegally, the Procuracy, citing glib and specious reasons, refused to conduct the case, and my KGB investigator could only shake his head and sigh dolefully. It was not surprising that the Politburo had to hold a meeting to decide whether to publish some elementary lies about this case in the papers. For me this fact is a kind of gold medal, or the award of a scientific diploma.

In all probability, generations that did not live in those times will find it hard to understand the practical significance of all this. The more so because we had practically no aims in the narrow, utilitarian sense—just like that Chinese man who smashed all the Japanese dishes at the Khabarovsk "mill." None of us thought that the Soviet regime would be brought down by our trials, by samizdat, or by tiny, purely symbolic demonstrations. Nor did anybody count on the "improvement" of the regime. It was paradoxical that our movement, which exercised such a significant political influence, was not in fact political—it was *moral*. Our main stimulus was not a desire to remake the system, but a refusal of complicity in its crimes. Everything else developed later as a logical extension of this position.

In its turn, the position of noncompliance arose in public reaction to Stalin's repressions, or rather to their partial, but still real, exposure under Khrushchev. The public, or in any case its better part, was tortured by the question, "How could such a monstrous crime have occurred? Who is to blame?" And the inevitable conclusion was that part of the blame lay on everyone, for practically everybody, voluntarily or involuntarily, passively or actively,

---

[89]Article 190-3 prohibited "violation of public order by a group, either in a coarse manner or in disobedience of the lawful demands of representatives of authority." It was introduced in 1966 to deal with public demonstrations.

was an *accomplice*. Not only those who executed and tortured, but also those who raised their hand at meetings and "unanimously approved" the massacres; not only those who issued orders, but also those who remained obediently silent.

> *Be silent and you'll be a hangman.*
> *Be silent, be silent, be silent....*

Just as in postwar Germany, this had a particularly strong effect on new generations, which were not party to their fathers' crimes; such is life that children always have to pay for the sins of their parents. And even though the Soviet leaders were never in the dock in Nuremberg, the verdict of this tribunal applied to us in full. Like our German contemporaries, we had to remember that neither the opinion of the surrounding majority, nor orders from superiors, nor even the threat to one's life relieved us of the responsibility for our choice. But unlike them, for us it meant confrontation with our not-yet-demolished Reich, our own SS—with whom, alas, the entire Western world strove for "peaceful coexistence."

So we could not dream of any practical aims. Probably nobody even tried to determine what could be considered a victory. Our task was making constant distinctions between the written law and its unwritten ideological interpretation, forcing the authorities to a broad exposure of its unlawful essence. It was better not to think of what it would mean for you personally. After all, the most you could get was the maximum term. For this reason, irrespective of practical results, you just had to do as much as you could to serve your sentence with a clear conscience. With time, this is how victory came to be seen—as the right to tell your descendants, *I did everything I could.*

Now, looking back over the Central Committee documents concerning our cases, I was simply amazed: just about any one of them could be placed on the table of a court, as if for many decades our movement had only occupied itself with preparing for this Constitutional Court trial of the CPSU. And this movement started, at least formally, with our first demonstration in 1965, under the slogan "Respect your constitution!"—and a demand for *glasnost.* You couldn't make it up![90]

• • •

---

[90]KGB head Semichastny reported to the Central Committee (6 December 1965, 2685-S^) that about fifty or sixty people gathered around the Pushkin monument that day. Thirty years later, his report was published in *Nezavisimaya gazeta* (5 December 1995).

At that time, in December 1965, we threw down our first gaunt-let to the regime. The reason was the "case of [Andrei] Sinyavsky and [Yuli] Daniel," which caused a great deal of noise—the case against two writers who had published their books clandestinely in the West. The curious aspect of the situation was that the country was expected, just as in Stalin's times, "to condemn renegades and turncoats" without ever having laid eyes on their books. And here was the first appearance of that word *glasnost.* Our foremost "lawyer," Alexander Esenin-Volpin, probably came across it in the Criminal Procedure Code of the Russian Federation in the section dealing with "publicity [*glasnost* in Russian] of judicial examination."

> Examination is open in all courts with the exception of cases that run counter to the interests of safeguarding state secrets.
>
> [...]
>
> In all cases, the sentences of the courts are publicly proclaimed.

The slogan would appear harmless to even the best-intentioned citizens: If you don't let us read the books in question, then at the very least conduct a public trial over them, so that we can find out everything for ourselves.

This demand caught the authorities unprepared; nothing like this had happened in the past, that a Soviet citizen would demand anything at all. So they had to invent their own glasnost.

The head of the KGB, Vladimir Semichastny, and Procurator General Roman Rudenko wrote the following in a report to the CC dated 23 December 1965 (with which the CC agreed benignly), *almost two months prior to the trial* (23 December 1965, 2843-S):[91]

> At present, the KGB, acting together with the Department of Culture of the Central Committee and the Union of Writers of the USSR, is preparing relevant publications for the press that shall expose the true nature of the "literary activity" of SINYAVSKY and DANIEL. In order to provide the public with more detailed information and put an end to similar activity by hostile individual elements, it seems feasible to try the case against SINYAVSKY and DANIEL in an open hearing of the Supreme Court of the RSFSR and sentence the criminals to imprisonment for the production and dissemination of literary works that contain slanderous allegations regarding the Soviet state and social system, under part 1 article 70 of the Criminal Code of the RSFSR. It is planned to conduct the trial at the beginning of February 1966 under the chairmanship of Comrade

---

[91] 5 January 1966* (St 132/11), pp. 6–7.

> L.N. [Lev Nikolayevich] SMIRNOV, the chairman of the Supreme
> Court of the RSFSR, with the participation of state prosecu-
> tor Comrade O.P. [Oleg Petrovich] TEMUSHKIN, assistant to the
> Procurator General of the USSR, in the courtroom for hearings
> of the Supreme Court of the RSFSR accommodating 100 per-
> sons, and to invite representatives of Soviet and party active
> functionaries as well as the literary community to the hearing.
> In our opinion, the participation of a public prosecutor from
> the sphere of literary workers in the trial would be advisable.
> To this end, we suggest that it is essential to instruct the Union
> of Writers to nominate a suitable candidate for the position of
> public prosecutor. After the trial, relevant publications should
> appear in the press and on the radio. We request consideration
> of the above.

These were but general desires. Specific development of the Soviet understanding of glasnost came from a totally different person,
who, twenty years later, became the architect of glasnost under Gorbachev, Alexander Yakovlev, but who at that time was head of the
Department of Agitation and Propaganda of the CC. He is now seen
as a historical figure, without knowing his background all the roots
of Gorbachev's glasnost cannot be comprehended fully. This was
his definition of an "open court" (5 January 1966*, St 132/11):[92]

> According to the plan, the court hearing will proceed in the
> presence of representatives of workers, active Soviet and party
> functionaries and Moscow writers and journalists; the proce-
> dure for their invitation shall be the concern of the Moscow
> City Committee of the CPSU.
>
> In connection with the forthcoming trial, it is deemed essential
> to issue suggestions concerning its coverage in the press and
> on the radio:
>
> 1. Reports from their own correspondents from the court-
>   room, and also special daily reports by [major Russian
>   news agency] TASS on the progress of the trial to be pub-
>   lished in the newspapers *Izvestia* and *Literaturnaya gazeta*
>   [*Literary Gazette*]. The editorial boards of the newspapers
>   *Komsomolskaya pravda* [*Komsomol Truth*], *Sovetskaya kul-
>   tura* [*Soviet Culture*] and *Sovetskaya Rossiya* [*Soviet Rus-
>   sia*] may publish material from their own correspondents
>   in the courtroom at their own discretion.
>
> All other newspapers shall publish only official TASS re-
> ports regarding the trial; in the course of the hearing, ra-
> dio shall broadcast TASS reports and certain newspaper
> correspondents concerning the proceedings.

---

[92] 3 February 1966, pp. 8–9 in 5 January 1966* (St 132/11).

Acting together with the KGB under the Council of Ministers of the USSR, APN [Novosti Press Agency] is charged with the preparation of relevant articles concerning the trial for publication abroad.

Correspondents of the indicated newspapers, TASS and APN shall enter the courtroom (without cameras) with official passes, issued by the KGB under the Council of Ministers of the USSR.

Foreign correspondents are excluded from the court hearing.

2. In order to prepare official reports and provide scrutiny of reports on the court proceedings, a special press group shall be formed of... [names from the Department of Culture of the CC CPSU, Department of Agitation and Propaganda of the CC CPSU, Department of Administrative Units of the CC CPSU and the KGB under the CM [Council of Ministers of the] USSR].

It would seem that Yakovlev gave careful consideration to all eventualities. The scrupulously selected public "greeted the verdict of the court with applause." The press, party organizations and the KGB were also not tardy in doing their bit, as the latter was proud to report (16 February 1966, 346-Z):

The sentencing of criminals SINYAVSKY and DANIEL was met with approval by Soviet society. In the course of the hearing, the court and the editorial boards of newspapers received numerous letters and telegrams from Soviet citizens, demanding strict punishment for the slanderers.

Yet despite all their efforts, thousands of sheets typed on onion-skin paper were spreading throughout the country, bearing the "final words" of the accused, and everyone knew that *they did not plead guilty!* Protests escalated, and the world at large was perturbed and indignant at the outcome of the trial. Our glasnost was at work.

Yakovlev had nothing to do but howl even louder:[93]

In order to clarify the substance of the trial of Sinyavsky and Daniel, and also expose the slanderous claims of the bourgeois press... it would be feasible to implement the following actions:

- conduct informative and clarifying presentations by authoritative activists in the fields of literature, the arts and

---

[93] 18 February 1966^, Yakovlev and Chauro note to Central Committee. See Politburo decision of 21 February 1966 (Pb 255)^.

sciences, in creative organizations, newspaper and journal offices, in publishing houses... [and] [...] in the humanitarian faculties of institutions of higher education;

- charge Politizdat [the political publishing house of the CPSU Central Committee] with the urgent publication of the materials of the trial (the conclusion to indict, the speeches of state and social accusers, the sentence, etc.) for the purpose of informing party and creative activists, and also the correspondents of newspapers in socialist countries and press bodies of communist parties in capitalist countries;

- publish a letter from the Secretariat of the Administration of the Union of Writers of the USSR that contains a response to the declarations of foreign writers and cultural activists regarding the trial in the Literary Gazette and Izvestia;

- instruct the editorial boards of the newspapers Izvestia, Komsomolskaya pravda, Literaturnaya gazeta and Sovetskaya kultura to publish readers' letters, and also prominent representatives of literature, the arts and sciences, approving the verdict of the court and condemning the anti-Soviet activities of Sinyavsky and Daniel...;

- instruct the editorial boards of the newspapers Pravda, Izvestia, Literaturnaya gazeta, Komsomolskaya pravda and the journal Kommunist to publish theoretical articles regarding the Marxist understanding of the question of freedom and the responsibility of the individual in socialist society.

The committee on radio broadcasting and television under the CM USSR is to draw up and send the following to foreign countries:

- declarations of support by representatives of Soviet society regarding the sentences in the case of Sinyavsky and Daniel;

- a talk by a prominent Soviet jurist substantiating the justice of the verdict from the point of view of Soviet legislation;

- materials exposing the slanderous nature of the writings of Sinyavsky and Daniel, their calls to terrorism and vile anti-Semitic statements, and the wide application of their works for the purposes of the Cold War....

- materials demonstrating the moral grubbiness and political double-dealing of Sinyavsky and Daniel;

- comments and talks on the freedom of creativity in the USSR and the persecution of progressive activists in the West.

The scandal spread far and wide. Just as under Stalin, meetings were held in all workplaces for the purpose of "unanimous condemnation" of the writers by those who had never read their books. Hundreds of thousands of Soviet citizens were forced to choose between their consciences and their well-being. Some refused, but the majority agreed, for after all, those who refused were "too few". . . and what was the point? To improve the Soviet system?

This served as the prototype of all our subsequent trials, a kind of model of party glasnost: "open" trials behind closed doors, with a handpicked audience, with a handful of friends of those in the dock and foreign correspondents at the court entrance. Always followed by the deafening roar of Yakovlev's propaganda after every trial, which still did not manage to silence our glasnost, but merely increased distrust of the official press. Was it really surprising that even children preferred to listen to foreign radio?

This was how the battle line was drawn from the start of the opposition: our glasnost versus their glasnost, the law versus ideology. How could anyone "not understand" or "not know" this, if the regime demanded not just wordless submission but full, active agreement from its subjects?

Of course they understood and knew everything, but after several years of "thaw," when it was even fashionable to talk about civil conscience and moral responsibility, the country reverted to its monkey-like status: hear nothing, see nothing, say nothing. People preferred to pretend to be blind, deaf, and dumb, so that later, as had happened after Stalin, they could feign dismay: *How could this have happened? Who is to blame?*

Strangely enough for such a philosophical-ethical position, its political effect was very great in the beginning. The trials that followed after that of Sinyavsky and Daniel, especially the case of Alexander Ginzburg and Yuri Galanskov,[94] caused an outbreak of turbulent protests inside the country, a sort of chain reaction. Direct repressions proved not just useless, but downright dangerous to the regime: the more trials took place, the more people protested. The atmosphere in the camps also changed: those incarcerated no longer vanished without a trace, were not expunged from life, but joined in the general resistance. Information about hunger

---

[94]The first issue of *A Chronicle of Current Events* (30 April 1968) reported on the Galanskov-Ginzburg trial (https://chronicleofcurrentevents.net/no-1-30-april-1968/) and the protests and numerous petitions that preceded and followed it.

and other strikes, petitions, and even literary works of political prisoners began to trickle out of the camps, cocking a snook at the idea
of isolation. Furthermore, the camps became a kind of link between various groups of the movement arising in different parts of
the country. It was also the place where we met one another, and
thus became known to each one's relatives and friends. The punishments meted out by the courts simply became futile; they contributed to the growth and consolidation of an originally scattered,
random movement into a serious political force.

This was a lesson the regime never forgot. The entire subsequent history of our mutual relations is a history of the regime's
search for other means to fight us, and ours a search for responses
to their new stratagems. Arrests and trials became their last resort, an enforced necessity, and being able to make them take these
steps frequently was like a victory for us. The authorities preferred
other means, from psychiatric confinement and defamatory campaigns ("compromising" people, as the *chekist*s called it) to expulsion abroad. Running true to form, in 1977 the regime even tried to
"codify ideology" in the new Constitution of the USSR, for the first
time in its history stating the following openly in article 6:

> The leading and guiding force of Soviet society, the core of its
> political system, state and public organizations, is the Commu-
> nist Party of the USSR. The CPSU exists for the people and
> serves the people.
>
> Armed with Marxist-Leninist teaching, the Communist Party
> determines the general outlook for social development and the
> line of internal and foreign policy of the USSR, steers the great
> creative activity of the Soviet people, providing a smooth, scien-
> tifically based character to the struggle for the victory of com-
> munism.

Thus they partly accepted the rules of the game we offered. Now
just try to cite the Constitution! All is in accordance with the law.
However, not even that helped them; prior to this we had already
begun to refer to the UN's Universal Charter of Human Rights, to
pacts concerning civil liberties, and subsequently to the Helsinki
Accords. You can always find something to cite if you try.

Curiously, the defense of rights — this seemingly difficult-to-
digest aspect of our philosophy—became unusually popular over
time. Looking through samizdat documents from the end of the
1970s, I was amazed by the precision of the references to all the
fine points of the law in petitions penned by even simple laborers.
"Asserting one's rights" suddenly became very fashionable.

The regime, tottering on the brink of doom, also made use of this trend. The system was ageing, it was on its last legs, and the "party elite" had to save itself somehow. This was when "liberal" Yakovlev, the foreman of perestroika, emerged. All of a sudden, newspapers became full of our slogans from twenty years ago: *rule-of-law state*, *period of stagnation*, and, naturally, *glasnost*. Whole chunks of our samizdat began to appear in the official press, and even party decisions, but without quotation marks or any mention of the original authors. Meanwhile the "liberated" people, studiously hiding their eyes, pretended that they had heard nothing of the kind until now. The West rejoiced, astounded by the freethinking of the party elite. Party *glaznozt*—as it was pronounced by entranced foreigners—suited them fine. It became the *dernier cri* of Western mode, even though nobody knew what it really meant. Under the circumstances, nobody remembered us—we could not even come to Moscow; up until 1991 our names were still on the blacklists of the KGB. Formally we still remained "particularly dangerous state criminals," "continually sluggish schizophrenics," and imperialist agents. But this did not trouble anyone.

Who did those birdbrains hope to fool? History? Logic? Themselves? Even without our names, glasnost could not be controlled, and the law was still incompatible with ideology. It took only a few years without repressions, a few years of relative freedom to exchange opinions, for the regime to collapse. Already by the beginning of 1990, a wave of strikes and massive demonstrations roared across the entire immense country like a mountain avalanche that grows in size along its path. These people did not demand bread or money, even though both commodities were in sufficiently short supply. No, they demanded the *repeal of Article 6 of the Constitution* —that very article affirming the supremacy of the CPSU over every social structure in the land, and of which I spoke at my 1967 trial, brandishing the KGB's copy of the Constitution. I admit that when I saw miners, covered in black coal dust like fiends from the underworld, half-starved people, whole families with old people and children who were calling not for vengeance, but for *a change to the Constitution*—I felt like crying. Like frames from a film, three decades of camp barracks, the cells of Vladimir Prison, carbolic-reeking corridors of psychiatric institutions, and the narrow Moscow streets in which I grew up, feeling myself even then as being behind enemy lines—all flashed through my mind. Suddenly all this made *sense*, found its place in the general harmonious symphony of images, sounds, smells.... The rest was a question of one or two years, not more. The subsequent fall of the regime, the disintegration of the Soviet Union was merely a logical conclusion.

As if waiting for this, the Supreme Court of the Russian Federation immediately sent me two notices about the quashing of my 1967 and 1972 sentences "in view of the absence of *corpus delicti*," the component elements of a crime. Both notices carried the same date: 5 December 1991, Constitution Day, on which we had staged our first demonstration twenty-six years earlier.

Yakovlev, however, has retired and does not engage in politics. He is now head of the Russian presidential commission on the rehabilitation of people who have been repressed. Almost like having Joseph Goebbels in charge of the rehabilitation of victims of Auschwitz in 1945.

• • •

Unsurprisingly, most of the CC documents concerning our trials did not tell me anything new. Some things we already knew, others we guessed, and some we learned later. Nonetheless, they made a strong impression: it is one thing to guess, but to see a document with all the signatures and seals detailing your guesses in black and white, expressed in the ineffable bureaucratic party language, is something else. The level at which these decisions were made was, as I have already said, much higher than we had thought. Clearly all decisions were made by the party, but to assume that our cases were discussed in the CC or even the Politburo would have struck us as immodest. Moreover, recalling the veiled, allusive language of the Nazi leadership in Germany, I was still unprepared for such blatant and cynical disregard of legal norms. Acting well in advance, at times several weeks before a trial, they would decide who should be imprisoned and who should be shown mercy, totally unconcerned by the constitutional principle of the independence of judges. Even sanctions for house searches emanated from the CC, and not the Procuracy. In the full sense of the term, they were above the law, not constraining themselves with any judicial reflections, and daily rewriting laws at their own discretion. All other agencies simply rubber-stamped their decisions.

In April 1968, shortly after the Ginzburg-Galanskov trial, the Politburo, infuriated by our friends whom they considered were too active in defending the condemned, decided to deal with us once and for all (15 April 1968, Pb 79/XI):[95]

> Acting as accomplices of the more reactionary representatives
> of bourgeois press and radio, they systematically supply them

---

[95]3 April 1968 (718-A), p. 2 in 15 April 1968 (Pb 79/XI). See also Issue 2 of the Chronicle of Current Events (30 June 1968): "The campaign against those who signed letters" (https://chronicleofcurrentevents.net/2013/09/28/2-2-certain-episodes-in-the-campaign-against-those-who-signed-letters/)

with slanderous materials, try to hold private press conferences for foreigners, incite antisocial elements to politically harmful activity, inspire the production and dissemination of hostile letters, declarations and "protests," and display provocative behavior toward bodies of power.

What, may one ask, is the problem? Put them in the dock; they had already done more damage than Ginzburg and Galanskov by defending those two. The more so, as is noted in the document:

Thus the behavior of the indicated group of persons is displaying an increasingly audacious nature, and the fact that their actions go unpunished dismays many citizens.

But imprisoning or judging them was not what the CC wanted right now:

... insofar as this measure may lead to a new wave of demagogic demands from antisocial forces within the country and incendiary actions by bourgeois propaganda.

Hence a complex decision to keep everybody happy. Send Pyotr Grigorenko for a psychiatric examination. Allow Alexander Esenin-Volpin to travel to the USA to attend a mathematical symposium, to which he has been invited numerous times, and then strip him of citizenship and "deny him reentry into the USSR" if "during his presence in the USA he compromises himself by improper conduct." Summon Yakir, Litvinov and Larisa Bogoraz-Brukhman to the Procuracy of the USSR and "demand, in categorical terms, the immediate cessation of their antisocial activities."[96]

Caution Yakir, Litvinov and Bogoraz-Brukhman that otherwise they shall be deprived of residential registration and removed from Moscow.

Pursuant to the above, we deem it necessary to make an addendum to the resolution of the Council of Ministers of the USSR dated 15 August 1966 N658-211, "On the reinforcement of the passport regime in the cities of Moscow and Leningrad and in the Moscow Region" (draft attached);

- instruct the Moscow City Council (if the caution is ignored) to make a decision on withdrawing Yakir and Litvinov's Moscow residential registration for a period of 2 years;

- instruct the Ministry for Protection of Public Order to remove Yakir and Litvinov from Moscow, relocating Yakir to

---

[96]No date (Pb 615), p. 7 in 15 April 1968 (Pb 79/XI).

reside in the Tyumen region and Litvinov to reside in the Guryevsk region of the Kazakh Soviet Socialist Republic;

- the question of depriving Bogoraz-Brukhman of residential registration and removal from Moscow shall be reviewed additionally, depending on her behavior after the application of the indicated sanctions to Yakir and Litvinov;

- prepare and publish a notice on this matter on the day the sanctions are applied to Grigorenko, Esenin-Volpin, Yakir, Litvinov and Bogoraz-Brukhman in the *Soviet Russia* [*Sovetskaya Rossiya*] newspaper.

A copy of the "addendum" to the law on residential registration was attached, allowing city councils to:

> ... without the preliminary imposition of an administrative sanction, annul the residential registration of individuals engaged in antisocial activity, voicing slanderous falsehoods that incite antisocial elements to politically harmful actions, who behave in a provocative manner toward state bodies. ... The removal of individuals indicated in the present resolution is to be carried out within twenty-four hours from the moment of the decision to annul residential registration.

At that time, none of these measures were legal. But why should they care? So the Politburo orders the drawing up of everything required within ten days,[97] without consulting anyone, not even for the sake of appearances. Millions of residents of Moscow and Leningrad and their city councils still know nothing about such unlimited powers, nor do the leaders of "sovereign" Kazakhstan know of Litvinov's impending exile to their republic. Equally ignorant of the new material destined for its pages is the editorial board of *Sovetskaya Rossiya*. The Council of Ministers of the USSR, allegedly the legal government of the country, dutifully signs the attached draft "resolution," and a new era begins, in which any person can be deprived of his residence, without trial or investigation, within twenty-four hours. And all this to drive three people out of Moscow, whom trying in court was inconvenient at the moment.

I have cited this example not because it was the most flagrant or cruel. On the contrary, it was one of the more benign. In the main, these measures were not implemented: a month later the "noise" in the West subsided and the opportunity arose to simply imprison citizens who had drawn the wrath of the Politburo, which

---

[97] 16 May 1968, Pb 81/XVI, pp. 6–8, Grigorenko activities in response to arrests of Ginzburg and Galanskov.

suspended its decision without informing any interested parties yet again (16 May 1968, Pb 81/XVI).[98]

So these duly signed and stamped "laws" lie in archives, never having seen the light of day. Litvinov and Bogoraz-Brukhman were actually exiled half a year later, but for totally different reasons and after a "lawful" trial. Esenin-Volpin was allowed to travel to his symposium... four years later, and five years later Yakir was sent into internal exile, also for a different reason. This example is striking in its absurdity and the monstrous indifference of the supreme power toward the most elementary legal norms. They called it "socialist legality."

It is interesting to note that on that same day, 15 April 1968, the Politburo reached a decision concerning two more people: Anatoly Marchenko and Ilya Gabay (15 April 1968*, Pb 79/XII). Despite identical formulations and accusations, they were to be stripped of Soviet citizenship and exiled abroad. Once again, the decision was made, and the order of the Presidium of the Supreme Soviet was signed, but a month later the Politburo changed its mind. A formal and judicial reason to arrest and throw them into the camps, as persons stripped of Soviet citizenship, turned up soon enough. But nobody remembered this.

Both of them were to die tragically: Gabay committed suicide, Marchenko died during a hunger strike in prison, in the times of "perestroika". What a game of chance that was: had they been sent into exile earlier, they would probably be alive today.

Naturally, this is how it was at first. With time, the regime learned to be more "accurate" in dealing with the law, and to prepare its "measures" more thoroughly. Here is a later example of how the CC prepared to deal with the members of the Helsinki Groups in 1977 (20 January 1977, 123-A)[99]

> Bearing in mind the political and operative situation, suppression of the more active anti-Soviets would be feasible by various means.
>
> With regard to [Yuri] ORLOV, an investigation should be made into the criminal case initiated earlier by the Procuracy of the City of Moscow, with the aim of charging him with criminal liability under Article 190 of the Criminal Code of the RSFSR at a later stage. ... Orlov is not to be arrested in the course of the investigation, unless he precipitates such arrest by his actions.
>
> It is deemed essential to arrest A.I. GINZBURG and bring criminal charges against him under Article 70 of the Criminal Code

---

[98] 16 May 1968, Pb 81/XVI, p. 1, handwritten annulment.
[99] 20 January 1977 (123-A), p. 5.

of the RSFSR, the investigation to be carried out at his place of residence in the Kaluga region.

Kiev resident N.D. RUDENKO is to be arrested and charged with criminal liability under Article 62 of the Criminal Code of the Ukrainian SSR (identical to Article 70 of the Criminal Code of the RSFSR), but the investigation is to be conducted not in Kiev, but Donetsk for procedural reasons.

With regard to [Tomas] VENCLOVA, born in 1937, former scientific worker in the Institute of History of the Academy of Sciences of the Lithuanian SSR, who is applying for a temporary exit permit to visit the USA on a private invitation, it has been decided to grant him permission for this trip. The issue of VENCLOVA'S future fate shall be decided on the basis of his behavior abroad.

Preparation for their trials was even more thorough and even further removed from the law. For a start, all political trials in 1977 were deferred for almost a year for purely propagandistic purposes (1 April 1978*, 785-A).

Completed investigations on criminal cases are to be forwarded to the courts. However, allowing for the various important political enterprises throughout the country (discussion and adoption of the new Constitution of the USSR, celebrations of the sixtieth anniversary of the Great October), as well as the situation concerning the Belgrade Conference,[100] the conduct of trials on the indicated matters was deemed unfeasible in 1977.

This was addressed to the CC not by *Pravda* pen pushers seeking approval, not even by the agitprop head Yakovlev—no, it emanated from the three senior jurists of the country: Procurator General Rudenko, chairman of the Supreme Court Smirnov and KGB head Andropov. What could be expected from the Politburo, the Central Committee, if those responsible for maintaining the law saw it only as an appendage of ideology? For them, the concept of *legality* did not exist; what they understood was *feasibility*—i.e. something consonant with ideological aims.

They certainly knew the laws; this was not a matter of ignorance. For example, a legal confusion occurred in the case of Anatoly Sharansky (who changed his name to Natan Sharansky upon arrival in Israel)—the *chekist*s almost overstepped themselves in accusing him of espionage:[101]

---

[100]the 1977 Belgrade Conference was arranged in compliance with the follow-up provisions of the 1975 Helsinki Final Act (technically the Final Act of the Conference on Security and Cooperation in Europe)

[101]11 January 1978 (26-A), p. 5 in 25 December 1977.

Pursuant to Article 9 of the Statute on Military Tribunals, this case should be examined by a military tribunal. However, this could lead to a strengthening of the anti-Soviet campaign being waged by Western reactionary circles in connection with SHARANSKY'S case. In view of the above, we deem it feasible to make an exception and alter the jurisdiction of the Sharansky matter, and have it examined by the Judicial Division for Criminal Cases of the Supreme Court of the RSFSR. The draft of the resolution of the Presidium of the Supreme Soviet of the USSR is attached.

The attached resolution of the country's highest legislative body would sound ludicrous to any lawyer:

As an exception, permit the Judicial Division for Criminal Cases of the Supreme Court of the RSFSR to examine, in the first instance, the criminal case of Anatoly Borisovich SHARANSKY, charged with treason against the Motherland in the form of espionage.

As the executive asked, so the legislature did, in compliance with "socialist legality," simply and easily, for they all knew that the accusation of espionage was too far-fetched by virtue of its "feasibility." Sharansky's real fault lay (25 December 1977, no number) in that he:

... provided the West systematically with slanderous information regarding the Soviet Union, which was actively used by special services in the USA under the guise of the "protection of human rights" in the USSR. These data were also put to use by pro-Zionist US congressmen upon the adoption of the discriminatory Jackson-Vanik Amendment to the "Trade Act of 1974."

3.6   "Without the consent of the latter..."

It is obvious that the most blatant violations of the law committed by the regime were due to its unwillingness to incarcerate us or "punish with the full severity of the law." The search for alternative means of vengeance led to glitches in their punitive machine. Ideological "feasibility" had no desire to be consistent with legality, thereby causing incredible paradoxes, obvious even to those who knew nothing of the law. For instance, our exiles, expulsions abroad, "exchanges," stripping of citizenship—was there anyone unaware of them? Did anyone doubt that these were simply political reprisals, deprived of any legal foundation? Did the authorities make any effort to maintain a semblance of legality? We had already seen how arbitrarily this question was decided regarding Gabay and Marchenko in 1968: The authorities decided to exile them, then changed their minds. They did not even bother to repeal the signed order that stripped the two of citizenship. But in all other cases decisions were no less arbitrary, beginning with Valery Yakovlevich Tarsis, the first person to be stripped of citizenship for political reasons in post-Stalinist times. Having allowed him to travel to England, the authorities had not yet decided what to do next. Then the KGB reported that it had managed to discredit Tarsis in the West (8 April 1966, Pb 238/132):

> The Committee for State Security is continuing measures for the further compromising of Tarsis abroad as a mentally ill individual. Due to Tarsis's anti-Soviet declarations abroad, and also the positive reaction of Soviet citizens to measures against him, we consider his return to the Soviet Union to be inadvisable and deem it feasible to deprive Tarsis of Soviet citizenship and bar his return to the USSR.

The Politburo agreed, and the Presidium of the Supreme Soviet issued the relevant order. One might ask whether, if Soviet citizens had expressed a negative reaction to these measures, Tarsis would not have lost his citizenship. And in what way should such a reaction have manifested itself?

Even more bizarre from a legal point of view were "exchanges", especially when the "exchanges" involved one's own for one's own (23 May 1979, 1012-A).[102] According to Andropov:

> Pursuant to the resolution of the CC CPSU NII129/44-оп; dated 16 November 1978, acting on 27 April 1979, the Committee for State Security deported criminals [Georgi] Vins, [Eduard] Kuznetsov, [Mark] Dymshits, [Valentin] Moroz and Ginzburg, all stripped of Soviet citizenship by the Presidium of the Supreme Soviet of the USSR, to the USA, and exchanged them for Soviet intelligence officers, comrades Chernyaev and [Valdik] Enger, who had been sentenced by the American authorities. At the same time, Jewish nationalists [Anatoly] Altman, [Hillel] Butman, [Sylva] Zalmanson, [Boris] Penson and [Leib] Khnokh[103] left the USSR after being granted exit permits for the purpose of sanitation of the operative situation in the country in connection with preparations for the Olympic Games in Moscow.

---

[102]23 May 1979 (1012-A), p. 8 in 24 April 1979 (Pb 150/129).

[103]Participants, with Eduard Kuznetsov, in the 1970 hijackers trial at which several of them received the death sentence. See *A Chronicle of Current Events*, Issue 17: "The Leningrad Trial of the 'Hijackers'" (31 December 1971, https://chronicleofcurrentevents.net/2014/08/05/17-6-the-leningrad-trial-of-the-hijackers/).

As if that were not sufficiently amusing, he added[104] the following:

> Data received by the Committee for State Security indicates that the expulsion of the abovementioned individuals from the USSR has been perceived by foreign anti-Soviet circles and antisocial elements in our country as a serious blow to their plans for "destabilizing socialism from within." Comments from abroad stress that in the persons of Vins, Kuznetsov, Altman and other anti-Soviets, the West has lost "reliable executors" of the hostile intentions of special services and subversive centers, and also sources of vicious slander concerning Soviet reality and the internal and foreign policy of the Communist Party and the Soviet government. ...
>
> ... The expelled evaluate the situation similarly. For example, Ginzburg and Vins state that they would have preferred to avoid exile, even to remain in prison, in order to preserve ties with the milieu in which they worked.

Mark you, all this was written at a time when tens of thousands were vainly trying to emigrate, and many of the "expelled" landed in prison because they wanted to emigrate to Israel. There was a cartoon in the *New York Times* in which one figure wearing a fur coat and a hat with earflaps, is standing in Red Square and saying to another, "Well, it's all clear now. Those who want to leave are not allowed, and only those who want to stay can go."

In actual fact, all those "expelled" were still incarcerated at the time of the exchange. So if "sanitizing" would have improved the "operative situation," it would have been easier to expel them straightaway, without the added burden of court hearings and investigations. And alongside them, all the other "reliable executors of hostile intentions" and indeed all those imprisoned. Especially if "subversive centers" would claim that this was a "serious blow" to them.

Recalling this now is amusing, but it was pretty much so at the time. I remember how, in 1970 and 1971, prior to my last arrest, I managed to assist several Jewish activists among those who, for one reason or another, the authorities did not want to allow to leave. Toward the end, my special ability regarding the "refuseniks" even acquired legendary status, but I kept my method a close secret. In fact, it was all done quite simply: feeling sorry for some of them, I suggested staging a performance for the KGB, as if I were making them my assistants. They were to phone me at regular intervals and utter mysterious phrases and come to visit me as if secretly.

---

[104]24 April 1979 (Pb 150/129), pp. 8–10.

From time to time they would appear with me in public and discuss seemingly very serious matters and, having received their "orders," disappear quickly. As a rule this performance would last less than a month, and my "assistant" would receive an exit visa without delay, although before that he may have spent years in futile efforts to emigrate. That was how we helped the KGB to "sanitize the situation."

Here is another example of Central Committee lawmaking (30 September 1986, 1942-Ch):

> Yu.F. Orlov, born 1924, former corresponding member of the Academy of Sciences of the Armenian SSR, was sentenced in 1978 to 7 years' imprisonment and 5 years' internal exile under part 1 article 70 of the Criminal Code of the RSFSR. At present, he is in exile in the Yakut ASSR, with the term expiring in February 1989. ... For purposes of a mutually acceptable resolution of the matter of [Gennadi] Zakharov and [Nicholas] Daniloff, we deem it possible to agree to the expulsion of Orlov from the country, relieving him of the need to serve the rest of his sentence, and strip him of Soviet citizenship.

Not the slightest effort was made to give this decision at least the appearance of legality. It was simply the case that the CC had to solve a problem that had no relation to Orlov whatsoever. He was a kind of makeweight to a different matter, something like small change from a large banknote.

In my case they merely "forgot" to strip me of citizenship and repeal my sentence, having "expelled" me from the USSR; they even gave me a five-year passport. The question of my exchange was discussed in the Politburo at least three times, the last time being three days before the exchange took place. It emerges that there was also an order issued by the Presidium of the Supreme Soviet of the USSR, which remained secret. The proposal was put forward by Andropov, Gromyko, and Ponomarev and grandly entitled "On measures relating to the release of comrade L. Corvalan" (14 December 1976, 2816-A):[105]

> The Soviet ambassador in Washington has reported the consent of the Chilean authorities to exchange L. Corvalan in Geneva. Bukovsky and his mother will be exchanged there as well.
>
> The Chileans propose to make the exchange on 18 December of this year (telegram from Washington N3130). We deem it feasible to accept this date.

---

[105] 15 December 1976* (Pb 38/46), p. 6.

It would be advisable to send a representative of the International Department of the CC CPSU and a doctor to greet comrade L. Corvalan.

A special aircraft should be assigned to transport comrade Corvalan from Geneva to the USSR. The same aircraft shall deliver Bukovsky to Geneva.

It is essential that prior to transferring Bukovsky to the Chilean side, the Presidium of the Supreme Soviet of the USSR should issue an order regarding his removal from his place of confinement and expulsion from the USSR. This will allow Bukovsky to remain unreleased and under guard, and without the consent of the latter, deliver him to Geneva.

How about that! So in order to avoid requesting my consent and to have the pleasure of transporting me in handcuffs, a special order was issued. At the same time, there was no need to repeal my sentence or to let me keep my Soviet citizenship: they could not keep a citizen, moreover one not convicted, under guard.

Sixteen years passed before I was able to see this order, and when the time came I simply threw up my hands and burst out laughing. Since when had they developed such niceties as to ask for our consent to be subjected to punishment? And mainly: why? What did they think, that I would resort to fisticuffs with them?

Laughter, however, is very relative—there is not much to laugh about in conditions of lawlessness and arbitrary tyranny. By such means, over the 1970s and 1980s, the country "rid itself" of the best, and often most talented, and certainly most honest figures in science, art, and literature.

An analysis of materials received shows that during their entire stay abroad in 1974, [Mstislav] ROSTROPOVICH and [Galina] VISHNEVSKAYA have engaged in antisocial activity, slandered the Soviet state and social system and committed other actions unworthy of the calling of a Soviet citizen.

By their provocative actions and slanderous declarations, Rostropovich and Vishnevskaya supplied material aimed at inflaming anti-Soviet insinuations in the West, including vicious attacks on the USSR regarding the notorious questions of "human rights" and "creative freedom" in our country. ... Such behavior by Rostropovich and Vishnevskaya shall create a precedent for emulation by other politically immature representatives of the creative intelligentsia. Acting on their example, a number of musicians, directors, writers, artists and sportsmen have lodged applications to travel abroad for lengthy periods.

In view of the above, it would appear feasible to strip M.L. Rostropovich and G.I. Vishnevskaya of Soviet citizenship and publish a relevant Order of the Presidium of the Supreme Court of the USSR in the Gazette of the Supreme Soviet of the USSR, with a brief note on this matter in *Izvestia*.

It is strange that this package (14 March 1978*, Pb 97/54) also contained earlier documents of the CC regarding the persecution of Rostropovich, including those forbidding him to visit the USSR in 1977[106] with the National Symphony Orchestra, whose conductor he was at that time. Here is yet another document (12 May 1977*, 958-A):

> According to information received, the "Association of International Meetings on Contemporary Art" in the West intends to conduct a competition for young cellists, named in honor of Rostropovich, in Paris from 27 June to 3 July 1977, which is one of the events in connection with his 50th anniversary. Preparations for this competition are widely advertised in the West.
>
> In this situation it is deemed feasible to instruct the Ministry of Culture of the USSR to inform the cultural bodies of the People's Republic of Bulgaria, the People's Republic of Hungary, The German Democratic Republic, Cuba, the Mongolian People's Republic, the Polish People's Republic and the Czechoslovak Socialist Republic of the undesirability of participation of representatives of socialist countries in this competition.

The Politburo examined all these documents while deciding the question of Rostropovich and Vishnevskaya's citizenship, and the Politburo should have seen that these people had more than enough cause to discuss not just human rights, but also systematic persecution. The Politburo itself had launched this persecution and then stripped them of citizenship, offended by their response. Yet what had it expected? Gratitude?

As if propelled by an urge to self-destruct, the Politburo paid no regard to anything in those years. If someone refused to bow before it, be he ever so famous, no matter how many achievements or awards he had, he would be thrown out of the country. Among the exiled were the sculptor Ernst Neizvestny, the director of the country's most famous theater, Yuri Lyubimov, and the famous cinema director Andrei Tarkovsky. Others, tired of relentless party scrutiny, either fled or refused to return from trips abroad—and were immediately branded "traitors" and "renegades," any mention of whom in the Soviet press was proscribed. Their books were confiscated from libraries, and any mention of their names in encyclopedias was expunged. Scientists and chess players, ballet dancers and

---

[106] 19 October 1977 (P78/57), p. 3.

writers suddenly became the regime's worst enemies. Not even nuclear physicists, whom Stalin himself did not touch, were spared (6 November 1978, No. 24348):

> The Ministry of Medium Machine Building proposed stripping senior scientific employee of the Unified Institute of Nuclear Research, [Sergei] M. Polikanov, of awards and medals of the USSR, the title of laureate of the Lenin Prize, and his academic degree of Doctor of Physics and Mathematics, and recommends his expulsion from the ranks of corresponding members of the Academy of Sciences of the USSR.
>
> The proposal was motivated by the circumstance that S.M. Polikanov has established contacts with foreign correspondents and supplies them with slanderous materials, used by the Western press for anti-Soviet purposes, has joined a group of individuals known for antisocial activity, and participates in their hostile enterprises.
>
> By order of the CC CPSU, Polikanov and his family are permitted to leave for permanent residence in a capitalist country.

The only one they did not have the courage to exile from the country was Sakharov—he was exiled to Gorky without trial (8 January 1980*, Pb 177/X), just like that, without citing any law and without any reference to the "legislation" the Politburo had devised regarding administrative relocation from Moscow and Leningrad for Yakir, Litvinov, and Bogoraz-Brukhman back in 1968.

> For the purposes of averting Sakharov's pernicious activities, criminal contacts with citizens of capitalist countries and consequent infliction of damage to the interests of the Soviet state, it is deemed necessary to relocate Andrei Dmitrievich Sakharov in administrative order from the city of Moscow to one of the regions of the country that are closed to foreigners.
>
> A living regime for A.D. Sakharov must be established that would preclude his contacts with foreigners and antisocial elements, or travel to other areas of the country without the specific permission of the Ministry of Internal Affairs of the USSR. The Committee for State Security and the Ministry of Internal Affairs of the USSR are charged with exercising control over A.D. Sakharov's observance of the established regime.

Can anyone explain to me why this regime could not do anything in accordance with the laws devised by itself?

• • •

In order to confer at least some kind of understanding of the workings of the minds of Politburo members in deciding such matters,

I shall cite the minutes of the meeting at which the question of Solzhenitsyn was decided (I quote from the publication in the newspaper *Russkaya mysl*):[107]

BREZHNEV. According to information from our representations abroad in France and the USA and the foreign press, it appears that Solzhenitsyn's new work—"The GULAG Archipelago" is about to be published.

I have been told by comrade Suslov that the Secretariat has decided to launch a campaign in our press aimed at exposing Solzhenitsyn's writings and the bourgeois propaganda associated with the publication of this book. As yet, nobody has read the book, but its contents are well known. It is a crude anti-Soviet lampoon. Therefore today we need to discuss what we should do next. Under our laws, we have grounds to imprison Solzhenitsyn, because he has raised his hand against what is most sacrosanct—against Lenin, our Soviet system, Soviet power, against all that is dear to our hearts.

At one time we imprisoned Yakir, Litvinov and others, sentenced them, and that was the end of the matter. Kuznetsov, [Svetlana] Alliluyeva and others went abroad. Some noise was raised at first, then everything was forgotten. But this hooligan Solzhenitsyn is still swaggering around. He does not care about anything, takes nothing into account. What should we do with him? If we apply sanctions against him at this time, will we benefit from the unleashing of Western propaganda against us? I am putting this question up for discussion. I simply want us to exchange opinions, confer and reach the right decision.

KOSYGIN. There is a note from comrade Andropov on this matter. The note suggests expelling him from the country.

BREZHNEV. I have discussed this problem with comrade Andropov.

ANDROPOV. I consider that Solzhenitsyn should be expelled from the country without seeking his consent.

BREZHNEV. It is clear that Solzhenitsyn would never give his consent.

KIRILENKO. Maybe we can remove him from the country without his consent.

PODGORNY. But is there a country that would agree to take him without his consent?

---

[107]"The Expulsion of Alexander Solzhenitsyn: Secret Politburo and KGB Documents of the year 1974"; First published in Russian as a Special Addendum to the Newspaper *Russkaya Mysl* No. 3998, 30 Sept–6 Oct, 1993. 4 pp. between pp. 10 and 11.

BREZHNEV. We must bear in mind that Solzhenitsyn did not even travel abroad to receive the Nobel Prize.

ANDROPOV. When he was offered the chance to go abroad to receive the Nobel Prize, he raised the question of guarantees regarding his return to the Soviet Union.

Comrades, I have been raising the matter of Solzhenitsyn since 1965. He has now reached a new level of hostile activity. He is trying to create an organization within the Soviet Union, putting it together with former prisoners. He speaks out about Lenin, against the October Revolution, against the socialist system. His work "The GULAG Archipelago" is not a literary creation, but a political document. That is dangerous. There are tens of thousands of Vlasovites in our country, UONovites[108] and other hostile elements. Overall, hundreds and thousands of people, among whom Solzhenitsyn will find support. Now everyone is waiting to see how we shall deal with Solzhenitsyn, if we shall apply sanctions or let him be.

Comrade [Mstislav] Keldysh phoned me recently and asked why we have not taken any measures regarding Sakharov. He says that if we continue to do nothing, then how shall other academics such as [Pyotr] Kapitsa, [Vladimir] Engelgardt and others conduct themselves?

All this is important, comrades, and we have to decide these questions now, no matter what is happening at the European Conference.[109]

I think we should take Solzhenitsyn to court and apply Soviet laws against him. Many foreign correspondents are going to see him now as well as other dissatisfied individuals. He talks to them, and even conducts press conferences. Let us say that we have a hostile underground and the KGB fails to uncover it. But Solzhenitsyn is acting openly, in an audacious manner. He abuses the humane attitude of Soviet power and conducts hostile activity with impunity. That is why we should employ all means, of which I wrote to the CC, in other words expel him from the country. First of all, we should ask our ambassadors to sound out the relevant governments as to whether they are prepared to take him in. If we do not expel him now, then he shall continue his hostile activity. You know that he has written the hostile novel "August 1914", then the scurrilous "GULAG

---

[108] *Vlasovite* is a term used to refer to Soviet POWs who agreed to work as unarmed auxiliaries for the German forces from 1942 to 1945; the Organization of Ukrainian Nationalists (OUN) was a controversial body engaged in wartime resistance to the Soviet regime.

[109] A reference to the Conference on Security and Cooperation in Europe, which ran from September 1973 to July 1975 and culminated in the signing of the Helsinki Accords.

Archipelago", and is now writing "October 1917." This will be a new anti-Soviet slur.

Therefore I suggest expelling Solzhenitsyn from the country by administrative order. We should instruct our ambassadors in the countries mentioned in my note to inquire about their willingness to take in Solzhenitsyn. If we do not take these steps now, then all our propagandistic work will yield no results. If we publish articles in newspapers, talk about him on the radio without taking steps, this will be an empty gesture. We have to decide what to do about Solzhenitsyn.

BREZHNEV. What if we expel him to a socialist country?

ANDROPOV. Leonid Ilyich, this is hardly a gift that socialist countries would welcome. Just think of what a specimen we would be sending them. Maybe we should ask Iraq, Switzerland, or some other country? Living in the West would be easy for him, he has the equivalent of eight million rubles in European banks.

SUSLOV. Solzhenitsyn has become unacceptably brazen, he spits on the Soviet system, the Communist Party, he has raised his hand against the holy of holies—Lenin.

What we should do with Solzhenitsyn is a matter of time: expel him from the country, or try him under our Soviet laws—this must be done. In order to apply this or that measure regarding Solzhenitsyn, we need to prepare our people by conducting extensive propagandist work. We made the right choice concerning Sakharov with a broad propagandistic campaign. There are now practically no hostile letters on the subject of Sakharov. Millions of Soviet people listen to the radio about these new books. All this has an influence on them. We need to publish a number of articles unmasking Solzhenitsyn. This really needs to be done.

In accordance with the decision of the Secretariat, the plan is to publish a couple of articles in "Pravda" and the "Literary Gazette." People are bound to know about this book of Solzhenitsyn's. Of course, there is no need to unleash a campaign about this, but several articles should be published.

KIRILENKO. This will only draw attention to Solzhenitsyn.

SUSLOV. But we cannot keep silent.

GROMYKO. Solzhenitsyn is an enemy, and I vote for the institution of the most severe measures against him. As for the initiation of propagandistic measures, they should be precisely dosed. They require careful thought. But we cannot reject the steps that comrade Andropov proposes. If we expel him from the country forcefully, without his consent, this is something bourgeois propaganda could use against us. It would be good if we could remove him from the country with his consent, but he will never agree to that. Maybe we should exercise a little more patience while the European Conference is in progress? Even if some country agrees to accept him, expelling him now is not feasible, because a huge campaign could be launched against us, and this will not help us toward the end of the Conference. I suggest waiting two to four months, but want to stress that in principle I agree with implementing severe measures. Solzhenitsyn must be cordoned off now, so he will be isolated during these months and be unable to see anyone through whom he could spread propaganda.

Leonid Ilyich shall be visiting Cuba soon. That is also not too good for us, as there will be numerous materials published against the Soviet Union. We must do everything possible to discredit Solzhenitsyn through propagandistic measures.

USTINOV. I would suggest starting work on implementing the proposals made by comrade Andropov. At the same time, we need to publish propagandistic materials exposing Solzhenitsyn.

PODGORNY. I would like to pose the question like this: what administrative measure should be applied to Solzhenitsyn: either we try him under Soviet laws inside the country and force him to serve his punishment here or, as comrade Andropov suggests, exile him from the country? Beyond doubt, Solzhenitsyn is a brazen, audacious and sworn enemy. The fact that he remains unpunished is also clear. Let us consider what would be most profitable for us, which measure: trial or expulsion. In many countries such as China people are executed openly; the fascist regime in Chile shoots and tortures people; the English in Ireland carry out repressions of the working people, while we have to deal with an arrogant foe and simply walk by when one and all sling mud at us.

I believe that our law is humane, but at the same time merciless with regard to enemies, and we should try him under our Soviet laws in our Soviet court and make him serve his sentence in the Soviet Union.

[Pyotr] DEMICHEV. Of course there is bound to be a lot of noise abroad, but we have already published several materials concerning Solzhenitsyn's new book. We need to continue propagandistic efforts, as we cannot remain silent. In his poem "The Feast of the Victors" Solzhenitsyn says that he writes like this because he is angry with Soviet power, but now in "The GULAG Archipelago," which he wrote in 1965, he rants against the Soviet system and the party with even greater ferocity and candor. That is why we must publish strong reactions in our press. In my opinion this will not affect international détente or the European Conference.

SUSLOV. Party organizations and socialist countries are also waiting to see our response to Solzhenitsyn's actions. The bourgeois press is trumpeting about this new book at full blast. We cannot remain silent.

[Konstantin] KATUSHEV. We are unanimous in our assessment of Solzhenitsyn's activities. He is an enemy, and must be treated as such. It looks as if we cannot get away from the need to make a decision on the question of Solzhenitsyn now, but it must be made systematically. On one hand, we must direct all our propaganda against Solzhenitsyn, and, on the other hand, we need to take measures consonant with comrade Andropov's note.

He could probably be exiled from the country by an order of the Supreme Soviet and this could be reported in the press. He has encroached on our sovereignty, on our liberties, on our laws, and should be punished.

Talks on exiling Solzhenitsyn will probably take some three to four months but, I repeat, this question must be resolved systematically and the sooner he is exiled, the better.

As for our press, articles need to be published.

[Ivan] KAPITONOV. I would like to consider this question from another angle: if we exile Solzhenitsyn, how shall it be perceived by our own population? Naturally there may be some omissions, gossip and the like. What shall we be displaying by this—our strength or our weakness? In any event, I do not think we shall prove our strength by this. To date, we have not unmasked him ideologically and have not said anything substantial about him to the people. Yet this is something that must be done. First of all we should start working on unmasking Solzhenitsyn, turn him inside out, and then our people will understand any administrative measure.

[Mikhail] SOLOMENTSEV. Solzhenitsyn is a seasoned foe of the Soviet Union. If it were not for the foreign policy initiatives currently performed by the Soviet Union, then the matter could be resolved without delay. But how shall any decision reflect on our foreign policy activities? It is clear that in any event we must tell the people all that needs to be told about Solzhenitsyn. We should make a harsh assessment of his activities, his hostile activities. Of course people will ask why measures are not being taken against Solzhenitsyn. For example, an article about Solzhenitsyn has already been published in the GDR, and in Czechoslovakia as well. I say nothing about the bourgeois press, but our press is silent. We hear a great deal on foreign radio about Solzhenitsyn, about his "GULAG Archipelago," but not a word on our radio.

I believe we cannot stay silent. The people expect decisive action. The press must publish strong materials exposing Solzhenitsyn for what he is. Obviously there should be agreement with socialist countries and the communist parties in capitalist countries regarding matters of a propagandistic nature that could be implemented in their lands.

I consider that Solzhenitsyn should be tried under our laws.

GRISHIN. Comrade Andropov should probably seek a country that would agree to accept Solzhenitsyn, and this search should be started immediately.

KIRILENKO. Whenever we speak of Solzhenitsyn as an anti-Soviet and vicious enemy of the Soviet system, it always seems to coincide with some important events, and we put off making a decision. This may have been justified at the time, but we cannot delay a decision on this matter now. The fact that something has been written about Solzhenitsyn is well and good, but as comrades here have pointed out, writing about him must be more solid, acute and well argued. For instance, Polish writer Krolikowsky wrote an excellent exposé of Solzhenitsyn. Now Solzhenitsyn is becoming increasingly brazen. He is not a loner, he is in touch with Sakharov. He has contacts abroad with the NTS.[110] So the time has come to tackle Solzhenitsyn seriously, but so that this will be followed by his expulsion from the country or the implementation of other administrative measures.

Andrei Andreyevich [Gromyko] asks how to avoid this measure turning against us. Yet however it turns against us, this question cannot be left hanging in the air. Enemies are trying to spike our guns, and we cannot remain silent. Even many bourgeois newspapers are now saying that in all probability Solzhenitsyn will be tried under Soviet laws, and that he now comes under the enforceability of the law regarding breach of the Convention on Copyright Protection [of Authors' Rights], to which we have acceded.

I support the proposal made by comrade Andropov.

Articles should appear in the press, but they must be substantial and well-argued.

KOSYGIN. Comrades, we are all of the same opinion, and I fully endorse all that was said.

For some years, Solzhenitsyn has been attempting to take over people's minds. It is as if we are afraid to touch him, yet at the same time, our people would welcome action against Solzhenitsyn.

Talking about public opinion generated abroad, we need to rea-

---

[110]National Alliance of Russian Solidarists, an émigré anti-Soviet organization. (see §3.9—What did they believe? for more on the NTS and the dissident movement)

son as follows: what shall cause less damage—either we expose him, try and imprison him, or we wait a few more months and then exile him to another country.

I think we shall suffer fewer losses if we act against him decisively and sentence him under Soviet laws.

Obviously, the press should carry articles about Solzhenitsyn, but they must be serious. Solzhenitsyn has been bought by bourgeois companies, agencies, and works for them. His book "The GULAG Archipelago" is a gross anti-Soviet lampoon. I have discussed this matter with comrade Andropov. Naturally, socialist countries will reject Solzhenitsyn. I think that comrade Andropov should sound out this question with capitalist countries and see which one of them would be prepared to accept him. But on the other hand, we should not fear to apply severe measures of Soviet justice to Solzhenitsyn. Take England, for example. Thousands of workers get killed there. The same happens in Chile.

We should try Solzhenitsyn and disclose everything about him, then he could be exiled to Verkhoyansk. No foreign correspondents will go there: it's very cold. We cannot keep this secret from the people. Articles must appear in the press.

PODGORNY. Solzhenitsyn is engaged in active anti-Soviet activity. In other times, we sent less dangerous enemies than Solzhenitsyn out of the country or put them on trial, but at the moment we cannot get close to Solzhenitsyn, we keep looking for an approach. Solzhenitsyn's last book gives no grounds for leniency toward him.

Naturally, the selected measure should not impede the conduct of other actions. Solzhenitsyn has many followers, but we cannot overlook what he is doing.

I think people will support whatever measure we employ. Papers should publish articles, but they must be very well argued and convincing. Much is known about him now and about his latest book as well. There are broadcasts by Voice of America, Radio Free Europe and others. Both here and abroad, people are wondering about the measures the Soviet government will employ against Solzhenitsyn. He, of course, is not afraid and assumes that nothing will be done to him.

I believe that European Conference or not, we must not abandon our position that measures against Solzhenitsyn need to be taken. Even irrespective of what is happening at the European Conference, we must put Solzhenitsyn on trial, and let them know that we are pursuing a principled policy in this regard. We give no quarter to our enemies.

I think we shall inflict a great blow on our common task if we take no steps against Solzhenitsyn, even if this causes a lot of noise abroad. There will be much talk, but the interests of our people, the interests of the Soviet government, our party, are paramount. If we do not move decisively, we shall be asked why we failed to do so.

I am for putting Solzhenitsyn on trial. If we exile him, then we shall be showing our weakness. We must prepare for the trial, unmask Solzhenitsyn in the press, institute a case against him, conduct an investigation and forward the matter to court through the Procuracy.

[Dmitry] POLYANSKY. Can he be arrested before the trial?

ANDROPOV. Yes. I have consulted Rudenko about this.

PODGORNY. With regard to exiling him to another country, it would be completely unfeasible to do so without the consent of that country.

ANDROPOV. We shall start working toward exile, but at the same time, initiate a case against him, isolate him.

PODGORNY. If we exile him abroad, he will continue to cause us damage.

GROMYKO. It looks as if we shall have to choose the domestic version.

ANDROPOV. I think that it will be worse if we continue to drag out the case against Solzhenitsyn.

PODGORNY. We can delay the matter with Solzhenitsyn, such as by stretching out the investigation. But let him spend that time in prison.

SHELEPIN. When we met three months ago with comrade Kosygin and discussed the measures that should be employed toward Solzhenitsyn, we decided against employing administrative measures. It was right at the time. Now the situation has changed. Solzhenitsyn has gone directly against the Soviet power, the Soviet state. I think it would benefit us to resolve the Solzhenitsyn issue before the end of the European Conference. That would show our consistent adherence to principle. If we initiate this action after the Conference, we shall be accused of insincerity when we made decisions at the Conference, that we are already starting to breach these decisions and so forth. We have a clean and correct line. We shall not allow anyone to violate our Soviet laws. In my opinion, exiling him abroad is an unsuitable measure. I do not think foreign states should be involved in this matter. We have judicial bodies, so let them start the investigation, then handle the trial.

BREZHNEV. The matter of Solzhenitsyn is not easy, but highly complex. The bourgeois press is attempting to tie the Solzhenitsyn issue with the conduct of our large actions aimed at global peaceful settlement. How should we deal with Solzhenitsyn? I believe that it would be best to act in compliance with our Soviet laws.

EVERYONE. Yes, that's right.

BREZHNEV. Our Procuracy can begin the investigation, prepare the indictment, give a detailed explanation of this indictment as to his guilt. Solzhenitsyn has already been in prison, served a term of punishment for crude violation of Soviet legislation and was later rehabilitated. But how was he rehabilitated? He was rehabilitated by two people—[Olga] Shatunovskaya and [Alexey] Snegov. In accordance with our legislation, he should be denied communication abroad while under investigation. The investigation should be conducted openly and show the people his hostile anti-Soviet activities, his desecration of our Soviet system, smearing the memory of the great leader V.I. Lenin, the founder of the party and state, profaning the memory of the victims of the Great Patriotic War, justifying counterrevolutionaries and blatantly violating our laws. He should be tried on the basis of our legislation.

There was a time when we did not fear facing up to the counter-revolution in Czechoslovakia. We did not fear allowing Alliluyeva to leave the country. We survived all that. I think we shall survive this too. We should publish well-argued articles, give a clear and precise response to the writings of such a journalist as Olson and publish articles in other newspapers.

I have discussed the influence of our measures against Solzhenitsyn at the European Conference with comrade Gromyko. I think this will have no great effect. It is probably unfeasible to exile him, as nobody will want to accept him. It was one thing when Kuznetsov and others fled by themselves, and quite another when we exile someone by administrative order.

For this reason I think it is essential to charge the KGB and the Procuracy with devising the sequence of bringing Solzhenitsyn to trial, allowing for all that has been said here, and approve the relevant measures of legal order at a meeting of the Politburo.

PODGORNY. He should be arrested and indicted.

BREZHNEV. Let comrades Andropov and Rudenko work out the whole procedure of indictment properly, in accordance with our legislation.

I consider it essential to charge comrades Andropov, Demichev and Katushev with preparing information for the secretaries of fraternal communist and workers' parties in socialist countries and other leaders of fraternal communist parties about our measures regarding Solzhenitsyn.

EVERYONE. Right. Agreed.

The following resolution was approved:

On measures for prevention of the anti-Soviet activity of A.I. Solzhenitsyn

1. A.I. Solzhenitsyn is to be brought to book for vicious anti-Soviet activity, expressed in supplying foreign publishers and press agencies with manuscripts, books, letters, interviews containing slander of the Soviet system, the Soviet Union, the Communist Party of the Soviet Union and their internal and foreign policy, that desecrate the bright memory of V.I. Lenin and other functionaries of the CPSU and the Soviet government, victims of the Great Patriotic War and the fascist German occupation, justifying the actions of both internal and foreign counterrevolutionaries and groups and elements hostile to the Soviet system, and also crude violation of the rules governing publication of his literary works by foreign publishers, established by the Universal Copyright Convention (Geneva).

2. Charge comrades Yu.V. Andropov and R.A. Rudenko with determining the sequence and procedure of the conduct of the investigation and trial of A.I. Solzhenitsyn in accordance with the exchange of opinions in the Politburo and their own proposals on this matter, to be submitted to the CC CPSU.

3. Charge comrades Andropov, Demichev and Katushev with preparing information for the first secretaries of the Central Committees of Communist and workers' parties in socialist countries and certain capitalist countries regarding our measures against Solzhenitsyn with mention of the exchange of opinions at the Politburo meeting and submit the same to the CC CPSU.

4. Charge the Secretariat of the CC with determining the date for sending this information to fraternal parties.

• • •

It is obvious that the leaders had no interest in legality, and if they ever recalled the law, it was only in connection with its severity. It appears that they genuinely believed that whatever they decided would be legal. It is highly unlikely that any of them thought, for example, that a decision on the institution of a criminal case can be made only by the Procuracy, or that "the order and procedure for the conduct of an investigation and a trial" are regulated by the Criminal Procedure Code of the RSFSR and thus cannot be determined by either the head of the KGB or the Procurator General.

Never mind the law, they had trouble coping with reality: their conviction that "thousands of workers get killed" in England is an illustrative gem. Or their claim that they "did not fear allowing Allilu-yeva to leave the country." There is also their unfounded conviction that the people support their repressions.

Significantly, at this very time the Western press was full of materials by "Sovietologists" about the struggle between the "doves" and the "hawks" in the Kremlin, and worse still, Western politicians believed these tales. Détente ruled—it was the most idiotic period in postwar history. But how easy it is to believe, on the strength of the above minutes, that the only "dove" was Andropov, and even he preferred to exile Solzhenitsyn. It was well and good for the Politburo to decide what others should do, shouldering no responsibility for the implementation of its decisions. Andropov knew that he would be blamed for all the negative consequences of an arrest and trial of Solzhenitsyn. So naturally enough, he found a way to reverse the Politburo's decision by 180 degrees or, rather, found a country that was willing to accept Solzhenitsyn without the latter's consent.

For Andropov, and to a degree Gromyko, the Politburo's decision on the criminal prosecution of Solzhenitsyn was extremely unwelcome. Not only had the Politburo disagreed with them and rejected their proposals—that defeat in itself did not bode well for the future —but all their crafty détente games came under threat. What else could they do but turn to their partners in this game—the German social democrats? And these partners did not let them down. We shall return to this subject in greater detail, regarding what all this meant and where it was leading. The whole of chapter 4 will be devoted to this issue. At this point it suffices to say that a solution was found within one month: the chancellor of the FRG, Willy Brandt, made the unexpected announcement on 2 February that Solzhenitsyn could work and live in the FRG without impediment. As Solzhenitsyn said later in his "The Oak and the Calf": "He said it—so he said it."

Andropov hastened to inform the CC (7 February 1974*, 350-A/ov) that:

> BRANDT'S announcement provided grounds for Solzhenitsyn's expulsion to the FRG pursuant to the Order of the Presidium of the Supreme Soviet of the USSR and deprivation of Soviet citizenship. This decision shall be legal and takes into consideration the materials available regarding SOLZHENITSYN'S criminal activities.

Moreover, in order to be sure of gaining his ends, Andropov took two further steps: first, he inspired the report by two subordinates, Viktor Chebrikov and Philipp Bobkov, on feelings within the country in connection with the Solzhenitsyn case, stating that Solzhenitsyn had numerous admirers even among the working class, who consider that he advocated the lowering of prices and "opposes the export of goods vital to the people under the guise of aid to Arab countries."

Second, he wrote personally to Brezhnev (7 February 1974*) that the Solzhenitsyn matter "presently falls outside the scope of a criminal case and has turned into a pressing problem, with certain political overtones."

> Dear Leonid Ilyich, before sending this letter, we in the Committee once again weighed up carefully all the possible losses that could arise with regard to the expulsion (to a lesser degree) and arrest (to a greater degree) of Solzhenitsyn. Such losses are certain to occur. Unfortunately, we have no other way out, as Solzhenitsyn's unpunished behavior is already causing us much greater damage inside the country than will arise in the international sphere in the event of Solzhenitsyn's expulsion or arrest.

In other words, Andropov got what he wanted, and he was quite right: less damage resulted from expulsion. This is why this method of political punishment became so popular toward the end of the 1970s. But there is another question regarding domestic damage resulting from the "unpunished behavior" of any one of us, and it should be noted that the fact that such damage was greater than the other costs to the regime was not disputed by any Politburo member. Such a high evaluation of the effectiveness of our activities is extremely interesting. It explains a great deal. The system could survive only on the condition of the monopolistic rule of the party and the ideology over the country—above the law, logic and common sense. The appearance of an opposition, no matter how insignificant in numbers, even one person, heralded its end. This is probably what one of them had in mind when he spoke of "sovereignty." The Politburo sensed this infringement of sovereignty from the very beginning of our movement.

Back in 1968, after the Ginzburg-Galanskov trial (26 January 1968, 181-A, p. 3), Andropov had written, "It is now quite clear that Western propaganda and the group of abovementioned individuals, being an instrument in the hands of our opponents, are attempting to legalize the conduct of anti-Soviet activity inside our country, to achieve impunity for hostile actions."

As far as he was concerned, our scrupulous openness, legality, and appeals to the law were much more dangerous than any underground conspiracies or terrorism (20 January 1977*, 123-A): "In recent years, the opponent's special services and propagandist agencies are attempting to create the impression of the existence of a so-called 'internal opposition' in the Soviet Union, undertake measures to support the inspirers of antisocial manifestations and objectively cooperate in the consolidation of participants in various spheres of anti-Soviet activity." He reported with concern on the appearance of the Helsinki Groups in 1976 (15 November 1976*, 2577-A): "While at this stage prioritizing the achievement of anti-Soviet aims by illegal methods of subversion, the enemy is simultaneously trying to incite hostile actions in legal or semilegal forms."

Of course, arrests and expulsions were not the only reactions of the regime to these attempts. The entire arsenal of measures, from psychiatric incarceration and slander campaigns ("compromising") to threats and blackmail was pressed into service. It is characteristic that in 1977, as we have seen, the party even tried to ensure its monopolistic status through the Constitution, openly expressing this for the first time in its history in article 6 of the new Constitution of the USSR.

That was how they defended their "sovereignty" from our "infringements," partially accepting the rules of the game that we offered. It cannot be said that the regime did not display a fair amount of flexibility. Nonetheless, despite all the "damage" incurred, it could not manage without the usual repressions (29 December 1975* (3213-A), p. 4):

> At the same time, it is currently impossible to abandon the criminal prosecution of individuals pitting themselves against the Soviet system, as this would lead to an increase in particularly dangerous state crimes and antisocial manifestations.

This was written by Andropov in December 1975, after the signing of the Helsinki Accords; he thereby accepts the inevitability of external "damage" from their future violation as the lesser of two evils. The "damage" in question was far from minor. Not only did the "bourgeois" public opinion turn out to be sharply opposed to the USSR (something that could still be ascribed to "imperialist schemes"), but also opinion in "progressive" circles. Even many Western communist parties, especially the larger ones that were therefore more dependent on public opinion in their countries, were forced—albeit with reservations and reluctance—to voice condemnation of such practices. However hypocritical these condemnations may have been, the threat of a schism in the communist movement, and especially the political isolation of the USSR, was real enough.

3.7 External damage

Needless to say, the Politburo was very concerned by this development. According to Andropov (29 December 1975*, 3213-A):

> In recent times, the subversive activity of hostile bourgeois propaganda regarding Soviet democracy and that of other socialist countries is exploiting certain statements made by the leaders of the French and Italian Communist Parties, aimed against the Soviet Union and other socialist countries on matters relating to Soviet democracy. ... The problem arising in connection with statements made by leaders of the French and Italian Communist Parties, apart from the ideologically theoretical aspect, also has a practical side affecting the matter of ensuring the security of the Soviet state. ... The thesis advanced by "Humanite" about granting freedom of action under socialist conditions to those who "assert their disagreement with the system embraced by the majority" offers objective support to opponents of socialism in their efforts to create a legal opposition in the Soviet Union and other socialist countries, to undermine the leading role of communist and workers' parties.

> Comrades voicing similar views, even after the events in Hungary and Czechoslovakia, refuse to see that under the conditions of developed socialism, despite the monopolistic and political unity of society, there are still anti-Soviet manifestations in one form or another, to a greater or lesser degree. ... Available data demonstrate the aim of enemy special services and ideological centers to unite the actions of hostile elements of all sorts. ... It is clear from the above that a refusal to put an end to the politically harmful activities of "dissidents" and other hostile elements, as advocated by French and Italian comrades, would result in extremely serious negative consequences. [...]

> It would be desirable to hold relevant high-level discussions with our French and Italian comrades at a suitable time and explain to them that the struggle against so-called "dissidents" is not an abstract question of democracy in general, but a vital need to safeguard the security of the Soviet state.

For this reason, starting at the end of 1975, the Politburo sent several lengthy missives to the leadership of "fraternal parties" in general, and the CC of the French Communist Party in particular. The first such missive, sent in December 1975, was very carefully and diplomatically worded (18 December 1975, Pb 198/93, p. 5):

Comrades, we quite understand that the French Communist Party is engaged in an unrelenting struggle for democracy in France, against the efforts of reactionary forces to encroach on workers' rights. This is a lawful endeavor, which has our full understanding and support. But one cannot defend freedom in France while tolerating frequent attacks on the Soviet Union, thereby damaging the relations between our parties. ...

Of course, just like other countries, we have our share of criminal elements, which the Soviet Union needs to isolate in places of confinement and corrective labor. But this has nothing to do with violation of the democratic freedoms of Soviet citizens. We can tell you in all conscience that very few persons, out of a population of 250 million, are convicted by Soviet courts and then only in full compliance with the Constitution and in observance of the norms of judicial democratic procedure, and only if they engage in hostile activity against the socialist system and the Soviet state.

Another, longer missive on the same subject followed hard on the heels of this one, in January 1976 (14 January 1976, Pb 201/44), addressed to all "fraternal parties," with a detailed rebuttal of the "fabrications of anti-Soviet propaganda." It was sent first to twenty-two parties, and around a month later, on 5 February 1976, to a further thirteen, including even the most insignificant, or those operating underground.[111] But after several months, diplomacy yielded to annoyance, and an alarmed Andropov reported the following to the International Department of the CC (25 October 1976*, 25-S-2025):

There has been a noticeable upsurge in the anti-Soviet campaign supporting "dissidents" sentenced by Soviet courts for hostile activity in a number of capitalist countries. To this end, organizers of such campaigns have attempted to lure representatives of progressive organizations into taking part in their activities in order to lend them the appearance of "objectivity," and also to "tie in" their words of support for "dissidents" with declarations of support for victims of abuse in capitalist countries.

On 21 October of this year, there was a meeting in Paris in support of Bukovsky, and simultaneously one in support of the Uruguayan communist Masser and a number of others. The meeting was attended by representatives of the French Communist Party, in view of which the CC CPSU sent a letter to the leadership of the FCP (resolution of the CC CPSU N030/43 dated 18 October of this year).

We deem it feasible to send orientation advice on these matters to Soviet ambassadors in countries where such attempts may be made (Italy, Great Britain, USA, FRG, Japan, Spain, Portugal, Belgium, Switzerland, Sweden and Norway). The text of telegrams to Soviet ambassadors in those countries is attached.

---

[111] 5 February 1976 (Pb 203/104).

Obviously this was not the end of the matter, and at the beginning of 1977 the Politburo sent another long missive to the French Communist Party, which was much more harshly worded.

It was not just a letter, but a full-blown theoretical discourse, aimed at explaining the class nature of democracy and human rights to errant French comrades. Work on this letter took more than a month; it was discussed by the Politburo several times, amended, and finally sent to the addressee (15 March 1977*, Pb 49/XV, pp. 6–7) and, at the end of March, to all the communist parties of the world.[112] Instead of the usual vituperation, the result was a fundamental "class" determination:[113]

> After all, the emergence of an insignificant handful of counter-revolutionaries, who broke away from the very basis of our system, entered on the path of struggle against it and, as a rule, were linked with imperialist circles, is by no means a lawful outcome of the internal development of the Soviet Union. Admittedly, in the past there were groups of people and even political parties that opposed the Soviet system openly. They frequently progressed from words to deeds—up to attempts to assassinate V.I. Lenin and other leaders of the communist party and the Soviet government. At that time, such groups leaned on as-yet-unliquidated, exploitative classes.
>
> We have no such classes now and, it follows, no social bases for anti-Soviet groups. However, there are isolated instances of anti-Soviet manifestations. This is not surprising. The development of political awareness of multimillion popular masses, their upbringing in the spirit of socialist ideology, morality and rectitude, overcoming private ownership ideology and morality, obviation of the remnants of capitalism in the popular consciousness are essentially slower than the restructuring of the material base of society. Moreover, they occur today against a background of massive, daily anti-Soviet propaganda and direct subversive activities of imperialist centers that are hostile to socialism and that have stepped up their work to a significant degree. Remnants of capitalism in the perception of certain individuals are systematically fed and encouraged from abroad by imperialist propaganda centers.
>
> [...]
>
> In trying to create the impression that there are numerous opponents of socialism in the USSR, our class enemies sink to tricks of all kinds. One of the most frequently employed is to call "dissidents" all those who for some reason have a personal

---

[112] 15 March 1977 (Pb 49/15), pp. 20–23.
[113] Ibid, pp. 6–10.

opinion on some matter that differs from a generally accepted view, even writers and actors who have professional differences with their creative organizations. The falsity of such stratagems is despicable.

[...]

The close bond between the activity of "dissidents" and the process of global class struggle can be seen in the following. The first of the people emerging as active opponents of the Soviet system declared themselves in the mid-1960s, that is at the beginning of the period of détente, when imperialism floated the slogan of the "softening" of socialism. Accusations addressed to the Soviet Union and other socialist countries, proclaimed by them then just as today, are exactly the same as those employed then and now by bourgeois propagandists. Their demands coincided with Western demands concerning the "softening" of socialism. Numerous facts indicate that this is not by chance, that in most cases the so-called fighters for the perfecting of socialism receive materials with slanderous claims from abroad —from bourgeois special services. [...]

When some "dissident" or other arrives in the West, he quickly sheds the false mask of a "fighter wanting to perfect socialism" and emerges as a dyed-in-the-wool reactionary, a monarchist (like Solzhenitsyn) or admirer of [Franz Josef] Strauss and [Margaret] Thatcher (like Bukovsky), urging Western leaders to undertake even more active confrontation with the Soviet Union and other socialist countries. This has already been noticed by many fraternal parties, including communists in Great Britain, Holland, Austria, Portugal, Greece, Finland and others. It is reported in their press. Strangely, certain leaders of the French Communist Party have remained silent. Furthermore, they appeal to us to allow such people "unlimited freedom of expression" and to enter into "discussion" with them!

Basically, this document was not really about us, it concerned the French Communist Party and its positions. It amounted to a virtual ultimatum, falling little short of a declaration of total severance of relations:

Recent interviews of representatives of the French Communist Party and anti-Soviet broadcasts on French television show critics of various aspects of socialist democracy in the Soviet Union and other socialist countries, in which representatives of the leadership of the FCP actually reach the point of attempting to cast doubt on the correspondence of the political system in the USSR and other socialist countries to the interests of their citizens. We are openly called upon to review or, in fact, to abandon the entire system of Soviet democracy in order to grant unlimited "freedoms" to all opponents of socialism. ...

Therefore this is not subject to discussion, and anyone insisting otherwise is an enemy of the USSR.

• • •

Tensions in relations with the Italian Communist Party were less obvious, less "public", but no less dangerous and also continued to rise. In August 1976, replying to a letter from Enrico Berlinguer, the General Secretary of the PCI, regarding my case, the Politburo was scrupulously polite and diplomatic. Citing the usual "information" concerning my anti-Soviet activities, they wrote (29 August 1976, Pb 24/25):

> It can be concluded from your letter that Italian comrades lack sufficient information about Bukovsky's anti-Soviet activity. ... As you can see, comrade Berlinguer, the point at issue is not about a way of thinking, but concrete anti-Soviet acts of a citizen who bears full responsibility for them. He is not in prison for his convictions and views, we do not try anyone for their ideas, but for acts committed that are punishable in judicial court.

Yet half a year later, the tone begins to change, and upon the PCI's continuing participation in various campaigns on human rights, becomes increasingly strident. Boris Ponomarev and V. Kuznetsov reported the following to the CC (27 September 1977* (St 74/6), p. 12):

> According to reports received, there is a new wave of an anti-Soviet and antisocialist campaign in Italy, the focus of which is on alleged "dissidents." There are active preparations for the so-called "Sakharov Hearings" in Rome (25–27 November), "discussions with dissidents" in Florence, the international arts exhibition in Venice (the Biennale) for propaganda about the activities of dissidents (15 November–17 December). These manifestations are masterminded by imperialist propaganda services and are timed to immediately follow our main events marking the 60th anniversary of the October [Revolution] and pursue the aim of discrediting real socialism. Preparations for these manifestations are being conducted with the full approval of the Italian authorities, which clearly runs counter to the Helsinki Accords. On a number of occasions, representatives of the Italian Communist Party have allowed themselves to be put on the leash of the organizers of the indicated initiatives, they have participated in some of them, and the party press has published various materials about "dissidents," thereby objectively increasing the interest of Italian society in them.

Their proposed "plan of informative and propagandistic measures for counteracting anti-Soviet actions in Italy" envisaged a collection of complex measures, from official embassy protests to publications in the Soviet press, to appearances on Italian television of Soviet journalists, writers, and cultural figures related to the "Week of Soviet Cinema" in Italy, to the sending of a delegation of Soviet writers to Italy for public appearances.

However, subsequent events were not conducive to the improvement of bilateral relations. On the contrary, trials of members of the Helsinki Groups, the invasion of Afghanistan, Sakharov's exile, the military situation in Poland—all these were causes for differences. By 1980 Moscow was already oriented toward a split with the PCI, supporting its internal groups that "maintain positions friendly to us, and critical of the erroneous actions of the leadership of the PCI."[114]

Granted, these were just part of the "damage" the regime inflicted upon itself by its repressive policies, but they are an indicator of how successful our campaigning in defense of rights proved in the West. European communist parties joined in, not because they were doing well, but because they simply could not stand aside without discrediting themselves. Public reaction was too strong for any politician to ignore. It is not surprising that soon afterward this campaign became a factor in intergovernmental relations (the Jackson-Vanik Amendment in 1974, the so-called third basket of the Helsinki Accords in 1975), and by 1977, with the election of Jimmy Carter as the president of the USA, it was almost a key question in East-West relations.

These developments were an absolute catastrophe for the USSR, threatening it with political isolation. The Politburo sent the following order to its ambassador in Washington (18 February 1977, Pb 46/10):

> Meet Vance and tell him that you have been instructed to bring the following to the attention of President Carter and his Secretary of State, and that such interference in our internal affairs on the pretext of concern for "human rights" does not alter the substance of the matter.
>
> It stands to reason that everyone has the right to have a personal opinion about anything, including on how matters stand regarding freedom and human rights in one country or another. We also have our own view on these questions and their status in the USA.

---

[114]Cf. Vadim Zagladin note, 2 September 1980 (St 226/3), p. 7.

But it is another matter to introduce such views into the sphere of interstate relations, thereby complicating them. ...

It is not hard to imagine what would happen if we acted on the basis of our moral values, and were to link the development of interstate relations with the USA and other capitalist countries with such genuine problems in those countries as widespread unemployment, discrimination against ethnic minorities, racial discrimination, female inequality, violation of the rights of citizens by state administrative agencies, persecution of persons with progressive convictions, etc.

My meeting with Carter exactly ten days after this démarche probably cast the Politburo into a panic. It did not know how to react, let alone how to inform the population. In the end the news agency TASS supplied a draft on instructions from the CC (1 March 1977*, St 46/15, p. 2):

RECEPTION AT THE WHITE HOUSE

WASHINGTON, 1 March (TASS). Today, President of the USA J. Carter received criminal Bukovsky, who was expelled from the Soviet Union, and who is well known as an active opponent of the development of Soviet-American relations.

A White House spokesman stated that the meeting lasted about an hour and was of an amicable nature (this phrase to be confirmed with the White House statement that will be issued after 2300 hours Moscow time).

This information went to the press without the final phrase—someone decided to remove it at the last moment.

However, the confusion did not last long. By May the entire gigantic Soviet machine of "ideological warfare" had gone into action. Everyone was pressed into service, all "friends" and fellow-travelers, employing all forms of blackmail and threats, promises and bribes. The regime was fighting for its life, for its sovereign right to throw us into prisons and psychiatric institutions, to exile and expel us. Signaling the attack, the Politburo issued a directive to "all Soviet ambassadors and Soviet representations" in the world on 19 May (19 May 1977*, Pb 56/68):

A sweeping and coordinated propaganda campaign has been launched recently in the West regarding alleged "violations of human rights" in the Soviet Union and other socialist countries. The instigators of this clamor, which is of an openly provocative and demagogic nature are, as has occurred frequently in the past, mainly reactionary anticommunist and anti-Soviet forces in the USA and certain countries in Western Europe. It is note-worthy that in this instance this has been joined actively by official Washington circles, moreover from the highest political ranks of the new American administration.

Embassies and Soviet representations are to conduct persistent work on decisively counteracting this hostile campaign, to ac-tively expose its demagogic and slanderous nature that threat-ens political efforts in the cause of peace, and denoting inter-ference in the internal affairs of other countries. ... This work should be conducted on a combative plane, with obvious al-lowance for the specific country of their location, the positions of its government and the political inclination of the audience or interlocutor, in close coordination with the embassies of fra-ternal countries.

[This is followed by twenty pages of instructions, counterargu-ments, specific undertakings and hidden threats.]

In the first place, stress that campaigns of this kind, which are undoubtedly incapable of shaking the socialist system by one iota, may, however, have a negative effect on détente and impede the positive processes occurring in international relations in recent years. ...

Dismiss assertions that the campaign advocating the "defense of human rights," which is hostile to socialist countries and, among other things, public statements on this matter by cer-tain highly-placed officials in the West, are in no way interfer-ence in the internal affairs of other countries, but a form of ide-ological warfare, allegedly acknowledged by socialist countries themselves. ...

Stress that we really stand on the point of acknowledging ide-ological struggle, a struggle for social and political perceptions of the world, which does not cease even in a period of interna-tional détente. However, this struggle has nothing in common with the methods and devices of ideological sabotage, with the creation and support of illicit organizations in other countries. ...

In view of the circumstance that the propaganda campaign in-spired by Washington elicits a negative reaction in the ruling cir-cles of a number of Western countries, it is advisable to make a point of exposing conditions in the USA itself in all discussions on human rights. It is advisable to make convincing use of ar-guments to discredit the USA's attempts to position itself as an example of democratic rights and the world's supreme arbiter. ...

It is essential to ensure that the entire operative staff of em-bassies and representations and correspondents be prepared for discussions on human rights, that they be capable of bringing facts to the attention of the greatest possible number of people capable of influencing state policies and public opinion in the country where they are located. ...

You must conduct systematic work on discovering the most vulnerable aspects in the policies and practices of Western countries in the sphere of ensuring human rights, drawing special attention to the relevant legislation and punitive legal practices in those countries, and supply the Center [Central Committee] with proposals for strengthening our propagandist counterattack on Western countries that try to exert political pressure on us under the pretext of "defense of human rights."

It stands to reason that Western politicians were unable to withstand such a massed attack, especially since the subject of human rights, despite Soviet assertions, was only a fashion for them, and not a long-term strategy. They feared a return to the Cold War, some tried to maintain détente, and Carter needed a strategic arms limitation agreement. In a word, by the end of the year, Western campaigns for human rights had not died completely, but had faded somewhat. In any case, at the November Belgrade Conference on monitoring observance of the Helsinki Accords, only public representatives were not afraid of censuring the USSR; governments chose to limit themselves to generalized, vague formulations.

We shall return later to how and why this came about. Nonetheless, regardless of this, it is inarguable that the regime was prepared to accept colossal outward "damage" if only to avert the emergence of a perfectly peaceful and law-abiding domestic opposition, knowing full well that it could not withstand even a symbolic opposition. It was another matter to attempt to reduce such damage to a minimum, employing repressions as a last resort, but mainly depending on less obvious forms of persecution (resorting to psychiatry, defamatory campaigns, expulsion abroad, etc.). This was how Andropov formulated these policies in 1975 (29 December 1975*, 3213-A, p. 4), immediately after the signing of the Helsinki Accords:

All the above confirms the correctness of our party line for decisive struggle for "the protection of Soviet society from the actions of hostile elements." To this end, bodies of state security shall continue their efforts to suppress any anti-Soviet activity on the territory of our country. It is feasible to carry out the proven line of a reasonable combination of prophylactic and other operative *chekist* measures with measures of criminal prosecution when necessary.

The KGB shall maintain a stringent watch to ensure that so-called "dissidents" will be unable to organize an anti-Soviet underground and conduct anti-Soviet activity, including from "legal positions".

3.8   The Psychiatric Gulag

I would say that my main search was for documents relating to the use of psychiatry for repressive purposes, and they proved to be the hardest to find. Was my search being sabotaged by former apparatchiks, or were there really no such documents? Time passed, and I would soon have to give evidence in the Constitutional Court, so I was beginning to panic quietly; these documents were to be the "highlight of the program," evidence of one of the most vicious crimes of the post-Stalin period, which, as Solzhenitsyn noted acutely, were "the Soviet version of gas chambers."

To me, this was especially important—it was relevant to my personal case, for which I served my last sentence, was driven out of the country, continued my fight in the West, and finally won. It goes without saying that I have no intention of ascribing this victory just to myself; on the contrary, the achievement lay in that an enormous number of psychiatrists, lawyers, and public figures from all over the world joined the campaign against punitive psychiatry. Despite the political situation, it continued to grow, reaching its apogee in 1977, when the World Congress of Psychiatry in Honolulu censured Soviet abuses in this sphere. This campaign did not dry up, as had happened with previous campaigns; it continued to be a permanent factor influencing public opinion worldwide. In 1983 the Soviet delegation was even expelled from the World Psychiatric Association— or, rather, the Soviets resigned themselves, realizing that expulsion was inevitable.

This was the most convincing victory of our glasnost. The problem was that having started this campaign and even while laying my life on the line, I nevertheless did not know whether I had been correct in my conjectures right until the very end. Of course, the materials I passed to the West in 1970 about six political prisoners who had been sent into psychiatric institutions were genuine, and there was no reason to doubt those people's sanity. But was that just a chance coincidence, or an arbitrary act on the part of the local authorities or the local KGB? Or was it the conscious policy of the regime? This was something I could not know. There were only guesses based on some indirect evidence. We knew that the first wave of psychiatric repressions began under Khrushchev, shortly after his declaration in 1959 that there were no political prisoners in the USSR, only mentally ill people. But again, we knew of this only empirically; I was incarcerated in a psychiatric institution in 1963 and was a witness to these repressions.

After Khrushchev was ousted, the wave receded for a while, and swelled again at the end of 1968 and beginning of 1969. In any case, many of our friends were thrown into psychiatric institutions in this period.

Moreover, it was not hard to perceive why these "waves" arose: on one hand there was growing dissatisfaction and protests, and on the other there was reluctance to increase visible repressions, to accept external damage in the period of détente. Everything was logical, everything coincided, but it all remained mere guesswork. The official explanation that the Politburo was ignorant of psychiatry and simply believed the doctors was not contradicted. What could I do in the absence of documents? They may not have existed at all, just as documents on the "final solution" of the Jewish question were not found in the archives of the Third Reich.

Yet what I finally found exceeded all my expectations. For a start, nothing was simple with our case in 1967. On 27 January, the day after our arrests, the then head of the KGB, Vladimir Semichastny, and Procurator General Rudenko reported to the Politburo on what they proposed to do with us (27 January 1967*, Pb 32/5, p. 3):

> As a result, a group was formed of some 35–40 persons engaged in politically dangerous activity by means of producing and disseminating anti-Soviet literature and organizing various kinds of protests and meetings. The participants in this group appeal to the Western press, which publishes the materials they produce and attempts to distribute them on the territory of the Soviet Union.

After giving a quite detailed description of our activities and listing our names, as well as the names of those who, in their opinion, "incited" us, they wrote, as if in passing, that "it is worth noting that some of these persons are suffering from mental illness." And further: "The hostile activity of those formerly brought to book on criminal charges and released due to mental illness, P.G. GRIGORENKO, born 1907, former major-general of the Soviet Army, and A.S. [Esenin-]Volpin, born 1924, are also documented."

This is followed by a more or less standard list of propagandistic and prophylactic measures:

> Considering the possibility that bringing the indicated individuals to book on criminal charges will cause a definite reaction within the country and abroad, we deem it feasible to instruct the Department of [Agitation and] Propaganda of the CC and the

[Moscow] City Committee of the CPSU to conduct the necessary clarifying work, including addresses by party functionaries, authoritative propagandists, leading functionaries of the Procuracy and State Security in workplaces, offices, and particularly among students.

For their part, the Committee for State Security and the Procuracy of the USSR intend to conduct prophylactic measures at the places of work and study of persons performing antisocial actions due to their political immaturity and insufficient life experience.

At the same time, it appears feasible to prepare detailed material for publication in "Izvestia" explaining the measures implemented, and also to charge the Ministry of Foreign Affairs of the USSR, the KGB and the Procuracy to inform our foreign representations abroad.

It looks as though the KGB and the Procuracy feared that there would be a worldwide reaction, just as there had been in the previous year after the trial of Sinyavsky and Daniel. They seemed more inclined to resort to the "psychiatric method," at least in regard to those "suffering mental illness." However—by some miracle—the Politburo disagreed with them (27 January 1967* (Pb 32/5), p. 1):

1. Withdraw the question from consideration.

2. Assign comrades M.L. Suslov, [Arvids] Pelse and V.E. Semichastny to reconsider the question, bearing in mind the opinions expressed at the Politburo meeting and, if necessary, submit them to the CC (including the responsibility of the authors for sending their manuscripts for publication abroad, etc.).

As it turned out, the Politburo did not make any further decisions on this matter, and three months later Semichastny was removed from his post to be replaced by Andropov, who was present at the February meeting. Several months later we were all sentenced and—*not a single one of us was declared insane.*

All that remains is to guess what had really happened at the Politburo meeting. What was the substance of the disagreement between the party leaders and the lawyers? The only explanation I can think of is that it was the leniency of the proposed measures. I can easily imagine Suslov saying, *What have we here, comrades? Do we fear bourgeois propaganda? It would seem that they won the case of Sinyavsky and Daniel, and we cannot bring ourselves to punish those who followed in their footsteps to publish their slander abroad with the full severity of the law.*

It is also quite possible that Suslov had long wanted to get rid of Semichastny, who had retained the post of head of the KGB since Khrushchev's time, so he could replace him with his protégé Andropov. Whatever the situation was (and we shall probably never really know), psychiatric measures were clearly rejected. For some time after Khrushchev they were presumably regarded as too lenient, too great a concession to the West.

However, several years later the situation changed significantly, and in 1969 and the beginning of 1970 several people (Grigorenko, Natalya Gorbanevskaya, Viktor Fainberg and others) were declared mentally ill. On one hand Semichastny proved to be right: our trials caused a colossal response; on the other hand détente with the West had begun and it was vital to find effective means for repressing the growing number of protesters, means that would not attract the attention of global public opinion. In any case, by 1970 the psychiatric method warranted serious discussion in the Politburo as a possible method for mass repressions. The Politburo documents on this matter are extremely interesting, if only because they were classified under the highest category of secrecy: this was not just a general file, but its margins bear an inscription the like of which I have never seen anywhere else (22 January 1970*, Pb 151/XIII):

FOR INFORMATION:

A comrade receiving secret documents may neither pass them, nor disclose their contents, to anyone else without a special provision by the CC.

Copying of the indicated documents or making excerpts from them is categorically forbidden.

A record and date of familiarization are to be made personally on each document by the comrade to whom it was addressed, accompanied by his signature.

The question of the Committee for State Security:

Instruct the Ministry of Health of the USSR, the Committee for State Security and the Ministry of Internal Affairs of the USSR, acting with the participation of Gosplan of the USSR and the Councils of Ministers of Union republics to submit proposals for the establishment, recording and organization of treatment, and in some cases isolation, of mentally ill citizens in the country, and submit the same for examination by the CC CPSU in the first half of 1970.

This initiative certainly came from Andropov, who sent Politburo members a memorandum (dated 15 December 1969) from the KGB of one of the regions, Krasnodar, as an example of what was occurring throughout the country:

Regarding the existence of a significant number of psychiatric hospitals caring for [those] harboring terrorist and other socially dangerous intentions. A similar situation exists in other regions of the country.

This unique document deserves to be cited in full:

The KGB under the Council of Ministers of the USSR in the Krasnodar region possesses materials that indicate that there is a significant number of mentally ill persons who exhibit socially dangerous and hostile signs, harbor criminal, politically harmful intentions, and have a demoralizing effect on the lives of Soviet people. Over the past two years, more than 180 such persons have come to the attention of the regional security service. Some of these issue terrorist threats, intentions to kill representatives of the security service or commit other crimes. G.L. Bychkov and G.B. Mikov made vicious anti-Soviet declarations and issued threats toward several party leaders and the Soviet government; A.P. Vorona also made terrorist threats, drew up a list of active functionaries of the Crimean region who are "subject to destruction" and attempted to form an anti-Soviet group; S.A. Soni raves viciously of intentions to visit Lenin's Mausoleum and, using a movie camera, bring the leader of the revolution to life, and then kill him again; G.V. Vatintsev visited the Mausoleum, where he committed an audacious, cynical act; O.V. Dmitriev attacked and wounded a government security sergeant in a woodland close to Sochi; V.M. Pikalov threatened one of the leading functionaries of the Anapa city party with physical violence in September 1969 and used photographic means to produce slanderous materials, which he then disseminated.

A number of the mentally ill commit dangerous crimes at the state border, attempting to board foreign vessels with the aim of escaping abroad. In 1969, 19 persons out of a total of 50 attempting to violate the state border or attempting to board vessels of foreign navigation turned out to be psychologically unstable. The following committed particularly dangerous crimes: P.A. Skrylev, who hijacked an AN-2 aircraft, flew off in the direction of Turkey and was shot down with the aid of advance air defense systems over neutral waters; N.A. Korotenko absconded from the recruiting office in the city of Kropotkin, reached Novorossiysk and attempted to board an Italian vessel; V.I. Pavlov attempted to commit high treason using a boat with an outboard motor in the Sochi area in 1968, and had been detained earlier for the same reason in Batumi; V.A. Grekalov made persistent attempts to cross the border.

Some of the mentally ill make their way to Moscow and, displaying fanatical persistence, attempt to meet foreigners or penetrate embassies of capitalist countries with delusional demands or requests for political asylum. In November of this year, P.L. Rybka visited the French embassy; A.I. Cherep tried to enter the US embassy on a number of occasions in 1968; S.V. Rezak attempted to penetrate the embassy of the USA; N.I. Lelyabsky met with English people at the "Inprodmash" exhibition and asked them for political asylum, and attempted to pass across some documents to them.

Many of those suffering mental illness attempt to create new "parties," various organizations and councils, prepare and disseminate draft charters, program documents and laws. N.S. Sheinin nurtures and tries to impose on others the delusional idea of creating "Councils for control over the activities of the Politburo of the CPSU and local party organizations," for which purpose he sought out and worked on fellow thinkers, traveled to Moscow in order to meet activists of Communist and Workers' parties to "discuss" this matter, blackmailed persons unwilling to support him, sent a threatening letter to the secretary of the Novocherkassk headquarters of the CPSU for the Rostov region regarding the known events of 1962;[115] A.I. Bekh attempted to create an illicit "party"; V.A. Pak engages in the systematic production and dissemination of documents with politically dangerous content and demands the creation of a so-called global government.

Many of the mentally ill write numerous letters to various regional and central organizations containing slanderous, anti-Soviet concoctions and threats. Of these, D.I. Mikhalchuk, who is attempting to emigrate, sent a letter dated 5 April 1969 and addressed to the Presidium of the Supreme Soviet of the USSR, in which he wrote: "Do you want all my actions to be identical to those at the Borovitsky Gate?" ... In a discussion with the chairman of the Belorechensk city executive committee, Mikhalchuk stated that he is not responsible for his actions and may commit a crime.

There are quite a few among the mentally ill who are inclined to commit attacks, rapes and murder, while some actually do attempt and commit such crimes. For example, during an aggravated period of their illness L.G. Buznitsky beheaded his ten-year-old son, B.M. Onelyan murdered her husband and A.M. Ponomarenko murdered his sister.

According to data from psychiatric institutions, out of the total

---

[115]A protest by hundreds of workers over price rises and food shortages in Novocherkassk in early June 1962 was dispersed by soldiers firing into the crowd, wounding dozens and killing twenty-four (according to the official death toll).

of 55,800 mentally ill persons, many are aggressive or malevolent and some 700 of them pose a danger to the public. The
majority of them reside in Krasnodar, Sochi, Novorossiysk,
Maykop, Gelendzhik, Yeysk and Crimean districts.

In order to prevent dangerous actions by the indicated category of persons, the regional state security bodies are forced to
implement necessary measures, which involve a great deal of
manpower and expense.

At present, according to data supplied by regional health authorities, eleven to twelve thousand persons stand in need of
hospitalization, but medical facilities of the relevant profile have
only 3,785 beds.

For the purposes of preventing dangerous manifestations by
persons suffering mental illness, in our opinion—one that is
shared by managers of health care agencies in the region—there
is a need for further improvement in the system of measures required for their identification, registration, hospitalization and
treatment, as well as for control over their behavior outside the
walls of medical facilities.

The regional party committee and the regional executive committee are to be informed of the above.

Head of the Administration of the KGB under the Council of
Ministers of the USSR for the Krasnodar region Major-General
V. Smorodinsky

15 December 1969

This amazing document is the acme of *chekist* duplicity. For
a start, it was doubtless inspired by Andropov himself; the head of
the regional KGB had no reason, nor was he obligated, to write such
generalized memoranda to his boss. Moreover, he had probably informed Andropov of every cited case in the past. Was it possible
that Moscow had not been advised immediately about the shooting
down of a plane "over neutral waters"? Did they not know in Moscow about visits by people from Krasnodar to foreign embassies or
Lenin's Mausoleum, even though an "audacious, cynical act" had
taken place there? If the sending of this memorandum was Major-
General Smorodinsky's own idea, he would surely have added the
sacred bureaucratic phrase *as I have already reported* after describing the situation. These words do not occur even once, as though
all these data had been collected by the poor general for two years,
until he could stand no more.

Furthermore, the selection of examples focuses consciously on
the danger of terrorist acts by the mentally ill. It is noteworthy that
the matter occurred at the end of 1969, that is, shortly after the
notorious attempt to assassinate Brezhnev—the act "at the Borovit-

sky Gate"—committed by Ilyin, who was immediately declared to be insane and confined in the Kazan special hospital with a "lifetime bed" (he was released only toward the end of the 1980s and showed no signs of mental illness). It appears that both the writer and the readers are perfectly aware of the substance of the matter. They know what is meant by "mental illness" and "danger to the public": they relate to people who have been driven to their breaking point and are no longer receptive to *chekist* "prophylactic measures."

Consequently it becomes clear why the Krasnodar region had been chosen as the origin of this document: it hosts numerous state health resorts and is close to the border with a capitalist country, Turkey. In other words, there were more desperate attempts there on average than elsewhere in the country. Andropov was certainly lying when he claimed in his accompanying note that "a similar situation exists in other regions of the country." This could not occur in regions that have no direct access to a border. Nobody would hijack a plane in the Ryazan region, because there was no way it could reach a capitalist country. Nor were there any "vessels of foreign navigation" to be found, or other objects likely to tempt a Soviet citizen. In such areas, the statistics on local "mental illnesses" would be incomparably lower.

Finally, let us look at the cited figures. The total figure of mentally ill people in the region was said to be 55,800, of whom 11,000 to 12,000 required hospitalization, and around 700 posed a "danger to the public." So the members of the Politburo would have no trouble understanding the scope of the problem, insofar as the situation was "similar" to everywhere in the USSR, which comprises about a hundred regions and districts. This meant that there would be some 70,000 "dangerous" individuals and 1.2 million requiring hospitalization. It meant, no more and no less, that there was good reason for the creation of a *psychiatric gulag*. The Politburo was agreeable to its creation, and in a short time at that: it planned to solve this problem within half a year!

It is not hard to understand why Andropov wanted to play it safe by forwarding his subordinate's memorandum to the Politburo, something that he did not usually do either before or after this occasion. After all, it was only three years ago that his predecessor Semichastny had been stung over the issue of psychiatry, having demonstrated his "leniency" toward enemies. Who could be sure that the Politburo would not kick up again? The more so because the issue related to such sweeping action—a shift in the entire punitive policy. So Andropov is trying to scare the old men of the Politburo by reporting a massive outbreak of insanity in the Krasnodar region, as though this situation had come into being only then, and for unknown reasons.

• • •

When I was released from a camp in January 1970, I did not have the slightest idea that right at that time the Politburo had reached a decision that would see me back in prison. None of us could have ever imagined such a state of affairs.

All we noticed was that the number of those declared insane in our cases had increased significantly. It was also obvious that psychiatrists were busily devising a special system of diagnosis, very well suited for mass application to political opponents and indeed to anyone dissatisfied with the regime. Questionable terms such as "reformist delusions" appeared, and Professor Andrey Snezhnevsky's "sluggish schizophrenia," which up to that time had been considered disputable, found acceptance. It was perfectly clear that we were earmarked for psychiatric repression, although we had no idea of the scope of preparations for it.

However, it turned out that our campaign had hit the bull's-eye. Half a year had not yet passed, and the Politburo had not reached a final decision, when my first interviews appeared in the Western press, and by summer they were on television, where the question of psychiatric repression became a top story. It was as though we had caught them red-handed at the scene of the crime, and quite by chance at that. It is probably like this in wartime, when a rogue shell hits the arsenal and scuppers the impending attack. The regime had to defend itself with all it had, and the decision to create a psychiatric gulag was shelved for two years at least. When discussion of this matter was resumed, it was only in January 1972, soon after my trial—and who can say whether this was coincidental or linked? After all, I had been tried and sentenced for slandering Soviet psychiatry. The atmosphere was too explosive. There had been too much talk of abuse of psychiatry to go back to the original plan without adding more fuel to the fire. What secrecy could there be if all the Western mass media were trumpeting Soviet psychiatric repressions?

In essence, the discussion was reduced to simply analyzing the state of psychiatry in the country. A special commission of the Council of Ministers was appointed to study the situation, the so-called Rakovsky Commission, which found, among other things, that all political considerations aside, the situation was highly unsatisfactory (22 February 1972*, St-31/19, pp. 3–5):

> According to the data of the Ministry of Health of the USSR, an increase in mental illness has been noted throughout the country. If at the beginning of 1966 there were 2,114,000 in-

dividuals on record receiving extramural treatment in psycho-neurological institutions, then at the beginning of 1971 this figure rose to 3,700,000, with a further 280,000 receiving in-house treatment in clinics.

The number of psychiatric hospital beds sufficient for the pop-ulation per capita is two and a half times below the required norm. The material bases of the majority of psychiatric clin-ics are unsatisfactory, most of them are located in unequipped premises that are unsuitable for the normal accommodation of patients. Numerous hospitals have only 2.0–2.5 square meters per patient, while the norm is 7 square meters. Quite frequently patients have to share a bed or sleep on the floor. Some hospi-tals have built two-tier bunk beds [...]

Difficulties with hospitalization of the mentally ill and their pre-mature discharge from clinics lead to the result that there are seriously ill and frequently dangerous people at loose in the community.

Data from the Ministry of Internal Affairs of the USSR and the KGB under the Council of Ministers of the USSR indicate an increase in the number of murders, robberies, thefts and other serious crimes committed by persons suffering mental prob-lems that have increased in recent times. In 1970 they commit-ted 6493 crimes, including 937 murders. Some of the indicated crimes were committed with particular cruelty and involved a large number of victims. [...]

The resolution of the CC CPSU and the Council of Ministers of the USSR dated 5 July 1968 N517, "On measures for the further improvement of health and development of medical science in the country," envisages the building and commissioning of no less than 125 psychiatric hospitals with a capacity of 500 beds each by 1975. The economic plan for 1971–1975 includes the building of 114 psychiatric hospitals and the commissioning of 43,800 beds.

In 1971 the Ministry of Health of the USSR and the Ministry of Internal Affairs under the Council of Ministers of the USSR submitted a draft resolution to the Council of Ministers on mea-sures for the further improvement of medical assistance to men-tally ill patients [...]

Overall, the business clogged up for a long time and passed into the sphere of purely professional problems, losing its political char-acter. Naturally, the number of psychiatric hospitals increased to-ward the end of the 1970s, as had been planned, but the number of people relegated to them for political reasons did not increase, not even in proportion with the number of hospitals. This is not surprising in view of the scope of the global campaign against the abuse of psychiatry, as Andropov reported to the CC (10 September 1976*):

> An anti-Soviet campaign containing crude falsifications alleging the abuse of psychiatry in the USSR as an instrument in the political struggle against "dissidents" is being waged in a number of Western countries. The ideological centers and special services of the foe are attracting mass media, use the podiums of scientific forums, inciting anti-Soviet "demonstrations" and "protests." ... The latest data show that this campaign is a thoroughly prepared anti-Soviet action. The organizers of slanderous declamations are apparently attempting to turn opinions toward the public condemnation of "abuse of psychiatry in the USSR" at the forthcoming [Sixth] World Congress of Psychiatry (Honolulu, USA) in August 1977, hoping to achieve a negative political resonance on the eve of the sixtieth anniversary of the Great October Socialist Revolution. [...]

Note that all this is written without a trace of irony, as if it were not Andropov himself who had sent this material and proposals regarding the creation of a psychiatric gulag to the same CC (22 October 1976, No. 2750):[116]

> The Ministry of Health of the USSR is working to locate progressively minded prominent psychiatrists in the USA, England, France and other capitalist countries and invite them to the USSR to participate in scientific conferences and symposia, informing them of the achievements of psychiatric help in our country. The aim is to use their positive reactions in propagandistic work abroad. [...]
>
> The Ministry of Health of the USSR and the Ministry of Internal Affairs of the USSR have organized inspections of special hospitals in which the enforced treatment of mentally ill persons is performed for purposes of improving medical service to this category of patients. It is presumed that where necessary, certain such hospitals may be shown to foreign specialists.

Undoubtedly, "progressive" Western colleagues would not be shown ordinary psychiatric hospitals, where there were not enough beds, so patients had to double up or sleep on the floor. Still, some of them might be "progressive" enough for this not to bother them, as Soviet "parliamentarian" Yuri Zhukov reported to the CC (16 November 1976):[117]

---

[116] 10 September 1976* (No 2066-A), pp. 6–7.
[117] 10 September 1976* (No 2066-A), pp. 12–13.

On the last day of the visit of the Portuguese parliamentary delegation to the USSR, a member of this delegation, which I escorted, [Antonio] Fernandes da Fonseca, a prominent specialist in the field of neuropathology and psychiatry, a deputy of the Socialist Party, told me the following in confidence. According to data in his possession, anti-Soviet-inclined American activists intend to use the forthcoming World Conference of Psychiatry in 1977 in Honolulu to organize a scurrilous anti-Soviet campaign in connection with widespread slanderous allegations in the West to the effect that our psychiatric hospitals are used for incarcerating "dissidents."

[...]

In connection with this, A. Fernandes da Fonseca asked to be supplied with relevant data for the preparation of his address at the Congress. According to him, these data would be used to acquaint prominent psychiatrists from other countries in which Portuguese is spoken. ...

[...]

A. Fernandes da Fonseca stressed that what is needed now is not general statements of a political nature that expose the absurdity of American accusations, but specific scientific material —diagnoses and information on the treatment of such individuals as Plyushch, Bukovsky and others, who are being hailed as "innocent victims."

How I would like to meet this Antonio Fernandes da Fonseca now, preferably in the presence of journalists or on television. But he would not dare, just like all our opponents during the Cold War. Even if he were to be brought by force, he would not repent. It is a given that he would whine that he "didn't know," that he "believed," and that it is all the fault of the Americans. In any event, neither Leonid Plyushch nor I ever received any apologies from him.

• • •

It need hardly be said how delighted Soviet psychiatrists were to obtain a voluntary assistant, one who would allow them to employ him "in the future also, and make use of his possibilities for disseminating information we find useful" (13 December 1976, No. 3193).[118]

They really had too much work to do: practically every year a "Plan of Measures for Exposing the Anti-Soviet Slanderous Campaign Concerning So-Called "Political Abuses" in Psychiatry" had to be drawn up and approved by the CC. These are impressive documents, containing a detailed scheme for an international countercampaign involving all possibilities: the press, television, Soviet

---

[118] 10 September 1976* (2066-A), p. 17.

diplomacy, and KGB measures. They set out tactics and strategy, both prior to condemnation in Honolulu and afterward. But if before Honolulu this scheme was mainly a complex of defensive measures of a propagandistic nature, then after Honolulu it was a desperate struggle for survival.

Condemnation in Honolulu was a cruel defeat for the regime, going far beyond the boundaries of psychiatry. First and foremost because even the most strenuous efforts of the Soviet foreign policy machine could not avert it.[119] Justifying itself to the CC, the leadership of Soviet psychiatry gave a detailed list of all the measures taken (21 November 1977, No. 3042):[120]

> In preparing for the Congress, the Ministry of Health of the USSR analyzed the main anti-Soviet publications, and reasoned counterarguments were drawn up; a number of symposia took place with the participation of prominent foreign specialists, and participation in the programs of the World Health Organization was activated. Shortly before the Congress, Soviet psychiatrists visited Bulgaria, Hungary, GDR and the Czechoslovak Republic to coordinate the positions of socialist countries.
>
> An authoritative Soviet delegation was picked to take part in the Congress, which, upon arrival, immediately established active contacts with delegations from socialist countries and other states (Mexico, Venezuela, Senegal, Nigeria, India, etc.). These contacts, and also the further conduct of the Conference, confirmed that although the Congress was officially organized by the WPA, all the actual preparations were in the hands of the American Psychiatric Association. ...
>
> The premises in which the meetings of the Congress took place were flooded with anti-Soviet trash, leaflets containing scurrilous attacks on Soviet psychiatry and its individual representatives. "Former Soviet psychiatrists," brought to the Congress deliberately, skulked in the corridors. ...
>
> In view of this, the Soviet delegation made consecutive vigorous protests from the very first day.
>
> But the main collision with anti-Soviets occurred at two meetings of the General Assembly of the WPA, where the organizers of the Congress moved for discussion of the "Declaration of Hawaii," drafted by the Ethics Sub-Committee of the Executive Committee, concerning general ethical principles of contemporary psychiatry (to which the Soviet delegation acceded), and

---

[119]Sidney Bloch and Peter Reddaway's *Russia's Political Hospital* formed part of this international campaign. *Russia's Political Hospital: The Abuse of Psychiatry in the Soviet Union.* London: Gollancz, 1977.

[120]21 November 1977 (No 3042), pp. 2–5.

also the provocative Anglo-Australian resolution "condemning the abuse of psychiatry in the USSR" and the American proposal to form a "Committee for investigating instances of the abuse of psychiatry."

The Soviet representative at the Assembly (E.A. Babayan) protested against the inclusion of these proposals in the agenda as clearly slanderous and contrary to the Charter of the WPA. He also spoke against the proposed procedure for the discussion of items on the agenda that do not warrant serious consideration. A categorical protest was made regarding the voting system, which is organized on the basis of the number of votes being proportionate to the monetary contributions made by national associations into the WPA budget (from 30 to 1-2 votes). However, these proposals were rejected due to unconcealed pressure by the President of the WPA, H. Rome,[121] and references to the Charter of the WPA. ... Subsequently the President of the WPA crudely violated the procedure for the conduct of the meeting and forced a vote without regard for the elementary rules of procedure. ...

As was widely noted in the corridors of the Congress and the press, despite the formal "adoption" of the slanderous Anglo-Australian resolution, the moral victory at the Congress was won by Soviet psychiatry.

Obviously this "victory" did not suit the CC, so work began immediately after Honolulu:[122]

Soviet academics (A.V. Snezhnevsky, [Georgy] Morozov, [Eduard] Babayan, [Nikolay] Zharikov, [Marat] Vartanyan, [Vladimir] Rozhnov and others) attended learned conferences on psychiatry in the FRG, Switzerland, GDR, and the HPR [Hungarian People's Republic], where they met with foreign colleagues and presented them with detailed information regarding the true nature of events at the recent Congress. A press conference on the results of the Congress was held (E.A. Babayan), which received objective coverage in a number of Swiss newspapers.

Consequently the campaign approved by the CC for 1978 and 1979 included an enormous number of propagandistic measures, the use of scientific contacts and publications, and tactical moves such as "Strive for the democratization of the WPA Charter and procedural rules of its highest body—the General Assembly."

---

[121] Harold Rome, also president of the US Psychiatric Association.
[122] 21 November 1977 (No 3043), p. 8.

There were occasional curious moments. Thus, before and after Honolulu, an important measure was deemed to be (13 April 1978, No. 1763):[123]

> To organize the receipt of information concerning the fate of mentally ill individuals, former citizens of the USSR who have left the country, for the purpose of using this information in acceptable form, allowing for the requirements of medical ethics, to expose the slanderous nature of accusations being levelled at Soviet psychiatry.
>
> Responsible entities:
>
> Ministry of Foreign Affairs of the USSR,
>
> Committee for State Security under the Council of Ministers of the USSR,
>
> Ministry of Health of the USSR.

The aim of this was to determine whether those of us who had been incarcerated in Soviet psychiatric hospitals ended up receiving psychiatric treatment abroad. And if there had been no such cases, they were to be invented. The KGB did not need to be asked twice, and shortly numerous Western left-wing publications announced that one or another of our friends had allegedly landed in Western psychiatric hospitals.

Among others, such information was published about Alexander Esenin-Volpin, who was living in the USA, but he did not waste any time and filed a suit in an American court against the publication in question for defamation. In dire panic Andropov, Kuznetsov, Leonid Zamyatin, and Lev Tolkunov alerted the CC (26 January 1977*, St 42/18, pp. 2–3):

> Reactionary Zionist circles in the USA, acting with undeniably provocative, anti-Soviet aims, have incited an appeal to an American court by the renegade Esenin-Volpin. He has filed a suit against TASS, APN and the American newspaper "Daily World" (an entity of the Communist Party of the USA) for insulting him through publication (defamation). The formal pretext is republished material in the "Izvestia" and "Sovetskaya Rossiya" [*Soviet Russia*] newspapers taken from the Italian left-wing journal "Ragione" (May 1976), exposing the slanderous reactionary propaganda alleging that healthy people are incarcerated in psychiatric hospitals in the Soviet Union for political reasons. The article in question stated: "As soon as he arrived

---

[123] 14 April 1978 (No 1644) p. 8.

in Italy Esenin-Volpin, who was so hotly defended by the Western press, had to be admitted to a lunatic asylum; at present, he is being treated by American psychiatrists."

TASS sent this to Soviet newspapers, APN carried it in one of its publications in the FRG, and the "Daily World" published its own piece on the basis of the "Ragione" article.

The American court sent summonses to the New York offices of TASS and APN demanding their appearance in court, and in the event of their nonappearance by 2 February of this year, TASS and APN will be found guilty automatically, and will each have to pay Esenin-Volpin two hundred thousand dollars in damages.

The claim itself is worded in an anti-Soviet, provocative spirit regarding the so-called repression of dissidents in the USSR, their incarceration in psychiatric hospitals and similar nonsense. All this is aimed at inciting yet another campaign against the Soviet Union in America through the mass media of the USA.

To suppress this process, the ambassador of the USSR in the USA had a discussion with the US deputy Secretary of State, drawing his attention to the inadmissibility and the unfounded actions of the American court. The State Secretary evaded making a direct response, claiming that "from a legal point of view this is not such a simple matter."

In order to obviate the need for representatives of TASS and APN to appear in American court and so these entities could avoid being drawn into this essentially provocative process, the Soviet ambassador was permitted to hire an American attorney and strive for dismissal of the case and its annulment with the aid of the attorney and the citing of American legislation.

The ambassador was also instructed to make representations to the State Department, demanding urgent measures for the termination of the matter of Esenin-Volpin's claim due to its unfounded nature and clear pursuit of political ends hostile to the Soviet Union, as ensues from the claim itself. The Soviet ambassador was further instructed to let the American side be aware that otherwise we shall take reciprocal measures against American press bodies and their Moscow correspondents, who frequently publish genuinely slanderous reports concerning the Soviet Union and its citizens.

Depending on the response of the American side and further developments, we deem it feasible to devise retaliatory measures in line with the Committee for State Security. We also deem it feasible to continue necessary measures to pursue our line through the State Department of the USA.

To avoid becoming involved with the matter in substance, which is the aim of Zionist circles that incited Esenin-Volpin's suit, we

believe that TASS and APN correspondents should not attend
the American court either now or subsequently. It appears feasible to coordinate our actions with friends in the matter of the
analogous suit against the "Daily World."

We request approval of the indicated course of action.

It is a given that the CC approved the "course of action," thus
covering up the obvious lies in which the hapless *chekists* were
trapped. In the interests of socialism, everything was "feasible."
The State Department, for its part, was afraid of confrontation. I
do not know how it was able to interfere in judicial matters—under
American law this is proscribed as criminal—but the case never
came to court.

That is a great pity. Had the West shown enough stamina to refrain from violating its own laws and procedures at least in order not
to bow to Soviet *diktat,* communism would have met its end much
sooner and would have inflicted less damage on the people. In any
case, the example of the praiseworthy conduct of most Western psychiatrists serves as the best proof of this. So the Soviet leaders were
unable to establish their psychiatric gulag, their grandiose plan collapsed without being born, and right up to 1989 they were forced to
make excuses before the whole world and implement endless "measures." They were unable to wash off this shameful blot completely.
Moreover, our glasnost proved to be so effective in this matter that
by the end of the 1970s the KGB came to fear any dissident being
placed in a psychiatric hospital even accidentally, irrespective of its
wishes. For example, it was due to this that Alexander Zinoviev
was not arrested—it was easier to throw him out into the West. Andropov reported to the CC in 1978 (28 June 1978, 1311-A, p. 3)
that

> materials in the possession of the Committee for State Security
> demonstrate that all the activities of ZINOVIEV are unlawful,
> and there are legal reasons to bring him to book on criminal
> charges. It is our opinion, however, that the application of this
> measure for terminating ZINOVIEV'S anti-Soviet activity is un-
> feasible for the reason that statements by persons closely ac-
> quainted with ZINOVIEV indicate that he had been treated for
> alcoholism in the past, is psychologically unbalanced and suf-
> fers from delusions of grandeur. These circumstances could
> (in the event of ZINOVIEV being brought to book on criminal
> charges) lead the court to find him mentally ill with direction
> for mandatory treatment. In view of the extensive Western cam-
> paign concerning psychiatry in the USSR, this course of action
> is deemed unfeasible.

It was only in 1989, when Gorbachev-Yakovlev glasnost was in full swing and it had become profitable to admit to past crimes, that the Politburo finally passed "On Improving Legislation Concerning the Conditions and Procedure for Rendering Psychiatric Aid" (15 November 1989, Pb 171/21), the resolution that introduced legal guarantees against the abuse of psychiatry. It is true that even then this measure was partly forced, enacted under pressure from the West.

There are now public groups of psychiatrists in Russia and Ukraine that are vigilant in watching for any signs of a resurgence of the use of their profession for political purposes. They investigate all suspicious cases, scrutinize every complaint, visit psychiatric hospitals, and where necessary petition the authorities for the review of suspicious cases. But such cases are now no more frequent than in any other country.

Striking changes have occurred in the field of psychiatry, much more than in many other spheres of Soviet life. Our times are now history. In the Leningrad Special Hospital where we met with Major-General Grigorenko, our "medical histories" are being shown to visitors, just like the cell in which Mikhail Bakunin was held in the Peter and Paul Fortress. And in 1992, preparing for my appearance at the Constitutional Court, I visited the Serbsky State Scientific Center for Social and Forensic Psychiatry with a Russian television crew. We were welcomed by a young, attractive woman, the then director of the institute, Tatyana Dmitrieva. "I have read your book and have long wanted to tell you that everything you wrote about our institute and about special hospitals is true," she said.

I knew she was not being two-faced; she had already said as much to the press.

Thirty years have elapsed since the day when I first stepped over the threshold of this once-notorious institution. Only two people who knew me as a "patient" were still alive: the old nurses' aide Shura and the "honorary director", "academician" G.V. Morozov, our very own Dr. Mengele—who, they say, prefers to stay away from there nowadays.

Yet are these changes really so final? Nobody has repealed our diagnoses, nobody has thought of apologizing for all the slander that was hurled at us for decades in the press and whispered behind the scenes in personal contacts. None of these "academics" ever stood before courts to answer for crimes against humanity, and none were stripped of academic titles for violating the Hippocratic Oath. On the contrary, many of them, such as Vartanyan and Babayan, continue to stand at the head of Soviet psychiatry and even represent it abroad. And if the current authorities do not

need the psychiatric method today, that does not mean it will not
be required by those in power tomorrow. Would it be so difficult
to revert to it? All it would take would be to demand the dismissal
of this nice young woman from her doctor's post and consign the
few remaining psychiatrists from public monitoring groups into the
camps. As for what ideology shall be served by psychiatry that cor-
rects the minds of its citizens—be it national socialist or international socialist—who cares?

3.9   What did they believe?

Undoubtedly, the misuse of psychiatry as an instrument in political repressions was the outstanding crime against humanity in
the postwar epoch. It shall be remembered by our descendants
for centuries to come, just as we remember the guillotine of the
French Revolution, Stalin's gulags, and Hitler's gas chambers. Furthermore, the documents cited above show clearly that this was
not happenstance, not a whim of the executor, but Politburo policy, without the will of which not a hair would have fallen from our
heads. Strange as it may sound, even having read all these papers, I can find no satisfactory answer to the question of whether
the Politburo understood what it was doing. Despite all its practi-
cality, did it really live in the dream bubble of socialist realism, in
which it was impossible to distinguish fact from fiction or information from disinformation? Especially as these were people for whom
truth (determined by class) was by definition arbitrary due to their
ideology. Like legality, truth also served the principle of "feasibility."

    In fact, are such concepts as good and evil, lies and truth, appli-
cable to these people? I don't know. Keep in mind that in communist newspeak such words, just like many others familiar to our ear,
had a completely different meaning. For instance, we were accused
of "slandering the Soviet state and social system" over and over
again like an incantation; in all their documents, decisions, and
missives, the term "slanderous" described our pronouncements,
publications, and samizdat materials. Did they really believe that
we were distorting reality, consciously or subconsciously? Of course
they didn't. But the very concepts of "reality" and "actuality" had
totally different meanings in their language.

    The ideology spurned everything that was common to mankind,
including the meanings of words: there could be no such things as
"reality" or "actuality" alone—things were either "bourgeois" or "socialist." Thus a "slander of socialist reality" translated simply into
the discrepancy between something said or written with the im-

age of the "real socialism" created by the Politburo itself. And this image, by definition, could not contain any "organic defects" or imperfections; there could only be "isolated shortcomings" or "growing pains."

It is easy to imagine to what level of absurdity all this could lead from a purely linguistic point of view. For instance, in a letter to Brezhnev concerning the exile of Solzhenitsyn, Andropov writes that the book *The Gulag Archipelago* "is definitely anti-Soviet, but the facts contained therein did actually take place" (7 February 1974*). Certain documents even speak of "slanderous facts," which is inexplicable outside the Soviet system.

The matter is complicated further because in time these concepts became formalized, and the language became simplified. Thus the adjective *socialist* stopped accompanying every word—it was self-evident. What else could a word mean? For this reason, for example, one could not say, "There is no democracy in the USSR," much less "There is no real democracy in the USSR"—because there is socialist democracy, which, unlike the bourgeois version, is the real thing. And if saying something like this caused you to be accused of "slanderous fabrications," it fell under article 190 of the Criminal Code, but "anti-Soviet fabrications" came under article 70, while the term "ideologically harmful" meant that you were in luck and might only lose your job and be expelled from the party, the Komsomol, or the institute and be subjected merely to "prophylactic measures." Just as in the 1930s, the term "first-category enemy of the people" meant death by firing squad, and "second-category" meant concentration camp or exile (4 February 1938*).

It is impossible to say what the members of the Politburo really thought. And what did they perceive to be real? There was no way out of the vicious circle of socialism. Not a single member of the Politburo could ask another: "You, Ivan Ivanovich, report that the wellbeing of the Soviet people is steadily growing. But what is the real situation?" To them, the supreme dispensers and curators of the imaginary world of socialist realism, "real" was what the party said it was. So if the wellbeing of the people had to grow steadily under socialism, it grew... in all reports.

Or, for instance, if the party decided in the 1930s that "class struggle is increasing with the building of socialism," then the number of "enemies of the people" increased correspondingly. Did they believe or not that their yesterday's colleague and friend has turned into an "enemy of the people" today? Were they surprised that these "enemies" are always calculated in round numbers—hundreds, thousands, tens of thousands?

This question is senseless. I am sure it was never discussed, and it probably did not even enter anyone's head. Other things were decided and discussed, such as the scope and feasibility of purges. And just as in our time, the party did not care whether we were mentally ill or not. Even the fact of a sudden increase in mental illness in the country—*by 42.8 percent in five years*[124]—did not seem to surprise party members or raise any doubts in their minds.

Having read so many documents written (or signed) by them, I still cannot be certain whether they believed in their ideology, at least, or whether it was all a complete sham. It may be said with a certain degree of probability that Lenin and his immediate entourage were believers. I would allow that despite all his cynicism, Stalin believed in the historic justifiability of his actions, even feeling himself toward the end to be a demigod, a personal embodiment of historical truth. It is also undeniable that Khrushchev had a somewhat naive, genuine peasant's belief in socialism. But tell me—in what did Brezhnev, Andropov, and Konstantin Chernenko believe? Yes, they were all people of small intellect, not inclined toward self-analysis, but they surely had to believe in something? They must have had aims in accordance with which they acted. Let us say that Lenin, in liquidating the bourgeois classes, acted in accordance with his aim of creating a classless paradise. Stalin considered anyone who, in his opinion, "objectively" impeded the cause of socialism was "subjectively" responsible as an accessory to the class enemy, and he considered anyone he imagined to be a personal foe as "objectively" hostile to the task of socialism. Even Khrushchev may have had a sincere belief that since under socialism no internal enemies could emerge, only mentally ill individuals could be hostile to the most perfect sociopolitical system in the history of mankind. They were all possessed of an admittedly inhuman, perverse logic, but with a certain congruity of personality and deeds, aims and actions. Yet what are we to think, say, in reading Andropov's report[125] in 1968 that Gabay and Marchenko "having lost the feeling of civil responsibility, disdain the interests of the state, and render direct support to our class enemies by their actions"?

Does he genuinely believe in the existence of "class enemies" after fifty-one years of Soviet rule? In the "class interests" of the Soviet state? In the duty of every citizen of the USSR to defend these interests? Or is this phrase just paying homage to the jargon party members employed?

Or, in sending the memorandum from the Krasnodar general to

---

[124]22 February 1972* (St 31/19), p. 3.
[125]1 April 1968 (718-A)^.

the Politburo regarding the epidemic of insanity in the region, did he not understand what he was doing? And did the Politburo really believe that anyone attempting to "commit high treason with the help of a boat with an outboard motor" must be mentally ill? That the idea of creating a "Council for control over the activity of the Politburo and local Party agencies" could only enter into the head of a madman? Only several years later that same Andropov informed the Politburo that there are hundreds of thousands of hostile persons in the country, and that the regime could not cope without repressions (29 December 1975*, 3213-A).

I was informed by very reliable sources back in 1977 (I have already described this episode in the book *To Choose Freedom*) that soon after my meeting with Carter, Brezhnev requested the file on my activities abroad and, after reading it, said to his aides:

"Comrades, what have you done? You told me that he was, *you know*"—here he made a circular motion around his temple—"but *he's not.*"

So it would seem that Brezhnev really did believe that we were mad.

Because I read so many of Andropov's memos and reports, or for some other reason, I became intrigued as to what Andropov really believed. If typical apparatchiks such as Suslov, having become accustomed to continual hypocrisy, were really incapable of distinguishing the difference between ideology and reality, and fossils such as Brezhnev and Chernenko were probably incapable of much thought even in their best years, Andropov did not create the impression of a fanatic or an idiot. Unlike his party colleagues, he did not come across as a man capable of believing his own disinformation. On the contrary, he even understood that ideologues (or even ideology) breed enemies of the system whom he, Andropov, would have to combat later. It is noteworthy that in attempting to reduce such manifestations to a minimum, he even interfered in matters concerning art and the party policy in the cultural sphere. He wrote the following to the CC in 1976 (8 October 1976*, 2280-A):

> Artist I.O. GLAZUNOV has been working in Moscow since 1957, and has acquired an ambiguous reputation among different creative circles. On one hand, GLAZUNOV has built up a group of supporters who see him as a gifted artist, while on the other hand he is considered totally untalented by others, a person reviving petit bourgeois tastes in depictive art. However, for many years, GLAZUNOV has been invited regularly to visit the West by prominent social and state personalities, who commission him to paint their portraits. GLAZUNOV'S reputation as a portrait painter is very considerable. He has painted the President of

Finland, [Urho] KEKKONEN, the kings of Sweden and Laos, Indira GANDHI, [Salvador] ALLENDE, CORVALAN and many others. Exhibitions of his work have taken place in a number of countries and were reviewed favorably in the foreign press. At the request of Soviet organizations he has visited Vietnam and Chile. The cycle of paintings completed there was displayed at special exhibitions.

This situation, in which GLAZUNOV finds enthusiastic support abroad but is viewed askance by Soviet artists, creates certain problems in his formation as an artist, and even harder problems in his outlook on life.

GLAZUNOV is a person with no clear convictions, and there are definite shortcomings in his art. He frequently portrays himself as a Russophile and often allows himself to express open anti-Semitism. His muddled political views do not only induce wariness on occasion, but also repel. His audacious nature and flashes of conceit do not promote the development of normal relations in creative circles. Nonetheless, it would be unfeasible to reject GLAZUNOV for just those reasons.

The demonstrative failure of the Union of Artists to acknowledge him merely reinforces all that is negative in GLAZUNOV, and could lead to undesirable consequences if it is borne in mind that Western representatives not only advertise him, but also attempt to influence him, among other things persuading him to emigrate from the Soviet Union.

In view of the above, it appears necessary to take a close look at the situation around this artist. It might be feasible to attract him to some socially useful endeavor, such as creating a museum of Russian furniture in Moscow, something that he and his supporters are anxious to do.

Thus yet another museum appeared in Moscow, and Glazunov's views became even more muddled, but there were no "consequences" considered "undesirable" by Andropov. Still, he was not always able to avert them—the system continued to breed enemies before he could interfere, and it was not always possible to overcome the stubbornness of the "ideologues" (10 October 1974*, Pb 55/12):

The Committee for State Security has received information that sculptor E.I. NEIZVESTNY, a member of the Union of Artists of the USSR, intends to go abroad for permanent residence in the near future. This decision stems allegedly from the circumstance that he is experiencing a certain degree of dissatisfaction with the lack of interest in his work by the relevant cultural organizations and departments, due to which he receives no commissions and is forced to accept occasional orders.

Available data suggest that NEIZVESTNY expects to receive an invitation from some influential individual in the West. It is suggested that this person may be American senator Edward KENNEDY, whose personal representative visited NEIZVESTNY during the senator's last visit to the USSR.

[...]

In the event of a refusal to grant NEIZVESTNY an exit visa, he intends to attract the attention of the international community. In this he relies on the support of individual members of the Italian and French communist parties and the Vatican.

In view of the above, it would be feasible to examine the possibility of offering NEIZVESTNY a state commission to create some monumental work on a contemporary subject which would match his creative plans.

But Neizvestny's thinking was not muddled, and persecution and proscriptions by party authorities continued. Although he did receive a few commissions following Andropov's letter, he preferred to leave two years later. As he says himself, not without Andropov's help.

And what about the earlier cited incident of the memorandum concerning Zinoviev, in which Andropov cautioned against imprisoning Zinoviev in case he might be found to be genuinely mentally ill and sent to a psychiatric institution? One might think that something like this could happen at the will of the court without Andropov's knowledge! As we have seen, even direction for an expert examination required a decision of the CC. But Andropov had to be rid of an extra case, so he frightened the Politburo with a possible scandal on an already sore topic.

These and many other episodes subsequently gave Andropov the reputation of a "liberal" in the West upon his accession to power in 1983, which mutated into the legend of a "covert liberal," also probably not without his help. In fact, he was no more a liberal than Lavrentiy Beria, who laid the foundations of the de-Stalinization process: just like Beria, he aspired to come to power, and was not at all keen on being branded the smotherer of the intelligentsia. Furthermore, again like Beria, he probably understood the need for some correction of the policies of his predecessors, who had led the regime into a dead end. Observing the "process of chain reaction" in 1968, when direct repressions only aided the growth of our movement, he made more recommendations for the employment of preventive, prophylactic measures, which by that time were more feasible under the foreign policies of the regime. By the 1970s, having become one of the main architects of Soviet foreign policy and thus the figure responsible for it, he became even more inclined to depend on "operative-*chekist* measures."

It was not just that these measures minimized damage to socialism both domestically and externally and helped to create a more civilized image of the regime. This was undoubtedly so. But after one has read his documents and seen his tricky games in the Politburo, the thought comes to mind that he simply liked these methods, he was psychologically inclined to them. It is not by chance that under him and his direct leadership there was a grandiose flowering of international terrorism, the system of Soviet disinformation, and "liberation movements" in the third world. Détente, that invention so ruinous to the West, flourished under him, allowing the Soviet regime to conduct a unilateral ideological war, and with Western funds at that. In the critical moment for détente in 1980, the wide-sweeping "peace movement" unfolded under his leadership. Finally, under him and his student and successor Gorbachev, the entire domestic and foreign policy of the regime became one gigantic operative-*chekist* measure under the name of perestroika.

It seems that he was a manipulator by nature who, if he actually believed in something, believed only that history is a continuous chain of conspiracies. Suffice to say that his 1978 report (which I was unable to copy, and barely managed to glance through), entitled "On Our Relations with the Vatican," gives serious consideration to the idea that election of Polish cardinal Karol Wojtyla to the papal throne is part of an international conspiracy aimed at splitting Poland from the Soviet bloc. In fact, the imperialists propel Poles into the front ranks: in Washington, Zbigniew Brzezinski; in the Vatican, Wojtyla. This cannot happen by chance, even though there is no known mechanism that would enable Brzezinski to have any influence whatsoever on the decision of the [Papal] Conclave. In all, as my KGB investigator used to say, "if there are more than three coincidences, then these are not coincidences." His boss does not seem to have departed far from this *chekist* wisdom. I do not doubt, even though I found no documents on this subject, that Andropov was behind the attempt to assassinate Pope John Paul II several years later: after all, he had been proven "right": Poland had begun to break away.

Actually, this belief in conspiracies is natural in all secret services to some extent, and Andropov's roots were rather in communist ideology. Only in abstract thinking does Marxism interpret history as an objective and inevitable struggle between classes. Just read the classics of this teaching, Marx, Engels, and Lenin analyzing the more concrete political situation in their contemporary world, and you will see that their entire "analysis" comes down to "unmasking" the latest bourgeois "conspiracy" against the proletariat. Even the political jargon they introduced speaks of belief in conspiracy: you will never see even one simple characterization of somebody, only words like *stooges, accomplices, lackeys, henchmen, hirelings*, and *provocateurs*. In extreme cases people were characterized as *renegades* and *traitors*. That's class warfare for you.

Communist ideology is definitely deeply paranoid, and even those who were merely pretending, not believing it for a moment (and I think that such were the party bosses of the 1960s and 1970s), inevitably acquired certain stereotyped forms of thought. It makes no difference that most of them, drowning in the routine of everyday concerns, gave no thought to the philosophical tenets of Marxism-Leninism—that was what the ideology was for, so there was no need to remember those tenets. It was sufficient for the practitioners, relying on developed reflexes, to simply follow the logic of struggle in accordance with the famous Lenin maxim: "who whom."

Moreover, as is habitual for dim-witted people who know little about life in the West, they ascribed their own methods, intentions and morality to their opponents, responding to imaginary "schemes" with real ones, and with slander against "slander." Like a boxer sparring with his own shadow, they could never win. Did they understand the absurdity of the situation? Yes and no. Like all Soviet people, they possessed the amazing ability to say one thing, mean another, and do a third. Seemingly immune to such splitting of the persona, they could believe and not believe in their ideology simultaneously, both love and hate the system that on one hand subjugated them and on the other endowed them with almost superhuman power.

Andropov was probably no exception. It was said that he did not like ideology, and especially "ideologues." This is not surprising: they impeded his work, limited his actions, or, on the contrary, created extra problems. Who likes overseers? However, this does not mean that he rejected the ideology consciously or comprehended its absurdity. More likely, like the majority of his colleagues, when he encountered the discrepancy between ideology and real life he was prone to ascribe this discrepancy to enemy schemes, and to solve them with schemes of "friends." It was easier this way, especially as "enemies" and "friends" can always be found, if you look hard enough. ... What other way out could there be for someone for whom belief in the infallibility of the ideology was mandatory? Either the idea is perfect, but its realization is hampered by enemies, or it is imperfect, in which case you become an enemy yourself.

Ironclad logic, just like the reasoning that turned the sails of the *chekist* "mill" near Khabarovsk (4 October 1956*, St 1061).

• • •

The emergence of our movement posed not just a practical problem for the Politburo, but a theoretical brainteaser. It was all very well for Lenin—he had to deal with a real "class enemy." Even Stalin managed somehow to make ends meet: at least his enemies had been born before the revolution and were formed "under the conditions of bourgeois society," which meant they were able to retain the "remnants of capitalism" in their minds. But how could the appearance of an "enemy" be explained in the classless socialist paradise? Most of us were born and raised under conditions created according to their recipes. Figuratively (and occasionally literally), we were their children.

It is not surprising that the regime was glad to seize Khrushchev's psychiatric thesis, although even Suslov would have to sweat copiously to devise an ideological basis for the implacable rise of insanity under socialism—neither Marx nor Lenin had foreseen such a thing. But even this loophole closed due to the powerful campaign against punitive psychology. The only thing left to do was to blame everything on imperialist schemes. The regime could hardly admit that people were personally capable of understanding the absurdity of the Soviet system. Hence the monotonous repetition of the formula regarding the schemes of enemy "special services" and "ideological centers" that allegedly controlled us in every document relating to our activities. From this source comes the more detailed "class" definition, made by the Politburo in missives to "fraternal parties" from 1975 through 1977, in which it ensues that since the "exploitative class" had been liquidated in the USSR,[126] then

> ... the emergence of an insignificant handful of counterrevolutionaries, who have broken away from the very foundations of our system and entered the path of struggle against it and, as a rule, are connected with imperialist circles, is by no means a natural product of the internal development of the Soviet Union.
> [...]
> ... Remnants of capitalism are systematically encouraged in the minds of some people from abroad, by imperialist propaganda centers. As for the intelligence and other subversive agencies of bourgeois countries, and allied émigré organizations, they are attempting to appeal to the outmoded ideas of certain individuals in interests hostile to socialism. And, as

---

[126] 15 March 1977* (Pb 49/XV), pp. 7–8.

should be clear to communists, this is inevitable while there are two juxtaposed systems on the world arena—the socialist and the capitalist; the main substance of global development is still class struggle between them.

Such was the policy within the framework in which the Politburo had to act. It was easy for the ideologues in the Politburo to think up "class" explanations, useable until history's end—they did not have to implement the policies that emanated from these explanations. It was not for them to answer if the policy did not yield results. Andropov was required to locate these mythical "centers" and defuse their schemes while knowing full well that no such "centers" existed. A brain-busting assignment, especially in periods of détente, and with Western governments bending over backward to demonstrate their friendship to the Soviet people. So what could he do but invent at least one "subversive center"?

This is how the notorious NTS entered our lives—the People's Alliance of Russian Solidarists—the KGB tried every trick to "stick" a connection with it to literally every one of us. Even the most innocuous book published by Posev, the NTS publishing house, could serve as adequate reason for such an accusation. At the very least, this fact would be spread all over the press as though it were the sole reason for your incarceration. How could one avoid of this if up to the 1970s there were practically no Russian publishers in the West? A manuscript passed abroad by even the occasional tourist would invariably end up with the NTS.

Consequently, KGB reports and the missives of the CC would cite the NTS as "one of" the subversive centers (naming no others due to their nonexistence), attributing the most sophisticated schemes to it, and Soviet propaganda exaggerated its activity to absolutely mythical proportions. As we recall even the Politburo, in deciding Solzhenitsyn's fate, did not omit mention of his "contacts with the NTS" as something particularly pernicious. Who can say whether they believed it or not? In the minds of the Soviet people—at the top or the bottom—the NTS was perceived as some gigantic super-octopus, omnipresent and omnipotent. A devil incarnate.

In reality the NTS was a negligible émigré organization with a dubious past, suspicious present, and indefinite future. Founded in Yugoslavia in 1930 by profascist émigré youth (at first it was called the National Labor Alliance of the New Generation and was strongly influenced by Mussolini's ideas), it cooperated with the Germans in the war years (through the Abwehr, the German intelligence service during WWII), including by publishing newspapers in German-occupied territories of Russia.

After the war, the NTS became, among other things, the property of the Americans and the English, and in the thick of the Cold War up to Stalin's death, it was used for sending reconnaissance groups into the USSR to recruit agents and collect information. By that time the failure of some of their groups raised suspicions that the NTS had been infiltrated by the KGB at the highest level. As a result there was a schism in 1955, practically destroying the organization. By our time, the remaining two to three hundred members eked out a living in poverty, artificially supported by both the KGB and the CIA as a double-agent organization.

It stands to reason that the majority of NTS members had no idea of the role played by their organization—this was probably known only to the leadership, something like their Central Committee. The organization was strictly secretive, built along principles somewhat similar to the Bolshevik party. As I was able to see for myself here, in emigration, most of the ordinary members were honest people, often deeply religious, devoted to their ideas and leadership to the point of fanaticism. In the main, they were representatives of the "second wave" of Russian émigrés, that is, those who had managed to survive the war, captivity, camps for displaced persons, and the forced repatriation of his runaway slaves to Stalin by the Allies after the war. For them, service to Russia and its future liberation was almost a religious mission, and it was impossible to explain to them what was really going on.

At first, in the 1960s, we did not know all of this either. Yet the KGB knew very well what it was doing. They were perfectly aware that we could have no relation to the NTS if only because in essence we were their direct opposites. If the NTS was a strictly clandestine organization, centralized and moreover setting itself the aim of armed war with the Soviet regime and calling for revolution, our position was markedly open, nonviolent, and even legalistic; furthermore, we had decided deliberately to refrain from creating an organization or even an organizational structure as a matter of principle. From the point of view of the KGB, tying us in with the NTS was the best possible way of compromising us.

To give us our due, it did not take us long to determine just what the NTS was, so we did not take the bait. Partly this was because of the differences in principle between our group and theirs, but more to the point, it was because the KGB was too assiduous in trying to attribute this connection to us, attempting to virtually force us into the arms of the NTS. Moreover, the NTS acted too clumsily, in an obvious attempt to complete the assignment. I recall my first glimpse of the truth when in 1965 some friend or other gave me an envelope from a visiting NTS courier. This occurrence was enough to put me on my guard, as I had never sought contact with them. But the contents of that envelope were an even greater shock: a closely typed sheet of instructions on how to create "groups of five" (underground groups consisting of five people, a favored tactic of the NTS), and a letter addressed to me with a request to... blow up Lenin's Mausoleum! There was also a sheet of "invisible" carbon paper for secret encrypted messages and instructions on how to maintain connection with the NTS. In a word, the full "gentleman's kit." Had the KGB chosen that moment to burst into my place, it would have made them a great present.

At that time all I did was laugh at the hapless conspirators and burn the gentleman's kit straightaway, but the thought of this episode bothered me for a long time. Whichever way I looked at it, it didn't bode well. First, I had just been released from the psychiatric hospital, which was probably known to my unexpected "instructor." He must have thought that I was really mentally ill, and that my insanity might prompt me to carry out his instructions. Second, who would want to blow up the mausoleum, and to what purpose? It was probably needed for someone to claim this as "their operation," and the attempt, if not the explosion as such, would be very useful to the KGB. Under this pretext not just I, but also all my friends would be arrested. What if I had really been insane?

Soon my suspicions became widespread, and in 1968, when the KGB made assiduous efforts to stick Alexander Ginzburg and Yuri Galanskov with a charge of connections to the NTS at their trial, it became overzealous. That was just the unfortunate case on which Semichastny blundered in trying, as we recall, to put a quiet psychiatric brake on the matter, but the Politburo balked at the idea. This was the first case in which Andropov had to prove his abilities, foreseeing all the desires of the CC. But the accursed case refused to come together: either his opponents in the CC were intriguing against him, or he was simply mistaken in his guesses. This is what he reported at the end of the investigation (22 November 1967, 2840-A):

> The preliminary investigation has been completed and the matter submitted to the Moscow City Court. It will be examined at a court hearing in mid-December. ... The investigation established that GINZBURG, GALANSKOV and [Alexei] DOBROVOLSKY maintained contacts with the foreign organization "National Alliance of Russian Solidarists" (NTS) through foreign visitors to the USSR, and sent anti-Soviet, slanderous materials abroad, which were published in the anti-Soviet press and were actively used by the NTS in propaganda hostile to the Soviet Union. Among other things, GALANSKOV sent the NTS the

anti-Soviet miscellany "Phoenix"; GINZBURG prepared the so-
called "White Book" containing slanderous materials regarding
the trial of SINYAVSKY and DANIEL, which GALANSKOV sent
abroad and which was published in the NTS journal "Grani."
... In view of the political nature of the trial, and also that
an anti-Soviet campaign is being waged in the West concerning GINZBURG and his confederates in the foreign press, the
advice is to hold the hearing behind closed doors. [We should]
issue information on the trial that is favorable to us for the foreign press through the channels of the KGB and APN. The outcome of the trial should be published in "Vechernaya Moskva"
[*Evening Moscow*] as a topicality report (text attached).

But the CC was still unsatisfied, and inscribed a severe resolution in the margins of the report: "Requires an exchange of opinions
in the Politburo. "Objections from ideologues are a very serious
matter (25 November 1967*, SF No. 4597):

The bill of indictment on the matter of Ginzburg, Galanskov
and Dobrovolsky in its present form, as formulated both in the
clauses of the indictment and the argumentation of the charges,
puts the investigation and the public prosecutor into an extremely unfavorable situation.

Conduct of the trial on the basis of the present version of the bill
of indictment may cause a new anti-Soviet campaign abroad,
similar to that after the trial of Sinyavsky and Daniel.

The problem is that the present version stresses charges relating to the collection and, in part, authorship of tendentious
(in substance anti-Soviet) materials for delivery abroad, pushing into the background better proven and, for both the Soviet
and foreign community, more convincing accusations. There
is a sufficient amount of convincing facts in the court case to
be used by the press for propagandistic exposure of the underhanded methods employed by American intelligence services
(through one of their branches—the "National Alliance of Russian Solidarists" (NTS), duplicitously referred to as "an independent political organization") to hoodwink the Soviet and foreign
communities.

As the bill of indictment has already been handed to the accused and their attorneys and cannot be amended, it would
be feasible for the state prosecutor, in the course of the court
hearing and his presentation, to construct the arguments in
the indictment and the hearing on the basis of the following
scheme, which may be confirmed by facts at the disposal of the
investigating authorities.

1. It would be feasible to explain why Ginzburg, Galanskov,
Dobrovolsky and [Vera] Lashkova became party to anti-

Soviet activity and where they became infected with anti-Soviet sentiments. ...

2. It would be feasible to focus attention on their connections with the NTS in evidence proving their guilt. ... At the same time, while stressing specifically these moments, it would be feasible to show that the accused may not have been fully aware of the true target of their activity, presented to them by NTS emissaries under the guise of the "struggle for freedom, democracy, struggle against injustice" and so forth. But in fact the accused performed the assignments of that branch of American intelligence and were being groomed to be used, in the final analysis, as agents of American intelligence under the umbrella of the NTS. ...

3. It would be feasible to reduce to a minimum any mention of dissemination of the so-called "White Book," the underground journals "Phoenix" and "Syntaxis" as well as various appeals and documents relating to the "struggle" for the release of Sinyavsky and Daniel from the bill of indictment and, if possible, omit any mention of them at all. This way, the prosecution will be able to concentrate on the one undeniable fact: the accused acted on the assignment of the NTS—a branch of American intelligence, under the cover of the flag of an anti-Soviet organization. ...

For the purposes of propagandistic coverage of the trial both in the Soviet Union and abroad, it would be feasible to perform the following work prior to the trial, which would be best limited to one day, omitting hearing the evidence of secondary witnesses:

1. Prepare an orientation circular to Soviet ambassadors, containing the abovementioned interpretation of the trial. This circular should be sent in good time (1-2 days before the opening of the trial) to Soviet ambassadors in a number of countries, to inform the leadership of fraternal parties.

2. Acting together with the appropriate administration of the KGB, departments of the CC CPSU are to prepare relevant versions of journal accounts regarding the progress of the trial for publication in the newspapers *Komsomolskaya pravda* [*Komsomol Truth*], *Moskovskaya pravda* [*Moscow Truth*] and the journal *Nedelya* [the *Week*]. Analogous versions are to be prepared for distribution abroad through the "Novosti" press agency and the radio.

Andropov tried to defend himself, claiming that this is exactly what he had in mind, and he even attempted to cite laws, among others those regarding the impossibility of conducting the trial in just one day, as the ideologues demanded (3 December 1967, 2949-A). But all in all, he did not dare argue; at that time he had been the chairman of the KGB for just six months, and his situation was probably insufficiently secure. In the main, the trial was conducted along the lines suggested by the CC. Moreover Andropov, following the instruction to stress the role of the NTS, outdid himself. The trial was scheduled for 11 December, but was suddenly deferred with no indication of dates or reasons, to begin only on 8 January 1968. During this time, an extremely important event occurred: as if on cue, an NTS courier arrived in Moscow bearing materials "in defense of Ginzburg and Galanskov" and was arrested and presented at the trial as either the main witness or as material evidence of the criminal connection. This move was so transparent that nobody was left with any doubt as to the connection of the KGB with the NTS. Either the KGB summoned this "courier", or it at least knew about his arrival and deferred the trial until that time.

However, this was not the end of the NTS epic. The KGB continued to stick us with this connection in every case, in order to have a pretext for displaying its heroic struggle with "subversive enemy centers." Furthermore, NTS cells were occasionally created by the KGB with a full complement of its agents as members—for purposes of "prophylaxis" aimed at "revealing ideologically immature" citizens, and at the same time, for playing "games" with the "foreign center." At times the KGB even succeeded in trapping some youth group using its self-created reputation of the NTS as the regime's greatest foe. But more frequently "evidence" was squeezed out of those who broke under investigation. The reward for such an "exposure" was almost immediate release, an appearance on television, and even permission to emigrate. This is what happened with Pyotr Ionovich Yakir and Viktor Krasin in 1973 (27 August 1974, 2436-A) —a tragic page in our history that would take too much space to recount.[127]

Meanwhile the NTS leadership, not at all abashed by its provocative role in these tragedies, continued the game. Moreover, they probably expected someone's gratitude, they even flaunted that role, stating in verbal and written form that "dissidents" were an "NTS creation." After Galanskov's tragic death in a camp in 1972, they declared him to have been a secret member of their CC—a rare display of cynicism even by them. I have no doubt that if it were not for my unexpected exchange and release, the same lot would have awaited me. I was later told by Alexander Esenin-Volpin that after

---

[127]See the reports of "Case No. 24" in *A Chronicle of Current Events* (issues 28, 29 and 30 https://chronicleofcurrentevents.net/no-28-31-december-1972-2/).

he left the Soviet Union in 1972, NTS representatives tried hard to persuade him to join their organization: "Your friend Bukovsky is one of our members," they told him, probably in the hope that Alik and I would never meet again. At that time I was on hunger strike in Vladimir Prison, and reports on my state of health were very grim.

They considered that lying, claiming nonexistent achievements and hundreds and thousands of members in Russia, was fully justified in the interests of the "highest aims." Such is the nature of an underground psychology—*devilry*, as we called it then, from which were saved by refusing to go underground as a matter of principle. In the same way we refuted all the other attributes common to bad crime fiction in the style of John le Carré.

None of this is secret now: in 1990 a former colonel of the KGB, Yaroslav Karpovich, declared in the press[128] that he had been a member of the "leadership circle" of the NTS, their "man in Moscow." According to him, this "operation" was monitored by Andropov, under the supervision of Brezhnev himself.[129]

So tell me now: what did they believe in?

3.10 The most powerful weapon of the Party

This was not the end of the "operative-*chekist* measure." Unlike the Khabarovsk "mill," the Andropov effort did not leave any leftovers. If an effort to stick us with connections to the NTS worked, fine; if not, that was fine too. The *chekist* imagination is always two jumps ahead of reality and invariably compensated for colleagues' errors, creating the requisite reputation with its own resources. They called this "compromising measures" quite openly.

Stretching a point, let us say that they managed to stick Ginzburg with the notorious connection, even though it was not he but someone else who delivered his manuscript to Posev, the publishing house of the NTS, where it was duly published. This "fact" must now be worked on and served up to the best possible advantage. That is not done by just some nameless apparatchik; the Politburo itself sends an "orientation" to all Soviet ambassadors in the world (22 December 1967*, Pb 63/122):

> Within the next few days there will be an open hearing in the Moscow City Court on the case of Ginzburg, Galanskov, Dobrovolsky and Lashkova.

---

[128]"Our man in the NTS," *Literaturnaya gazeta*, No. 49, 5 December 1990, p. 13; Karpovich interview with Yuri Shchekochikhin.

[129]Karpovich interviewed by Dmitry Volchek on Radio Liberty in 1992 (a total of 9 broadcasts).

There is the usual anti-Soviet uproar abroad concerning the forthcoming trial, the accused are billed as "talented young writers," "freedom fighters," etc.

In fact, Ginzburg, Galanskov, Dobrovolsky and Lashkova have no relation to writers or to literary endeavor at all: the first two are office workers, Dobrovolsky is a bookbinder and Lashkova is a typist. They do not have any literary works to their credit.

At various times, they entered into contact with agents of the NTS—a notorious branch of the CIA—whose aim was to recruit them for the performance of espionage assignments. For a start, foreign intelligence agents instructed them to recruit members into the NTS, supplying them with instruction materials on forms and methods of combating the socialist system, equipment for duplicating leaflets of an anti-Soviet nature and maintaining secret correspondence abroad. ... Soviet security agencies deemed it necessary to terminate the ties Ginzburg, Galanskov, Dobrovolsky and Lashkova had with hostile intelligence organizations, and to prevent them from being drawn into committing serious crimes linked to espionage.

Only in the event of a query to the leadership by friends, clarify the above to them.

Notice: This message is sent to ambassadors of the USSR in European socialist countries (apart from Albania), also Austria, Australia, Argentina, Belgium, Brazil, Great Britain, Denmark, Italy, Canada, Norway, Syria, USA, Uruguay, FRG, Finland, France, Chile, Ceylon and Sweden.

This can be regarded as quite modest—they were probably afraid to make too much noise and hoped that everything would pass off quietly. Usually the scope would be much wider, and measures would be implemented much more aggressively. But now they would only be shared through ambassadors of the listed countries and "friends" upon their special request, should enquiries arise. Everything else was grist to the mill—diplomacy, the press, and the resources of the KGB.

However, it is typical how easily the *chekist* imagination made the leap from the NTS publishing house to "crimes linked with espionage." There could be a plethora of such leaps, until the desired artistic conclusion of the required "compromising" was complete, but no matter how hard the KGB tried, it was unable to stick me with connections to the NTS.

Such an accusation was never made to me officially, and it did not even figure in "compromising measures" aimed at me up to 1976. It is curious that it appeared for the first time in a Politburo letter to Enrico Berlinguer (29 August 1976, Pb 24/25), head of the Italian Communist Party, four months prior to my exchange:

> Upon discharge from psychiatric hospital, Bukovsky has continued his anti-Soviet activity. In November 1965 he founded a "five-man storm group" with the aim of preparing an armed attack against Soviet authorities. At the same time Bukovsky entered into contact with the notorious anti-Soviet organization NTS.

One cannot but wonder how the Politburo came to know about the instructions contained in the gentleman's kit I burned so carefully back in 1965. And why now, almost eleven years later, should they recall that failure? They were probably already aware of my forthcoming exchange, and were taking care to create a suitable image of me. It's always a pity to part with certain goods; were their 1965 efforts to be wasted?

So I was followed by a really powerful fusillade of propaganda: I was a criminal (what else? We "do not have any political prisoners"), and "a dropout student" (they should know, they were the ones who drove me out), and, of course, there was that "five-man storm group" (at the time I was at a loss as to where they got these groups from). And although their fire had no effect in the West—the Western press merely laughed about these five-man groups—the image of a half-mad terrorist was to follow me for many years. The leaders were never confused by such failures, for they believed firmly that a lie repeated hundreds of times becomes a truth in the end, in line with the principle proclaimed by Pierre Beaumarchais: "Defame, defame.... In the end, something will remain."

At times I thought that this principle worked for them too, and that they had begun to believe the lies they repeated to each other and had originated themselves. In any event, I can find no explanation for this amazing Politburo document dated 1979, entitled "On a response to the proposals made by the Minister of Justice of the USA" (1 November 1979*, Pb 172/113):

> In a discussion with the ambassador of the USSR, US Attorney General [Benjamin] Civiletti touched upon the holding of the Olympic Games in the USA and the USSR and spoke of the possible activation of terrorist activity, the smuggling of drugs and other criminal actions in that period. In his opinion, it would be feasible to establish a tacit working contact between the corresponding security services of the Soviet Union and the USA for the "purpose of exchanging ideas regarding possible concrete concerns on these matters," and then create "special working groups for the exchange of information and implemen-

tation of various means by the parties." Civiletti said that he would appreciate a preliminary response to his proposal.

It is clear that we and the Americans have different approaches to the question of terrorism. For instance, this is demonstrated with regard to national liberation movements and their organizations.

Furthermore, there has been a halo of "martyrdom" created in the USA for convicted Soviet criminal terrorists such as Kuznetsov, who intended to hijack an aircraft with a group of accomplices and kill the crew.[130] Kuznetsov and the renegade Bukovsky, another advocate of terrorism, were received in the White House by the President of the USA. ...

On the basis of the above, the Committee for State Security of the USSR considers it inadvisable to establish contacts along the line of the administrative agencies of the USSR with American services as proposed by the Minister of Justice of the USA. At the same time there could be agreement that on the basis of mutuality, the parties could share information through the usual diplomatic channels regarding presumptive terrorist or other criminal acts connected with the Olympic Games.

Thus the first "terrorists" about whom the US administration received a warning from their Soviet colleagues were Kuznetsov and I. It remains unknown what was said about us in confidence, if this went through "the usual diplomatic channels." I was able to gain some idea about this quite unexpectedly and not long ago, in 1985, when the Soviet journal *Novoye vremya* [the *New Times*], which is published in the West by APN in ten languages and distributed practically worldwide, carried an article under the mysterious headline "Who Killed Jessica Savitch?" (No. 37, September 1985). Jessica Savitch was an American TV journalist who was known for her pro-Soviet views and who had died recently in a car accident; imagine my amazement when I glanced through this article out of curiosity and discovered that it was... I who had killed her! Yes, yes, in the literal, not metaphorical sense—killed her. Bumped her off, and that's it. Naturally, not with my own hands, admitted the journal, but in cahoots with the notorious terrorist Meir Kahane and the forces of his organization, the Jewish Defense League.

The death of Jessica Savitch shows that the criminal world of the USA has acquired a new gang, which is headed by Bukov-

---

[130]Imprisoned for his part in the open-air readings at Mayakovsky Square, Eduard Kuznetsov took a leading role in the attempted hijacking of a plane in Leningrad, see *Chronicle of Current Events*, Issue 17: "The Leningrad Trial of the 'Hijackers'" (31 December 1970) https://chronicleofcurrentevents.net/2014/08/05/17-6-the-leningrad-trial-of-the-hijackers/.

sky. From childhood, he had dreamed of becoming a terrorist chieftain, yearned for terror and was particularly appreciative of murderous inclinations in others. He was tried and sentenced to imprisonment for organizing a terrorist group, whose members were preparing to "destroy physically, hang from lamp posts, shoot and strangle" (these are Bukovsky's own words, quoted from the court record). Having become a CIA agent in the West, Bukovsky was free to give full rein to his criminal tendencies. One former acquaintance of Bukovsky in Paris describes him as being "vainglorious, cruel to the point of sadism. Pathologically greedy for money. A criminal who has no greater pleasure than taking someone's life."

Partnership with the terrorist rabbi Kahane and his League and protection by the Jewish community of the USA make Bukovsky invincible before the police.

I must admit that I was taken completely aback—this was really something new. I was accustomed to being reviled as an "agent of imperialism," "slanderer," "renegade," and even "agent of the CIA"— I was used to these accusations and paid no attention. But here not abstractly, but quite specifically, it was claimed that I had *killed* a certain person! What could this mean? Could the KGB be planning to involve me in a criminal situation, and even kill to do so? It always followed the line: action is accompanied by propaganda, and propaganda by action.

Quite unexpectedly, I became infuriated and asked a friend, a prominent American attorney, to file a suit with the New York court against the authors, publishers, disseminators, and in general all accessories. At least, I thought, once they have to give evidence under oath, these swine may let something slip. And whatever their intentions, continuing the "operation" when facing a court suit might give them pause. Not in a hundred years! There was no chance of bringing the authors and publishers to court; they were all in Moscow. All that remained was the distributor—that very Kamkin bookshop set up and maintained with Soviet money for the distribution of communist propaganda. But taking Kamkin to court also proved impossible because under American law, he was responsible for the distributed slander only if we could prove that he had known the contents of his goods: "If a bookseller offers sale of a newspaper or journal that constantly contains articles of a scandalous nature, distribution of such a publication may pose the risk that the articles therein do contain slanderous attacks of some kind."

• • •

The matter ended with that, having dragged on for more than two years without coming to court.

"It's not worth the worry", I was told. Soviet propaganda is so glaringly ludicrous that nobody believes it.

"On the contrary, it is worth worrying about, and the West should know more about Soviet propaganda", said others; it exposes the regime better than any of us could.

Alas, that would be so in a normal, morally healthy world, in which every invention of the agitprop or Chief Administration "A" of the KGB would really make people roar with laughter, be mocked in the press, and rouse the indignation of politicians. We had to live in the real world, in which most people wanted to believe in the Soviet regime—because of ideological sympathies, fear of a nuclear disaster, faith in "stability," in a "pragmatic approach," in Divine Providence, or who knows what else.

Be that as it may, Soviet propaganda and disinformation were much more effective in the West than in the USSR. To be convinced of this, it is enough to recall, for instance, the multimillion-person "peace movement" that emerged as if by magic at the beginning of the 1980s, or the jubilation in the press caused by the coming of "covert liberal" Andropov to power in 1983 (to say nothing about the joyous bacchanalia unleashed by Gorbachev and his perestroika). Generally speaking, people, by their very nature, tend toward a selective choice of the information they expect or really want to receive; this tendency is further reinforced by emotions, desires, and beliefs. The best example of this with regard to Gorbachev is the Chernobyl disaster, which did not affect the rapture surrounding Gorbachev, who tried to conceal it at the cost of the health of millions of people; it did not shake the bright belief in socialism, but was seen only as an example of the danger of nuclear power plants wherever they might be, and whoever built them.

As for the dissidents, just about anyone was ready to believe whatever dirt was flung at us; despite all the outward admiration of our "courage," the Western elite hated us fiercely. Our very existence threatened the illusions of some and sounded a reproach to the deeply-buried consciences of others. Even their admiration was sickening, as if stressing that our activity and our position presumed the possession of some superhuman qualities and was thus alien to "normal" people.

You might think that the emergence of our movement in the USSR would be considered the best, the most optimistic news in the post-Khrushchev period, heralding the prospect of the possible peaceful riddance of the Soviet threat. No, it was not. We were declared—first with admiration and then with anger—to be an "exception" to the general rule with no significance for Western policies, nothing but an unwanted headache. No matter how stupid, absurd, and infamous the Soviet campaign to "compromise" us was, it usually did not raise a laugh or provoke indignation. On the contrary, it gave the West an excellent excuse to wrap up the campaign for the defense of human rights in the USSR at the most decisive moment, as Andropov reported to the CC in March 1977 (24 March 1977, Pb 50/71):

> The Committee for State Security reports that the materials published with the sanction of the CC CPSU in "Izvestia," exposing the hostile and incendiary activity of US special services among "dissidents" in the USSR, played a certain part in discrediting the anti-Soviet "human rights" campaign in the USA.

The matter in question was the publication of a letter from one Lipavsky containing the usual "exposure" by a usual KGB informer, a nonentity unknown to anyone. Such "exposure" by persons who had broken under investigation or were broken by some other means numbered dozens, and usually made no impression. Only an idiot would not know that the regime was capable of squeezing out such "exposures," or even worse ones. If Nikolai Bukharin could "confess" to sabotage, what could be expected of some Lipavsky? But the campaign for human rights was already beginning to bore the West, forcing it to change all its long-term policies, all its priorities. The resistance of the Western elite to such radical changes was enormous. Hence the sudden effect of disinformation, essentially very primitive, concerning the as-yet-unarrested Anatoly Sharansky (24 March 1977*, Pb 50/71):

> According to information received, the implemented measure aroused a serious reaction in the USA and other Western countries. Reports in American newspapers, radio and television express public concern regarding the line taken by the CARTER administration in support of "dissidents" and open interference in the internal affairs of the USSR and other socialist countries. It is noteworthy that commentaries in American media contain no serious arguments in defense of this line.
>
> The materials published in "Izvestia" have cast American diplomats and journalists accredited in the USSR into confusion and have had a restraining effect on their contacts with "dissidents." Following instructions from Washington, they are refusing to make any comments and limit themselves to bald rejections of the facts contained in the open letter and article.
>
> However, within their own circle, US embassy staff express fears that the Soviet side may demand the expulsion of diplomat [Joseph] PRESEL, who has compromised himself by links with the CIA. It is planned to hold a press conference with the author

of the open letter and publish exposing materials in other newspapers. There has also been definite confusion in the ranks of
pro-Zionist sympathizers and "dissidents" who maintain active
links with American representatives in the USSR.

Elated by the unexpected success of a rather run-of-the-mill
disinformation action, Andropov proposed (and the Politburo approved) a plan for expanding his campaign:

> The Committee for State Security deems it feasible to implement
> the following measures for discrediting the role played by US
> special services in the anti-Soviet campaign after the visit of
> US Secretary of State VANCE to our country:
>
>   • organize interviews with the author of the open letter, S.L.
>   Lipavsky, with an American or other Western correspon-
>   dent with the participation of a Soviet journalist for sub-
>   sequent publication of this interview in "Izvestia" and the
>   foreign press;
>
>   • with the resources of TASS, APN and Gosteleradio [the
>   USSR State Committee for Television and Radio Broadcast-
>   ing], use the articles prepared by the Committee for State
>   Security pointing out factual data in reports and foreign
>   broadcasts... that the occurrence with Lipavsky is not
>   an isolated incident in the work of special services of the
>   USA, employing "dissidents" in intelligence and subversive
>   activity against the USSR;
>
>   • with the resources of the Committee for State Security, for-
>   ward letters from ordinary Soviet citizens and collectives
>   protesting against the interference of the USA in the inter-
>   nal affairs of the USSR to Washington and the US embassy
>   in Moscow;
>
>   • to avoid provoking retaliatory measures by the American
>   authorities toward staff in Soviet representations in the
>   USA, it is deemed sufficient to limit our actions to com-
>   promising the first secretary of the US embassy PRESEL
>   and the correspondent [Peter] OSNOS, without resorting
>   to measures for their official expulsion from the USSR.

It is certain that had the American administration shown sufficient stamina at that time, and the Western public sufficient indignation to cause Andropov to quiet down, Sharansky would not have
been stuck with an accusation of espionage. Instead, Carter began
to make excuses, apologize, swear that he had checked with the CIA
to ensure that Sharansky had not been their agent. An even more
ingratiating position was adopted by Vance on a visit to Moscow.

After all, détente must be saved! Western Jewish organizations also took fright—dear oh dear, what if this should impede emigration?

In a word, the West went weak at the knees, like a newcomer at a KGB interrogation, and something that had been an ordinary *chekist* provocation blossomed into a grandiose victory for their propaganda. As Andropov reported, flying high on the wings of victory (29 March 1977*, 647-A):

> The Committee for State Security has received information that American diplomats and foreign correspondents in Moscow are assessing articles and commentaries in the Soviet press, radio and television debunking the Western anti-Soviet campaign around "violations of human rights" as evidence of the firm resolve of the Soviet Union to allow no interference in its internal affairs, especially on the eve of the visit to the USSR of the State Secretary of the USA, Vance. In their opinion, the "culminating moment in these Moscow measures" was the arrest of "dissident" Sharansky by the Soviet authorities, affirming the inflexible intention of the USSR to apply the relevant legal means to such renegades.
>
> According to journalist [Jay] AXELBANK, the publication of revelatory materials in "Izvestia" and the subsequent arrest of SHARANSKY have placed the American side in an extremely embarrassing position. If this situation reveals more evidence of the use of "dissidents" by US special services for the purposes of espionage, this shall be a serious obstacle for Western propaganda "in defense of human rights" in the USSR, and will reinforce Moscow's position in this matter.
>
> REZINI, another American journalist, expressed the view that punishment for espionage to the benefit of another state raises no doubts in anyone's minds, including American lawyers. Fears of offending VANCE are unfounded, although he may express displeasure. ... After SHARANSKY's arrest, "dissidents" headed by SAKHAROV organized an improvised press conference on March 16 of this year in a private apartment, to which they invited several American and other Western journalists and handed them prepared statements of a slanderous nature. According to data received, in its report to the State Department concerning this press conference, the US embassy in Moscow made special reference to SAKHAROV's statements that "in the current critical situation of the Soviet movement for defense of human rights, it would be helpful if the American Congress and president would voice a reaction to SHARANSKY's arrest. Any relaxation in pressure from abroad in such a critical moment is undesirable."
>
> Replying to a question from one of the foreign journalists as

to whether he intended to meet VANCE during the latter's visit to the USSR, SAKHAROV said that he did not wish for such a meeting if it would place the state secretary in an awkward position and does not intend to seek any meeting.

At a closed press conference in the US embassy on March 18 of this year, an embassy spokesman was evasive in comments regarding the appeal by SAKHAROV and other "dissidents" for support, stating that he did not know how the government of the USA would react.

In reply to a question from another correspondent as to whether SHARANSKY's arrest would complicate VANCE's visit to the USSR, the embassy spokesman said that the CARTER administration did not link human rights with détente.

Information received indicates that US media admit that "a specific serious charge of high treason" has been leveled at SHARANSKY, which places those attempting to support him in a difficult situation.

Cutting to the chase, the West not only betrayed Sharansky, but also undermined achievements that the West had done nothing to win in the first place. It was the laughable, Politburo-inspired definition of dissidents as instruments of "imperialist subversive centers" that, unexpectedly for its authors, carried the day and was legitimized. A year later, building on this success, they made short work of the entire Helsinki movement in the USSR, nimbly juggling its trials with trials of genuine spies, and the entire Western campaign for the defense of human rights practically ended. As we recall, the Politburo did not venture to try the "Helsinki monitors" (1 April 1978*, 785-A) for a long time, deferring their trials for a year and engaging in thorough preparation of this "measure." The damage to the party could be too great in view of the global fever pitch around the question of human rights at that time. It is likely that had the West displayed more stamina, the Politburo would not have dared to throw such an open challenge.

> The current situation is conducive to resolution of the question of conducting trials in court. Among other things, recent enemy attempts to discredit measures taken against criminals exhibit signs of wavering. There is a lowering in the tone of assertions that the investigation allegedly has no substantial proof of the culpability of the accused. Furthermore, the administration and agencies of US propaganda, while not actually denying the criminal connection of SHARANSKY and American intelligence, wish to prevent new revelations concerning the CIA and try to convince the public that his activity was only in the cause of the defense of "human rights." A similar line of justification of

criminal activity is being pursued with regard to other individuals.

It is also borne in mind that at present the formerly exposed intentions and arguments of the opponent in organizing various campaigns in the West for the defense of criminals warrant fuller consideration, and can be used for propaganda purposes.

The above and other favorable circumstances enable the development of effective tactics for the organization of court trials and their propagandistic support.

This is followed by a detailed plan of how, in what order, and with what accompanying disinformation these trials are to be conducted. The key tactic for them in this matter was the deliberate alternating of trials of Helsinki monitors with those of numerous individuals arrested for genuine espionage and totally unrelated to the Helsinki monitors. There would also be a precise rotation of trials of those who had not broken under investigation with those who had. All this was discussed quite cynically, with no circumlocution or hints:

Bearing in mind that the opponent shall concentrate mainly on discrediting the investigation of the cases of SHARANSKY, GINZBURG, [Yuri] ORLOV and [Zviad] GAMSAKHURDIA, it seems feasible to commence the organization of trials with the publication of materials exposing the activity of US special services in the collection of espionage information and creation of a hotbed of organized anti-Soviet activity on the territory of our country. Among other things, publish materials from the trial of RADZHABOV, an unmasked agent of American intelligence, in "Trud."

The implementation of revelatory measures shall ensure profitable conditions for the simultaneous holding of the trials of [Miroslav] MARINOVICH and [Mykola] MATUSEVICH in the second half of March in the city of Vasilkov in the Kiev region, and [Leonid] LUBMAN in Leningrad. Such a combination in the order of examination of cases shall enable some neutralizing of the noise around the trials of MARINOVICH and MATUSEVICH and at the same time facilitate exposure of the interference of American intelligence in the internal affairs of the USSR.

The conduct of the remaining trials is envisaged for the second half of May–beginning of June. It is feasible to begin them with the examination of the ORLOV case in Moscow, correlating it in time with proceedings in the cases of GAMSAKHURDIA and [Merab] KOSTAVA in Tbilisi. Tactically, such a correlation shall be justified insofar as GAMSAKHURDIA has made a full confession of his crimes. GAMSAKHURDIA is the son of the prominent Georgian writer and has extensive contacts in creative intelligentsia circles, in view of which his revelatory declarations, including those about the underhanded role of established American spies acting under the aegis of the US embassy in Moscow, shall produce a favorable resonance for us. Revelations made by GAMSAKHURDIA shall, in their turn, ensure conditions for the trial of GINZBURG, and then SHARANSKY.

As SHARANSKY is charged with high treason, his trial must be correlated profitably with the trials of [Anatoly] FILATOV and [Alexander] NILOV, which shall create additional significant positions for exposing the espionage activities of the CIA on Soviet territory. These trials shall be preceded by the publication of materials confiscated from American spies [Martha] PETERSON and [Vincent] CROCKETT upon their being caught red-handed in 1977, demonstrating the subversive activity of US intelligence on the territory of the USSR.

This was a full debacle, a total surrender of its positions by the West at the most critical moment of our history. As a result, the so-called Helsinki trial became senseless, degenerating into an empty talking-shop. Despite the provisions of the Helsinki Accords, the West no longer "linked human rights with détente." Certainly there were many reasons for such a turn in the policy of the West (we shall examine them in chapter 5), but it is unlikely that anyone could deny the role played in this by Soviet disinformation and, no matter how ridiculous it was, the astounding readiness, even desire, of the West to believe it.

Our movement never recovered fully after this rout. A year later, in 1979 and the beginning of 1980, with no particular outcries or protests, the last of us were picked up, Sakharov was dealt with, and Afghanistan was invaded—all to the approving roars of the crowds at the Moscow Olympic Games. The West could not stop even this exceptionally cynical show—the Soviet style of thought triumphed everywhere. Their "truth" won, their concepts of good and evil. As for the détente so dear to the heart of the West—it vanished just as imperceptibly and ignominiously; unlinked with human rights it was meaningless, turning into an ordinary capitulation.

It is characteristic of the Soviet leaders that they played their game unflinchingly to the very end. Even many years later, at the height of glasnost and perestroika, they did not drop their legend and remained adamant that Sharansky be released as a genuine spy—in exchange for a real Soviet spy—on the bridge in Berlin that served as the place for such exchanges. These guys never let up. As for the West, it wiped the spittle off its face, and rejoiced in its new friend Gorbachev.

As the English say, with friends like these, who needs enemies?

• • •

Without doubt, if this primitive KGB disinformation could still play its fateful role in such an important question, then it was all the more effective in less pressing issues that attracted much less public attention. Especially as *chekist* "compromising measures" frequently centered skillfully on purely human traits, human frailty, irregular relations, using people's ambitions, their lack of rights, and their insufficient awareness of the West. The *chekists*' scheming was incredibly unwholesome. For instance, in Sharansky's case, it was not enough for them to brand him a spy; they had to pry into his private life as well (14 December 1977, 2643-A):[131]

> In connection with the circumstance that the official US authorities are actively using former Soviet citizen [Natalya, changed Natalya to Avital upon arrival in Israel] Stiglitz, purportedly Sharansky's wife, in their anti-Soviet campaign, instruct the Soviet ambassador A.F. Dobrynin to pass President Carter materials exposing Sharansky's immoral nature, including letters written by Stiglitz's father that categorically refute his daughter's marriage to Sharansky and condemn her provocative activity. These materials can be handed over subsequently for publication in the foreign press.

The rationale behind this act is as simple as it is reprehensible: it was well known that Carter was a deeply religious Baptist, and held much stronger views on the morals of marital relations than was customary. And these materials are delivered shamelessly through "normal diplomatic channels," through the Soviet ambassador in the USA. One can only guess at what scurrilous information passed via the channels of the KGB in the wings (5 November 1969*, 2792-A):

> According to data at the disposal of the Committee for State Security, the opponent is considering a new publication of S. ALLILUYEVA's book "Only One Year" as one of the means for expanding the anti-Soviet campaign timed to coincide with the centenary of V.I. LENIN's birth. ... In view of the above, for purposes of distracting the international community from the slanderous campaign being waged by the opponent with the aid of S. ALLILUYEVA's book "Only One Year," the following measures are proposed:
>
> In connection with the letter of Iosif ALLILUYEV and Ekaterina ZHDANOVA to the Politburo of the CC CPSU, which expresses indignation regarding their mother's treacherous behavior, we

---

[131]25 December 1977, p. 3.

deem it possible to prepare and publish abroad the open letter of S. ALLILUYEVA's children, addressed to prominent political observer [Harrison] SALISBURY, assistant managing editor of "The New York Times," who interviewed S. ALLILUYEVA on numerous occasions and regards her personally with a measure of contempt.

This action shall be underpinned by publication of the indicated letter and an interview with S. ALLILUYEVA's children in one of the leading European journals.

Put forward a suggestion to the Western press that S. ALLILUYEVA's new book is the result of a collective effort by [George F.] KENNAN, [Harold] FISHER, [Milovan] DJILAS, [Georges] FLOROVSKY, [Arkadiy] BELINKOV and others, who are known to be virulent foes of the USSR and who specialize in falsifying the history of the Soviet state. At the same time, include materials that personally compromise the aforementioned individuals from materials in the possession of the KGB.

Send S. ALLILUYEVA a letter from prominent representatives of the Soviet intelligentsia (writer [Vladimir] SOLOUKHIN, screenwriter [Alexey] KAPLER, senior editor of the journal "Sovetsky ekran" [*Soviet Screen*] [Dmitry] PISAREVSKY, Professor [Georg] MYASNIKOV — S. ALLILUYEVA's research manager when she defended her thesis—and others) expressing a motivated protest regarding the falsifying of facts from Soviet history and slandering of V.I. LENIN. This letter could be delivered to S. ALLILUYEVA through the resources of the KGB and with the intention that it becomes known to the Western press.

Such "compromising measures" accompanied just about any event, from the publication of books to arrests and trials, from escapes abroad of figures in the sphere of arts to large-scale international occurrences. It stands to reason that not all these "measures" were successful, but denying their significance would be the height of naivety, as the result was the creation of an enormous machine of disinformation, a whole system of "agents of influence" against whom the West had no defense. On the contrary, democracy was forced to defend the right of its sworn enemies to disseminate arrant lies. In many countries, for example the USA, the law practically fails to defend you from being slandered in the press; you must prove to the court that the slanderer acted deliberately. And if you, God forbid, are a known personality, slandering you is seen as the divine right of the press.

Moreover, the majority of these "agents of influence" were not KGB agents in the strict sense of the term. Some disseminated Soviet disinformation out of purely ideological motives, some to repay an old debt to that authority or because they expected a reciprocal favor or service, while others simply knew not what they did. After all, the "information" desired by the KGB could frequently be of equal interest to your competitor, someone jealous of you, or simply an unpleasant person, while the task of the KGB was to merely convey it on to an interested party.

The possible scenarios were unlimited. For instance, most Western specialists on Russia—Sovietologists, Slavists—were dependent on the regime by virtue of the fact that they needed to travel to the USSR from time to time. Otherwise a specialist in the Western world was not considered a specialist. Anyone could reproach him for becoming "disqualified" by breaking away from reality. Any travel to the USSR in those days was under the firm control of the Lubyanka. Yet there was also a corresponding mechanism, a much mightier one: a Soviet citizen of any profession could not travel abroad for, say, an academic conference, a guest performance, or a competition without the sanction of the KGB. Having lost the right to travel, that person became practically worthless, and could even lose his job. Thus the "resources of the KGB" were practically boundless.

Tell me now that the KGB was stupid, that their disinformation did not influence anyone. Far from it! For years, with rare patience, they built up their channels, frequently playing with people the way a cat plays with a mouse. And woe betide anyone who entered into these games with the naive expectation of outsmarting them: one can fool an individual or a group, but not the system (30 September 1968, 2281-A).[132]

> [Andrei] SINYAVSKY, sentenced in February 1966 by the Supreme Court of the USSR to seven years' imprisonment under Article 70 part 1 of the Criminal Code of the RSFSR, is serving his sentence in the Dubrava corrective labor camp.
>
> Monitoring of his behavior in the corrective labor camp shows that in recent times he has spent an increasing amount of time considering his future life, although he continues to deny his guilt. Unlike DANIEL and his family members, SINYAVSKY and his wife do not take part in any anticommunist actions.
>
> For the purposes of terminating Western use of the fact of sentencing SINYAVSKY and DANIEL for anticommunist propaganda, we deem it feasible to continue work with SINYAVSKY aimed at inclining him to petition the Supreme Soviet of the RSFSR for clemency. Upon receipt of such a petition, we would deem it possible to satisfy SINYAVSKY's request.
>
> Approval is requested.
>
> Chairman of the Committee for State Security ANDROPOV

---

[132] 14 January 1969*, Pb 111, p. 2.

Memorandum from Yu.V. Andropov dated 30 September 1968 (re Sinyavsky)

(Comrades Suslov, Andropov, Polyansky, Shelepin, Demichev)

Two years later, the following report was submitted (19 May 1971*, Pb 4/48):

Permit comrade Yu.V. Andropov to continue work, allowing for the opinions expressed at the meeting of the Politburo of the CC.

Writer A.D. Sinyavsky, author of books with anti-Soviet content, published in the West under the pseudonym "Abram Terts" and sentenced by the Supreme Court of the RSFSR to seven years' imprisonment, has served two-thirds of his term to date.

Monitoring of Sinyavsky's behavior shows that he observes the established regime in the corrective labor camp, reacts negatively to the efforts of individual prisoners to draw him into antisocial activity and has given no cause for the use of his name abroad for aims hostile to our state.

His wife [Maria] Rozanova-Kruglikova, who resides in Moscow, has also committed no prejudicial acts. Nonetheless, Sinyavsky continues to take the position of denying his guilt and the anti-Soviet nature of his activities, continues to consider his trial to be unlawful. However, with his consent, Sinyavsky's wife has petitioned for clemency, the motivation for which is difficulty in raising their small son.

Having examined this petition and analyzed the materials, and also bearing in mind that Sinyavsky's term expires in September 1972, we deem it possible to reduce his term as a measure of clemency by one year and three months.

In our view, this measure could promote Sinyavsky's disengagement from antisocial elements and exercise a positive influence on his future behavior.

Drafts of the resolution of the CC CPSU and the Order of the Presidium of the Supreme Soviet of the RSFSR on this matter are attached.

We request their examination.

Yu. Andropov, R. Rudenko, L. Gorkin

12 May 1971

Sinyavsky was pardoned on 19 May 1971. In 1973, Andropov submitted another report. (26 February 1973*, 409-A):

Regarding granting clemency to A.D. Sinyavsky

Approve the draft of the Order of the Supreme Soviet of the RSFSR on this matter (attached).

SECRETARY OF THE CC

The Committee for State Security is continuing work toward exercising a positive influence on Andrei Donatovich SINYAVSKY, released prematurely from his place of deprivation of liberty, creating an atmosphere promoting his distancing from antisocial elements.

Pursuant to measures employed, SINYAVSKY's name is currently somewhat compromised in the eyes of that part of the creative intelligentsia that had supported him. Some, according to available data, consider that he is allied to KGB agencies. SINYAVSKY is adhering to the mutually agreed-upon line of behavior upon his return to Moscow, leads a reclusive life, and is engaged in creative work related to aspects of XIX-century Russian literature and the history of ancient Russian art.

By employing SINYAVSKY's influence through his wife ROZANOVA-KRUGLIKOVA, it became possible to exercise a positive influence on the positions of DANIEL and GINZBURG pursuant to their release to our satisfaction, as a result of which they are making no attempts to play an active part in the so-called "democratic movement" and avoid contacts with YAKIR's group.

However, it is clear that SINYAVSKY, while adhering to our recommendations, remains essentially on his former idealistic creative positions and does not accept Marxist-Leninist principles in matters of literature and art, and therefore his new works cannot be published in the Soviet Union.

Various bourgeois publishers are attempting to exploit this situation, offering their services in publishing SINYAVSKY's works, which might lead to the formation of an unhealthy atmosphere around his name.

On 5 January 1973 SINYAVSKY petitioned the visa office of the GU MVD of Russia in Moscow, requesting permission to travel to France with his wife and son, born 1965, for a period of 3 years on a private invitation from CLAUDE FRIOUX, a professor at the University of Paris.

In view of the above and bearing in mind SINYAVSKY's desire to retain Soviet citizenship, we consider it possible not to hinder the SINYAVSKY family traveling from the USSR.

The favorable resolution of this question would lessen the probability of SINYAVSKY being drawn into a new anti-Soviet campaign, as it would deprive him of the status of "an internal émigré," remove him from the creative community and finally relegate SINYAVSKY to the ranks of "writers abroad" who have lost public resonance.

It may be possible to decide in the future whether SINYAVSKY's return to the Soviet Union would be feasible after the expiry of his stay in France.

We request approval.

Chairman of the Committee for State Security ANDROPOV

(26 February 1973*, 409-A).

3.11   The suffering intelligentsia

I have cited almost the whole of this drama in documents, because it illustrates in great detail how step by step, how patiently and precisely the Politburo worked in preparing its "operative-*chekist* measures." Say what you like, but it had an excellent understanding of its domestic intelligentsia, knowing full well how to balance reward and punishment. And even better, how to play on the intelligentsia's narcissism. It is not my task to expose anyone personally, or even judge, especially as for most of us, there is nothing new in these documents. The fact that Sinyavskaya played complicated games with the KGB is something she never concealed.

I still remember how, having returned from camp in January 1970, I met her at a dinner with mutual friends. Curiously, this was our first and last meeting in Moscow; we had never met before, but Mrs. Sinyavskaya simply never closed her mouth. She spoke —as always—with great aplomb, saying that "we—the writers" do not need all this noise, this so-called "movement," all this "politics." They only hinder "us—the writers," and we should sit still and keep quiet. And most of all, we should not get involved with all these Yakirs and similar lovers of turmoil. Observing my highly negative reaction to her "writers" line, she never sought any further meetings with me. "Sinyavsky's authority to influence" failed—and that was that. This was all she needed to see me for, and it was the reason for dragging herself to dinner with friends on the same day I was supposed to turn up.

But that is neither here nor there. I do not care whether she used "Sinyavsky's authority" on her own initiative or as part of an "achieved agreement," just as it does not matter now whether she provoked endless squabbles in emigration (including constant attacks on Solzhenitsyn) in accordance with the "mutually devised line" or simply because of a quarrelsome nature. Either way, Andropov did not miss his guess. There is another amusing fact: mention of these documents in the Russian press evoked the unbridled fury of Madame Sinyavskaya. Not abashed for a moment by the amusing contradiction, she immediately—and as always, dictatorially—declared (in *Moskovskiye novosti*, the *Moscow News*) a) that the documents "are stolen," b) that the documents "are forged,"

c) that Andropov distorted everything. It was just like that joke about the overzealous provincial lawyer who claims that his client is innocent, as he has an ironclad alibi, but at the same time deserves leniency because he had an extremely difficult childhood. Then again, without pausing for breath, she went ahead and published those same documents herself—here it is, the "whole truth," neither stolen nor forged. Finally, in a long, drawn-out article in *Nezavsimaya gazeta* (the *Independent Newspaper*) taking up two full pages in two issues, she imparted an account of her astounding exploits—how she, a clever and fearless woman, snookered the stupid and cowardly KGB, and defeated it at its own game. You see, she blackmailed the KGB, falsely accusing it of stealing some valuable books during a house search. What resourcefulness! What courage! What could the poor *chekist*s do but allow them to depart to Paris in peace?

This would not have mattered—you will find much worse in the Russian press these days. As they say, if you don't want to listen, then don't, but don't stop me from lying. Had it never occurred to them that Sinyavsky is as pertinent to the Sinyavsky-Daniel case as Kirov is to the case of Kirov's killing? Or Alfred Dreyfus is to the Dreyfus affair? Preparing for our first demonstration in 1965, we had never seen Sinyavsky or read his books (I was later unable to get past the first twenty pages). The issue did not lie with him; the issue was to see if the public would tolerate political repressions in post-Stalin times. Would we go back to the times of the terror, or will people finally come to a sense of their civil courage? It was just a test of maturity, which only a few passed. The majority remained as Soviet as before, including Sinyavsky. A voice from the chorus—and a flat one at that.

What stands behind the leaden language of Andropov's reports is comprehensible only to the initiated. Let us say, what does "reacts negatively to the efforts of individual prisoners to draw him into antisocial activity" mean? It means keeping your mouth shut when your cell mate is being bullied, going to work when your fellow camp inmates are striking, shamefully gobbling camp porridge when the zone has declared a hunger strike. Or what does "petition for clemency" mean? It is an admission of guilt, no matter how often you declare later that you deny your guilt. That is all the regime wanted from us—at first. Should one of us agree, then—home, freedom, warmth, food. A loving wife and fractious children. But the dying Galanskov did not agree and Marchenko preferred to die. On the other hand, the "pardoned" Gamsakhurdia made it to president of Georgia. Yet we know: the regime never rested on its achievements, it levied the debt even many years later.

> On 24 July 1969, Anatoly Vasilyevich KUZNETSOV, born 1929
> in Kiev, member of the CPSU since 1955, responsible secre-
> tary of the Tula chapter of the Union of Writers of the RSFSR,
> deputy secretary of the party organization of that chapter, mem-
> ber of the editorial board of the journal "Yunost" [*Youth*] from
> June 1969, traveled to England for the purpose of conducting
> research for a new work on V.I. LENIN.
>
> According to information from the embassy of the USSR in Eng-
> land, on the evening of 28 July KUZNETSOV left his hotel and,
> as was later advised by the Home Office of England, applied for
> permission to remain in the country. KUZNETSOV's request
> has been granted.

This story (4 August 1969, 1926-A) made waves at the time not
just because Kuznetsov was a well-known writer, but mainly because of his sincere admission of cooperation with the KGB. To give
him his due, he admitted it at once, at the first opportunity, and insisted on the publication of this admission in English newspapers
in full detail, thereby hoping to expunge his guilt. Nonetheless,
the story is an amazing one: according to him, he "played with the
KGB" for more than a year and even wrote false, fantastically absurd reports on his friends and colleagues, prominent writers and
artists, who were allegedly members of a conspiracy against the
Soviet authorities—all in order to gain an opportunity to go abroad
and remain there. He declared that he could no longer live in the
USSR, where his talent was suffocating for lack of creative freedom.

This is not the worst example by far. At least Kuznetsov did
not demand any heroic laurels, did not expect sympathy, and recounted the whole story quite truthfully. At least he felt that he
had done something dishonorable. The majority felt nothing of the
kind. Cultural functionaries who received permits for trips abroad
were later obligated to write reports on what they had seen and
heard, and occasionally to carry out a KGB assignment. They saw
this as completely normal, just like informing on foreigners arriving
in the USSR.

The point at issue is not the connection with the KGB *per se*; I always regarded that with total indifference, just as one would regard
ordinary informers. I once met one of the latter by chance in the
street: a quarter of a century ago he had reported such dirt about
me to the KGB that I could have perished. Yet I felt nothing except
a bit of pity for him. No, this is something completely different.
Those I mean elicit no pity and never feel guilty. On the contrary,
they fancy themselves. I don't know, maybe I'm too subjective, but
I am physically revolted by them, like at the sight of a wood louse.

As I was writing these lines, the second BBC channel showed an unusual documentary about the new hero of our times, Vladimir Vladimirovich Pozner. Yes, yes, that very same Pozner who spent years convincing Western television viewers in America, England, and France in impeccable English and French of the advantages of the Soviet system, talking about peace-oriented Soviet policies, that Sakharov was rightly exiled, that the invasion of Afghanistan was just, and that nobody but the genuinely insane are placed into psychiatric hospitals. Now, with equal conviction and a catch in his voice, he describes how terribly he suffered all those years. He —dreadful thought!—was not permitted to travel abroad for a very long time, while all his productions were "for export." He—*he!*— was not trusted, he was unable to be the anchor of any program on his beloved Soviet television! And in what lay his talent? In that he was the best liar in his impeccable English and French.

It must be said, the BBC worked extremely hard; to create a hero out of very poor materials is a difficult job—something like making a heroic film about Ezra Pound in the 1940s. But they wanted this ever so much—it was probably being done by similar Pozners, only Western ones. The camera panned lovingly over Pozner taking a morning jog, Pozner with his American twin Phil Donahue, Pozner at home, Pozner young and Pozner old. Here is "his" school in New York, where he studied until repatriation to the USSR; here is the Pozner house in Greenwich Village, in the heart of liberal New York. The house is not bad at all, at current prices it would fetch several million, and it was probably pretty much the same at the time of purchase. But all this joy was lost forever due to the accursed McCarthyism; Pozner senior was a communist by conviction and a Soviet citizen by passport, who did not wish to part with the "hammer-and-sickled one" and he—what injustice!—lost his job in a large Hollywood company. There was no option but to go to the USSR—and suffer. Now, at the sight of his childhood photograph Pozner... weeps. Yes, yes, weeps with real tears.

Then came the culmination: August 1991, tanks on the streets of Moscow, *Swan Lake* on Soviet television and—the liberation of Pozner. Clips from Forman's *One Flew over the Cuckoo's Nest*: the ever-obedient giant Indian rips a stool out of the floor and hurls it through the window. Freedom! He decided, he broke the bonds.

"I shall not allow myself to believe, neither in man, nor in the government, nor in ideology. Never again!" Convincing as ever, in his impeccable English, Pozner speaks from the screen in conclusion, like an old, raddled whore swearing that she will never "give" anything to anyone, never, for any price. Just as well nobody is asking. What has belief got to do with it? We already heard the explanation: he did not believe in anything, and he lied and suffered all his life.

• • •

But come, they all suffered, struggled, were persecuted—that was the essence of the Soviet regime that never changed from Stalin's time. Like those academics who elbowed their colleagues aside to sign the letter against Sakharov—because those who did not get to sign would not figure among the names of "leading Soviet scientists." There was also a chance-met person who was "exiled" as an ambassador to some rundown Western country for freethinking. Even Andropov—just think how much he had to bear from the Politburo ideologues! They all struggled and suffered. One lot persecuted another, were executioners and victims at the same time. But now everyone remembered being a victim, and nobody wanted to admit to being an executioner.

The intelligentsia was the most suffering of the lot, "making sacrifices" daily to preserve its talent, its science, art, literature. It was *sine qua non* in our days for a writer to suffer a little to attract attention to his talent, so that it would shine and sparkle. Not too much, of course; as Vladimir Vysotsky wrote: "to be crucified at thirty-three, but not too much." Who could be a writer worthy of that name if he had not been persecuted even a tiny bit? Tell me who would know, especially in the West, of the existence of such a "poet" as Yevgeny Yevtushenko, a member of the CC of the Komsomol, without his "authority" as a disgraced, persecuted "angry young man"? It didn't cost him much:

> The chief administration for protecting state secrets and the press under the Council of Ministers of the USSR reports that N6 [No. 6] of the journal "Yunost" for 1977 has typeset a poem by Yevtushenko entitled "The Northern Bonus." The hero in that poem is Pyotr Schepochkin, who has worked in the north for a long time and, having stitched his "northern bonus" of ten thousand rubles into a money belt, goes on vacation. He dreams of boarding the "Vladivostok-Moscow" train, where on arrival he will "fill his belly" with beer. ... After several "blurred" days in the capital and being lighter by "three bills of credit and heavier by a hundred bottles of beer," he goes to visit his sister, Valya, who works as a nurse in the town of Klin in the Moscow region. He, who had become accustomed to throwing around thousands of rubles, is "shocked" by the meeting with his sister, who lives with her husband and child in an "edge-of-the-town" barrack on a salary of 150 rubles.
>
> He "formulates" his "conclusion" in words addressed to an old watchman: "You're scared of thieves? Go tell who is a thief...,"

thereby hinting ambiguously that people living on a "hundred-ruble wage" and inhabiting "ten-meter homes" are, in fact, being robbed.

These moments that we find unacceptable in Yevtushenko's poem "The Northern Bonus" have been drawn to the attention of the editor of "Yunost," [Andrey] Dementyev, in a discussion at the Chief Administration on 6 May. Comrade Dementyev agreed with these comments but said that the editorial board will probably be unable to enter the necessary amendments to the poem as the poet has allegedly said that he will not change a single line.

It stands to reason, though, that the CC sorted everything out and made the required corrections.

Glavlit of the USSR [General Directorate for the Protection of State Secrets in the Press under the Council of Ministers of the USSR] (comrade [Grigory] Romanov) reports that Yevtushenko's poem "The Northern Bonus" is being prepared for publication (in N6 1977) of the journal "Yunost," and that it contains serious ideological-artistic blunders that distort our way of life.

In accordance with the directive to the departments of propaganda and culture of the CPSU, a meeting was held with the editorial leadership of "Yunost" (comrade Dementyev) and the Union of Writers of the USSR (comrade [Sergei] Sartakov). Comrade Dementyev reports that prior to clearance for publication, substantial corrections have been made to the text, bearing in mind the comments made by Glavlit.

The matter was limited to a scolding, a slap on the wrist—no more than that. The poem was published, nobody was convoyed anywhere, but the outburst of indignation, the noise—imagine, the Politburo itself intervened! Now the reader shall immerse himself in the journal until it falls apart at the seams, and articles shall appear abroad by sympathetic journalists extolling Yevtushenko's commitment to truth. Naturally this will increase his "authority" in intelligentsia circles: he's in disgrace, he's angry.

In reality, they were all just complementary cogs in the same machine, some working for export and others for domestic consumption. Therefore the CC decreed (16 January 1981, St 246/49):

The leadership of the French Communist Party (PCF) has requested that some representatives of the Soviet intelligentsia, whose names are known in France, send a letter expressing solidarity and sympathy with French communists. This action is linked to a meeting of French democratic intelligentsia that will take place in Paris on 30 January 1981 and is regarded by

friends as a manifestation of support for the General Secretary
of the PCF, [Georges] Marchais....

Falling over one another, they rushed to sign the letter —
which was composed by some semiliterate apparatchik from the
international division — the most progressive and most liberal:
Yury Trifonov, Valentin Katayev, Sergei Yutkevich and even Andrei
Tarkovsky. What of it? Debts must be paid, "exportability" carries
a price:

> We express our fervent solidarity with your struggle for the flow-
> ering of national culture, the development of international cre-
> ative ties between cultural workers in all countries, for peace,
> democracy and socialism. In our time, ideas of liberty, equality
> and fraternity are irrevocably bound with the ideas of social-
> ism, which renders all forms of culture and the achievements
> of human genius available to the workers.

So they signed, and without even wincing; yes, the style is stulti-
fying and "we—the writers" could have done better. They know that
as a reward for this, they will be forgiven certain stylistic lapses in
their own works. The censorship shall overlook them benignly: an
omission here, a hint there. The Soviet "art" and "literature" they
have created remained on the level of games with censorship, the
level of half hints, comprehensible only to the enlightened, who were
supposed to admire the courage of the authors with bated breath.
All these people were phony "authorities" whose works did not, and
could not, survive the regime. Yet those whose works have survived
it never considered compromising their consciences for the sake of
"saving their talent." This would never have entered the heads of Mikhail Bulgakov and Andrei Platonov, or Anna Akhmatova and Osip
Mandelstam, or Solzhenitsyn and Joseph Brodsky.

Yes, they were outcasts, outsiders, and—with the exception of
the last two—did not live to see their main works published in their
own country. But they did not sit in presidiums, did not save humanity from war, did not sing in chorus. I remember when, as
I child, I was taken by my father to visit Platonov (they knew each
other from their days at the front) in his watchman's hut. My mother
was very upset. "What are you doing! He's got extrapulmonary tuberculosis, and you're dragging the child to see him."

"Never mind," Father cut her off drily, "when he grows up, he'll
be proud."

And I am proud: I saw a man who worked as a watchman at the
Institute of Literature, but refused to lie in the frightening Stalin
years. I later read all his books that I could find. Yet what was

written by those he swept pathways for is of no interest to me. It was incredible: the sight of Platonov with a broom and a spade in his hands taught them nothing, although he was certainly the best visual aid in their academic program.

Listening now to the keening and wailing of the intelligentsia about how they suffered, how they were forced to lie, I am deeply puzzled: Why was it necessary to become writers, professors or academics at any price? As we can see here, talent has nothing to do with it; talent survives being a watchman. Everyone has a choice. But no, nobody was prepared to become a watchman, everyone wanted to suffer in comfort. Everyone needed an honorable justification for their own conformism.

I remember how, emerging from the psychiatric hospital in 1965, I suddenly discovered that all my "thaw-time" friends had disappeared somewhere, as if they had melted away. When we met by chance in the street, they would hurry away, clutching folders or briefcases or, even better, wheeling a pram. *Sorry, old man,* they would mutter without stopping, eyes lowered, *I have to defend my diploma, dissertation, get my candidate's application approved.* Or *I need to raise my children first.* Then they would speed off, looking neither left nor right. It seemed as though the whole generation of my contemporaries had fenced itself off from life with briefcases and baby buggies, with academic degrees and books. Who did they think they were fooling? Themselves, the regime, their children? Did none of them realize or understand that in our time, unlike the 1920s and 1930s, any talents and achievements they might have would be used by the regime purely to people's detriment? Was it not clear that failing to resolve these problems, it was unconscionable to burden their children with them? With time their children too would become either executioners or victims—the monstrous conveyor belt produced nothing else.

And so it was: some twenty years later those same children, conceived in deception, were packed off to Afghanistan as justification for their parents' shamelessness, to kill or be killed. The country was dumbly silent, those parents trotted off to work with their books and dissertations; even such a sacrifice did not seem too great to disturb their accustomed small world with its sufferings and authorities. That was the cost of their self-admiration: now all those books and doctoral theses, those vehicles of self-expression that they used to justify themselves, flooded the country, and the country was sinking. But there is not even a shadow of repentance in them. Whatever for? Everyone else is to blame, not them.

3.12   The new Chichikov and his "dead souls"

It is impossible to describe the ecstasy of the Soviet intelligentsia at the appearance of Gorbachev and his "glasnost." At the height of glasnost, in the spring of 1987, ten of us—writers, artists, and dissidents living in the West—fuming over this fantastic lie, and especially over Western euphoria, wrote a collective letter to the newspapers in the hope of introducing at least some sobriety into public opinion. This letter, which later came to be known as the "Letter of the Ten,"[133] was published in the newspapers of most Western countries—in *Le Figaro*, the *Times* of London, the *New York Times* ("Is 'Glasnost' a Game of Mirrors?"[134]) and even, to our surprise, in *Moskovskiye novosti* (*Moscow News*), the most "progressive" perestroika-oriented Soviet publication at that time. All we said, and in a very restrained way, was that it was too early to rejoice over Gorbachev's "reforms," especially as they were still merely promises, and very vaguely worded promises at that. The more so while the cannibalistic system of Marxist-Leninist ideology continued to reign supreme. This letter was addressed to the West, not to them, but ye gods! How much vituperation these domestic "liberals" flung at us! Even *Pravda* had not reviled us to such an extent in the old days—we were "renegades" and "dyed-in-the-wool anti-Soviets" and, naturally, "CIA agents." They published the letter of their own accord (to demonstrate the genuine nature of their glasnost), then took fright and, having taken fright, took to abuse, unashamedly resorting to hoary KGB stereotypes. I was also reminded of the "five-man storm groups."

It stands to reason! We had dared to question their glasnost! We were renegades and traitors, émigrés who sought an easy life, while they stayed on to suffer and struggle. We were enemies of the Motherland, and they were fighters for her betterment. Incredible! Here they were, explaining the meaning of human rights to us!

The more they fretted and fumed—because they had nothing significant to say—the farther our letter spread throughout the country, rewritten by thousands of hands and photographed from the street display stand of *Moskovskiye novosti* outside the newspaper's building. This was probably the first case in our history of material from official publications entering samizdat. The party had to take

---

[133]Apart from me, the Letter of the Ten was signed by writers Vasily Aksyonov, Vladimir Maximov, sculptor Ernst Neizvestny, journalist Eduard Kuznetsov, physicist Yuri Orlov, professor of philosophy Alexander Zinoviev and his wife Olga, stage director Yuri Lyubimov and mathematician Leonid Plyushch.

[134]"Is 'Glasnost' a Game of Mirrors?", New York Times, 22 March 1987 https://www.nytimes.com/1987/03/22/opinion/is-glasnost-a-game-of-mirrors.html

a serious look at its defenses. Now not only *Moskovskiye novosti*, published primarily for foreigners and a small circle of reliable "perestroika stalwarts,"[135] but all the other "progressive" publications —that is, those who had Politburo permission to run a little way ahead of events, demonstrating their courage—were forced to enter the fray, featuring "letters from workers" and "round tables" on their pages. *Ogonyok*, and *Novoye vremya* and finally *Pravda* all acted in the best traditions of the Alexander Yakovlev propaganda at the times of our trials.[136] The scandal stretched over many months, but the more they floundered, the more they became stuck like flies to flypaper. Was this not an omen of what their games with glasnost could lead to? Meanwhile, just when the perestroika acolytes showered us with curses on the pages of their "liberal" publications, we were receiving private messages with quite different reproaches through mutual friends:

Why have you people let us down like this? You provoked us into printing your letter, for which we got it in the neck. There's a threat that Moskovskiye novosti is going to be closed down. How could you do this to us? We are not harming anyone, just fooling the West. We and you know what is really going on.

What could you say to them if "fooling the West," just like informing on foreigners, is normal from their point of view? It turns out that we are guilty because we let them down, we provoked them. As one of my school friends said to me many years later: "You have no idea how you let us all down!"

"How?" I asked.

"What do you mean, how? It was because of you that we started taking an interest in samizdat and some got caught, they were barely able to graduate from university, defend their dissertations...."

"Sorry, ..." was all I said. What else could I say? Yes, their lives would have probably been much happier, if it were not for my example at the backs of their minds.

Starting their crafty game of glasnost, Gorbachev and Yakovlev knew perfectly well that they could rely on the Soviet intelligentsia. If anything bothered them at that time, it was the possibility of our influence; that was why they took great care to isolate us, cut us off. These concerns, as shown in documents, began long before our "Letter of the Ten" and, indeed, long before glasnost. Viktor

---

[135]See *Moscow News* 13, (April 5–12), p. 10 and 15 (April 19–26), p. 8 for the subsequent discussion of the Letter of the Ten.

[136]See *Ogonyok* (No 13, March 1987), *New Times* (3 April 1987), *Pravda* (25 March 1987), *Sovetskaya kultura* (1 April 1987) and *Leninskaya smena* (*Lenin Shift*), (April 1987).

Chebrikov, head of the KGB, reported the following in June 1986 (1 June 1986*, 1135-Ch):

> Materials received by the Committee for State Security of the USSR indicate that targeted subversive actions are being carried out with the aim of discrediting the party line for acceleration of the socioeconomic development of the country and further perfection of the social process, in which the opponent is paying special attention to representatives of the Soviet creative intelligentsia, first of all to figures in the literary and arts spheres. In view of the upsurge of activity in the political and work aspects in the life of our country, Western special services and centers of ideological subversion are updating their methods of undermining activity, aimed at the "ideological deformation of the socialist system" and promotion of revisionist and oppositional moods, and they are attempting to lead Soviet literary figures on to the path of divergence from the principles of socialist realism and the party orientation of literature. In order to achieve its hostile intentions, the opponent attempts to infuse the consciousness of the creative intelligentsia with a nihilistic evaluation of the entire socialist construction in the USSR. Political retrogrades such as Solzhenitsyn, [Lev] Kopelev, [Vladimir] Maximov, [Vasily] Aksyonov, [Georgi] Vladimov and suchlike are being "reanimated" and moved into the arena of ideological warfare, entering the path of active hostile activity. Many of them have become direct participants in and executors of anti-Soviet provocations and extensive propagandistic actions. On assignments of the special services they search for fellow thinkers and try to establish contact channels with negatively minded people among the creative intelligentsia in our country.
>
> In view of the party line for the further democratization of Soviet society, the opponent has the primary aim of a mass cultivation of those literary figures who have displayed ideological wavering in the past, not always passed the test of civil maturity and class conviction, directly or indirectly raised doubts about the correctness of the party line regarding collectivization, the actions against kulaks, the struggle against Trotskyism, the national policy of the CPSU, have made claims about the lack of social justice and creative freedom in our country, have demanded the "abolition of censorship" and the removal of literature and the arts from the control of party agencies.
>
> It is worth noting that it was just these issues that were expounded by Solzhenitsyn in 1976 in his provocative letter to the Fourth Congress of Soviet Writers, which received the support of eighty members of the Union of Writers of the USSR. They included [Anatoly] Rybakov, [Felix] Svetov, [Vladimir] Soloukhin,

[Bulat] Okudzhava, [Fazil] Iskander, [Boris] Mozhayev, [Mikhail] Roshchin and [the poet Vladimir] Kornilov.

Available data indicate that during the entire subsequent period these writers were under the close scrutiny of the special services and the ideological subversive centers of the opponent. In recent times, their ideological cultivation has increased considerably both from the position of representatives of capitalist countries in Moscow and in the course of their visits abroad within the framework of international cultural exchange. ...

The opposition is attempting to position the matter in a way that implies that at present "in Russian literature, as in the Russian social consciousness, a new epoch has begun that is much less dependent on the ideological policy of the party. ... Social thought has moved to a cardinal reevaluation of the entire spiritual and historical situation." With this in view, the special services have advanced a thesis on the so-called "unity of global Russian culture" that they try to impose on representatives of the literary community of the USSR, promoting its idea of merging on the basis of "common spiritual orientation and aims" of the creative process of the creative intelligentsia in our country and former representatives who are actively engaged in anti-Soviet activity and have been assigned the status of "geniuses of Russian literature in exile."

According to available data, individual Soviet literary figures have advocated the review of relations regarding the personalities and works of various renegades in public and private appearances, and insist on the timeliness of a review of their works as an integral part of a "united Russian culture." Among other things, [Valery] Roschin and [Anatoly] Pristavkin express an opinion on the possible return of Solzhenitsyn to the USSR and the feasibility of an imminent publication of his "works" in our country. At a meeting of the Moscow branch or the All-Russian Union of Poets in April of this year, [Vladimir] Leonovich publicly called for a review of attitudes toward [Vladimir] Voinovich and Brodsky, renegades who reside abroad. At an evening in the State Museum of V.V. Mayakovsky in March 1986, he gave a positive appraisal of the works of the anti-Soviet [Alexander] Galich, expressing dissatisfaction with the circumstance that we do not publish his courageous works. Speaking at the All-Union Seminar of Academic Slavists in Narva-Joesuu in the Estonian SSR, Leonovich called Galich "the leading light among significant bards of Russia."

In recent times, various agencies have received requests and letters in defense of certain persons sentenced for unlawful activity who were actively used by the West for purposes hostile to the USSR, and their libelous productions are now being declared

"an integral part of Russian literature." ... The Committee for
State Security of the USSR is implementing the necessary measures to counteract the subversive aims of the opponent within
the creative intelligentsia community.

That really worried the CC. It was not by chance that Gorbachev
added the following resolution to the abovementioned report:

1. To be forwarded to all members of the Politburo of the CC
   CPSU, candidates for membership of the Politburo of the
   CC CPSU and secretaries of the CC CPSU.
2. Comrades [Yegor] Ligachev and A.N. Yakovlev. Please discuss this with me.

All the tens of thousands of Soviet pen pushers—be they "left"
or "right" or "progressive" or "reactionary"—with their eternal bickering and sham nonconformity suited the authorities down to the
ground, even in any combinations that might be required by the
party (26 June 1986*, Pb):

GORBACHEV. Let us hear information from comrade A.N.
Yakovlev on the progress of work at the Congress of writers of
the USSR.

YAKOVLEV. All in all, the congress is proceeding in compliance
with party decisions, but with some contentions. Harsh char-
acterizations are being given in some of the working groups. At
times this goes to extremes. The poet [Stanislav] Kunayev had a
physical fight with one writer. The question of periodic changes
in members of the board of the Union of Writers is being raised
in debates. It is proposed that they be elected for a maximum
of two terms. The current leaders of the Union of Writers are
being described as "children of their time" who should retire
along with that time. The audience greets such declarations
with enthusiastic applause.

The leadership of the Union of Writers is being criticized for
opacity, lack of democracy and bureaucratism. ...

[...]

... [Georgy] Markov is presently in the hospital. Maybe this version warrants consideration: Markov—chairman of the board,
[Yuri] Bondarev—first secretary. But at the same time a working bureau could be created in the composition of comrades
[Dmitri] Bykov, [Sergei] Zalygin, [Vladimir] Rasputin, [Chingiz]
Aitmatov and several other writers. It would not be advisable
to discount comrades Yevtushenko, Voznesensky and [Robert]
Rozhdestvensky. It should also be borne in mind that the overall mood is such that the old composition of the leadership may
be blackballed.

GORBACHEV. I do not think that we should focus on one person, there is no need to fight over drawing a line for nominating candidates for its leadership.

YAKOVLEV. If ten additional candidates' names go on the ballot paper, the old leadership may be blackballed. In that case, it would be possible to have a reserve version: chairman of the board—comrade Zalygin, and first secretary—comrade Karpov. But even in this case, it would be feasible to create a working bureau.

[Andrei] GROMYKO. Which version are the writers favoring?

YAKOVLEV. As for the first version, the election of comrade Markov as chairman, it must be borne in mind that he has been in the leadership of the Union of Writers for a long time, and this may come under criticism.

GORBACHEV. Of course, comrade Markov's election would be the best option. How is Bondarev's candidacy regarded?

GROMYKO. He is a prominent writer.

[Mikhail] SOLOMENTSEV. He sticks to the right line.

[Vitaly] VOROTNIKOV. Comrade Bykov could be included in the composition, and several others.

MEDVEDEV. Will comrade Bondarev be blackballed?

YAKOVLEV. He shouldn't be.

GORBACHEV. Maybe if comrade Markov is not elected, comrade Zalygin would be a suitable choice. But he's old and rather frail. It looks like we should steer in the direction of comrade Bondarev.

[Mikhail] ZIMYANIN. And what should be done about the secretariat of the board of the Union of Writers?

GORBACHEV. Let it stay.

YAKOVLEV. If we are setting our sights on comrade Bondarev as first secretary, we should discuss it with comrade Markov.

GORBACHEV. Everything should be discussed with comrade Markov. He should receive his due. And even if he is not elected, he deserves to be treated well.

YAKOVLEV. Is it necessary to talk to comrade Bondarev?

LIGACHEV. After his election to the board of the Union of Writers.

GORBACHEV. Agreed. In any case, the choice will be from those who are elected to the board. Philipp Denisovich, what do you think?

BOBKOV (deputy chairman of the Committee for State Security of the USSR). If information gets out about our attitude toward Bondarev, he may not be elected. So this is something that should not be voiced prematurely. As for comrade Bondarev, he is a good candidate.

[...]

GORBACHEV. Yes, there is no need to put comrade Bondarev into a tight spot.

LIGACHEV. Generally speaking, a change of the leadership of the Union of Writers is very timely.

GROMYKO. We should not take the change of leadership in the Union of Writers hard. The main thing is that it should be creative and authoritative. After all, there was a time when the Union of Writers did not exist, but there were still always authorities in literature.

GORBACHEV. Of course, the general mood toward a change of leadership should be taken into account. There is no need to dramatize the situation. Egor Kuzmich is quite right, the question is timely. Let us decide firstly to orient toward comrade Markov being elected chairman, and comrade Bondarev secretary. For this, we need to exercise our influence. There are sure to be meetings of party groups at the congress?

YAKOVLEV. Yes.

GORBACHEV. Let us proceed on that assumption, and let comrade Yakovlev get back to the Congress.

As a result, comrade Markov became chairman, and the backup candidate—reserve colonel and patriot comrade Vladimir Karpov, who had the reputation of being a great liberal—became secretary. But how much rejoicing followed—in the East and in the West— regarding these revolutionary changes! This marked the start of a new era—their glasnost.

• • •

Beyond doubt, glasnost and perestroika were a diabolical invention. It was not bought by just the Soviet intelligentsia, which was always up for grabs; the whole world bought it. And how could one not buy a young, energetic General Secretary, though he had not even started talking about reforms, after a procession of dull, unsmiling Kremlin oldsters, their endless funeral processions, and moreover, after the tensions that had resurfaced as the Cold War at the beginning of the 1980s, with its arms race, peace movements, and crises. Who would not wish that all this were in the past? And no matter how much you try to explain to people that the Soviet system is not a monarchy, and the General Secretary is not the tsar, who at that time did not wish the best of luck to the new reformist tsar? Out of hundreds of thousands of politicians, journalists and academics, only a tiny handful retained sufficient sobriety not to yield to temptation, and it was an even tinier one that had the courage to voice their doubts aloud.

But did anyone want to listen to them?

Meanwhile, it was enough to just look at Gorbachev, hear his incorrect, stilted, and senseless speech, the endless drivel of a small-time party functionary—he benefited greatly from translation—to shed any illusions and pipe dreams once and for all. It was enough to have even a cursory knowledge of the Soviet system to harbor no illusions from the start; it was impossible for a liberal reformer to climb to the top of the party ladder. Such miracles do not occur.

But everyone yearned for a miracle!

Skeptics were attacked viciously, like enemies, like destroyers of future humanity: Keep quiet! Don't scare him off. . . .

It was as if we had all suddenly become accomplices in a huge global conspiracy, and mentioning it aloud meant betraying the conspirators, waking the dreaming foe. *Shhhh. . . quiet. He might wake up. . . .*

This was just how the Soviet press (and the Soviet intelligentsia) assessed our "Letter of the Ten": as a "denunciation of our own people" (*Pravda*), as "an attempt to kill perestroika" (*Moskovskiye novosti*). This begs the question: What is this perestroika that it can be killed unexpectedly with one word of doubt? A denunciation of whom? Where has this unseen foe concealed itself? In the East? In the West? Whom were we to fool by a love for our country? Certainly not the Politburo—it was a child of their own making.

It was the genius of this invention that no logical arguments had any effect on people. It was a kind of mass psychosis similar to the irenic hysteria of the early 1980s, and what's more, one inspired by the same Kremlin manipulators. Certainly not by Gorbachev himself, that provincial apparatchik, capable only of petty crookery at best. Brilliant director Yuri Lyubimov, with his professionally sharp eye for typical characters, noted the amazing likeness of the new General Secretary to the epitome of a classical Russian swindler:

"But he's a typical Chichikov—a gentleman pleasing in all respects! And truly, just for fun, take a look at Gogol's description of his immortal hero: 'The gentleman in the chaise was not particularly handsome, but of a pleasing appearance, not too stout, but not too thin, not really old, but not too young.'"

It was this all-around pleasantness that marked Gorbachev as a suitable candidate for carrying out the grandiose "operative-*chekist* undertaking," planned and developed by that master of such things, Andropov, toward the end of Brezhnev's reign. Not for nothing did the *chekist*s confide in specially trusted members of the "liberal" intelligentsia of the time: *Wait, don't be in a rush. We'll finish off*

*the dissidents, Brezhnev will die, and the time of great changes will
start.*

Gorbachev himself admitted this toward the end, when the process had spun out of control and many began to blame him for the
poorly planned nature of the reforms. *What do you mean, poorly
planned?!* he fumed. The planning was thorough: long before 1985,
110 studies were submitted to the CC by various brain trusts. "They
all relate to the period when the April Plenum was far in the future," said Gorbachev, speaking to a group of so-called activists in
the fields of culture and science in January 1989. (The text was
printed a year later for all to read on the front page of *Literaturnaya
gazeta,* 11 January 1989.)

And really, could the secretary of an obscure regional committee,
who made it into the CC only in 1978 and was charged merely with
the duty of curator of agriculture, devise such a devilish plan so
ably aimed at the psychology of the Western establishment? He
had never visited the West until 1984—before the time when the
Party apparatchiks started grooming him actively for the part of
General Secretary. No, the hand of the master of disinformation
was clear to see, his fifteen-year experience as the head of the KGB
and his belief that conspiracy was the moving force of history. Who
else could have thought up the staging of the Moscow hybrid of
the "Prague Spring" and Lenin's New Economic Policy? Who else
could have created the appearance of political pluralism through
the means of the KGB?

That very word, *perestroika,* was also a masterstroke of propaganda. What does it really mean? Whole libraries of books and
studies were written on this subject in the West, and the whole
world, like a flock of parrots, dutifully intoned, *pe-res-troika!*

Yet it would seem plain: constructing perestroika was the same
as turning a garment. It did not promise anything new; just the
same material turned to show a still-clean lining. The same socialism, but with a new facade. So they "rebuilt" the concentration
camp of socialism into a huge Potemkin village. To be sure, such
an operation could not be devised by a specialist on agriculture;
Potemkin villages yield no harvests.

Now, when the edifice of this measure came crashing down, it
emerged just how these fictional parties, KGB-inspired national
fronts and various ultranationalistic bogeymen such as the neo-
Nazi group Pamyat were created. A.N. Yakovlev admitted recently
that even Zhirinovsky was a creature of the KGB, approved by the
CC in 1989. But the greatest chef d'oeuvre had to be the legend
of the struggle within the Politburo between the reformers and the
conservatives, thanks to which the entire world saved Gorbachev

for a whole seven years! And how he was saved! In loans and credits alone, Gorbachev milked the West—that is, Western taxpayers—to the tune of $45 billion. To say nothing of the Nobel Peace Prize, which he managed to get for himself. And now the question arises—where did all that money go? God alone knows in which Swiss banks it settled.

Recalling that time, I cannot rid myself of a feeling of physical nausea. The world was prepared to forgive everything: the Moscow-provoked Nagorno-Karabakh conflict, the April 1989 slaughter in Tbilisi, and even the provocations of Soviet special forces in the Baltics in January 1991, although anyone could watch the latter two on television screens. As though nobody even dimly aware of the Soviet system could not see that not a single one of these events could have occurred without the approval of the General Secretary. But anything to hang on to the golden dream of perestroika, anything to prevent the "conservatives" from devouring the "reformers" in the Politburo! Thousands of people died, but the world was concerned solely with the dread that this might hurt Gorbachev.

It is astounding that a man who had concentrated more power in his hands than Stalin and Mao Zedong together was seen as a victim, a driven opponent. Does history have another such example? The subject was practically inexhaustible: his could be "a struggle for succession" or "a struggle for power"; one lot of names or another of "enemies of perestroika" would be dutifully spread abroad by hundreds of thousands of journalists, observers and "experts." Whether they knew or not that they served the channels of disinformation, this shall remain a heavy sin on their conscience. Even now, when all has become clear, not one of them has recanted. On the contrary, they are now at the top of the pyramid; consider Strobe Talbott, who elevated Gorbachev to "man of the decade" in *Time* magazine and is currently the main architect of Clinton's relations with the East.

Where is that so-called struggle? I look at the minutes of the Politburo meeting on 11 March 1985, at which Gorbachev was elected General Secretary (11 March 1985, Pb). Elected, you should note, *unanimously*. This is a lengthy and boring document, full of panegyrics uttered by all those present in turn. For that reason I shall not quote it in full, but cite only the words of those who were frequently pointed out as Gorbachev's competitors for the post, enemies of his policies, "conservatives" and "reactionaries": Grishin, Romanov, Chebrikov, Demichev, and Ligachev.

[Viktor] GRISHIN. We have to reach an extremely important decision today. The issue is the continuation of the party line, the succession of the leadership. The General Secretary of the CC is the person organizing the work of the Central Committee. So this post should go to the one who satisfies the highest demands. He should have knowledge, a principled position and relevant experience and, moreover, a great degree of tolerance. Last night, when we heard about the death of Konstantin Ustinovich, we had predetermined this question to some extent in agreeing to confirm Mikhail Sergeyevich as the chairman of the funeral committee. In my opinion, he has all the qualities required for the post of General Secretary of the CC. He is a man of great erudition. He graduated from the law faculty of Moscow State University and the economics faculty of an agricultural institute. He has extensive experience of party work. So I believe that there is not and cannot be a better option than to nominate him for election to the post of General Secretary of the CC of the CPSU. As for us, we shall all actively support him in our respective posts.

ROMANOV. Mikhail Sergeyevich has a wealth of life experience behind him. He started from the bottom in the Komsomol and progressed to party organizations. This where he displayed his abilities as a mass organizer. I can say on the basis of my previous work that the party active has a high opinion of M.S. Gorbachev's activity. He is an erudite man, he was able to sort out numerous highly complex matters of scientific and technical progress. Not only did he sort them out, he began to seek solutions to many other problems connected with the implementation of the achievements of science and technology in industry. Nikolai Alekseyevich Tikhonov has spoken of Mikhail Sergeyevich Gorbachev's work in the Commission charged with improving the agricultural mechanism. The tone of this commission is set by comrade Tikhonov, and Mikhail Sergeyevich, leaning on the sectors of the CC, tactfully introduces his suggestions, most of which are approved by the commission.

Mikhail Sergeyevich is very demanding in his work. But this trait combines actively with genuine assistance to people, with confidence placed in him. Therefore I am convinced that he shall ensure fully the succession of the leadership of our party and will cope with those obligations that shall be entrusted to him.

CHEBRIKOV. Andrei Andreyevich Gromyko has set the tone of today's discussion. He said rightly that we must look to the future. The ability to look forward is probably the most important issue at present. I was also impressed by A.A. Gromyko's observation concerning the need to preserve and reinforce the unity of the Politburo, the Central Committee, our entire party. In today's consideration of the General Secretary of the CC CPSU, we must define clearly the man capable of fulfilling this difficult task. I am certain that Mikhail Sergeyevich Gorbachev will handle this task honorably. These qualities in Mikhail Sergeyevich Gorbachev were highly rated by L.I. Brezhnev, Yu.V. Andropov and K.U. Chernenko.

The leader of our party must possess a sound theoretical and practical basis. One could cite a number of M.S. Gorbachev's articles and addresses. I shall only refer to his recent address at the All-Union Scientific-Applied Conference. I am sure that we all noted what a courageous and strong address this was.

Mikhail Sergeyevich is a very contactable person. He is able to listen to the opinions of others and treat problems raised with understanding. And there are numerous problems in our country. Their solution requires a man who has a good grasp of these problems, a man possessed of great capacity to work and erudition. M.S. Gorbachev has both these qualities in abundance.

On my way to the plenum today, I consulted my work comrades. Our department is such that it must have a good knowledge of not just problems of external policy, but also issues of an internal, sociological nature. So allowing for all the abovementioned circumstances, the *chekists* instructed me to nominate M.S. Gorbachev to the post of General Secretary of the CC CPSU. You know that the voice of the *chekists*, the voice of our body, is the voice of the people. As for us, we shall do our utmost to work at the top level of the tasks faced by the Committee for State Security. The united *chekist* collective shall do all it can to work even more effectively under the Politburo of the CC CPSU headed by the General Secretary of the CC CPSU, M.S. Gorbachev.

[Pyotr] DEMICHEV. I will be very brief. I am certain that we are making the right choice. Mikhail Sergeyevich Gorbachev is well known in our country. He is also quite well known abroad. The fact that he is able to work abroad has been demonstrated amply by his trips to England, Canada and the People's Republic of Bulgaria.

GROMYKO. Italy as well.

DEMICHEV. Mikhail Sergeyevich Gorbachev has a feeling for the novel, broad erudition and organizational talent. He is a charming person. It is no secret that after Yu.V. Andropov's death, he undertook dealing with all the questions relating to the work of the Central Committee, but especially in the field of our agricultural and industrial complex. It is no exaggeration to say that he attracted our scientists, the creative intelligentsia and writers. He is very worthy of occupying this high post.

LIGACHEV. First of all, I would like to note the very important introduction made by A.A. Gromyko. Undoubtedly, Mikhail

Sergeyevich Gorbachev has all the attributes of an outstanding
political personality. Furthermore, he is endowed with an excellent reserve of intellectual and physical stamina. It should
also be noted that M.S. Gorbachev is always keen to work and
aims to organize matters to the best advantage in small and
large problems. As you know, this is extremely significant with
regard to all party organizational work, the improvement of its
style and methods. That work embraces the cadre's policy, the
activity of the Soviets, trade unions, the Komsomol, so familiar
to Mikhail Sergeyevich Gorbachev, who enjoys the great respect
of party, trade union and Komsomol organizations, the active
functionaries of our party and the nation as a whole. I have
heard this today from many secretaries of regional and district
party organizations. The nomination of M.S. Gorbachev shall
make our people proud and augment the authority of the Politburo of the CC CPSU.

And so spoke all the present members of the Politburo, secretaries of the CC (with the absence of Vladimir Shcherbitsky, who
was on a visit to the USA and thus unable to attend). So where is
the struggle for succession? Not a hint of it, not a shade of doubt.
What was the origin of the rumors (and even assertions) that Gorbachev was elected with a bare minimum of votes? Maybe the idea
of perestroika struck them without warning? Maybe it precipitated
the subsequent struggle for power? On the contrary, they were perfectly informed of the plan the new General Secretary was to carry
out; therefore they stress the energy, the innovativeness of their
candidate, the problems facing the country. The issue of succession appears to have been settled well in advance, possibly under
Andropov, and the proceedings of 11 March were a mere formality.

Moreover, having studied dozens of Minutes of meetings of Gorbachev's Politburo, I found no mention at all of any "struggle." Of
course there were differences of opinion, doubts and even arguments regarding specific problems, just as there were in Brezhnev's
time. In fact, they were fewer and less acute than those Andropov
had with ideologues. If there were any "conservatives" among them,
Gorbachev was the real conservative, as he always adopted a cautious approach. But unpleasant problems were charged quite consciously to those who were labeled conservatives, while the pleasant
ones were allotted to the "reformers." There are numerous examples
of this, some of them quite amusing (20 March 1986*, Pb):

GORBACHEV. I have deferred one matter. It was raised on my
assignment by comrade [Vladimir] Dolgikh. Here is his memo
[reads]. This is on the question of returning its former name

"Arktika" [Arctic] to the icebreaker "L. Brezhnev." The new ice-breaker can be called "L. Brezhnev."

[Lev] ZAIKOV. They already have the nameplate "L. Brezhnev" installed.

[Heydar] ALIYEV. Launch "L. Brezhnev" without publicizing it.

[Nikolai] RYZHKOV. This should be done in one day, without any televising.

GORBACHEV. Let us instruct comrades Ligachev and Zaikov to think the matter over and report their proposals.

There is another question. [Reads letter from Alliluyeva.] Of course, there was much haste in making a decision on her arrival. The first desire was, to let her come, but maybe without undue speed. It should be discussed.

CHEBRIKOV. The first letters were good, expressing gratitude. But here she fails to address fifty percent of the problems raised. She was taken to hospital yesterday with a heart attack.

GORBACHEV. We need to hear her daughter's opinion and have a high-level meeting. It may fall to me to make determinations concerning Stalin, Stalingrad, and so forth. I'm from a family like that myself. My uncle's health was destroyed. My mother had to raise five children in extreme poverty. I received a medal for my essay on "Stalin is our military glory, Stalin is the flight of our youth!"[137] So may it be advisable to assign such a meeting to comrade M.S. Solomentsev?

GROMYKO. Or possibly comrade Y.K. Ligachev?

GORBACHEV. Let us assign this to comrade Ligachev.

It emerges that Gorbachev was himself unable to determine just what kind of a family he came from—the one that suffered, or the one that remained eternally in the realm of "the flight of youth."?

In fact, little is really amusing in this business. Their games cost us all a high price.

3.13 Live souls

It stands to reason that in such a massive imitation of democracy, the first question the authorities had to tackle was whether to keep the initiative or allow the real opposition to consolidate. The example of the Polish trade union Solidarność (Solidarity) would have been a grim reminder always at the back of their minds. That is why, before establishing their fronts, it was necessary for them to

---

[137]"Tempered in battle and labor / on the expanses of our wonderful Motherland / we wrote a joyful song / about our great Friend and Leader." (1938).

finish off, once and for all, the opposition groups that had formed over twenty years of struggle against the regime. First and foremost, they had to break the stubborn *zeks*, destroy their moral authority, force them into ideological disarmament. At the same time, it was impossible to count on success in the West while the problem of political prisoners remained unresolved; it was far too obvious.

This was a problem to which the future winner of the Nobel Peace Prize turned his hand immediately after coming to power. On the surface, 1985 was not distinguished by any high degree of mercy; on the contrary, arrests and persecutions increased. This is understandable: the first task was to "cleanse" the country of all potential opposition. In the personal report of KGB head Chebrikov to Gorbachev regarding work carried out by his department for 1985, Chebrikov noted the following, among other things (19 February 1986*, 321/Ch-ov; italicized figures are entered by hand):

> Over the reporting period, agencies of state security have intensified the struggle against ideological saboteurs of the class enemy. . . .
>
> [. . .]
>
> The actions of several hundred emissaries and functionaries of foreign anti-Soviet nationalist, Zionist and clerical organizations have been prevented and suppressed in Moscow, Leningrad and the capitals of other Union republics. Of these, 300 were deported and 332 refused entry into the USSR. . . .
>
> Twenty-five illegal nationalist groups were uncovered and liquidated in Ukraine, the Baltic republics and some other places at the stage of inception. Attempts to create a number of illegal groups by pro-Zionist elements were averted successfully. Twenty-eight of the more active inciters of hostile activities were brought to book on criminal charges. Timely measures prevented the formation of ninety-three youth groups based on ideologically harmful leanings.
>
> Eleven leaders of illegal religious sects were brought to book on charges of hostile activity and other actions, the illegal activities of many other religious extremists were averted, and several printing shops, transit depots and stores of literature were liquidated. The measures taken put an end to activities on the territory of Central Asian and north Caucasian republics of around 170 underground "schools" teaching children religion, and a number of sectarian communities were advised to seek registration.
>
> 1,275 authors and distributors of anonymous, anti-Soviet and slanderous materials were uncovered, 93 of whom have been brought to book on criminal charges. . . .

KGB bodies have played an active role in party and state activity in educating the Soviet people toward high political awareness and respect for legislation and the law, and have conducted comprehensive work on preventing criminal, antistate actions, politically harmful processes and manifestations. Preventive and prophylactic measures have been applied to *15,271* persons.

Humane treatment of erring Soviet citizens was combined with firm and decisive prevention of criminal actions by hostile elements. The following were charged with criminal liability: for particularly dangerous state crimes—*57*, other state crimes—*417*, other crimes—*61*. Investigation of cases was conducted in strict compliance with criminal procedure norms, under the supervision of bodies of the Procuracy.

At the same time, pressure was stepped up on prisoners for the purpose of forcing them to repent, to recant their convictions. This pressure continued to increase in 1985 and 1986, reaching its apogee in 1986. Gorbachev was clearly in a hurry; the problem had to be solved urgently with the inception of glasnost (25 September 1986*, Pb):

CHEBRIKOV. According to our legislation, these crimes are particularly dangerous state crimes. A total of 240 persons were charged with criminal liability and sentenced for such crimes. These are people charged with espionage, violation of state borders, distribution of hostile leaflets, machinations with foreign currency and suchlike. Many of them have declared their refusal to participate in further hostile activity. They base these refusals on the political changes following the April Plenum of the CC CPSU and the XXVII Party Congress.

It appears possible to release at first one-third, and then half of these persons from penal confinement. In that case, only those who continue to maintain positions hostile to our government shall remain imprisoned.

GORBACHEV. It is possible to support this proposal.

CHEBRIKOV. We shall do this prudently. In order to be certain that the indicated persons do not continue to engage in hostile activity, they shall be kept under surveillance.

SHCHERBITSKY. What is the reason that comparatively few persons charged with committing particularly dangerous state crimes face criminal liability? Is it perestroika?

CHEBRIKOV. It is explained by the emphasis placed on prophylactic measures by KGB bodies. Many people are, if one can say so, on the brink of committing a punishable crime. In order to influence them, all KGB and social resources are invoked.

GROMYKO. Which crimes are the most dangerous, and what punishment do they envisage?

CHEBRIKOV. Espionage. This is punishable by execution by firing squad, or 15 years' imprisonment. [Lev] Polischuk was shot for espionage. [Adolf] Tolkachev was executed yesterday.

GORBACHEV. American intelligence paid him well. He was found to have 2 million rubles.

CHEBRIKOV. That agent supplied our enemies with very important military technical secrets.

GORBACHEV. Let us agree that the proposals made by comrade Chebrikov are approved in principle. Let the KGB submit proposals in the established procedure.

POLITBURO MEMBERS. Agreed.

Note how craftily foreign currency dealers, spies, and political opponents are lumped together. As if they did not know the difference between them. The supposition is ludicrous. Who refused to "continue to engage in hostile activity" due to the political changes introduced by the April Plenum? Hardly the foreign currency dealers and spies. But it was probably easier this way—not to call things by their real names.

Thus, toward the end of the year, "proposals" were submitted "in the established procedure." Chebrikov, Alexander Rekunkov, Vladimir Terebilov and Boris Kravtsov reported the following to the leadership in December 1986 (26 December 1986*, 2521-Ch; italicized figures are entered by hand):

In recent years... it was possible to paralyze the illegal activity of the organizers, inciters and active participants of illegal groups: the "Helsinki Groups," the "Free Inter-Industrial Workers' Association," the Russian chapter of "Amnesty International," the "Fund for Aid to Political Prisoners" and others, whom the opponent regarded as "forces capable of leading to a change of the state and social system of the USSR." In the period 1982–1986, more than *100* persons renounced further participation in illegal activity and entered the path to reform. Some of them... appeared on television and in the newspapers with public declarations, exposing the Western special services and their former fellow thinkers.

In 1986, the Presidium of the Supreme Soviet of the USSR and the Presidium of the Supreme Soviets of Union republics acted on submissions made by KGB bodies and the Procuracy, and sanctioned the release of *24* persons from further incarceration. The sentences of *4* persons were commuted to internal exile. The majority of them accepted the justice of their sentences to imprisonment, with the exception of [Irina] Ratushinskaya who, having arrived in the West on personal matters, continues to make hostile public declarations.

At present, *301* persons imprisoned under the indicated articles are serving their sentences, and *23* are under investigation.

Available data indicate that social changes in our country pursuant to the April (1989) Plenum of the CC CPSU and the XXVII Party Congress have influenced the thinking and behavior of some of those who had previously succumbed to bourgeois propaganda and hostile elements, committed crimes and borne punishment. Some have come to realize the harm they caused to social interests, others are maintaining a wait-and-see attitude. Some have not altered their anti-Soviet views.

In the current conditions of democratization at all levels of social life, the growing unity of the party and the people, it appears possible to consider the question of release from imprisonment and exile as a measure of clemency for some of those sentenced, and also relief from criminal liability for persons under investigation for committing the crimes mentioned above.

Persons from the indicated category may be offered the chance to petition the Presidium of the Supreme Court of the USSR regarding the refusal of future participation in hostile or other illegal activity. Upon receipt of petitions, release simultaneously such persons from serving their sentences or criminal prosecution upon submissions from the Procuracy of the USSR, the Supreme Court of the USSR, the Ministry of Justice of the USSR, the Ministry of Internal Affairs of the USSR and the KGB of the USSR in the clemency procedure of the Presidium of the Supreme Soviet of the USSR. ... Particularly dangerous recidivists, and also persons continuing to adhere to hostile positions and refusing to give written assurances of cessation of antisocial activity, are not subject to release.

These measures would enable those who have refused to participate in further antisocial activity to resume their place in society, and on the other hand expose those who had previously hidden their anti-Soviet aims under the guise of struggle for "democratization" and "human rights."

A positive decision on this matter shall yield political gain and stress the humane stance of the Soviet authorities yet again. In implementing the indicated measures, we may encounter recidivist antisocial activity, but in our opinion this would not lead to serious negative consequences.

This is how Gorbachev's "democratization" began—by twisting the arms of political prisoners to the accompaniment of laudatory Western dithyrambs. Admittedly, it is hard for an uninformed public to understand what all this meant: three months in an unheated "cooler" in midwinter, fourteen ounces of bread a day, hot food every second day, and several times a week a KGB officer with the invariable question: *Well, have you come to your senses about the April Plenum of the CC?*

And that was not all by far; relatives came under pressure, a new term was threatened. There were cases of beatings. The *chekist* imagination was unlimited—some people would be changed into civilian clothes and taken home, just to show them how good it was to be free. And at the end, the same question: *Well, are you ready to write a petition?*

This vicious game infuriated Anatoly Marchenko so much that he declared an unlimited hunger strike, demanded the unconditional release of all political prisoners, maintained this hunger strike for more than three months, and died (4 February 1987*, 206-B). Yet even this extreme form of protest did not sober up the West. Unprecedented, shameless times were upon us.

However, Marchenko's death did alarm the Politburo: murder was not part of their plans. There was also an effect on the West, such as it was. The process of releases had to be stepped up; pressure was decreased, demands lowered. Releases were granted upon any petition, even without an undertaking "to abstain from antisocial activity," the main concern being that clemency was requested. Chebrikov and Procurator General Rekunkov stated the following in a personal report to Gorbachev in February 1987 (1 February 1987*, 183-Ch):

> On 15 January 1987, 288 persons were serving sentences under articles 70 and 190 of the Criminal Code of the RSFSR and corresponding articles in the criminal codes of the Union republics. Of these, 114 persons were sentenced to corrective labor camps for anti-Soviet agitation and propaganda (article 70), 119 persons were sentenced for dissemination of deliberately false concoctions, slandering the Soviet state and social system (article 190), and 55 persons in internal exile were sentenced under the indicated articles.
>
> In executing the resolution of the CC CPSU N47/54 OΠ dated 31 December 1986, the Procuracy and the Committee for State Security of the USSR organized the required work among this category of persons.
>
> As a result, 51 persons gave written assurance of abstaining from illegal activity in the future. The Presidium of the Supreme Soviet of the USSR approved their release as an act of clemency.
>
> Another 13 applications for review have been received. Work is continuing with other prisoners and will be concluded in Febru-

ary.

Furthermore, the cases of 4 persons being investigated under article 70 have been dismissed. The cases of 17 persons being investigated under article 190 have also been dismissed.

In corrective labor institutions and exile there are 25 particularly dangerous recidivists, sentenced under the abovementioned articles, none of whom are eligible for release from punishment in accordance with the established order.

It appears feasible to conduct corrective work with them on a strictly individual basis. Those who have entered the path of reform, condemned their past activity and undertaken to desist from such in future can be presented for clemency on general grounds. ...

With regard to those who are serving sentences under article 142 of the Criminal Code of the RSFSR and corresponding articles in the criminal codes of union republics (breach of laws concerning the separation of the Church from the state and the school from the Church)—10 persons, who organized illegal underground printing shops, incited antisocial acts among religious believers and conducted illegal religious instruction of children—it would seem feasible, in the present case, to present materials concerning clemency on general grounds on the condition of their undertaking to abstain from such illegal activity in the future.

A separate category is comprised of persons (96) who committed crimes envisaged by the abovementioned articles of the criminal code in a state of criminal incapacity and were directed by the courts for mandatory medical treatment. In accordance with the established procedure regarding medical reviews twice every year, those who no longer pose any danger to the community are transferred to general psychiatric hospitals or released into the custody of their relatives. At present, among other things, a number of persons ([Vladimir] Gershuni, [Vasily] Pervushin, [Vladimir] Klebanov and others) have been released from mandatory treatment pursuant to medical assessment.

Reports like this, reminiscent of body counts from a battlefield, continued to land on Gorbachev's desk practically every month until the middle of 1987. The last I was able to look at was dated 11 May—among others, it contains the following figures:[138]

Pursuant to the decision of the relevant agencies, 108 persons sentenced for anti-Soviet agitation and propaganda were released on the basis of individual clemency petitions in March–

---

[138] 11 May 1987 (6/2140)^.

April, as well as 64 persons sentenced for crimes envisaged under article 190 of the Criminal Code of the RSFSR and corresponding articles in the criminal codes of other union republics.

On 1.05.1987, 98 persons from this category of prisoners (78 in penal institutions and 20 in exile) continued to serve their sentences, including 24 recidivists and 74 who have so far refused to promise to desist from criminal activity in the future.

Toward the end, the outcome we had feared most came to pass: those who were released (even with no promises) were prisoners who had support in the West. They were the ones driven abroad and usually stripped of citizenship. But this provoked no interest or indignation. On the contrary, everyone was delighted by Gorbachev's liberality, his endless struggle against the "conservatives." That is how it will go down in history, that Gorbachev the reformer freed political prisoners. Not all of them at once, gradually, because he had to overcome the endless "resistance of the conservatives" in the Politburo, but he managed it.

In fact, the last political prisoners were freed by Yeltsin in February 1992.

• • •

Of course Gorbachev could not fool a willing West indefinitely without resolving the question of Andrei Sakharov, who was still in internal exile. This was another problem he tackled soon after coming to power, long before any proclamation of his glasnost (29 August 1985*, Pb):

GORBACHEV. At the end of July this year, I received a letter from the notorious Sakharov. He requests permission for his wife [Yelena] Bonner to go abroad for medical treatment and to visit relatives.

CHEBRIKOV. This is an old story. It has been dragging on for 20 years. Different situations have arisen in that time. The relevant measures were employed, both in relation to Sakharov and to Bonner. But throughout all this time, no actions were taken that would breach the law. This is a very important point, and needs to be stressed.

At the moment, Sakharov is 65 years old, Bonner is 63. Sakharov's health is not very good. He is currently undergoing an oncological examination, as he has lost a lot of weight.

With regard to Sakharov, he has lost his standing as a political figure and has not said anything new lately. Possibly Bonner should be allowed to go abroad for 3 months. Under our legislation it is permissible to suspend exile (and Bonner, as is known, is in exile). Of course, once in the West she might make some kind of declaration, receive some award or other, and so on. It is quite possible that she might travel to the USA from Italy, where she intends to receive treatment. Allowing Bonner to go abroad would look like a humane act.

There are two possible versions for her further behavior. The first is her return to Gorky. The second, she remains abroad and begins to raise the issue of reunification of families — in other words, that Sakharov should be given an exit visa. In this event, there could be appeals from state leaders of various Western countries and certain representatives of communist parties. But we cannot allow Sakharov to go abroad. The Ministry of Medium Machine Building [i.e. the nuclear industry] is against this, because Sakharov has detailed knowledge of the development of our nuclear arms.

Specialists agree that if Sakharov is given a laboratory, he could continue working in the field of military research. Sakharov's behavior is under Bonner's influence.

GORBACHEV. That's Zionism for you.

CHEBRIKOV. He is 100 percent under Bonner's influence. We are counting on the possibility that his behavior may change. He has two daughters and one son from his first marriage. They bear themselves well, and may exercise a certain influence on their father.

GORBACHEV. Is it possible for Sakharov to state in his letter that he understands that he cannot travel abroad? Can we get a statement like that from him?

CHEBRIKOV. I would say that this is a matter we need to decide now. If we make a decision on the eve of, or immediately after your meetings with Mitterand and Reagan, it will be interpreted as a concession on our part, which would be undesirable.

GORBACHEV. Yes, we must decide now.

ZIMYANIN. There is no doubt that Bonner will be used against us in the West. But a rebuttal of her efforts to gain reunification with family can be made by our scientists in relevant declarations. Comrade [Efim] Slavsky (Minister of Medium Machine Building) is right — we cannot allow Sakharov to go abroad. There is no cause to expect decency from Bonner. She's a beast in a skirt, an imperialist stooge.

GORBACHEV. Where shall we suffer the greater damages — allowing Bonner to go abroad, or refusing to do so?

[Eduard] SHEVARDNADZE. Naturally, there are serious reservations about allowing Bonner to go abroad. But we still stand to gain politically. The decision must be made now.

DOLGIKH. Can Sakharov be influenced?

RYZHKOV. I am for letting her go abroad. It is a humane act. If she remains there, it will cause a lot of noise. But we will also gain the opportunity of influencing Sakharov. He's now running away to hospital in order to feel freer.

SOKOLOV (Minister of Defense of the USSR). I think we should proceed with this action, it will not make anything any worse for us.

KUZNETSOV. It is a difficult question. If we do not allow Bonner to travel for treatment, it could be used in propaganda against us.

ALIYEV. It is hard to give an unambiguous answer to this question. At present, Bonner is under control. Her anger has increased over the years. She will let it all out once she is in the West. Bourgeois propaganda will have a specific person for the conduct of all sorts of press conferences and other anti-Soviet actions. The matter will become more complicated if Sakharov raises the question of traveling to see his wife. So there is an element of risk. But we will have to take that risk.

[...] [Ivan] KAPITONOV. If we let Bonner out now, the story will drag on and on. She will have an excuse for demanding family reunification.

GORBACHEV. Maybe this is what we should do: confirm receipt of the letter, say that it has been taken under consideration and that the relevant orders have been issued. We should let it be understood that we might grant her permission to leave, but everything will depend on what she will do abroad. It would be feasible to limit the matter to that for the moment.

The result was, as is known, that Sakharov promised not to request permission to go abroad, and Bonner promised to make no political statements, and the trip went without incident.

This is just one episode in the game played by the Politburo around Sakharov. Throughout 1985 and 1986 Gorbachev kept a vigilant eye on everything that concerned the exiled scientist: he personally received all the KGB-tapped telephone conversations and pieces of the *Recollections* stolen by the KGB that Sakharov tried to write at that time (31 December 1985, 1776-B). In June 1986 the Politburo returned to the question of Sakharov in connection with his letter to Gorbachev, criticizing the entire practice of political persecution. Explaining this issue, Chebrikov reports the following, among other things (7 June 1986, 1163-Ch):

It should be noted that the number of persons charged with criminal liability for the indicated crimes is negligible, and is tending to decrease. At present, 172 persons are serving time in corrective labor camps and exile for anti-Soviet agitation and propaganda, 179 persons for dissemination of deliberately false concoctions slandering the Soviet state and social system, and 4 persons for breaching legislation on the separation of the Church from the state, and the Church from the school. The 12 persons mentioned by Sakharov in his letter ([Anatoly] Marchenko, [Alexey] Osipov, [Ivan] Kovalev, [Viktor] Nekipelov, [Yuri] Shikhanovich and others) were sentenced for committing concrete criminal acts, that come under the norms of criminal legislation, and in strict compliance with the law. ... Certain persons among those serving sentences, including Kovalev, Osipov and Shikhanovich, mentioned by Sakharov, have denounced their actions pursuant to systematic educational work, and have declared their repentance and refusal to take part in any future illegal activity. ...

The questions raised by Sakharov appear to be misunderstandings, which are fostered by the constant negative influence of his wife, Bonner.

Allowing for the above, we deem it inadvisable to send Sakharov a response. A responsible representative of the Procuracy could be directed to conduct a substantial talk with him, and give reasoned replies to the questions raised in the letter.

The problem of Sakharov and the problem of political prisoners were inextricably bound: it was impossible to resolve one without the other, and the resolution of one would automatically assume resolution of the other. So the basic principle of the decision—to release only the "ideologically disarmed"—was also retained in this instance. Presenting the CC with his proposals regarding Sakharov, head of the KGB Chebrikov, Politburo member Ligachev, and the president of the Academy of Sciences of the USSR, Gury Marchuk, wrote (9 December 1986*, 2407-Ch):

The need to prevent Sakharov's hostile activity was due to his lengthy subversive work against the Soviet state. He incited aggressive circles in capitalist countries to interfere in the internal affairs of socialist countries and to military confrontation with the Soviet Union, and he inspired protests against the policy of the Soviet state that are aimed at international détente and peaceful coexistence. At the same time, Sakharov took steps toward the organized rallying of anti-Soviet elements within the country, incited them to extremist actions, attempted to establish contacts with anti-Soviet groups in the Czechoslovak SSR, declared solidarity with the Czechoslovak "Chartists" and representatives of the Polish so-called "Committee for Public Self-Defense," urging them to organized unification for the conduct of anti-socialist activity.

But now, due to the influence exerted by the sage KGB, having cooled off in Gorky and mainly in the absence of his wife, Sakharov resumed his interest in science, "criticized the American 'Star Wars' program, commented positively on the peaceful initiatives of the Soviet leadership and gave an objective assessment of the events at the Chernobyl nuclear power station."

> The indicated changes in Sakharov's behavior continue to meet with stubborn opposition by Bonner. In fact, she tries to persuade her husband to abandon scientific activity, directs him toward the preparation of provocative documents and makes him keep diaries with a view to their publication abroad. However, despite this, it is feasible to continue efforts to attract Sakharov to scientific work, which would be useful in itself, and could restrain him from active participation in antisocial activity.
>
> To this end, it seems possible to make a decision now regarding Sakharov's return to Moscow, as his continued residence in Gorky may encourage him to resume anti-Soviet activity, taking into account his wife's negative influence and the continued interest in the "Sakharov problem" in the West.
>
> I admit my reluctance to believe that Sakharov stated that he would abstain from public activity upon return to Moscow.
>
> Sakharov's return to Moscow may result in some negative moments, considering Bonner's anti-Soviet stance, her clear desire to provoke Sakharov into confrontation with us, and her blatant desire to cooperate with Western circles that wish to counteract our policy. Their apartment may again become a place for all kinds of press conferences with the participation of foreign journalists, a meeting place for antisocial elements, the preparation of negative declarations and demands. It is unlikely that Sakharov will resist the temptation of participating in matters of so-called "defense of human rights." But regardless of the above, Sakharov's return shall cost us less political damage than his continued isolation in Gorky. It should be borne in mind that measures shall be enacted along the line of the Committee for State Security to neutralize possible negative behavior.

In the end, both Sakharov and the "pardoned" political prisoners returned not as conquerors and not even as repressed innocents, but as the neutralized and generously forgiven. There was no word about rehabilitation, as there had been, for example, under Khrushchev. The decision was dictated, once again, by party "feasibility," the need to minimize damage. There can be no talk of a "victory for democracy"—it was a victory of the Politburo, a victory of their glasnost.

The "pardoned" themselves knew that this was defeat; those who wrote appeals, no matter for what reasons, acknowledged the *chekist* "feasibility." "Refusing activity" meant that one could have avoided imprisonment in the first place. The regime wanted nothing else from us. Those who did this were rewarded and became deputies, "political activists," while those who refused remained "antisocial elements." Was there anyone who did not understand what had to be denounced if this opened the way to public activity? Did Gorbachev remind Sakharov of his promise to "abstain from public activity" when he magnanimously invited the latter to open his Congress of People's Deputies of the USSR in the spring of 1989?

This was the end of our movement, which split into those who undertook to support Gorbachev and those who refused to serve as a screen for the General Secretary of the CPSU in his games. Even those of us who were exiled to the West were divided quickly into "good" and "bad" dissidents: those who "acknowledged perestroika" and those who refused to recognize it. (As with the émigrés of the 1920s, those who "accepted" the revolution and those who did not.) Those who accepted were able to visit the country and print articles in newspapers about their heroic pasts; there was silence regarding those who refused acceptance, as though we had never existed. Only Soviet diplomats, upon encounter, would smile invitingly and be honestly offended by our stagnant distrust.

Naturally, one of the first to hurry back was Sinyavsky, who explained to the public with an importance typical of "us—the writers" that "all I had were stylistic differences with the Soviet authorities." (*Russkaya mysl*, 27 January 1989)

My God, how much coyness there was in that phrase, how much snobbery and villainy. He was talking about the bastards who tortured millions of people and, as we see now to our sorrow, destroyed the country. It would be interesting to know if he would have had similar stylistic differences with Hitler. And what would be their substance? In what style would "they—the writers" prefer to kill people?

There were clearly no differences regarding syntax and grammar with Gorbachev, whom he proclaimed to be "Dissident No. 1."

Tell us, why do you not go back? perestroika-oriented journalists asked me with genuine surprise. And it was hard to decide whether there was more stupidity or infamy in that question.

3.14   Last-ditch efforts

It was not enough to break the old opposition; it was also vital to prevent the formation of a new one (4 December 1987*, St 45-09):

> A group of persons... is attempting to hold a so-called "seminar of independent public organizations of participant countries of the Helsinki process on humanitarian issues" on 10–14 December in Moscow. ...
>
> ... [Sergei] Grigoryants, [Sergey] Kovalev, [Larisa] Bogoraz-Brukhman, [Vyacheslav] Chernovil, [Parur] Harikan and others intend to head this seminar. They have all been sentenced in the past for anti-Soviet activity and were pardoned this year by an Order of the Presidium of the Supreme Court of the USSR. [Lev] Timofeyev has declared himself chairman of the "preparatory committee."
>
> An "appeal" is being distributed in which the organizers of the "seminar" make a demagogic declaration, calling among other things for the establishment of international guarantees that would ensure observance by the member countries (the Conference on Security and Cooperation in Europe) of their obligations in the sphere of human rights, and also "the development of international control over the observance of decisions on the humanitarian aspects of the CSCE." ...
>
> ... Questions for the preparation of this "seminar" are discussed constantly at meetings of the indicated persons with the participation of foreign journalists. The attendant "Glasnost Press Club" makes no secret of its intention to unite all antisocial elements in our country, and its ambition is to play a leading role in the proceedings.

This is not in 1968 or 1977, but in 1987, at the height of the perestroika so favored by the West, with the same Alexander Yakovlev, the inventor of the party's glasnost, in charge of "preventive measures."

> On the whole, it is clear that the issue under discussion concerns the preparation of a provocation, which in the plan of the organizers and their foreign instigators must yield dividends in any scenario: if the "seminar" is successful, it will add weight to "glasnost" and create a precedent of some kind; if the enterprise is prevented, it will give rise to anti-Soviet clamor, the more so because the event is scheduled to coincide with Human Rights Day on December 10 and also the holding of the top-level Soviet-American meeting.
>
> In view of the above, the following measures are proposed:

- Refuse the application of the organizers of the "seminar" to the executive committee of the Moscow City Council for the rental of premises, pointing out that until the development of relevant legislation, the Provision of the executive committee of the Moscow City Council dated 11 August 1967 remains in force. [This Provision] was adopted in the interests of ensuring state and public order envisaging, among other things, the obligation to observe the Constitution of the USSR and other legislative acts. Furthermore, the "Glasnost Press Club" is not an officially registered entity, and it is not clear on what grounds it aspires to the right of organizing international events. It is assumed that after the refusal of rental of premises, the "seminar" will meet in private premises so its propagandistic effect will be considerably diluted;

- An analogous motivation should be implemented in refusing entry visas to foreign citizens wanting to attend the "seminar." It is probable that a certain number of foreigners will arrive as tourists, and that certain Western journalists, accredited in Moscow, will participate in the meeting;

- Bearing in mind that one of the main aims of the organizers of the "seminar" is to provoke a scandal, refrain from implementing preventive measures at this stage;

- If the organizers ignore the decision of the Moscow City Council, serve them a warning along the lines of the Procuracy concerning the illegality of the putative enterprise.

At the same time, there is the question of not just administrative, but also political means for neutralizing the activity of such antisocial elements. As shown by the first trial of action in the situation of democratization, the most effective method is scrupulous individual work conducted by Soviet, party and public organizations, including at places of residence, with the implementation of a differentiated approach if necessary, exposure of the true face of these "defenders of rights" in the media.

So what changed? The same Yakovlev, the same KGB, the same "measures," the same abuse of power. Only now the sympathy of the West is not on our side; our glasnost is not winning. Nobody wants to see that this is not democracy triumphing, but "democratization," that there is no market, just so-called market socialism. Not even Margaret Thatcher or Ronald Reagan saw this. The Western press is full of praise in writing about all these *chekist* fronts and similar "public organizations," and their Western colleagues hasten to establish bilateral business contacts and Western funds to supply them with technology and means. It is useless to argue and explain: you are regarded as an imposter, a swindler seeking to rob honorable people who, unlike you, are struggling against the "conservatives" for democracy in their own country. And who are you, anyway? What are you doing here in the West?

What is the sense of trying to explain anything? That Gorbachev's glasnost and perestroika is a gigantic operative-*chekist* sham? That all these fronts are merely *chekist* games? At best, you will be considered a lunatic: even Reagan and Thatcher do not think like that. Even "Sakharov himself" supports Gorbachev....

What can you say in reply to them? That the game is calculated for that purpose? That its aim is to prevent the formation of genuinely independent social forces? This is quite acceptable to the Western establishment: "independents" are its greatest fear. That is the reason why dissidents did not have the real support of the West—neither before, nor during, nor after perestroika:

You are uncontrollable, I was told quite frankly by those on whom such support depended. Such touching unanimity of the Western establishment and the Politburo: they all wanted a controlled revolution, so they bred puppet "revolutionaries."

Without doubt, Gorbachev's Politburo had an excellent understanding of this. It was for that purpose that they created their "public organizations" to ensure a "neutralizing" effect. So in connection with the seminar on human rights they proposed the following measures, to name just a few (p. 5):

> The Municipal Committee of the CPSU (comrade [Yuri] Karabasov), acting together with the Committee for international cooperation on humanitarian problems and human rights under the Soviet Committee for European Security and Cooperation (comrade [Fedor] Burlatsky), are to attract party, Komsomol, soviet and other organizations to conduct systematic work on neutralizing the activity of antisocial groups such as the "Glasnost Press Club," including the exposure of the true face of these "champions of rights" in the media."

This was the reason for the creation of all these commissions and committees headed by party "liberal" Burlatsky, ensuring that no Helsinki activity would get out of control. Here is the proud report of their success to the CC by the main architects of perestroika—Yakovlev, Shevardnadze, Chebrikov, [Anatoly] Dobrynin and others (19 December 1987, 2594-Ch):[139]

> Pursuant to the adopted resolution, measures have been implemented to counteract the conduct of the so-called "seminar of

---

[139]4 December 1987* (2451-Ch), pp. 6–9.

independent public organizations—participants in the Helsinki process on humanitarian matters," which has the support of imperialist special services and foreign subversive centers and is organized by antisocial elements for the creation of a standing controlling body monitoring the observance of human rights in the USSR. For the purposes of localizing this political provocation, representatives of a number of foreign anti-Soviet formations, former Soviet citizens who are renegades living in the West, members of Polish Solidarity, "The Initiative for Peace and Human Rights" group (GDR) were refused entry into the USSR, as well as instigators of nationalist and other antisocial manifestations Harikan (Armenia), Chernovol... [Mikhail] Goryn, [Ivan] Gel (Ukraine), [Nijole] Sadunaite (Lithuania) and others.

The implemented measures facilitated a certain narrowing of the circle of participants of the so-called "seminar" and prevented the unification of hostile persons with antisocial elements in other socialist countries and frustrated the formation of an organized standing center in the Soviet Union. Failing to receive permission for the use of state premises for conducting the seminar, the provocateurs dispersed to private apartments and formed sections. ... They were headed by Timofeyev, Grigoryants, Bogoraz-Brukhman, Kovalev, Gamsakhurdia, [Alexander] Ogorodnikov and others, formerly sentenced for anti-Soviet activity. On the whole, they managed to draw around 150 Soviet citizens into this provocative manifestation (including more than 40 persons from 30 different cities in the country). It has been established that the majority of them had participated previously in provocative activities, for which they were charged with criminal liability, and maintained and continue to maintain contacts with foreign subversive organizations.

What did these criminals, enemies of progress, talk about? Why, even under the conditions of Gorbachev's glasnost, were they unable to conduct their seminar? Maybe they supported the "conservatives" and spoke out against democratization?

Meetings in private apartments were of an anti-Soviet nature. For example Timofeyev ("Glasnost Press Club") stressed in his address that "The seminar should demonstrate to the world that there are many people in the USSR who are against the socialist system...." [Gennady] Krochik ("Trust Group") called for the formation of "free trade unions" in the country. Ogorodnikov ("Bulletin of the Christian Community") asserted that "the USSR is a totalitarian state" and spoke of the need to increase the role of the Church in the political and social life of the country. [Valeriya] Novodvorskaya ("Democracy and Humanism Seminar") declared: "There must be a nonviolent political struggle against the government of the USSR. The main aim of our movement is constant opposition to the government. Demand a multi-party system in the country." [Georg] Myasnikov ("Glasnost" bulletin) claimed that half the population of the USSR lives in poverty, that there are millions of unemployed in the country, that there is slave labor and 25% of the population has no roof over their head. He alleged that not a single constitutional right is observed in the USSR.

The addresses of a number of participants called for struggle for the unrestricted right of exit and entry into the country, refusal to perform military service, the free transfer of any information abroad. Resistance to bodies of Soviet authorities, the policy of the CPSU, the creation of a mechanism of influence over the internal and foreign policy decisions of the government were also discussed.

In other words, nothing new was said in comparison with what the perestroika press was already writing. But these were the wrong people, they were "uncontrollable." As the authors of the report admit, "the provocative action passed largely unnoticed by Soviet citizens" and [such actions] should be prevented in the future because "without doubt, its organizers shall continue their seditious activity."

The propaganda department and the International Department of the CC CPSU, acting together with the Ministry of Internal Affairs and the KGB of the USSR, envisage developing new measures for exposing the hostile and provocative nature of the activity of the organizers and participants of the indicated enterprise, and also for the prevention of similar actions in the future.

This was probably the only serious effort to unite the independent opposition in the country. What could they do—a handful of people faced with the gigantic machine of strangulation, with no means, surrounded by the total indifference (or even hostility) of the West and their own people? Who needed their homemade journals, their limited-circulation newspapers, if every perestroika-sponsored publication had print runs of millions of copies? The times when one word of truth was more powerful than a nuclear superpower had gone with the wind: now everybody spoke "the truth," many different "truths," and all at the same time. Just keep your ears open! The Soviet propaganda of perestroika learned to lie even inconsistently, creating the glossolalia of "socialist pluralism." No matter how hard you strained your vocal cords, your voice would remain only one of many, your truth one of many. Was there any chance of shouting them down?

Furthermore, there was now no need to seek any justification in order to avoid a clash with the authorities. Why look for trouble, place yourself in the way of special forces' truncheons, for the sake of 100 percent truth, if it took only 75 percent to become a public servant with a private car? Why hurry if what is forbidden today may be permitted tomorrow? A specific feature of Gorbachev's "democratization" was that the controlled protestors were allowed to do much more than the uncontrolled, who the minions of the law dispersed with unparalleled severity.[140]

> The Committee for State Security of the USSR has received data indicating that extremist-minded participants of the so-called seminar "Democracy and Humanism"... are planning to stage a provocative demonstration on October 30 of this year.
>
> They intend to hold this demonstration under the slogans "We demand the release of all political prisoners," "We demand a political amnesty," "Rehabilitate prisoners of conscience," "Stop stifling free thought," "Repeal articles 70, 72 and 1901 of the Criminal Code of the RSFSR."
>
> For the purposes of lending this provocation a mass character, the organizers plan to distribute an "Announcement" and a "Declaration by the participants of the demonstration for the release of political prisoners in the USSR." Its organizers count on the presence of persons formerly punished for anti-Soviet activities and sentenced by people's courts to mandatory psychiatric treatment. They have informed foreign correspondents of the time and place of the event. The appearance of Western tourists is also expected.
>
> The Committee for State Security, acting together with the Ministry of Internal Affairs, are implementing measures to avert the planned provocation.

It appeared that political prisoners were being freed, there was alleged discussion about a review of the Criminal Code, but holding demonstrations for that reason was "an extremist provocation", it was prohibited by the Moscow City Council, it was dispersed by the militia. (According to a report in *Russkaya mysl* dated 6 November 1987, some twenty-five persons were detained before the demonstration and delivered to various precincts where they were held for more than three hours). The man in the street could only wonder, why fight the police in city squares over something that can be published in the official press? The intelligentsia took fright: "Oh, hope-

---

[140] 11 May 1987 (6/2140)^.

fully this won't hurt Gorbachev!" The West threw up its hands in perplexity, ascribing everything to the chicanery of "conservatives" in the Politburo. What hope could there be for the emergence of a unified, firm opposition? Even those few who tried to create such an opposition, knowing that acting alone meant death, retreated to their republics, split into small groups. The regime could not countenance them even in such a practically harmless form. In the turmoil of the perestroika years, despite all Gorbachev's zigzags, only one thing remained unchanged and consistent: prevention of the formation of genuinely independent social structures and stopping the consolidation of a genuine opposition. Just two years before the collapse, recommending the creation of a special "Administration of the KGB for the protection of the constitutional system," the then head of the KGB, Vladimir Kryuchkov, reported the following to his commander-in-chief (11 August 1987, Pb 164/87):

> The special services and subversive centers of the opponent are transferring their activity against the USSR to a new strategic and tactical platform. ... By activating nationalism, chauvinism, clericalism... they attempt to instigate hotbeds of social tension, antisocialist manifestations and mass disorder, and to incite hostile elements to actions aimed at the violent overthrow of Soviet power. Displaying stubborn persistence, they attempt to form legal and illegal groups of an anticonstitutional orientation, exercise direct control over them, render material and ideological support, and inspire extremist acts. ...
>
> The same can be said of anti-socialist elements in their illegal activity. Using some of the groups formed spontaneously under the influence of the political activity of our citizens, under the cover of slogans calling for democratization and the renewal of Soviet society, they conduct anticonstitutional work aimed at the creation of *structures opposing the CPSU* (italics mine—*V.B.*) [and] other organized groups.

Even the repeal of article 6 of the Constitution, as a result of which such attempts ceased to be "anticonstitutional," the Gorbachev reforms did not deviate from this general line. Right up to the end, any independent groups were under pressure from the KGB, including those that were quite prepared for some degree of cooperation with the perestroika authorities. You say it could be a coincidence? And that Mikhail Sergeyevich, duped by the "conservatives," knew nothing about this? Not in a million years (27 July 1988*, 1541-K):

> According to data received, antisocial elements, encouraged from abroad by so-called "defenders of rights" and Jewish na-

tionalists, plan to hold a seminar in Moscow in the first decade of September on the subject of "the KGB and perestroika."

The organizers of the seminar, hiding behind the process of glasnost and democratization, have the aim of "discrediting the Committee for State Security of the USSR" by attracting the attention of wide circles of the Soviet and international communities to its "activity and crimes." It is envisaged that among others there shall be a public discussion of the following addresses: "The function of the KGB in an era of new thinking," "The role of the KGB in the national-democratic movement in the USSR," "The monopoly of information," "Overcoming the mystery and fear of the KGB," "The KGB and antisemitism." Sponsorship is sought from such organizations as "Amnesty International" and the "International Helsinki Federation [for Human Rights]" that have proved themselves sufficiently in the capacity of "defenders of human rights in socialist countries."

There are plans to invite prominent Western politicians and Sovietologists, including [Zbigniew] Brzezinski and [Richard] Pipes, and also our former citizens [Ludmila] Alexeyeva, Bukovsky, [Alexander] Ginzburg, [Yuri] Orlov, [Leonid] Plyushch and others, who are engaged in anti-Soviet activity in the West. It is likely that the seminar will be attended by prominent "defenders of rights" Grigoryants and Timofeyev, representatives of "national-democratic" movements of Azerbaijan, Armenia, Georgia, the Baltics and Ukraine, and "authorities" from among Crimean Tatars and religious activists.

The organizers of the seminar intend to send invitations to Chebrikov, Kryuchkov, Alexander Sukharev, the head of the Management of Visas and Registration of the Ministry of Internal Affairs of the USSR, people's deputies of the USSR [Ales] Adamovich, [Yury] Afanasyev, [Yury] Vlasov, [Telman] Gdlyan, Ivanov, [Vitaly] Korotich, the writer [Yulian] Semenov, the poet [Andrey] Dementyev, former chairmen of the KGB [Vladimir] Semichastny and [Alexander] Shelepin, [...] the editor of the newspaper "Moskovskiye Novosti" and the television programs "Vzglyad" [*Outlook*] and "Pyatoye koleso" [*Fifth Wheel*].

The report bears the following resolution:

This enterprise must be aborted. M. Gorbachev.

3.15   The agony

What are these "subversive centers"? What are these "schemes"? This was an iniquitous time: the more the regime lied, the more sophisticated it became, the greater was the applause of the West.

Yesterday's hangmen boasted of their former crimes and the world melted: what honesty, what changes! Yet the regime still continued to kill people, suppress the opposition, harass prisoners with impunity, while the world worried that this might harm the main hangman. Just like Fonvizin's character Mitrofanushka ("Little Mitrofan") who felt terribly sorry for Mummy because she was so tired from beating Daddy.

I was asked at lectures, "Why don't you want to acknowledge the obvious? Everything has improved, hasn't it?"

"Sometimes someone who is fatally ill feels much better just before death," I would joke, not knowing what to answer for the first time in my life. If they still did not understand the meaning of the communist system, it was too late. These were the hardest, most bitter years of my life. I had always found betrayal the most difficult thing to bear, even the betrayal of one person; but now we had been betrayed by practically the whole world, which had been seduced by a lie, by a promise of a miracle cure from a common ailment, and even worse, by a promise from a small-time con man. One by one, they disappeared—people who had been allies, friends, people on whom I depended in difficult times and who—so I thought—would believe me just as unquestioningly as I did them. We had borne so much together, gone through so much. But now it was as though they had been stricken by some virus of madness and preferred to believe someone they had never met, never looked in the eye."

"Well, you dissidents have a jaundiced view of Gorbachev," they would say.

What is happening? I would think in despair. Have I done something despicable in my life, or at least dishonest? Have I ever betrayed anyone or let them down?

Fairly or not, I took this as a personal insult:

"Who do you believe? Me or Gorbachev?"

They did not believe me.

Involuntarily I began to compare our biographies: in 1963 I landed in prison, and he was the secretary of the district committee of the Lenin Komsomol; in 1966 I was incarcerated in a psychiatric hospital for organizing a demonstration, and he became the secretary of the city committee of the CPSU; in 1967 through 1971 no sooner was I released than it was back to prison, and he climbed the party ladder, step by step, making it to secretary of the regional committee; he became a member of the CC when I received my last sentence. Finally he rose to the post of secretary of the CC just at the time when I, exiled from my country, was tearing myself in half between studies at Cambridge University and the need to conduct a campaign for the defense of my political prisoner friends, and published my first book; then he became a member of the Politburo just as Soviet troops invaded Afghanistan and Sakharov was exiled to Gorky. It is an amazing comparison, because we are contemporaries, participants in the same events, and the difference in our ages is a mere eleven years. It could not be that he did not know what I knew, that he had not faced the same problems, not had to answer the same questions. But he chose the path of serving lies, chose it quite consciously, negotiating all the steps of party slavery, and I made the equally conscious choice of prisons and camps, psychiatric incarceration and exile for the simple reason that I refused to lie. And now the world believed him, not me. Now tell me, what must one do to be believed?

"You suffered too much under this regime," I was told in editorial offices, "it's hard for you to be objective." And my articles would be rejected.

How did I suddenly acquire the reputation of a fool who is incapable of objectivity? I would torture myself. All that I'd said and written was in front of their very eyes. One can disagree with my views, but I have never written anything stupid or dishonest in my life.

These were the hardest years, years of crisis and an acute sense of the total senselessness of my existence. I knew full well that this was the time when the fate of the world was being decided, the fate of the country, but what could I do? How could I help the handful of people attempting to counter this epidemic of lies? There remained only two or three publications in the world where I could express my point of view.

Moreover, everyone started seeing us as some kind of "splinters of the Cold War", who were "impeding the process of democratization." The world, losing all its sanity, tried to "save" the policy of the CPSU from us! From us!

Naturally, the regime did not miss the chance of exploiting this state of affairs: after all, its disinformation was believed just as willingly as its propaganda. KGB head Chebrikov reported the following to Gorbachev (31 July 1986*, 1503-Ch):

> According to available information, a new anti-Soviet campaign is being launched in the USA on questions concerning human rights, promoted in the first place by reactionary political and Zionist circles in the USA with the participation of certain renegades who left the USSR and were stripped of Soviet citizenship. For the purposes of countering hostile propagandist actions, it would be feasible to prepare and implement a number of measures to disrupt it. For example, point out to certain US political, commercial and social circles that are interested in fos-

tering contacts with the USSR that this new anti-Soviet campaign would complicate the general political climate in Soviet-American relations, and will cause the USA to suffer considerable political and certain economic damage.

Implement propagandistic measures to expose the unlawful activities of certain members of the US embassy in the USSR and foreign journalists accredited in our country, as well as emissaries from foreign subversive centers and organizations who use their stay in the USSR for the collection and dissemination of anti-Soviet materials, and instigation of individual Soviet citizens to commit state crimes and other antisocial activities.

Create conditions for the receipt of documentary materials by foreign journalists accredited by the Ministry of Foreign Affairs, exposing the false concoctions of bourgeois propaganda regarding the alleged facts of breaches of human rights in the USSR, and factual data compromising renegades whose names are actively used by Western media in the conduct of anti-Soviet campaigns.

The "Provision" adopted by Gorbachev's CC on this subject consisted of six points regarding demarches and publications, including the following:

4. TASS, APN, Gosteleradio of the USSR, KGB of the USSR are to prepare and send abroad materials compromising the renegades whose names are actively used by bourgeois propaganda for anti-Soviet purposes, and also materials exposing the role of the US embassy and foreign journalists accredited in the USSR.

5. The Ministry of Foreign Affairs, APN, the KGB of the USSR are to prepare and implement a number of measures for the information of journalists accredited by the Ministry of Foreign Affairs of the USSR and supply them with documentary materials exposing the concoctions of bourgeois propaganda about alleged "facts of breaches of human rights" in the USSR. Among other measures, hold a press conference for Western journalists clarifying our policy regarding the emigration of Soviet Jews from our country; acting together with the Council for Religious Affairs under the Council of Ministers of the USSR, organize interviews for journalists Walker (Great Britain), Lederichs (FRG), [Cyrus] Eaton (USA), An-Hauman (Kuwait) and other foreign correspondents who write more or less objectively about Soviet reality, with Metropolitans Yuvenaly and Alexy [Russian Orthodox Church hierarchs], the president of the All-Union Council of Evangelical Christians–Baptists Logvinenko, the General Secretary of the Council Bychkov,

religious functionaries [Konstantin] Kharchev and pastor [Mikhail P.] Kulakov, Mufti [Shamsuddin] Babakhanov, in the course of which point out the unfounded assertions made by Western media concerning "violations of believers' rights in the USSR."

6. The Ministry of Foreign Affairs of the USSR, Gosteleradio of the USSR, the KGB of the USSR shall offer assistance to Western television journalists in television broadcasts to West European countries concerning the political contribution of the USSR and other countries to the reanimation of the process of détente in Europe, bearing in mind the anti-American slant and with the participation of leading Soviet political observers.

I did not check whether the named journalists interviewed the metropolitans and the mufti. What would be the difference? The overwhelming majority of the writing fraternity in those years "wrote objectively about Soviet reality." Those who tried to be more restrained were censored by their editors. It was *de rigueur* in those times to write only enthusiastic babble about the USSR, to the extent that it was surprising that the paper on which it was written did not go up in smoke out of shame. For instance, I recall the following headline in one Western (conservative) newspaper: "Is there life after Gorbachev?"

Authors, step forward! No, they won't respond, won't admit it. Even if you stick their noses into it, they will disclaim all knowledge. It would not be bad now to make them eat all the literary garbage they scribbled in the perestroika years.

As for measures for "compromising the renegades," they were pursued as inevitably as rain after frogs have croaked and, naturally, contributed to the isolation to which the Western "Gorby-mania" consigned us. An article here and an article there, a rumor, and before you knew it, most doors were closed to us. Finally the last coppers on which the remaining independent publications in the USSR survived were taken away. This was done with the aid of KGB "measures." The American fund issuing these coppers, the "National Endowment for Democracy," had been founded under Reagan, upon a decision of the Congress of the USA, as an independent public organization devoted to the global spread of democracy. In order to avoid any rumors, the board of directors was made up of representatives of both US political parties, trade unions (AFL-CIO) and the Chamber of Commerce, with its financial support being assigned openly and consciously "balanced." The money was given to, say, black trade unions in South Africa, and to Polish Solidarity; to human rights organizations in Argentina or El Salvador, and to us.

As I have said, all this was done quite openly: the list of organizations receiving aid, their projects and moneys given were published in the fund's annual report and sent to the press, public organizations, and congressmen. The moneys at their disposal were negligible: the fund disposed of around $3.5 million a year worldwide, and the USSR merited only about $200,000 per annum—while Gorbachev received billions. The money received was barely enough to sustain the last independent publications such as *Glasnost* magazine and the newspaper *Ekspress-khronika* [*Express Chronicle*], paying for the translation of their materials and their dissemination in the USA. That proved to be too much for Gorbachev's glasnost.

Then, suddenly, in March 1988, the obscure left-wing (not to say communist) weekly *Nation* (I had never heard of its existence) published an article in the best traditions of the KGB entitled "U.S. Funds for Soviet Dissidents." No, the authors had nothing against dissidents, on the contrary they are concerned that "American money" should not cause us any harm. After all, Soviet "conservatives" are famous for their paranoia, and might seize on this matter to the detriment of glasnost. The authors are even more worried that we émigrés, living in the West and receiving money from "the government of the USA" are conducting business in such a way that it "looks more like intelligence activity... than defense of human rights."

To put it plainly, that is what is called insinuation. As if it were not they—two genuinely concerned honest American journalists—who had thought up these allegations or pulled them out of a hat, but that they worried that the "conservatives" in Moscow might interpret this situation as such. And we Russian émigrés do not take care, either through mercenary motives or through negligence. But halfway through the article the tone changes: subjunctive turns of phrase and "conservatives" disappear, the public fund becomes "the government of the USA," and we turn into heartless exploiters of unsuspecting Russian dissidents, concerned only with how to "use Soviet human rights defenders to gather political and military information regarding the USSR."

This was just what the KGB needed, what it had tried to link us with for the past twenty-five years. As is customary with KGB measures of this kind, this article was reprinted with lightning speed in the Soviet press and leftist publications all over the world. In Denmark, a similar newspaper, *Dagbladet Information*, published the article a week ahead of the *Nation* original without any hints, but cutting straight to the bone: "Soviet Dissidents Employed as Spies for the USA," with a large photo of me in the center (although at first I was given only a passing mention in the article). This Danish version was reprinted immediately (removing all the authors' "concern" for the fate of dissidents) by *Sovetskaya Rossiya* (24 March 1988) under the challenging headline "Bring Out Information—It's Paid For," while the *Nation* version was published just as speedily by *Za rubezhom* (*Life Abroad*) (No. 13, 1988) with an equally sensational heading: "Espionage Under the Guise of 'Struggle for Human Rights,'" with the subheadings: "The New Contemporary NTS," "All the secrets become clear" and so forth.

So off it went—Soviet "glasnost" in full cry, from newspaper to newspaper, with references to one another, each more trenchant than the last. The campaign lasted half a year, alongside which the KGB trashed the editorial offices of independent publications, beat up the staff, and wrecked equipment.

Literaturnaya gazeta (23 March 1988) was first off the starting line, in the person of its New York "correspondent" Iona Andronov, who wrote the lengthy article "Pawns in Someone Else's Game." I put "correspondent" in quotes because his cooperation with the KGB was already well known, and now I found documents confirming this cooperation from at least May 1972, when he was the New York correspondent for the *chekist* journal *Novoye vremya* (27 January 1972, St 28/11). Either he had been in too much of a hurry with the article or he was too keen to boast of his luck, but it emerged that it was he who inspired the whole measure, and he may have even edited the article by the two "concerned" American authors:

> I learned the secret and the truth about the New York editors of the faux *Glasnost* from a local journalist, Kevin Coogan. He interested me earlier with the inside story of the new anti-Soviet journal and unearthed some semiconfidential information about it. In this respect he worked together with a staff member of the liberal weekly *Nation*, Katrina vanden Heuvel. Their joint article for "Nation" is already typeset, but meanwhile Coogan agreed to share his information with *Literaturnaya gazeta*. ...

A whole history unrolled. The authors refuted the text and protested against the "use of their article to the detriment of dissidents," even though they did not deny contacts with Andronov, nor that he had seen their article prior to its publication, almost in draft form. Even the *New York Times* came to our defense,[141] to say nothing of more friendly publications, which printed indignant

---

[141] Richard Bernstein, "Exiled Soviet Dissidents' Group in Dispute Over Threat to Dissenters," the *New York Times*, 12 April 1988.

responses by dissidents.[142] But what was the use? The money was lost in any case.

In this respect, America is an amazing country. On the one hand, publishing slander is recognized as the sacred right of the press, protected by the First Amendment to the Constitution of the USA. On the other hand, America is a country of extreme conformists, where any criticism in the press, even if it is genuinely slanderous, renders a person unacceptable, especially when it comes to the receipt of public funds—"too controversial," as they say in such cases. Note that it is the victim of slander who becomes "controversial" and not the slanderer. It is not surprising that this is widely used by all kinds of leftist rabble: it appears that money cannot be received without their approval.

In any event, we were already hanging by a thread, and our pitiful aid to dissidents was a fly in the ointment of the leftist establishment. Then the perfect excuse cropped up: we had become "too controversial."

So what was to be done? Armed with the bitter experience of my "killing" of Jessica Savitch in the journal *Novoye vremya*, I did not try to achieve anything in an American court. But due to the fact that a tiny part of the *Nation* print run (no more than one hundred copies) was distributed in England, I tried to take them to court there.

My God, what incredible excuses were thought up by the "respondents" to prevent the case from coming to court, to drag it out, delay submission of papers. I shall not weary the reader by listing them all—suffice it to say that the matter dragged on for *more than five years*, passing from one authority to another. The action was terminated quite recently by... the House of Lords, no less, as the respondents complained about the excessive length of the proceedings.

I had the pleasure of reading their petition—it was a masterpiece of cynical and brazen lies: Oh, they wrote, we are suffering such nervous tension after waiting for the hearing for five years. We do not even recall all the details of the matter—it would be unfair to try us now under oath. Moreover, everything has changed, there is no more USSR and no more KGB. What is there to dispute? Why dig up the past?

---

[142]Joshua Muravchik, "'Glasnost', the KGB and the Nation," *Commentary*, vol. 85, Iss. 6, (Jun 1, 1988), pp. 47–49. See also the ten letters of protest from Sergei Grigoryants, Irina Ratushinskaya, Eduard Kuznetsov, Vladlen Pavlenkov, Nadezhda Svetlichnaya, Leonid Plyushch, Mykola Rudenko, Ivan Kovalyov and Tatiana Osipova, in *Commentary*, vol 86, Iss. 5 (Nov 1, 1988), pp. 16–21.

So I was unable to make them answer before the law, or even receive an apology. I could not even spit in the eyes of this human trash. If you ever meet one of them by chance, please do it for me.

• • •

What else do I have to hope for at the end of this too-long chapter, and my life into the bargain, apart from wishing to spit in the eyes of all these evil spirits—be they in the East or in the West,—that deprived my life of meaning, and deprived the world of recovery? Rejoice now in the work of your hands, rejoice in how ably you fooled everyone. I say *everyone*, because you fooled yourselves as well. It is unlikely that you will be comfortable in this decomposing world that is drowning in lies, for even a thief only really feels safe when surrounded by honest people, as does a liar among the truthful; otherwise we shall have to steal from one another and fool one another. What sense is there in that, what gain?

Yet everything could have been so different had people possessed just a grain of conscience—no, this is something for which I dare not hope—but at least a drop of farsightedness, just a tiny measure of calculation beyond momentary triumph. It would seem that we should possess this ability, we who walk erect on two legs and differ from our closest kinsmen who, finding a handful of seeds, stuff it in their mouths immediately and are ever so happy that their stomachs stop rumbling. Our forefathers planted the seeds in the earth, watered them and endured hunger, but harvested tenfold. Is this not how our civilization began? And shall it not end with a complete unwillingness to think about the future for just one minute? However fantastic this may sound today, it is quite possible that we might, given such inclinations, wake up one day in a jungle, amid the ruins of our ancient temples, which have become home to screaming monkeys.

Rejoice, those who walk erect, at the onset of monkey civilization! No extra effort is needed, you don't even need to wear pants: you can scamper around on all fours, flashing a bright red behind.

What can you expect from a macaque, you will say; its forehead is so small it could not hold a large thought. Not like the one Mikhail Sergeyevich Gorbachev has, and with a birthmark as well, a Socrates, no less. And is he content now, with a forehead like that and with a Nobel Prize, to walk on his feet? Yet what cunning he possessed, what intrigues he wove—the mind boggles. Just one more day, but in power, even on the edge, but still on the throne. He managed to outsmart everybody, and only the servants remained. And then—oops!—the servants snookered him. There is nobody to blame; he made the choice, he promoted those who were the most treacherous, stamped on those who were more honest, spun his schemes and finally became entangled in them.

And what about our intelligentsia? You can't help but spit in disgust. God did not shortchange them with foreheads—oh, what foreheads you can see in Russia! Nurtured over hundreds of years. And still to no avail: they spun in circles, fidgeted this way and that, guessing which side to approach in order to get the best bit of the pie, to grab it so that it seemed uneaten. All that filled their big foreheads and thoughts was how to elbow their way forward to the big, smelly trough. Then look—there is no pie, no trough. Emptiness. Now they sit in their cold apartments, feeding an iron stove with volumes of Lenin's works. Only the blizzard outside wails *un-fai-un-fai-airrrrr* down the chimney. . . .

Gogol was right when he wrote nearly one hundred years ago: wherever you look, nothing but snouts in the trough on all sides. What could I do if this situation had not improved in a hundred years? In all honesty I can say that if you gave me a second or third life, I would be unable to do anything, because I would not seek victory, I would come to understand too soon:[143]

"Poor country, in which simple honesty is seen as heroism at best, and at worst as a mental disorder, for in such a country the earth will not yield a harvest. Woe to that people that has lost a sense of dignity, for its children shall be born monsters. And if in that country, among its people, there shall be at least a handful, even one, willing to take upon himself the common sin, the wind shall never return to its quarters."

Oh, Russia. . . . I admit that I, an old codger—having witnessed so much—also believed that it wasn't the end yet. No, I told myself as I warmed the prison's cement floor with my bones, just wait—let the horses toss their manes, grab the reins, throw your arms out wide and break into song, and—the *versts* will fly past until your eyes blur! Hooves flying, snow blinding—then the road will leap, and a frightened passer-by will let out a cry of fear.

What else was there to give warmth, if not such a vision? And there was a moment when the horses would seem to shudder and an unknown force would sweep you up on its wing and take you far, far away. . . . O, horses, horses, where are you? Where is that land that brooks no nonsense? Where is that jaunty people that birthed us to our misfortune? And the horses—are nags, and the coachman—is no coachman: no beard, no mittens, no yoke, no harness, he sits on the devil knows what, and instead of singing a rousing song, just moans:

---

[143]In Russian, Bukovsky's 1978 memoirs are entitled *And the Wind Returns.* . . . See Ecclesiastes 1:6–7 (ESV) ("All is Vanity").

I could do with some German jackboots.
Where are you, troika Russia? Do you still live? Answer me.
Silence.

Part II

In the West

Chapter Four

Betrayal

4.1   Stupidity or treachery?

"What do you think about détente?"

This was one of the most frequent questions I was asked immediately after my arrival in the West. I recall that at first I did not understand what was meant by this question; instead of the word détente, the Soviet press usually employed the clumsy construction "relaxation of international tension" or simply "defusion". Nor did I know anything about Western debates on this subject. But as soon as I reacted negatively to this matter, or the allied issue of "socialism with a human face," I could feel an instant coolness or even hostility from the centrist press, to say nothing of leftist publications. Subsequently, at first tentatively and then with increasing aggression, attempts were made to "compromise" me:

"Oh, he's fallen under the influence of right-wingers. . . ."

What right-wingers? I wondered, looking around and seeing none.

"He sounds like Solzhenitsyn. . . ."

Ah, we got you there! Caught with your hand in the till at the scene of the crime.

But several years later, when my protective wave of "publicity" began to recede, the need to be careful disappeared. I was now referred to as a "right-winger" and even an "extremist." And why not? I reject "moderate" improvements of the communist system; I do not even want socialism with a human face!

Admittedly, attempts were made at first to adapt me, break me down, and the methods used—in the civilized West at that—differed little from those of an average camp godfather. Shortly after I arrived I had dinner with the directors of the Ford Foundation. They listened attentively, and for a moment I thought that I could explain something to them, and they would do something sensible after hearing how things really stood in the Soviet Union. After all, they had hundreds of millions of dollars in their hands to be used for social projects. But at the end, the chairman asked one question only: What would you do if on one hand, you had information about the flagrant persecution of one individual, and on the other hand, publication of this information placed the reaching of an agreement on arms limitation under threat?

My God, if this was a camp godfather talking, it would be just the moment to tell him where to go. Hardly believing my ears—after all, this was the West!—I started to explain as politely as possible that the Soviet game of "arms limitation" was not worth a brass farthing, it was deceit from start to finish... and I saw the eyes of the formerly attentive foundation directors begin to glaze over. I did not receive any funds from them, or even a Christmas card.

How many such dinners and lunches I was to have. Even with Rockefeller. And they all openly measured me, adapted me—not to listen to what I had to say or learn something new, to understand the meaning of the system that was aiming rockets at them, but to readjust me to say what they wanted to hear. In any audience I addressed I waited, like a condemned man on the eve of his execution, for the inevitable question:

"Won't a noise in the West harm those who remain in the USSR?"

And no matter how many hundreds of times I explained, poking myself in the chest, that I was the best example of the opposite, the same question would crop up again in the same audience. Finally, one of us would be found who cracked, unable to resist the temptation of "success," who would confirm what everyone wanted to hear:

"Yes, it will. . . ."

And this would be spread on the front pages of all newspapers. In case no sufficiently well-known Russian dissidents could be found to speak in favor of "socialism with a human face," dissidents to suit the purpose were created on the spot. Some dubious Czechs, still hoping for a Prague Spring on a global scale, or some random émigrés from the Soviet Union, who were still paying their party dues a week ago—here they were, "real dissidents." Good ones. Whole newspaper pages were devoted to them, they became professors. . . .

Imagine for a moment Nelson Mandela, released as the result of a lengthy public campaign, facing this question at his first press conference: "How do you feel about apartheid with a human face?"

And imagine how annoyed everyone would be if Mandela replied negatively regarding both apartheid with a human face and any peaceful coexistence with it.

"Well, he's an extremist, so what can you expect?"

Moreover, imagine that every television appearance by Mandela was to include a moderate "apartheidologist" from an American university—for balance. Or even better, a collaborationist from Pretoria: after all, you cannot show the public only extremist views, you must have balance!

"You suffered too much from apartheid," he would be told sympathetically. "Of course you can't be objective."

"Objectivity" prompted helpfully by "moderate specialists on apartheid" would conclude that the black population of South Africa had no "tradition of democracy" (in other words, they are ignorant savages) so apartheid could not be repealed just like that, it needed to be reformed gradually. Therefore open condemnation of apartheid, introducing boycotts and creating obstructions is not only useless, but downright harmful. The right thing to do is to develop cooperation with it, exercise a "civilizing influence" on it while striving for changes by way of "covert diplomacy"....

It is impossible to imagine anything like this with regard to Nelson Mandela. And if at least one crazy Western public figure were to dare say something to this effect—naturally not to Mandela's face, that is inconceivable, but at least behind his back or by implication—that kamikaze would disappear off the face of the earth, destroyed by public anger. He would be branded a racist, a lapdog of apartheid. Despite all the fine talk about freedom of speech and the press, no newspaper, no television channel or radio station would allow him to say so much as a word of self-justification.

Yet what is apartheid by comparison with communism? A local abomination, posing no threat to anyone outside South Africa. It aimed no nuclear weapons or columns of tanks at the heart of Western Europe; it did not try to impose on anyone its version of a bright future for all of humanity; it did not attempt to export its model elsewhere; it had no dedicated allies (secret or open) in every corner of the globe.

It would seem that the desire to rid the world of communism should take precedence over the perfectly humanitarian desire to see the end of apartheid. But it was we, not Nelson Mandela, who had to bear the offensive nonsense of the Western elite. It was we who had to force our way through the brick wall of resistance of the local establishment, defend ourselves from slander, put up with unconcealed hatred as if we were the only ones who wanted to be rid of communism. As if this were our local problem, which had nothing to do with anything else in the world.

Of course this was no Western naivety, as it was put politely in those days, nor even stupidity, as we sometimes said in exasperation. It was the conscious policy of the Western establishment, "stupid" only in the broad sense of the word, as stupid as the idea of socialism itself. To my amazement, the Western establishment was, and remains, pro-socialist; at best moderately social democratic. It does not really matter who is in power at any given time: the press and the money (funds such as the Ford Foundation) remain in the same hands as before. The establishment does not change, and its power in a democracy is much greater than the power of the government, especially in the life of the intelligentsia.

Moreover, it does not really matter what this or that political party calls itself; in our century, due to the fashions of the intelligentsia and the concentrated propaganda of socialists, the political spectrum has shifted so far to the left that today's "conservative" in England is practically undistinguishable from the social democrat of the beginning of the century. Margaret Thatcher was an exception, representing not even the main body of her party, but a very small part thereof, and that of recent origin. Sir Edward Heath was and is a typical contemporary conservative—a colleague and fellow-thinker of Willy Brandt in the grandiose idea of transferring Western wealth to the "poor" South. This idea is so flagrantly socialist that one cannot but wonder how it could merit serious discussion anywhere apart from a congress of the Socialist International. Yet not only was it discussed seriously, it came about somehow that at this very time (the early 1970s), Western banks actually shelled out more than a billion dollars to third world countries in the form of loans, credits, and so on, knowing full well that this money would never be repaid. Now, in our time, these fantastic funds have simply been written off as "bad debts," with no acknowledgement that this money belonged, in fact, to investors and taxpayers, whose consent to this socialist affair was never sought. In a word, suspecting nothing, we turned up with our human rights concerns, our prisons and psychiatric abuses, in a world where socialism as an idea had already won, while the only arguments behind the scenes were regarding which particular form of socialism would be the leading one. It would be as if you, seeing a house being burgled, reported this to the police, not knowing that they are in league with the burglars. Some picture, isn't it?

"Soooo. . ." drawls the duty sergeant, "veeerry interesting. Are you sure the people you saw are burglars? Maybe they were the owners of the property simply moving house? Maybe it's all in order. Anyway, who are you? A relative?"

I plead guilty that it took me a couple of years before I realized what was actually happening. At first I could not understand why I seemed unable to explain everything properly. Maybe it was my insufficient knowledge of English or something, but nobody understood. Or maybe I did not understand them? It was as though we were speaking in different languages, in which the words were the same but their meanings were completely different.

I was astounded by the habit of treating concepts in the abstract, out of context, thereby rendering them into senseless words or brief slogans, acting on the local public like a signal on one of Pavlov's dogs: the gastric juices start flowing for no visible reason. For instance, the words peace and cooperation. They immediately produce radiant smiles—the gastric juices are at work. Yet neither word has any meaning outside a specific context. In an abstract sense, the most peaceful place on earth is a cemetery, while cooperation with, say, a criminal is deemed complicity and is punishable by law in any country. It's simple, isn't it? Yet I could not explain these simple truths to my interlocutors. The Pavlovian conditioned reflexes, developed over decades, proved impossible to overcome. To this day there is such an absurdity as the Nobel Peace Prize. Peace with whom?

In fact, that notorious détente, all that "defusion of international tension"—what does this dream mean? Why should one struggle with tension rather than its source? It has to come from somewhere. What sense is there in defusing it all the time if it is going to continue building up? But logic is powerless here; all you get in reply is yet another signal phrase: "There is no alternative to détente."

And your interlocutor's gastric juices make themselves felt.

You start to worry. "Wait a moment, what do you mean, there is no alternative? There is an alternative to everything in the world. After all, that is the very art of politics, to create alternatives."

In reply you hear, "Political realities have to be acknowledged."

Buzzzz... another signal. I remember spending an hour trying to convince another person that "political realities" have to be created, not acknowledged. In my case, for example, acknowledging the political realities in the USSR would have entailed joining the party, cooperating with the KGB. Instead of that, I created reality; and here I am sitting next to you in the West. It made no difference. Finally, his stomach rumbling, he retorted: "We need peace and cooperation."

Do you think that I am exaggerating or simplifying? I am not. Our arguments with the local establishment about détente were just as ludicrous—like a dialogue between two deaf people—because none of the "détentists" even tried to substantiate their doctrine. They lied, fidgeted, tried to get away with slogan-like phrases, but could not manage to give a clear explanation of why détente was so necessary. In any case, it is impossible to explain why, for instance, you should supply credits, goods and technology to a totalitarian regime whose declared intention is your destruction. There are no adequate arguments in human logic to justify such a state of affairs. All that remained was to lie.

"The idea is to make it easier to influence the USSR and make them respect human rights," the détentists would say, winking conspiratorially. "We will tie them to us, make them economically dependent on the West and exert influence."

But as soon as the time came to "exert influence"—such as when the USSR breached the Helsinki Accords or invaded Afghanistan—it would emerge suddenly that "we depend more on them than they do on us." Never mind that we cannot so much as boycott them, or introduce any embargo; on the contrary, they are in a position to blackmail the West.

What is this? Stupidity? Happenstance? Neither one nor the other, because straightaway, without pausing for breath, the offer came to enter into an even greater dependency on the USSR by building a pipeline to bring Soviet gas to Europe.

What concern can there be for human rights if the entire Ostpolitik of German socialists reduced the problem to trafficking in people. A whole industry came into being: for every released political prisoner the authorities of the GDR received 40,000 marks, thereby stimulating more unmotivated arrests.

"We Germans have to care for our eastern brothers above all else."

So they "cared"—in exchange for massive injections into the economy of the GDR, certain selected individuals would be granted merciful permission to visit their relatives in the East. It was enough to make one shed a tear, to see old men and women meeting each other thanks to détente... while at the same time, "eastern brothers" were being shot at the Berlin Wall, were blown up on mines, had dogs set on them. It was not even the done thing to notice the Wall in the middle of the city, let alone mention it. Heaven forbid! That would be "Cold War rhetoric."

"Détente is peace and cooperation."

What was this? Stupidity? Cowardice? No; treachery.

4.2   Who invented détente?

I had always thought that the détente of the 1970s was the brainchild of the Kremlin, but I was wrong; it was thought up by German socialists. My error was understandable: the rotation of periods of "tension" and its "defusion" are typical of the entire history of East-West relations and were always initiated by the Soviet side. Starting with Lenin's New Economic Policy (NEP) through the years of the "great alliance" of the Second World War and ending with Khrushchev's "peaceful coexistence," decisions about "defusion" and "pressure" were made in Moscow, while the West simply accepted its role in the game by default. In essence, it would always be ideal for the regime to keep up this kind of relationship with its "capitalist surroundings" when in reply to "increasing class struggle", the West would react with increased friendliness. But this did not work out: frightened by the growth of Soviet influence, the seizure of new territories, increase of subversive activity, the West bristled, generally not for long, and a period of cold war would set in, to the curses of all of progressive humanity.

No matter what was claimed in leftist propaganda, Western policy toward the USSR was always passive, defensive rather than aggressive. Even at the height of the Cold War, the overriding doctrine of the West was containment, which left all the initiative in the hands of the Soviet leaders. Therefore, having tired of opposition and having exhausted most of its resources, but having played significantly on the nerves of its opponents, the Soviet regime would begin a "peaceful advance" for the purpose of receiving a pause for breath in the arms race, Western credits and technologies, and a more conducive atmosphere for the further expansion of its influence. There was no instance of the West rejecting this unsolicited "friendship," although the regime never made any secret of the fact that its essence had remained unchanged. Khrushchev's promise, "We shall bury you!" worried the West much more than the Berlin Wall, even though Khrushchev had not said anything really new; he had simply affirmed the Marxist dogma that "the proletariat is the grave digger of capitalism." Unlike Khrushchev, Brezhnev, who never repeated anything in his own words, nonetheless stated time and again that "détente does not in any way change, nor can it change, the laws of class struggle."[144] But this sounded somewhat vague, so it did not upset anyone.

Naturally, all these "détentes" ended the same way—with the latest invasion, the Soviet seizure of this or that country, undisguised hostility toward the West, and threats. Just like a troop of monkeys when one of its members is carried off by a hungry tiger, Western countries would go into a brief period of unhealthy agitation and then calm down. Then it would all start over again, with the sole difference that with the passage of time the cycles became shorter. The regime was increasingly unable to cope with the pressure, its economy increasingly unable to survive without Western infusions. However, the periods of "rest" became increasingly dangerous, as without "tension" control would start to slip over various parts of the empire.

---

[144]See L. I. Brezhnev, Speech at Twenty-Fifth Congress of the CPSU, Moscow: *Politizdat*, 24 February 1976. http://xn--80aagr1bl7a.net/index.php?md=books&to=art&id=1355

In other words, there were more than enough reasons to believe that the détente of the 1970s also came about on Soviet initiative. Moreover, it came in very handy for the Brezhnev leadership that had just crushed Czechoslovakia and found itself isolated as it commenced the "Kosygin reforms," in other words just as it was in dire need of Western support. But facts are stubborn things. The little I was able to find in the archives on this matter amazed even me.

Let us go back to the document cited at the beginning of the first chapter (see §1.1—Who cares?), the one dealing with a meeting between a "KGB source" and an authorized representative of one of the leaders of Egon Bahr's SPD, the beginning of "unofficial contacts" between the German social democrats and the KGB (9 September 1969*, 2273-A).

They started this shameful policy in a shameful manner—concealed from their own people, like a conspiracy, and through KGB channels to boot. But this is not the main issue—after all, I will be told, there are many examples throughout history when necessary matters were dealt with in secret; rather, the main issue is that the document in question refutes all the lies conjured up later by the social democrats as justification for their new policy.

For example, the dependence of the FRG on its Soviet neighbor, which they later called a "reality" they had to "take into account," was, as we were to see later, instituted by them quite consciously. Or look at their cries about how they are saving humanity from nuclear war with the aid of their Ostpolitik, all their assurances that there is no alternative to détente. But there was nothing really threatening Germany in 1969 (at least, nothing threatening it more than usual), and the notorious "international tension" had not yet taken a grip on the world. There was no need to seek any "alternative." On the contrary, the tension escalated as a result of détente when, making use of Western goodwill, the USSR started to build up its arms toward the end of the 1970s.

Finally, let us not forget the simple fact that Germany is a member of NATO, and in 1969 the social democrats—members of the ruling coalition of the FRG—were actually committing treason in conducting such negotiations with Moscow behind the backs of their allies. Being a democracy, it stands to reason that nobody could forbid them from changing their former stance of supporting NATO or even from becoming allies of Moscow, but in order to do this they would be obligated to quit the coalition and openly declare their new choice. By doing neither of these things they became, essentially, agents of Moscow influence in NATO. As a result of this policy Germany did not achieve anything substantial, but East-West relations became infected by the virus of capitulation for a long time.

Meanwhile, the Andropov-recommended line of a balanced approach to relations "with both parties" was no more than a game. At that time, in May 1969, the KGB forwarded the following document to the CC (27 May 1969*, 231-Z):

> Pursuant to the decision of the Secretariat of the CC CPSU (St-57/59) in October 1968, the Committee for State Security of the Council of Ministers of the USSR forwarded photocopies of archive documents to the Ministry of State Security of the GDR regarding the Nazi past of the West German chancellor, [Kurt] KIESINGER.
>
> At present, the Ministry of State Security of the GDR is requesting the loan of original documents for use in preparing measures for the compromising of KIESINGER.
>
> We find it feasible to grant the request of our German friends and lend them the indicated documents concerning the Nazi past of the chancellor of the FRG, KIESINGER, that are stored in the State Archive Administration of the Council of Ministers of the USSR.

Moscow's game is perfectly clear: if Chancellor Kiesinger refuses to cooperate under threat of blackmail, it can dispose of him by placing its stake on his "big coalition" partners, the social democrats. As we now know, that is exactly what happened, and in the same year Willy Brandt became chancellor while Kiesinger retired as a result of "measures" implemented to "compromise" him (not without the assistance of his social democratic "partners," who instigated an artificial government crisis). It is much harder to understand the motives of the social democrats who willingly stuck their heads in the Soviet noose. It stands to reason that later they said a great deal about their honorable intentions to protect human rights, which was allegedly impossible without making certain concessions to the USSR, without a "mutually beneficial" game with Moscow. . . . Yet this is all just a smoke screen, if not to say an outright lie, as the main concessions to Moscow were precisely in the sphere of human rights. It suffices to recall that this entire game was devised a mere half year after Soviet tanks crushed the Prague Spring and the world was still voicing its indignation about it. At such a moment the very offer to establish "special relations" with the aggressor were a solid concession, if not outright betrayal. It is not surprising that, starting on such a note, the new Ostpolitik betrayed the cause of human rights, turning the Germany of the early 1970s into a second Finland. For example, here is another document illustrating

the activities in "defense of human rights" of the FRG government
by 1972, Andropov's report to the CC (30 April 1972*, 1176-A):

> On 5 March 1972, senior academic employee of the Institute
> of General History of the Academy of Sciences of the USSR,
> Doctor of History Mikhail Sergeyevich VOSLENSKY, born 1920,
> Russian, not a party member, single, traveled to Germany at
> the personal invitation of the president of the FRG, [Gustav]
> HEINEMANN.
>
> On April 29 of this year, the state secretary of the Ministry of
> Internal Affairs of the FRG, [Paul] FRANK, advised [Valentin]
> FALIN, the Soviet ambassador in Bonn, that VOSLENSKY had
> applied to the authorities of the FRG for a 2-3 year extension
> of his visa, and requested support in obtaining an extension of
> his Soviet passport for the same period. VOSLENSKY based his
> request on a desire to engage in academic activity, without ex-
> pressing any political motives. According to FRANK, VOSLEN-
> SKY'S behavior raises certain suspicions, pursuant to which
> the government of the FRG is not interested in an extension of
> his stay in that country. At the same time, the West German
> side is unable to make an unequivocal refusal of extending his
> visa, as it fears that VOSLENSKY may make a public appeal
> and, as a desperate measure, apply to the police, asking for
> political asylum with all the resulting consequences.
>
> In the complex political situation in the FRG at the moment,
> such a course of events, in FRANK'S opinion, would be highly
> undesirable. On this basis, FRANK states that in the West Ger-
> man view it would be feasible to extend the validity of VOSLEN-
> SKY'S West German visa for 2-3 months. ...
>
> Allowing for the fact that VOSLENSKY is in the FRG on the per-
> sonal invitation of President HEINEMANN, it would seem feasi-
> ble to take up FRANK'S suggestion regarding the extension of
> VOSLENSKY'S visa on the condition that the West German au-
> thorities shall take steps to prevent any undesirable actions on
> his part.
>
> At the same time, acting through the Soviet ambassador in
> Bonn and with recourse to the possibilities of the KGB to pose
> the question of the unpublicized removal of VOSLENSKY to the
> Soviet Union should such a need arise.

   In other words, in 1972 the German leadership was in an active
conspiracy with Moscow and against its own people, even the police, with regard to those very same "human rights."[145] By 1974 the

---

[145]Voslensky remained in West Germany and four years later was deprived of his
Soviet citizenship (5 November 1976, Pb 33/2). See the 31 December 1981 document
in the Bukovsky Archives online (in Russian).

"confidential cooperation" was so strong that the forced expulsion of Solzhenitsyn from the USSR, for example, was practically decided together by the Politburo and the socialist leaders of the FRG (and seemingly in secret from their coalition partners) (7 January 1974* (Pb). The reader will recall what a headache the matter of Solzhenitsyn was to the communist leadership: on one hand, the Politburo seemed to support the idea of dealing with the matter in court, and on the other hand they all (especially Andropov and Gromyko) understood that such a blatant violation of human rights would undermine their successes in international affairs. They were particularly worried by the imminent conclusion of the contract of the Helsinki Accords, whereby in exchange for the "recognition of postwar borders" (i.e., legalization of the Soviet occupation of a good half of Europe) they were to give all kinds of guarantees regarding the protection of human rights—naturally with no intention of honoring them. But it is one thing to breach agreements after they have been signed; what to do before this is another matter. Solzhenitsyn's arrest at that time could have ruined their entire game, and expelling him against his will (as Andropov suggested) would be difficult without a country willing to accept him. That is where they thought of Brandt—who better to ask for help than the party most interested in détente? Andropov reported the following in a personal message to Brezhnev (7 February 1974*):

As I reported to you by telephone, Brandt has declared that Solzhenitsyn may live and work freely in the FRG. Today, on February 7, comrade [Boris] Kevorkov will fly for a meeting with Bahr for the purpose of discussing the practical issues relating to Solzhenitsyn's expulsion from the Soviet Union to the FRG. If Brandt does not fail at the last minute and Kevorkov's negotiations are concluded satisfactorily, by February 9–10 we should have an agreed-upon decision, of which I shall advise you immediately. If the indicated agreement is reached, then I believe that no later than February 9 it would be feasible to adopt an Order of the Presidium of the Supreme Soviet of the USSR depriving Solzhenitsyn of Soviet citizenship and his expulsion abroad (a draft of the Order is attached). The implementation of Solzhenitsyn's expulsion in that case could be carried out on February 10–11.

All this must be done as quickly as possible, because according to operative documents, Solzhenitsyn is beginning to guess our intentions and may issue a public document, which would place both us and Brandt in a very awkward situation.

Two days later he was able to report success:[146]

> On February 8, our representative had a meeting with
> BRANDT'S authorized representative to discuss the practical
> issues linked with SOLZHENITSYN'S expulsion from the Soviet
> Union to the FRG.
>
> *As a result of this discussion, the following decision was reached
> upon the suggestion of the representative of the FRG* [italics mine
> —V.B.]. On the evening of February 12 comrade FALIN, the So-
> viet ambassador in Bonn, will call Secretary of State P. FRANK
> (specifically him), requesting a meeting on an urgent matter at
> 8:30 a.m. on February 13.
>
> On February 13, comrade FALIN will be received by FRANK and
> advise him of SOLZHENITSYN'S expulsion. (The text of the ad-
> vice is forwarded separately simultaneously with the Ministry
> of Internal Affairs.) The cabinet meeting will start at 10 a.m.
> BRANDT will instruct BAHR, FRANK, and the representative of
> the Ministry of Internal Affairs to make a positive decision. At
> the request of the West German authorities, SOLZHENITSYN
> should arrive on an ordinary passenger aircraft to Frankfurt
> by 1700 hours local time on February 13.
>
> From the moment SOLZHENITSYN disembarks from the air-
> craft, the Soviet representatives have no further involvement in
> the action. . . . *If at the last moment BRANDT, despite all his as-
> surances* [italics mine.—V.B.], changes his mind for whatever
> reasons, then SOLZHENITSYN will remain under arrest and the
> Procuracy will institute proceedings on his case.

Such "cooperation" merits the name only in the sense of the way
agents "cooperate" with their center. What we see here is collusion,
a conspiracy.

It stands to reason that when the Helsinki Accords were signed,
the German social democrats knew full well that the USSR had no
intention of fulfilling its obligations regarding human rights, and
they were not inclined to protest against this. Without doubt, despite all their public declarations, détente was not tied up with human rights in their eyes. The change of chancellors in 1974 brought
about no alteration of this policy. The point was not who was chancellor, but what party he belonged to. Moreover, by 1977, at the
culmination of the global campaign for human rights in the USSR,
when it had been joined by the new president of the USA, Jimmy
Carter, the German social democrats were refraining from mentioning this problem as fundamental to Ostpolitik. Carter and his

---

[146]9 February 1974 (388-A)^.

stance frightened them half to death: what if the problem of human rights really became central to relations with the USSR?

The leadership of the Social Democratic Party experienced great concerns with the start of Carter's activities. The lack of clarity regarding the course of the new administration to the USSR in matters of détente, bilateral relations with the USSR, and the key areas of economic and financial policy hampered the development of the program of the social-liberal coalition and exerted a negative influence on the commencement of the activity of [Chancellor Helmut] SCHMIDT's cabinet, advised the Soviet embassy in its report for 1977 (21 June 1977).[147]

Brandt and Bahr hastened to Washington to instruct Carter in the intricacies of European politics, and every mention of the accursed human rights was accompanied by endless caveats. The Soviet ambassador in Bonn, FALIN, reported the following to Moscow (2 March 1977*, No. 74):[148]

> On the one hand, [the Americans] are obliged to be seen as champions of "human rights" and cannot allow themselves to be outshone by either their internal competitors or their allies. After the publication of Carter's letter to Sakharov, Chancellor Schmidt (20.02.77) declared that the motives of the president are the same as those of West Germany, and that the government of the FRG "shall continue to take all adequate steps to ensure that persons expressing differing views shall not be subjected to discrimination and persecution." In the same vein, German statesman Hans-Dietrich Genscher described the implementation of human rights "global in scope" as the central concern of the liberals and reiterated his suggestion to institute an "international court on human rights."

> On the other hand, according to reliable data, the leadership of the SPD of Germany was alarmed by Carter's crusade regarding the question of dissidents. If Schmidt spoke of "adequate steps," then Bahr, who was going to the USA, was charged with giving the new administration a comprehensive explanation of the social democrats' perception of such "adequate steps" that would not throw détente overboard. This subject will probably be raised by Brandt and [Horst] Ehmke in their forthcoming meetings with Carter and [Cyrus] Vance. ... Even more frank concern regarding the developing situation was expressed by West German politicians from the government camp in unofficial discussions. ...

---

[147] 21 June 1977*, p. 3.
[148] 2 March 1977 (No 74), pp. 3–4.

It is easy to understand that it was they and their European socialist allies spreading the lie that noise in the West would harm dissidents, despite the opinion of the dissidents themselves, just like other lies about us, thereby becoming KGB channels for "compromising measures." Moreover, they hurried to tell their Soviet "partners" about their successes in this field (21 June 1977):[149]

> For your information, Schmidt, Brandt, and Werner have done useful work with H.-D. Genscher, bringing him closer to a better acceptance of social democratic foreign policy concepts. The social democrats stress that under this influence the foreign affairs minister has shown greater restraint in making hostile statements regarding the USSR.

So all the forces of European socialism were brought to bear to save détente from... problems of human rights. Simply speaking from us, a handful of people prepared to sacrifice our liberty (and occasionally our lives), who defended those rights. These forces are still powerful enough, but in those days they were gigantic. It is enough to recall that in 1977 and 1978, when our campaign reached a critical moment[150] and our arrested friends—members of the Helsinki Groups—were hanging by a thread, most European governments were socialist. To say nothing of the press, the intelligentsia, trade unions, and business circles.

Is it surprising that they "won"? Or, to put it more succinctly, betrayed us and the idea of human rights? It cost them little effort to join forces and make Carter turn away from his human rights line regarding the USSR. But that was not all. Long before the Belgrade Conference, which was to examine observance of the Helsinki Accords in the fall of 1977, European socialist parties met in Amsterdam behind closed doors and decided not to demand too much from the USSR at that conference. And half a year later in Belgrade, they did not demand anything. The conference, on which many placed great hopes in expectation of a firm line by the West, got away with a communiqué that made no mention of repressions in socialist countries.

This betrayal was a blow from which our movement never recovered completely. Dozens of Helsinki monitors were incarcerated in

---

[149]21 June 1977*, p. 4.

[150]Issue 44 of *A Chronicle of Current Events* (16 March 1977) led with "Reprisals against the Helsinki Groups" (https://chronicleofcurrentevents.net/no-44-16-march-1977-2/), dealing with the arrests of Alexander Ginzburg, Yuri Orlov, Mykola Rudenko, Alexei Tikhy, and Anatoly Sharansky and with searches at the homes of Ginzburg, Ludmila Alexeyeva, Lydia Voronina and Orlov.

prisons and camps, and many died there,[151] paying with their lives for the deceit called the Helsinki Accords—for the solemn promise of the West to tie together questions of security, cooperation, and human rights in its relations with the East.

Actually, they betrayed not just us and not just the idea, but their own countries, their own civilizations. And in the end themselves: unaffected by the struggle for human rights in socialist countries, détente turned into a simple capitulation, and the idea of "socialism with a human face," now that the face had been sacrificed, turned from Utopia into a conscious deception. Who did these Bahrs and Franks expect to become with the reinforcement of Soviet influence in Europe? Moscow's quislings and gauleiters? Such naivety. For purposes like that, the Kremlin leaders had their own Erich Honeckers in reserve. But following in the footsteps of all socialists who helped the communists seize power, these Bahrs and Franks would have ended their days in the gulag.

As I said by the Berlin Wall on 9 May 1977, "There were no machine-gun toting convoys standing behind the delegates in Amsterdam, they were not menaced by guard dogs: they chose to relinquish their freedom willingly."[152]

4.3 Mensheviks and Bolsheviks

Yet another "human rights"–oriented excuse for détente—care for the "eastern brothers," which may have been quite sincere at the start—was sacrificed very soon to that very détente and turned into a propagandistic camouflage. I am willing to concede that in signing the Moscow and Warsaw pacts in 1972, the social democrats showed that they still believed their slogan of "influence through rapprochement." However, it soon became clear that that it is one thing to come to power through various manipulations, and another to retain that power while preserving your aims and principles. Socialist ideas are only good in theory. In practice, the popularity of the SPD soon began to fade, and by 1977, according to the assessment of the Soviet embassy in Bonn (21 June 1977*), "its authority was at its lowest ebb since coming to power."

> In political circles there were unending discussions about the future of the West German social democracy, and also about the survivability of the social-liberal coalition as a whole. As

---

[151]In March 1978 *A Chronicle of Current Events* (Issue 48) reported on no fewer than seventeen cases being investigated (https://chronicleofcurrentevents.net/no-48-14-march-1978/) in Moscow, Ukraine, Lithuania, Georgia, and Armenia.

[152]The text was reprinted in the *Times* (London), 9 May 1977.

can be seen from the numerous meetings and discussions of representatives of the Soviet embassy in social democratic circles, the leadership of the SPD was doggedly seeking ways to achieve positive results in its foreign and domestic policy and increasing the trust of the electorate in its political course. In these circumstances foreign policy activity... is seen by the leadership of the SPD as one of the decisive prerequisites of increasing the influence of the party in the country.

Simply speaking, the social democrats became hostages to their own Ostpolitik, the success of which was wholly in the hands of Soviet leaders. Naturally, such "rapprochement" suited Moscow, allowing it to not simply "influence" the FRG government, but dictate its own policy to the Germans. Even Brezhnev's visit to the FRG was turned into an event that that NATO country awaited with much greater trepidation than would have been the case in Warsaw (21 June 1977*, p. 3.):

> The leadership of the SPD has great hopes regarding the successful visit of L.I. Brezhnev to the FRG. It expects that new impulses for further improvement in Soviet–West German relations shall dispel the unfavorable impression that in the activity of Helmut Schmidt's cabinet since May 1974 there has been little discernible movement in the political sphere of these relations. Soviet-American dialogue regarding the conclusion of the second agreement on strategic arms limitation, the visit of comrade L.I. Brezhnev to the FRG, and the constructive passage of the Belgrade Conference must, in the view of the SPD leaders, become important mutually linked stages on the path of the further deepening of détente.
>
> It is worth noting that in preparing for comrade L.I. Brezhnev's visit, the social democrats are avoiding active participation in noisy anti-Soviet campaigns around the issue of "human rights" and criticize their organizers from the CDU/CSU.

Remember that at that time even certain communist parties (French, Italian) were not particularly reticent in criticizing repressive Soviet policies. Therefore the SPD was much more reliant on Moscow than European communist parties, and the FRG was somewhat like Bulgaria. But why speak of Moscow? Even the insignificant marionette GDR was able to dictate policy to its "Western brother." (21 June 1977*, pp. 4–5):

> The SPD leadership is working hard to deprive the opposition of one of its main arguments that the government headed by Schmidt has "painted itself into a corner" in German affairs and has demonstrated its total lack of efficacy. The chancellery

is using various channels to inspire the GDR to discussion on a wide range of measures, achieving success which would allow it, acting in the interests of the FRG, to "create a positive balance" in relations with the GDR. The political and ideological aim of these measures is characterized quite frankly—the creation of such a close net of intermixed mutual interests that the GDR would be unable to break it without losses to itself under any circumstances. As H. Werner declares, "so that the opposition between the FRG and the GDR shall gradually grow into good-neighborly existence, into relations between loyal neighbors."

The chancellor is fully aware of all the difficulties in resolving this matter and does not nourish any great illusions. The leaders of the SPD continually stress the need to show care and patience in relations with the GDR, and most importantly not to jeopardize the already existing "fundamental changes" by demonstrative and senseless actions. What is meant here in the first place is the increased possibility of meetings between FRG and GDR citizens. Visits by FRG citizens to the GDR rose to 8 million in 1976, which is seen by the SPD leadership as "an improvement of the situation of people in a divided Germany" and one of the main achievements of FRG policy in German affairs since 1969.

Thus, care for "eastern brothers" devolved into a rather paradoxical situation wherein the model of successful socialism in the GDR was sustained by the money of West German taxpayers, eight million of whom were allowed to pay one annual visit and see it for themselves. It is easy to see whose "influence" prevailed in this "rapprochement." Even the Soviet embassy report does not conceal the irony of this "main achievement" of the social democrats over seven years of détente.

Toward the end, when neither human rights nor the influencing of the GDR could be advanced seriously as a basis for policy, as a rational reason for détente, they proclaimed a different scheme altogether: peace and disarmament. But this also sounded unconvincing: in 1969, when the social democrats devised and began to implement their Ostpolitik, the threat of war in Europe was much less than it was as a result of that policy by 1980. Nonetheless, even despite such results, they continued to champion détente with obsessive stubbornness, always attempting to ensure the spread of Soviet influence in the country, within the party, often with their own money (16 March 1977, No. 99/360)[153] by using such means as the following:

---

[153] 7 April 1977 (No 99/3), p. 2.

> A propaganda channel such as the social democratic Friedrich
> Ebert Fund, which may enable, using its lines and funds, trips
> to the USSR by an additional number of journalists from the
> FRG, and arrange appearances by Soviet lecturers before West
> German audiences. It could also be possible to establish neces-
> sary contacts with the SPD. As was noted by the SPD chairman,
> W. Brandt, the activity of the fund has been fully reviewed in
> recent years. It no longer engages in activities that may be per-
> ceived by the GDR as infringing on its interests, and functions
> under the supervision and instructions of the SPD government.
> In Brandt's opinion, the fund could serve as a channel for con-
> tact between countries under the control of the SPD and the
> CPSU.

Not even the Soviet invasion of Afghanistan, which exercised a
sobering effect on Western public opinion, had much influence on
the policy of the German social democrats. Their main aim remained saving détente. Saving it from whom? Brezhnev? No, from
(1 February 1980*, Pb 182/2): "thoughtless and hypertrophic reaction, which does not correspond to events and would thereby precipitate an even worse situation." It was not by chance that the
Politburo applied directly to Brandt with a personal message immediately after the invasion, expecting justifiably to overcome the
arising political isolation with his assistance "The main issue," they
wrote, "is to find a common language in the matter that has long
been your and our concern—how to save the matter of reinforcing
international security."

However, this search for a "common language" was conducted
in the most unexpected spheres. By 1981, for example, the theoretical journal of the SPD, *Neue Gesellschaft*, and the editorial
board of the CC CPSU journal *Kommunist* were cooperating on
questions concerning the theory of building socialism (27 January
1981, St 247/13). What for? What bearing does this have on peace
or international security?

In fact, what was this policy of détente, Ostpolitik or whatever?
It can hardly be explained simply by stupidity, cowardice, or even
infiltration of the SPD by the KGB (although all three surely played
their part), if only because this policy was accepted not only by the
Germans. Practically all the socialist and social democratic parties of Europe supported it to some extent. Moreover, even nonsocialist governments, for example those of France (Valery Giscard
d'Estaing) and the USA (Richard Nixon and Henry Kissinger), saw
no alternative to détente. To be more precise, they did not even seek
it, accepting fully the game and arguments of the socialists.

What were the aims of the European socialists in creating this game and trying to force it on the world? After all, it was not like the harmless games of leisured politicians, but an extremely dangerous adventure that could have cost the peoples of Europe their freedom. It prolonged the life of communist regimes in the East for at least ten years. Hundreds of thousands of people did not have to lose their lives in Afghanistan, Ethiopia, Central America, and the Middle East. Why were they condemned to die? In the name of "socialism with a human face," a Utopia into which they intended to herd an unsuspecting humanity, the socialists sentenced the peoples of the USSR and Eastern Europe to ten years of slavery. They did it for the sake of "convergence," as a result of which, they thought, Soviet communism would acquire a human face, and the West would become socialist. Generally speaking, they did it for the eternal dream of Mensheviks to return the Bolsheviks to the bosom of social democracy, the wish of an idiot for a hybrid of a kindergarten and a labor camp.

Yet as we know from the history of their relations, the Mensheviks propose, and the Bolsheviks dispose. History knows of no instances of the former outsmarting the latter and countless examples of the use of the former by the latter. As I was once told rightly by an old social democrat, a man of exceptional honesty, social democracy only has the right to exist while the basis of its policy is consecutive anticommunism—otherwise it mutates into "Kerenskyism." That is why the first stage of the Cold War in the 1940s and 1950s was so successful for the West, as European social democracy maintained strict anti-Soviet positions. It is said that Brandt —until then a firm anticommunist, mayor of the "frontline" city of Berlin—"broke" when he saw that the Allies were prepared to sacrifice Berlin and take no action against the raising of the Wall in 1961. He writes about this himself:[154]

> "In the following years my political views were under the significant influence of this event, and as a protest against the situation in which this event occurred gave birth to my so-called East policy beginnings in the field of détente."

Maybe it was so — I was not there, and do not presume to judge. But even then, he should have thought about the example of Alexander Kerensky, whose "détente" with Lenin ended up bringing the Bolsheviks to Berlin.

No matter how, by the end of the 1960s the positions of European social democracy had begun to drift to the left, toward cooperation

---

[154]Willy Brandt, *People and Politics: The Years 1960–1975*. London: Collins, 1978.

with communists. That was also influenced by purely tactical considerations (joint campaigns against the Vietnam War, apartheid in South Africa, Augusto Pinochet's regime in Chile), the Khrushchev "thaw," and the schism between Moscow and Beijing, as a result of which the Soviet model of communism began to seem like the lesser evil. The temptation to cooperate became even stronger with the appearance of "Eurocommunism," which reawakened the socialists' old dreams regarding the evolution of communism toward social democracy. But I believe that the main role was played here by cynical, conjunctural reasons: it was only the growth of communist influence, just like the growth of Soviet influence, that made social democracy acceptable, if not an alternative in Western eyes.

In fact, by the 1960s they should have become convinced that socialist ideas, remaining the religion of the elite, found no resonance among the general public and thus their favored "third way"—to maneuver moderate social democracy between the "extremes of communism and capitalism"—was chosen by the West merely as the "lesser evil." Only the growth of Soviet influence could make them desired middlemen in East-West relations, "saviors of mankind" so to speak, allowing them—as they thought—"to influence both sides," gradually ironing out the ideological inconsistencies and thereby bringing opposing worlds to peace and cooperation —to "convergence."

This way, declaring that the aim of their policy of détente was to ensure peace and security, improve the situation of people in the East, and respect human rights and other benefits, the socialists lied only in part. Yes, these were their dreams, but not entirely disinterested dreams, because they made no mention of the fact that realization of the dream required involuntary acceptance of their version of socialism and of them as our more or less permanent ruler-saviors.

Furthermore, by keeping silent about all this, and realizing that the majority of people would not accept their Utopia willingly, they practiced the deliberate reinforcement of Soviet influence, in secret from their people and allies, as well as from their partners in various government coalitions. Like some of our intelligentsia, who with naive self-confidence engaged in games with the KGB—"We're smarter, we can outplay them"—European social democracy embarked on secret games with Moscow and, as was to be expected, got tangled in the web.

Understandably, Moscow was only too happy to take part in these games: if the Bolsheviks had learned anything from their history, it was how to use the Mensheviks to their own ends. In essence, all the "breathers," beginning with the New Economic Policy (NEP), were gained by them at the cost of drawing in various "reforming" leftist movements to implement their policies, frequently by means of creating "united fronts" with them—naturally under communist leadership. By a clever combination of official cooperation with unofficial infiltration of its agents and leftist radical activists into the ranks of "moderate" movements, Moscow simply manipulated them. It was the same this time.

On one hand, Soviet leaders were extremely enthusiastic in greeting such cooperation in the name of peace, progress and socialism. Even Brezhnev, speaking at the Twenty-Fifth Congress of the CPSU, stressed the enormous significance of closer relations with Western socialists. The head of the International Department of the CC, Boris Ponomarev, writing in the journal *Kommunist*, was even more enthusiastic about positive changes in the social democratic movement resulting from a number of international debates.[155] In a special article devoted to the conference of the Socialist International in 1976 (appearing in *World Marxist Review*), he wrote,[156] "The permanent and broad-scale cooperation between communists, socialists and social democrats may become one of the decisive factors for peace and social progress."

On the other hand, the KGB received a special assignment to concentrate its activity on these parties. The then head of the intelligence administration of the KGB, General Kryuchkov, instructed all his residents in Western Europe as follows (I quote from the English edition of the book by C. Andrew and O. Gordievsky) (26 August 1977*, No. 644/54):[157]

> The new correlation of forces on the international stage, the development of the process of détente and far-reaching changes in international circumstances have obliged the leaders of the Socialist International (SI) along with its constituent parties to take the appropriate corrective measures with regard to their political course and tactics.

> The latest Congress of the Sotsintern (November 1976) on the whole endorsed the results of the Conference on Security and Cooperation in Europe (CSCE) and expressed its intention of promoting the implementation of the Final Act.

> A resolution of the Congress dealing with international détente stated: "It is possible and necessary to broaden, strengthen and consolidate détente on a wider scale."

---

[155] *World Marxist Review*, May (5), 1976.

[156] *Kommunist*, November 1976.

[157] See also Christopher Andrew and Oleg Gordievsky (ed.), *Instructions from the Centre: Top Secret Files on KGB Foreign Operations, 1975–1985*. London: Sceptre (pbk), 1993, Chapter 8, "The Socialist International," pp. 244–249.)

In general terms the Congress took up a constructive position on questions of disarmament. The resolution stated: "Disarmament and the imposition of controls on armaments and arms deals is of vital importance for the whole world with regard to an escalation of the arms race and a worsening of the economic situation in most countries."

The Congress spoke out in favor of a prompt conclusion to the talks between the USA and the Soviet Union with the aim of obtaining agreement on a qualitative and quantitative reduction of strategic arms, and underlined the great importance of the talks taking place in Vienna on the mutual reduction of arms and armed forces.

In contradistinction to the period of the "Cold War", the leadership of the Socialist International now refrains from unilateral and oversimplified treatment of the foreign policies of the countries of the socialist community and acknowledges the positive role of the Soviet Union in developing the process of détente.

On the other hand, the social-democratic leaders of the important Western European countries which play a leading role in the Sotsintern, are adhering to their previous line regarding the need to consolidate NATO. They are also playing a part in the conversion of the EEC [the European Economic Community] into a military-political alliance, promoting in this context the demagogic slogan: "Let the Europe of monopolies be transformed into a Europe of workers." [. . .]

An analysis of the activities of the new leadership elected at the latest Congress of the Socialist International (BRANDT, CARLSON) enables us to conclude that it is making active efforts to develop its new program. [. . .]

In particular, by widely promoting the theory of "Democratic Socialism as a Third Way" (in contradistinction to capitalism and communism) for the development of Society, the Social Democratic leaders have put forward a "Socialist Strategy for the Third World" and have launched a new campaign to increase their influence in different sections of the national liberation movements in Asia, Africa and Latin America.

[. . .]

. . . The question of the normalization or the development of collaboration with the communist and workers' parties was sidestepped in the Congress resolution. As is well known, on this question there are deep differences of opinion within the international Social-Democratic movement. Nonetheless the Sotsintern has been compelled of late to refrain from imposing sanctions against those on the road of contacting or collaborating with the Communists.

[...]

In the process of studying these problems, it would be expedient to consider and evaluate the possibilities open to you for initiating active measures, the purpose of which would be to support and increase the operations of those leading activists and functionaries who are speaking out in favor of widening and strengthening the process of détente, curbing the arms race, and in favor of international cooperation.

[...]

The Centre would be interested to have ideas from Residencies on how we can exploit to our advantage:

- divergences between the parties of the Sotsintern on individual questions of ideology and tactics (differing approaches to the solution of economic problems, to capitalist monopolies, to the political concept of a "United Europe," to cooperation with Communist Parties);

- rivalry between leaders of the German Social-Democrats, the French and Australian Socialist Parties, the Swedish Social Democratic Workers' Party and the British Labour Party for the leading role in the Socialist International;

- contradictions between the pronouncements and the actual policies of Social-Democracy;

- specific examples of selfish neo-colonist policies by the social-democrats of the industrially developed countries towards Third World countries etc.

In other words, the entire gigantic machine of communist secret services in Europe was ordered to open a hunting season on the heads of socialists and social democrats, in order to turn these movements into a tool of Soviet policy:[158]

> Submit proposals for a wider and more purposeful exploitation of existing agent-operational resources with a view both to obtaining the necessary intelligence and to implement the active measures. In particular, ideas should be submitted on the direction in which further work with existing agents and confidential contacts from within the ranks of the Social-Democrats should proceed; information should be communicated to us which might open the way to us to recruit either as an agent or as a confidential contact other prominent, active figures in the movement, whom we can use to penetrate its leading bodies and means of propaganda and information.

---

[158]Andrew, Christopher M; Gordievsky, Oleg, *Instructions from the Centre: Top Secret Files on KGB Foreign Operations, 1975–1985*. London: Sceptre, 1st ed, p. 248.

How could the loose-mouthed intelligentsia from socialist parties withstand such formidable pressure? In the words of Vladimir Vysotsky, it was like "a schoolboy fighting a gang of rabble."

4.4 "Quiet diplomacy"

However, I do not intend to reduce the entire problem of the betrayal of European social democrats to KGB infiltration, leaving them the morally easy position of simpleminded idealists. General Kryuchkov was right when he spoke of the Mensheviks' traditional "gulf between words and deeds," which they, in his view, "are unable to bridge." More specifically, they do not even want to bridge it; not for nothing did Lenin brand them "social traitors." This gap is not accidental; it arises from a tendency of the intelligentsia as a whole, and especially the left, to cover up its far-from-disinterested aims with fine words. Let us assume that the problem of human rights in communist countries was not a peripheral issue, a humanitarian problem of détente that could be ignored for the time being on the road toward "convergence." Yet as we recall, the ideas of the social democrats presumed changes on both sides of the Iron Curtain; the mandatory condition for its realization was, therefore, the appearance of the "human face" in the Soviet model of socialism. And even the most simpleminded idealist should have understood that if the Soviet regime refuses to acquire that face, the entire idea of détente becomes meaningless. Just as the Helsinki Accords become meaningless, making a substantial concession to Moscow—by legalizing its postwar territorial expansion—precisely in exchange for respect for human rights.

Meanwhile, the key moment of the test of the Helsinki deal was the repression of Soviet Helsinki monitoring groups headed by Yuri Orlov, although the text of the Helsinki Accords envisaged the right to public monitoring of their observance.[159] By arresting Orlov and his colleagues, the Soviet Union threw an open challenge to the whole world—and the West, having swallowed this pill, capitulated. Even the same simpleminded idealist could not fail to understand that by continuing the policy of détente after this, continuing its cooperation with the USSR as though nothing had happened, the West betrayed its own principles. No KGB infiltration could change this situation, nor excuse such behavior.

---

[159]The author would like to acknowledge a debt to the book *The Orlov Affair*, where many of the sources cited in this section were originally found. Ludmila Alekseeva, *Delo Orlova* (in Russian, *The Orlov Affair* in English). Khronika Press, 1980.

It must be said that the West understood this dilemma perfectly. For instance, the British Daily Mail on the eve of the sentencing wrote:[160]

> The trial of Yuri Orlov in Moscow for the 'crime' of monitoring his country's fulfilment of its obligations under the Helsinki Agreements to further human rights shows what a farce those agreements were, and how naive the faith of so many Western politicians in a détente which is only respected on one side of the Iron Curtain. ... The British Foreign Office finds the fact that the trial of Professor Orlov is taking place 'very disturbing'. ... It would be much better if the Western nations showed that the era of gutlessness is over in those areas where it counts. ... It is not by gestures but by resolute action that the global chess-players in the Kremlin are likely to be impressed."

Usually moderate circles were just as condemnatory.
The Financial Times:[161]

> In retrospect, it now appears that not just the trial of Dr. Orlov but the Helsinki agreements themselves were a kind of play in which the Soviet authorities pretended that an ideological system imposed through force could honor solemn human rights commitments without undermining its own existence. ...
>
> The challenge to the Western signatories of the Helsinki agreements in the trial of Dr. Orlov has been laid down.... It is now up to the Western powers to decide how to react.

The Economist:[162]

> The cruel pretense of a "trial" inflicted on Yuri Orlov in Moscow this week, ending with the maximum sentence of 12 years of jail and banishment, sheds a fierce light on the Soviet regime's cynical view of its international obligations.
>
> "Nobody imagined, in 1975, that the Soviet government would meet all its Helsinki obligations immediately. But it was reasonable to hope for signs of movement in the right direction. At the Belgrade review conference Russia had ample opportunity to display such signs; and entirely failed to do so.

---

[160]"Too much wetness in the west," *Daily Mail*, 17 May 1978, p. 6.

[161]"The Yuri Orlov Case: An 'Open' and Shut Trial," David Satter, *The Financial Times*, Friday, 19 May 1978, p. 2.
(https://archive.org/stream/FinancialTimes1978UKEnglish/May%2019%201978%2C%20Financial%20Times%2C%20%2327563%2C%20UK%20%28en%29#mode/2up)

[162]"What Orlov Means to You," *The Economist*, May 20, 1978.

"The most blatant of its anti-Helsinki actions has been its persecution of the groups of Soviet citizens who have undertaken to monitor its compliance with the 1975 promises.

"But the sentencing of Mr. Orlov, the Moscow group's former head, serves sharp notice that Mr. Brezhnev sees no present reason to even feign a minimal compliance with his 1975 promises.

"To all who hope to see the eventual emergence of a true east-west détente, it should now be clear that non-communist Helsinki signatories—governments and peoples alike—have a duty to use all possible means to induce the Soviet regime to start complying.... Every Western scientist or other professional person now faces the question: Should I ignore the persecution of among the bravest of my Soviet colleagues, or should I help to end it by suspending all professional contact until their government stops flouting its Helsinki promises?"

And in fact, hundreds of scientists all over the world declared their boycott of the USSR, refusing official contacts and exchanges. Public indignation regarding the punishment of the Helsinki monitors was so great that, as we recall, even communist parties could not disregard it. Not just the larger parties such as the French and Italian, but even smaller ones that were much more dependent on Moscow expressed their open disagreement. It was only the social democrats and socialists, who at that time headed most European governments, who limited themselves to expressing "concern" as in the statement issued by the European Community:

With regard to the recent sentencing of Soviet citizens monitoring observance of the Final Act signed in Helsinki, including the case of Yuri Orlov, the governments of nine countries—members of the European Union, wish to declare the following:

"These nine countries have joined efforts in a persistent aim to support détente in Europe. They have demonstrated their decisiveness by active participation in the Conference on Security and Cooperation in Europe and after that conference.

"These nine countries that consider that the Final Act of the Conference on Security and Cooperation in Europe is a program for action for achieving détente reiterate that this document, signed by the heads of these countries or governments, obligates the participating countries to observe human rights and fundamental freedoms, and affirmed the right of the individual to know his rights and obligations, and to act accordingly.

"For this reason, the governments of the nine countries find that an individual being persecuted and sentenced for demanding observance of the Final Act in his own country to be a breach of the Final Act."

Even the Labour government of Great Britain, which was seen as the most conservative by its socialist colleagues, did not exceed verbiage. Foreign Secretary David Owen stated that "Orlov's sentence is 'severe and unfounded' and that this threatens the entire policy of détente." Baroness Llewelyn-Davies, speaking on behalf of the government of Prime Minister James Callaghan in the House of Commons,[163] said:

> Her Majesty's Government have stated that they regard the treatment of Professor Orlov as harsh and unjustifiable and are concerned at its effect on the good relations between East and West which are so important to us all.... The Soviet Union is one of the two great States of the world and... we must not cut off relations with her, however strongly and rightly we feel about human rights. To contemplate the alternative is really too horrible and we must not give up easily on this matter.

However, such a dramatic posing of the question had nothing to do with reality. Nobody declared war on anybody. On the contrary, just at that time a Soviet trade delegation was visiting England.

"Mr. Vladimir Kirillin, the Soviet deputy premier now in Britain with a trade delegation, yesterday called on Mr. Callaghan, Prime Minister, to discuss Anglo-Soviet trade relations and the progress of détente," reported the *Daily Telegraph* on 20 May, three days after the sentencing in Moscow.[164] "Mr. Callaghan expressed disapproval of the treatment and sentencing of Dr. Yuri Orlov, founder of the Moscow Helsinki group, while maintaining the need for normal state and trade relations with the Soviet Union."

This was too much even for the *Sunday Mirror*, which traditionally supported Labour:[165]

> So great was the severity and illegality of the trial that even the British Communist Party was shocked. It has asked the Soviet authorities to rescind the sentence. That is one better than the British Government. We have made no formal protest though we are parties to the Helsinki Agreement and the United Nations Covenant on Human Rights. Our position is clear. We

---

[163]"Dr Yuri Orlov's trial," Historic Hansard, House of Lords, 24 May 1978. (https://api.parliament.uk/historic-hansard/lords/1978/may/24/dr-yuri-orlovs-trial

[164]By Our Communist Affairs Correspondent, "Soviet leader in talks with Callaghan," *The Daily Telegraph*, May 25 1978, p. 1.

[165]Woodrow Wyatt, "Why is Britain silent on the Orlov brutality?" *The Sunday Mirror*, May 21, 1978, p. 14.

are frightened of the Soviet Union, so we do not wish to offend them. We also think that official protests would do no good.... Also, the bullies in the Kremlin are not always as resolute as they look.... The Kremlin caved in. The Russians respect only strength and determination. There is no more point in appeasing the Kremlin than there was in appeasing Hitler. There is no difference between the barbaric dictators of Moscow and the fascists.

And this, I repeat, are English Labourites, considered to be moderate socialists. What could be expected from the others? Of course, they did express "concern" and hinted at "damage to détente," naturally in deprecatory tones. Some even received replies via Soviet ambassadors, depending on past good behavior (3 July 1978, St 114/39):

> A telegram addressed to comrade L.I. Brezhnev has been received from the chairman of the Norwegian Labor Party, R. Steen,[166] and the General Secretary, I. Leveros, requesting a review of the case of Soviet citizen Yuri Orlov, sentenced for anti-Soviet agitation and propaganda.
>
> R. Steen belongs to the moderate circles of the party, which supported the establishment of official contacts with the CPSU for the development of good-neighborly relations and cooperation between Norway and the USSR.
>
> We deem it feasible to send R. Steen and I. Leveros a reply through the Soviet ambassador in Norway regarding the indicated question.

And in fact the inquirers were sent several pages of bare-faced, shameless lies, which seemed to have satisfied them.

Others, like the head of the Austrian socialists, Bruno Kreisky,[167] did not get even this much. He sent Andropov an incredibly obsequious letter (4 August 1983, 110-A):

> I have received, and continue to receive, numerous appeals from friends and acquaintances to intercede for Soviet citizen Yuri Orlov, who has been incarcerated since the beginning of 1977. ... Naturally, I am far from wanting to interfere in the internal matters of the USSR. So if I make this request, it is only out of compassion and in the firm hope of your magnanimity. I presume that such a goodwill gesture at this time of increasing

---

[166]Reiulf Steen (1933–2014), chairman of the Norwegian Labor Party between 1975 and 1981.

[167]Bruno Kreisky (1911–1990) led the Austrian social democrats, and from 1970 to 1983 was chancellor of the Republic of Austria.

> tension in this matter will have a positive effect in which, as I
> know, we are both interested.

"Yuri Vladmirovich," writes an assistant, "I believe that Kreisky's
intercession for the dissident Orlov should remain unanswered."
And lower, in Andropov's hand: "I agree. Andropov."

In all honesty, I too would leave such a servile request "unanswered"—simply out of a feeling of revulsion. Explain to me, why
did he prostrate himself like that, as if asking for a loan of money?
In other words, *My friends are driving me crazy; I would never have
dared on my own accord. I ask for your magnanimous pardon for
bothering you with such a trifle. We have a full understanding of
your "internal affairs,"* and so on. Is this any way to ask, especially when international agreement requires that you demand an
answer? So Andropov treats him accordingly, as the master would
a lackey catching at his sleeve in the doorway: "Can you spare a
coin, kind sir?"

Not for nothing did the "détentists" insist so stubbornly on "quiet
diplomacy" with Moscow in matters concerning human rights;
speaking publicly would have required expressing oneself more honorably, pretending to be an equal partner in the game, which is
something Moscow would never have tolerated. They hoped that
this way, nobody would recognize the nature of their master-and-
lackey relationship; at the same time, when they occasionally rescued someone's head from the block as a gratuity, it could be
boasted of to all and sundry as a "an achievement of détente."
Something was needed to justify their "special relationship" with
the Kremlin.

On the other hand, following its *chekist* habit of subverting a
partner, Moscow also insisted on this "quiet diplomacy," perfectly
aware that confidentiality in relations is the first step toward subversion. Let us say that in September 1973 the CC responds through
its ambassador to the General Secretary of the British Labour Party,
Ron Hayward, that his appeal to Mikhail Suslov on behalf of refuseniks Eugene Levich, Alexander Lerner, and Vladimir Slepak
shall not be granted—their cases will not be reviewed for another
two or three years. But—take comfort—the question of two others
shall be decided at the end of 1973 or the beginning of 1974. So
Hayward will not remain empty-handed; he will have something to
boast about.[168] However, the CC instructs its ambassador, "Stress
the confidentiality of this information." *Only for you, boys! See that
you justify our trust.* And the other side, glad to serve, keeps his

---

[168]18 September 1973 (St 97/61)^.

honorable silence. One may, of course, boast secretly to interested parties. But—hush!—not a word to anyone, don't spoil the game.

It stands to reason that the Labourite brothers did not realize just how delicately and professionally they were being had by Moscow. And they did not seem to try very hard. After all, at that time they were holding talks about establishing "special relations" with the CPSU. Their delegation (members of parliament William Simpson, Edward Short, and Ian Mikardo, headed by Hayward) was telling Moscow enthusiastically of its aim to "achieve a turn for the better in relations with the USSR" and that it was "critically evaluating certain aspects of the former policies of the Labour Party leadership." On behalf of all the delegates, Hayward spoke of striving toward détente, especially in relations with Moscow. The aim of the visit was ". . . to establish contact with the CPSU, exchange views on international problems. Similarity of views was noted, as well as the closeness of positions regarding matters of détente (economic cooperation, the all-European Conference on Security and Cooperation, the significance of agreements with the GDR and Poland, aid to Vietnam, support for developing countries, support of Allende in Chile)."

Naturally, ideological differences were also noted—on the matter of the invasion of Czechoslovakia, and the "lack of clarity in positions regarding the People's Party of China." But these were mere trifles by comparison with the similarities. Enthusiasm was unbounded. Even such Soviet demands as Labour's closer cooperation with the British Communist Party and its refutation of "anti-Soviet slanderous campaigns" did not meet with any serious objections from the Labourites. It is hard to cooperate with the British Communist Party, they said, but they were prepared to maintain "good personal relations with the communists."

"The tone of the response is much softer than before," noted Moscow in a detailed report to. . . the General Secretary of the British Communist Party,[169] John Gollan.

With such a "similarity of views," what price human rights? Even a mention of this problem or a public intercession for someone was viewed as an "anti-Soviet campaign." Moscow did not allow anyone to look good on their own account (26 December 1980*, St 243/57).

> The chairman of the Social Democrats of Denmark (SDPD), Prime Minister Anker Jorgensen, sent a telegram to the International Department of the CC CPSU in which, on behalf of his party, he requests consideration of the "family reunification" of

---

[169] 15 June 1973 (St 84/58)^.

Soviet citizen Victor Brailovsky, recently arrested and undergoing investigation on charges of systematic dissemination of slanderous claims and defaming the state and social system of the USSR.[170]

In view of the circumstance that the leadership of the SDPD and the CPSU have interparty links, we would deem it unfeasible to leave A. Jorgensen's telegram without a reply. The reply can be made through the Soviet ambassador in Denmark.

In view of the fact that Jorgensen's telegram was reported widely in the Western media, it must be borne in mind that our reply might be publicized similarly.

After giving Jorgensen a detailed "explanation" regarding the kind of miscreant he is championing, the CC did not refrain from issuing a rebuke:

At the same time, we cannot but express regret that the fact of the sending of your telegram, before we received it, has already caused speculation in the media of some countries.

Remember who the master is! Do not expect favors if you do not want to play by our rules.

Thus Moscow quickly turned human rights into an instrument for subverting European socialists, by selective rewards only for those who had moved to closer "rapprochement" with them. And what of the socialists? Can it really be that they did not understand where their games with Moscow were leading? If at the start of détente this might be accepted by stretching a point, then by 1977 the "gulf between words and deeds" would have been obvious to the village idiot. And really, after the demonstrative punishment of the Helsinki Groups—can you still maintain "quiet diplomacy"? Continue "rapprochement", seeing that your "influence" is nonexistent? Yet note that under the guise of talks regarding the need to improve interstate relations, the rapprochement was actually interparty, with the CPSU. By the beginning of the 1980s, most socialist and social democratic parties had established special interparty relations with the CPSU, meaning, apart from all else, very extensive contacts at the level of regional and even local party units. How much closer could they be? And the result? At the very least it facilitated greater KGB infiltration, which reached a fantastic scope in some parties: for example, in the cases of Finland and Germany

---

[170]For Brailovsky see issue 56.14 (30 April 1980) https://chronicleofcurrentevents.net/no-56-30-april-1980-2/ and 60.6 (31 Dec 1980) https://chronicleofcurrentevents.net/no-60-31-december-1980/ of *A Chronicle of Current Events*.

it would be hard to say where the KGB ended and social democracy began. The Japanese socialists, as we recall, became so close to the CPSU that they even conducted their electoral campaigns with Soviet money (3 March 1972, St 33/8). And after all that—to continue to believe in rapprochement-influence?

Of course, by 1978 it was not just in the leadership, but among the party rank and file that there could be no more simpleminded idealists. What was there to do? Make an honest rejection of détente, admit its failure?

On the contrary, in April 1978, several weeks prior to the trials of the Helsinki monitors, when there were no doubts as to their outcome, the Socialist International conducted a conference in Helsinki (what better place for it?) devoted wholly to disarmament, and even invited a Soviet delegation headed by Boris Ponomarev to attend. Not a word about human rights, not a hint of the imminent trials; from now on, détente had only one meaning—disarmament. As might have been expected, many high-flown words were spoken —but now about "saving humanity from a nuclear catastrophe." Those attending listened sympathetically to Ponomarev's blaming the arms race on "NATO countries, headed by the USA" and offering salvation through... dialogue with Brezhnev.[171] And what do you think? The following year, in October, a delegation of the Socialist International actually went to Brezhnev to discuss disarmament! The trouble was, it was too late to disarm: two months later Soviet troops invaded Afghanistan. A period of "black reaction", and Cold War began, so unbearable for the progressively minded part of humanity, and the détentists lost power in practically all European countries. They had to retreat into deep opposition and take up the so-called struggle for peace.

So they did not manage to establish socialism in all of Europe, having sold it to the Soviet regime. They were unfortunate, just like the gypsy in the old joke who decided to stage an experiment —stop his horse from eating. The amazing outcome is that success seemed so close, and the horse practically refused to eat of its own accord, but then... it died.... Practically everyone forgot about the Helsinki Accords that were so triumphantly signed by thirty-five countries in 1975. Certainly they were never formally revoked, and the 1980 Madrid conference to "check" them dragged on for almost five years. But who except us paid any attention to that? The condemned Helsinki monitors remained in prisons and camps (by then four of them had already perished), and the Soviet Union

---

[171]Boris Ponomarev, *Selected Speeches and Writings*. Oxford [etc.]: Pergamon Press, 1982. Pergamon Press was a publishing house run by Robert Maxwell.

continued to make use of the unilateral advantages granted to it by those accords. Finally, toward the tenth anniversary of their signing we—a large group of dissidents—issued an appeal for the termination of this mockery of common sense and a denunciation of the accords that had become a farce.

"We have done our best to make the Helsinki Agreement serve peace and democracy. However, we can no longer associate ourselves with the agreement which not only failed to serve its humanitarian purposes, but even to protect its most sincere supporters, an agreement which has turned into a repressive tool in the hands of Soviet authorities. We appeal to the Western governments to make the Helsinki Agreement null and void.

"We still believe that peace can be and must be based on human rights. Therefore, until the Soviets prove by concrete actions their readiness to observe these basic rights, any peace or arms control agreement with them would be self deception."[172]

Need it be said what indignation our appeal aroused among all of progressive humanity?

4.5 The American aspect

Any picture of the détente of the 1970s remains unclear and incomplete unless we touch upon—if only briefly—the role of the USA in this game. It is impossible to understand this role without at least a general understanding of American political culture and the psychological atmosphere prevalent at the time. I must admit that I may not be very objective; I did not like America from the very first moment I found myself there. It was enough for me to see, at one of my first appearances in one of the universities in February 1977, all those eternally shining eyes, burning with enthusiasm, to realize that I would never be able to explain anything to these people.

Later, having lived there for several years, I specified and supplemented my first impression, but did not reject it. On the contrary, when I was finally leaving America, I explained to my friends that I constantly felt myself overqualified to live there. And this, strange as it may seem, creates an additional burden on the nerves, just like having to live in an institution for mentally retarded adolescents.

In saying such negative things about American society, I am not claiming in any way that they are true of all Americans. It is an enormous country, composed of people of many ethnic origins, with a

---

[172]"Exiles: Nullify Helsinki Pact," *Wall Street Journal*, Eastern Edition; New York, N.Y. 8 May 1985: 1.

large number of relatively recent migrants who still retain their former culture. Even among bedrock Americans you will find all kinds of people. Furthermore, as we shall see later, it was in America that there were those who were able to withstand the spread of Soviet influence throughout the world. The problem is that they themselves were somewhat besieged, on the periphery of social life as a heterogeneous minority, while the main herd dominated (and continues to dominate) the life of the USA.

Apparently it takes living in America for a while to get a sense of Europe and its culture as a distinct and integrated entity. Normally, living in Europe, we do not feel this, do not notice anything that is common to the French and the English, Italians, and Germans; but once in America you rejoice to meet a Chinaman, and will find more in common with a Japanese than with the locals. The cause does not lie in that, as is usually said, Americans are a young nation that has not yet built up its own culture; I do not think they will build it up even in a thousand years' time. For this is not what they are doing; they are engaged in what their Declaration of Independence defines with the quaint expression the "pursuit of happiness." I do not undertake to translate this expression correctly. In any event, in a literal Russian translation "pursuit of happiness" sounds too mocking, presuming the futile nature of such a pursuit, and totally unsuited to be classed as akin to constitutional law.

Meanwhile, it was this senseless "pursuit" of the phantom of happiness in which that eternally young America was engaged. It was back in Roman times that cynical Europe reached the conclusion that you cannot run away from yourself and can only better your lot through persistent labor. The ones who fled to the New World did not believe this, blaming Old Lady Europe for all their misfortunes. Is it any wonder that their descendants have a sacred belief in the "American dream"—that is, that you can start your life afresh, from scratch, like turning the page of a book? And if happiness is not found, pack your gear, saddle up, and "go west, young man!" The average American family does not live in one place for more than five years. So what "accumulation of culture" can there be if the past in America means two weeks ago, and the preceding five years are considered antiquity? Every five years America rediscovers the world, life, sex, religion—all this without any link to the discoveries of the past five years. It is an ensorcelled country, where life is three-dimensional with the fourth dimension unknown—moving forward in a state of permanent amnesia. There is a feeling that your footsteps produce no echo, and your body casts no shadow. Even applying the greatest efforts, you are unable to change anything or even leave any tracks, as if you had spent your life walking along the water's edge at the seashore.

And if one's only purpose in life is to pursue happiness, success at any price, then one cannot have any principles or concepts; after all, they exist only in time. In fact, what is the worth of a reputation if a person is reborn every day? What is the worth of concepts if every five years the world is reinvented once more? A person speaking of principles and concepts is looked upon as a madman. It is deemed normal, good, and successful to be a "pragmatist," an opportunist, a conformist.

America is really a land of conformists, ruled by constantly arising epidemics of a feverish nature; all of a sudden, everyone starts jogging, because it is allegedly good for one's health. It does not matter that the man who invented this craze died at the age of 55 while jogging—40 million Americans continue to jog, making the earth shake. Or salt is suddenly declared to be the source of all ailments —so just try getting salt on the table in any American restaurant. Should you ask for it, you will be suspected of suicidal tendencies. I do not know, but it is quite possible that at the beginning of the century America was truly "the land of the free," but hearing this today is laughable. It is hard to imagine a nation more enslaved by any craze, even the most idiotic ones, by any petty charlatans who thought it up. In the final instance, enslaved by its pursuit of success. Yet even success, perceived so three-dimensionally, temporally, can only be purely material, not going beyond the framework of the old Russian saying, "It is better to be healthy and rich, than sick and poor."

But while we say this ironically, it is not perceived as funny by Americans; such is the program of their lives. Health is their main concern, or rather obsession, reaching absurd heights, as if death is not the inevitable end of human life, but only the result of one's sins: failure to follow the right diet, exercise, and doctor's orders. And wealth is the natural measure of success, that someone who has "made it in America" (another obscure expression in Russian eyes—made what?) immediately buys a limousine one and a half blocks long, and if he "made it big," a whole skyscraper.

The American mass media is aimed at the most primitive crowd, the rabble, first by artificially creating celebrities, blowing them up from nothing, and then just as artificially bringing them down by trumpeting a scandal—again out of nothing. It is all false, fake, empty, wavering like a mirage in a desert, and there is nothing real, genuine, and stable that could continue to exist, even if you close your eyes for just one minute. Or switch off the television.

Is it surprising that in the midst of this pursuit of happiness, most Americans are very unhappy people, dissatisfied with their fate, frequently burdened by problems they have created them-selves, endlessly trying to "find themselves" and finding nothing? Hence the preponderance of various gurus, psychoanalysts, sects, and similar saviors of people from themselves, which are regarded as essential by a good third of the American population. At times it seems that Americans, unable to bear the burden of freedom, simply seek someone to enslave them.

In a word, this is an anticulture that no evolution, no "accumu-lation" shall develop into a culture. This is also due to the circum-stance that America has no social stratum that usually promotes culture—no intelligentsia—and that its replacement, "intellectu-als," are simultaneously the most illiterate and the most repellent part of society. I do not undertake to judge what it was like earlier (after all, this country gave the world numerous outstanding writers and scientists in the past), but what I encountered was truly awful. It is not enough that they possess all the abovementioned specific features of American anti-culture in full, if not in excess, but apart from these delusions, and with no justification at all, American "in-tellectuals" suffer from all the sins of the European intelligentsia: overweening narcissism, belief in their "enlightening" mission, and the right to a privileged, elite position. And invariably, leftist ten-dencies of the most primitive variety. At least the European intel-ligentsia with its leftist sympathies, apart from its "class interest," are supported by concepts from a two-hundred-year-history of pub-lic debates, revolutions, and wars, so it is possible to polemicize with them. Their American counterparts have nothing to lean on except bare emotions that can reach hysterical levels. To hell with debates, beware of having your eyes scratched out; for they are, naturally, the voice of conscience and their opponent is an enemy of the people by definition. They sympathize, while you are hard-hearted and merciless. The only catch is that for some reason their sympathy is always very selective, which is why in their purview "some animals are more equal than others," as was noted keenly by George Orwell.

I do not think that communist ideology would ever have been able to conquer the USA—simply because this ideology is too complex, too conceptual, and presumes at least some knowledge of history. It is a sickness of culture, of intellect, and there is simply not enough of either in America to produce an epidemic. (However, if it were to establish itself, a totalitarian system would remain there forever be-cause of the Americans' incredible conformism). The American left, like the American subculture, is three-dimensional. Imported, one may assume, at the time of the French Revolution, it remains on the level of the ideas of the age of the Enlightenment, unaffected by anything new over two hundred years. The American elite still believes the myth of the "noble savage," the innate good nature of Man, ruined by bad institutions. It professes some kind of completely antediluvian egalitarianism, but probably only one in a thousand can name the original source. As followers of a socialist Utopia in the most general, masonic version, they know nothing of the subsequent development of socialist ideas, especially not their downfall. It is like a sanctuary in honor of Jean-Jacques Rousseau, in the same sense that North Korea is a sanctuary in honor of Stalin.[173]

Then again, it is just as hard to say whether they believe all this nonsense as it is to determine whether Andropov really believed in communism. It is advantageous to profess these views in today's America, and for people in intellectual professions it is simply vital for career advancement. For however our Utopian rebels may position themselves as opponents, protectors of popular interests, they mutated into the establishment long ago and wield more power than the authorities, the government. Unity of interests has turned them into a deceitful, brass-necked clique, holding on to their positions and privileges with the same tenacity as the Soviet *nomenklatura.* And woe betide the daredevil who seeks to defend his own opinion against the will of this intellectual mafia.

It is amusing that European leftists still have not realized to what extent their fellow thinkers have subjugated America, and by inertia continue to criticize it for something it no longer represents. In their imagination it is still a land of cowboys, "cops and robbers," and "tough guys" who shoot anything that moves, while their leftist ideas and formations, attitudes, and social benefits have triumphed there since the 1960s, much more so than in old, conservative Europe. What talk can there be of "tough guys" if the generations that have grown up since then are unable to cope with stress, a traumatic situation, or themselves without the help of a psychoanalyst. Even the death of a neighbor's dog can plunge them into deep depression.

All this would be of mere academic interest to us if the USA, by virtue of its geographic specifics, had not become "the leader of the Western world" at the most critical moment of confrontation with communism. And although America honorably withstood the early period of the Cold War at the end of the 1940s and the beginning of the 1950s (the creation of NATO, the Berlin blockade, the Korean War, etc.)—by the end of the 1960s it was creaking at the seams.

As it happened, American "intellectuals" of the 1940s and 1950s

---

[173]"News from the Lavrenty Beria memorial park", was a famous samizdat publication by Ukrainian dissident Valentin Moroz.

were leftists, a significant part of them were even pro-communist
(although they had not yet managed to enslave all society, as happened later). The outburst of dismay among the American establishment at the recently published memoirs of Stalin's main butcher
and super-spy, Lieutenant-General Pavel Sudoplatov, provides am-
ple evidence of this. The most amazing aspect of this situation is not
so much the names of famous physicists—J. Robert Oppenheimer,
Enrico Fermi, Leo Szilard and others—who willingly shared atomic
secrets with Stalin, but rather the ease with which Soviet intelligence was able to operate in American leftist circles. Agents from
their midst were not sought, but selected.

As for the physicists, I see the current indignation of their colleagues as spurious: as if their pro-Soviet sympathies were not
known before the general's revelations. It is sufficient to recall that
the entire Manhattan Project was their initiative: the possible fear
that the atomic weapon could end up in Hitler's hands worried them
to such an extent that they, forgetting their pacifism, simply forced
the American president to sanction the creation of the atom bomb.
But the real news that the weapon fell into Stalin's hands did not
concern them at all: on the contrary, from that moment they became pacifists again and "opponents of atomic weapons"—Western
ones, of course.

However, despite all the evil they perpetrated, I am more dis-
gusted by their current protectors than by Oppenheimer and company. The latter at least believed in what they did and were prepared
to risk their lives for their convictions, while their protectors are
simply preserving their cozy position in the elite, totally unashamed
of barefaced lies. They are certainly not concerned about the good
name of their late colleagues, but the need to take responsibility for
the common fault. The participation of American leftist intellectuals in Soviet atomic espionage is just one example of their complicity
in the communists' crimes. And to admit this would mean admitting that the anticommunist campaign of the late 1940s and early
1950s, popularly known as "McCarthyism," was no witch hunt. It is
regrettable that, like everything in America, it took on a hysterical
nature, but in fact it is indisputable that it was fully justified.

The bogey of McCarthyism, shamelessly exploited by American leftist intellectuals for a good fifty years, was the instrument
whereby the self-proclaimed elite became the establishment, occupying a practically dictatorial position in American society. It
was akin to emotional blackmail: they had suffered unfairly, so everyone now owed them. Nobody could dare to challenge them or
even remind them of their responsibility for the past: this would be
declared renewed persecution, renewed McCarthyism. Everything

was turned upside down: being pro-Soviet, or even a communist, became respectable, if not to say mandatory; being an anticommunist was shameful and practically criminal.

So the present turmoil in the American establishment is not surprising: its very legitimizing of its supremacy has come under question, the whole myth of its unfair suffering. And is that suffering not a myth? After all, at a time when their spiritual brothers were enslaving entire peoples, destroying millions to the benefit of their common ideology, all these people had to face were questions, moreover public ones, in the presence of their lawyers, the press, and with observance of all procedural formalities, such as: "Are you a member of any communist group?"

That was all. I remember how glad I was in 1967 to finally say to my judges' faces everything I thought of their political system, thereby earning three years in the camps. I never thought of myself as a sufferer. They, however, faced no threat of camps, or torture, or destruction. At worst a loss of their jobs. It's curious how the majority of them broke so shamefully, pointing fingers at their friends and neighbors and lying under oath. Only a few refused to speak. Suffering heroes indeed! But for a good forty years their "tragedy" featured in the press, on television, in the cinema. Dozens of Hollywood films were made on this subject, the last one as recently as 1990: *Guilty by Suspicion* starring Robert De Niro.

Not a word about the tragedy of hundreds of millions who really suffered under the communist yoke. Just look at the productions of this citadel of the American left—Hollywood—for the past forty years from this angle, and you will see that there has not been a single film that gave an honest and serious depiction of the main tragedy of our century. These are either open Soviet apologetics, or a more refined, sophisticated lie, relying on the ignorance of the general public. A historian forced to judge our times by Hollywood films will not understand anything. Most likely he will reach the conclusion that we spent the entire century under the permanent threat of fascism, or the threat of crazed American generals. And if communism existed in our world at all, it was very distant, as an innocuous background. Even the ageless James Bond does not fight the KGB, but is most frequently in an alliance with them against some mythical super-corporation headed, as a rule, by a lunatic capitalist. There is no hint that communism itself could threaten mankind in any way—just our reaction to it. Not the opponent, but our resistance to the opponent.

As for the opponent, he only elicits sympathy. At the very least compassion, a feeling of fellow suffering, as a "deluded idealist" or "Red"). Even Pasternak's "Doctor Zhivago", the penalty for reading which was imprisonment in the USSR, was turned into a sloppy tearjerker. There is no sympathy for the millions of victims of these idealists, let alone remorse. Where it is impossible to avoid mentioning victims, there are not just lies, but monstrous lies. The best example of this is *The Killing Fields*, a film about the best-known communist crime in our time, in Cambodia. You cannot hide the skulls, but you can avoid explaining to viewers who killed a good half of their countrymen. So try and guess: where did they come from, and why do they murder people? Throughout the entire film you cannot determine that they were simply communists, and seemingly even greater idealists than their Moscow (or Vietnamese) colleagues: at least those shamefacedly buried their victims in the ground, they didn't display them for the entire world to see.

The whole purpose of the film is pure disinformation. First, to justify the occupation of Cambodia by Vietnam. As though the fault does not lie in communism, because Vietnamese communists put an end to the slaughter in Cambodia. Rejoice and be glad. Second, to justify the treacherous role of the American left in this tragedy. So we have as the hero a left-liberal correspondent of a left-liberal press saving a Cambodian family. Forget that it was they who facilitated the victory of communism in Southeast Asia by their hysterical antiwar campaign, due to which three countries vanished off the face of the earth, and the red killers were able to create pyramids of human skulls. All this is negligible compared to a marvelous human feat—the rescue of one family. Tears cloud the eyes of viewers; what an honorable act! Even Goebbels would have shed a tear watching this film.

Having formed on the basis of lies and betrayal, and even been raised on this propaganda, the American elite was a natural ally of the USSR long before détente. In the USA, as distinct from Europe, the basis was not merely ideological sympathies—the overwhelming majority of American intellectuals had no idea what communist ideology consisted of, even those who proudly proclaimed themselves to be Marxists—but rather stemmed from opposition to their own government. The Vietnam War, which did not differ substantially from the Korean War one half to two decades earlier, served as the catalyst for such social attitudes. Paradoxical as it may sound, America was pro-Soviet at the end of the 1960s and the beginning of the 1970s because it became anti-American: the antiwar hysteria, blown out of proportion by the leftist elite to the degree of paranoia, divided the country, making anti-American sentiments more widespread than in Europe. But if the elite needed this hysteria for self-affirmation, to seize leading positions in society, millions of young Americans, like the biblical herd of Gadarene swine possessed by devils, followed meekly in their wake out of simple conformity. Marijuana, rock, eternally open mouths, clear eyes shining with idiotic enthusiasm, and "protest." "Rebellion" became the fashion, necessary for success, which later changed to jogging in the morning, ecology, and the obsession with health.

For the rest of the world this was a catastrophe: not only was it left without a leader—which was neither here nor there—but it was betrayed by that leader.

4.6 Peaceful offensive

Naturally, all this did not occur without Soviet help and would not have escaped their attention. Both the war in Southeast Asia and the antiwar hysteria were fanned and supported by Moscow, and with success in both directions, the time had come for decisive action. The game of détente suggested by European social democrats came in very useful: there remained practically no obstacles in the path of the Soviet "peace offensive." As Brezhnev said, launching his "Peace Program" at the XXIV Party Congress in March 1971: "The balance of forces on the world arena has shifted to the side of socialism."

It must be remembered that in communist Newspeak, "peace" has nothing to do with what normal people take it to mean, but with the victory of communism throughout the world. The CC documents leave no doubt that the class nature of the foreign policy of the USSR did not change in the period of détente—which in their conception "is a form of class struggle, aimed at reinforcing global socialism, the international communist, workers', and national liberation movements, the entire anti-imperialist front" (24 July 1973*, St 88/1).

Despite existing opinion, a purely military victory over the class enemy was never considered preferable by Moscow. The doctrine demanded "liberating humanity from the shackles of capitalism" in the process of "class struggle," not in the process of nuclear destruction. It presupposed revolutions and even revolutionary wars, but those that would result in power passing to the "victorious proletariat," i.e., their fifth column. And from a purely pragmatic point of view, if they needed something from the West by the start of the 1970s, it was industrial potential and not endless expanses of scorched earth. Thus "liberation" should start with local forces, "friends," and the glorious Soviet army could only put a brilliant end to it, coming to the assistance of "class brothers."

Correspondingly, the aim of Soviet foreign policy has always been the "reinforcement of the positions of global socialism, creation of favorable possibilities for the activities of the international communist, workers' and national liberation movements." Soviet sights were always set on gaining Europe and its industrial base. Strictly speaking, the Bolshevik revolution in Russia occurred by mistake: according to Lenin's plan (and that of Marx even more) it should have happened in the industrially developed countries of Europe, which would ensure the subsequent victory of socialism worldwide. While planning his revolution in St. Petersburg, Lenin was actually trying to speed it up in Europe, but was mistaken. The workers' unrest in Germany, Italy, and France did not amount to a revolution, and the Red Army was still bogged down near Warsaw. It remained for Russia to build socialism "in one separately taken country."

Nonetheless, Lenin's pupils and successors knew full well that without European industry there could be no serious talk of socialism. They could "create favorable possibilities for the activities" of their European friends only by the destabilization of a Europe that had calmed down by that time. Hence the seemingly contradictory acts by Stalin, supporting Hitler in his coming to power and in the creation of the Wehrmacht on one hand, and on the other giving assistance to republican Spain in the civil war. In Stalin's estimation, Hitler should become the "icebreaker of the revolution": having broken the "old order" in Europe and produced a political polarization (the consolidation of antifascist forces under the leadership of "friends") he should have ensured the Red Army the honorable role of the liberator of the European continent from Nazism and the shackles of capitalism at the same time.[174] But as a result Hitler upstaged Stalin, who had to engage in a long defense (for which he was unprepared), and in the meantime the Americans entered the war (and acquired the atomic bomb at the end). Although Stalin put an end to the war in Berlin, he had no luck in achieving a glorious liberation of all Europe.

The postwar confrontation, while not changing the substance of Soviet aims, shifted the emphasis of Soviet foreign policy; it was pointless to think of destabilizing Europe while its stability was assured by the American presence, the nuclear umbrella, and economic influence (the Marshall Plan). It may be stated without any exaggeration that this is what saved Europe from communism—which is why the USA became the number one enemy of all of progressive humanity, and the "struggle against American imperialism"

---

[174]Viktor Suvorov, *Icebreaker: Who Started the Second World War?* London: Hamish Hamilton, 1990 (published in Russia in 1992 as *Ledokol.* Moscow: New Times).

its main concern (just as the "struggle for peace" and nuclear disarmament were directed against the real advantages of the USA). The purpose of this struggle was not just to change the social system in America itself or to undermine its influence in other parts of the world, but to make it leave Europe. But global confrontation has its own rules, and if, as it emerges now, Stalin precipitated the Berlin crisis in order to deflect American forces from the Korean War,[175] then the Vietnam War, although not pursuing the same aim, did decrease American influence in Europe.

To be more precise, not that war as such, but the antiwar frenzy around it: this factor brought about the narrowing of the gap between socialism and communism, just like the spread of pro-Soviet attitudes in America itself. The USA ceased to be an effective counterbalance to the USSR, enabling the latter to launch its "peaceful offensive." But if its allies in Europe were social democrats, in the USA they were the left-liberal circles, which Soviet policy deliberately aimed at. Long before the adoption of the "Peace Program," Soviet official delegations were instructed as follows (23 April 1970, St 96/126^):

> Use the stay in the USA to further contacts with liberal and opposition circles that are promoting the normalization of relations on the basis of the USA's rejection of the policies of the "Cold War" and the arms race... activate the interest of business circles... and criticize as widely as possible the obstacles set by the USA along the path of improved relations, firstly the arms race, intervention in Southeast Asia and support of Israel.

This was also the time of the (28 April 1970*, 1128-A; §1.4— Intellectual Shenanigans) "measures to support [the Negro protest movement]," which interested the Kremlin leaders only because it would "create certain difficulties for ruling US circles and shall distract the attention of Nixon's administration from the conduct of an active foreign policy". Everything was calculated to force America into détente, or, at least, into self-isolation. By 1973, with the ceremonious signing of the "Basic Principles of Relations Between the United States of America and the Union of Soviet Socialist Republics" (1972) and the "Agreement between the United States of America and the Union of Soviet Socialist Republics on the Prevention of Nuclear War" (1973) the situation had become even more acute: the Arab oil boycott dealt a huge blow to the economic situation of the West, and the war in Southeast Asia grew more hopeless.

---

[175]Pavel and Anatoli Sudoplatov, *Special Tasks: The Memoirs of an Unwanted Witness—A Soviet Spymaster*. Boston: Little, Brown, © 1994, 1995.

"The turn toward the relaxation of international tension is occurring at a strategically profitable moment for us," reasoned the CC (24 July 1973*, St 88/1),[176] "under the conditions of the deepening of the general crisis of capitalism, the enforced adjustment of contemporary capitalism to circumstances resulting from numerous defeats of aggressive imperialist policies, the crisis of the monetary system of capitalism, relative weakening of the positions of American imperialism throughout the world, the fall of the prestige of the political system of the USA, in the situation of the sharpening of internal class, national and also interimperialist contradictions, and the growing interest of capitalist business circles in establishing trade and economic relations with the Soviet Union."

So after Brezhnev's visit to the USA, the CC adopted "a broad program of propagandist measures" in which its strategy is reflected quite precisely. At an emergency meeting called by the CC for all leaders of "Soviet public organizations and Soviet representatives in international democratic organizations," the following instructions were issued "regarding the purposes of their work under contemporary conditions, and also on questions of the development of links with public organizations and movements in the USA for strengthening our influence on broad circles of the American public" (24 July 1973*, St 88/1, pp. 7–8):

> All organizations conducting information and propagandistic work are charged with an all-round increase in the advance of our propaganda. Highly significant changes in the international situation should not give rise to unsubstantiated illusions, complacency, and passivity. It is necessary to point out that there are certain forces in the world that oppose the defusion of international tension and that there are still dangerously explosive pockets of aggression and war. Avoiding stereotypes inherited from the period of the "Cold War," concentrate attention on a comparative analysis of both systems. In every possible way, explain the advantages of socialism, socialist ideals, its moral and spiritual values and ideas, without ignoring the actual difficulties of our development. . . .
>
> Conduct a decisive advance against anticommunist, anti-Soviet, Zionist, and militarist forces, all those who oppose détente and support a return to the "Cold War" and the arms race, and those who sow the seeds of discord and distrust between nations.
>
> Constant attention must be paid to exposing the attempts of hostile ideological centers to revive concepts aimed at encouraging the "erosion" of socialist ideology (including "theories" of

---

[176]24 July 1973* (St 88/1), p. 3.

convergence and deideologizing in their various versions). Rebuff any attempts to interpret international détente as an affirmation of such theories. At the same time, consistently instill the thought of the unacceptability of mixing the "Cold War," which is a definite but far from fatally unavoidable stage in interstate relations, with ideological struggle, which is a form of the class struggle of the proletariat against the bourgeoisie, stemming from the difference between two social systems.

Exposing by argument the provocative meaning that bourgeois propaganda attributes to the well-known thesis of "the freedom to exchange ideas, information, and people," indicate that the Soviet Union has always championed the development of cultural contacts that facilitate the mutual spiritual enrichment of people, and has achieved considerable success in this field.

. . .

In all spheres of propaganda, expose the inadequacy of various forms of petit bourgeois leftist movements that have found favor among some young people in the capitalist world, the pointlessness of the so-called "rebellion of youth" unconnected with the liberating work of the proletariat, and attempts to ignore the real problems and contradictions of capitalist society. Stress that only socialism opens the way to the genuine liberation of the younger generation. Rebuff firmly "technocratic" and other theories and views aimed at providing grounds for the pretensions of the intelligentsia to a special role in the leadership of contemporary society and various forms of speculation regarding "creative freedom" under socialist conditions.

This plan was approved, embracing practically all spheres of the activity of mutual relations.[177] The most important feature of it was the extensive use of Western mass media to spread Soviet propaganda.

The USSR State Committee for Television and Radio Broadcasting (Gosteleradio) received the following instructions:

- Employ the new opportunities for increasing contacts and links with the television and radio organizations in the USA, France, and the FRG, among other things for the promotion of Soviet TV materials and the preparation of joint programs, paying special attention to the establishment of direct contacts with local TV and radio stations;

- Organize the invitation of prominent American TV and radio journalists to the USSR for the purpose of preparing radio programs and TV films about the Soviet Union under the aegis of the State Committee;

---

[177]24 July 1973* (St 88/1), pp. 12–22.

- Upon agreement with the Department of Propaganda [and Agitation] of the CC CPSU... conduct consultations with television and radio organizations of fraternal socialist countries on questions of coordination, including propagandist appearances in the USA and other capitalist countries of Europe, determinations of the basic propagandist directions with allowance for the specifics of individual European countries, and clarification of the time schedule of broadcasts;

- Organize regular counter-propagandist appearances exposing the conjectures and insinuations of bourgeois radio propaganda of Maoist, Zionist, and revisionist views.

The Novosti Press Agency was instructed to:

- Prepare articles by party, state, and public figures of the USSR for influential American publications, explaining various aspects of the domestic and foreign policy of the CPSU;

- Cooperate with prominent American journalists in preparing materials at their request;

- Continue joint cooperation with American TV and radio organizations ABC, CBS, NBC, and also the television service UPI [United Press International] in the preparation of reports, informative materials, and TV programs devoted to the achievements of the Soviet Union and the lives of Soviet people. Prepare and promote the TV films *The 'Pravda' Newspaper*, *The Supreme Soviet*, *Secretary of the Party Committee*, *Progress and Protection of the Environment*, and others.

The State Cinema Committee was assigned a task: "Develop specific offers of the joint staging of Soviet-American productions."

The State Press Committee was to "perform the systematic translation into Russian of books by progressive American writers and publicists and collections of addresses by prominent public figures and journalists that give an objective description of political and socioeconomic processes and who support cooperation with the Soviet Union."

The Academy of Sciences of the USSR fared even worse:

- Study the possibilities of attracting leading American scientists to the Pugwash movement, envisaging the possibility of individual approaches by prominent Soviet scientists;

- Expand studies of the economic, political, and social situation in the USA, the problems of the struggle of workers', communist, nationalist, and other mass movements in the USA, increase study of the contemporary state of American philosophical, economic, historical, sociological, legal, and psychological sciences, literature, and literary criticism, and also the ideological struggle in the field of science and the arts;

• Prepare a situational analysis on issues of Soviet-American relations, on the basis of the new stage of their development and influence on the global situation, and also the relations of the USA with West European allies in new circumstances;

• Activate contacts with scientific institutions in France, the FRG, Japan, and other countries concerned with American Studies.

In other words, this was simply an intelligence-gathering and analytical role, as if the Academy of Sciences were a KGB department. Intelligence academicians Georgy Arbatov, Yevgeny Primakov (recent head of the intelligence service of Russia, currently risen to the post of Minister of Foreign Affairs), Inozemtsev, and Mikhail Millionshchikov were charged with regularly working on the American elite, and for this purpose Soviet-American "scientific" colloquiums and symposiums were held on problems of bilateral relations and other "various problems of sociological and humanitarian knowledge."

This was a massive offensive of Soviet propaganda and disinformation, using all channels and methods, public and state structures. This included sister cities, and work "on the creation of a broad public organization in the USA calling for the development of friendly relations with the Soviet Union." Everything was grist to the mill: youth and women's organizations, associations of war veterans, and professional unions—all these were invoked to the achievement of that aim.

Even the main tourist administration was obligated to ". . . implement measures for a comprehensive explanation to tourists from the USA and other countries of the achievements of the Soviet people in communist construction and the practical steps of the CC CPSU and the Soviet government in the implementation of the Peace Program, making active use of propaganda lectures, meetings with the Soviet public, showings of Soviet films, and visits to cultural and visual events."

As for Soviet tourists to America, they were obligated to participate ". . . in informative-propagandistic work among the American population, bearing in mind the organization of meetings with the

American public, press conferences, and the presentation of lectures and addresses on radio and television."

At the same time, stringent measures were in force to prevent any Western influence on the Soviet population. Any "cultural exchange" became a deception under the unrelenting control of the Ministry of Culture over its ideological content; Soviet propaganda was exchanged for Western "progressive culture." Repressions of dissidents did not diminish. The rules of the game set by Moscow really were, as noted by Ronald Reagan, "a one-way street." Soviet propaganda, disinformation, and subversive activity appeared to be legalized under the guise of the free exchange of people and ideas, and were legitimate aspects of the "ideological struggle." Any attempts by the West to counter this or conduct its own ideological struggle were unacceptable as "interference in the internal matters of the USSR" and "a return to the practices of the 'Cold War.'"

It is easy to imagine the confusion in the minds of clear-eyed Yankees created by this avalanche of deceit, moreover, sanctioned by their own government in the name of the honorable cause of protecting peace. Its influence on the American elite is beyond doubt.

4.7   Defeatists

In 1980, when détente was a thing of the past, one of its architects, former US president Richard Nixon, wrote:[178]

> The Soviet Union today is the most powerfully armed expansionist nation the world has ever known, and its arms buildup continues at a pace nearly twice that of the United States. There is no mystery about Soviet intentions. The Kremlin leaders do not want war, but they do want the world. And they are rapidly moving into position to get what they want.
>
> In the 1980s America for the first time in modern history will confront two cold realities. The first of these is that if war were to come, we might lose. The second is that we might be defeated without war. The second prospect is more likely than the first, and almost as grim.

It is a pity that he had this epiphany too late, when his policy of détente had already borne the aforementioned fruits. Moreover, in 1980 he was still unwilling to acknowledge the link between détente and this result. Were it not for the tragedy of the situation, his explanations would have sounded comical. On one hand, he seems to

---

[178]*The Real War.* New York: Simon & Schuster Inc. (pbk), 1990, pp. 2–3.

understand that the substance of the communist system, its ideology and aims, have not changed, that, as he writes,[179] "Neither Brezhnev nor his predecessors engaged in negotiation to achieve peace as an end in itself. Rather they sought peace so that they could use it to extend communist domination without war in all areas of the world."

Yet addressing the Congress of the USA upon returning from Moscow in 1972—speaking almost like Chamberlain in 1938—he declared,[180] "... We did not bring back from Moscow the promise of instant peace, but we do bring the beginning of a process that can lead to lasting peace."

After that he blames all his misfortunes on the "unjustified euphoria" of Western society. But what else could have been expected of it if even the president of the USA, moreover one with an anticommunist reputation, believes in the likelihood of establishing a firm peace with the USSR by means of agreements? Having conceded all possible Western positions, he tries to justify himself by claiming that he had been misunderstood, that détente had not been deemed an alternative to the Cold War but a supplement to it:[181]

> The meaning of détente, as originally envisaged by my administration, has become so distorted, both by Soviet behavior and by misunderstanding in the United States, that the term has lost its usefulness as a description of Soviet-American relations. When détente is said to be the "alternative to the Cold War" it even becomes an obstacle to clear thought.

So who is guilty of this "misunderstanding" that almost cost humanity its future? The Soviet leaders with their improper behavior? But Nixon himself writes the following on the next page:[182]

> If the Russians think they can get away with using détente as a cover for aggression, either direct or indirect, they will try. In recent years they have not only tried but succeeded, just as they have succeeded in using aggression as a cover for shifting the military balance in their favor.

In other words, nothing else could have been expected of them. Then was it the fault of the "misunderstanding" that arose in the USA? But it was precisely Nixon and Kissinger who created that misunderstanding.[183]

---

[179]Ibid., p. 49.
[180]Ibid., p. 267.
[181]Ibid., p. 285.
[182]Ibid., p. 287.
[183]Ibid., p. 5.

The hope arose that if the United States limited its own arms, others—particularly the Soviets—would follow. But the Soviets did not perform according to theory. In fact, during the same period when this arms-control doctrine was winning favor among American theorists, and the theorists were winning influence, the Soviet five-year plans were charting ever greater increases in military spending, clearly guided by coherent strategic objectives. The Soviets were not bogged down in theory; they were driving toward supremacy.

Yet who but Kissinger and Nixon fielded all these theories, this lunatic philosophy of arms control by means of treaties, agreements, and similar nonsense that did not oblige the Soviets to do anything?[184]

Whether directly or indirectly, trade with the Soviets strengthens them militarily. Even trade in nonstrategic times frees resources for them to use in other ways. We must never forget that doing business with the Soviets includes these costs; it is only justified when the benefits outweigh the costs. Trade with the Russians must be used as a weapon, not as a gift.

But in 1980 he was still trying to argue that his attempts to grant the USSR most-favored-nation status in trade was fully justified, even though that status would allow the Kremlin practically unlimited access to cheap credit. Then, probably trying to confuse us utterly, he adds:[185]

As long as the Soviets continue on their present aggressive course... we should remember that trade is something they want which we can give or deny, depending on their behavior.

The paradox of the Nixon-Kissinger strategy lies in that on one hand, they seem to comprehend the total absurdity of détente and even realize the danger of these games, but on the other hand, they crawl into the python's jaws like mesmerized rabbits:[186]

The primary purpose of arms control is to reduce the danger of war. But arms control by itself cannot do this. Political differences, not arms, are the root causes of war, and until these are resolved, there will be enough arms for the most devastating war no matter how many arms control agreements are reached.

[...]

---

[184]Ibid., p. 207.
[185]Ibid., p. 208.
[186]Ibid., p. 269.

> Trade and arms control must be linked with the settlement of
> political differences if the danger of war is to be reduced. Only
> if we use linkage in this way will we be attacking the root causes
> of war.

It might be possible to agree with this, but only if it is remembered that the main "political difference" in this case is Marxist-Leninist ideology, and that Soviet leaders have no intention of abandoning it in exchange for any benefits. It appears that Nixon understands this; in any case, he mentions it constantly throughout his whole book. Then what, in the perception of the Nixon administration, was the main benefit of a détente that outweighed the "losses"? Where is the *quid pro quo*? I fear the reality was much more transparent than all those dialectics that the former president of the USA produced to justify himself: simply speaking, finding itself in a difficult situation, America tried to buy off the Soviet aggressor.[187]

> It was during the transition period between my election in
> 1968 and my first inauguration in 1969 that Henry Kissinger
> and I developed what is now widely called the concept of link-
> age. We determined that those things the Soviets wanted—the
> good public relations that summits provided, economic cooper-
> ation, and strategic arms limitations agreements—would not be
> gained by them without a quid pro quo. At that time the prin-
> cipal quid pro quos we wanted were some assistance in getting
> a settlement in Vietnam, restraint by them in the Middle East,
> and a resolution of the recurring problems in Berlin.

We should note that the danger in all these places was created quite consciously by Soviet aggression, which means that any payment for its removal was no smarter than paying racketeers. The idea was even more suicidal in that the payment in question gave the USSR strategic advantages: military advantage, credits, technologies, the appearance of a peace-loving, respected partner of the West. Such a strange deal, which, even if it may have granted the West a short breather, placed the future of mankind into the hands of the Kremlin bandits.

But as happens in dealings with racketeers, they did not even allow the promised breather: having received their ransom, the Soviet leaders did not even think of fulfilling their promises. The USA had to drink the bitter cup of its defeat in Southeast Asia and flee, practically abandoning its allies to the mercies of the enemy; Soviet influence in Europe reached its apogee in those years, and the terrorist movements supported by the USSR threatened political

---

[187]Ibid., pp. 167–168.

destabilization. It is impossible to say that in those years the USSR showed any "restraint" in the Middle East: it suffices to recall the massive Soviet aid to Syria, Iraq, and the Palestinian terrorists, the role played by the USSR in the destruction of Lebanon and the war against Israel in 1973. The Berlin problem, needless to say, simply became a permanent source of hard currency for the GDR.

In fact, let us calculate what price humanity had to pay for détente in that decade:

- If by the end of the 1960s there was a relative degree of parity in strategic arms between the East and the West, then by the end of the 1970s the USSR had gained a clear advantage;

- If the Soviet empire was experiencing a crisis in the two post-war decades and was forced to suppress unrest in Eastern Europe (the GDR in 1953, Hungary in 1956, Czechoslovakia and Poland in 1968), then it was able to stabilize over the decade of détente;

- If in that same period communism spread to only two countries—Cuba and North Vietnam—then during the decade of détente a plethora of noncommunist states was wiped off the face of the earth (Angola, Ethiopia, Afghanistan, South Yemen, Somalia, Mozambique, Laos, Cambodia, South Vietnam, Burma, Nicaragua), not counting pro-communist regimes in little-known countries at that time, such as Grenada, the Cape Verde Islands, and Madagascar, and "national liberation" movements became active in another ten countries (Salvador, Guatemala, Lebanon, Namibia, Chile and others). A good hundred million people.

But the worst result of détente was the loss of the will to resist that afflicted the West. It could be likened to an epidemic of moral AIDS, due to which seemingly healthy countries lost immunity to harmful bacteria. And this was not least due to the positions of the USA—the European social democrats could not have managed it alone, as Nixon writes:[188]

> Other nations have much longer experience than we have in the use of power to maintain the peace. But they no longer have the power. So, by default, the world looks to the United States. It looks today with nervous apprehension, as the bulwarks against Soviet expansion crumble in one nation after another, and as the United States appears so lost in uncertainty

---

[188]Ibid., p. 3.

or paralyzed by propriety that it is either unable or unwilling to
act.

Despite all their errors, it would be unfair to place all the blame
on just Nixon and Kissinger. Coming to power in the thick of the
antiwar hysteria, or, to be more precise, in the thick of the rebellion,
when the old elite had all but capitulated and the new was trying
to occupy leading positions at any price, the Nixon administration
tried to stabilize the situation by compromise, first of all with the
new elite. Even Soviet expansion in Europe, let alone in third world
countries, moved to the back burner. They were simply sacrificed.
America, which was literally being torn apart, had to be saved—
hence the fractured nature of American foreign policy at that time.
This led to Nixon's downfall as a symbol of the total victory of the
new elite and the subsequent destruction of the old institutions of
presidential power, the army and the CIA.

Power switched to the institutions traditionally controlled by the
left: to the press, television, public organizations, and—to the extent that it was controlled by the new elite—to Congress.[189]

Naturally, the sinfully conceived anti-American campaign—conceived in the sin of betrayal of Western interests in general and its
own country in particular—this new elite was pro-Soviet (which,
God forbid, cannot be said aloud in America even now without
arousing the cry "McCarthyism again!"). Even Nixon, who did not
curb his tongue all the time in describing the new elite, did not go
that far:[190]

> If America loses World War III, it will be because of the failure of
> its leadership class. In particular, it will be because of the atten-
> tion, the celebrity, and the legitimacy given to the "trendies"—
> those overglamorized dilettantes who posture in the latest idea,
> mount the fashionable protests, and are slobbered over by the
> news media, whose creation they essentially are.

Everything would seem in order, but for some reason these "fashions" correlated invariably with Soviet interests, and frequently the
basic directions of the massive Soviet propaganda described above.
It does not really matter whether it is called a conspiracy or not;
if the majority followed fashion out of conformity, the trendsetters
certainly knew what they were doing. Their lies are too obvious,
pro-Soviet "theories" were too persistently drummed into the heads
of Americans, with the purpose of justifying any communist crime.
Pick up any book about the Cold War at random and you will see

---

[189]Ibid, p. 245.
[190]Ibid, p. 242.

it for yourself.[191] Even the beginning period of "cold" after the war, when Stalin not only swallowed six European countries (not counting the Baltic states and one-third of Germany), but was preparing actively for the next round of "liberating" Europe, is interpreted by them as "Western paranoia." Poor Stalin, you see, was only practicing defense, and was misinterpreted by Harry Truman and Winston Churchill.

"So what?" they say without a blink. "If the communists falsified the elections in Poland or Czechoslovakia, the Western allies did the same in Italy and Belgium."

And in the period of détente they portrayed Soviet love of peace in response to the paranoia of the USA. At best they described the situation as the struggle between two superpowers for global supremacy, and not as the resistance of humanity to the communist infection, by which both sides seem to be equalized, and the writer appears as some kind of sage, floating above the conflict like an ethereal spirit over a vale of tears. Here is perhaps the most glaring example, quoted at random:[192]

> Despite the ramifications of the Sino-Soviet split, the war remained essentially a bi-polar conflict between the Soviet Union and the United States. The elite of each country—the dominant political and economic groupings, with their bureaucracies—were blinkered by universalist assumptions about their respective systems. While they used a variety of means, such as their alternation of tension and détente, their goal was always the triumph of their own ideology. In pursuit of that end they sought to control the behavior of their own populations and their satellites and client states. Armed with ideological fervor for either the "Free World" or the "Communist World", they had no scruples about misleading their citizens and manipulating their alliances.

This lying ploy, which was subsequently dubbed the "doctrine of moral equivalence," is very typical of the left, especially in academic circles. (The same method was used, for instance, in the 1980s for equating the Soviet occupation of Afghanistan with the American operation in Grenada.)

The unwillingness of the left to admit, even now, the simple fact that there can be no "moral equivalence" with the totalitarian mon-

---

[191]I, for one, bought the book *The Cold War* by Hugh Higgins, vice-principal of Kingsway Princeton College, to which I refer the reader. Hugh Higgins, "Détente and Beyond: The End of the Cold War," Heinemann Educational, Jordon Hill, Oxford, Third Edition, 1993.

[192]Higgins, op. cit., p. 123.

ster, that the only result will be the gulag and destruction, is indicative in itself. If in the 1920s and 1930s one could still speak of their naive faith in the ideals of socialism, their unwitting delusion, then after the war and more so in the 1970s and 1980s, we are faced with deliberate lies and falsifications. The difference is just as substantial as that between a murder in a fit of temporary insanity and a cold-blooded murder for gain. I think that this watershed came right in the years of détente, after which there were no more honest left-wingers.

4.8   The Jackson amendment

Recalling that time and looking through the CC documents, there is no doubt that détente was the most dangerous period for our civilization. Full supremacy of communism over the world was but half a step away. Confident of their ultimate victory, the Kremlin leaders were sure that time was on their side, and there was no need to hurry; they were waiting patiently for their moment and removing the final obstacles. Strangely enough, our campaign for human rights was almost the only obstacle in their path at that time. This was all the more regrettable, since in their eyes it really was an insignificant one: from a Marxist point of view (and they had no other), the West was in their pocket because the "capitalists" and "their subservient ruling circles" had already capitulated.

However the game was a delicate one, it required care to avoid waking the victim — something like hypnosis, in which just the buzzing of an insect nearby might jeopardize all efforts. We were like a wasp buzzing around the head of the unconscious victim: you cannot risk swatting it, but leaving it alive is dangerous. Furthermore, we drove them from advance into defense, which was an absolute miracle in view of how few we were. The communists were never any good at defense. In any case, what defense can there be in an ideological struggle? The one who becomes defensive has already lost.

Another factor was their lopsided "Marxist" understanding of Western democracy, which took practically no account of such a classless force as public opinion or human conscience. No matter how strange it may sound in our cynical or downright shameless time, then, in the 1960s and 1970s, there were still enough people for whom the words "human rights" were not a meaningless noise. Moreover—and this may be even more important—such idealists were found both on the left and the right, and above and below, and were totally unpredictable from either the class or the political viewpoint. No matter how cynical, say, the leaders of the European social democrats were, especially the communists, their parties' electorate also contained such idealists, and in sufficient numbers to make party leaders pay attention to them.

Our movement at that time was a very colorful mix, which did not fit into the customary definitions of "leftists" and "rightists." If the rightist French government of Giscard d'Estaing threw itself into Brezhnev's arms, the French leftist intelligentsia proved to be our closest ally. France was probably the first Western country in which the intelligentsia began to give thought to its responsibility for the crimes of communism because of a group of the "new philosophers" under the influence of *The Gulag Archipelago*. In the summer of 1977, during Brezhnev's visit to Paris, this movement reached its culmination, marked symbolically by the "handshake of the century": at a reception organized by the intelligentsia in the Theatre Recamier, Jean-Paul Sartre and Raymond Aron shook hands for the first time in many decades.

Yet in Germany or England, where the governments were leftist, our allies were instead the Conservative opposition, although they were not alone. There are always honest people of any political convictions whatsoever.

The most outstanding example was Italy: even Italian communists deemed it their duty to demonstrate their disapproval to Moscow. The liberals, the socialists, and later the radicals—all made their contribution to our task. In this war, public opinion was on our side, whether the establishment liked it or not.

In the USA, as we recall, the "elite," who yearned for friendship with Moscow, also had to acknowledge this force. The question of human rights became the catalyst of differing forces and tendencies, and the struggle concentrated around the so-called Jackson-Vanik Amendment, forbidding the government to grant the USSR most-favored-nation status in trade specifically because of the civil-legal problem of emigration from the Soviet Union. Although the problem was a sufficiently narrow one, concerning a specific group of people, everyone understood its importance in principle. On the one hand this status, giving the USSR unlimited access to credit, would serve to strengthen Soviet military might, which was highly undesirable as such. On the other hand, the idea of somehow linking détente with political changes in the USSR was in the air, and requiring an obligation to observe human rights before there could be an increase in contacts between the East and West, especially in the economic field, was common sense. No matter how the establishment and the Soviets tried, they did not manage to quash the Jackson amendment.

Both sides tried with great persistence: the fate of détente seemed to hang on the outcome of these debates. At the height of the struggle, shortly before the final Congress vote, our old friend Zhores Medvedev put in an appearance as if on order.[193] His ideas, as we recall, frequently coincided with those of Andropov by pure coincidence, and he was invited immediately to give evidence before the Senate Committee on Foreign Relations by its chairman, the well-known liberal senator J. William Fulbright. Stating straightaway that he was not speaking on his own behalf but "actually representing a certain group of liberals in the Soviet Union" (who on earth could he have meant? Maybe his brother?), Zhores Alexandrovich proceeded to tell the senators that:[194]

- pressure on the Soviet leadership is effective only when it proceeds from a "friendly" country that is an important trade partner of the USSR;

- the dependence of the USSR on foreign aid is greatly exaggerated, and limitations on trade shall mainly create difficulties for ordinary people; and

- the Jackson amendment, therefore, shall be seen by the Soviet government and the greater part of the population as a deliberate insult.

It will be considered by the Soviet Government to be some kind of provocation to stop all the good developments which have resulted from American policy over the last few years.

Therefore, I think that this amendment, if it becomes law, will not make the Soviet Union inclined to make further concessions, but will make the Soviet Government retreat from the position which it now has and emigration would slowly be diminished to an almost zero level. Other liberal reforms would be much more difficult, and I think that results in the Soviet Union will be more negative than positive.[195]

---

[193]In the preface to his written testimony Medvedev was described as a distinguished and courageous Soviet scientist: "Officially stateless since the Soviet Government deprived him of his citizenship in August 1973, Dr. Medvedev now lives in London and travels with British documents."

[194]"Détente: Hearings Before the Committee on Foreign Relations, United States Senate," Ninety-Third Congress, Second Session on United States Relations with Communist Countries, August 15, 20, and 21, September 10, 12, 18, 19, and 25, and October 1 and 8, 1974. United States Congress. Senate Committee on Foreign Relations. Washington D.C.: U.S. Govt. Print. Off., 1975 (Reprint by the University of Michigan Library, 2018), pp. 415–418.

[195]Ibid, pp. 417–418.

Furthermore, Zhores Alexandrovich told the senators, talk about political repressions in the USSR was also grossly exaggerated

> ... simply because foreign countries are paying much more attention to the domestic problems of Soviet life and want to support those who are repressed, and so even use some minor cases as examples of totalitarian practices of the Soviet Union. ... The fact that the Soviet Union is not a democratic system is well known, and as such, the Soviet Government still uses force and repression against some groups of dissidents. But we cannot ignore the fact that other dissidents who also criticize the Government from a political and scientific and economic point of view, which was unimaginable some years ago, have been given the chance to freely express their criticisms and publish their works abroad in the foreign press without any serious consequences for themselves."[196]

(And who might that be except his brother?) All this, naturally, is due to détente, which

> would improve the liberal attitude of the government to opposition, and people who are in trouble now will find it less dangerous to criticize the government on political issues.[197]

Even censorship, which was still raging unabated,

> is less and less effective and as soon as relations between the Soviet Union and other countries can be improved, the censorship will be even less efficient.[198]

He claimed further that the entire purpose of détente is to improve the standard of living of ordinary people:

> The ruling group which dismissed Khrushchev made more serious steps to improve the economic situation in the Soviet Union and raise the standard of living within the country. I think this is the main reason why the Soviet Government wants to improve trade relations with the United States and other countries.[199]

As for communist ideology, it exists only for domestic consumption, as a means of control over the population:

---

[196]Ibid, p. 419.
[197]Ibid, p. 420.
[198]Ibid, p. 421.
[199]Ibid, p. 421.

The party as a whole is not as monolithic now as it was 10 years ago or during Stalin's time. Even in the party you could find different attitudes on international and domestic policy. You could find liberals, conservatives, and new Stalinists, therefore, even in the party you could find different approaches to international and domestic issues. ... I think that the Soviet Union now is a country where the political situation is changing, and it is changing mainly in the direction of some kind of democratization, slowly, very slowly, and the fact that this process is slow is disappointing. This disappointment is realized in the form of outcry from the West and from Russian liberals who want very quick changes. But I think that quick changes are unrealistic, and we must agree that even slow democratization of the Soviet Union is a very good sign of progress in the world, and the only hope that the relations between the Soviet Union and America can be improved in the future.

I hope that I will witness these results because I think that they are slow, but not hopelessly slow, and I think that within 3 or 4 or 5 years we will witness more serious changes within the Soviet Union. I think that if the obstacles to this development are not created by the other party, unnecessary obstacles which are neither in the American national interest nor Russian, I think that relations between our countries will be improved slowly.[200]

But if such unnecessary hindrances (for example, the Jackson amendment) shall be created, "failure in this direction could result in the emergence of more hard-line people"[201] upon a change of the Soviet leadership.

Zhores Alexandrovich is even more frank in his written statement to the Senate committee:[202]

The limits on democracy that exist in the Soviet Union, cases of repression and persecution of dissidents, hypersensitive action by censors and other sad developments are not a necessary aspect of socialism as a system, but are a hangover from the past —the result of inertia. The pathological fear of communist aggression sometimes noticeable in the United States is also the result of inertia from the years of the "Cold War," when even in America many democratic principles were violated. [...] The inertia of the past, and especially the inertia of fear of closer cooperation among these countries, will weaken in the future. It is impossible to ignore the idea which is often put forward by the critics of the natural development of normal trade relations between the Soviet Union and the United States. This

---

[200] Ibid, pp. 421–422.
[201] Ibid, p. 418.
[202] Ibid, pp. 432–433.

is the notion that the U.S.S.R. will receive great benefits from this development, and will thus strengthen its military potential, and that this amounts to strengthening an uncontrollable military enemy. Specifically, this idea was suggested by Andrei Sakharov in an interview with Western correspondents that he gave on August 21, 1973.

This idea is too abstract. [...] Is it possible to call the current Western policy toward the Soviet Union a "new Munich"? I think this is a mistake.

Without regard to the Soviet Union, one can find numerous historical examples which show that when a totalitarian society meets economic problems "which it cannot solve for itself," that this situation leads to militarization and, eventually, to military conflicts. A country that can solve its economic and other internal problems cannot be aggressive.

Could anything be clearer than that? But it was not enough for Senator Fulbright:[203]

The Chairman: If I may make an observation. You feel that better overall relations between the Soviet Union and this country will gradually tend to a democratization, I believe you said, within the party. There will be no opposition, but the party itself will undergo changes which lead to a less repressive internal policy, if I correctly understood you.

Dr. Medvedev: Yes, I think that if the policy of détente fails, this would create a more negative development within the ruling group of the Russian Soviet Communist Party in the Soviet Union. [...] Therefore, I think that improvements between the Soviet Union and America would encourage those groups in the party who are more liberal than others.

[...]

The Chairman: You are saying within the Party, and even within the highest areas of the organization, there is considerable diversity? They are not all the same? It isn't a monolithic government at all?

Dr. Medvedev: Yes. Second, it is not a monolithic government. ... In the Politburo you could find some kind of moderate people who could be considered as pro-American, pro-détente persons, and some more hardliners who still believe that the Soviet Union must have a strong leader and must have a monolithic party.

[...]

---

[203]Ibid, pp. 434–445.

The Chairman: You lead me to believe the Soviet Government is not interested in revolution in other countries; they are not a revolutionary country. They want stability in other countries; is that correct?

Dr. Medvedev: Yes, I think that they want stability in other countries.

[...]

The Chairman: I believe that not too long ago Erich Fromm said that the Soviet Union was reactionary, conservative. Do you think that is an accurate portrayal of it?

Dr. Medvedev: The Soviet Union is reactionary?

The Chairman: Reactionary, conservative, is the way he characterized it, I think. [...] He was speaking of foreign relations. In other words, his view was inconsistent with what you said. They do not seek to inspire instability. They prefer friendly countries to have stable governments. They are not trying to generate revolution within those countries.

Dr. Medvedev: Yes, I think this is the case. They would prefer a stable government but would prefer the stable government mostly of a democratic kind of government, stable government, like, for example, Britain or America or others. They do not prefer stability like exists in Spain or—

The Chairman: Portugal?

Dr. Medvedev: Yes, or in Uganda or in other dictatorship countries. [...]

The Chairman: Since emigration has been such an important issue here in this country, you said a good deal about the effect of our great interest in emigration. If I understood you correctly, you said emigration was not so important; it was the overall freedom to go and come, and especially to return. You considered that far more important. I would gather that you felt that what has taken place in the Congress has been negative in its effects upon the Soviet Government, that the Jackson amendment has been provocative and that they feel that this does not promote better relations, nor does it even encourage or promote greater freedom of emigration. Is that a correct statement?

Dr. Medvedev: Yes, this is correct.

[...]

The Chairman: Do you think that most-favored-nation status is all that important to the Russians? Is it important to them in a trade sense or is it a matter of prestige?

Dr. Medvedev: I think it is a matter of prestige and prestige not only for the Soviet Government but also for Russia, for the Soviet official description of the American Government. [...] If this amendment is passed, this would be considered not from an economic point of view, but as a victory of conservative and reactionary forces in the American policy toward the Soviet Union. [...]

[...]

The Chairman: To return to a question we discussed some moments ago, you feel that the concept of what we call détente—more normal relations between our country and Russia—would not lead to greater repression in Russia, as some have alleged, as those who oppose the movement toward détente have said. I believe you think that more normal relations would lead to greater internal freedom and greater freedom for trips, for example. Is that correct?

Dr. Medvedev: Yes; this is correct and I think that this would mean you could enjoy more influence on this issue, and your institutions like the American Academy and others could have more influence when they protest against some repressions of intellectuals in the Soviet Union, but worsened relations could influence the Soviet Union to become a more closed country where repression is much more likely as a means of internal policy, not to mention the possibility of increasing power for more conservative circles.

Now that subsequent events are known, it is amusing to read this testimonial—it is no more than a curiosity. But then, at the height of the struggle, there was little to laugh about: this was not said by Arbatov or Primakov, but a prominent "dissident scientist" who did not avoid making occasional references to his friendships with Sakharov and with Solzhenitsyn. And he did not say this just anywhere, but in the Senate of the USA, on which the fate of détente depended.

4.9   We held out

This was exactly what the left-liberal establishment of the USA wanted to hear. The Sovietologist brotherhood hastened to start writing about the "doves" and "hawks" in the Politburo, about the struggle between them, so God forbid doing anything that may hamper the "doves." However, just who these "doves" and "hawks" were was unclear; even Dr. Medvedev did not venture this information. Having read the minutes of the debates in the Politburo, we now know that the number one "dove" was Andropov. He was also the number one "hawk."

Luckily there were other people in America apart from those who wished to achieve a radical improvement of human nature in cooperation with the Kremlin. It was through their efforts that the Jackson amendment was passed, and the campaign for human rights in the USSR escalated. For this reason, the Helsinki Accords of 1975 included the mandatory obligation to observe human rights.

This seeming concession to public opinion was undoubtedly mere hypocrisy; both sides were perfectly aware that these promises would remain on paper. As we recall, at that same time Andropov was informing the Politburo that the Soviet regime could not survive without repressions, and several years later the arrests of members of the Helsinki Groups caused only "concern" to Western governments. But the degree of public disapprobation was so great that it was impossible to omit human rights from the Accords.

Furthermore, in the post-Vietnam and post-Watergate USA, the idea of human rights was the only topic uniting a divided country, at least this is how it was perceived to be by the success of Carter's electoral campaign, who declared it from his platform. Even the new American elite, which formed under the influence of the black civil rights movement, could not ignore it. The result was a paradoxical situation: the arrest of a small group of Helsinki monitors posed a challenge to the whole world and threatened the entire process of détente and all its "achievements."

"What the Kremlin is signaling to the West is: Human rights are our business," wrote the *International Herald Tribune*.[204] "The Kremlin may be making a mistake here.... By simply canceling a third of it [the Helsinki Accords], the Kremlin is wiping out the rest of the agreement and forming an unbridgeable gap between the Soviet Union and the West."

Thousands of Western scientists declared a scientific boycott of the USSR, parliamentary resolutions proliferated, and the US Congress gave serious consideration to the withdrawal of the USA from the Helsinki Accords, the termination of cultural exchanges and even the suspension of negotiations regarding nuclear arms limitation (SALT II).

"Let me say at the outset that though I was skeptical at the time of Helsinki, I firmly believe that it was worth a try," stated Senator Bob Packwood.[205] "For Helsinki represented a *quid pro quo*. We, with great reluctance, agreed to that in the volatility of the frontiers

---

[204]Leopold Unger, "Orlov: The Kremlin's Dreyfus Affair," *International Herald Tribune*, Friday, June 2, 1978. P. 4. (https://archive.org/stream/InternationalHeraldTribune1978FranceEnglish/Jun%2002%201978%2C%20International%20Herald%20Tribune%2C%20%2329614%2C%20France%20%28en%29#page/n3/mode/1up)

[205]'News from Bob Packwood,' July 11, 1978, Robert W. "Bob" Packwood Papers, Williamette University Archives, Box No. 753, Folder 7

of all signatories in all states in Europe. The Soviets dearly wanted that, for it meant international recognition of the boundaries they established by force at the end of World War II. . . . The Soviet Union has not lived up to their side of the bargain. Therefore, the US should take the lead, and in concert with our allies, declare the Helsinki Accords what they have, in fact, always been—null and void."

Finally the American Senate accepted Senator Jackson's suggestion and nominated the arrested Helsinki monitors for the Nobel Peace Prize, a move that was supported by the parliaments of numerous countries.[206] The reaction in the USA was much stronger than in Europe, and American representatives at the Belgrade Conference were practically isolated: they were the only ones to demand an open condemnation of the USSR. Sol Chick Chaikin, a representative of the AFL-CIO in the American delegation, became the target of vicious attacks by the Soviet representatives for "attempting to poison the atmosphere": all he did was pass on an invitation for Sakharov from the head of the AFL-CIO, George Meany, to attend the forthcoming congress of American trade unions and—what impudence!—demanding a reply.[207] The Europeans were not too pleased, either; everything had been going so smoothly, so properly without that Yankee. . . .

No, it was not the capitalists, nor the "reactionaries," who stood in the way of détente in America, but ordinary people—trade unionists like George Meany, who was the first to issue a verdict regarding this policy of capitulation and betrayal:[208] "Détente is a confidence trick."

This mighty old man, who started out as an ordinary plumber and finally came to head the association of sixteen million American workers, was to me the epitome of all that was good and deserving of respect that had once created a great country—a leader of the free world. At the same hearings of the Senate Committee on Foreign Relations at which Zhores Medvedev spoke of the "doves" in the Politburo, Meany said the following:[209]

> We live in strange times. We live in a time when a man whose
> whole political career was built on rabid anti-communism can
> become President and overnight be transformed into the chief

---

[206]Leopold Unger, "Orlov: The Kremlin's Dreyfus Affair," *International Herald Tribune*, Friday, June 2, 1978. P. 4.

[207]Sol C. Chaikin, *A Labor Viewpoint: Another Opinion.* Monroe, N.Y.: Library Research Associates, 1980, p. 165.

[208]Archie Robinson, *George Meany and his Time, A Biography.* New York: Simon & Schuster, 1981, p. 401.

[209]Ibid, p. 398.

advocate of unilateral concessions to the Soviet Union. We live in a time when the President of Pepsi-Cola is transported into ecstasy by Leonid Brezhnev, about whom he says he was tremendously impressed, "By the candor and sincerity of this man and by his clear commitment to pursue not only peace, but also... the enrichment of life in his country."

Strangely enough, Meany—with no university degrees or academic titles under his belt—understood international politics much better than all American professors combined:[210]

I'm not blaming all the world's troubles on Henry Kissinger, but I'm saying, in the final analysis, the cause of human rights in this world is dependent on the strength, the economic strength, the military strength, the moral strength of the United States of America. If we falter, freedom is shaken everywhere....

Alas, our success did not last long: by the end of 1979 both the Soviet and the Western establishments had rallied. Carter was unable to resist such pressure from all sides and "moderated" his course. The *Washington Post* wrote:[211]

That thrust has since been moderated, partly out of a growing recognition in Washington that the Kremlin would not shrink from taking vengeance on the intended beneficiaries of American concern. [...] But there must also be acceptance of a requirement to match the promotion of human rights abroad with the particular foreign context in which they are necessarily worked out. This demands a measure of self-discipline at odds with the outrage Americans feel for foreign abuses, particularly for Soviet abuses. The United States cannot be in the business of helping create martyrs. It can only do what it can to widen the scope for individual liberty. It ought to strive, in so doing, to keep open prospects for progress on other fronts.

Thus we see the triumph of a viewpoint not too unlike the ideas of Zhores Medvedev and his "liberal" friends. But the crux of the matter was not in ideas, but in the coincidence of the interests of the left American establishment, their socialist "allies" in Europe, and the Soviet leadership. Carter simply capitulated under their combined pressure.

---

[210]Ibid, p. 399.

[211]"The Kremlin's War at Home," *The Washington Post*, May 20, 1978, Saturday, A14, Final Edition. (https://archive.org/stream/ InternationalHeraldTribune1978FranceEnglish/May%2022%201978%2C% 20International%20Herald%20Tribune%2C%20%2329634%2C%20France%20% 28en%29#page/n5)

Even the scientists' boycott, which was unprecedented in its scope, began to be evaded by 1979: a resolution of the CC admitted (3 April 1979, St 153/13)[212] that it was "unfeasible to enter into polemics with the organizers of the new anti-Soviet campaign," as "many leading American scientists and scientific centers are displaying an interest in Soviet science and cooperation with our scientific institutions."

At the end of 1978 and the beginning of 1979, the Academy of Sciences of the USSR held talks with the leaders of the National Academy of Sciences of the USA, the US National Bureau of Standards and the Phillips Petroleum Company. There were also talks between the USSR and the US on world oceans. At these talks the American side noticed the constructive approach to the further development of scientific cooperation. New long-term agreements were signed.

Meanwhile, the Western "human rights" organizations that had played such a vital role in our campaign were quietly taken in hand by the local left *nomenklatura*, which for the cause of more objectivity turned its attention to human rights—mainly in nonsocialist countries. An entire "human rights" field of bureaucracy sprang up, to which we were denied access because of our "lack of objectivity." It became impossible to say anything critical of the Soviet Union without saying ten times more about South Africa, Chile, or Iran. Before you know it, some "Helsinki Watch" or other would issue a portentous report on violations of human rights in the world, on quality notepaper and for good salaries: three violations in the USSR and eleven in the USA. One can only guess where all these "defenders of human rights" came from.

The establishment adjusted, found ways to bury the whole subject, filled it with its fictitious activity: committees proliferated on the rights of American Indians, women, Mexicans, Micronesians and other "minorities," real or imagined (in the report on the hearings in the Helsinki Committee of the Congress of the USA for 1979,[213] I counted a good two dozen such organizations, leagues, funds, associations, and societies). "Human rights" as a subject was hijacked and became the banner of the left for a long time. We were no longer admitted there.

It is easy to imagine how the 1980s could have turned out without the annoying buzzing we provided which made the Soviet strate-

---

[212]3 April 1979 (St 153/13), p. 3.

[213]"Hearings before the Commission on Security and Cooperation in Europe," Ninety-Sixth Congress: First Session on implementation of the Helsinki Accords, Vol. VIII, U.S. Compliance: Human Rights, April 3 and 4, 1979.

gists waste so much time on us, and most importantly, lose the initiative in their "peaceful advance", even if only briefly:

- Torn by internal conflicts and forced to quieten "revolutions" in their Latin American backyards, the USA would have been unable to guarantee security in Europe;

- The oil resources of the Persian Gulf and mineral resources in South Africa would have come under Soviet control through the assistance of surrounding pro-Soviet regimes;

- Finally, a defenseless Europe, socialist and "neutral," ruled by Soviet quislings, would have become the industrial base of the global paradise.

Generally speaking, what Lenin failed to achieve with his "global revolution," or Stalin with his "war of liberation," could have been managed by Brezhnev with his détente. But it was too late, the worst times had passed. Then came the occupation of Afghanistan, followed by the Polish events of 1980 and 1981 that shook the world. Détente was over. We were on the threshold of a new era—the epoch of Thatcher and Reagan, with their arms programs, active anticommunism, and dismantling of socialism in the West. The world entered the last lap of the stage of opposition.

And another ten years down the road, it was hard to believe that we had stood at the edge of the precipice and had not fallen into it due to a handful of people who refused to compromise their conscience.

Chapter Five

The Watershed Years

5.1   Afghanistan and the end of détente

The Soviet invasion of Afghanistan in December 1979 shocked the world, as if there had been no Soviet expansion in practically all parts of the globe. This amazement, shock, and bewilderment were something disgustingly deceptive, as in a man who marries a prostitute and then finds out—horror of horrors!—that she is not a virgin. Sovietologists and politicians tripped over one another offering their theories aimed at explaining Soviet behavior by any means to hand. The left, as was customary, saw this as a "hyperreaction to the hostile behavior of the West"—NATO's decision to place new rockets in Europe. The right muttered something about "Russian imperialism", and the "grandiose drive of Russia toward warm seas." Poor things, they're freezing in their Siberia and want to get warm. Meanwhile it was perfectly clear that this occupation was just the latest (and not at all obligatory!) stage of the usual Soviet scenario of "liberation"; it merely showed that the Soviet strategists did a bad job with the scenario and had to send in troops to correct the miscalculation. By the time of the occupation, Afghanistan had already been practically swallowed by the Soviet Union, something the West had stubbornly refused to notice. And it would not have "noticed" if it were not for the Kremlin's miscalculation or, to be more precise, the desperate resistance of the Afghan people.

The history of relations between the USSR and Afghanistan is probably the best illustration of the fact that the Soviet system was incapable of existing peacefully with the rest of the world, and is an excellent picture of what would have happened in Europe if détente had triumphed. Actually, of all the world's nonsocialist countries, Afghanistan was probably the country most friendly to the USSR: it was one of the first to establish diplomatic relations with Soviet Russia and was a kind of Asian Finland for six decades. The Kremlin was in no hurry to export revolution there, knowing that Afghanistan would not escape, and simply "promoted progress" in that country: roads were built, industry was created, and specialists were trained. From a Marxist point of view, it was impossible to demand that a backward, feudal state become socialist immediately. First of all, the relevant social prerequisites had to be established: industrialization, the growth of the proletariat, and, naturally, its "avant-garde." Just so, a careful householder does not slaughter a piglet too soon but fattens it up so it will be ready for the table in time for the feast.

The feast was on its way: the Soviet "peaceful advance" of the 1970s, having neutralized the opposition of the "forces of imperialism," brought a whole lot of third world countries into the bosom of the socialist commonwealth. Now it was Afghanistan's turn to embark on the path of progress, having thrown off the shackles of monarchy. This historical "change of social formations" occurred in the summer of 1973 by means of a virtually bloodless palace *coup d'état*, performed with Moscow's approval by Mohammed Daoud Khan, a relative of the king. Having proclaimed a republic and become its president, Daoud Khan was not a communist but rather a moderate social democrat, no more radical than European socialists. Moscow saw him as a sort of Alexander Kerensky: his historical role was to prepare political conditions for further progress. Once more, the Kremlin strategists were in no hurry—Daoud Khan suited them fine for a transitional stage, especially since communist groupings were quarrelling continually among themselves and could not unite. The International Department of the CC reported this in June 1974 (21 June 1974, 25-S-1183):[214]

> Leaders of progressive political organizations in Afghanistan, Karmal Babrak [sic] (Parcham) and Nur Taraki (Khalq), who maintain unofficial contacts with the CC CPSU through the resident of the Committee for State Security of the Council of Ministers of the USSR in Kabul, acting shortly after the establishment of a republican regime in July 1973, advanced progressively minded elements in the CC of the republic, the government, and the army and started an unprincipled internecine struggle for reinforcing the positions and influence of their groupings for the right to "represent the communist party" in the land.

In its message to its Afghan "friends" the CC wrote:[215]

> The interests of reinforcing the national independence of the country call for closing ranks between forces, united currently in Parcham and Khalq, in order to serve the interests of workers, peasants, and all strata of Afghan society on the basis of cooperation with the republican regime and the government of the republic headed by Mohammed Daoud.

However, four years later the "plans allegedly made by leftist forces" were implemented with the full support of the Soviet Union

---

[214]26 June 1974 (St 129/11), p. 5.
[215]26 June 1974 (St 129/11), p. 3.

in the Saur [April] Revolution. The incessant infighting of communist groupings received short shrift: the stake was placed on one of them (Khalq), leaving the second one (Parcham) at the mercy of their class brothers. Its leader, Babrak Karmal, was appointed ambassador to Czechoslovakia and thus escaped repressions, which descended immediately on the heads of his colleagues, but he did not give up and, just like Trotsky, continued his struggle in exile.

In fact, these were just trifles. The main purpose had been achieved: yet another progressive "people's democratic republic" had appeared on the map of the world, thereby confirming the thesis of the replacement of the balance of forces in the global arena in favor of the forces of peace, progress, and socialism. The next step was a "Friendship Treaty", massed economic aid, military advisers, supplies of "special property" (armaments)—all of this gratis, or at a quarter of the actual price. The progressive regime began decisive construction of a "new life" after destroying thousands of "reactionaries," "religious believers," and "revisionists." And nobody, you will note, was concerned by the movement of communism "toward warm seas," just as there was no particular worry in the world about its progression in South Yemen, Somalia, or Ethiopia.

Yet there was one small detail overlooked in the heat of class struggle: the attitude of the Afghan people toward progress and socialism. Suddenly, like a bolt from the blue in March 1979, came the news that Herat, the third largest city in Afghanistan with a population of two hundred thousand, was in the hands of "insurgents."

5.2   Turmoil in the Kremlin

The news clearly caught Moscow by surprise. Nobody really knew what was going on. Brezhnev was ill, so an emergency meeting of the Politburo was called in his absence on 17 March under the chairmanship of Andrei Kirilenko. Andrei Gromyko reported the following (17–18 March 1979*, Pb):

> It is worth noting that I had a conversation at 11 a.m. today with [Hafizullah] Amin, the Minister of Foreign Affairs and Taraki's deputy, and he did not express any particular concern about the situation in Afghanistan, but said with Olympian calm that the situation is not all that serious, that the army is in control, etc. In a word, he made it clear that their situation is stable.
>
> [. . .]
>
> As for Kabul, the situation there is generally calm. Afghanistan's border with Pakistan and Iran is closed, or, to be more

accurate, half-closed. Large numbers of Afghans who previously worked in Iran have been deported and are naturally very dissatisfied. Many of them have already joined the insurgents.

The measures we intend to implement to aid Afghanistan are outlined in the papers you have before you. I would like to say that we have assigned Afghanistan an additional 10 million rubles in currency for the purpose of guarding its borders.

As Pakistan is the main entry point for terrorists to cross into Afghanistan, it would seem feasible for the Afghan government to send a protest note to Pakistan or make a declaration, that is, to issue a document of some kind. But the Afghan government has not done so. This does seem very strange.

I asked Amin what measures he considers to be necessary for us to take. I told him approximately what aid we could render. He made no other requests, merely said that he has an optimum evaluation of the situation in Afghanistan, and that Soviet aid shall be of great assistance and that all the provinces are under the control of the legitimate government. I asked, "Do you not expect any unpleasantness emanating from neighboring countries or the internal counterrevolution by religious activists and so forth?" He replied firmly that there is no threat to the regime. At the end he sent his regards to the members of the Politburo and personally to L.I. Brezhnev. That was my conversation with Amin today.

Some two or three hours later we received information from our comrades that disorder has broken out in Herat. One regiment, as I have already said, the artillery one, opened fire on its own forces, and part of the second regiment has gone over to the insurgents. Consequently, government forces are left with around half of the 17th division. ... Our comrades also report that tomorrow and the next day new masses of insurgents, backed by Pakistan and Iran, may enter Afghanistan.

About half an hour later our comrades informed us that the senior Soviet military adviser, comrade Gorelov, and the charge d'affaires, comrade Alekseyev, have been invited to meet with comrade Taraki. What was the subject of the meeting with Taraki? First, he made a request for military technical equipment, ammunition, and rations, all of which are envisaged in the existing documents we have circulated to the Politburo for consideration. As for military aid, Taraki said in passing that assistance on the ground and in the air may be required. This can be interpreted to mean that we shall have to send in our troops, both ground and airborne.

I think that first of all we have to proceed from the main issue in rendering aid to Afghanistan. We have lived alongside them for 60 years in peace and with good-neighborly relations. If we lose

Afghanistan now, and it distances itself from the Soviet Union, it will be a severe blow to our policy. Of course, it is one thing to resort to extreme measures if the Afghan army remains on the side of the people, and quite another if the army refuses to support the legitimate government. And finally, if the army opposes the government and thus our forces, the matter will become very complex. Comrades Gorelov and Alekseyev report that the attitude of the leadership, including comrade Taraki, is not particularly accommodating.

[Dmitry] USTINOV. ... We have advised comrade Taraki that certain forces should be sent to districts where insurgency has occurred. He replied that this would be difficult, as there is unrest in other places as well. In a word, he expects significant action by the Soviet Union with both ground and airborne forces.

ANDROPOV. They hope that we shall hit the insurgents.

KIRILENKO. The question is who our forces will be fighting if we send them there. With the insurgents, and they have been joined by a large number of religious adherents, they are Muslims with numerous ordinary people in their midst. So in the main, we shall have to fight these people.

KOSYGIN. What is the Afghan army like, how many divisions does it have?

USTINOV. There are ten divisions, numbering more than 100 thousand men.

ANDROPOV. We know from operative data that around three thousand insurgents are heading for Afghanistan from Pakistan. They are mainly religious fanatics drawn from the ordinary people.

KIRILENKO. If the people rise up, then apart from those coming in from Pakistan and Iran and who are mainly terrorists and insurgents, the bulk that our forces will be fighting shall be ordinary Afghans. Admittedly, these are religious adherents, followers of Islam.

GROMYKO. At present, it is hard to determine the correlation between government supporters and insurgents. Judging by everything, the events in Herat erupted very violently, more than a thousand people were killed. But even there the situation is not sufficiently clear.

ANDROPOV. Of course, the insurgents that have penetrated into Afghanistan shall first of all rebel and try to attract the Afghan people to their side.

KOSYGIN. I consider that the draft resolution that has been submitted requires serious amendment. First of all, there is no need to put off the supply of arms until April; it should be done immediately, now, in March. That is the first issue.

The second is that it is necessary to give the Afghan leadership some moral support, and I suggest implementing the following measures: advise Taraki that we will raise the price of gas from 15 to 25 rubles for one thousand cubic meters. That will enable them to cover the losses they have with regard to the acquisition of armaments and other materiel. I believe we should supply arms to Afghanistan free of charge without naming any 25 percent.

ALL. Right.

KOSYGIN. Thirdly, we envisage giving them 75 thousand metric tons of grain. I think this should be revised and raised to 100 thousand metric tons. These measures, in my opinion, should be included in the draft resolution and thereby show the Afghan leadership moral support. We need to fight for Afghanistan as, after all, we have lived in perfect harmony for 60 years. Of course, the struggle with the Iranians, the Pakistanis, and the Chinese is powerful, but Iran shall render assistance to Afghanistan, it has the means to do so, the more so that they profess the same religion. This must be borne in mind. Pakistan will also agree to such a measure. No need to say anything about the Chinese. So I believe we should adopt a comradely resolution and render serious aid to the Afghan leadership. As I have said, there is no need to talk about payment at this stage, especially, as is noted here, in freely convertible currency. Whatever hard currency they have, we will still get nothing from them. . . .

There is another question I would like to raise: whatever you might say, both Taraki and Amin are concealing the true state of affairs from us. We still have no detailed knowledge of what is going on in Afghanistan. How do they assess the situation? They continue to draw a picture in bright colors, but we really see what kind of events are occurring there. They are probably good people, but they still hide quite a lot from us. It is hard to understand why. . . .

Furthermore, I think it is necessary to send an additional number of qualified military specialists there and let them find out in detail what is going on in the army.

I also consider it necessary to find a broader political resolution. Maybe the draft of such a resolution could be drawn up by comrades from the Ministry of Foreign Affairs, the Ministry of Defense, the KGB, and the International Department. It is obvious that Iran, China, and Pakistan will come out against Afghanistan and resort to all means and measures to hinder the legitimate government and discredit all its actions. This is precisely where our political support of Taraki and his government shall be needed. Naturally, Carter shall also speak against the Afghan leadership.

If the need arises to send in forces, whom will we be fighting, who will rise up against the current Afghan leadership? They are all Muslims, people of the same faith, and their faith is so strong, religious fanaticism is so prevalent, that they may unite on that basis. I think we should tell Taraki and Amin straight out about the mistakes they have made in this period. After all, they are still executing people who disagree with them; almost all the leaders of not just the top, but also the middle level of the Parcham party have been done away with. Of course, it is hard for us to formulate a political document right now; that will be the task of the comrades I have mentioned, say within three days.

USTINOV. Everything Alexei Nikolayevich has said is quite right, it must be done faster.

GROMYKO. Documents should be prepared faster.

KOSYGIN. I think we should not encourage the Afghan leadership to ask us to bring in our troops. Let them form special units that could be sent to hot spots to quell the insurgents.

USTINOV. I believe we should not mix our forces with the Afghans in the event that we do send in troops.

KOSYGIN. We need to form our military units, devise appropriate instructions for them, and send them in on a special command.

In this way the basic decision was made by the Politburo regarding the sending of Soviet forces into Afghanistan back in March 1979—that is, nine months before the NATO decision to place new rockets in Europe and with no hankering after "warm seas." If they had any geopolitical aim, it was fully covered by the simple formula "we cannot yield Afghanistan to the enemy" (that is, the Afghan people). However, the atmosphere changed rapidly, new information continued to flood in regarding the situation in Afghanistan, and the "extreme measures" had to be delayed. This was influenced particularly by Kosygin's conversation with Taraki, which took place through an interpreter the next day, 18 March, at the insistence of the Politburo, and was fully read out to the Politburo by Kosygin upon its completion (18 March 1979*, No. 242):

KOSYGIN. Please tell comrade Taraki that I want to pass on greetings from Leonid Ilyich and all the members of the Politburo.

TARAKI. Thank you.

KOSYGIN. How is comrade Taraki, does he not get too tired?

TARAKI. No, I don't. There was a meeting of the Revolutionary Council today.

KOSYGIN. That's good, I'm glad to hear it. Please ask comrade Taraki to describe the situation in Afghanistan.

TARAKI. The situation is bad and getting worse. [...]

[...]

KOSYGIN. Do you have support among the workers, the city bourgeoisie, and officials? Is there anyone on your side?

TARAKI. We have no active support from the population. They are almost all under the influence of Shia slogans. "Do not believe the ungodly, but follow us"—that is the basis of their propaganda.

KOSYGIN. What is the population of Herat?

TARAKI. 200–250 thousand. They behave according to circumstances. They'll go wherever they're led. Now they are on the side of the opposition.

[...]

Propaganda should be mixed with practical aid. I suggest that you put Afghan markings on your tanks and aircraft, and nobody will be any the wiser. Your forces could advance from the direction of Kushka and of Kabul.

KOSYGIN. Kabul still has to be reached.

TARAKI. It is not far from Kushka to Herat. Troops could be airlifted to Kabul.

KOSYGIN. If troops are sent to Kabul and they advance on Herat, we do not want to disappoint you, but this would be impossible to conceal. The whole world will know about it within two hours. Everyone will start screaming that the Soviet Union has launched an intervention in Afghanistan. Tell me, comrade Taraki, if we airlift weapons and tanks to Kabul, will you be able to find crewmen or not?

TARAKI. Very few.

KOSYGIN. How many?

TARAKI. I have no precise data.

KOSYGIN. And if we were to make a quick airlift of tanks, the necessary ammunition, and mortars, will you be able to find specialists capable of using these weapons?

TARAKI. I cannot answer this question. You can get an answer from Soviet advisers.

[...]

KOSYGIN. We have decided to send you emergency military materiel, to undertake repair of helicopters and aircraft—all of this gratis. We have also decided to send you 100 thousand metric tons of grain and to raise the price of gas from 21 dollars per one thousand cubic meters to 37.82 dollars.

TARAKI. That is fine, but let us talk about Herat.

KOSYGIN. Very well. Would you be able to form several divisions in Kabul comprised of advanced people, on whom you can depend, and not just in Kabul but other places? We would supply the necessary arms.

TARAKI. We have no officer corps. Iran sends soldiers to Afghanistan in mufti. Pakistan also sends its men and officers into Afghanistan in Afghan dress. Why can't the Soviet Union send in Uzbeks, Tajiks, and Turkmens in civil clothing? Nobody would recognize them.

KOSYGIN. What else can you say about Herat?

TARAKI. We want you to send us Tajiks, Uzbeks, and Turkmens so that they could drive tanks, as all these ethnic groups exist in Afghanistan. Let them wear Afghan clothes and Afghan badges, and nobody will recognize them. In our opinion, this is very easy work. Judging by Iranian and Pakistani experience, this work can be done easily.

5.3 "Some Marxists..."

Needless to say, this discussion and the next (not believing his ears, Kosygin rang again) depressed the Politburo. It seems as though for the first time they realized what an unpleasant situation they had landed in in Afghanistan. The more so as in the second call Taraki was even more frank (17–18 March 1979*, Pb):[216]

KOSYGIN. Talking about Kabul, today's telegrams show that the situation there is practically the same as in Iran: there are protests, people are gathering in groups. Large numbers of men armed with Chinese weapons are passing into Afghanistan from Pakistan and Iran. ...

USTINOV. With regard to Tajiks, we have no such separate units. It is hard to say at this time how many of them serve in the tank units of our army. ... When I spoke to Amin, he also requested bringing troops into Herat to crush the opposition. ...

The Afghan revolution encountered many obstacles in its path, said Amin in his conversation with me, and its preservation depends only on the Soviet Union.

What is the matter, why did things turn out like this? The fact is that the Afghan leadership underestimated the role of Islam.

---

[216] 17–18 March 1979* (Pb), pp. 12–17.

It is under the banner of Islam that soldiers are deserting to the other side, and the absolute majority of them, with maybe a few exceptions, are religious believers. That is why we are asked to help in routing the attacks of the insurgents in Herat. Amin said, with no great certainty, that they can rely on the army. But just like comrade Taraki, he appealed for help.

KIRILENKO. So they have no guarantees regarding their army. They are hoping for a single solution, specifically our tanks and armored vehicles.

KOSYGIN. Naturally, in reaching a decision about aid, we must give serious thought to all the possible consequences. This is a very serious matter.

ANDROPOV. Comrades, I have thought about this question in depth, and reached the conclusion that we must give very, very serious consideration to the question of the purpose of bringing our troops into Afghanistan. It is quite clear to us that Afghanistan is not ready to reach a socialist decision on all these matters. Religion is very powerful there, the rural population is virtually illiterate, the economy is backward, and so on. We know Lenin's teachings about a revolutionary situation. But what situation can one talk of in Afghanistan? There is no such situation in that country. For that reason I consider that we can retain the revolution in Afghanistan only by force of our bayonets, but that is unacceptable to us. We cannot take that risk.

KOSYGIN. Maybe we should instruct comrade [Vladimir] Vinogradov, our ambassador in Iran, to see prime minster [Mehdi] Bazargan and point out the inadmissibility of interference in the internal affairs of Afghanistan.

I support comrade Andropov's suggestion regarding the exclusion of such a measure as taking our forces into Afghanistan. The local army is unreliable. Therefore our army, entering Afghanistan, will be the aggressor. Whom shall it fight? The Afghan people first of all, and it will have to shoot them. Comrade Andropov noted rightly that the time for revolution in Afghanistan is not yet ripe, and all that we have done with such difficulty over the past few years toward international détente, arms reduction, and much more—all that shall be wasted. Of course, this would be a great gift for China. All nonaligned countries will be against us. This action will have serious consequences. The meeting between Leonid Ilyich and Carter would be canceled, and Giscard d'Estaing's visit at the end of March would come into question. I ask you, what do we have to gain? Afghanistan with its current government, a backward economy, and an insignificant rating in international affairs? On the other hand, we must also bear in mind that sending in troops would be legally unjustified. According to the UN Charter, a

country may appeal for help, and we could send in troops if
that country faced aggression from without. Afghanistan is not
threatened by any aggression. This is their internal matter, a
revolutionary civil strife, battles between one group of the population with another. It must also be said that the Afghans have
made no official request to us regarding the sending of troops.

[...]

ANDROPOV. We should not delay in publishing an article about
Pakistan and its support of the insurgents.

USTINOV. I assume that we shall implement measures of support as we agreed yesterday.

ALL. Right.

USTINOV. Only excluding the sending of troops.

KOSYGIN. In other words, we are not changing anything regarding aid to Afghanistan, apart from the matter of sending
troops. They should be more responsible in deciding questions
concerning state affairs. If we do it all for them, what will be
left for them? Nothing. We have 24 advisers in Herat. They will
have to be evacuated.

ZAMYATIN. As for the propagandistic reinforcement of this
measure, we have a prepared article about Afghanistan. There
is also an article about Pakistan and support of the Afghan insurgents by China. These articles should be sent to the press
today.

ALL. Right.

CHERNENKO. Comrades, we need to decide who will invite
comrade Taraki.

KIRILENKO. That should be done by comrade Kosygin. Let
him phone Taraki and invite him to either Moscow or Tashkent,
whichever he prefers.

And the machine went into action. On the next day, an extended
meeting of the Politburo was called[217] with all the secretaries of the
CC (including the still-young secretary for agriculture, M.S. Gorbachev). By some miracle Brezhnev was reanimated and, reading
visibly from a piece of paper, expressed approval of "... all those
measures that were envisaged by the draft decision of the CC CPSU,
introduced on Saturday, all the measures that were implemented on
Saturday and Sunday." He recited them in order. "The question was
raised regarding the direct participation of our forces in the conflict
in Afghanistan. I believe the members of the Politburo determined
correctly that at this time we should not be drawn into this war."

---

[217] 17–18 March 1979* (Pb), pp. 18–28.

5.4   The breath of doom

That was the end of the first phase of the Afghan crisis. The situation stabilized somewhat (two days later the insurgent regiments in Herat were ruthlessly crushed by tanks and air strikes, hastily sent from other towns), and then, by the summer, the atmosphere began to worsen once more. However, from that moment and up to the day of the Soviet invasion, all the efforts of the Soviet leadership were directed at... avoiding this invasion. Reading through their documents now, you can almost feel the breath of doom; the old men in the Kremlin felt instinctively that the Afghan adventure would be the beginning of the end of their regime, and resisted to the last. This collective wisdom was even set out in their "political document," which analyzed the reasons for the March crisis (12 April 1979, Pb 149/XIV):

> Therefore our decision to reject the request of the DRA leadership to send Soviet military units into Herat was correct. This line should be continued also in the event of new antigovernment manifestations in Afghanistan, the possibility of which cannot be excluded.

But the situation began to slip out of the old-timers' hands, and the more they dug in their heels, the closer they slid to the edge of the precipice. Like an incantation, they repeated all the arguments against an invasion, sinking deeper and deeper into the quicksand of the crisis.

Brezhnev offered Taraki a whole range of measures to strengthen the regime in Afghanistan, from the creation of a "united national front" headed by the People's Democratic Party of Afghanistan (PDPA), the expansion of "political work among the masses", up to work with the clergy for the purposes of its "stratification" so that at least part of the clergy, even if it gave the government no open support, would at least refrain from attacking it. As an old party worker, Brezhnev instructed Taraki as follows (20 March 1979, Pb 486):

> It is important for the command personnel to be sure of the stability of its position. You cannot expect much from the army if commanding cadres are changed frequently. This is understandable, especially if changes in command are accompanied by arrests. When many commanders see their colleagues arrested and disappearing, they naturally begin to feel unsure of their own future.

But on the matter of Soviet forces, he was adamant:

> Regarding the question you posed in a telephone conversation with comrade Kosygin and later here, in Moscow, about the possibility of sending Soviet military units into Afghanistan. We have studied this question thoroughly, weighed up all the pros and cons, so I will tell you directly: this should not be done. It would only be to the advantage of the enemy—yours and ours. ... I would like to hope that you will show an understanding of our position.

> Obviously, no public statements should be made — either by you or by us—that we have no intention of doing this, for clear reasons of feasibility.

Everything was in vain: Taraki listened, thanked Brezhnev for received aid and for the good advice, then went back to pleading for Soviet forces. If not forces, then tank drivers and helicopter pilots. If not supplied by the Soviets, then maybe by some other countries? Kosygin lost his temper, and probably snapped at Taraki (20 March 1979, Pb 499):

> I cannot understand this harping on about pilots and tank drivers. To us, this is a totally unexpected question. And I very much doubt that socialist countries will be forthcoming. The issue of sending men who will climb into your tanks and shoot at your people is a very acute political matter.

Yet a month later, upon the supply of Soviet military helicopters, the question arose again, and once more the Politburo was forced to adopt a special resolution: "On the Unfeasibility of the Participation of Soviet Military Helicopter Crews in Suppressing Counterrevolutionary Manifestations in the Democratic Republic of Afghanistan" (21 April 1979, Pb 150/93), with the following instruction to the chief military adviser:

> Convince Amin that the available military helicopters manned by Afghan crews, acting together with units of land forces and combat aviation, are capable of solving issues concerning the suppression of counterrevolutionary manifestations. Supply the Afghan command with the necessary recommendations on this matter.

In May, due to the "activation of counterrevolutionary activities of reactionary forces," the Afghans requested assistance again. And again they were offered "special equipment" to the sum of 53 million rubles (for 1979 through 1981). The Politburo reported through the Soviet ambassador in Kabul (24 May 1979, Pb 152/159) that what they were given was to include:

... 140 cannons and mortars, 90 armored personnel carriers (of these, 50 to be rapidly dispatched), 48,000 small arms, around 1,000 grenade launchers, 680 aviation bombs, and also to be rapidly dispatched in June–July 1979, medicines and medical equipment to the sum of 50 thousand rubles. ...

As immediate aid in May of this year, 100 incendiary tanks and 150 single cluster bombs were supplied. Obtaining gas bombs with a nonlethal toxic substance does not appear possible.

Nonetheless, by June there were some Soviet units in Afghanistan, although they took no part in combat activity. The situation had deteriorated so much that Boris Ponomarev had to make an emergency flight there. On 28 June, Gromyko, Andropov, Ustinov, and Ponomarev reported to the Politburo that (29 June 1979*, Pb 156/IX):

> The situation in the Democratic Republic of Afghanistan (DRA) continues to deteriorate. The actions of insurgent tribes are increasing and acquiring an organized nature. Reactionary clerics are stepping up antigovernment and anti-Soviet agitation, and preach the idea of the creation of "a free Islamic republic" in the DRA, similar to that in Iran. ...
>
> [...]
>
> Send an experienced general with a group of officers to assist the chief military adviser for direct work in the ranks (in divisions and regiments). The main task of this group shall be providing assistance to commanders of compounds and units in organizing combat actions against the insurgents and improving the management of units and subdivisions. Additionally, post-Soviet military advisers to the battalion level, including to the governmental brigade of guards and to tank brigades (40–50 persons, including 20 political advisers), as well as military counterintelligence advisers to all the regiments of the DRA.
>
> For the purposes of ensuring security and protection of the aircraft of the Soviet air squadron at the Bagram Airfield, and with the consent of the Afghan side, send a paratrooper battalion disguised in the uniform (overalls) of aviation technicians. To ensure security of the Soviet embassy in Kabul, send a special squad of the KGB of the USSR (125–150 persons) in the guise of embassy service personnel. In August of this year, upon completing their training, send a special squad of the GRU of the Central Command of the armed forces to the DRA (Bagram Airfield) for deployment in the event of a sharpening of the situation to guard and defend particularly important government sites.

Using the channels of the KGB of the USSR and the GRU of the General Command, send targeted information to the Indian leadership regarding plans for the inclusion of Indian Kashmir, as well as Afghanistan, into a "global Islamic republic," in order to stimulate the Indian government to take active steps toward countering the anti-Afghan activity of Pakistan.

Increase propaganda in the Soviet media condemning attempts at interference in the internal affairs of Afghanistan by Pakistan, Iran, China, and the USA under the slogan "Hands off Afghanistan." Assist with the publication of such materials in the press of other countries.

Whether the Soviet leaders wanted it or not, the Rubicon had been crossed. In making this decision they undertook complete responsibility for life and death in Afghanistan. After this, the question of the Soviet invasion of Afghanistan became purely academic.

5.5   Change of course

By an ironic quirk of fate, the need for invasion arose, but not for the reason expected. By the fall, the "insurgency" began to subside, as though it had exhausted its force, and did not threaten to overthrow the regime. There was even a degree of stability, but the Afghan "leadership" fought among itself. In September, Taraki was deposed by his faithful deputy and minister of foreign affairs Hafizullah Amin and soon killed, despite the will of Moscow. This was followed by purges among the leadership, punishments, and, the Kremlin felt, changes in the political orientation of the new leaders. Gromyko, Andropov, Ustinov, and Ponomarev reported on this at the end of October (29 October 1979, No. 0937):[218]

The situation in Afghanistan after the events of 13–16 September of this year, as a result of which Taraki was removed from power and liquidated physically, remains highly complex. Aiming to ensure his retention of power Amin, while making such cosmetic gestures as starting the development of a draft constitution and releasing some previously arrested persons, is in fact increasing the scope of repressions in the party, the army, the state apparatus, and public organizations. His plain intention is to clear the political arena of practically all prominent party and state activists whom he perceives to be his real or potential opponents.

[...]

----

[218]See 31 October 1979* (Pb 172/108), pp. 2–7.

Alarming signals have been received regarding Amin's setting up of contacts with representatives of the rightist Muslim opposition and chiefs of tribes that are hostile to the government, in the course of which he exhibits readiness to reach agreement with them regarding their cessation of armed conflict against the current government on conditions of "compromise," which would be detrimental to the progressive development of the country.

It has been noted recently that the new leadership of Afghanistan intends to conduct "a more balanced policy" toward Western countries. Among other things it is known that representatives of the USA, on the basis of their contacts with the Afghans, are reaching the conclusion that there is a possibility of a change in the political course of Afghanistan in a direction favorable to Washington.

Amin's conduct in the realm of relations with the USSR clearly exposes his insincerity and duplicity. He and his entourage claim that they wish for further expansion of cooperation with the Soviet Union in various spheres, but in fact allow actions counter to such cooperation. Agreeing outwardly with the recommendations of Soviet representatives, including with regard to the preservation of unity in the PDPA and the DRA, and declaring readiness to reinforce friendship with the USSR, in practice Amin not only refrains from taking measures to suppress anti-Soviet attitudes, but actually encourages them. For example, on his initiative, word is being spread about the participation of alleged Soviet representatives in an "assassination attempt" on him during the events of 13–16 September this year. Amin and his closest cronies do not hesitate to make slanderous allegations about the participation of Soviet representatives in the repressive actions taking place in Afghanistan.

Amin is a power-hungry and exceedingly cruel and dishonest individual. In view of the organizational weakness of the PDPA and the ideological ignorance of its members, it is quite possible that Amin may attempt to change the political orientation of the regime in order to secure his personal power.

[...]

There are still rational forces in the People's Democratic Party of Afghanistan and the Afghan army who express serious concern regarding the present situation in the country, which may lead to the loss of the achievements of the April Revolution. But these forces are isolated and actually find themselves in an illegal position.

It is hard to say now to what extent Moscow's fears regarding Amin's "more balanced policy" toward the West were justified, and its involvement in his "assassination attempt" was an invention. One thing is certain: Amin was not the Soviets' candidate, he was not trusted, and he behaved too independently. Not only did he slip out of control, but he seemed to believe that he could dictate his own rules of the game to Moscow. After the invasion and the killing of Amin they declared him a CIA agent, which cannot be taken seriously. Maybe he simply tried to stabilize the situation by demonstrating his independence, a certain distancing from Moscow, while conducting talks with the opposing side—who knows? In the situation of the time this may have been a sensible approach. But the prospect of surrendering Afghanistan, and not just to some "insurgents" but to their bitter enemies, was too frightening for the Soviet leaders. It was one thing to lose the revolution, and quite another for their ideological enemies to have a base on their borders, posing a lethal threat to their power in central Asia. Without doubt, Amin's fate was sealed from that moment, and invasion became inevitable. This can be seen from the decisions made by the Politburo in October pursuant to the aforesaid report (31 October 1979*, Pb 172-108, p. 4):

> Continue working actively with Amin and the current leadership of the PDPA and the DRA, giving Amin no reason to think that we do not trust him and wish to have nothing to do with him. Use the contacts with Amin to exert the relevant influence on him, and at the same time determine the true nature of his intentions.

In other words, Moscow set about forming a new crew of "leaders" out of the "rational forces" in the party, the army, and the state apparatus, and—to give it its due—went about this with great skill. Babrak Karmal was taken out of mothballs, still continuing his intrigues in Prague, and even managed reconciliation between Parcham and Khalq, then—lo and behold!—the "government of national unity" emerged. By December, in record time, everything was ready, including the development of the plan for the military part of the operation. I do not undertake to judge Amin's treachery, but the Soviet leaders were certainly guilty of the height of treachery in this instance, easily outstripping their Eastern brothers: on 6 December the "personal guard" Amin had asked for in vain since the summer arrived on the doorstep without warning. As Andropov and Ogarkov reported to the CC without batting an eye (6 December 1979*, Pb 176/82):

> ... H. Amin, has lately been insisting on the need to send a Soviet army infantry battalion to Kabul to guard his residence.

In view of the existing situation and H. Amin's request, we deem it feasible to send a specially trained squad of the GRU of the Central Command of the armed forces to Afghanistan, numbering around 500 men in a uniform not disclosing its affiliation to the Armed Forces of the USSR. [...]

As the question of sending the squad to Kabul was agreed upon with the Afghan side, we deem it feasible to transport it by aircraft of the military transport aviation in the first ten days of December of this year.

This was the *spetsnaz* (special forces) squad that, on the night of 28 December, stormed and took Amin's palace. So after all, Tajiks and Uzbeks were found in the ranks of the Soviet army, and it was not difficult to dress them in Afghan uniforms.

5.6   Operation Storm-333

When it came to really delicate issues, the Soviet leaders displayed incredible secrecy, trusting nobody, even their closest allies. Very frequently there was no trace of these issues whatsoever in their documents. It is not surprising that there was not a single paper in their secure archives containing the resolution regarding the invasion of Afghanistan in black and white, and even less so that there was nothing about Amin's removal. Yet these decisions were made by the entire Politburo—it could not be otherwise in the Soviet system, in which every crime was bound by a "bloody surety," as in Dostoyevsky's *Demons.*

The decision regarding the invasion of Afghanistan by Soviet forces and the *coup d'état* in this "democratic republic" was made on 12 December 1979 by Politburo members Brezhnev, Andropov, Ustinov, Gromyko, Chernenko, Arvids Pelse, Mikhail Suslov, Kirilenko, Viktor Grishin, and Nikolai Tikhonov, with the participation of nonvoting candidate-member to the Politburo Ponomarev. But even those who for reasons of distance or illness could not be present had to sign this resolution at a later time: Dinmukhamed Kunaev on the twenty-fifth, Grigory Romanov and Vladimir Shcherbitsky on the twenty-sixth. The document itself, if it warrants that name, is an ordinary sheet of paper on which someone (probably Chernenko) wrote by hand an insignificant text, in which the word *Afghanistan* is not mentioned at all. It runs as follows:

Regarding resolution "A"

1. Approve the reflections and measures presented by comrades Yu.V. Andropov, D.F. Ustinov and A.A. Gromyko.

> Permit them to make amendments to these measures that do not alter them in principle.
>
> Questions requiring CC decisions should be submitted to the Politburo in a timely manner.
>
> Implementation of all these measures shall be the responsibility of Yu.V. Andropov, D.F. Ustinov and A.A. Gromyko
>
> 2. Instruct comrades Yu.V. Andropov, D.F. Ustinov and A.A. Gromyko to keep the CC Politburo informed of the accomplishment of the intended measures.

Secretary of the CC L.I. Brezhnev

This is the historic decision of the Politburo (12 December 1979*, Pb 176/125) that led to the deaths of hundreds of thousands of Afghans, starting with unfortunate president Hafizullah Amin, as well as tens of thousands of servicemen drawn from all the corners of the multiethnic Soviet Union.

However, it seems that they conferred again about Amin on 26 December at Brezhnev's dacha (as usual, he was unwell) in a closer circle. This was followed by yet another meaningless piece of paper with the following typewritten text, certified by the signature of K. Chernenko dated 27 December:

> At a meeting on 26 December 1979 (at the dacha) attended by comrades L.I. Brezhnev, D.F. Ustinov, A.A. Gromyko, and K.U. Chernenko, comrades Ustinov, Gromyko, and Andropov reported on the progress of the implementation of CC CPSU resolution No. 76/125 dated 12/XII-79.
>
> Comrade L.I. Brezhnev expressed a number of wishes while approving the plan of action scheduled by the comrades for the nearest future.
>
> It was deemed feasible that the same composition of the Central Committee of the Politburo of the CC should act according to the reported plan, giving careful thought to every step of action. On matters requiring decisions, the CC CPSU should be advised in a timely manner.

Who knows what details of the operation they were itemizing on the eve of the coup in Kabul? It was only in 1992, when the Soviet regime fell and tongues became loosened, that the Russian press began to carry detailed accounts by participants in these events—out of work KGB and *spetsnaz* officers and former "advisers."

We now know that the operation went under the code name "Operation Storm-333" and was carried out by the special battalion of the GRU and two special groups of the KGB. Ironically enough, Taraki's requests did not disappear without trace: the *spetsnaz* battalion, comprised almost exclusively of Central Asians (which is why it became referred to commonly as Muslim), began to be formed immediately after the March 1979 events, at the beginning of May. The personnel were recruited mainly from intelligence and tank units. The main criterion was knowledge of Eastern languages and physical fitness. Only the leader, Colonel Vasily Kolesnik, was a non-Asian.

On 10–12 December the entire battalion, some five hundred strong and dressed in Afghan uniform, was delivered to Bagram Airfield, and on the twenty-first it was sent to "guard" Amin's Tajbeg Palace, where he had moved even before the first assassination attempt.

The "Muslim" battalion and its attendant KGB special units were located in the gap between the lookout posts and the Afghan battalions. Commanders were summoned to the Soviet embassy by the senior military adviser, General [Soltan] Magomedov and head of the KGB apparatus in Afghanistan, one General [Alexander] Bogdanov. Only there were they informed of the aim of their sudden redeployment:[219]

> Bogdanov was interested in the guard plan of the palace and then, as if in passing, suddenly suggested we think about a plan of action if we were not to guard, but seize the palace.
>
> The planning of combat operations lasted all night. Everything was considered at length and in scrupulous detail. It was clear that this was the real purpose of their presence in Kabul.
>
> On the morning of December 24 colonel Kolesnik set out a detailed plan for seizure of the palace. After long discussions, the battalion command was told to wait. The waiting took quite some time. It was only in the second half of the day that word was received that the decision has been affirmed. The plan was not signed. All that was said was—act!

Meanwhile, on 25 December at 1500 hours Moscow time, the incursion of Soviet forces into Afghanistan began.

The first to cross the Amu Darya River were scouts, and then the rest of the units of the 108th motorized rifle division crossed the bridge. Forces were moved through Pul-e-Khumri and Salang Pass toward Kabul. At the same time, military transport aircraft began to airlift the main forces of the airborne division and the airborne regiment of the special-purpose guards to the Kabul and Bagram airfields. The transportation of personnel and technology required

---

[219]A Lyakhovsky, "Operation Storm," *Sovershenno Sekretno*, No 8, 1992. This and subsequent quotations.

343 flights over 47 hours. In all, 7,700 personnel, 894 units of combat technology, and 1,062 metric tons of miscellaneous cargo were delivered to Kabul and Bagram. This was the invasion watched by alarmed Americans via their satellites. But the main part of the operation could not be seen from space:

> On 26 December, a reception was held for the purpose of establishing closer relations between the command of the Afghan brigade and the "Muslim" battalion. Pilaf was prepared and all sorts of herbs were purchased at the market. Admittedly, there were problems with liquor. The KGB men came to the rescue. They had brought along a case of "Posolsky" [Ambassadorial] cognac and various delicacies. In other words, it was a grand spread. Fifteen men from the guard brigade arrived, led by the commander and the political officer. Attempts were made throughout the reception to get the Afghans talking. Toasts were raised to Soviet-Afghan friendship and to combat cooperation. The hosts drank considerably less. At times the soldiers serving the tables at the reception filled the Soviet officers' glasses with water. [...] When the time came to part, if it was not as close friends, then at least as good acquaintances.

> Direct preparations for storming Amin's palace began on the morning of 27 December. The KGB personnel had detailed plans of Tajbeg. So by the start of operation "Storm-333", the spetsnaz personnel from the "Muslim" battalion and the KGB group had a precise knowledge of seizure object NI [...], the best approaches, the duty regime of the guard service, the general number of guards and Amin's bodyguards, the location of machine gun "nests", armored vehicles and tanks, the layout of rooms and labyrinths in the palace and the radio and telephone communication center [...] The personnel of the "Muslim" battalion and the special units of the KGB were told that H. Amin was guilty of mass repressions, thousands of perfectly innocent people were killed on his orders, he had betrayed the cause of the April Revolution, entered into collusion with the American CIA, etc. This version did not fool many, because in that case it would have made more sense for Amin to invite in Americans, and not the Soviets.

And what of the duplicitous Amin? Although in September he had deceived Brezhnev and Andropov (promising to let Taraki live when the latter had already been strangled, as a result of which the Soviet leaders had spent two or three days haggling with Amin over the already dead leader of the April Revolution), strangely enough, he believed them. Or perhaps he reasoned that winners are not judged, that one makes friends with them. Maybe, like the *Sunday Mirror*, he did not doubt that Russians "respect only force." For whatever reason, though, he surrounded himself with Soviet military advisers, he only fully trusted Soviet doctors, and in the end he depended on Soviet forces, calling constantly for their presence in Afghanistan. He had even less faith in "his own" Afghans.

> At that time Amin, suspecting nothing, was in a state of euphoria over finally achieving his aim—Soviet forces had entered Afghanistan. During the day on 27 December he held a dinner for the members of the Politburo and ministers with their families in his opulent palace.
>
> [...]
>
> Quite suddenly, in the middle of the dinner, the General Secretary of the PDPA and many of his guests began to feel ill. Some lost consciousness, as did Amin. His wife immediately summoned the commander of the President's guard..., who began phoning the Central Military Hospital... and the clinic of the Soviet embassy for help. The foodstuffs and pomegranate juice were sent off for testing. The Uzbek cooks were detained. When a group of Soviet doctors, who were working as advisers, arrived at the palace... they were unexpectedly searched. The officers were harshly ordered to surrender their arms. What had happened? They realized just what when they saw people lying in unnatural poses in the vestibule, on the stairs and in surrounding rooms. Those who were conscious were writhing in pain. The doctors knew at once that this was a mass poisoning. They started to render assistance, but at this point an Afghan medic came running up to them. [...] He took them with him—to Amin. He said that the General Secretary was in a very bad condition. When they went up the stairs Amin was in one of the rooms, undressed to his shorts, his mouth hanging open and his eyes blank. Dead? They felt his pulse—it was barely discernible. Dying?
>
> (The doctors), having no idea that they were upsetting someone's plans, bent their efforts to the task of saving the life of the head of a "country friendly to the USSR." Injections, gastric lavage, more injections, a drip.... It was a considerable time before Amin's eyelids fluttered; he regained consciousness, and then asked in surprise: "Why did this happen in my home? Who did it? Was it an accident or sabotage?"

One KGB officer was to reminisce later:

> ... At first only KGB personnel stormed the palace. We yelled in fear, mainly swearing, which helped us not just psychologically, but practically. The soldiers of Amin's guards took us first to be part of their own mutineers, but when they heard Russian speech, surrendered to us as to a higher and more just

force. It emerged later that many of them had been trained at the Higher Airborne Command School in Ryazan, and probably remembered Russian swearwords for the rest of their lives.

The Soviet doctors did all they could. Those who had tried to resuscitate Amin huddled behind a bar. They were probably the last to see him alive:

> The palace shuddered under continuous explosions. Along the corridor, illuminated by flames, came... Amin. He was wearing only white shorts and held jars of isotonic solution as if they were grenades in upraised hands that were wound around with tubing. It is hard to imagine what effort this must have cost him, and how painful the needles stuck in his veins must have been.
>
> —Amin?!—cried the doctors, not believing their eyes. [One of them], jumping out of concealment, started pulling out the needles and steered him over to the bar. Amin leaned against the wall but tensed up immediately, as if hearing something. The doctors also heard a child crying—from one of the side rooms, knuckling the tears streaming down his face, came Amin's five-year-old son. Seeing his father, he rushed forward and clenched his arms around Amin's legs. Amin pressed the child's head to him, and they both sat down against the wall. This was such a dreadful, heart-rending sight that [one of the doctors] turned away and stepped from the bar: "I can't bear to look at this, let us leave."

After the storming, Kabul radio broadcast a recording of Babrak Karmal's address to the people of Afghanistan: "Today has seen the breaking of the torture machine of Amin and his henchmen—savage butchers, usurpers and murderers of tens of thousands of our fellow countrymen—fathers, mothers, sisters, sons and daughters, children and old people...."

But these were just words. The new regime differed little from the previous one. Karmal himself was at Bagram Airfield under the eye of an airborne regiment. At 0030 hours on 28 December he was phoned by Yu.V. Andropov. Speaking on his own behalf and "personally" from L.I. Brezhnev, he congratulated the new chairman of the Revolutionary Council of the DRA on the victory of the second stage of the revolution.

It is amazing how many events hid behind one unprepossessing sheet of paper bearing the signatures of the members of the Politburo.

5.7   Temporary measures

This has become known only now. The Politburo committee (the same Andropov, Gromyko, Ustinov, and Ponomarev), which was charged to "inform," naturally did not choose to describe what actually happened in its report, but set out the official version of events (31 December 1979, 2519-A):

> Under incredibly difficult conditions that threatened the achievements of the April Revolution and the interest of ensuring the security of our country, it became necessary to provide additional military aid to Afghanistan, especially because we had received such a request in the past from the government of the DRA. Pursuant to the terms set out in the Soviet-Afghan treaty of 1978, a decision was made to send the required contingent of the Soviet army to Afghanistan.
>
> On the wave of patriotic feelings of quite broad layers of the Afghan population at the arrival of Soviet forces, which occurred in strict adherence to the terms of the Soviet-Afghan treaty of 1978, forces opposing H. Amin staged an armed military attack on the night of 27–28, ending with the deposition of H. Amin's regime. This action had the support of the laboring masses, the intelligentsia, a significant part of the Afghan army, and the state apparatus, all of whom welcomed the creation of a new leadership for the DRA and the PDPA.

Exactly in the same spirit (and often using the same expressions) were all official Soviet declarations and messages (reports from the TASS news agency, instructions to all Soviet ambassadors and, separately, to the Soviet representative at the UN, the closed letter of the CC to party organizations of the CPSU, missives to heads of socialist countries, the letter from the CPSU to communist and workers' parties in nonsocialist countries), which had been prepared and approved by the Politburo back on 27 December (27 December 1979, Pb 177/151), presumably while Amin was still alive (or maybe at the very time when Amin and his guests were imbibing pomegranate juice). Without exception everyone was told that this was a "temporary" matter and that the Soviet contingent that had been brought into the country was "limited." The only difference was that "outsiders" were told nothing about Amin, as if he had never existed. "Insiders" were given the version about "healthy forces" among communists who had brought down the usurper for the purpose of rescuing the April Revolution. The *most* inside insiders—that is, members of the CC, the CCs of the union republics, and local and district committees, were informed additionally that:[220]

> In implementing the indicated measures, the Politburo of the
> CC bore in mind the strategic situation of Afghanistan. The
> country is directly beside our borders, is a neighbor of the Soviet
> republics of Central Asia, has a lengthy border, and is not far
> from China. Therefore it is vital to guard the security of our
> socialist Homeland and observe our international duty.

Then the entire Soviet propaganda machine was instructed as
follows: "Give a firm and well-argued rebuff to any possible insinuations regarding alleged Soviet interference in Afghan internal affairs."

A particularly brazen and even insulting response was sent by
Brezhnev via direct hotline to US president Carter: it suggests
that the Kremlin psychologists intended to overwhelm or possibly
frighten their critics with deliberate rudeness (29 December 1979,
Pb 177/220):

> Your claim that the Soviet Union played a part in the overthrow
> of the Afghan government is totally unacceptable and untrue.
> I stress categorically that the changes in the leadership of Af-
> ghanistan were brought about by the Afghans, and only the
> Afghans themselves. You can query the Afghan government on
> this issue. ... I must also inform you in all clarity that the So-
> viet military contingents played no part in any military actions
> against the Afghan side, and we have no intention of doing so.
> ...
>
> [...]
>
> And here is our advice to you: the American side could have
> made its contribution into halting military incursions from out-
> side into Afghanistan.

No wonder that Carter was to say later that in those December
days he learned much more about the Soviet Union than over his
entire life. This was followed by the embargo on sales of grain to
the USSR, the limitation of cultural exchanges, and subsequently
the boycott of the Olympic Games in Moscow and the increase in
the military budgets of NATO countries. The Western reaction was
quite strong, not least due to the arrest and internal exile of Andrei Sakharov, which astounded many no less than the invasion of
Afghanistan. The détente of the 1970s with its rotten atmosphere
of dreams about "socialism with a human face" and "convergence"
receded into the past. The new decade began in a much healthier

---

[220]27 December 1979 (Pb 177/151), pp. 17–18.

climate of resistance and the "conservative revolution." The world was swinging rapidly to the right, socialist governments in Europe were disappearing one by one, and the forces of peace, progress, and socialism suddenly found themselves on the defensive.

It took a long time for Moscow to understand the scope of this catastrophe, pretending that nothing special had occurred. Let the West fret and fume. It's happened before, then things will quieten down, and it will be back to the beginning, to détente. A plenum of the CC was held in June. The high vaults of ancient Kremlin halls resounded again with forceful speeches about the unconquerable might of the Soviet Union to deafening, lengthy applause.

Gromyko rhapsodized as follows:[221]

> It is impossible to see certain tendencies in a proper perspective without taking fully into account the decisive factor of global development—the unswerving reinforcement of socialist positions, including those in the international arena.

As for the USA—what could one expect from those imperialists?[222]

> The normal progress of Soviet-American relations is not assisted by presidential elections in the USA. Once every four years these elections, as a rule, result in an anti-Soviet witch hunt. The candidates, unable to offer any real programs for changing the serious faults of foreign and domestic policy and its obvious failures, compete in attacking and slandering the Soviet Union.
>
> Incidentally, the choice of presidential candidates is poor. The foremost of them, Carter and Reagan, leave little to choose between them. No wonder there is a grim joke circulating among Americans: "The only good thing is that Carter and Reagan can't be in the White House at the same time." [Laughter in the audience.]

Brezhnev gave the following summary, which was followed by lengthy applause:[223]

> We shall continue to spare no efforts in order to preserve détente, all the positive gains of the 1970s, to achieve a turn toward disarmament, support the right of peoples to free and independent development, protect and reinforce peace.

The following resolution was adopted in closing:[224]

---

[221]23 June 1980, Central Committee Plenum, p. 3.
[222]Ibid. p. 8.
[223]Ibid, p. 2.
[224]Ibid, pp. 25, 28.

The plenum of the CC expresses full approval of the measures taken for rendering comprehensive aid to Afghanistan in repelling armed attacks and outside interference, the purpose of which is to stifle the Afghan revolution and create a pro-imperialist bridgehead for military aggression on the southern borders of the USSR.

The plenum charges the Politburo of the CC, acting in the current situation, in which the adventurous actions of the USA and its flunkeys have caused an increased military danger, with pursuing the course of the XXIV–XXV Congresses of the CPSU toward the overall strengthening of ties between socialist states, support for the just struggle of peoples toward freedom and independence, peaceful coexistence, deceleration of the arms race, the protection and development of international détente, and mutual cooperation in the economic, scientific, and cultural fields.

At the same time, the plenum considers that the schemes of imperialists and other enemies of peace require unrelenting vigilance and the all-round strengthening of our country, in order to frustrate imperialist plans for achieving military supremacy and creating a global *diktat*.

Thus, to thunderous and lengthy applause, the Kremlin concluded the latest cycle from a cold war to détente and back: the program of the last stage of the Cold War, with its "arms race" and "struggle for peace," was adopted.

5.8   Pages of shame

However, their immediate and most important concern was to prevent a boycott of the Moscow Olympics, which were to open in July. Essentially, the problem was not new: the decision made at the height of détente in 1974 by the International Olympic Committee to hold the 1980 summer Olympics in Moscow had been debated hotly in the West for some years. The continuing Soviet expansion in the third world and, especially, the growth of political repressions in the USSR troubled the consciences of those who still retained them. There were inevitable comparisons with the 1936 Olympics in Berlin, which had given the Hitler regime a semblance of respectability and international acknowledgement. Maybe it was for this reason that the question acquired a symbolic significance: would humanity permit a repetition of its mistake forty-four years later? Would it enter, once more, onto the path of conciliation with a totalitarian regime and betrayal of its victims, or would it find the courage to oppose it?

The atmosphere became even more heated in 1978 after the trial of Yuri Orlov and the Helsinki Monitors, when public indignation tried to find a way out with some symbolic gesture at least. This is when the first voices were raised calling for a boycott of the Olympic Games, which was widely echoed by the press and public organizations. Committees and groups in support of this campaign sprang up in practically all Western countries, although not all of them insisted on a boycott; some of them advocated various conditions regarding the observance of human rights.

By 1979 there was a mighty chorus of voices that could not be ignored. Andropov reported the following to the CC (25 April 1979*, No. 819-A):

> In order to discredit the XXII Olympic Games in Moscow, the special services of the opponent and foreign anti-Soviet centers are continuing to issue all kinds of insinuations regarding "violations of human rights in the USSR." In individual cases they manage to inspire provocative actions by antisocial elements inside the country, to push them toward making irresponsible declarations of a slanderous nature aimed at increasing anti-Soviet hysteria in the West. Thus the notorious anti-Soviet Sakharov advises each foreign sporting delegation to hinge its participation in the 1980 Olympics on the release of one or two so-called "prisoners of conscience in the USSR." A group of antisocial elements have sent information to the West regarding the creation of a so-called "Association for Olympic Guarantees in the USSR," full of slanderous concoctions and provocative appeals.

I recall that the entire year of 1979 was devoted to this campaign, in endless public debates and declarations,[225] which did not remain unnoticed by Moscow. It is quite amusing to read about this now in Andropov's reports; as was his wont, he saw the hand of "the opponent's" special services behind our busy activity, and would never have believed that alas, there was nobody involved but us—a handful of exiled dissidents (30 July 1979, No. 1455-A). Unfortunately, even among us there was no unity: some thought that the Olympic Games should be "used", while others supported a boycott. I was among the latter, believing that a totalitarian state has sufficient control over the population, entry into the country and, moreover, the media to avoid being "used."

---

[225]Bukovsky articles: "How Russia Breaks the Rules of the Games," *Daily Telegraph*, 2 October 1979; "Games Russians Play," *Wall Street Journal*, 6 October 1979; "Do Athletes Want the KGB to Win the Olympics?" *News of the World*, 20 January 1980.

And so it turned out: from the very start, the KGB was preparing for possible "use."[226] In the summer of 1979, a year before the games, the CC adopted a resolution, "On the Introduction of Temporary Limitations on Entry into Moscow and the Moscow Region in the Olympiad 80 Period and Inclusion of Citizens of Moscow and the Moscow Region in Construction Brigades, Sports and Pioneer Camps, and Other Leisure Facilities in the Summer of 1980" (24 July 1979, St 168/6).

In effect, Moscow became a closed city: there were to be no conferences, competitions, excursions, or business trips to the capital during the Olympic Games. All roads were blocked off; special detours were set up for transit transportation and transit passengers. Children were sent to summer camps in good time; even entry exams to higher educational institutes in the capital were deferred. The stadiums were to be filled only with reliable spectators, mostly soldiers from the Moscow garrison in plain clothes. An ordinary citizen could not get close to any Olympic objects; apart from the forces of the Moscow militia and state security agents, a further thirty-seven thousand persons from other parts of the country were sent to Moscow. Additionally, more than four thousand soldiers from the forces of the Ministry of Internal Affairs of the USSR (MVD USSR) were assigned to guard the airports and railway stations (20 May 1980, No. 1/3110):

> The Olympic Village will be guarded by 4,100 persons. These include: 900 to guard the perimeter; 1,086 for hotel and economic services; 691 to ensure special control at checkpoints; ... to ensure security and supervising public order at the 22 sports complexes, 21,758 persons; in 60 training facilities, 1,474 persons; in 9 hotels housing the foreigners accredited at the Olympic Games, 6,813 persons; in 120 places of residence for tourists, 3,482 persons; ...

Even cleaning out the Olympic stables was to be done by state security personnel.[227] At the same time, however, a much more serious "cleanup" was underway, as Andropov reported (12 May 1980, 902-A):

> Six thousand foreigners deemed to pose a threat of mounting hostile actions during the Olympics have been refused entry into the USSR. Work on detecting foreigners of this category and refusing them entry into the USSR is continuing.

---

[226] 16 June 1978 (1213-A).

[227] 20 May 1980 (No 1/3110), p. 3.

Alongside this, operative-*chekist* and prophylactic measures are being implemented for the purpose of reinforcing public order in Moscow and the Moscow Region, as well as stepping up the struggle against antisocial elements.

In order to prevent flagrant antisocial manifestations by mentally ill persons with aggressive tendencies, MVD USSR agencies and health authorities are implementing measures to isolate such persons for the duration of Olympiad 80.

In fact, there was no secrecy regarding this matter even at the time: arrests began in October 1979 and continued until summer, as was reported quite widely in the West. I wrote a good dozen articles on the subject myself, which were published in practically all Western countries (for example, "Cleansing for the Olympics," *The Observer*, 18 November 1979). Moreover, I sent my letter addressed to all the sporting associations in England and to the most prominent athletes whose addresses I managed to obtain. Much was said on this question on television and numerous discussions that were subsequently broadcast on the radio.

I insist that none of them could have been unaware of what was going on. But they either remained silent, or replied to the effect that they could do nothing, as all decisions were made by the IOC. Some were even aggressive, defending sport from politics. Very few individual athletes responded to our appeals and refused to participate in the Soviet "witches gathering." The remaining, overwhelming majority pretended ignorance. Only one of them told me frankly that the professional life of a sportsman is short, and the Olympic Games are too important for his career for him to jeopardize it by political gestures. Dozens of our friends went into prisons, camps, and psychiatric incarceration for these people to enjoy jumping and running in Moscow.

So the campaign against the Olympic Games began long before the Soviet invasion of Afghanistan, which only whipped up more agitation, and Carter's decision regarding a boycott gave the sporting world an unexpected opportunity to be positioned as heroes, nonconformists, and staunch opponents of the dictates of politicians. Naturally, the leftist press was quick to seize this useful moment.

In England, the main heroes were two famous runners, Steve Ovett and Sebastian Coe, whose rivalry was keenly observed by the whole world. The self-satisfied faces of these "heroes" filled television screens as they manfully prepared to compete despite pressure from reactionary forces. For England at least, the Olympics in Moscow automatically became a great event if these two were taking part.

Of course I appealed to them both, but received no reply. Publicly they made proud declarations of their indifference to politics, as if this were something deserving of praise. I think neither of them would have turned down a chance to run at Auschwitz for the sake of their medals. Yet many years later I read with surprise that Sebastian Coe was running for Parliament, and as a Conservative candidate at that! Still, I suppose this was not really unexpected: the Conservatives were in power, and his success in the elections was guaranteed. If the communists had been in power, it is likely that he would have stood for election from their platform. So nowadays the apolitical Conservative Sebastian Coe, hero of the Moscow Olympic Games, sits in Westminster.

As for using the event, the scenario ran true to form: those who were its most enthusiastic advocates did nothing. The only ones to exhibit an unexpected initiative were the Italians: the representative of their radical party staged a demonstration in support of gay rights on Red Square. Another group of young Italians decided to have some fun and prepared a fake copy of *Pravda*, which they distributed in Moscow at the height of the Olympic Games. The fake newspaper was extremely well done; at first glance it was impossible to distinguish it from the central press organ of the CC CPSU. Only on the first page, directly under the title of the newspaper, there was a very realistic montage of Suslov's head and the body of a criminal with a tattoo of Stalin on his chest.

This Italian *Pravda* carried a quite prophetic report about a military coup coinciding with the Olympic Games, according to which the power of the CPSU had been overthrown, the Russian Federation had seceded from the USSR, and "all the other Soviet republics [had] proclaimed their autonomy, after which each of them was able to pursue its own path of development at last."

Nonetheless, the boycott of the Moscow Olympics, announced by Carter and supported by a number of countries, had its positive points: the problem became an interstate issue, forcing the Soviet Union to mount a serious defense. Many associations, deprived of the support of their governments, had no option but to join the boycott at the last moment. As the CC reported in January 1980 (29 January 1980*, St 195/3):

> US president Carter, acting on the pretext of the Soviet Union's aid to Afghanistan, has issued a demand for the boycott of the summer Olympic Games in Moscow. The Congress of the USA has passed the relevant resolution on this matter. This hostile action by the US administration has found the support of nine governments (Great Britain, Canada, Chile, Saudi Arabia,

Egypt, Australia, New Zealand, Pakistan, and the Netherlands).
Carter's direct pressure on the National Olympic Committee of
the USA has forced that Committee to decide to request the
IOC to relocate the 1980 summer Olympics elsewhere, to defer
them, or to cancel them completely.

Carter's administration is trying to encourage other countries
to support the idea of a boycott. Carter has sent the relevant
personal appeal to the heads of state of more than one hundred
countries.

The only organization in the Olympic movement that can decide
to cancel or relocate the Games is the International Olympic
Committee (IOC). To date, not a single one of its eighty-nine
members has expressed support for Carter's proposal. Most of
them, including the IOC president [Michael Morris, 3rd Baron]
Killanin, see no grounds for the cancellation or relocation of the
Games from Moscow.

Decisive condemnation of the current hostile campaign of the
US administration has been expressed by the International
Olympic Committee, the leaders of twenty-one international
sports federations, and the national Olympic committees of
most countries, including those whose governments publicly
announced support for Carter's proposal. The governments of
the FRG, Japan, and several other countries are waiting on
events. There is a suggestion that the whole question should
be discussed within the framework of NATO and the EEC [Eu-
ropean Economic Community].

After the February session of the IOC reaffirmed the invariability
of its decision concerning the terms and place of conduct of the
Games, the Politburo adopted a resolution, "On the Measures for
Supporting Olympiad 80" (29 February 1980, Pb 186/2). The entire
gigantic machine of Soviet propaganda and manipulation, pressure
and coercion went into action (29 February 1980, Pb 186/2, p. 3):

> In order to neutralize the hostile actions toward the Olympic
> movement by the US administration, work is to be carried out
> in support of the XXII Olympic Games with state and business
> circles, the foreign public and international organizations. . . .

Detailed instructions were received by Soviet ambassadors
throughout the world, with precise formulations of who was to say
what.

This was a fantastic machine, with nothing to equal it in all of
human history. It is not even possible to explain its workings to
someone who has never lived under communism. Is it possible to
conceive how an entire country, and with it almost half the world,

served aims established by a dozen elderly men who had not been elected by anyone?

A month later, the CC was informed that over 140 exhibitions on the 1980 Olympic Games had been displayed in sixty countries. Twenty documentary films were issued. Preparations were underway for an international photo competition devoted to the Moscow Games. More than 1,300 meetings were held with foreign journalists, and ninety press conferences (1 April 1980, St 204/14) were conducted in the USSR and abroad. A quick search located an American company interested in making a series of documentary films about the cultural program of the Moscow Olympics for public US television. They not only located this company (Foreign Transactions Corporation), they paid it for the rendering of "production and creative services" (3 April 1980, St-205/31). Rights to show the Games were presold immediately to the American TV company NBC, again for currency and equipment (all this, you will note, despite the official boycott of the Games by the government of the USA and strong public disapprobation for such actions). Soviet ambassadors were adjured as follows (15 April 1980, St 206/16):

> We report for your information that the Soviet side renders aid in the form of providing discounted (to the amount of 50 and 100 percent) transportation of athletes from a number of countries to the Moscow Games and will cover their maintenance in the Olympic Village.

Only agree to come, and Aeroflot aircraft shall deliver you gratis to Moscow, where you will not have to spend so much as one cent (27 May 1980, St 212/83). Even the director general of UNESCO, Amadou-Mahtar M'Bow, and "attendant persons" were brought to Moscow and maintained free of charge.[228]

> Another solution, bearing in mind the extreme sensitivity of M'Bow regarding matters of protocol, may elicit a reaction unfavorable to us. M'Bow is sympathetic toward the Soviet Union and—despite the USA—supports the participation of UNESCO in the struggle for peace, détente and disarmament.

Then, suddenly, a new calamity: upset by overall condemnation, president of the IOC Lord Killanin, the mainstay of the Soviets in the entire campaign, decided to resign almost a month before the opening of the Moscow Games. This was to be avoided at all costs! The CC issued an immediate order (4 June 1980, St 214/1):

---

[228] 27 June 1980 (No 554/GS)^.

> In view of Killanin's decision to resign from the post of president of the IOC, he should receive urgent recommendations to refrain from any such announcements before the session of the IOC in Moscow, as Killanin's plan to resign his presidency shall be seen by opponents of the Olympics as evidence of the disintegration and demoralization of the IOC.

In order to cheer up the disappointed lord, it was decided to award him the Order of Friendship of Peoples "for active work in developing the international Olympic movement and a great contribution to the preparation and conduct of the Olympic Games 1980 in Moscow" (15 July 1980, Pb 219/31). You think he refused? Not for a moment! Brezhnev personally pinned the well-deserved medal on his chest at the end of the Games. It's not just the Senegalese who have an "extreme sensitivity to matters of protocol."

Finally, at the last moment, literally a few weeks before the opening of the Games, a new opportunity presented itself (1 July 1980, St 217/8):

> Pursuant to agreements with the Afghan government regarding the withdrawal of certain unnecessary units of Soviet military forces back to USSR territory, it is deemed feasible to use this measure to exercise additional influence on the national Olympic committees of a number of countries for the purpose of a wider representation at the Games in Moscow.

Yet again a new "plan of measures" — instructions to all Soviet ambassadors, all representatives and delegations, missives and telegrams indicating, *See? We're leaving, we're leaving....* A unique machine, knowing no fatigue, no obstacles—and no defeats. The CC reported the following to fraternal communist and workers' parties (19 August 1980*, St 224/7):

> Generally speaking, the idea of boycotting the Moscow Olympics that the US administration and some of its allies tried to implement has failed for all intents and purposes. Sporting delegations from 81 countries numbering more than 8,300 individuals took part in the Olympic Games. The Games hosted 3,500 honored guests and officials, as well as 200,000 foreign tourists from 72 countries. The competitions were attended by some 5 million viewers. [...] The Moscow Olympic Games drew the broad attention of the global community. 5,529 representatives of the media were accredited at the Games, including 3,500 from abroad. Television reports on the Games were beamed to all the world's continents, viewed daily by more than 1.5 billion people.

> It can be affirmed that it was possible on the whole to over-
> come the anti-Olympic and anti-Soviet Western propaganda
> and break through the "information blockade" surrounding the
> Games. ... Many Western journalists did their best at first to
> seek out "negative materials," but were soon forced to acknowl-
> edge the precise organization of events, the first-class state of
> the sporting facilities, the efficiency of Soviet information ser-
> vices, etc.
>
> It is a fact that the vast majority of the participants and guests
> of the Olympics among those who came to the USSR with prej-
> udiced conceptions of socialist reality subsequently gave short
> shrift to the slanderous concoctions of bourgeois propaganda.

So it can be said that the Kremlin celebrated victory. Those who
had distinguished themselves particularly were rewarded with honors and medals (12 August 1980, St 223/17). Five thousand workers and officials, 300 military personnel, 1,500 MVD USSR personnel, and 850 from the KGB. And one lord—with the Order of
Friendship of Peoples medal.

5.9   Rescue measures

Now Afghanistan and its problems moved to the back burner. The
main concern was to save détente and emerge from political isolation. It stands to reason that this had not been unexpected by the
Soviet leaders: back in March 1979 they had been quite realistic in
their assessment of the consequences of their intervention. By the
end of January the Politburo adopted the resolution "On Further
Measures to Ensure the State Interests of the USSR with Regard to
Events in Afghanistan," which, apart from measures aimed at stabilizing the situation in Afghanistan itself (including "measures of a
specialized nature on disuniting Afghan émigré organizations and
discrediting their leaders"—the source of future fratricidal slaughter after the withdrawal of Soviet forces), set out the general plan of
a political campaign: "The need to ensure the broad political interests and security of the USSR," wrote Gromyko, Andropov, Ustinov
and Ponomarev (28 January 1980*, Pb 181/34), "requires maintaining the offensive nature of measures being implemented by us
in connection with the Afghan events."

The complex plan of measures they proposed covers practically
all aspects of international politics:

> • In relations with the USA, to continue countering the
>   provocative steps of the Carter administration with a bal-
>   anced and firm line in international affairs. ...

- Strengthen influence on individual allies of the USA in NATO, primarily France and the FRG, making maximum use to our advantage of the differences between them and the USA in their chosen responses to the actions of the Soviet Union in Afghanistan.

- Bearing in mind that the events in Afghanistan are exploited by the USA and China as a convenient excuse for further rapprochement on an anti-Soviet basis, plan long-term measures to complicate the ties between Washington and Beijing within the context of the development of relations within the framework of the so-called tripartite alliance, USA-China-Japan. . . .

- Within the nonaligned movement, use the possibilities of Cuba and the Socialist Republic of Vietnam, as well as states of the progressive wing of DN [Independence Day]; inspire protests in support of the Afghan government. . . .

- The main efforts to counter the hostile activity of the USA and their allies should concentrate on the Islamic countries of the Near and Middle East. . . .

- Implement measures aimed at preserving the anti-imperialist, in the first place anti-American, aspects of Iran's foreign policy. . . .

- In conducting foreign policy and propagandistic measures, make greater use of the thesis that the provision of military aid to Afghanistan by the Soviet Union should not be seen out of context of the longtime provocations of the USA aimed at achieving unilateral military advantages in strategic areas important to the USSR.

Practically the entire future development of Soviet foreign policy was determined by this document.

In fact, the "Cuban initiative" in the nonaligned movement (which was chaired by Cuba at that time) was "on the political settlement" of the problem of Afghanistan by means of bilateral talks with Pakistan and Iran (subsequently the Geneva talks). Propaganda directed at Iran was stepped up, including radio and television transmissions from Uzbekistan and Azerbaijan (8 July 1980, St 218/6). A campaign was launched "on stimulating protests by international society against the aggressive actions of the USA in the area of the Persian Gulf." South Yemen was given the task of launching the campaign, but the "plan of measures" affected practically all the countries in the region, if not all of Asia and parts of Africa, but implemented through Soviet organizations such as the Soviet Committee of Solidarity of Asian and African Countries, the

World Council of Churches, and their progressive allies (13 March 1980, Pb 187/55).

All progressive regimes, organizations, and forums, all the strongholds of socialism in the region of the Indian Ocean were pressed into service. By April, when the campaign was well underway, the Politburo adopted a resolution, "On Countering Plans for the Expanded Presence of the USA in the Near and Middle East and the Indian Ocean" (5 April 1980, Pb 191/8), which was sent to all Soviet ambassadors and contained a special task for the "friends of the people" (5 April 1980, Pb 191/8, p. 1):

> Instruct the KGB of the USSR to employ special channels to facilitate the activation of protests against the American military presence and the threat of American intervention in developing countries, especially Arab states and in Iran

The Politburo adopted at least two resolutions regarding China, attempting to "counter American-Chinese military cooperation" and "expose the pro-imperialist course of Beijing" in the eyes of third world countries.

Despite such scope, all these were ancillary measures: the main campaign of an "offensive nature" was to be launched in Europe and the USA. This is why the first people to whom the Politburo turned after the invasion of Afghanistan were their partners in détente, the European social democrats, including Willy Brandt and the head of the Finnish social democrats (16 December 1980*, St 241/108), whom we know all too well—the former Finnish prime minister and minister of foreign affairs Kalevi Sorsa, the one who enjoyed "confidential cooperation" with Moscow on matters of détente and disarmament. By that time Brandt was already chairman of the Socialist International, and Sorsa one of its vice presidents, head of the special group coordinating the activity of the Socialist International on questions of détente and disarmament. The sense of these messages was, first and foremost, the affirmation that there is no causal link between the Soviet invasion of Afghanistan and the resultant international tension: the latter, maintained the Politburo, resulted from the aggressive policy of the West in general and the USA in particular. Here the mention of the "December session of the NATO Council" is raised for the first time as the main source of all the troubles, which later became the favorite argument of the forces of peace, progress and socialism in the West. As the Politburo wrote to Brandt (1 February 1980*, Pb 182/2):

> In recent times, especially in connection with the December session of the NATO Council, events have occurred that have

brought about a tangible sharpening of the international situation. As is well known, the Soviet Union has frequently warned that if NATO adopts its decision in December, it will destroy the foundation of negotiations, destroy their basis. Our agreement to negotiate in the face of the NATO decision would result in dealing with a reduction of just the Soviet defensive potential, while the USA forges ahead with the production of new missile and nuclear systems.

All this, writes the Politburo, "exposes the course of the current American administration, which was not devised overnight, but in connection with events in Afghanistan." This course became obvious a long time ago and "merely acquired its more obvious expression in the 'Carter doctrine'."

It is clear that Carter and [Zbigniew] Brzezinski are aiming at intimidating the USSR, isolating our country, and creating difficulties whenever possible. This line is bound to fail, because it is impossible to intimidate the Soviet Union or shake its firm position.

Meetings with the working group of the Socialist International in Moscow discussed the question of where the course of president Carter is leading. Now this has been confirmed. The aim is simply the destruction of the gains of the past decade, gains achieved through the efforts of people of good will, including the social democrats.

This was first and foremost. Second, whatever the reasons for the increase in tension, the main task was to save détente.

In the present situation it is vital to affirm the policy of détente. It is important to note declarations that it is necessary to "keep a cool head and continue the process of negotiations," that "nervousness is no substitute for a thought-out policy," that "it is essential to avoid impulsive and hypertrophic reactions that do not correspond to the substance of events and can precipitate an even worse situation."

As for the events in Afghanistan, which are, naturally, unrelated to the matter, they should be regarded without prejudice and nervousness and with the understanding that they were provoked by the undeclared war of the CIA and Beijing.

5.10   "On the offensive" campaign

The message to the "confidential cooperator" K. Sorsa contained the same ideas, and often the same expressions, the only difference being that it smacked strongly of an instruction (1 February 1980*, Pb 182/2):

International social democracy could play a role here. In a few days' time there will be a meeting of leaders of social democratic parties in Vienna, at which K. Sorsa shall be making an address. In view of the trust that has developed in recent years between us, would you consider it possible—naturally, at your own discretion—to raise some of the following ideas?

This is followed by a point-by-point list of what Sorsa should say to his colleagues:[229]

1. Although it would not be right to speak of "the end of a decade of détente" (as some of its detractors do), there is no denying that the process has clogged.

2. It is particularly worrying that there has been no forward movement in the field of military détente: the Vienna talks have stalled, Carter has deferred the ratification of SALT II, and the decision of the December session of the NATO Council makes it impossible for the USSR to continue talks on the limitation of medium-range weapons in Europe.

3. Both superpowers—the USA and the USSR—have different explanations for the sharpening of the international situation, but it important to examine what they both offer. Carter, citing a nonexistent Soviet threat, is stubbornly steering the matter toward increasing US and NATO military strength. . . .

4. No matter how differently the reasons for the sharpening of the international situation may be viewed in Europe, "there is a prevailing opinion regarding the need to safeguard détente." [. . .]

Naturally, this would require a more active policy both in matters of disarmament and in other areas of cooperation.

5. International practice shows that the line of the Socialist International toward a more active participation in examining and deciding questions of disarmament was correct. This line. . . has demonstrated that social democracy also possesses greater possibilities for exercising a positive influence on the governing circles of those countries on which, first and foremost, success in moving along the path of military détente depends.

In conclusion, the Politburo wrote:

---

[229] 1 February 1980, Pb 182/2, pp. 16–20.

An analysis of the existing situation points to the following recommendations:

It would be feasible for the Socialist International to continue its
line in matters of disarmament. It is particularly important to
complete the development of all positions on the entire complex
of problems of disarmament and its adoption by the Socialist
International as its document ....[230]

Need it be said that "confidential cooperator" Comrade Sorsa
fulfilled the instructions of his Moscow comrades conscientiously?
His address in Vienna on 5 February 1980 contains practically all
their recommendations, and even borrows some of their phraseology. This was the conclusion to his long address:[231]

Comrades! I think that in this meeting we have every reason
to remind ourselves and the world that social democracy has
always been and continues to be a peace movement. Broadly-
based work for peace and disarmament is now needed even
more than under favorable international conditions. Our movement is in a strategic position to influence developments both
within our countries and societies as well as between states. In
the present tension-charged situation, we should not do anything that would irreversibly hurt our interests in the long run.
Above all, we must work for the public opinion that sees the
possibilities and the necessity for peace and disarmament and
is not moved by expedient political acts and demonstrations of
public policy.

Who can say what the leaders of European social democracy
thought upon hearing the impassioned appeal of their Finnish colleague, and whether they guessed whose wishes he was espousing
with such fervor? By that time even the Italian communists had
condemned the invasion of Afghanistan, and of the socialists, the
only party not to do so was the Greek PASOK (Panhellenic Socialist
Movement) party. Moreover, many of them at that time were in the
governments of NATO countries. So there was no chance of avoiding a resolution in Vienna calling for the withdrawal of Soviet troops
from Afghanistan. One thing on which they were unanimous was
the aim of saving détente, to which—for them—there really was no

---

[230] 1 February 1980, Pb 182/2, p. 20.

[231] Kalevi Sorsa, Speech to the Socialist International Party Leaders Conference in
Vienna, Feb 5, 1980. See Socialist International Archives, ##236–239, International
Institute of Social History, Amsterdam and SWE/ARBAK SAP 1889/E/5/80 (*Arbe-
tarrörelsens Arkiv och Bibliotek* [Archive and Library of Labor Movement, Sweden];
http://www.arbark.se/en/archival-catalogue/?refkod=1889/E/5/80&lang=en.

alternative. The Socialist International adopted Sorsa's recommendations with practically no discussion.[232]

> The member parties should create the necessary organizational and financial conditions for efficient and continuous work for disarmament.
>
> Member parties should cooperate with appropriate organizations such as the trade unions and fraternal organizations, especially in the field of training and education as well as the mobilization of public opinion.
>
> Member parties should be active in the work for disarmament also at the national level by cooperating in suitable forms with other non-governmental organizations in their own countries. ... The UN week for disarmament should be made a broadly-based national event encompassing various political, civic and research organizations in all fields of life. Socialist and social democrats work actively for the success of this week.
>
> Citizens! The Socialist International, a free grouping of the world's socialist and social democratic parties, calls every person all over the world to work. ... to make a contribution to efforts for disarmament, peace, détente and international cooperation.

● ● ●

The Soviet "struggle for peace" campaign that swept across Europe at the beginning of the 1980s would not have had even half of its success if it were not for the participation of social democrats, socialists and their subservient trade unions, and youth, women's, and similar organizations that chose to cooperate with communist parties in this matter. The most astounding fact was not so much the campaign's openly pro-Soviet orientation as its scope: when all was said and done, this was the measure of its success. If at the end of 1979 and the beginning of 1980 their demonstrations gathered no more than ten or twenty thousand, by the end of 1980 the figures had risen to between eighty and one hundred thousand, and by the fall of 1981 the ground shook under their marches: three hundred and fifty thousand in Bonn, two hundred and fifty thousand in Brussels, up to two hundred and fifty thousand in London, around half a million in Rome, four hundred thousand in Amsterdam, some one hundred thousand in Copenhagen, thirty to forty thousand in Bern, and no fewer than ten thousand even in little Norway. Then came the culmination of the campaign, December 1983,

---

[232]"Conclusions of the study group on disarmament," Congress of the Socialist International, 13–16 November 1980, Madrid. In *Akademiya Nauk SSSR, Institut Nauchnoy Informatsii po Obshchestvennym Naukam* (Academy of Sciences, USSR, Institute of Scientific Information on the Social Sciences), *XV Kongress*, pp. 142–185.

with the deployment of new missiles in Europe: up to a million in West Germany, six hundred thousand in Rome, three or four hundred thousand in London, and up to half a million in Brussels and The Hague.[233] The figures had a hypnotic effect on the crowds that seemed to convince them of their rectitude, making the crowds grow and grow. These figures gave pause even to the well versed; surely Moscow could not have so many agents and "fellow-travelers"! The figures were frightening: it seemed as though nothing could halt this epidemic of antinuclear hysteria. A little more and some government or other would be unable to hold out, surrender, agree to a compromise, split NATO, and grant the USSR an unlimited *diktat* in a nuclear-free, neutralized Europe. After that, a chasm on the edge of which there would be no foothold for a babbling socialist with his vain hopes for an intermediary between East and West, his Utopian dreams of "socialism with a human face" and convergence; after that it would be Moscow deciding which latter-day Alexander Kerensky in which European country was due for replacement by a staunch Leninist. . . .

Now that the decorative facades have fallen, exposing the vicious squalor of the essence of the Soviet regime, it is hard to believe that only some ten or twelve years ago millions of people in Europe saw no other way out than capitulation. It is hard to imagine that a commonplace Soviet "measure of an offensive nature," which would not have fooled even a Soviet schoolchild, evoked mass hysteria among the adult population of a safe, free, well-protected Europe. And this population, forgetting Afghanistan and other communist crimes, demanded unilateral disarmament from its governments! And how they demanded: storming missile bases, surrounding them with human chains; in Holland even military servicemen declared their refusal to accept nuclear arms. No logic, no reasoned arguments had any effect.

"*Protest and survive!*"[234]

Protest—against what? Against the Soviet invasion of Afghanistan? Against the already-deployed Soviet SS-20 medium-range missiles? No, against NATO's intention to deploy its Pershing and cruise missiles in Europe.

"*Our deterrent doesn't deter anymore!*"

What happened? Why? Had war broken out?

---

[233]April Carter, *Peace Movements: International Protest and World Politics Since 1945*. London: Longman, 1992, pp. 120–121. (A Fellow of Somerville College, Oxford, from 1976 to 1984, Carter served as CND secretary from 1970 to 1971.)

[234]The title of a peace movement brochure in which E.P. Thompson and others mocked Protect and Survive, a multimedia series containing the official advice for coping with a nuclear attack.

"There has never been such a great threat of the nuclear destruction of the world," howled the pro-Soviet World Peace Council.

"We are entering the most dangerous decade in the history of mankind," echoed "independent" Western pacifists.

Why? What was the reason for such a sudden danger? Was it because for the preceding decades there were games of détente with the Kremlin or, rather, a giveaway? It is frightening to think what the outcome could have been if the game had lasted another five years.

But neither the leaders of the movement nor their followers occupied themselves with such complex questions. Their arguments, if one can use that word for their hysterical ravings, were so contradictory at times that it was hard to see how they could all form part of a single movement. The only thing that united them was an irrational fear, a readiness to capitulate without being asked to do so. "Better red than dead", the more so as most of them were already, if not red, then certainly a very bright pink.

I must confess that I cannot stand hysterics; they infuriate me and fill me with an almost irresistible desire to issue a few good slaps in the face (the best way to stop hysterics). Seeing a mass pro-Soviet hysteria was absolutely intolerable. I was overcome by sheer desperation: I had sacrificed half of my life trying to explain the essence of the Soviet system to people, and it had seemed that they did understand. But no, someone in Moscow pulled a string, did a bit of scaremongering, and it was back to the drawing board, as if there had never been a gulag, or our trials, or our books. Never mind us—the entire history of the twentieth century seemed to have disappeared into some dark hole, disappeared from the consciousness of millions of people, and we, like a theater audience, had to watch—not for the first time!—a repeat performance of a familiar tragedy. It was as if once more, as in 1917, there was an unbridled thirst for peace—at any price, and right this minute—that could sweep countries from the face of the earth to the joy of the Bolsheviks. Or as in 1938, when an identical seizure of pacifism opened the door to Europe for their brown-shirted brothers.

What could be done? Lacking the physical opportunity to slap all their faces, I selected the closest equivalent—I wrote a large, deliberately scathing article for the London *Times* ("Better Red than Dead Is Not Good Enough," 4 December 1981) and then expanded and published it as a separate booklet ("The Peace Movement and the Soviet Union"[235]) in practically all Western countries:[236]

> So now, despite all their errors, useless adventures and eco-
> nomic disasters, the Polish crisis and the stubborn resistance
> of Afghan peasants, Reagan's plan for rearmament and UN reso-
> lutions, the Soviet leaders celebrated a significant victory: they
> found millions of useful idiots to implement their bankrupt pol-
> icy. They were no longer in isolation, and the big question was
> whether they would allow the Americans to deploy their mis-
> siles in Europe. Undoubtedly the ranks of the peace movement
> contain an enormous number of sincerely concerned, fright-
> ened people whose intentions are for the best. I am absolutely
> sure that the overwhelming majority of them are sincere, honest
> people. But just as in the 1950s, there are also enough commu-
> nists, fellow travelers, misled intellectuals, hypocrites seeking
> popularity, professional political speculators, frightened bour-
> geois and young people prepared to rebel for the sake of re-
> bellion; of course, there are also indestructible Catholic priests
> with a dubious "mission" and many deeply religious people who
> are convinced that God has chosen them to be a force for peace
> on earth. But there is also no doubt that this disparate crowd is
> manipulated by a handful of scoundrels, receiving instructions
> directly from Moscow."

It is easy to imagine the roar of fury that exploded, how the leftist intelligentsia hated me. Especially as at that time I had no direct evidence to back up my thesis; all I had were official Soviet
publications, some materials from the World Peace Council, and
a thorough knowledge of my beloved homeland. Like anyone who
had grown up in the USSR I knew that the "struggle for peace"
formed an integral part of the Soviet ideological battle with the outside world or, to be more precise, one of its mutations, because
according to communist ideology, peace is possible only with the
full victory of socialism worldwide. In communist Newspeak, these
concepts became synonymous a long time ago, and the expression
"struggle for peace" simply meant the struggle of the USSR for the
expansion of its influence. This was true for Soviet citizens, all departments and organizations, many of which—committees for the
protection of peace, "friendship" societies with all sorts of countries
(and their counterparts in those countries), the Soviet Committee

---

[235]"The Peace Movement and the Soviet Union" (1982), https://www.
commentarymagazine.com/article/the-peace-movement-the-soviet-union/

[236]Vladimir Bukovsky, "'Better Red than Dead' is not good enough," *Times* (London), 4 December 1981; *Les pacifistes contre la Paix*, France, 1982. US and Dutch
editions were published in 1982; Swiss, Polish, and Greek editions followed in 1983,
and a Swedish edition in 1984.

of War Veterans, the Committee of Soviet Women or the Foreign Relations Department of the Moscow Patriarchate—were created for that purpose. Their task, like the task of any Soviet organization coming into contact with foreigners, was to hoodwink those foreigners, infiltrate international organizations and movements with similar profiles, find fellow travelers in them, promote "our" line in all matters—in general, to struggle for peace.

This was a gigantic machine that worked without stopping, simply mutating depending on the requirements of the moment. The usual wavering of Soviet foreign policy from the Cold War to détente and back needed only minimal adjustments to its functioning. So the need to overcome the shortfall in nuclear arms and counter the creation of NATO, and the general increase of fear in the West at the beginning of the 1950s called for an aggressive campaign for disarmament in general and nuclear arms in particular. Hence the explosion of peace-loving activity of the time, the famous Stockholm Appeal, Pablo Picasso's *La Colombe* (*The Dove*), etc. However, the turn towards détente in the 1970s did not mean the cessation of this activity; the cultivated Western structures and personal contacts did not disappear but, on the contrary, became stronger. Now their orientation switched to the current problems of Soviet policy (23 March 1976, No. 235)—the campaign against the war in Vietnam, solidarity with the Chilean people or the people of Palestine, the struggle against apartheid, etc. The turn toward the Cold War of the 1980s just meant a change of emphasis in this incessant "war." In fact, nothing changed: the same World Peace Council with its immortal chairman Romesh Chandra, with its headquarters in Finland and offices all over the world, had the same offstage director, head of the International Department of the CC Boris Ponomarev, and the same clients, mostly false "peace-loving" organizations created by local communist parties. Even the financing remained the same—mainly through the Soviet Peace Fund, into which every Soviet citizen was obligated to contribute part of his salary. The financing was not miserly: according to my very approximate calculations at the time, based solely on official Soviet sources, the Peace Fund collected around 400 million rubles, of which at least one-third (140 million, $35 million at the unofficial exchange rate at that time) was spent in the West to "render financial support to organizations, movements and individuals fighting for peace and disarmament, and to finance international congresses, symposiums, festivals and exhibitions, that grant these organizations and people the possibility of coordinating their activities on an international scale."[237]

I repeat that all this was known even then, at the beginning of the 1980s and from perfectly accessible Soviet publications. Furthermore, from time to time the Western press would mention scandals connected with Soviet manipulation of the peace movement; for example, an activist in Denmark, Arne Petersen, was caught with Soviet money he'd received for publishing paid announcements and petitions of his movement; Soviet diplomats in Switzerland turned out to be party to organizing antinuclear demonstrations;[238] and West German Greens, having quarreled with their communist allies, accused the latter of total manipulation of antinuclear rallies.[239] The extremely high percentage of communists in antimilitary organizations in England,[240] Holland, and Germany,[241] to say nothing of Italy, was a convincing fact that spoke for itself.

However, at that time I did not have more direct evidence, and knew nothing about many aspects of these "measures of offensive nature." I remember how I cudgeled my brains to determine when specifically the Politburo had made the decision to launch its campaign for disarmament. Before or after the invasion of Afghanistan? I was inclined to think that it was before, somewhere in mid-1979, around the same time as the decision concerning Afghanistan. It emerged that I was not quite right; history proved to be much more interesting. For one thing, this decision in itself had nothing to do with Afghanistan, and was made back in 1975, at the Twenty-Fifth Congress of the CPSU, "as part of the general Program of further struggle for peace and international cooperation." The achievements of détente had to be affirmed, as well as the Helsinki Accords which legalized the subsequent Soviet expansion in Europe, to camouflage the rapid build-up of arms and, most of all, to prevent retaliatory measures by Western governments. There were concerns about Soviet military supremacy even then. Andropov reported the following to the CC in December 1975 (14 December 1975*, 3088-A):

> In recent times, the attention of the military and political circles

---

[237]Vladimir Bukovsky, *Soviet Hypocrisy and Western Gullibility* (with Sidney Hook and Paul Hollander). Washington; London: Ethics & Public Policy Center, 1988.

[238]John Vinocur, "KGB officers try to infiltrate antiwar groups," *New York Times*, 26 July 1983.

[239]John Vinocur, "Antimissile group in Bonn is divided," *New York Times*, 6 April 1982.

[240]Douglas Eden, "The story of who is behind Britain's CND," *Wall Street Journal*, 22 February 1983.

[241]Wynfred Joshua, "Soviet manipulation of the European Peace Movement," *Strategic Review*, Winter 1983.

in various NATO countries has been drawn to the problem of so-called tactical nuclear weapons, the development of which, according to prognoses, may cause a change in the structure of armed forces and result in a future serious influence on the development of the international situation. The main feature of such weapons, with their high autonomy and mobility, is their capability of hitting their target with practically one shot, irrespective of distance and in any weather conditions at any time of the day or night. Examples of these weapons are bombs with laser or television guidance, already deployed in the war in Southeast Asia; various types of missiles and shells guided by laser beam (the Hellfire antitank missiles being produced in the USA and the homing 155-millimeter artillery shells), or by the relief of a locality (the "Pershing-2" tactical missile with a targeting margin of error of 20–40 meters), unmanned aircraft, etc.

All this, continued Andropov, would introduce a raft of both stabilizing and destabilizing factors into the international situation. On the one hand:

The appearance of weapons such as these can lead to the abandonment of certain types of contemporary expensive aviation and armored vehicle technology, to an increase in the role of cheap tanks, armored vehicles, and unmanned aircraft in the future conduct of military actions with small, highly mobile units.

But on the other hand:

It is assumed in NATO military circles that the threat of a guaranteed defeat of targets with the new weaponry shall involve a number of measures for the dispersal of military industrial objects, arsenals, and large military bases. Stabilizing factors are seen in the high efficiency of the new weapons, which lessens the likelihood of the possible use of nuclear weapons and increases the ability of the defending side to oppose even the superior forces of the opponent.

... NATO military and political circles deem it feasible to arm one-shot system weapons with low-yield nuclear warheads. In their opinion, such weapons systems can destroy large targets with practically no damage to civil objects and no significant numbers of civilian victims. These features of the new weapons are used by NATO leaders as an argument for the need for simplified procedures in reaching a decision on the combat employment of tactical nuclear weapons.

The United States is attempting to exploit new possibilities linked with the appearance of tactical weapons to reinforce

NATO and "raise the confidence of their West European allies
in their ability to counter the forces of the Warsaw Pact."

This was something that Moscow could not accept: the entire
meaning of the "peaceful offensive" was to make Europe vulnerable, dependent on Soviet dictates, i.e., totally incapable of countering the forces of the Warsaw Pact countries. It could be said that
this was the aim of all their military maneuvers since Stalin's time,
but the appearance of nuclear arms at the end of the war had interfered badly with their plans. In view of the enormous numerical
superiority of the socialist camp, Moscow would have been satisfied with full disarmament: communist hordes could have crushed
Europe with their bare hands. But nuclear disarmament was the
height of their dreams: the weapons at the disposal of democratic
Europe had no chance of catching up with those of the totalitarian monster. In order to achieve this, the population of the whole
continent would have to be militarized, all resources would have to
be mobilized; i.e. Europe would have had to become a totalitarian
state like the Soviet Union. For this reason, Truman and Clement
Attlee depended on nuclear weapons from the moment NATO was
created: they allowed Europe to enjoy democracy, develop economically, and remain independent. But there were certain minuses:
nuclear weapons could not be used without destroying half of Europe in the process of repulsing a Soviet attack. All that could be
relied on was the deterrent force of nuclear arms, i.e. to live under
the perpetual threat of a nuclear catastrophe, and this served as
the source of the shameless Soviet exploitation of fear. Whether the
West would resort to using them at a critical moment was the main
problem of European security, arising with every change in the political situation. This was the root of the infamy of détente with its
temptation of peace and cooperation (in particular the infamy of its
Western advocates, who knew perfectly well what they were playing with), its premise that when faced with an impossible choice
between capitulation and nuclear suicide, that is, whether to become "red" or "dead," people were inclined to the former, unwilling
to even contemplate the horror of communist slavery. Moreover, it
was considered improper to talk about such a horror in the midst
of détente—it would be dismissed as "Cold War rhetoric"!

The appearance of strategic arms, the neutron bomb, and, later,
the idea of the Strategic Defense Initiative (SDI, better known as
Star Wars) were the answer to this problem. It unleashed such a
fury in Moscow because it neutralized the USSR, rendering its enormous numerical superiority (by the end of the 1970s about 3:1 by

comparison with NATO in ground forces, tanks, and aviation[242]) completely useless, depriving the Soviets of their main ace—the ability to threaten. Should this come about, Europe would not have to make the torturous choice between slavery and death. Europe's ability to ensure its full security unilaterally, without the participation of the USSR or any "collective agreements" (which could be interpreted later to the USSR's own benefit), was a source of constant anxiety in the Kremlin. It would have put an end to all their dreams of getting their hands on Europe and its industrial potential without a single shot being fired.

For this is how they saw the future: they had no plans to occupy Europe or destroy it with nuclear arms. Especially as we saw in Andropov's report, they did not fear for their security with the deployment of new weapons by NATO counties; the Kremlin knew perfectly well that their function was purely defensive. It stands to reason that the demonstrative emplacement of hundreds of SS-20 missiles at the end of the 1970s was a direct response to NATO's new weapons, but only in the sense that it deprived the West of new defense advantages mentioned in Andropov's report. It was as if Moscow was telling the West: *Do not even dream of any "clean" nuclear defense, reducing civilian casualties to a minimum, because any use of your strategic arms will be met by our SS-20 missiles with nuclear warheads.* There is only one explanation for these missiles —a desire to make Europe face, once again, the terrible choice between suicide and capitulation. There was no explanation for the unconcealed placement of these missiles, at the rate of about one every week by 1979, no attempt at camouflage. After all, if they wanted, the Soviets were perfectly capable of concealing from American satellites such things as the ongoing modernization of their missiles since at least 1974. In the Central Command of the Soviet army there was even a special department for that purpose—the Chief Directorate of Strategic Deception, which was very good at its work.

In fact, the notorious "Soviet paranoia" was well-enacted Soviet disinformation, seized upon willingly by the leaders of peace movements and similar "Sovietologists." After all, in view of the enormous system of Soviet intelligence and the mightiest army in the world, what did they have to fear? But being experienced players, Soviet leadership calculated soberly that a sharp change toward hostility after decades of demoralization, the sudden Western awareness of the colossal military advantages of the East that gave

---

[242]Winston S. Churchill, *Defending the West*. Sydney: Doubleday Australia, 1982, © 1981 p. 87.

NATO no chance of defense, would make Europe's choice to "redden" inevitable. This is just what I wrote in my booklet:[243]

> From that moment you will gradually start to lose your freedom, finding yourselves subjected to constant and unstoppable Soviet blackmail.
>
> You may like or dislike your trade unions, but would you want them to be afraid of a Soviet invasion every time there was the possibility of a big strike (as happened in Poland over 16 months)? You can like or dislike your press, but would you want it to be controlled by stringent censorship in order to avoid an angry reaction of a powerful neighbor (as occurs in Finland)? You can like or dislike the parliamentary system, but you are at least free to cast your vote for whoever you want without having to consider the desires of a foreign state. Nobody threatens to move in and enforce an alien government on your country (as happened in Afghanistan). The nature of the Soviet system is such that it will calm down only when you become identical to it.

5.11   The machine in action

So the disarmament campaign was already planned in 1975, but was not considered urgent; it was something for the future. The placement of the medium-range SS-20 missiles was planned for the end of the 1970s, and the American missiles were not expected any sooner. As Andropov stated at the end of his report (14 December 1975*, 3088-A):

> At present, work on creating strategic missiles at the stage of installation of tested samples, study the accrued experience of their practical deployment, and also the development of new experimental systems. At an unofficial meeting of representatives of NATO military and industrial circles in March 1975 in the FRG, a conclusion was reached regarding the reality of a wide distribution and possible application of strategic weapons by the beginning of the 1980s.

The beginning of the 1980s was earmarked for the launch of the "struggle for peace" in all its glory. Preparations for it were not hurried, but substantial. In the summer of 1975 the World Peace Council issued its appeal for disarmament, coinciding with the twenty-fifth anniversary of the Stockholm Appeal.[244] It was only

---

[243]Vladimir Bukovsky, "The Peace Movement", (1982).   https://www.commentarymagazine.com/article/the-peace-movement-the-soviet-union/

[244]Viktor Suvorov, *Inside the Soviet Army*. London: Panther, 1982, pp. 102–105.

in May 1976 that the CC resolution "On the Procedure in the USSR for a Campaign Calling for a Halt of the Arms Race, for Disarmament" was finally adopted, and the plan for the main events was approved. The CC wrote the following (21 May 1976, St 9/4):

> The conduct of a global campaign for cessation of the arms race and for disarmament is an important sociopolitical undertaking, making it possible to acquaint foreign society with the peace-loving foreign policy of the USSR and the countries of the socialist commonwealth, the creation of a broad social foundation of support for Soviet initiatives in the field of halting the arms race and [promoting] disarmament, and isolating the bellicose forces of imperialism and Maoism, which are striving to undermine the process of decreasing international tension.

The main event was the mass collection of signatures under the appeal of the World Peace Council issued a year earlier, allegedly to mark the twenty-fifth anniversary of the famous Stockholm Appeal.

> The collection of signatures under the WPC Appeal is being conducted among citizens of the USSR with a minimum age of 16 on a strictly voluntary basis. Foreign citizens located on the territory of the USSR may sign the appeal at their own discretion. ...[245]

This was accompanied by evenings, meetings, exhibitions, festivals, the publication of special Soviet posters, brochures, stained glass, and even a special postage stamp—all "for halting the arms race and [promoting] disarmament." It was only at the end of the programs that there was a modest addition:

> TASS, APN, Gosteleradio [the USSR State Committee for Television and Radio Broadcasting], and the editorial boards of central newspapers and journals shall all give broad, regular coverage of the campaign in the USSR and abroad. In work aimed at foreign countries, special attention must be paid to propaganda showing the essence of Soviet positions on questions of disarmament, coverage of the mass nature of the campaign being conducted throughout the country.[246]

A special announcement was sent to every communist and workers' party in the world. The leaders of socialist countries were informed additionally in confidence of the following (8 July 1976, St 11/5, p. 3):

---

[245]21 May 1976, St 9/4, p.4.
[246]Ibid, p.6

The mass nature of the campaign in support of the WPC Appeal
in socialist countries will serve as an added stimulus to activate
participation in the campaign by the public in capitalist and
developing countries.

One can just feel how slowly and ponderously, like millstones,
the wheels of this gigantic machine of "fraternal" countries, their
associates and branches, friends and fellow travelers began to grind
on all continents, with the possible exception of Antarctica. Their
work was adjusted, financial aid was increased to various foreign
structures—such as in Scandinavia (8 June 1976, St 11/7)—positions in international organizations were reinforced, coordinated
meetings and briefings were held. The scope of the planned campaign and its putative terms can be assessed if only from the fact
that the USSR and its clients achieved in 1978 a special session of
the UN General Assembly on disarmament, the final document of
which proclaimed:[247]

> Alarmed by the threat to the very survival of mankind with the
> existence of nuclear arms and the continuing arms race, and
> recalling the devastation inflicted by all wars,
>
> Convinced that disarmament and arms limitation, particularly
> in the nuclear field, are essential for the prevention of the dan-
> ger of nuclear war and the strengthening of international peace
> and security and for the economic and social advancement of
> all peoples, thus facilitating the achievement of the new inter-
> national economic order,"

Let us not forget: all this is in 1978, at the height of détente,
when there did not seem to be any direct threat of a nuclear war.
But there was rapid Soviet expansion in the third world, there were
heavily-armed communist hordes in the center of Europe, the only
defense against which remained nuclear arms, and it was unclear
whether it would be used as a last resort. What was the threat to the
world perceived by the UN, what worried the General Assembly so?
Why, the very existence of this last resort against communism. Why
did the UN recommend nuclear disarmament, which would result
in the global triumph of "a new international economic order"—to
wit, socialism?

---

[247]Final Act of the General Assembly's session on Disarmament (23 May
to 1 July 1978), Office of Public Information, United Nations.   (https:
//search.archives.un.org/special-session-of-general-assembly-devoted-to-
disarmament-to-be-held-may-june-1979)

> It must be emphasized, moreover, that this special session
> marks not the end but rather the beginning of a new phase
> of the efforts of the United Nations in the field of disarmament.

And in fact, the Politburo-approved program of action made the
UN and all its endless structures an appendage to the "struggle for
peace," although all this was done with Western money.

The 1980s were declared the "Decade of Disarmament," and entire states and regions were openly called upon to declare themselves to be "nuclear free."

At the same time, the CC ordered "steps toward raising the role
of the Soviet Union in UNESCO, an increase in the numbers and ac-
tivities of Soviet employees in the secretariat of that organization"
and reported on the success already achieved in the development of
UNESCO's USSR-initiated Declaration on Fundamental Principles
Concerning the Contribution of the Mass Media to Strengthening
Peace and International Understanding, to the Promotion of Human
Rights and to Countering Racialism, Apartheid and Incitement to
War. These achievements were really noteworthy: the special reso-
lution of the CC "On Further Increase of the Activity of the USSR in
UNESCO Matters" summarizes the result of this work over twenty-
five years (28 August 1979, St 173/6):

> Due to the principled line of the USSR and fraternal socialist
> countries, UNESCO has taken a firm course for its active par-
> ticipation in current international problems, first of all in the
> struggle for peace, détente, and disarmament, and against colo-
> nialism and racism. ...
>
> Despite the opposition of Western countries, UNESCO cond-
> ucted and received broad international approval of events dedi-
> cated to the 150th anniversary of the birth of K. Marx, the 100th
> anniversary of the birth of V.I. Lenin, the 50th and 60th an-
> niversaries of the Great October Socialist Revolution, the 50th
> anniversary of the formation of the USSR, etc.
>
> Important political decisions adopted at the 220th session of
> the General Conference (October–November 1978), create fa-
> vorable conditions for a more active orientation of UNESCO to-
> ward more active support of the attempts of the Soviet Union
> and other socialist countries for an enhancement of the inter-
> national situation, countering the schemes of militarist forces
> and opponents of détente, including the Maoists.
>
> The Soviet Union's participation in UNESCO activities has not
> just a foreign policy and ideological effect, but also gives a con-
> siderable boost to the national economy. Through UNESCO,
> Soviet scientists receive access to information valuable to our
> science, national economy, and defense.

However, the possibilities for strengthening our positions in UN-
ESCO and increasing our receipt of scientific and economic information are not being exploited to their full potential. This
applies to both the scientific and technological programs of UN-
ESCO and receipt of the relevant information, and the propaganda channels as well as the Organization's publishing activity
(its publications are distributed in 140 countries).

All this, you will note, was being conducted with Western money,
and the generous annual budget of UNESCO in 1979 amounted to
$151.6 million! Years passed before the USA and England termi-
nated their participation in financing UNESCO, seeing finally that
this organization had become a mere instrument of Soviet policy
and a hotbed of espionage. But this situation was common to most
international organizations, including the UN itself. Just listing
them all would fill several pages, and all of them were full of Soviets with their clients and fellow travelers, employing their "possibilities": channels, finances, and prestige. Together with the "peace
movement" of all leftist forces, they became a formidable weapon for
influencing public opinion, allowing the use of any subject, any excuse for broadening their campaign and creating its infrastructures.
For example, 1979 was proclaimed as the International Year of the
Child by UNESCO, which seemingly had no relation to the Soviet
campaign for the nuclear disarmament of the West. But this would
fool only an ignorant Western citizen (14 August 1979, St 171/5,
p. 8):[248]

> Pursuant to the Resolution of the CC CPSU and the Coun-
> cil of Ministers of the USSR N139-44 dated 5 February 1979,
> the Committee of Soviet Women, the VTsSPS [All-Union Central
> Council of Trade Unions], and the Central Committee of the
> Lenin Communist Youth League [Komsomol] are authorized to
> conduct a World Conference: "For a Peaceful and Secure Fu-
> ture for all Children" in Moscow in September 1979 with the
> participation of up to 700 foreign delegates.

Without taking a closer look, this appears to be quite innocuous.
Children, as they say, are the flowers of life. Who does not want a
peaceful and happy future for children? One can only thank the
Soviet Union for all the trouble and expenses required by such an
honorable cause. And the expenses were quite impressive: 1.5 million rubles and 80,000 hard foreign currency rubles. All for the
sake of children?

---

[248] 14 August 1979 (St 171/5), p. 8.

> The organization of the global conference in Moscow opens up new possibilities for explaining the peace-loving policy of the Soviet Union and its efforts in the struggle for disarmament and international détente, for propaganda concerning the advantages of socialism in creating conditions for a happy childhood. The conference shall lend a new impulse to the development of cooperation among the extensive forces of the global society in the struggle for children's rights.[249]

The main right of children turned out to be "to live in peace."

• • •

The Afghan adventure actually hindered rather than helped the Soviet campaign for unilateral Western disarmament by mixing their cards and upsetting all their plans. In any event, prior to the invasion of Afghanistan the global political atmosphere was much more favorable for their plans. The moot point is whether the West would have managed to stand fast if the situation had lasted a few more years. The first real test of their strength was the campaign opposing Carter's idea of arming NATO with neutron weapons—one of the technical innovations calculated to reinforce European defense against the superior forces of the Warsaw Pact (especially in tanks), as mentioned in Andropov's report. And although these weapons were clearly defensive and no threat to peace in Europe, and the campaign of opposition was just as clearly pro-Soviet, it was extremely successful. All it took was a few protests in Holland, Denmark, and Norway between 1977 and 1978 to scare Carter and force him to reconsider his attitude toward neutron weapons. Without doubt, this was a defeat for NATO and a victory for Moscow, moreover an easy and confidence-inspiring one, as shown in the proud report of the International Department of the CC (26 September 1978, St 126/8):[250]

> The significant stepping up of the activity of the World Peace Council (WPC), particularly in the field of struggle for the cessation of the arms race and against neutron weapons has enabled the recent increase in the level of mobilizing the masses and broadening the sociopolitical base of antimilitarist manifestations, primarily in capitalist countries including the USA and West European states.

The "struggle for peace" continued to grow and spread throughout the late 1970s, according to plan and totally independent of world conjuncture. Even the signing of the 1979 agreement on the

---

[249]Ibid, p. 15
[250]See 26 September 1978 (St 126/8), pp. 7–8, 27 August 1978 (227).

limitation of nuclear weapons (SALT II) by Brezhnev and Carter in Vienna (29 May 1979, St 160/5) and the top-level meeting did not slow it down. On the contrary, the Soviet Union continued to force the issue, including by the continuous issue of "peace initiatives" and proposals unilaterally advantageous to the USSR and unacceptable to the West (non-use of nuclear weapons, means for reinforcing "trust" by a unilateral withdrawal of a small number of Soviet forces in Germany, etc. (16 March 1979, Pb 147/8). Thus the artificial (and not unsuccessful) impression was created of the tireless work of Soviet leaders devoted to peace and, to a lesser degree, the indifference of NATO and the US government, forced to reject these "initiatives." By the end of 1979 the Soviet Union was winning the campaign rganizationally, psychologically, and strategically and, it can be assumed, would have won completely in a few more years were it not for Afghanistan.

Probably the most important aspect of this adventure was not even the concrete Soviet aggression (this had happened in the past) but its surprising untimeliness, which brought about a change in the general world situation, and the entire political context. It would be hard to imagine a more colorful illustration of what "peaceful coexistence" with the Soviet regime could lead to, especially for a small neutral country. This illustration was all the more impressive at the height of the Soviet campaign for disarmament, for a peaceful coexistence based upon trust. There could be no better advertisement for NATO—even Switzerland began to doubt the usefulness of its traditional neutrality. At the very least, none of this could promote the "growth of the sociopolitical base" of the Soviet peace movement. On the contrary, this moment widened the split between the Western left and right wings regarding questions of defense, with the latter achieving a clear and well-founded position. This played a considerable role in the West's move to the right in the 1980s, bringing Ronald Reagan to power, then Helmut Kohl in the FRG. Polarization also increased in European socialist and social democratic parties, in which the more moderate pro-Atlantic wing in the leadership either broke away (such as the British Labour Party), or restrained their parties from a more radical position (Chancellor Helmut Schmidt in the FRG and Prime Minister Bettino Craxi in Italy).

On the other hand, the Soviet leaders had to force their campaign, alter their plans and terms, and overload their resources in trying to overcome the resultant political isolation. Even a decrease in "cultural exchange" due to boycotts and protests against their policy undermined their possibilities seriously, especially in the USA. The very necessity of overcoming such isolation raised doubts about all their campaigns. Not by chance, even I had the impression that such a turbulent "struggle for peace" was much more closely tied to events in Afghanistan than it was in reality.

In view of this, the success of their campaign is all the more astounding. The April 1980 resolution of the CC "On Additional Measures for Activating Public Manifestations against the NATO Decision to Manufacture and Deploy New American Missiles in Western Europe" (15 April 1980, St 206/15) affirms the new plan of action in the resultant atmosphere. All mass media received the following instruction:

> Reinforce argumentative criticism of the US-influenced decisions of the Brussels session of the NATO Council as one of the main causes of the sharpening of the international situation, explain the significance of the proposals of the Soviet Union regarding medium-range weapons in Europe and general military détente on the continent for a radical decrease in tension concerning relations between states.[251]

> Soviet public organizations should make full use of planned contacts and exchanges with West European countries, and also the additional proposals of Soviet embassies in these countries for the purpose of ensuring that the campaign against the NATO military continues to grow and reach maximum intensity by the time of the spring session of the main agencies of that bloc (May–June of this year).[252]

Sure enough, by June, demonstrations were springing up in Europe.[253] The task was made easier by the fact that many protests and events had been planned and prepared in advance, so all they needed was to be reinforced and broadened, to receive more financing and not have to start from scratch. For instance, the International Association of Parliamentarians for Peace in Helsinki in May 1980 (23 May 1980, St 212/57), the international conference for a ban on nuclear arms in Japan in August (28 July 1980, St 221/35), and the World Parliament of Peoples for Peace in September in Sofia, of which I wrote in 1982, had all been planned about a year ahead.[254] The latter, as I guessed correctly in my brochure, was really the central event in 1980, calling for[255] "... activation of protests against the adventurist policy of imperialist circles in the

---

[251] 15 April 1980, St 206/15, p. 2
[252] Ibid, p. 1–2
[253] See Carter (1992), p. 120.
[254] For "World Parliament", see 12 September 1979 (St 176/1).
[255] 11 August 1980 (St 223/53), p. 3.

USA, NATO, and the Beijing hegemonists, for the preservation and continuation of the process of international détente in the 1980s."

Initially, this "parliament" was planned as a more modest, commonplace measure of the WPC, and had the original title World Congress of the Supporters of Peace. But the activation of the "struggle" required additional financing, so preparatory work was stepped up (especially regarding the inclusion of noncommunist organizations), help was received in accordance with Sorsa's recommendations from socialists and social democrats, and the enterprise mutated into a "parliament of peoples." Its role was manifold: in the first place it was to lend its authority to Moscow's decisions (just the way dubious banks launder dirty money), as shown by the Soviet Peace Committee's report to the CC:[256]

> The political preparation for this central enterprise of the public movement for peace, called upon to determine the main directions of the efforts of peace-loving people for the next couple of years, is conducted in cooperation with international and national organizations of various political orientations. It is expected that the work of the World Parliament shall include 1,500–2,000 delegates and guests from more than a hundred countries, from the UN, UNESCO, UNCTAD, and other international governmental and nongovernmental organizations.[257]

However, the reality exceeded all expectations: the event was attended by 2,260 lovers of peace from 137 countries representing 330 political parties, 100 international and more than 3,000 national nongovernmental organizations, 200 members of various parliaments, around 200 trade union leaders, 129 leading social democrats (33 of whom were members of the executive bodies of their parties), 150 writers and poets, representatives of 33 liberation movements, 83 communist and workers' parties, women's, youth, and religious organizations, 18 representatives of various committees and specialized services of the UN, etc.[258] Naturally this "parliament" unanimously adopted the Soviet program of actions, the appeal and other documents.

Secondly, this gathering was convenient for deciding numerous organizational questions regarding future actions and reinforcement of ties with various Western organizations of the required tendency, i.e., for the further development of infrastructure. To this end, for example, some of the delegates (some six hundred persons!) were taken from Sofia to Moscow on their way home, where

[256]See 11 August 1980 (St 223/53), p. 6.
[257]Vladimir Bukovsky, Soviet hypocrisy (1987), pp. 23–24.
[258]Daily reports in Pravda, 23–29 September 1980.

a further week was devoted to the development of "bilateral relations" and "acquaintance with Soviet reality" at the same time (15 September 1980, St 228/44).

After all, fulfillment of the decisions of the Parliament of Peoples had to be ensured—to guarantee that its participants, upon returning home, incorporated the relevant resolutions into their organizations, adopted the program of actions, and implemented it unfailingly. The special resolution of the Secretariat of the CC "On Measures for the Further Activation of Manifestations by Peace-Loving Peoples in Light of the Results of the World Parliament of Peoples for Peace" (18 November 1980, St 237/101) set out the basic directions of this work and the main measures. All Soviet agencies and public organizations, for instance, were instructed to

> ... coordinate their actions with the relevant organizations in fraternal socialist countries and progressive organizations in the nonsocialist parts of the world and achieve an active antiwar direction for forthcoming large international enterprises:
>
> Meetings of the participants of the Brussels public movement on questions of security, cooperation, and disarmament (Brussels, November 1980), the Congress of the International Union of Students (Berlin, November 1980), the World Forum of Youth and Students for Peace, détente and disarmament (Helsinki, January 1981), the sessions of the General Council of the Soviet Committee of Solidarity of Asian and African Countries (Aden, March 1981), the Congress of the International Democratic Federation of Women (Prague, October 1981).
>
> Special attention must be paid to the forthcoming extended meeting of the leadership of the World Forum on contacts with peace-loving forces in Vienna in January 1981, striving for reinforcement and development of the established cooperation between various political parties and mass organizations based on an antiwar platform, and steering the matter, among other things, toward reaching a decision to conduct an authoritative global conference on disarmament and détente in a capitalist country. ...
>
> [...]
>
> ... this work should be carried out in close contact with the relevant organizations in socialist countries and international democratic organizations;
>
> [...]
>
> The All-Union Central Council of Trade Unions is to take steps toward the convening of an international conference on the socioeconomic problems of détente in 1981 in accordance with the decision of the Twentieth Congress of the International Feder-

ation of Trade Unions, and to cooperate in the implementation of the proposals of the British National Union of Mineworkers regarding the conduct of a global miners' conference against the arms race.

The Central Committee of the Komsomol and the Committee of Youth Organizations of the USSR shall participate in the activity of workers' agencies launched in October 1980 at the Budapest meeting of the All-European structure of cooperation of youth and students for the purposes of reinforcing the antiwar direction within the framework of its enterprises.

The gigantic flywheels of this diabolical machine spun faster, nuts and bolts did their job, piston rods and cranks hurried into motion, and off it went to crush countries and continents in a cloud of dust. Congresses and forums, marches and protests, "nuclear-free zones," and missives from scientists — all was accomplished practically to the letter. And in front lay a whole ten years, previously designated by the UN as "the decade of disarmament." It seemed as though nothing could stop this epidemic of peace loving, until the whole world turned red. As the wise rabbi said in a Soviet joke of the 1950s, "There will be no war, but there will be such a struggle for peace that not a stone will be left standing."

5.12   Doves of peace

Even now, with hundreds of documents before me attesting to Soviet manipulation of Western peace movements, when there would seem to be answers to all questions in these piles, I still cannot find an answer to the question that occupied me more than anything else: what really made these "peaceniks"—stupidity or infamy? If it was a bit of both, then in what proportion? I recall being asked at a press conference at the time, *What should one do in order to avoid becoming a "useful idiot"?* My answer was, *Do not be a fool in the first place.* If this circumstance cannot be changed for purely biological reasons, then one should follow this simple rule: never be useful to the USSR or its policies. If even this is too hard to grasp, it is probably better to abstain from public activity altogether. And certainly avoid participation in any enterprises with the Soviets and their clear friends.

A simple rule, one that should be understandable even to a fool. But no, our peacemakers painted themselves into a corner by proclaiming themselves ready to cooperate with *all* "antiwar" forces: how can we, they reasoned, demand disarmament from the USSR if we are not prepared to disarm ourselves? We should set an example of "dialogue" to the rest of the world. And so they did. So what was this, naivety or pretense, stupidity or convenient self-justification? I do not know. I remember only what burning indignation my brochure evoked among the leading peacemakers: is it impossible to have dealings with Soviet or local communists, and remain "independent" at the same time?

"There is not a shred of evidence that the peace movement received Soviet funding," wrote one of them in a tone of injured innocence,[259] as if the crux of the matter were money and it was impossible to be a Soviet flunky gratis. Some even refused demonstratively to take part in any events of the World Council of Churches, being fully aware of the odious nature of that Soviet structure. *Look at us: we're independent!*

But even this was foreseen by the sages in the CC. The subject arose at a special coordination meeting of the secretaries of the central committees of all fraternal socialist countries in Budapest on 14–16 July 1980, convened on the initiative of Erich Honecker, at which, among other questions of international politics, the issue of "matters of coordination of international mass public peace movements" (9 June 1980*, St 214/74) was discussed. Before the meeting began, the German insisted that

> the achievement of our common aims apart from diplomacy requires the support of a broad mass movement. However, the breadth and efficacy of this movement depends greatly on how we shall be able to achieve the action of the broadest possible action by supporters of peace—far beyond the framework of the movement directed by the World Peace Council—aimed at the solution of the core task, which is the continuation of détente and liquidation of the threat of nuclear war. ... We deem it feasible to come to an agreement between our parties on the key issues of the strategy and tactics of a global movement in support of peace and to agree on the most important international actions.[260]

> We are naturally proceeding on the assumption that the World Peace Council must retain its important role and continue to augment it. Yet it is an acknowledged fact that the World Peace Council falls far short of reaching all the political forces prepared to struggle for peace, détente, and disarmament. Numerous reformist trade union organizations, religious groups of Christian, Islamic, and Buddhist confessions, many national

---

[259]Paul Oestreicher, Bruce Kent and Theo McEvoy, "Mr. Bukovsky and peace in Europe," *The Times* (London, England), Dec. 9, 1981, Issue 61103, p. 11.
[260]9 June 1980*, St 214/74, p. 7.

action committees representing millions of people, refuse to join the World Peace Council or to cooperate with it. ... It is a fact that numerous important actions (the Dutch movement "No to the neutron bomb!", the Brussels demonstration against NATO missiles, the international peace rally) took place without the involvement of the World Peace Council and even despite the initial resistance of individual representatives of its leadership.[261]

Of course, write the East Germans, such enterprises as the World Parliament of Peoples in Sofia are very significant, but:

> The preparatory committee... consists mainly of representatives of the World Peace Council. The fact that the Dutch movement "No to the neutron bomb!", the British Labour Party Campaign for Nuclear Disarmament, the Belgian Action Committee for Peace and Cooperation and also the Danish Committee for Cooperation are still not involved in the preparations is clearly due to the known position of these organizations that decline direct cooperation with the World Peace Council, and the International Parliament for Safety and Peace is still openly declared to be a creation of the World Peace Council.[262]

Understandably, the East Germans' proposal for more flexible tactics and greater coordination with the social democrats and socialists received full support in Budapest. So it was possible to bring many more "moderates" to Sofia than expected, and individual work with them began to bear fruit, as the CC's International Department reported in August 1980 (11 August 1980, 25-S-1395):[263]

> The prominent Belgian public figure, former minister, and member of the socialist party [Albert] De Smaele, who played an active role in the Brussels movement for European security, informed Soviet representatives of his intention to put forward the idea regarding reinforcement of the security of the non-nuclear states of Europe. He stressed that the main motive for proposing this initiative is the deep concern of the European public in the face of the increase in nuclear missiles foisted by the militarist circles of the USA and NATO on Europe.

Amusing, isn't it? Neither the triple supremacy of the troops of the Warsaw Pact or the already-deployed Soviet SS-20 missiles aimed at his country perturbed this former Minister of Economic Affairs. Furthermore, he hurried to advise Moscow of his intended initiative before declaring it publicly. And what was the substance

---

[261]9 June 1980*, St 214/74, p. 10

[262]Ibid, p. 11

[263]2 September 1980*, St 226/4, pp. 3–5.

of the "initiative"? How would it "reinforce the security of the non-nuclear states of Europe"?

> De Smaele's proposal was that the public of European countries without nuclear arms should attempt to achieve the status of non-nuclear states for their countries. His primary motivation is that countries that already have nuclear arms on their territories should reject their increase and the deployment of new types of missiles, to be followed by efforts toward the reduction and subsequent withdrawal of existing nuclear arms.

> The Belgians intend to discuss this initiative with representatives of the public of other socialist countries, and also the neutral and nonaligned countries of Europe in the near future.

Naturally, the initiative of Belgian "public circles" delighted Moscow:

> Such a public discussion would reinforce the stepping up of the struggle against the deployment of new types of American medium-range missiles in Western Europe.

Admittedly, there was a small hitch:

> The present formulation of this proposal for guarantees of the security of nonnuclear states diverges from the positions agreed upon between socialist countries.

Simply speaking, it was unacceptable to the Warsaw Pact countries, but was perfectly acceptable in relation to Western Europe. It was therefore deemed feasible to

> ... use the discussion of the De Smaele idea for advancing our known proposals to the political circles of the West. ...

There was more to come. Exhilarated by the mighty support of the Soviet Union, the former minister plunged into frenzied activity as a result of which his initiative became wholly "aimed at increasing public resistance of the nonnuclear states to the increase in nuclear missiles being foisted on them by the militarist circles of the USA and NATO" (17 November 1980, 237/76) and received the "full support of the leadership of both socialist parties and Catholic circles of Belgium as well as Holland and other neighboring countries." In this form it became a pan-European movement, seized upon and reinforced by the Soviet machine.

Following instructions to lend the campaign total support, the Central Committees of fraternal communist parties used it to

> ... advance the proposals of L.I. Brezhnev in Western polit-
> ical circles to examine the question of medium-range nuclear
> missiles in Europe together with the organic ties with the issue
> of American forward-deployed nuclear arms at the commenced
> Soviet-American talks on the nuclear question....

and the contents of:

> ... the presentation by comrade A.A. Gromyko at the XXXV
> session of the General Assembly of the UN proposing guaran-
> tees of the non-use of nuclear weapons against countries not
> possessing such weapons, nor having foreign nuclear weapons
> [on their territory].

Tell me no more tales about "independent" movements for a nuclear-free Europe, nuclear-free zones, cities, municipalities, or villages. It is amazing that Western peacemakers refused stubbornly
to see how they were being used by the Soviet machine for its purposes—refused mainly to see that no treaties, agreements, or especially cooperation with this machine on equal terms were possible.
So how can one tell whether this was due to assumed naivety or
natural stupidity?

Take, for example, "nuclear-free zones" and municipalities—yet
another "independent movement" launched by the Soviets through
the system of "twinned cities." This was approved by the CC CPSU
on 15 January 1980[264] in a special resolution. The system of "twinned cities" had existed since the times of the Second World War and
was used by the Soviet regime for "propaganda concerning Soviet
reality, the achievements of communist construction, the peaceful
foreign policy of the CPSU and the Soviet state." Over the years this
degenerated into an empty formality: delegations were exchanged
from time to time, as well as exhibitions, collective artistic amateur
talent events and the conduct of friendship "days" and "weeks." The
deterioration of relations had its effect on all these links. As the
chairman of the Presidium of the Association of Soviet Friendship
and Cultural Societies for ties with foreign countries stated in a report to the CC (12 March 1980, No. 418):[265]

> The governing circles of a number of Western countries oppose
> friendly relations between cities. The British government is
> keeping strict control over these ties, up to the point of pro-
> scribing them; contacts have broken off between Soviet and
> Egyptian cities; Zionist circles in the USA are opposed to the

---

[264]15 January 1980 (St 193/2)^, mentioned in 8 July 1980 (St 218/8), p. 7.
[265]8 July 1980 (St 218/8), pp. 19–20.

establishment of such ties. Over the past two months there have been attempts by reactionary, anti-Soviet forces to bring discord into the friendly ties between Soviet and foreign cities. For instance, letters have been received from the municipalities of certain cities in the USA, Norway, and England indicating their decision to sever or suspend ties with Soviet cities due to "the invasion of Afghanistan by Soviet army forces." The municipalities of some Italian cities, including those headed by communists, have granted Sakharov "freedom of the city" status and sent protests concerning the "exile" of this "champion of human rights" to Gorky. It should be noted that great efforts to establish ties with cities in Japan, the USA, and Italy are being made by the Chinese for use in their hegemonic aims.

The CC had no intention of surrendering such "channels of external influence on various social strata in foreign cities" to the enemy (14 July 1980, St 219/96).

A plan of special measures was developed to boost this activity, financing was increased, party control was improved as well as the selection of cadres, supply of propaganda materials, coordination with fraternal socialist countries, and a "conference of mayors of European capitals devoted to cooperation and disarmament" was envisaged. The number of such cities was rapidly augmented. In other words, the machine roared into action.

Responding to the call of Soviet cities, a number of their foreign partners issued protests regarding the deployment of new American nuclear missiles in Europe.

In November 1980, the first city to declare itself "nuclear-free" was Manchester (twinned with Leningrad), followed by Sheffield (twinned with Donetsk). It is not surprising that by mid-1980, in Great Britain alone, 180 municipalities had declared themselves to be "nuclear-free zones," as well as 17 in Norway, almost 400 cities in Spain and Portugal, and the entire Quebec province of Canada, while entry into Japanese and New Zealand ports was severely restricted for navy vessels with nuclear arms on board. The first international conference of "nuclear-free" municipalities took place in Manchester in 1984, and one year later there was another in the Spanish city of Cordoba, twinned with Bukhara.[266]

Can it be that all these mayors and municipal advisers did not understand, after decades of very limited contact, that life in their "twins" differed vastly from life in the West; that those twins, for instance, were totally controlled, and their "appeals" were in no way spontaneous? Finally, did they not find it strange that despite all

---

[266]Carter (1992), pp. 132, 133, 142, 168, 175.

fraternal appeals, not a single Soviet city became "nuclear-free"? Even one stay in Donesk or Bukhara would have been sufficient for someone of the meanest intelligence to shed such illusions forever.

5.13   Payment in kind

Meanwhile, just the material aid to these movements was quite significant. Admittedly, it was rarely in monetary form—the episode in Denmark was rather an exception to the rule. The reason was that the GRU (military intelligence) and the KGB played only an auxiliary role in the "struggle for peace"; the main director was the International Department of the CC, which had no need to send banknotes directly to Western peace organizations—this was done through local communist parties along well-established channels (8 January 1969*, Pb 111/162). This procedure not only had purely technical advantages that lessened the chances of failure, but was also dictated by an organizational need: it affirmed the influence of communist parties in peace movements. It also enabled the peace-makers' leaders to "sincerely" reject accusations regarding their financial dependence on Moscow. Nonetheless, it is hard to believe that they did not know what part of their organizations' expenses were covered from the party strongboxes of their communist allies. It was equally easy to guess the source of contributions to these strongboxes.

Material aid was also rendered by means of free transportation by Aeroflot (and airlines of fraternal countries) of hundreds of delegates to international forums (especially from third world countries), payment of their maintenance (especially if the forums took place in socialist countries), or, for instance, the provision of simultaneous translators. These forms of aid were rendered regularly, at times even if Soviet organizations or the organizations of their allies were not the actual hosts of a given enterprise in the West, and certainly if the Soviets were among the organizers. At the very least, this ensured the required majority of votes to avoid undesirable decisions. Consider, for instance, this report from the first female cosmonaut, Valentina Nikolayeva-Tereshkova, chair of the Committee of Soviet Women, to the CC in July 1980 (2 July 1980, No. 76):[267]

> A forum of nongovernmental organizations will be held in Copenhagen on 14–24 July, which shall be conducted simultaneously with the World Conference of the United Nations

---

[267]See 11 July 1980*, 219/59, p. 4.

Decade for Women. It is assumed that some ten thousand people will participate in the forum. Preparations for the forum show that reactionary forces are attempting to exploit it for their own purposes. ...

It can be expected that such problems as Afghanistan, Cambodia, refugees, human rights and so on will be raised with hostile aims.

[...]

At the request of the WIDF [Women's International Democratic Federation], the Committee of Soviet Women shall pay for the return travel to Copenhagen for forty representatives from a number of Asian and African countries (Afghanistan, Vietnam, Cambodia, Laos, Angola, South Africa, Ethiopia, and others) in Soviet rubles, as well as the travel for progressive US forces. However, the living expenses of these delegations in Copenhagen will require additional funding in foreign currency.

The ceremonial opening of the conference by the Queen of Denmark was rudely disrupted: there were even fights before the police intervened.[268] Need it be added that undesirable subjects were effectively blocked, despite this not being a Soviet event? It is not hard to imagine what would have happened if it were. For example, the event that was to be one of the most important at the World Forum of Youth and Students for Peace, Détente and Disarmament on 19–23 January 1981 in Helsinki was organized on the initiative of the Komsomol. Preparations for it went perfectly, as noted by the head of the Komsomol, Boris Pastukhov, in a report to the CC (18 December 1980, No. 01/1281):[269]

The entire preparatory process was encouraged by the activation of joint protests for peace by young people and students at the national and international levels. Preparatory work in Finland is conducted by the National Committee of Finnish Youth Organizations (SNT) with the support of President of the Republic of Finland [Urho] Kekkonen.

The enterprise was really unusual: up to six hundred delegates from more than a hundred countries were expected, including representatives of international associations of young social democrats, liberals, centrists, demo-Christians, and other political tendencies, along with representatives of the UN, UNESCO, UNCTAD, and so on.

---

[268]See, for example, report in *Politiken*, 8–31 July 1980.
[269]6 January 1981* (St 244/11), pp. 9–11.

At the same time, in view of the broad spectrum of political
forces in the preparations for the forum, there were attempts
by certain organizations, mainly conservative ones, to force discussions of "violations" of human rights in socialist countries,
about the situation in Afghanistan, Poland, etc., and to include
participants in a number of reactionary youth organizations in
the forum. These attempts met with no support from the overwhelming majority of participating delegations.

But such things were no joke, and it was best to take early steps
to ensure "the positive political balance of forces to the advantage
of progressive youth organizations from liberated countries." Unfortunately, "allowing for the difficult financial situation" of many
of them, additional financial outlays were required for Aeroflot to
bring 110 delegates to Moscow and back and for up to 150 delegates to be taken by train from Moscow to Helsinki and back, "up to
18 thousand convertible rubles to cover the travel of groups of delegates from places not served by Aeroflot and to send a group of up
to 15 Soviet simultaneous translators for work at the forum." The
results were not long in coming as Pastukhov reported one month
later (6 February 1981, 01/118):[270]

> The vast majority of speakers, including representatives of so-
> cial democratic, centrist, and liberal organizations, supported
> the continuation of the policy of détente and the further devel-
> opment of the process of limitation of strategic weapons, and
> spoke positively of the contribution of the Soviet Union and
> other socialist countries to the cause of ensuring peace and
> security. They censured NATO plans for the deployment of new
> American medium-range nuclear missiles on the territory of a
> number of West European countries and criticized the concept
> of a "limited" nuclear war. Numerous delegates stressed the
> threat to peace from the hegemonic policy pursued by Beijing
> leaders. . . .
>
> The behavior of right-wing youth movements at the forum ex-
> posed their intention to undermine the cooperation of various
> political forces that has developed over the past decade, pri-
> marily to alienate the social democrats and socialists from joint
> actions with the VFDM and IUS [International Union of Stu-
> dents]. . . .
>
> The Soviet delegation, leaning on the VFDM and MSS, took
> steps to isolate the right-wingers and to consolidate the fo-
> rum on an antimilitaristic basis. This work was complicated by
> the komsomols of the "Eurocommunist" tendency (Italy, Japan,
> Sweden, and Spain), who spoke out against Soviet military

---

[270]6 January 1981 (St 244/11), pp. 14–17.

aid to Afghanistan. A positive role in discussions was played by member organizations of the VFDM and MSS from Asian, African, and Latin American countries.

It is true to say that this forum reflected the entire political spectrum of that time, but not in the proportions existing in the world. Therefore all the efforts of right-wing forces, moreover lacking even a tenth of Soviet experience in such matters, were in vain:

> The final document, approved unanimously by the participants of the forum, reflected the most important foreign policy initiatives of the Soviet Union and fraternal socialist counties. Among other things, the final document contains a demand for the soonest possible ratification of the SALT II treaty and continuation of the process of limitation of strategic arms, condemns the concept of a "limited" nuclear war, stresses the need to prevent the deployment of new American medium-range nuclear weapons on the European continent, and declares support for the conducting of a conference on military détente and disarmament in Europe.

One can only guess how much all this struggle for peace cost Moscow, including the direct and indirect financing of Western peacemakers. For 1981 alone, more than two thousand persons were to have free transportation by Aeroflot.[271] Apart from these, there were whole crowds of those who came "for rest and medical treatment," and for "acquainting themselves with Soviet reality"— mainly at holiday resorts. There was also the constant aid to friendship societies and solidarity committees. ... Other groups solicited invitations that looked more like a desire to have a good time on a "freebie" (8 April 1980, St 205/10):

> The Soviet Peace Committee, the Central Committee of the Komsomol, and the Committee of Youth Organizations of the USSR have received a request from the French peace movement to receive a group of 50 activists of the youth committee of the movement for the purpose of conducting a seminar in the USSR on questions of the struggle for peace, détente, and disarmament. The youth committee of the French movement includes representatives of various progressive French youth organizations, such as the Young Communists Movement of France[272] young people from the General Confederation of Labor [CGT], Working Christian Youth, and others. The visit to the USSR by representatives of the youth committee of the movement shall contribute

---

[271] See also 15 January 1980 (St 246/22).

[272] *Mouvement Jeunes Communistes de France* (MJCF), commonly simply called JC.

to intensifying the committee's activity, augmenting its authority, and allow us to broaden our cooperation with various forces
in France that advocate peace, détente, and disarmament.

Expenses required for travel—12,000 convertible rubles—and
for maintenance—30,000 rubles—were covered by the Soviet Peace
Fund. These sums were quite considerable at the time. The average
monthly wage in the country was 150 rubles, 5 rubles per day.
Every Soviet citizen was obligated to work one day every year to the
benefit of this fund, whether he wanted to or not. It is noteworthy
that this fact was not concealed from anyone; on the contrary, it
received broad coverage in the press and was reported in numerous
Soviet peace publications,[273] and therefore Western peacemakers
could not be unaware that their "struggle" was being financed by
the forced labor of the Soviet population. But did that worry them?

5.14   The oldest profession

People in general, and the intelligentsia in particular, are extremely
arrogant, egotistic animals, considering themselves smarter than
anyone else in the world, and certainly smarter than their governments. I can think of no occasion on which the intelligentsia admitted that it had been wrong, especially when it came to disputes
with the lawful authority. The reason for this is probably the intelligentsia's belief that its real abilities remain unwanted. Terrible.
After all, they are the elite, and that means that they should rule
the world or, at least, rule people's minds. But life, that unfair
judge, has condemned them to more humble pursuits: teaching
children the alphabet, curing our aches and pains, studying bacteria through a microscope, being bored in provincial courtrooms,
or giving communion to parishioners and listening to their endless complaints about the injustice of life. And all around, out in
the big world, completely different people make important decisions
that determine the fate of mankind. Moreover, those people are not
brighter, better educated, or morally worthy. How can one accept
that? So a member of the intelligentsia cannot simply force himself
to do his job without contrivances and pretensions. He cannot just
teach children to read and write—no, he has to "raise future generations"; he cannot just prescribe pills for a patient and ease his
suffering—no, he needs to concern himself with the health of all
mankind. A priest, meanwhile, is convinced that God Himself has
put him in the pulpit for the salvation of one and all.

---

[273]See *Pravda*, 30 April and 31 May 1982, and *Sputnik Monthly Digest*, February
1982.

The intelligentsia is the most dissatisfied layer of any society, and that is why it is the source of endless heresies: socialisms, communisms, feminisms, ecologisms, and similar Utopian ideas about universal happiness, which can be achieved only under their leadership (something that is not usually acknowledged openly). This is the source of their most common feature—lying. A member of the intelligentsia will never admit that the basic motive of his boisterous social activity is a desire for power. Certainly not! He will reject this until he is blue in the face, invariably advancing the most honorable, most altruistic reasons. He will bluster and wind himself up to the extent of believing in his own unselfishness.

Yet what he is really excels at is the art of interpretation—that is, the ability to shuffle and combine certain facts while omitting and "overlooking" others, or, on the contrary, rejecting them as false and even describing them indignantly as arrant lies. He is the unparalleled master of context; by changing it, unnoticed by anyone, he can come up with any highly unexpected conclusion by mixing totally unsuitable facts, like a magician pulling a rabbit out of a hat. No matter how hard you argue with him, no matter how closely you drive him to the wall, he will always slip away, like a cake of soap in a bath. His main evidence—the real, practical result of his ideas —is usually relegated to the future, and he is totally uninterested because he will bear no responsibility for it. It will be up to other people to pay the price, maybe in another epoch, and he will remain blameless; his ideas are honorable and wonderful, and it is not his fault that nature turned out to be flawed, useless for his brilliant ideas. Like the legendary Frankenstein, he feels no guilt for the acts of the monster he created, for he is less concerned with the end result than the process that allowed him to feel himself to be God, for a short time at least.

Such were our peace activists, mostly primary school teachers, nurses, parish priests, and similar semi-intelligentsia, all those Alexander Solzhenitsyn acutely labeled *smatterers*, possessing a smattering of knowledge. The same can be said of their leaders, for many of whom the process of "leadership" was more important than the essence of the cause. So how can one determine whether they were fools or villains? Did they understand that they were playing to Moscow's advantage or not? No, they were simply not interested; they did not want to know. Even their notorious fear of a nuclear disaster was originally contrived, self-induced rather than spontaneous. What can one say? Of course, saving mankind is a much more rewarding occupation than spending years teaching children multiplication tables. It adds a certain panache to one's movements and notes of honorable indignation to one's voice. A mob acquires the *power* to decide global problems, and the leaders acquire *power* over the mob. And who cares what will happen in the distant future? They will not be responsible in that future; even if nothing turns out the way it was supposed to, who shall call upon them to answer for it? Their intentions were noble, but our world is imperfect.

Such were, to use the term loosely, the "nuclear debates" of the 1980s in the West: logic, arguments, and facts played no part in them. Can it be that nobody really understood that it is impossible to "try" unilateral disarmament? Can it be that somebody did not know that this would be irreversible? Western governments tried in vain to explain the complexity of the situation, they showered the public with figures regarding missiles, warheads, tanks, and aircraft to no effect—their figures were not believed, because nobody wanted to believe them, and the general theme of the debates merely confused the man in the street even more, as though all these missiles and tanks had already opened fire on Europe.

The mobs may have been hysterical, but their leaders were not. They were the embodiment of incredible arrogance and ignorance combined, and the greater the ignorance, the greater the arrogance. For instance, most of them lacked the required education to understand the extremely complex technical aspects of nuclear missiles, strategy, or geopolitics. Nevertheless, they confidently rejected the data and expositions of acknowledged experts, labelling them "propaganda." In return, they created their own "experts" who said what they wanted to hear. An enormous number of dubious institutes, research groups, and committees were created, many of which included, naturally enough, pro-Soviet "experts" or simply Soviet representatives. For some reason, it was they who were to be believed.

Let us say that the overwhelming majority of the leaders of antiwar movements at that time had no idea of the nature of the Soviet regime, the reality of Soviet life, history, or even communist ideology, although questioning this would have been legitimate. At least half (and in fact almost 100 percent) of their claims depended on the USSR, its intentions, and its behavior. But the majority declared this to be "irrelevant," openly trusting the official declarations of the USSR or such "experts" as Georgy Arbatov. As far as they were concerned, the opinion of Vadim Zagladin from the International Department of the CC was sufficiently objective for them to cite him as a source of information about the USSR in the Western press and as an authority for rejecting my "prejudiced" opinion.[274]

---

[274]Nicholas Humphrey, "The Rat's a Rat for a' that," *The Guardian*, 29 March 1982, p. 9.

Our views, just like any negative information concerning the USSR, were dismissed as "propaganda" and "Cold War stereotypes."

Generally, absurd as it may seem, "the other side"—the Soviet Union and its satellites, its arms and intentions—did not worry anyone at all in these "debates." The threat of nuclear war and the need to prevent it were declared to be somehow outside the context of real life, as if they had emanated from nowhere—from God or sheer chance. For instance, from a mad general (invariably an American one). In the USA, where the "struggle for peace" was led by the leftist establishment (which had secured its positions in the campaign against the war in Vietnam and reached the peak of its power in the period of détente), mass brainwashing became particularly audacious, open, and gigantic in scope. It was a deliberate campaign to instigate mass hysteria, concentrated exclusively on one side of the question—the horror of nuclear war. Liberal foundations (such as the Ford, Rockefeller, Carnegie, MacArthur and George Gund) assigned literally *billions of dollars* so that, in the words of the president of the Rockefeller Foundation, "the prevention of nuclear war in the 1980s would be what the movement for human rights was in the 1960s."[275]

At that time Hollywood and television produced dozens if not hundreds of documentary and feature films about the consequences of a nuclear explosion, of the end of civilization. Suddenly, all American intellectuals became "concerned": concerned scientists, concerned teachers, and concerned doctors.

The groundwork was done by doctors, with their widely advertised letter of appeal to their Soviet colleagues under the eloquent heading "Danger—nuclear war."[276] I do not know whether they had thought up this profound headline themselves or whether they were prompted by some Pugwash committee with a suggestion from the sage CC. But I will never believe that they did not realize they were appealing not to their colleagues in the USSR, but to the Soviet government, providing it with a marvelous propaganda opportunity. Health Minister Boris Petrovsky reported the following to the CC (4 April 1980, No. 1099):[277]

> Pursuant to the decision of the CC CPSU dated 20 March 1980, the Ministry of Health of the USSR submits a draft reply by leading Soviet medical scientists to American physicians, composed with allowance for suggestions made by the Academy of

---

[275]Kathleen Teltsch, "Philanthropies Focus Concern on Arms Race," *The New York Times*, 25 March 1984, A.1.

[276]*The New York Times*, 2 March 1980

[277]See 15 April 1980 (St 206/19), p. 12.

Sciences of the USSR, the Ministry of Foreign Affairs, the Ministry of Defense and the KGB of the USSR. At the same time we report that there has been a meeting with one of the organizers of the American movement "Physicians for Social Responsibility" [Bernard] Lown, who reported that American scientists intend to organize a broad international movement in the medical community against nuclear war and, among other things, plan to hold a conference in the USA at the end of 1980, with the participation of Soviet and Japanese physicians. The final decision on the venue of the conference remains to be decided.

The CC was only too pleased to enter this game; it was not every day that such an opportunity cropped up to promote their positions through independent American scientific institutions, especially through physicians, with their considerable influence on health-obsessed Americans. It replied (15 April 1980 (St 206/19), p. 18.):

> Regarding the signatures of Soviet physicians under the answering letter, it appears feasible to collect a significant number of signatures, limited to those of comrades who represent the larger scientific organizations.

It stands to reason that these included the inevitable Yuri Ovchinnikov, and academician Nikolay Blokhin (as he was director of the oncological center), but there was still the need for a cardiologist: after all, the initiator of the whole enterprise, Bernard Lown, was an American cardiologist. This saw the arrival on the scene of academician Yevgeny Chazov, chairman of the All-Russian Scientific Society of Cardiologists. As Chazov reported to the CC a few months later (17 December 1980, No. 3457):[278]

> Pursuant to the decision of the Secretariat of the CC CPSU, a Soviet delegation headed by academician Y.I. Chazov went to Geneva in December of this year, comprised of academics from the USSR Academy of Medical Sciences [Leonid Andreyevich] Ilyin and [Mikhail] Kuzin. The delegation took part in a meeting with American scientists representing the "International Physicians for the Prevention of Nuclear War" movement. The American delegation was headed by Professor Bernard Lown, a prominent cardiologist of the Harvard school (Boston), and president of the American movement "Physicians for the Prevention of Nuclear War." The delegation also included Dr. Eric Chivian, a psychiatrist at the Massachusetts Institute of Technology (Cambridge) and the society's secretary, Jim Muller.

---

[278] 13 January 1981* (St 245/14), pp. 8–9

The meeting was of a consultative nature and was devoted to discussing the possibility of creating an international movement, "Physicians for Nuclear Disarmament." A memorandum outlining the principles of such a movement was composed at the meeting, which is basically acceptable to us, as it arises from the concept of prohibiting nuclear war.

Agreement was reached on the conduct of a Soviet-American conference of physicians and doctors advocating the prevention of nuclear war on 19–26 March 1981. On this occasion, the American side will be the organizers, and will invite ten prominent Soviet men of medicine as well as three experts specializing in the field of nuclear weapons and problems of disarmament.

It is envisaged that at the end of the conference appeals will be issued to all doctors of the world, to governments and peoples in various countries, as well as to the heads of state of the Soviet Union and the USA, which will stress the grievous consequences to all the peoples of the world from the occurrence of a nuclear war, and a call to the limitation and prohibition of nuclear arms.

We request that the composition of our draft documents be referred to the Ministry of Foreign Affairs of the USSR, the Ministry of Health of the USSR, the Academy of Sciences of the USSR, and the Ministry of Defense of the USSR. It is envisaged that the delegations shall implement a timely exchange of the indicated documents and conduct a preliminary discussion regarding them so that there will be agreed texts at the conference itself.

What a find! Practically all the appeals of the "concerned" physicians would be composed by Soviet generals and diplomats—after all, the American side is too independent to seek the advice of the Pentagon or the State Department, let alone accept the instructions of its government. Soviet "experts on nuclear weapons and disarmament" will certainly explain everything as it needs to be explained at the conference. The average American, if the doctor has prescribed that smoking, cholesterol, and nuclear war are bad for one's health, shall demand immediate nuclear disarmament from its congressmen and senators. Is it surprising that the "struggle for peace" in America, a country inclined to hysteria, should assume an even more hysterical nature than in Europe? The most popular campaign there was the one that seized upon Brezhnev's peace initiatives in 1979: "Nuclear freeze," "No to the first nuclear strike," and so forth, and the most active—crowds of frenzied people storming military bases or munitions factories. One such group even tried to physically fulfil the biblical precept of turning swords into plowshares: its members stormed the workshop where missiles were assembled and threw their bodies against them until they drew blood.[279] This is where the psychiatrists from the University of Massachusetts and cardiologists should have directed their efforts. But no, this had nothing to do with them, at that time they were receiving the Nobel Peace Prize in Oslo together with their colleague Yevgeny Chazov, although in all fairness it should have probably gone to the sagacious CC.

• • •

It was not just doctors; practically the entire educated class of America mobilized. How could it lag behind its enterprising colleagues? Even bishops made an effort and issued "A Pastoral Letter on War and Peace," in which, speaking on behalf of the Lord God, they declared nuclear weapons to be "absolutely amoral," leaving everyone to guess how amoral tanks and cannons had been in, say, the Second World War. Learned men from other professions joined in. However, they had a problem: the exile of honorary member of the American National Academy of Sciences Andrei Sakharov from Moscow to Gorky practically led to a boycott of the Soviet side by American scientists. Still, that was not an insurmountable problem: the noble cause of saving mankind justifies anything, even betrayal. The president of the Academy of Sciences of the USSR, A.P. Alexandrov, stated the following in a report to the CC (16 December 1980*, St 241/9):

> As we have already reported, at a meeting between the Academy of Sciences of the USSR and the National Academy of Sciences (NAS) of the USA in Moscow in June of this year, the Americans put forward a proposal for organizing bilateral exchanges of opinions on questions of reinforcing peace, international security, and disarmament. The NAS secretary for international affairs, [Thomas] Malone, assumes that such exchanges shall be one of the ways to restore bilateral meetings of scientists, suspended at the start of this year by the American side. In May 1980, the National Academy of Sciences of the USA set up a 16-member committee within the framework of the academy, headed by the president of the California Institute of Technology, Marvin L. Goldberger, to address issues of international security and control over armaments. The committee intends to establish and maintain contacts with Soviet scientists, and also academic circles in West European countries and Japan. The committee members consider that matters of international security should not be examined solely in the field of government channels, but also along the line of contacts between scientists searching for approaches to resolving problems in the sphere of

---

[279]Carter (1992), p. 164.

security and submitting the relevant recommendations to their government without undue publicity.

The CC was only too pleased to approve this initiative, as declaring "the right to live in peace" to be a basic human right was the main slogan of their "struggle for peace." Getting rid of the boycotts and embargoes caused by their repressive policies was one of the main tasks of the campaign for the resumption of détente. So whence this agitation among academics? Is it not clear that if your lawfully elected government requires your input on questions of state security, it will ask you? But no, the intelligentsia is always smarter than the government, nothing should occur without it. But what of colleague Sakharov?

The president of the NAS of the USA, Frank Press, told journalists, "Despite our continuing deep concern for Sakharov, there are some issues of such deep importance to the future of mankind that we have felt it necessary to continue talking about them with our Soviet counterparts. In this regard, arms control and international security are certainly of high priority. Our members feel very strongly about this issue."[280] This was said at the very time when it was being reported in the Western press that Sakharov was on the brink of death as a result of his hunger strike. Will you say again that American men of science did not know what they were doing?

Whatever anyone says, I cannot bring myself to believe in the naivety of these people. Possibly the only exception was the leader of the small but influential elite organization, the END (European Nuclear Disarmament), the Marxist historian E.P. Thompson. Even with all his fuddled leftist intelligentsia views, he did not deny that, say, the process of disarmament requires changes in the policies of both sides, and a popular disarmament movement is meaningful only if there is an analogous (i.e., independent of its government) movement on the other side of the Iron Curtain. Furthermore, he was sincerely dismayed by the Soviet manipulation of Western movements, something he wrote about quite frankly, calling his less discerning colleagues in the movement "lunatics."[281] Yet even he was unable to comprehend completely that dealings with the Soviet machine should be avoided at all costs.

"We are willing to engage in discussion with official organizations over there, provided that the discussion is on honest and equal terms, and not on terms which co-opt us into some pro-Soviet the-

---

[280] Frank Press, "Scientific exchanges must go on," Letters to the Editor, *The Washington Post*, 11 May 1984, P. A22.

[281] Edward Palmer Thompson, "The nuclear debate: Peace and the east," New Society, (Jun 2, 1983), Vol. 64, (Issue 1072), p. 347.

ater of propaganda," he wrote rather naively, although several paragraphs earlier he seemed to discern the total impossibility of fair and equal relations with Moscow. "To the Russians, we are background music only, and music not even loud enough to swing a German election."

He seemed to be a sincere person, but befuddled in his thinking. Moreover, he had his own domestic "expert on Soviet life" in the person of our good old friend Zhores Medvedev, that very same Dr. Medvedev whose ideas, as we recall, coincided amazingly with those of Yuri Andropov. Naturally, Zhores Alexandrovich was one of the coauthors of the END appeal for "a nuclear-free Europe from Poland to Portugal" in 1980 which, allegedly on behalf of "Soviet dissidents," was signed in Moscow by his twin brother Roy Alexandrovich.[282] Probably it was these two who explained to Professor Thompson that there are different kinds of dissidents: a) bad ones, and b) good ones. The bad ones do not believe in socialism and serve the forces of reaction, while the good ones believe in socialism and can certainly support the appeal. For several years, Professor Thompson searched vainly for "good dissidents." Alas! Whoever he found turned out to be "bad." The Czech Charter 77 and the Polish Workers' Defense Committee rejected any ideas of unilateral Western disarmament as pro-Soviet. The cunning Jacek Kuron, himself a first-class manipulator, managed to get a letter out of prison in 1984 to the END conference, where he suggested a joint struggle for the repeal of martial law in Poland and the full demilitarization of Central Europe. A year later, an extremely polite Vaclav Havel attempted an intelligent explanation to Western peacemakers that their Utopianism would not find understanding among a willy-nilly skeptical East European public. It was all in vain. Finally, though small, rather purely symbolic groups of activists for peace began to appear in the GDR and even the USSR. But—what bad luck!—as soon as they appeared, their members would be expelled to the West, or imprisoned. So E.P. Thompson did not manage to find any good dissidents in the East, right up to the collapse of communism.

Astounding, is it not? Here was a man who was no fool, who was honest, who was yet unable to grasp the simple truth (as Jacek Kuron wrote to him) that the whole of the threat to peace in Europe emanates from the Soviet bloc, that it is necessary to fight not *for peace*, but *against the Soviet regime*. Lost in socialist delusions, he, like thousands of West European socialists, was unable to comprehend *that the very idea of peace and disarmament, torn out of the context of the general political context of Europe, was already*

---

[282]Carter (1992), pp. 117–118.

a pro-Soviet one. And if there was a need for a mass movement in the East, it had already come into being in the human rights movement, without which there could be no hope for peace or any other independent public movement. Is this so difficult? Is this not what we all wrote about, Andrei Amalrik and Solzhenitsyn and Sakharov? Is this not what the Helsinki Groups spoke of again and again, stressing the link between the first and third baskets of the accords—between security in Europe and human rights? Is this not what I wrote about in my brochure in 1982? "Two sides of the Soviet regime—internal oppression and external aggression—are inextricably linked."

Paradoxically enough, this was the weak link in their campaign, which became a question of party politics; the question of Western disarmament could be resolved by the standard democratic mechanism of elections. Moscow and its allies were able to achieve success only with the aid of manipulations, machinations, hysterical propaganda, and blackmail. But it took just bringing the question to the judgment of the electorate, and their entire crafty campaign was doomed. Hysterical mobs and falsified "public opinion polls" regularly indicating a growing support for the idea of unilateral disarmament vanished. The British Labour Party, which had made nuclear disarmament its main platform in the 1983 election, suffered a crushing defeat for this very reason. In the FRG, despite all the efforts of Chancellor Schmidt to restrain the radicals in his party, in the minds of the electorate it was firmly associated with the anti-nuclear campaign and, like its British colleagues, lost the 1983 election. Only in Holland and Belgium, where the proportional election system condemned any government to exist as an unwieldy and unstable coalition dependent on the dictate of even the tiniest political groups, was the deployment of new missiles deferred for several years. In the rest of Europe the deployment began as scheduled, which undermined the campaign of the peacemakers even further, because despite their prophesies, this did not precipitate a nuclear war. This was definitely the tipping point—after 1983 the campaign dwindled markedly, and it petered out by the middle of the 1980s.

That was the end of this shameful page in the social life of the West. As we have said, the threat of a new world war and a nuclear holocaust disappeared with the collapse of the Soviet regime. Nowadays nuclear bombs, missiles, and warheads are stockpiled in arsenals, causing nobody any concern, in Russia and the USA and even Kazakhstan and Ukraine. This would seem to be just the time for concerned intelligentsia to demand their destruction, especially as it would be quite easy now. There they are, these "absolutely amoral" objects—so start demonstrating. But there are no indignant peacemakers on the streets of European capitals, no raging protests surrounding military bases such as the infamous women's "peace camps" at Greenham Common in the UK. Where are they? Where have they gone?

Look, there they are, they haven't disappeared anywhere. Nowadays those same eternally concerned preach lies about an inevitable ecological catastrophe, about the greenhouse effect, with the same aplomb and passion in their voices with which they once frightened the nervous bourgeoisie regarding the horrors of nuclear war.

5.15   Poland and the beginning of the crisis

Yet even before the 1983 elections and the deployment of new missiles, the biggest setback to the peacemakers' campaign was the events in Poland. Their effect was immediate and visible: as was noted by E.P. Thompson,[283] for example, crowds of demonstrators snowballed in October and November 1981, comprising over two million people throughout Europe.

So why, in the spring or fall of 1982, were there no demonstrations by three to four million people? The answer: the introduction of martial law in Poland and the persecution of Solidarity.

It is hard to say which aspect of the Polish crisis had the greatest effect on the peacemakers: the threat of a Soviet invasion, which hung over Poland for almost a year and a half, the crushing of a peaceful popular movement by the army, or that movement itself, which extended to practically the entire working population of the country. My own opinion is that this latter fact was not unimportant to our peacemakers, most of whom belonged to various Western left-wing parties and organizations. Perhaps for the first time, many of them paused to think about real life in the socialist paradise, and there was no way they could—at least externally, for the sake of appearances—not sympathize with the trade union movement. The need to make a political assessment of this event inevitably brought about dissent in their ranks: on one hand, the communists (such as the Italians) seemed to support Solidarity; on the other hand, the socialists (such as the Greek PASOK) supported the Jaruzelski regime and martial law.

It is true that it would have been difficult to imagine a more deadly situation for communist demagogues than a unanimous

---

[283]Edward Palmer Thompson, "The nuclear debate: Peace and the east," New Society, (Jun 2, 1983), Vol. 64, (Issue 1072), p. 347.

mutiny by workers against a proletarian state. Even Soviet propaganda did not dare to label Solidarity a reactionary organization, but preferred to speak of "individual anti-socialist elements" inside it. The Polish crisis could not have come at a worse time for them: right at the height of the "struggle for peace," when they had just managed to climb out of political isolation after the invasion of Afghanistan. The oldsters in the Kremlin simply did not have enough strength to cope with all the crises and campaigns that coincided in one year.

Poland had always been a weak link in their socialist chain. The main tasks had not been accomplished even while Stalin was still alive: the Catholic Church remained unbroken, there were still individual peasant owners, and alongside that there was the rebellious spirit of the Poles, thanks to which Poland survived three partitions, the Second World War, Nazi occupation, and Soviet "liberation." Rebellion is a truly Polish trait; it surfaced every three to five years, beginning with 1968, then again in 1970 and 1976—and every time, although at times with the shedding of blood, they managed to wrest certain concessions from the authorities. Moscow pretended not to notice—the main concern was to avoid a serious uprising. So Poland was, according to a joke of that time, the merriest barrack in the socialist camp. Almost a third of all workers were employed in the private sector—small trade and the service sector. This alone allowed a greater degree of personal freedom than any other state reforms (something anyone who has not lived under real socialism may find hard to appreciate). And there were just as many reforms in Poland as there were rebellions. By 1980 all versions of models of socialism had been tried, and not a single one of them worked.

The final crisis arose from the most prosaic reason, but one very characteristic of socialism: mired in external debts, the government was forced to raise food prices, including meat products, knowing full well that a similar attempt had resulted in the rebellion of 1976. But what could the government do? The country was bankrupt, incapable of paying even the interest to Western banks. . . .

On the other hand, former rebellions were not complete losses for the Poles: they accrued experience, and dissident structures were growing under the relative softness of the regime. After the events of 1976, the Workers' Defense Committee (KOR) came into being—a kind of coordinating center for dissident activity, ensuring contact between the workers' movement and the intelligentsia as well as an independent system of communication among various groups and parts of the country. The KOR played a key role in the events of 1980: it assisted in the synthesis of spontaneous, scattered strikes into a general strike that mobilized the whole country.

The workers had also learned from the past, and instead of the customary rebellion, demonstrations, bloody clashes with the police, now resorted to an original form of protest—they occupied their plants, mines, docks, and factories. This innovation caught the authorities in Warsaw and Moscow quite unprepared—only this can explain the unusual acquiescence of the Polish authorities, which practically sanctioned the creation of the independent Solidarity trade union, besides making a number of other concessions to the workers. Faced with the impossibility of employing their usual weapon—police force—they were prepared to agree to anything for the sake of calming the country (with the view of taking everything back quietly later).

But the Soviet authorities were also learning something. The crisis in Poland did not really come as such a great surprise to them. On the contrary, they had been preparing for it since at least April 1979,[284] being fully aware that raising food prices was inevitable. The situation was discussed frequently at meetings between Brezhnev and Edward Gierek, first secretary of the Polish United Workers' Party (PZPR), through July 1980—that is, after the rise in prices and the beginning of strikes, when Brezhnev was particularly concerned that the economic crisis would spill over into a purely political movement. His advice to Gierek was to do the following:[285]

- Suppress decisively all attempts to use nationalism for the imposition of anti-socialist and anti-Soviet attitudes, to distort the history of Soviet-Polish relations and the nature of the cooperation between the USSR and the Polish People's Republic;

- Launch irreconcilable counterpropaganda against attempts to blur the class content of socialist patriotism under the slogan "all the Poles in the world are brothers," and also idealize Poland's prerevolutionary past;

- In political struggle with anti-socialist elements, do not be on the defensive, but conduct a vigorous advance against them.

What did come as a surprise to the Kremlin was the weakness of their clients, Polish communists, who were clearly incapable of coping with the crisis. Even years later, Moscow could not understand the *nationwide* nature of the opposing movement. It seems

---

[284] 4 October 1980 (St 231-5), p. 5, mentions a Central Committee decree of 10 April 1979.
[285] 3 September 1980* (St 213/38), p. 7.

as though they really believed that the case concerned only certain "elements" that the Polish comrades treated far too liberally.

A hastily appointed Politburo committee on Poland (25 August 1980, Pb 210/11) began the immediate development of instructions to the Polish leadership on measures to "reinforce the role of the party in society," as though the matter concerned a region of the USSR in which naughty schoolchildren had gone too far. The Gdansk agreements were given an uncompromising assessment by the Politburo, which they sent to the Polish leadership on 3 September 1980 (3 September 1980*, St 213/38):

> The agreement of the government of the PPR, approved by the plenum of the CC PZRP [Central Committee of the Polish United Workers' Party], is a great political and economic price for the achieved "settlement." Of course, we understand under what conditions you had to make this difficult decision. Essentially, the agreement means the legalization of the anti-socialist opposition. An organization arises that aspires to extend its political influence over the whole country. The difficulty of fighting it lies mainly in that the opponents position themselves as defenders of the working class, the workers.

> The agreement does not remove the root causes of the critical events; moreover, resolution of the current problems of the Polish economy and Polish society becomes complicated.

> Insofar as the opposition intends to continue the struggle for the achievement of its aims, and the healthy forces of the party and society cannot accept the backsliding of the Polish people, the agreed-upon compromise shall, most likely, be of a temporary nature. It must be borne in mind that the opposition expects outside aid, and not without reason.

> Under the pressure of anti-socialist forces that have managed to delude a significant part of the working class, PPR had to retreat into defense. Now the problem is to prepare a counterattack and win back lost positions in the working class, the people.

> In this counterattack, displaying flexibility, it would be advisable to use all the resources of the ruling party, its firm and healthy core, state power, mass public organizations with the necessary reliance on the front ranks of the working class, and, if necessary, calculated administrative means.

> The party must give a principled political assessment of the August events and facilitate its own program of actions, including questions of improving workers' living conditions.

Moscow considered it particularly important to strengthen party control over information in the mass media, primarily regarding radio and television, which had been penetrated by the Church for the first time in accordance with the Gdansk agreements. They wrote:

> Under such conditions, the limits of what is permissible must be clearly defined, stating openly that the law on the press excludes any speechifying against socialism. ... The mass media should show that the events in Poland were not precipitated by any deficiencies of the socialist system, but by errors and miscalculations as well as certain objective natural factors (natural disasters, etc.).

Gierek was sent into retirement and replaced as General Secretary of the PPR by Stanislaw Kania, but that did not improve matters. The Politburo decided to invite the Poles to Moscow for talks in October (29 October 1980*, Pb):

> BREZHNEV. Tomorrow we have the arrival of the first secretary of the CC PPR, Comrade Kania, and the chairman of the Council of Ministers of the PPR, comrade [Jozef] Pinkowski. The committee of comrades—[Mikhail] Suslov, Gromyko, Andropov, [Dmitry] Ustinov, [Konstantin] Chernenko, [Mikhail] Zimyanin, and Rusakov—has prepared materials for talks with the Polish leaders. I have studied these materials in detail. I think that the comrades have covered all the main questions. If anyone has anything to add, please let us discuss it now.
>
> USTINOV. I have also read the materials carefully. I believe they are very substantial and cover the necessary points. It is important that all the questions are posed very acutely, just as they should be put to the Polish leaders.
>
> BREZHNEV. There is really a counterrevolution in full swing in Poland, but the Polish press and Polish comrades say nothing about this, nothing is said about the enemies of the people. Yet these are enemies of the people, direct accomplices of the counterrevolution and the counterrevolutionaries themselves are acting against the people. How can this be?
>
> (Omission in the text, ANDROPOV?) ... Now they are criticizing Gierek, the CC, the party, and at the other end anti-socialist elements, which are running amok unimpeded.
>
> Comrade Jaruzelski is a very reliable man, but is starting to speak without any particular zeal. He even says that the army will not go against the workers. I think we should say all this to the Poles in a very harsh manner.
>
> BREZHNEV. When Jaruzelski was talking to Kania about who should play the role of first, he flatly refused to be the first secretary and suggested that Kania should be the first. That also tells us something.

GROMYKO. I believe that the prepared materials set out the basic questions quite correctly. As for the introduction of martial law in Poland, that must be borne in mind as a measure for rescuing revolutionary achievements. Of course, it may not be necessary to introduce it immediately, especially straight after Comrades Kania and Pinkowski return from Moscow; some time should pass, but they must have it pointed out to them and given support. We cannot lose Poland. In the fight against Hitler the Soviet Union lost 600 thousand of its soldiers and officers to liberate Poland, and we cannot allow a counterrevolution. [...]

SUSLOV. I think the materials are well prepared and balanced. The current leaders of the PPR are insufficiently strong, but they are honest, the best in the leadership core. [...] They must launch a counterattack instead of retreating into a defensive position. This position is mentioned in the materials we are studying today.

BREZHNEV. They need self-defense units.

[ANDROPOV, SUSLOV, and USTINOV say that this measure is a necessity. Defense units should be formed and should be stationed in barracks and, possibly, be armed in a timely manner.]

SUSLOV. We once wrote to [previous first secretary of PZPR Wladyslaw] Gomulka that he should not use weapons against workers, but nobody paid any attention, and the Polish leadership resorted to arms.

[Boris] PONOMAREV. The documents prepared for talks with the Polish leaders are consecutive and realistic. The materials make our concern quite plain. We must stress this concern to the Polish leaders.

GROMYKO. Maybe we should give copies of these documents to the Polish leaders?

ANDROPOV. If we do that, it is possible that they shall end up in the hands of the Americans.

BREZHNEV. That could really happen.

RUSAKOV. Let them pay attention to Leonid Ilyich and take notes.

[Viktor] GRISHIN. Leonid Ilyich, you should start the talks by voicing our concern. Let them answer later. The documents are well prepared.

[Nikolai] TIKHONOV. Of course, Leonid Ilyich, you should open your address on this material and expound all it contains. We have invited them to express our concern regarding the situation that has developed in Poland. The materials set everything out very clearly. In Poland today, there are obvious actions by counterrevolutionary elements. Let them tell us what is going on, explain how things have come to such a pass. Communists are leaving the party in fear of anti-socialist elements. That is how bad the situation has become. [...]

[Andrei] KIRILENKO.   It is three months since the strikes started, and they are not becoming fewer. We have done a great deal for Poland, we gave them everything and advised them in order to resolve arising issues. So far they have not drawn the military into the struggle against anti-socialist elements, and do not even expose them, as present comrades have pointed out. Now they are having problems with young people. The Komsomol has practically ceased to exist. There are no youth units. Maybe military personnel should don civil clothing and go out into the working masses.

Resolution: Approve the materials for the friendly working visit of Polish leaders to the USSR.

• • •

Maybe all that sounds comical, but constant pressure from Moscow on the Polish leadership had its significance. No matter how the influence of the Polish United Workers' Party (PZPR) had weakened, its apparatus was enormous, and the structures of a totalitarian state put powerful means in its hands to control and suppress. In fact, the Kremlin strategists were right: the totalitarian system is calculated to be at constant war with the people, and all depends on its skillful use. The watching eye of Moscow forced the Polish leadership to act more energetically, putting aside doubts and wavering. The watching eye was ever keener: Brezhnev spoke by phone to Kania practically every week, and other Politburo members monitored their equivalent Polish colleagues, top-level Soviet delegations traveled to Poland periodically for on-the-spot investigations. Moscow virtually took over the leadership of the entire situation, down to the smallest details: just as in Afghanistan, special advisers and groups of experts on all matters were sent to Poland, without whose consent (or at least the consent of the ambassador, Averky Aristov) nothing was done. Even the economic program of PZPR, adopted at the congress, had first been studied and developed in Moscow (19 January 1981, St 246/79). Everything was exploited, right down to the smallest disagreements in the Solidarity leadership, their smallest miscalculations. The KGB presence in Poland increased.[286]

Finally, a formidable psychological pressure on the population was the deliberately circulated threat of a Soviet invasion of Poland, although no real preparations had been carried out for that purpose. For example, military maneuvers were staged on Polish terri-

---

[286]See 15 January 1981 (St 246/17).

tory, deliberately inflated, as a demonstration of readiness to "render international aid." However, from the very beginning of the crisis, this was no more than a bluff: "decisive actions" were demanded of the Poles, repressive measures were enacted and martial law was declared, but the option of an invasion was never even considered.

One way or another, by the beginning of 1981 the situation had stabilized. This was possible because the leadership of Solidarity had not expected such success, being more prepared for repressions, and was not quite sure how to handle it. As one of the top-level visitors reported (22 January 1981):

> The country is in a state of permanent discussion both in party organizations and at enterprises. This discussion also appears in the media, with frequent debates about the Polish model of a socialist society, about liberalization, revision of Marxism-Leninism, political pluralism, and so forth.

But this situation did not satisfy Moscow either—there was no breaking point, the crisis remained, and its negative results were beginning to be felt in the West and even in the USSR (2 April 1981*, Pb):

> BREZHNEV. We are all extremely concerned regarding future events in Poland. The worst of it is that our friends listen, agree with our recommendations, and then do practically nothing. Meanwhile the counterrevolution is advancing on all fronts.
>
> Politburo members have been informed of the content of all previous discussions with Polish leaders. I shall advise you of my latest telephone conversation with Kania on March 30.
>
> Kania reported on the recent plenum of the CC of the Polish United Workers Party and complained that they were severely criticized during the plenum. So I said to him, "Rightly so. You not only deserved criticism, they should have taken a stick to you. Then maybe you would understand." These were my very words.
>
> Comrade Kania admitted that they are acting too leniently and should have taken a harder line.
>
> I answered: "How many times did we try to convince you that decisive measures must be taken, that you cannot go on yielding to Solidarity? But you keep talking about a peaceful way, not understanding or unwilling to understand that the 'peaceful way' you are following may cost you in blood. So it is vital to draw the correct conclusions from the criticism at the plenum."
>
> Our friends managed to avert the general strike. But at what cost? The cost of yet another capitulation. Kania himself ad-

mitted in a discussion with the ambassador that the new compromise is a great mistake. ...

It seems that among other things it may be worth fulfilling our friends' request and allow comrades Andropov and Ustinov to go to Brest for a meeting with Kania and Jaruzelski. This will be a chance to get a detailed picture of the situation in the country, assess the intentions of our friends and set out our position to them once more.

We have the fallback measure of a new top-level meeting of the seven on the Polish question.

We have a committee on Poland. Maybe the comrades from the committee monitoring events in that country would care to say a few words?

ANDROPOV. I consider that the proposals put forward by Leonid Ilyich regarding future steps concerning Poland and the assessment of the situation there are perfectly accurate. We are saying that it is time for us to exert some more influence, apply more pressure to our friends' leadership. I believe the proposal for a trip to Brest by comrade Ustinov and me to meet with Kania and Jaruzelski is right. [...]

[USTINOV supports the proposals in practically the same words.]

GROMYKO. Allow me to inform you briefly of what we are hearing through the Ministry of Foreign Affairs. There is a great deal of incoming information on Poland. But it must be said that the situation in Poland is being watched closely in the USA, the FRG, and other countries, and the real state of affairs is greatly distorted. It stands to reason that the coverage of information concerning the situation in Poland by the USA and the FRG is tendentious. It shows the "justice" of demands by Solidarity and anti-socialist forces in Poland and the inability of the Polish leadership to settle an internal matter. There is also much said about the Soviet Union, as though warning us that the Soviet Union should not intervene in Polish affairs with our armed forces. Clearly this is mere bourgeois propaganda that has always assumed hostile positions toward the Soviet Union and now serves up this information in a tendentious manner, as I have already said.

I wish to add that the condition of both Kania and Jaruzelski is not good. There are even hints that Jaruzelski is deeply depressed and does not know what to do next. This is very bad. The fact that the leadership of the Polish Republic backed down in negotiations with Solidarity is also very bad. Even Polish leaders themselves say that the latest agreement with Solidarity is a mistake.

As for the attitude to Rural Solidarity, it can be said that it is already legalized. ... How can the situation in Poland be assessed after the plenum of the CC? I think we would not be mistaken in saying that there has been no improvement. On the contrary, there has been further deterioration, because the leadership is retreating. But as Leonid Ilyich has said, Kania has asked that Comrades Andropov and Ustinov come to Brest for an exchange of views with Comrades Kania and Jaruzelski. I think we should do this, especially as this will be an opportunity to say all we want to the comrades at a face-to-face meeting. In my opinion this meeting will be a kind of interim step and it must be used to the full. If they agree, as they say they will, to a partial introduction of emergency measures, they must be asked if they will be certain that the army, the Ministry of Internal Affairs, and state security agencies will back them. I think it would be advisable to conduct a deep analysis by our military people of what the situation is within the Polish armed forces, if the army is the main power, and if it is reliable.

The Politburo of the CPSU must have a clear picture of the distribution of forces in Poland. We must know this. The Polish command asserts that the army will do its duty. Is this really so? In any case, we have to urge our Polish comrades to take harsher, I would say extreme measures to restore order and that further backtracking is totally unacceptable, they must not retreat any more.

USTINOV. With regard to the military, the situation is as follows. The military leadership meets today at 2000 hours with Comrades [Viktor] Kulikov and [Vladimir] Kryuchkov and other comrades. The Polish army, according to Comrade Jaruzelski, is ready to do its duty. But to speak frankly, we must bear in mind that neither Kania nor Jaruzelski will go as far as confrontation, bearing in mind the conflict in Bydgoszcz.[287] The results of that conflict showed that it only took touching two members of Solidarity to bring the whole country to its feet—in other words, Solidarity was able to mobilize its forces in rapid order. Of course, there is still some hope if the army, the security agencies, and the militia form a united front, but it will still only get worse. I think it will be impossible to avoid bloodshed, it will happen. And if that is feared, then there is no option but to surrender position after position. And that could lead to a loss of all the achievements of socialism.

I also wonder whether we should implement some measures of an economic nature. What do the Polish comrades think? We

---

[287] On 19 March 1981, activists with Rural Solidarity were beaten up by the police in Bydgoszcz. Widespread indignation led to a nationwide four-hour strike on 28 March in which thirteen million took part.

help them, we tear things away from ourselves and our friends in order to give to Poland, but the Polish people do not know that. No Poles know that it receives all its oil, cotton and so on from us. If all the aid the Poles receive from the Soviet Union were to be counted up and considered seriously, if this were revealed on the radio and television, I believe the Polish people would understand who supplies their basic economic aid. But not one single Polish leader has appeared before the workers and revealed this.

As for the Polish leaders, I think it is difficult to decide which of them is better. At one time we considered Comrade Jaruzelski to be a firm leader, but he turned out to be a weakling.

[...]

BREZHNEV. We should tell them what proclaiming martial law means, explain it properly.

ANDROPOV. Yes we should explain that martial law means the establishment of a curfew, limiting movement along city streets, and reinforcing the guarding of governmental and party premises, enterprises, and suchlike. Jaruzelski has crumbled completely under pressure from Solidarity, and Kania has started drinking more and more lately. It's a sad situation. I believe that we have enough reasons to advance in talks with Kania and Jaruzelski. They should probably hear them.

At the same time, I would like to say that the events in Poland are having an effect on the western areas of our country. Among others, in Belorussia many villages get good reception of Polish radio and television broadcasts. Moreover, there have been spontaneous demonstrations in other areas such as Georgia, groups of loudmouths gather on the streets in groups, as happened in Tbilisi, shouting anti-Soviet slogans and so forth. We need to implement strict internal measures here too.

And it is true that from the very beginning of the crisis, very radical measures were taken in Moscow to prevent the spread of the Polish disease. Tourist exchange with Poland was reduced almost by half (28 November 1980, St 239/36); measures were implemented for additional censorship of the Polish press delivered to the USSR for retail sale (22 December 1980, St 242/61) or by subscription, and propaganda was stepped up.[288] Attempts were made to undermine the authority of Solidarity abroad, especially among friendly organizations and parties. Ponomarev reported (13 January 1981, 18-S-62):[289]

---

[288] 4 October 1980 (St 231/5)
[289] 14 January 1981* (St 246/1), pp. 11–12.

A Solidarity delegation (eighteen persons headed by L. Walesa) shall be in Italy on 14–18 January at the invitation of local trade unions. The delegation will also include representatives of the anti-socialist-inclined political opposition. According to available information, bourgeois parties and the mass media intend to provide broad coverage to the presence of this delegation in Italy in order to discredit the socialist system in the Polish People's Republic in support of a line aimed at destabilizing and finally liquidating the socialist achievements in Poland. To this end, reception of the members of the delegation is planned to take place at sufficiently high trade union and political levels. Apart from a meeting with the Pope in the Vatican, L. Walesa and his delegation will be received by the leadership of the United Federation of Trade Unions and will organize meetings with workers' collectives. Despite the original intention of the leadership of the Italian Communist Party to refuse a meeting with L. Walesa, the leadership is still hesitating and does not exclude the possibility of certain contacts with him.

We deem it feasible to approach the leadership of the Italian Communist Party, which has strong positions in the Italian trade union movement and exercises significant influence on the political circles of the country.

We could also instruct the Soviet ambassador in Italy to meet with [Enrico] Berlinguer or his deputy to point out the need to take all possible steps to ensure that L. Walesa's trip to Italy does not result in support for the political anti-socialist opposition.

East European leaders (especially Honecker) had expressed great concern regarding the possible spread of the infection while visiting Moscow for the Twenty-Sixth Congress of the CPSU (12 March 1981, Pb).

Unfortunately, the leaders of Solidarity themselves did not comprehend the importance of exporting their experience into other "barracks." It was only much later, at the first Solidarity congress in September 1981, that the famous "Appeal to the Workers of Eastern Europe" was adopted, and even then, it is said, it was quite by chance, on the initiative of rank-and-file members. Yet it was this that drew attention as the most mature political act. As can be imagined, the Kremlin was absolutely infuriated (10 September 1981*, Pb):

BREZHNEV. Yesterday I saw the "Appeal to the Peoples [sic] of Eastern Europe," which was adopted by the congress of Polish Solidarity. It is a dangerous and provocative document. The words are few, but they all hit the same target. Its authors wish to provoke unrest in socialist countries and stir up groups of all kinds of renegades. I do not think criticism in the press is sufficient response to this brazen challenge. What if this demagogy is refuted by the collectives of our large enterprises, such as the Kirov Plant, Magnitka, KamAZ, and others? Their letters addressed to Solidarity would be hard to hush up. Particularly if we give them prominent coverage in our mass media.

If the comrades agree, let us charge the committee on Poland with determining suitable enterprises and assist them in preparing a qualified rebuff to Solidarity. . . .

ZIMYANIN. I would inform the Politburo of the publications that are planned in connection with the Solidarity congress. It can be said that the congress demonstrates the increasing deterioration of the situation in Poland. It is already known that they have appealed to the parliaments and people of several countries, including socialist ones, with their "renewal" program. For that reason, relevant responses are being prepared along the line of our press and TASS. These materials shall expose the activities of the Solidarity trade union. I support Leonid Ilyich's proposal regarding the possibility that these materials shall expose the activities of the Solidarity trade union. I agree with Leonid Ilyich that we should give a voice to some of the collectives of our leading enterprises. We shall also try to prepare these [documents].

TIKHONOV. We have to react somehow, and react specifically to the acts of these hooligan elements in Poland, against whom the government is taking no steps. Apart from the fact that statues to our soldiers are being defaced, the leaders of our party and government are being lampooned, insulting the Soviet Union in as many ways as possible and more of the same. In other words, they are laughing at us. I do not think we can remain silent any longer, and we must lodge a protest to the Polish government along state or other lines. In my opinion, it is impossible not to react.

GROMYKO. This needs careful thought. We are talking about a friendly country.

GORBACHEV. I think that Leonid Ilyich's proposal regarding a reaction by collectives of our large enterprises in the press and exposure of the actions of Solidarity is quite correct.

GRISHIN. Such declarations should be organized and published in *Pravda* and other papers. We shall call upon such collectives as ZiL, the Hammer and Sickle [*Serp I molot*], and other large industrial plants.

So the plan went out to all the plants and factories in the country: workers' meetings, angry tirades, and resolutions of condemnation. But no matter what the intentions were of the sage leaders, the information blockade of events in Poland was thereby lifted, people started to talk and think, and who knows what conclusions they might have reached had this process started sooner? Unfortunately, the Solidarity leaders were too cautious, wary of provoking such a powerful neighbor, although it would seem clear that Big Brother would do whatever he wanted even without any additional provocation.

5.16   The intervention myth

Let us return to the secret meeting of comrades Andropov and Ustinov with comrades Kania and Jaruzelski in Brest. It was really this meeting that was to resolve the matter of future martial law. Upon their return, the comrades reported the results to the Politburo (9 April 1981*, Pb):

> ANDROPOV. Comrade D.F. Ustinov and I traveled to a meeting with our Polish comrades in Brest, and met in a railway carriage just outside the city. The meeting began at 9 p.m. and ended at 3 a.m. so that the Polish comrades would remain undetected and nobody would know they had been away.
>
> Our task was to listen to the Polish comrades attentively and give our relevant thoughts, as agreed at the Politburo meeting.
>
> Our general impression from this meeting is that our comrades were very tense, highly nervous, and it was clear that they were under great stress. Comrade Kania admitted candidly that they are finding it very hard to manage affairs and that they are under constant pressure from Solidarity and anti-socialist forces. However, they claimed that after the Twenty-Sixth Congress of the CPSU, the situation in Poland is stabilizing. Kania said that they had carried out membership and election meetings in most grassroots party organizations, and it is worth noting that not one single member of Solidarity was among the delegates, that is, our candidates were elected for the congress. Then Kania was forced to admit that subsequent events, including the warning strike and events in Bydgoszcz, showed that "the counterrevolution is stronger than we are". They were particularly fearful of the warning strike and even more of a general strike and were doing all they could to avert a general strike. ...
>
> These are the problems we face, said Comrade Kania. The first priority is restoration of the trust of the people in the party, straightening out the economy, and ending strikes and idle time at industrial enterprises. Of course, the Polish comrades have no experience in combating these negative manifestations, so

they do not know what to do and lurch from side to side. With regard to the entry of armed forces, they stated directly that this was totally impossible, as is the declaration of martial law. They say that they would be misunderstood, and they would be powerless to do anything. The comrades stressed that they would use their own resources to restore order. They mean the Ninth Congress, preparations for which are underway, will not allow Solidarity to include its candidates as delegates. Good workers are elected by party organizations to attend the congress as delegates. ...

As for martial law, it could have been declared a long time ago. What would this mean? It would help them to smash the advance of counterrevolutionary elements and all kinds of rabble-rousers and to put an end to strikes and anarchy in the economy once and for all. Our comrades have drawn up draft documents concerning the declaration of martial law, and these documents should be signed. The Polish comrades responded, "How can we sign these documents if they must first go through the Sejm?" and so on. We said, "There is no need for anything to go through the Sejm, this would be the document according to which you will act when you declare martial law, and now it is necessary for you—Comrades Kania and Jaruzelski—to sign them personally so that we shall know that you are in agreement with it and will know what to do during martial law. If martial law has to be declared, there will be no time to waste in devising measures for implementing martial law, they must be prepared in advance. That is what we are talking about."

After our clarification, Comrades Kania and Jaruzelski said that they will study and sign the document on 11 April.

We then asked about the content of Jaruzelski's address to the Sejm. Jaruzelski spoke at length and not very coherently. He said that he would indicate a two-month prohibition of strikes. We asked what he meant by two months, and what was supposed to happen after that? "Two months will fly past, and the strikes will resume. You promise your workers a lot, then fail to deliver, giving more reasons for distrust of the party."

The question of implementing widespread political measures is particularly important at present. For instance, regarding the issue that you have shortages of bread and other foodstuffs. Why is this happening? Because strike after strike has disorganized the national economy and this is the reason for shortages. Every strike costs the country millions upon millions of zlotys, but the average worker does not know this and blames everything on the government, the CC of the party, and the Politburo, while the instigators, the organizers of the strikes, stand aside and appear to be the protectors of workers' interests. But, we say, if you look at the matter in its entirety, then the main guilty party for all the economic ills is Solidarity and the strike organizers. That is the crux of the problem. Why not bring that to the attention of the workers?

There is much talk of creating a national front for the salvation of Poland. Discussion of this is being conducted in several districts. It is envisaged that such a front would include veterans of the revolutionary movement, military leaders such as Rola-Zymierski, and others. This could be written in. Or, for instance, there is now talk in the FRG about the return of Silesia and Gdansk, territories joined to Poland, to the FRG. Why not play up this question? I believe that the people would close ranks on such issues. The people must be stirred up.

We said that we have no objections to the formation of a national front for the salvation of Poland. But this front should not be a substitute for the party and the government. ...

The Polish comrades mentioned the possibility of bringing three workers into the Politburo. They cited Lenin, who suggested bringing workers into the Politburo. We replied that we have never had workers in the Politburo. But if you really have such a need, then there could be an introduction of not necessarily three, but maybe one worker into the Politburo. An additional number of workers could be brought into the CC in order to facilitate the rallying and unity of the party. For instance, you have mentioned recruiting workers into popular control. Not a bad measure.

[...]

We said directly to Kania, "You keep retreating every day, but action is needed, military measures and emergency measures must be affirmed." ...

As for the support of the Politburo. On whom can the Politburo depend for support? The army numbers 400 thousand men, the MVD [Ministry of Internal Affairs] of the USSR has—100 thousand and 300 thousand reservists, making that 800 thousand in all. Kania said that tension has eased and they managed to prevent a general strike. But it is hard to say how long this calmer situation will last.

What are they doing after our meeting? It must be admitted that they are doing something. Kania is on his way to Gdansk. Jaruzelski is revising his address to the Sejm. However, Kania and Jaruzelski hold very different views on specific questions. Comrade Jaruzelski repeated his request to be relieved of the post of Prime Minister. We made it clear to him that he must remain at that post and perform his duties honorably. We stressed that the opposition is gathering forces to seize power.

On the other hand, other Politburo members—Comrades [Stefan] Olszowski and [Tadeusz] Grabski—have a somewhat different, more hard-line position than the leadership. We need to work with them. Among other things, they propose to create a clandestine Politburo and carry on work. They say that they got this idea from Comrade Zhivkov. I do not know how true that is, but they claim comrade Zhivkov gave them this advice. We should also realize that if the leaders of fraternal parties are making such recommendations to our Polish friends, we shall have nothing to gain, but can only lose.

SUSLOV. Maybe we should prepare information for fraternal parties.

GROMYKO. Under no circumstances should it become known that this meeting took place.

ANDROPOV. Speaking about the meeting is absolutely impossible.

USTINOV. Yu.V. Andropov has given a comprehensive report, so I would just like to mention something briefly. First, the first thing we noticed was the depressed state of our partners. But I feel that despite everything, we need these two—retain Kania and Jaruzelski and reinforce relations between them. The situation is that they have disagreements in the Politburo. In the first place, they are shaken by strikes; they are very frightened of them. We asked why they had changed their decision regarding Bydgoszcz. Initially they had not wanted to give up in the Bydgoszcz conflict, and then they retreated. They assured us that they'd had the threat of a general strike hanging over their heads. We then asked why they pay workers during strikes. They said that this was demanded by Solidarity. That means you are on Solidarity's leash, we said. They have reached no decision regarding rural Solidarity, but have in fact acknowledged the existence of this organization. ...

In order to dispel their fears regarding the declaration of a state of emergency or martial law, we cited the example that in many countries, the moment there is an uprising or disorders of some kind, a state of emergency or martial law is proclaimed. Take Yugoslavia, when there were demonstrations in Kosovo; a state of emergency was declared, and nobody objected. We cannot understand why the Poles are so afraid of it.

Yuri Vladimirovich spoke very well about declaring a state of emergency. We said that the plan drawn up by our comrades should be signed.

Then I told them straight out what we agreed on in the Politburo, what will happen in Poland if things begin to boil over, and in what kind of an economic situation the country will find itself. "After all, at the moment Poland receives all its oil at almost half price from the Soviet Union. It also receives cotton, iron ore, and many other goods. What will happen if these supplies cease? Why is this fact not known, not clarified to the workers? After all, this is a powerful weapon. This must be pointed out to the workers and to Solidarity. At this time, Solidarity has dug in at the largest industrial plants. These plants must be taken back from Solidarity. You have excellent plants and factories in which the workers support the leadership. For example, the plant manufacturing television sets. You can and must support branch trade unions, work actively with them." Afterwards Jaruzelski told me privately once more that he cannot work, he does not have enough strength, and pleaded to be relieved of his post.

• • •

The question of just how real was the threat of a Soviet invasion was the key issue of the Polish crisis. The behavior of the leaders of Solidarity, the reaction of Poles to the declaration of a state of emergency, and the stance of the West all hinged on it. It also remained the subject of heated debates after the collapse of the regime, in the period of "round tables" between Solidarity leaders and the party's top figures in the spring of 1989, which determined the current situation in Poland. Even now, when some of the minutes cited above have been published in Poland, public opinion inclines toward seeing Jaruzelski as a hero of some sort, who saved the country from the horrors of a Soviet occupation and the attendant shedding of blood, national humiliation, and even a loss of statehood. Even after it became clear that Moscow had no intention of invading, the Poles still seem to believe that Jaruzelski knew nothing of this and, therefore, was a hero who saved Poland. Need it be said that this is a typical self-serving lie that suited the majority—both former communist activists and numerous Poles who, one way or another, saw the state of emergency as the lesser evil? Even the former leaders of Solidarity used it as justification for their reaching an accommodation with the party leaders at the round table. As a result, the savior of the homeland and father of the people General Wojciech Jaruzelski lives peacefully in Warsaw.

I do not know whether all the CC documents were published in Poland, but the ones in front of me leave no doubt: Moscow had prepared no invasion of Poland, and Jaruzelski knew this perfectly well. Furthermore, having no great trust in the Polish army, by the end of the 1980s he had made numerous requests for the entry of Soviet forces and received a decisive refusal from the Kremlin. He proclaimed an emergency situation only when he realized that no military aid from Moscow was forthcoming.

A detailed analysis of the situation in Poland and Soviet strategy relating to it was made by the Politburo of the CC CPSU in April 1981, soon after the secret meeting in Brest. They wrote (23 April 1981*, Pb 7/VII):

> The internal crisis in Poland has assumed a protracted, chronic nature. The Polish United Workers' Party has lost a significant amount of control over the processes occurring in the country. At the same time, Solidarity has become an organized political force, capable of paralyzing the activity of party and state agencies and actually seizing power. If the opposition is refraining from this, it is mainly because of fears that Soviet forces will enter the country and because they hope to achieve their aims without loss of blood by means of a creeping counterrevolution.
>
> However, it is perfectly clear that the calm after the Sejm session will be short-lived. The opposition has accepted it for tactical reasons while continuing to gather strength to strike new blows at the party. [. . .] Solidarity as a whole and certain sections of it in particular are preparing to blackmail the authorities again by issuing new demands of a predominantly political nature. The signs of emerging differences in the layers of this professional association provide insufficient grounds to expect any substantial change in its overall orientation. Even if there were to be a schism between Walesa and extremists from the CBS-CDF, Walesa and the Catholic clergy backing him have no intention of relaxing their pressure on the party. There is also the possibility that the extremists may seize control of Solidarity with all the inevitable consequences.
>
> A new tactical consideration has emerged lately, which unites practically all the variegated opposition. Realizing that the geopolitical situation of Poland precludes its participation in the Warsaw Pact and the principle of the leading role of the communist party, these forces have obviously decided to attempt to destroy the Polish United Workers' Party from within, bring about its rebirth, and then seize power "on legitimate grounds."
>
> [. . .] In view of the above, we need to weigh our attitude to the policy of the Polish leadership again and reach a clearer idea of which forces can be relied on to preserve the achievements of socialism in Poland.

As the document goes on to say, on one hand, there was the "right wing," composed mainly of "revisionist-minded" activists, closer to social democratic ideas and actually linking with Solidarity. On the other hand, on the "left wing" were comrades "closest to our positions," made up mainly of old party members.

> Unfortunately, representatives of this inclination are far from being in the majority. They create the impression that they see

the way out of the crisis in the form of a frontal attack on Solidarity, without taking the current juxtaposition of forces into account. Moreover, they see no chance for an improvement in the situation without the entry of Soviet forces into the country. Objectively, this results in their growing isolation in the party and in the country.

The Politburo saw a way out of the crisis in supporting Kania and Jaruzelski, who occupied a "centrist position." Even though they displayed "insufficient firmness and experience in the struggle against counterrevolutionary forces and make unjustified concessions in confrontation with them," that was the best option available.

> Both of them, especially Jaruzelski, have authority in the country. At present there are practically no other activists to exercise party and state leadership.

Therefore the Politburo came to a decision to:

> ... continue political support of Comrades Kania and Jaruzelski, who, despite obvious wavering, are coming to the defense of socialism. At the same time, it is necessary to strive to make them take more consecutive and decisive actions in the interests of resolving the crisis on the basis of preserving Poland as a socialist country that is friendly to the Soviet Union.

Apart from this and other recommendations regarding reinforcement of the unity of the Polish United Workers' Party, ties with the working class, economic measures, and suchlike, the Politburo advises to:

> ... make more active use of the putative differences between Solidarity leaders, expose the anti-socialist, antinational activity of the CDS-CDF and their leaders, and strive toward the isolation of these counterrevolutionaries. Take decisive steps against efforts to raise a wave of anti-Sovietism among the population.
>
> Encourage the Polish leadership to show constant care regarding the condition of the army and MVD USSR agencies, their moral and political stability, and their readiness to do their duty in defense of socialism. [...] Make maximum use of the factor reining in the counterrevolution of the fear of internal reactionaries and international imperialism regarding the possibility that the Soviet Union may bring its forces into Poland. In external policy declarations, stress L.I. Brezhnev's statement at the Twenty-Sixth Congress of the CPSU concerning our firm

intention not to abandon Poland in its time of trouble and to
allow nobody to injure it.

So it is obvious that the Soviet threat was nothing more than
a bluff, raised to the level of government policy. What was really
planned was an emergency situation on which the bets were placed
(as well as on a possible schism in the Solidarity leadership). Furthermore, this was a decision that was never rescinded; only minor adjustments were made from time to time. By September 1981
it was obvious that Kania was unable to handle his task despite
Brezhnev's threats to have him dismissed (18 June 1981, Pb). It
got to the point that Honecker suggested holding a meeting of fraternal parties in Moscow, inviting Kania, and urging him to resign
in favor of Olszowski (17 September 1981, Pb). But even here the
Politburo decided not to change its line: it appointed Jaruzelski.
The latter understood full well why he had been made First Secretary as well as Prime Minister and Minister of Defense. This was
something of which Brezhnev reminded him in a phone call on the
day of his "election" (19 October 1981*, Pb 1942):

> BREZHNEV. Hello, Wojciech.
>
> JARUZELSKI. Hello, deeply respected, dear Leonid Ilyich.
>
> BREZHNEV. My dear Wojciech, we have already sent you a
> congratulatory message, but I would like to congratulate you
> personally on your election to the post of First Secretary of the
> CC of the Polish United Workers' Party.
>
> You did right to agree to this decision. There is nobody in the
> party with authority equaling yours—the votes at the plenum
> make that plain. We realize that you are facing a very difficult
> task. But we are certain that you will cope with it and do every-
> thing possible to overcome the rampant disease affecting your
> country.
>
> I think the main thing now is for you to find reliable assistants
> from among devoted and committed communists, bring them
> together, stir the entire party into action, and inspire them with
> a combative spirit. That is the key to success.
>
> It is vital to implement your intentions regarding decisive action
> against the counterrevolutionaries without wasting time. We
> hope that everyone—both in Poland and abroad—will feel that
> things are going to be much different now. That the situation
> is on the mend.
>
> I wish you good health and success!
>
> JARUZELSKI. Thank you very much, my dear Leonid Ilyich, for
> your greetings and first of all for your confidence in me. I tell
> you frankly that I agreed to take up this post after a lengthy

inner struggle and only because I knew that you would support me and support this decision. If that were not the case, I would never have agreed. This is a very heavy, difficult task in the current situation in the country, of which I am now Prime Minister and Minister of Defense. But I realized that this is all right and necessary if you think so personally.

BREZHNEV. Wojciech, we have thought so for a long time. We have spoken about this with friends on numerous occasions.

JARUZELSKI. That is why I agreed. As a communist and a soldier, Leonid Ilyich, I shall do my best to make things improve, to reach a turning point in the country and the party. I understand and agree with you that this is a decisive moment— the selection of leadership in the party, and the government. That is why I have deferred the decision on cadres to the next plenum, which we shall conduct in a few days, in order to think carefully, to consult, so that this will be a complex decision, and not just individual measures concerning cadres.

BREZHNEV. Cadres are very important, both in the center and locally.

JARUZELSKI. This question will also have to be decided locally. Of course, this must be done in parallel with reinforcement of the party in the spirit of active struggle. In suitable circumstances, resolute measures should be employed to do battle where there is certainty of success.

I am off now to a meeting of the General Staff of the Polish Armed Forces in the Ministry of Defense. I shall outline the tasks facing us. We shall include the army in all spheres of the life of the country.

After yesterday's plenum, I had a meeting with the first secretaries of local committees and said that they should not be concerned that we shall include the armed forces in carrying out certain procedures, we shall increase meetings between officers in meetings with the working class in order to have direct influence on workers and alienate them from the influence of Solidarity. Naturally we are not changing our general direction in the sense that struggling for the healthy forces of the people who have misguidedly joined Solidarity, we shall attract them to our side and at the same time strike the opponent in a way that will bring results.

I shall be meeting your ambassador today. I will try to discuss certain matters with him in more detail and ask for your advice on questions that he will report to you.

In informing you of all the decisions that we make, we shall report at the same time on what grounds these decisions were reached.

Our greatest difficulty at the moment is the market. This is the cause of numerous strikes and protests, including those organized by Solidarity, but some are purely spontaneous. This complicates the implementation of some inevitable measures and complicates our work, as the mood of the population is not the best. But we shall do everything possible to improve the situation.

This is what I wanted to report to you immediately, to keep you informed. Thank you again for your kind words.

BREZHNEV. Once more, Wojciech, I wish you good health and success.

JARUZELSKI. Thank you. Goodbye.

Can you say that these are the words of a man who does not understand what is happening? Everyone understood everything perfectly. The Politburo awaited the results tensely. A mere ten days had passed since Jaruzelski's appointment, but the men in the Kremlin began to worry that there were no noticeable changes (29 October 1981*, Pb).

GROMYKO. With regard to Poland, I have just spoken with Ambassador Aristov. He said that the one-hour strike was very impressive. Solidarity is virtually in charge at many enterprises. Even those who want to work cannot do so, as Solidarity extremists block those who want to work, issuing threats of all kinds to them.

As for the plenum, comrade Aristov reports that it went by normally and an additional two secretaries were elected. At the Sejm, which resumes work on October 30, they shall pose the question of limiting strikes. How this law will work out is too early to say, but at least efforts are being made to limit strikes by legislation. Comrade Jaruzelski's address at the plenum was not bad at all.

BREZHNEV. I do not believe that Comrade Jaruzelski did anything constructive. I think that he is not sufficiently brave. ... In one conversation Schmidt let slip that the situation developing in Poland is very dangerous and may affect my visit to the FRG, which may not take place.

ANDROPOV. The Polish leaders are talking of military aid from fraternal countries. But we must stick firmly to our line: our troops shall not enter Poland.

USTINOV. In any case, we must say that our armed forces cannot go into Poland. They, the Poles, are not prepared to accept our forces. At the moment, there is a demobilization of servicemen who have completed their terms. Moreover, the demobilized are allowed to return to their homes to collect civilian clothing and then return for service at work for another two months. This is when they are worked on by Solidarity. As we know, Jaruzelski organized operative groups of around 3 persons. But these groups have done nothing so far. This probably calls for a meeting with the Polish leadership, including Jaruzelski personally. The question is, whom shall we be meeting?

RUSAKOV. The Sejm starts work tomorrow, and will tackle the question of granting the government something like emergency powers to decide certain matters. Jaruzelski would really like to come to Moscow.

Jaruzelski did not get his trip to Moscow, but Brezhnev sent him a "verbal missive" through the ambassador, which stated among other things that (21 November 1981, Pb 37/21):

In many discussions with our side, we have stressed the same thought repeatedly: we are not opposed to agreements. But they must not contain concessions to opponents of socialism. The main thing is that the business should not focus on mere agreements: alongside measures to win broad popular masses and various political forces over to your side, resolute measures must be implemented against open enemies of the people's system. You have agreed with this view and said that you intend to fight for the workers and strike the class opponent at the same time. ... Now it appears that the emphasis is placed only on the first part of that dual formula. We know that there are leaders who are placing their hopes on Kania's bankrupt course. It would be dangerous to listen to their persuasions. It is clear now that without a decisive struggle with the class enemy, it will be impossible to save socialism in Poland. In essence, the question is not whether there will or will not be a confrontation, but who will start it, by which means it shall be waged, and who will seize the initiative.

As we see, not a word about Soviet troops.

5.17 "There can be no entry of Soviet forces into Poland"

Finally, on 10 December—three days before the proclamation of martial law in Poland—the Politburo still did not know for certain what Jaruzelski would do (10 December 1981*, Pb). This is perhaps the most interesting and convincing document:

RUSAKOV. The day before yesterday there was a meeting of the secretaries of the Voevodship committees. Comrade Aristov has reported that the secretaries are at a loss to understand Comrade Jaruzelski's address, which gave no clear, precise line. Nobody knows what will happen in the next few days. There was talk of "Operation X." At first it was said that this would take place on the night from the eleventh to the twelfth, then from the twelfth to the thirteenth. The latest indication is that it will be around the twentieth. The plan is that the chairman of the Council of State [of the Republic of Poland], Jablonski, shall declare martial law on radio and television. At the same time, Jaruzelski stated that the law on the declaration of martial law can be implemented only after it has been discussed in the Sejm, and the next session of the Sejm is scheduled for 15 December. This complicates everything. The agenda of the Sejm session has been publicized. It contains no mention of martial law. But in any case, Solidarity is perfectly aware that the government intends to declare martial law, and is taking all necessary steps to prepare for it.

Jaruzelski says himself that he intends to make an address to the Polish people. But he will not talk about the party; he will appeal to the nation's patriotic feelings. Jaruzelski speaks about the need to declare a military dictatorship, as happened under Jozef Pilsudski, indicating that the Polish people will understand this better than anything else.

Jaruzelski also cites Comrade Kulikov, who, he claims, said that the USSR and allied states will render military aid to Poland. As far as I know, Comrade Kulikov did not say this directly; he simply repeated the words once said by L.I. Brezhnev, that we would not desert Poland in its time of need.

As for what is occurring in the Voevodships, it must be said that the power of party organizations there is nonexistent. Administrative power is still present, but only to a certain degree. In fact, all power is in the hands of Solidarity. It looks as though Jaruzelski is simply giving us the runaround, as his words do not reflect any proper analysis. Unless they organize themselves quickly, and do not repel the pressure from Solidarity, there will be no success in improving the situation in Poland.

ANDROPOV. From discussions with Jaruzelski, it is clear that they still have no firm decision to introduce martial law, and despite the unanimous approval of the CC of the Polish United Workers' Party and the Politburo of the CC of the party regarding the proclamation of martial law, we have seen no concrete measures implemented by the leadership to date. Solidarity extremists have the party leadership by the throat. In recent days, the Church has also made its position clear. It has virtually joined the side of Solidarity.

It stands to reason that in such circumstances the Polish comrades need to prepare quickly for Operation X and set it in motion. At the same time, Jaruzelski says that they shall implement Operation X only if forced to do so by the actions of Solidarity. This is a very alarming symptom. Especially in view of the fact that the last meeting of the CC of the party and the decision it adopted regarding the introduction of martial law shows that the Politburo is much more decisive. All the members of the Politburo spoke out in favor of more resolute action. This decision pinned Jaruzelski to the wall, and he is now forced to find a way to wriggle out of the situation. I spoke with [Miroslaw] Milewski yesterday and asked him what measures are intended, and for when. He said that he knows nothing about a specific date for launching Operation X. This would appear to indicate that Jaruzelski is either hiding the plan for specific actions from his comrades or is simply trying to evade taking this action.

I would like to note now that Jaruzelski is giving us quite demanding economic requests as a condition for conducting Operation X and, I would say, poses the matter of military aid, albeit indirectly.

If we look at the list of goods the Polish comrades want us to provide, let us say that it gives rise to serious qualms about how necessary the provision of these goods really is. For example, what can the provision of fertilizers and certain other goods have to do with Operation X? In connection with this I would say that our position, as formulated at the last meeting of the Politburo, and on numerous earlier occasions expressed by Leonid Ilyich, is correct and there is no need to deviate from it. In other words, we stand on the position of international aid, we are concerned by the situation in Poland, but the implementation of Operation X is a matter for the Polish comrades to decide, and whatever their decision is, so be it. We shall not insist on it, or try to talk them out of it.

As for economic aid, we shall find it difficult to provide the requested amount. It looks as though something should be provided. But I repeat that the supply of goods in the form of economic aid is a brazen one, and this is all being done so that if we fail to supply something, we shall be blamed. If Comrade Kulikov really did speak of bringing in troops, I think he made a great error. This is a risk we cannot take. We do not intend to send troops to Poland. This is the right decision, and we must stick to it to the end. I do not know how events will develop in Poland, but even if it falls under the power of Solidarity, that will be one matter. But if capitalist countries pounce on the Soviet Union, and they already have relevant agreements on economic and political sanctions, it will be very hard for us. We have to take care of the needs of our country, to strengthen the Soviet Union. This is our primary line. . . .

As for communications from the Soviet Union to the GDR through Poland, we need to do something to guard them.

GROMYKO. We are now discussing the situation in Poland very harshly. I doubt that we have done so before. This is because we have no idea what turns the situation in Poland might take. The Polish leadership realizes that power is sliding out of its hands. Kania and Jaruzelski were expecting support from neutrals. Now there are really no neutrals left. The position has emerged quite clearly: Solidarity has declared itself as a definite counterrevolutionary organization, aiming for power and stating openly its intention to seize that power. The Polish leadership must decide whether to surrender its positions if it fails to implement resolute measures, or take such measures, proclaim martial law, isolate the Solidarity extremists from Solidarity, and restore order. There is no other way.

What is our attitude to events in Poland? I quite agree with the opinions expressed by the comrades present. We might tell the Poles that we look upon events in their country with understanding. This is a standard formulation, and we have no grounds to change it. At the same time, we should try to douse the aspirations of Jaruzelski and other leaders regarding sending in armed forces. There can be no such thing. I think we can instruct our ambassador to visit Jaruzelski and inform him accordingly.

Despite the sufficiently unanimous decision of the Politburo of the CC of the Polish United Workers' Party regarding the proclamation of martial law, Jaruzelski is wavering again. At first he seemed to take heart, and now he has weakened. Everything he once said remains in force. If they continue to waver in the fight against the counterrevolution, there will be nothing left of socialist Poland. The introduction of martial law would show the firm intentions of the Polish leadership to the opposition. If the measures they intend to implement are carried out, I think we can expect positive results. ... I believe that at this time we should abstain from any harsh instructions that would force them to take certain actions. I think that we shall take up the right position in this case: restoring order in Poland is the task of the Polish United Workers' Party, its Central Committee, and its Politburo. We told our Polish friends, and will continue to do so, that firm positions must be maintained and that they should not feel disheartened.

Of course, if the Poles strike a blow at Solidarity, the West will probably refuse them credits and will provide no aid. This is what they have in mind, and this is something we should be aware of also. So Leonid Ilyich is quite right to suggest that we should charge a group of comrades with considering this question, allowing for our ability to provide Poland with a certain measure of economic aid.

USTINOV. The situation in Poland is definitely very bad. The situation becomes more complex with every passing day. The leadership, including the Politburo, lacks resolution and unity. All this affects the overall situation. At the last Politburo meeting there was a unanimous decision regarding the proclamation of martial law. Now everything is up to Jaruzelski, and how he will go about implementing it. Frankly speaking, nobody can say anything about Jaruzelski's actions. We do not know anything either. I spoke with Siwizky and he said directly that none of them know what the general is thinking. So the man actually performing the obligations of the Polish Ministry of Defense does not know what will happen next, what actions shall be undertaken by the chairman of the Council of Ministers and the minister.

As for what Kulikov allegedly said regarding bringing troops into Poland, I can affirm with certainty that Kulikov said no such thing. He simply repeated what we and Leonid Ilyich said, that we shall not desert Poland. He knows perfectly well that the Poles themselves have asked that troops be not brought in.

With regard to our garrisons in Poland, we are reinforcing them. I am inclined to think that the Poles will not initiate confrontation, unless Solidarity takes them by the throat, in which case they will proceed.

[...]

SUSLOV. It is clear from what has been said here that we share the same opinion regarding events in Poland. Over this entire period we have been restrained and coolheaded. This was mentioned at the plenum by Leonid Ilyich. We said this openly to the people, and our people have supported the policy of the Communist Party.

[...] This made it clear to all peace-loving countries that the Soviet Union advocates a policy of peace firmly and consistently. That is the reason we cannot change our position concerning Poland, one we adopted from the very start of events in Poland. Let the Polish comrades determine what actions they should take. We should not push them toward more decisive measures. But we should continue to assure the Poles that we regard their actions with understanding.

It seems to me that Jaruzelski is being rather cunning. He wants to protect himself by the requests he is making to the Soviet Union. Naturally, we cannot physically fulfil these requests, and Jaruzelski can say later that he asked the Soviet Union for aid, but did not receive it.

At the same time, the Poles say directly that they are opposed to the entry of military forces. If forces are brought in, that will precipitate a catastrophe. I think we are all agreed that there can be no question of bringing in troops.

On the matter of rendering aid to Poland, we have provided it to the tune of over a billion rubles. Quite recently we decided to send Poland 30 thousand metric tons of meat, of which 16 thousand metric tons have already been delivered. I do not know whether we shall be able to supply the total thirty thousand metric tons, but in any case we should probably add a certain number of metric tons of meat in the form of aid. ...

GRISHIN. The situation in Poland is heading for further deterioration. The line of our party regarding the events in Poland is quite correct. ... There is no question of sending in troops. Economic problems should be considered, and see what can be given to the Poles.

SUSLOV. We should expose the schemes of Solidarity and other counterrevolutionary forces in the press.

CHERNENKO. I agree with everything said by the present comrades. It is a fact that the line of our party and the Politburo of the CC regarding the Polish events, formulated in the addresses of L.I. Brezhnev and the decisions of the Politburo, is perfectly correct, and should not be changed.

I think we should decide today to:

1. Take note of the information provided by Comrade [Nikolai] Baibakov.

2. In our relations with the Polish Republic continue to pursue the general political line of the CPSU, also the instructions of the Politburo of the CPSU dated 8 December 1981 and the exchange of views at the meeting of the Politburo of the CC on 10 December 1981.

3. Instruct comrades Tikhonov, Kirilenko, [Vladimir] Dolgikh, [Ivan] Arkhipov, and Baibakov to continue studying the question of economic aid for Poland, allowing for the views expressed at the meeting of the Politburo of the CC.

BREZHNEV. What is the opinion of the comrades?

ALL. Comrade Chernenko has formulated all the proposals correctly, they should be adopted. ...

The resolution is adopted.

5.18   Operation X

No doubt about it, the Soviet leaders were first-class players. Even I breathed a sigh of relief when I heard about martial law in Poland: Soviet intervention had seemed extremely likely at the time, the bloody consequences of which were hard to imagine. The well-equipped and trained half-million-strong Polish army, unlike its Czech colleagues twelve years earlier, would hardly have remained neutral. The reaction of the population needed no guessing. The point at issue was a war in central Europe with a population of thirty-five million that was famous for its stubbornness, decades of partisan activity, and hundreds of thousands of victims. In fact, a European version of Afghanistan. *Is it possible that they do not understand this in the Kremlin?* I wondered gloomily. *Will they really unleash this madness?*

Yet they ventured into Afghanistan, they crushed Hungary. As for "surrendering Poland," that was surely something they could not countenance. Moreover, the matter was not limited to mere threats or Brezhnev's words that they would not "desert Poland in its time of need"—no fewer than forty-four Soviet divisions were brought up to the Polish border. How must it have been for the Poles to live with this constant threat hanging over their heads? It is not surprising that the introduction of martial law offered them some relief—the lesser evil—and they tended to justify their army and Jaruzelski (now being hailed as the savior of the country). The enormous pressure of those days was probably best expressed in the Polish anecdote about a man drowning in the Vistula River and shouting at the top of his voice, "Help! Help!"

The crowd on the bridge above his head shouts in reply, "Quiet! Quiet! Do you want the Soviets to hear you and come to render 'international aid'?"

Only this purely neurotic reaction can explain the amazing success of the martial law, the introduction of which passed almost without bloodshed. What can one say? The ability to make a situation they created seem like the lesser evil was something the Soviet regime had developed into a fine art. They were always the lesser evil—lesser than the typhoid and starvation of a civil war, lesser than Hitler, lesser than a nuclear war and even being invaded. And if there was nothing worse to be found, they made up "hawks" and "conservatives" in the Politburo who allegedly posed a threat to the "doves" and "reformers." Other scares were devised under Gorbachev: the neo-Nazi Pamyat society, Zhirinovsky. ... This stratagem was repeated dozens of times and, amazingly enough, it always worked.

It must be said that the Solidarity leaders were unprepared for martial law. The threat of repression had hung over them for too long and they were accustomed to it, and stopped preparing. With few exceptions, all their structures were seized practically in the first few days, and most of the leaders were arrested. This is understandable from a psychological point of view; what you wait for usually catches you unawares. It is amusing to recall now that during the night of introduction of martial law, I had been speaking on the phone with Polish dissident Adam Michnik. I said jokingly that judging by photos, he had gained a lot of weight and it was time to go on a diet—at which point the connection broke. I had no idea that at that moment all the telephones in Poland had been silenced, and poor Adam was fated to lose a great deal of weight during the next six months.

There is no avoiding making mention of eternal Polish carelessness: nobody had bothered to set up parallel "shadow" structures during the one and a half years of the crisis. Solidarity, with its millions of supporters and activists, simply ceased to exist overnight.

All in all, the Soviet calculations proved justified. Having done what they intended, they informed fraternal parties, acting like impartial observers (13 December 1981*, Pb 40/26):

> As friends are aware, the Polish leadership declared martial law in the country, announced the creation of a Military Council of National Salvation and isolated the more extreme elements in Solidarity, the Confederation for an Independent Poland and other anti-socialist groups.
>
> W. Jaruzelski's address to the people leaves a good impression; in our opinion it places the right accents on the basic questions. Among other things it is especially important that the leading role of the Polish United Workers' Party and the fidelity of Poland to its alliance obligations to the Warsaw Pact are confirmed.
>
> The success of the operation was made possible by the Polish comrades' maintaining strict secrecy. It was known only to a very limited circle in Jaruzelski's entourage. Due to this the opponent was caught unprepared, and the operation is proceeding satisfactorily at this time.
>
> On the eve of implementing the plan, Jaruzelski advised Moscow. He was told that the Soviet leadership views this decision by the Polish comrades with understanding. At the same time, we are proceeding on the assumption that our Polish friends will decide these matters with internal forces.
>
> Our preliminary assessment is that the actions of Polish friends are an active step in rebuffing the counterrevolution and thereby echo the general line of fraternal countries.
>
> These conditions raise the question of rendering political and moral support to Polish comrades, as well as economic aid. The Soviet leadership will continue to remain in contact with fraternal countries regarding the Polish question.

This was an inarguable success of the Soviet regime, but not a victory. It was too soon to celebrate: a Poland driven into the underground continued to resist; Western reaction, although less than it would have been in the case of an invasion, still undermined the Soviets' positions. The main point was probably that martial law did not facilitate resolution of the reasons for the crisis in Poland—on the contrary, the crisis worsened and became even more hopeless. "Rescued Poland" became an unbearable burden for the Soviet regime. It is curious that at about this time the Politburo began to realize the hopelessness of its position (14 January 1982*, Pb):

> BREZHNEV. ... There has been martial law in Poland for a month. The first results are obvious. As Jaruzelski says, the backbone of the counterrevolution has been broken. However, more serious problems lie ahead.
>
> Having restored relative order in the country, the Polish comrades must now address problems that may be called strategic—what to do with the trade unions, how to get the economy back on its feet, how to achieve a reversal in the consciousness of the masses, etc.
>
> The most important question is the situation in the Polish United Workers' Party. Friends are seeking the best approach to resolve it. It appears that Jaruzelski has no intention of dissolving or renaming the party, but intends to make use of the martial law situation to conduct a substantial purge. Maybe that will yield results.
>
> It appears that the general has developed as a political figure and usually makes the right decisions. At times he seems too cautious, and acts with a wary eye on the West and the Church. But in the present circumstances, a frontal attack may ruin everything. In matters of principle, firm, harsh measures should go hand in hand with flexibility and circumspection. It is good that Jaruzelski is studying the Hungarian experience of fighting the counterrevolution.
>
> We all understand that the main condition for the full stabilization of the situation in Poland must be the revival of the economy. After 1968, the return to normality in Czechoslovakia occurred so quickly because this sector was practically untouched by the counterrevolution. This situation is the reverse.
>
> Consequently, we are facing a difficult question—we are already at the limit of our possibilities with rendering aid to the Poles, but they keep sending new requests. We may have to do something, but we cannot give them large advances.
>
> We have to answer Jaruzelski's letter, telling him in a comradely

spirit what we can and cannot do. Under all circumstances we have to make our supplies in the first quarter according to schedule, in the hardest winter months for the Poles. ...

Incidentally, the Poles' situation regarding food is not all that desperate. There is enough bread in the country; the peasants need to be approached in order to gain their interest, to establish, as we used to say, a link between the city and the village.

The Polish leadership also continues to rely on help from the West. In principle we cannot oppose this, although it is doubtful that the West will support a military power willingly. They will probably continue to try for concessions, and this is where we shall have to be particularly vigilant.

Jaruzelski also poses another question: Should aid be accepted from the Chinese? Why not? That will mean that China diverges from the USA with their economic sanctions.

In conclusion it can be said that the Polish question will remain at the center of international politics for a long time. Therefore our commission on Poland should keep on working as actively as before.

TIKHONOV. On the issue of building an underground railway, the Council of Ministers has already drawn up the relevant proposals and they have been submitted to the Politburo.

CHERNENKO. The proposal concerning our participation in building the underground railway in Warsaw is to be voted on in the Politburo. ...

BREZHNEV. ... As you see in his letter, Comrade Jaruzelski expresses deep gratitude for the fraternal aid rendered by the Soviet Union to the Polish People's Republic. At the same time he requests the Soviet side to confirm the scope of supplies for 1982, as contained in the draft protocol for the coordination of plans of both countries for 1981 through 1985 concerning oil, gasoline, and petrochemicals. The scope of oil supplies in 1982 remains at the level of 13 million metric tons, and petrochemicals at 2.94 million metric tons, to ensure maximum supplies of fuel in the first quarter of 1982.

Comrade Jaruzelski also reports that he has appealed to the general secretaries of the CC of the Hungarian Communist Party, the GDR, Bulgaria, Romania, and Czechoslovakia, asking them to render Poland essential economic aid, including providing the domestic market with basic agricultural and industrial goods.

We have returned to the question of additional aid measures for Poland on numerous occasions. I have brought up this matter now for a simple exchange of opinions. It is obvious that this time again we will be unable to supply Poland with everything, but something must be found and something must be given. For this reason, on one hand, I ask the relevant comrades to speed up consideration of these questions and submit the corresponding materials to the Politburo. On the other hand, attempts must be made to resolve certain positions positively.

[...]

BAIBAKOV. Leonid Ilyich, I would like to raise two questions. The first concerns additional supplies of oil. I have taken a careful look at our resources, and there is no way to provide these additional supplies of fuel to Poland. I consider that we already provide Poland with an adequate amount of petrochemicals and they should manage with what they get.

The second question concerns the supply of grain for bread production. They have sufficient supplies of grain. They had a fairly good harvest this year, but the preparations for bread production are considerably lower than last year despite the good harvest.

ANDROPOV. They are requesting a certain amount of grain in order to return it in the second quarter.

SUSLOV. In other words, they are not making an additional request for grain, but one with return.

[...]

KIRILENKO. Of course it is hard for them to get any amount of grain from other countries, although they have bought some from Canada.

BREZHNEV. If there are no objections, we could adopt the following resolution:

Charge the Council of Ministers of the USSR, the Gosplan of the USSR and the Ministry of Foreign Trade with examining the requests in Comrade Jaruzelski's letter, bearing in mind the exchange of opinions at the past meeting of the Politburo. And submit the relevant proposals to the CC CPSU.

The proposal is approved.

5.19 Who can supply thirty thousand metric tons of meat?

It can be said that the Polish crisis was the first considerable demonstration of the general economic collapse of socialism, a harbinger of its future. After all, the question was not the appearance of Solidarity but the inability of the system to supply the country with necessary goods, and as the Politburo became increasingly aware, the entire socialist camp could not ensure the provision of even a temporary sufficiency of goods to Poland. The Polish crisis aggravated these problems, turning them into political issues: the question of whether Poland should or should not be a Soviet satrap came down to the point, strictly speaking, of whether the USSR could supply Poland with the required amount of oil, meat, grain, cotton, etc.

At first, this situation annoyed the Soviet leaders intensely, creating friction between those who were answerable for the economy and those who were answerable for politics, security, and ideology. Naturally, the reason did not lie in differing convictions, or in that one group was more dogmatic than another, but in that one group would speak of political *expediency* while others spoke of economic possibility (26 March 1981*, Pb):

> ARKHIPOV. Regarding the situation in the national economy, Comrade Jaruzelski has reported that the 1981 plan is 20 percent below the preceding one for 1980. There are particular difficulties with coal. As you know, they export coal as a source of hard currency. Instead of the 180 million metric tons envisaged by the plan, they shall extract only 170 million metric tons under optimum conditions. The production of meat is falling by 25 percent, sugar by one and a half. Instead of 1.5 million metric tons they shall gather 950 million metric tons at the most.
>
> Poland is now facing the rationing of bread and flour.
>
> As for the financial situation, the Polish debt, mainly to capitalist countries, stands at $23 billion, of which $9 billion was received under guarantee from the relevant states. The remaining credit was taken by the Poles from private banks. There are four hundred such banks. Now our Polish friends face the fact of the purchase of $9.5 billion worth of various goods from abroad. All this will be at the cost of loans. Exports will comprise only $8.5 billion. Western countries are dragging out decisions on whether to grant Poland credit. They now need to pay $1.5 billion, mainly interest on loans. They ask us for $700 million. Of course, we cannot raise such a sum. We are currently supplying Poland with oil, gas, iron ore, etc.
>
> In the course of the discussion, the Polish friends asked whether they should declare a moratorium on loans or join the International Monetary Fund and ask for additional loans from Western countries. Of course, in both cases this would be a concession to Western countries. It would have no economic effect. The Poles have no common opinion on these matters. They ask us for additional cotton and synthetic fibers. We have decided on a certain increase in cotton and synthetic fiber supply.
>
> GROMYKO. The Polish comrades have stressed the acute nature of the question of the import of goods, as they cannot pay for them. It is characteristic that they show no serious appreci-

ation of the supply of raw materials from the Soviet Union. It is as if they consider this a trifling matter. But in reality, all their cotton and iron ore come from us, as does oil.

ARKHIPOV. We supply Poland with 13 million metric tons of oil at 90 rubles per metric ton. If you take into account that the world price for oil is 170 rubles, we are short by 80 rubles for every metric ton. We could sell all that oil for hard currency, and the profits would be colossal.

In the meantime, things on the oil front were getting worse, and oil was the USSR's main source of hard currency, just as coal was for the Poles. In order to rescue Poland, supplies to the other East European brothers had to be reduced, a measure they did not take well (29 October 1981*, Pb):

RUSAKOV. In the course of negotiations, the leaders of fraternal countries touched upon economic matters. The main issue is the reduction of energy carriers, primarily oil. Comrades [Janos] Kadar, [Gustav] Husak and Zhivkov did say that even though this will be hard for them, they treated our proposal with understanding, saying that they would seek ways out of the situation and accept our measures. For greater clarity I asked the comrades if I could advise the Politburo that they agree with the proposal I have put before them. They replied that yes, I could go ahead.

The conversation with Comrade Honecker was a different matter entirely. He said immediately that such a reduction in oil supply was unacceptable, that this would cause serious losses to the national economy and to the GDR as a whole, that it would be a serious blow to the economy of the GDR and they would have no way of making ends meet. He stated that the GDR may refuse, and asked for a written response to the two letters sent to Comrade Brezhnev. The matter became extremely complicated and remained undecided. Comrade Honecker pointed out once more that the GDR supplies us with bismuth and uranium, supports the Group of [Soviet] Forces, and that they are experiencing difficulties because Poland is not supplying the coal which should be delivered along our line. As a result of all this, as Comrade Honecker expressed it, the standard of living of the German people will be lowered, and the authorities will not know how to explain it. The leadership will be forced to review all its plans.

BREZHNEV. ... As you know, we have decided to reduce oil supplies to our friends. They did not take this easily, especially Comrade Honecker, who, as you see, expects answers to the letters sent to us. The others do not expect an answer, but probably feel that we have changed our decision somehow.

Maybe at the next meeting with our friends on this matter, we should say that we are doing all we can to fulfil and even exceed the plan of oil supplies, and hope that we can accomplish this. In that case, we could make some changes to the planned supplies of energy carriers, but on no account create the impression that we are now retreating from our decision. ...

With regard to oil supplies, I am particularly concerned about the GDR. I must say that socialist countries have taken our proposals hard. ...

I simply do not know what our decision should be.

[ANDROPOV, SUSLOV, and KIRILENKO all say that they have to agree with what BREZHNEV just said.]

ARKHIPOV. We will also have difficulties with fuel. The miners will fall short of coal extraction by 30 million metric tons. How can that be compensated for? The oil industry will not exceed the plan, so we will have to cover this shortfall of 30 million metric tons somehow. Moreover, we are short 1.5 million metric tons of sugar, it will also have to be purchased, and 800 metric tons of vegetable oil, without which it is impossible to get by.

As for a reply to Comrade Honecker, I think comrade Rusakov's proposal is the right one. We have to affirm that we cannot change the decision of which comrade Honecker has already been apprised.

As for the supply of uranium mentioned by Comrade Honecker, the uranium we receive from the GDR is not an answer to a problem, it comprises only 20 percent of the amount we use. Comrade Honecker does not take into account the fact that we are building nuclear power plants for the GDR, and that this is no small undertaking.

RUSAKOV. I would like to add that the Poles ask us to maintain the same supplies of oil and gas that they have this year.

ARKHIPOV. We are holding talks with the Poles and believe that our economic relations with them should be conducted on the principle of the balancing of plans. Of course, this will result in a significant reduction in oil supplies, insofar as they are not supplying us with coal and other products. Still, if all goes well, we are including the supply of oil at the current level in our calculations.

BAIBAKOV. All the socialist countries are trying to probe us now, taking their cue from the GDR, waiting to see how we will deal with the GDR. If Honecker manages to breach the wall, they will try to do the same. In any case, nobody has sent written replies yet. Over the past few days I have talked with the chairmen of all the State Planning bodies of socialist countries. They all want to retain the overall amount of oil supplies, with division into years. Some propose that oil could be replaced with other energy carriers.

It was not just oil, which was the mainstay of the empire; there were other problems as well. The most basic: meat. The problem with meat was what had started all the unrest in Poland, and it would seem that a year later an effort could have been made to swamp Poland with it. But no, there was nowhere to get meat, and that was that. A huge totalitarian empire, in which the word of the leaders is law, struggles but fails to provide thirty thousand metric tons of meat.

> BREZHNEV. Have we sent the meat regarding which we adopted a resolution, and have we informed Jaruzelski about it?
>
> RUSAKOV. Jaruzelski was informed, and he was the one who named the figure of thirty thousand metric tons.
>
> ARKHIPOV. We shall send Poland meat from our state reserves.
>
> BREZHNEV. Have there been any contributions of meat from the republics into the union reserve after my telegram?
>
> ARKHIPOV. So far there has been nothing, Leonid Ilyich. Admittedly, not enough time has passed. I have talked to all the republics and can report that measures are being implemented everywhere to ensure fulfilment of the plan of supplies of meat to the state. Among others, such plans have come into force in Estonia, Belorussia, and Kazakhstan. The Ukrainians have not yet sent instructions to their regions.
>
> CHERNENKO. But we sent our telegram to all the regions of Ukraine.
>
> ARKHIPOV. We shall receive data by Monday, then we shall report how matters stand.
>
> GORBACHEV. Leonid Ilyich, your telegram played a great role. First, all the republics and regions are giving serious consideration to measures that would ensure fulfilment of the plan. At least, according to data at our disposal as a result of phone calls to regional, district, and township committees, and the CCs of the communist parties of union republics, so the question is being discussed at the bureau level. We shall give an estimate on meat deliveries for 1 January.
>
> BREZHNEV. I keep thinking that even though we gave the Poles 30 thousand metric tons of our meat, it is not really likely to help them. In any case, it is still unclear what will happen to Poland. . . .

The Politburo discussed these thirty thousand metric tons of meat over several more months: one day it might appear, the next day not. Telegrams flew hither and thither, runners rushed all over the place, telephone wires ran hot with furious bosses' curses, but there was still no meat. Anyway, what are thirty thousand metric tons of meat compared to world revolution? Even at Western market prices they were unlikely to fetch more than $30 million. All of Poland should not be lost over such a trifling matter. But on 10 December, three days before the proclamation of martial law, Gosplan chairman Baibakov returned from Warsaw and reported the following (10 December 1981*, Pb):

> As is known, we are assisting Poland with a delivery of thirty thousand metric tons of meat pursuant to the decision of the Politburo in response to a request from our Polish comrades. Of these thirty thousand, sixteen thousand metric tons are on their way abroad. It must be noted that the product—in this instance meat—is being sent in dirty railway wagons that have not been cleaned after transporting ore, and is of a disgusting appearance. When this meat is unloaded at Polish stations, there is real sabotage. The Soviet Union and the Soviet people are referred to by the Poles in unspeakable curses; they refuse to clean the wagons, etc. There is no limit to the insults directed at us.

Jaruzelski's new requests on the eve of martial law were, as Andropov put it, "brazen." But wasn't Poland worth it? Moscow would gladly have parted with even more, but it had nothing to offer.

> BAIBAKOV. ... It must be said that the list of goods they include as our aid to their country comprises 350 items to the sum of 1.4 billion rubles. It also includes 2 million metric tons of grain, 25 thousand metric tons of meat, 625 thousand metric tons of iron ore, and numerous other goods. Allowing for what we were going to give to Poland in 1982, the total amount of aid to Poland shall comprise around 4.4 billion rubles with inclusion of the requests submitted by the Polish comrades.
>
> The time is at hand for Poland to repay loans issued by Western countries. For this, Poland needs at least 2.8 billion convertible rubles. When I heard the Polish comrades ask for it and to what it amounts, I raised the issue that we should conduct our mutual economic relations on a balanced basis. I also pointed out that Polish industry is not fulfilling the plan to a significant degree. The coal-mining industry, which is the main source of hard currency, is in total disarray, no appropriate measures are being implemented, and the strikes continue. Now, even though there are no strikes, the mining of coal is still at a very low level.
>
> Or, for example, peasant produce; they have grain, meat products, vegetables, and so on. However, they give nothing to the

state; they are waiting to see what happens. Trade at private markets is fairly brisk at highly inflated prices.

I told the Polish comrades to their faces that they need to take more resolute steps in these circumstances. Maybe something like a surplus appropriation system should be introduced.

When it comes to grain, Poland harvested 2 million metric tons this year. The people are not starving. City dwellers go to markets and villages to buy the products they need. These products are all available.

... Realizing the state of the payments balance, the Poles want to introduce a moratorium on repayment to Western countries. If they do this, all Polish ships in the waters or docks in any country and all their assets in countries to which Poland is in debt will be seized. For this reason, the Poles have ordered captains of ships to leave port and remain in neutral waters. ...

RUSAKOV. Comrade Baibakov has given a very precise picture of the state of the Polish economy. What should we do? I think that we should supply Poland with the goods envisaged by the economic agreement, and this must not exceed the amount of goods that we supplied in the first quarter of last year.

BREZHNEV. Are we able to do this now?

BAIBAKOV. Leonid Ilyich, this can be done only by drawing on state reserves or by reducing supplies to the domestic market.

So how much did the "Polish crisis" cost the USSR? Of course, it is impossible to calculate all the expenditures, but economic aid alone, including loans for the purchase of goods and settlement of foreign debts, delayed payments, and gratis aid, comprised $2.934 billion in 1980–1981. And no subsequent year cost much less.

Nothing had changed in Poland four years later: the Politburo kept racking its brains about how to restore the leading role of the Polish United Workers' Party, and how to quash the counterrevolution once and for all. Top-level Soviet delegations flew to Warsaw and gave valuable advice on "increasing work among the masses"; Jaruzelski appeared in Moscow from time to time—requesting additional aid. By 1984 even the most thick-skinned member of the Politburo realized that the situation was hopeless. As one of them said (25 April 1984, Pb):

It must be taken into account that Poland, calling itself a socialist country, was never socialist in the full sense of the word.

5.20   The global crisis of socialism

It is unlikely that any of the Soviet leaders could say for certain
what "in the full sense of the word" means, or which fraternal country would qualify as such. Any of them could recite parrot-fashion
what it means theoretically, but the practical side of the question
upset all the schemes. One can only guess at which moment in history various leaders should have realized that the "model" they'd
created was dysfunctional. Presumably Lenin understood this by
1921, when it became clear that there would be no worldwide socialist revolution. Stalin certainly would have reached this conviction
in 1941, seeing the crash of his empire under the blows of the German army. Khrushchev probably never gave such questions much
thought until he was deposed, but the enforced inactivity of his final years opened his eyes. But for Brezhnev, Andropov, Gromyko,
Chernenko, Ustinov, Suslov and others, the Polish crisis was for
them what 1941 was for Stalin.

It is true to say that the beginning of the 1980s exposed the
putrefaction of the system. Afghanistan on one hand and Poland
on the other, the increasing hostility of the West, the unsuccessful
disarmament campaign, and in the center growing economic deterioration, mass disaffection, technical backwardness, and the all-
pervasive corruption of the ruling apparatus. In total, this signaled
the crisis of the system. After Poland, the Soviet leadership took
a look at its own country through different spectacles (24 October
1980, St 233/8):

> As instructed, the departments of the CC CPSU have analyzed
> the information coming into the Central Committee concerning
> the mistakes and conflicts between workers and administra-
> tions in individual enterprises, which have caused some down-
> ing of tools and other negative manifestations.
>
> We deem it essential to report that the number of such negative
> occurrences in recent times has increased, which is a matter
> of serious concern. Analysis shows that most of them are due
> directly to breaches of the procedure of the established review of
> norms and wages, incorrect accrual and late payment of wages,
> especially of bonuses, poor working conditions, and careless
> treatment of workers' complaints.

The symptom was malignant, even though strikes did not turn
into mass occurrences. As a rule, the issues in question were local conflicts, affecting one shop floor or a shift, caused by brazen
breaches of labor legislation by the administration. In 1979 there

were around three hundred such occurrences. But the situation in Poland had a definite influence on the mood of workers.

> It must be noted that in recent weeks there has been a growing number of refusals to work. In a number of places, refusals to perform work duties were not limited to the collective of one shift but spread to the next ones, involving a significant number of workers.

Predictably, the trade unions were reprimanded and ordered to take better care of their members. But how could this help if the trade unions, the administrations, and local party authorities had long fused into one apparatus whose primary responsibility was to ensure fulfilment of the plan? Moreover, the strikes were just the culmination of a growing dissatisfaction that had nothing to do with any specific labor dispute. First and foremost, there was the shortage of even the most basic products. It was all very well for the Poles to revolt over meat shortages; Soviet workers did not even dream of meat, they hardly had enough bread.

"Letters from citizens from various places have been received; they write, often in very harsh terms, about periodic irregularities in supplies of bread, the decrease in the assortment of available breadstuffs, and their low quality," reported Chernenko (17 February 1981, St 250/9). How could workers not strike if "their attitude results from irregularities with bread supplies, in some places no bread is to be had for up to four days? Children rarely see white bread or rolls. There is no flour available for sale."

Naturally, he pointed an accusing finger at inefficient local managers, and also peasants who were allegedly buying up grain to feed their personal livestock. But even Chernenko began to comprehend that there was something wrong with the system itself, if only because of the widespread nature of the phenomenon. In any case, managers had been replaced, bread was sold here and there with coupons and according to lists (in order to prevent it being bought to feed livestock), but there were still shortages of bread. How could this be?

Chernenko quoted from another letter (17 February 1981 (St 250/9), pp. 5–6):

> The newspapers publish reports about the successful fulfilment of socialist obligations of the tenth five-year plan regarding the sale of grain to the state by republics and regions, but in our working town it has been impossible to buy a loaf of bread for the second day in a row. By 2–3 p.m. the shelves in the shops are empty. This has caused the circulation of negative rumors.

It is really somewhat mystifying: the plans were met and exceeded, tens of millions of metric tons of grain were purchased from Canada and the USA, but there was still no bread. The cause could not be ascribed to mere negligence, the more so that the situation with bread was just one of many examples:[290]

> It is worth noting that alongside reports concerning interruptions in bread deliveries and certain other consumer goods, complaints are being received from certain republics and regions about shortages of salt and table vinegar.

The story with salt is even more intriguing than the disappearance of bread. There are whole lakes of salt in Russia, and it does not need to be grown or harvested; it is gathered by excavators and loaded directly into wagons. What could be simpler? The mystery of the vanished salt occupied the CC as a separate issue, but this riddle was never fully solved. The letters department of the CC reported as follows (17 February 1981, St 250/10):

> Among letters addressed to the Central Committee by workers from certain parts of the country on the question of providing the population with foodstuffs, there are complaints with increasing frequency about difficulties with acquiring table salt, its limited range and low quality. ... [One letter] states: "In recent times, trade in our town has been in a 'feverish' condition. This affects everyday consumer goods. A short while ago, table salt disappeared from sale. This causes all kinds of nervous reactions."
>
> "Our region produces salt," writes [another comrade]. "What can explain the fact that there are constant interruptions in the sale of this commodity? It has reached the point that children from the orphanage go around from door to door, asking for a pinch of salt. Inevitably, this has an effect on our productivity at work and our attitudes."

Curiously enough, the CC did not learn about these shortages from its own apparatus or control agencies or even the omniscient KGB, but from complaints made by ordinary citizens. The infuriated CC conducted investigations, guilty officials were brought to book on "strict party responsibility" or even imprisoned, but the situation did not improve. Local managers became more vigilant in ensuring that no further complaints reached Moscow, and particularly persistent complainants were put away in psychiatric institutions, imprisoned, or hounded to death. As for the party's economic

---

[290] 17 February 1981 (St 250/9), p. 10.

apparatus, it merely reported on the fulfilment of plans with excess at all levels, and no matter how hard the CC fought against these write-ups, it could not eradicate them. A special article was introduced into the Criminal Code, envisaging a punishment of up to three years' imprisonment, all in vain. Finally the leaders had no idea of what the country was producing, in what quantity, or of what quality....

By the beginning of the 1980s, corruption within the apparatus had reached epic proportions, even though since Khrushchev's times economic crimes had carried the heaviest penalties, up to execution by firing squad. The most fantastic matters were exposed only occasionally: entire sectors of the economy were riddled with corruption, and the scope of theft involved hundreds of millions of rubles (4 January 1980, St 191/12). On the other hand, this led to the appearance of an entire shadow industry: a system of clandestine enterprises and manufacturers totally unconnected with the state economy. Indestructible private initiative turned out to be much more efficient than the unwieldy state machine (4 October 1980, St 231/9). But this surfaced very rarely: as a rule, local party authorities were hand in glove with the wheeler-dealers, and even the KGB proved unable to fathom things out to the end. Entire regions, and at times republics, were ruled by these new mafia-like personal principalities (the best-known example being the notorious "Uzbek case", which saw even Brezhnev's son-in-law jailed). But very often the threads led to Moscow, into Brezhnev's entourage, so these cases were closed. As time went by, the leaders found it harder and harder to fight corruption: after all, their sole weapon of power—the party-administrative apparatus—was simultaneously the main source of corruption. It was a vicious circle. Subsequently this process contributed to the disintegration of the USSR much more than ethnic conflicts: the fragmentation of the USSR was caused primarily by the fragmentation of the party-administrative apparatus, while local "nationalism" was exploited only by local authorities. This explains why in 1992 all the breakaway "independent" republics ended up under the rule of the local party *nomenklatura.*

Nationalism *per se*, "ethnic conflicts"—all this was a commonplace matter; these things could not be rooted out in the Soviet empire either by propaganda about "friendship of the peoples" or by repressions. By the 1980s, with a weakening of the CC's control over local apparatuses, the situation began to become more acute. Andropov reported on this in December 1980 (30 December 1980*, St 243/8):

Materials received by the KGB of the USSR indicate that in re-cent times there have been increasing negative nationalist pro-cesses and crimes committed on this basis among certain cate-gories of the indigenous population of the Karachay-Cherkessia Autonomous Region. The nature of these processes, alongside other factors, is influencing hostile elements among the older generation that participated in armed struggle against the So-viet system. Idealizing the past moribund traditions and cus-toms of their people, they use all means to incite feelings of "grievance" toward Soviet power in their milieu for alleged "per-secution of Karachays," speculating on the fact of their ban-ishment to Central Asian republics in the years of the Great Patriotic War.

The situation is further influenced negatively by existing firm familial ties and religious anachronisms. Self-proclaimed mul-lahs (of whom more than 100 have been detected) attempt to affirm Islamic positions. ...

The existence of such moods among young people often grow into open hatred of Russians, which leads to incidents of brazen hooliganism, rapes, and group brawls that could turn into mass disorder at any time. In 1979 alone, law and order agencies in the region recorded 33 cases of rapes of Russian women and those of other nonlocal nationalities; over 9 months of this year there were 22 analogous crimes and 36 cases of assault. Such occurrences are frequently accompanied by cynical shouts such as: "... This will happen to all Russians!", "Kill the Russians!", "Get out of our country!" and suchlike.

The situation in the region is also negatively influenced by shared economic interests and parochialism. There are many known instances of certain Karachay managers going to any lengths to get rid of workers of other nationalities and replac-ing them with their own relatives or close cronies. This results in the frequent misuse of official positions and similar negative social manifestations, which paints a picture of lawlessness.

Naturally, the CC ordered "improvement of the organizational party and educational work among the population." What else was there to do?

It was a really amazing system: it was easier for it to occupy a neighboring country, suppress a full-fledged national rebellion in another, or, on the contrary, incite a revolution on the other side of the globe than to supply its own people with salt. In accordance with the CC's secret instructions, millions of Western simpletons turned against their governments, but it proved unable to control its own administrative apparatus. As for managing the economy of their own country, this was something it never learned over seventy years. All the CC was capable of doing was ordering, issuing instructions to "increase," "raise," "broaden," and vote "yes" unanimously. It could also raise prices (11 June 1979*, St 162/67), and if these "feasible measures" failed to yield the required results, it could seek out scapegoats and subject them to "strict punishment."

The Secretariat of the CC of the CPSU advises that it has been decided to raise retail prices as of 1 July 1979 for the following (on average):

Articles made of gold—by 50 percent;
Articles made of silver—by 95 percent;
Articles made from natural fur—by 50 percent;
Carpets and carpet articles—by 50 percent;
Light passenger automobiles—by 18 percent;
Imported furniture—by 30 percent.

Councils of Ministers of union republics, the Ministry of Trade of the USSR, and ministries and agencies owning public catering establishments are simultaneously ordered to increase markups in restaurants, cafés, and similar establishments by an average of 100 percent in the evenings, and to raise the prices for beer sold in restaurants, cafés, and other public catering establishments by an average of 45 percent.

The CC of the CPSU and the Council of Ministers of the USSR have been forced to adopt these measures due to difficulties balancing the growth of the financial incomes of the population with the volume of production of consumer goods and services, and the need to regulate the trade in scarce commodities as well as to increase the struggle against speculation and bribery.

Despite previous rises in prices for gold and silver articles, carpets, fur articles, automobiles, and imported furniture, demand for them exceeds supply. Trade in these commodities involves lengthy queueing and frequent breaches of trade regulations. Subpurchasers and black marketeers use this situation for personal gain and corrupt salespeople with bribes. In their letters to the CC CPSU and the Council of Ministers of the USSR the working people criticize such occurrences, and call for the restoration of order. The most effective means of solving this problem is increasing productivity and regulating the sale of scarce goods. Significant efforts are being made to this end. For example, the manufacture of carpets has risen from 30 to 67 million square meters, that is by 2,2 times, since 1970. The sale of automobiles to the population for that period increased by 9.5 times. However, the production of a number of commodities still fails to meet demand, and with regard to others, market funds cannot be increased in the necessary amount due to insufficient currency means (imported goods) or natural resources (natural furs, articles made from precious metals).

Therefore raising prices is a regrettable but necessary measure to regulate trade. In order to minimize the impact on the vital interests of workers, prices are only being raised on articles that do not constitute primary needs. Furthermore, the old prices for gold dentistry disks remain unchanged, and in view of the higher prices, compensation is increased for wedding rings for couples being married for the first time (up to 70 rubles per person). With the rise in prices for articles made of natural fur, retail prices for children's items and items made from rabbit fur or sheepskin remain unaltered (with the exception of fur coats).

[. . .]

The announcement of the changes in prices shall be made by the State Committee on Prices of the USSR in the press on 1 July 1979. Party committees should provide timely information to party activists and establish control over the implementation of means for the review of prices and organize the necessary clarifying work to the population. Should various conjectures and rumors arise regarding mass rises in retail prices, as has occurred in the past, refute them decisively. Activists must be oriented firmly and the population must be made aware that there will be no rise in prices other than those listed in the report of the State Committee on Prices.

In view of the forthcoming rise in retail prices, the CC CPSU considers it necessary to stress the extreme importance of the maximum expansion of the production of consumer goods, ensuring the precise fulfilment of confirmed plans for their manufacture and improved quality, the timely commissioning of new capacities, broadening the sphere of consumer services and improvements in the organization of trade.

I don't know about "maximum expansion," but every party activist took the prior warning to heart and stampeded to buy up gold, fur articles, carpets and other scarce goods. They made the most of their "affordable demands" as quickly as possible. How else could it have turned out?

Later, after the official announcement, a fully predictable speculation began in gold disks for dentures and the alteration of children's fur coats into adult attire. The CC's care about old people, children, and young folks is even rather touching, but did it not realize what boundless possibilities its care was providing for the abuse of office and ideal conditions for the black market?

This is just one relatively small example of how a party-ruled state is incompatible with economics.

5.21 Bankruptcy

So much has been written about the Soviet economy that there is no need to dwell on it here, especially as I have devoted numerous pages to this subject in a previous book.[291] The essence of the matter is sufficiently simple: either the party manages economic processes, or the market does. There is no possible third way, for these two versions are incompatible: either the welfare of the people depends upon persistence in work and demand for production, and career success—based on their own abilities (where there is no place for the party), or it depends on loyalty to the party and connections with the management (in which case there is no room for economic development). Yet even now, when this simple truth has been proved beyond all doubt by the collapse of the Soviet economy, there are still people who refuse to face that fact. For example, there is talk about some "Chinese model." There is no such thing as a "Chinese model"; there is a period of disintegration of party power in China. Just look at how many party functionaries are executed in China every year for corruption. How else could it be? The more influence market forces have on people's lives, the less power is exercised by the party. Corruption is the only way the party can participate in the economy, the market manifestation of its power. But this signals the beginning of the disintegration of the party, and of the entire system alongside it. Therefore, even knowing practically nothing about China, I can make a confident prediction that the communist system will disappear there just as it disappeared in the USSR and its satellites. And soon enough at that.

The Western leftist intellectual "elite" did not want to accept that the crisis of the Soviet system in the 1980s was first of all a crisis of socialism. On the contrary, this intelligentsia even took heart, and prosocialist forces went on the attack after the Soviet collapse; you see, the "bad" Soviet model only impeded them, throwing the shadow of totalitarian crimes over them, but now the time was ripe for the "good" model. But there are no "models" of socialism, there are only various scenarios for the failure of the economy. A country can be brought to ruin either quickly and radically, or slowly and irreversibly (with all versions of "models" between these extremes). The very expression "socialist economy" is a contradiction in terms. The basic idea of socialism is the idea of "fair distribution" of a product and not its creation, due to which any model works toward attrition: it distributes while there is something to distribute. When all

---

[291]Vladimir Bukovsky, *USSR: From Utopia to Disaster*, published in France (1990), in Germany and Italy (1991), and in Mexico (1992).

the wealth accrued over centuries has been distributed and those capable of generating wealth have been destroyed one way or another, the result is the attrition of natural resources and increase in the national debt up to the point of bankruptcy.

The Soviet model of socialism was radical: the principle of distribution was taken to its logical limit, where the state carried out the central planning of both demand and supply. It lasted so long simply because Russia is a fabulously rich country. Even now, after seventy-five years of the most rapacious robbery of its resources, it is still immensely wealthy with oil, gas, coal, ores, gold, diamonds, timber, and God knows what else. The laziest ruler could rule over it without a care in the world and with no crises. It required an "idea" to bring about an economic collapse. Socialism was just such a profound idea; it did not so much drain as bankrupt the country, causing an incredible delay in development. The "fairer" the distribution of profits and the less competition, the less intense production became and the less need there was for modernization. The economy arising on this principle was extremely extensive: it grew solely in breadth, consuming disproportionately huge resources. Consequently it proved incapable of intensifying its exploitation of these resources. Thus by the 1960s there was an insufficiency of manpower, by the 1970s of arable land, and by the 1980s of fuel, energy and oil, although all these existed in nature. But the system proved unable to exploit its own natural resources effectively.

This plus fantastic military expenses (according to current data, more than half the economy was engaged in work for military needs), the growing cost of the empire, and foreign policy adventures show that the collapse of the Soviet system was only a question of time. Knowing how all accountability in the USSR was built on write-ups, it is ridiculous to cite official Soviet statistics. Nevertheless, by the 1980s even these indicators began to show alarming signals. No matter how the administrative apparatus quibbled, the fact was that the growth of the economy and the productivity of labor had fallen to zero at a time when investments were beginning to make losses: by 1978 one ruble of investment yielded a return of a mere eighty-three kopecks.[292]

By comparison, the 1980s were years of tempestuous economic growth in the West due to the so-called "conservative revolution." For the first time in postwar history there were leaders of a definite antisocialist tendency (Reagan, Thatcher), and they made the dismantling of socialism the foundation of their program. The lowering

---

[292]Vladimir Yegorov, *Out of a Dead End into the Unknown: Notes on Gorbachev's Perestroika.* Chicago, IL: Edition q, 1993.

of taxes and expenditure in the state sector, privatization of enterprises and entire branches of industry formerly nationalized by socialists, the dismantling of social security systems and strict monetarism—all these factors together brought about an intensification of production and economic growth. Moreover, after these reforms, other countries had to follow whether they liked it or not. Otherwise they would lag behind. In those years, let us note, not only the USSR and its clients faced insolvency—all the socialist countries in Europe and the third world went bankrupt. Even countries with socialist governments had to abandon their traditional policies and follow in the footsteps of the hated Thatcher.

It is a curious phenomenon that despite the rabid, almost pathological hatred of the intelligentsia, the overwhelming majority of the people in the USA and the UK voted stubbornly for Reagan and Thatcher, even though the reforms they initiated proceeded far from smoothly. People realized that these reforms were in their interest, as they freed them from the power of the "distributive elite," from state leveling. Socialism as an idea was finished; it did not even attract the unemployed.

This meant that the intelligentsia began to lose their influence. The changes in attitudes and discretization of the intellectual "elite" was caused, in no small way, by the explosion of new communications technology, especially the appearance of cable and satellite television and private television and radio stations. If the leftist "elite" could still control three or four television channels (mainly state-run ones), the appearance of hundreds of commercial channels ruled out ideological control over information. And in what else lay the power of the intelligentsia, apart from its ability to manipulate public opinion?

Paradoxical as it might sound, it is impossible to dispute the fact that the "conservative revolution" actually expanded democracy, allowing the lower strata of society a wider freedom of choice, and with it power. Naturally, there were some minuses to this state of affairs, some costs. For example, a direct result of the commercialization of life was a fall in culture, even its bankruptcy. This is undoubtedly regrettable, but the fault was evident: the "carriers" of culture were too deceitful and egotistic. Yet because of the drop in culture its eternal parasite, leftist utopianism, that ersatz religion of the intelligentsia, also lost power. It has not yet died completely; it is in its death throes, taking on increasingly absurd forms such as trendy ecological concern and feminism. It will still inflict harm on many people, but it will have no place in the next century, just as there is no place left for socialism in the current one. It seems to be the end of that period in our history when the "elite" lorded over everything, because the same thing has occurred in the sphere of ideas, culture, and information as happened in the economy: the dictatorship of the producer became the dictatorship of the consumer.

These changes were like a death knell to the Soviet leaders. Their clients were bankrupt, their ideological allies were losing influence, and global development, making a mockery of Marxism, brought about a crisis of socialism instead of a crisis of capitalism. Even technological progress changed from an ally into an opponent of their system: they had enough trouble jamming Western radio stations, yet now there was the threat of the direct satellite transmission of television. The mushrooming spread of video recorders created a new form of ideological sabotage—pirated cassettes of Western films (19 April 1982, 782-A). For the rest of the world, the appearance of personal computers was a step forward, but for the Soviet regime it was a new headache; halting the flood of information from the outside world and restraining the circulation of samizdat became even harder. But progress was unstoppable. I recall a turbulent discussion in the Soviet press in 1985 and 1986: Does a Soviet citizen need a personal computer? The ideologists were against, the military was for. Contemporary military technology is based entirely on digital control, the military pointed out, but if a Western conscript is computer-savvy since childhood, a Soviet one is not. The military won.

The threat of the military falling behind, which arose in the 1980s due to Reagan's rearmament program, was the main argument in favor of the need for reform. Nothing would have forced the Soviet leaders to venture on reforms apart from the threat of losing their superpower status, and with it their influence in the world. This threat arose mainly because of the very nature of socialism: its economic base is incompatible with its global ambitions. The USSR had entered the "arms race" with an economy that was already creaking at the seams, and now they burst completely. Only when there was nothing left, when ruin was inevitable, did they take the desperate step toward "reform." As I wrote in my 1982 brochure:[293]

> Once you get on the back of a tiger, it is almost impossible to get off again. The effort at an internal liberalization may prove fatal. The amount of hatred that has built up in the country over 65 years of the socialist experiment is immense, the results of any reform are so unpredictable and the more so the destruction of the power of that clique and their unbelievable privileges (or

---

[293]"The Peace Movement and the Soviet Union" (1982), https://www.commentarymagazine.com/article/the-peace-movement-the-soviet-union/

even their physical annihilation) are so probable in a weakening of the central authority, that it is hard to imagine the leaders toying with liberal ideas. Only the threat of an unavoidable and imminent demise could force the Soviet rulers to implement serious internal reforms.

This fact is indisputable; it has been acknowledged openly by former Soviet leaders, workers in the apparatuses of the Central Committee, the KGB, leading economists and generals.[294] But it will never be acknowledged by the Western establishment, because admitting that the hated and accursed "arms race" brought about the full destruction of the threat of a world war, a global confrontation, and the very partition of the world into conflicting camps would be equal to their suicide.

The situation was paradoxical: if information from West to East used to be blocked by any means, now information going in the opposite direction was blocked just as thoroughly. Russian books, articles, information in the press confirming the above were not published in the West. Even the declaration of the last Soviet Minister of Foreign affairs in communist times, Bessmertnykh, made at Princeton University in the USA claiming that President Reagan's Strategic Defense Initiative hastened the end of the USSR,[295] was barely reported by the American press (a single article in the *Washington Post*[296] that was largely ignored by all other newspapers). Yet how much noise, what screams broke out in that same American press when that program was announced! The scientific establishment blocked any development of this program, and those few nonconformist scientists who agreed to participate in it were ostracized by their colleagues. But in this instance, total silence. The "free" press remained mute and the scientific world pretended that nothing had happened. The establishment remained the establishment, the nonconformists remained nonconformists and "renegades." It would seem that if there were to be any sense in the Nobel Peace Prize, it should be awarded now to those who devised the SDI, who were not afraid to take part in it. But no, the Nobel Peace Prize would go to "concerned" physicians, whose only merit was that they frightened the populace with the horrors of nuclear war under the guidance of the sage CC.

---

[294]Yevgeny Novikov and Patrick Bascio, *Gorbachev and the Collapse of the Soviet Communist Party: The Historical and Theoretical Background*. New York: Peter Lang cop. 1994. pp. 66, 125–126.

[295]Alexander Bessmertnykh, "Retrospective on the End of the Cold War," a conference held at Princeton University, 23 February 1993.

[296]https://www.washingtonpost.com/archive/politics/1993/02/27/sdi-chernobyl-helped-end-cold-war-conference-told/

However, the SDI is the most vivid and best-known example of Reagan's policy in the first half of the 1980s. A book published recently in the USA by Peter Schweitzer, *Victory: The Reagan Administration's Secret Strategy That Hastened the Collapse of the Soviet Union.*[297] gives us a first look at the strategic plans of his administration in those years and shows that the arms race, Star Wars, etc. was only part of a general strategy directed quite consciously at bankrupting the Soviet regime. This included the campaign against Western financing of the Soviet gas pipeline to Europe, the tightening up of control over the leakage of scientific and technical information to the East (CoCom) and financial measures against the Soviet Union receiving Western loans. The same aims were served by a massive program of aid to Afghan mujahideen, underground Solidarity, the Nicaraguan Contras, and similar anticommunist movements all over the world: apart from purely moral or political considerations, the "Reagan doctrine" (as it was known at the time) saw its own task as making the cost of the empire intolerable for the USSR.

Even the arms race launched by Reagan's administration concentrated deliberately on weapons calling for an ever-higher technological level—that is, the field in which Soviet lagging was particularly hopeless. The SDI was only the culmination of this process, its most outstanding feature, one might say—its symbol. Nobody could even say for certain whether this program could be implemented or not from a purely technical viewpoint, but both sides—the USA and the USSR—focused on it, understanding perfectly that if the USA commenced on it, the USSR would have to join in this race, which was completely beyond its capability.

Finally, the most important aspect of this undeclared economic war—from my point of view at least—was manipulation of the oil market performed by the USA through Saudi Arabia. Oil and natural gas were the economic bases of the Soviet empire, its main source of hard currency. Problems with their extraction began by the end of the 1970s, and in the 1980s the drop in their yield had become marked.[298] The reasons for this were purely internal: insufficient investment in infrastructure and equipment alongside increasingly rapid rates of extraction caused a drop in the yield from oil fields, especially in the Tyumen region. However, the catastrophe came in 1985–1986, when the sharp decline in oil extraction in the USSR coincided with an equally drastic fall in oil prices on

---

[297]Peter Schweizer, *Victory: The Reagan Administration's Secret Strategy That Hastened the Collapse of the Soviet Union.* New York: Atlantic Monthly Press, 1994.
[298]20 April 1978 (Pb 101/VII)^; 22 June 1979 (St 164/60)^.

the international market. As a result, the Soviet Union lost more than a third of its hard currency income in one year—a shock that a healthy economy in a prosperous Western country would not have survived.

As the aforementioned book indicates, the drop in oil prices was not by mere chance;[299] it was the result of the lengthy and purposeful efforts of the Reagan administration. Back in 1983 the US Department of the Treasury submitted a report to the president recommending efforts toward achieving falling global oil prices:[300]

> A drop in international oil prices to $20 a barrel would lower U.S. energy costs by $71.5 billion per year. That would be a transfer of income to American consumers amounting to 1 percent of existing gross national product....
>
> A lower oil price would occur with either a drop in demand (not very likely) or a dramatic increase in production. Concerning the latter, the report noted that if Saudi Arabia and other countries 'with available oil reserves should step up their production and increase world output by... about 2.7 to 5.4 million barrels a day and cause the world price to fall by about 40%, the overall effect on the United States would be very beneficial.'

For Moscow, this would be a disaster:

> The report noted Moscow's heavy reliance on energy exports for hard currency. By Treasury Department calculations, every one-dollar rise in the price of oil meant approximately $500 million to $1 billion in extra hard currency for the Kremlin. But the reverse was also true: dropping prices meant plunging incomes. And Moscow, unlike other producers, could not raise production to increase earnings.

Over all subsequent years the Reagan administration's task was to convince the Saudis to do just that: increase production in order to bring oil prices down to the desired level. Intensive lobbying of the Saudi royal family included such measures as reinforcing their defenses by selling them the latest military hardware (frequently against the wishes of Congress), American guarantees of security, and economic privileges. It must be said that the Saudis did not

---

[299]Peter Schweizer, emphVictory: The Reagan Administration's Secret Strategy That Hastened the Collapse of the Soviet Union. New York: Atlantic Monthly Press, 1994, pp. 140–144, 154–155, 179–181, 189–190, 203–205, 217–220, 232–233, 237–238, and 242–243.

[300]Schweizer (1994), pp. 141–142.

try too hard to resist: increasing oil production was in their interests. It brought money into their coffers, helped friends and ruined
enemies—Iran, Libya and the USSR.[301]

> August 1985, a stake was driven silently through the heart of
> the Soviet economy. ...
>
> In the first few weeks of the Saudi push, daily production jum-
> ped from less than 2 million barrels to almost 6 million. ...
>
> For the United States, the coming drop in oil prices was a boon
> —the equivalent of tens of billions of dollars being given to Amer-
> ican consumers. For the Kremlin, any drop in oil prices was
> damaging to the economy. But in 1985 it was cataclysmic. So-
> viet hard currency reserves were strapped. Gold sales had been
> doubled in 1985 to keep the hard currency coming at the nec-
> essary level. Energy, being the bread and butter of the Soviet
> hard currency–earning machine (almost 80 percent), mattered
> more than any other commodity to the health of the economy.
> ...
>
> Shortly after Saudi oil production rose, the international price
> of oil sank like a stone in a pond. In November 1985, crude oil
> sold at over $30 a barrel: barely five months later it stood at
> $12. For Moscow, over $10 billion in valuable hard currency
> evaporated overnight, almost half its earnings.

This blow, from which the Soviet economy never recovered fully,
came at the most unpleasant moment: income from oil was earmarked to cover the first phase of Gorbachev's reforms, the so-called
"acceleration"—intensifying the economy by the purchase and commissioning of new equipment from abroad. Only such a massive
modernization program could help the Soviet leaders to retain the
status of a superpower, cope with the arms race and the increasing
cost of the empire, and prevent the "Polish disease" on the domestic front. The economic collapse turned them immediately into "reformers," "liberals," and "democrats." They needed an NEP, just like
Lenin in 1921: an alliance with the West, just like Stalin in 1941;
and détente, just like Brezhnev in the 1970s. Simply speaking, they
badly needed a respite in the Cold War, without which they would
not get Western loans and technology. In order to achieve this, help
was needed from old allies: the leftist establishment of the USA and
European Mensheviks—so that once more, for the umpteenth time,
they could make the West believe in the sudden metamorphosis of
the Soviet regime.

But its Western friends were also keen for "reforms" of the
regime, for a new liberal image of the USSR. However much they

---

[301]Schweizer (1994), pp. 242–243.

now talked of "bad" and "good" models, the collapse of socialism in the West was a catastrophe for them, too, exposing their traitorous role in the half-century-old battle of humanity against the threat of totalitarian enslavement. Just as the defeat of Nazi Germany exposed the "peacemakers" and collaborationists of that time, the collapse of the USSR destroyed all the cunning self-justifications of its apologists and fellow-travelers, all the theories of the "moderates" and the "prudent":

- So there was no need to "coexist" with evil, if it took so little effort to conquer it?

- So there was no need to "struggle for peace" if it could be won without a single bullet being fired?

- So all that was needed was to throw aside demagogy and begin serious opposition to evil in order to bring it down?

- If so, why was this not done twenty years earlier? How many countries could have been saved from ruin, how many millions of human lives could have been preserved, how many misfortunes could have been averted?

It goes without saying that those Western circles that would have been required to answer these unpleasant questions were not overjoyed by this possibility. For them, and the Soviet leaders, there was only one way out: prevent the total collapse of the communist regime. There is no other explanation of the absurdity of the next five years, when communism was suffering obvious agonies while the whole world tried to prolong its existence. This seeming absurdity was fueled by the exaggerated "Gorbymania" in the press, the mass euphoria regarding glasnost and perestroika, multimillion-dollar loans—all this was not stupidity or naivety, but a well-planned campaign. The result was almost unbelievable: a criminal regime, feared by the whole planet for more than half a century, drowning in the blood of entire peoples, disappeared without a trace, and those who had served it—both in the East and in the West—remained in power.

The regime was certainly doomed; it would not have lasted out the century, first of all because its basic idea was absurd, unnatural, a creation of the intelligentsia. It fell because of those who dared to challenge it, who refused to accept its dictates, be they in the mountains of Afghanistan or in the White House, on the Gdansk docks or in the Vatican, in the jungles of Africa or Soviet prisons.

And in the final account because of ordinary people who rejected the power of the rotten elites of the East and West.

While these elites continue to cling to power, this simple truth will not be acknowledged universally. General Jaruzelski shall remain the acclaimed savior of his homeland, Soviet-nurtured terrorists shall receive Nobel Peace Prizes, and war criminals who soaked Afghanistan in blood shall command the Russian army. More than anything, this will be sustained by the Gorbachev myth—the myth about "courageous reformers" in the Kremlin who saved the world from themselves. Something akin to the tale about the good king Louis XVI, who rescued France from the monarchy.

Chapter Six

The Revolution That Never Was

6.1 "Acceleration"

There are so many lies around Gorbachev and his "reforms" (not least those issuing from him), lies so fantastic that only documentary evidence can be believed. Even so, it must be remembered that the documents relating to his period in power have been painstakingly cleansed: after the failure of the August putsch in 1991, his cohorts destroyed as much as they could get their hands on. At the time of the Constitutional Court hearing, documents of this period were hidden and protected from us with special zeal. When I was writing this chapter almost twenty years ago, I did not have the documents on many of these subjects, and I had to describe a whole range of aspects of his rule using mainly open sources and indirect data.

Getting anything later was not easy, either. The archives remained closed, and I was barred from entering Russia for fifteen years after the publication of this book. Nonetheless, there were researchers — Russian and Western, — who continued this work. For example, an immense collection of secret documents of the Gorbachev period was copied and brought out of Russia by Pavel Stroilov. The story of this archive and its "hijacking" has been described in the press, so there is no need to go into details. Although the originals of these documents remain in the Presidential Archive (the former archive of the Politburo) and are top secret to this day, Gorbachev and his assistants, upon leaving the Kremlin, copied and stored them in the Gorbachev Foundation for "friendly" researchers. After a while, the existence of this archive became known to the Kremlin, and in 2003 Gorbachev received a demand to black out those documents once again. But there were several years in the interim when control was lax, and Pavel made good use of it. He likes to say that he was my "spy" in the Russian archives, which he really was. For a whole year, practically on a daily basis, he sent me huge files of Gorbachev documents, so we now have much more material relating to this period than ever before. It is another matter that when he came to the West, Pavel came up against the same wall of resistance that I had encountered in my time. The world stubbornly refuses to hear about the secrets of the Cold War, especially its final years.

In any event, even those few documents that were initially at my disposal were enough to overturn the myth of Gorbachev the courageous reformer, a liberal and a democrat, who turned the tide of history despite the opposition of reactionaries and dogmatists (19 February 1986*, 321-Ch/ov):

> The activity of the Committee for State Security of the USSR was fully subordinated to fulfilling the demands of the Communist Party in terms of reliably ensuring the security of the Soviet state and society.
>
> State security agencies implemented a complex suite of measures using *chekist* resources to ensure universal cooperation in implementing the decisions of the April and October (1985) Plenums of the CC CP for accelerating the socio-economic development of the USSR, the overall progress of Soviet society, reinforcing the positions of the USSR in the international arena and counteracting the aggressive policies of imperialism.

Such annual reports on the work of the KGB were submitted to the General Secretary from time immemorial. In fact, this was a simple formality—the measures recorded there were reported to the General Secretary both when they were planned, and when they were implemented. For us, this formality is useful in that it gives us precise information on the main directions of Soviet policy at a given time.

For instance, looking at the priorities set for the KGB in 1985 by the new General Secretary, we see exactly what his real intentions were. The most important point in Chebrikov's report is intelligence, which is indicative in itself (19 February 1986*, 321-Ch/ov):

> The main efforts of intelligence were aimed at improving the quality and operative delivery of information on the policies of the ruling circles in the USA, other NATO countries, Japan and China concerning the international positions of our country and the peaceful initiatives of the Soviet state.
>
> The main focus of attention was on information regarding the military and strategic plans of our opponent, its plans for achieving military superiority over the USSR, signs of preparations for a possible sudden launching of a missile and nuclear war and other problems affecting the vital interests of the Soviet Union and other socialist and friendly countries.
>
> ... On the basis of the party's demands for accelerating the scientific and technological development of the Soviet economy, measures were implemented to raise the effectiveness of scientific and technological intelligence gathering. A significant amount of documented information has been obtained regarding new achievements and inventions in the spheres of science,

equipment and technology in leading capitalist countries. Great attention was paid to the acquisition of new materials and samples, preferably of an applicable nature. More than 40 thousand items of information and 12 thousand samples were obtained. Allowing for the main tasks and under instructions from the State Committee of the Council of Ministers of the USSR on military and industrial issues, more than 15 thousand materials and more than 6500 types of samples were obtained. The Ministry of Defense and the General Staff of the Armed Forces of the USSR have been sent 1610 materials and 309 types of samples. [...]

Intelligence has carried out systematic measures of cooperation with the implementation of the foreign policy initiatives of the Soviet state and its allies, and exposure of the aggressive policies of the USA and their allies. Active measures were taken aimed at discrediting the American "Star Wars" plan, sharpening and deepening inter-imperialist contradictions, and activation of the anti-war movement in Western counties.

It is obvious that the emphasis is placed on a more energetic implementation of the former policy of scientific and technological espionage, disinformation campaigns and the "struggle for peace." This is quite in tune with the course proposed by Gorbachev to his colleagues upon his election as General Secretary (11 March 1985, Pb):

GORBACHEV. First of all I would like to say that the most important issue for us is that today's meeting of the Politburo is taking place in a spirit of unity. We are going through a very complicated and crucial time. Our economy needs much more dynamism. This dynamism is vital for our democracy, the development of our foreign policy. [...] I see my primary task in our common search for new decisions, ways of promoting the future development of our country, ways of enhancing the economic and defensive might of the Motherland, and improving the lives of our people.

[...]

We do not need a policy change. It is the right, correct and genuine Leninist policy. We need to step up the tempo, move forward, pinpoint inadequacies and overcome them, and have a clear view of our bright future. (Italics mine—V.B.)

In other words, "acceleration" was in order, as the party announced a month later at the April Plenum. Correspondingly, in matters of ideology and foreign policy it actually envisaged a hardening of the old course rather than its liberalization.

Counter-intelligence has directed its efforts toward the timely discovery and frustration of the intelligence-subversive intentions and actions of the opponent's special services against the USSR. Successful measures have been carried out regarding the broadening of operative positions in its agencies and foreign anti-Soviet formations.

[...] An end has been put to the espionage activity of a number of staff members of various residents under the cover of diplomatic representations of the USA, UK and France, eight of whom have been expelled from the USSR. One hundred and thirteen intelligence-gathering trips over the country by military agents have been aborted, as well as efforts by 29 spies to penetrate zones with particularly important defense and other objects.

[...]

A great deal of attention was paid to measures for protecting the Soviet economy and science from subversive schemes of the opponent's special services. A number of successful measures were carried out to prevent the attempts of the USA and their partners to disrupt the foreign economic and scientific-technical ties of the USSR. [...] The criminal activity of certain officials in foreign trade organizations, who had been bribed by foreign firms to supply trade secrets and harm our economy, has been uncovered and terminated.

... Agencies of military counter-intelligence have rendered all-round assistance to the commanding and political sections in supporting the constant combat readiness of the Armed Forces of the USSR and ensuring the preservation of military secrecy. [...] The KGB of the USSR has pursued a consistent policy for strengthening international cooperation with the security agencies of fraternal socialist countries, which enabled the successful resolution of intelligence and counter-intelligence tasks. A great deal of assistance was rendered to Afghanistan in crushing armed counter-revolution and stabilizing the situation in the country, and also to Nicaragua—by improving the effectiveness of the struggle against American mercenaries. There has been further strengthening of cooperation with the special services of a number of developing countries.

There was a marked increase in political repressions, or "the struggle against the ideological diversions of the class enemy" as Chebrikov called it. This included reinforcing border security (1646 "violators" were detained), the "prevention of subversive ideological actions by emissaries of foreign anti-Soviet, nationalistic, Zionist and clerical organizations" (300 expelled, 322 forbidden entry into the USSR), the liquidation of nationalistic organizations in Ukraine and the Baltic states (25), and the "prevention of the formation of 93 youth groups on an ideologically detrimental basis." Just the number of "authors and disseminators of anonymous and anti-Soviet materials" caught was 1275 people, of whom 97 were imprisoned. Indeed, the "harvest" was unusually high in 1985:

> Indicted on criminal charges: for especially dangerous state crimes—57 persons, other state crimes—417, other crimes —61. [...] Preventive-prophylactic measures were conducted with 15274 persons.

This deliberate "hardening" had many purposes, including preparing public opinion for a more grateful reception of the subsequent "liberalization" (should such be required), and ridding the country of those who might make use of it. Apart from that, the regime appeared to be raising the stakes before beginning dialogue with the West, in order to make insignificant concessions in exchange for vitally important ones. Before entering into any dangerous games, the leaders seemed to be making a last attempt to probe the West for weakness: maybe there would be no need to take any risks?

But achieving their aim—the reanimation of détente—would probably require a much more delicate game, as they were well aware. At the same time, as if by chance and unrelated to the "hardening", was what Chebrikov referred to as "a complex suite of measures using *chekist* resources to ensure universal cooperation" with the plans of the Kremlin strategists. Thus, several months before Gorbachev's election as General Secretary, the Western press was flooded with materials hailing him as "young", "energetic", "liberal", "pro-Western" and so on. After his election, these praises knew no bounds. Gorbachev was served to the West as the best, if not last chance to "reach agreement", and his entire image was calculated to appeal to the Western consumer, especially the moderate left.

Not surprisingly, this campaign was promptly taken up by the leftist press, the socialists and social democrats. One of the first meetings of the new General Secretary was with a delegation from the Socialist International, and in April the counter-intelligence administration of the KGB instructed all its European residents to resume, with all speed, their somewhat faded contacts with their former partners in détente (9 April 1985*, 473/PR/54):[302]

---

[302] Christopher Andrew and Oleg Gordievsky, *Instructions from the Centre: Top Secret Files on KGB Foreign Operations 1975–1985*. London: Sceptre (pbk), 1993, Chapter 8, "The Socialist International", pp. 253.

Serious exacerbation of the international situation and the intensifying threat of war, evoked by the sharp increase in the aggressiveness of imperialist—above all, American—policy, the consistent peace-promoting line adopted by the Soviet Union, and the broadly based anti-war movement developing especially in West European countries, have combined to confront the Socialist International with the necessity of putting forward its own program to fight for peace and disarmament.

Such a program was announced in its most complete form at the sixteenth SI Congress, held in 1983, which declared that the "most fundamental" task of social democracy was to "ensure the survival of the human race". This task was, however, formulated as an appeal to the two "superpowers"—the USA and the USSR.

The Congress called on the USSR and the USA to reach agreement on the question of stopping the arms race, virtually repeating many of the specific proposals previously put forward more than once by the Soviet Union: for limiting and reducing strategic weapons; on nuclear weapons in Europe; on stopping the production of new kinds of weapons of mass destruction, banning chemical and biological weapons, demilitarization of the seabed and space, and establishing nuclear-free zones, etc."

[Cited here and further from the book by C. Andrew and O. Gordievsky in reverse translation].

This is precisely what the Politburo asked for in 1980 from the leaders of the Socialist International—Willy Brandt and Kalevi Sorsa (1 February 1980*, Pb 182/2). At that time, "blaming both superpowers" was acceptable as a convenient form of disguising the substantially pro-Soviet position of the Socialist International. Now such subtlety was unnecessary. The more so that the camouflage of "impartiality" did not save the Socialist International from a split between the northern "radical" wing (British Labourites and the German and Scandinavian social democrats) and the more pro-Atlantic "Roman group" (French, Italian and Portuguese socialists) (9 April 1985*, 473/PR/54).

While the Americans are speeding up the arms race and implementing their missile plans in Europe, differences between the member parties of the Socialist International on questions of war and peace became increasingly obvious. Different views between the leaders of the Socialist International, their waverings and inconsistencies on current key questions are firstly due to the truly opportunistic nature of the parties in this organization, as well as the presence of various groupings in their midst professing rightist, centrist and leftist views. [...] Nonetheless, despite these differences within the Socialist International and the outside pressure to which it was subjected, contemporary social democracy retains considerable political power and influence. Objectively, it makes a certain contribution to the struggle for peace and disarmament and a return to the policy of détente. Its representatives participate in various forums of protagonists of peace and frequently adopt close or identical positions to socialist countries.

All this provides certain possibilities for exercising a positive influence on the formation of the views of the Socialist International and its member parties regarding important international matters, firstly on questions of war and peace, thereby ensuring effective support in the struggle of our party for improving the international situation and terminating the arms race. With this purpose in sight, you must do everything in your power to expand our work with the leaders and prominent activists of socialist and social democratic parties in the countries where you live.

The proposed program envisaged a number of "active measures" aimed at sowing discord among NATO countries, increasing the influence of the "left wing" of the Socialist International in the campaign for the resurrection of détente by implementing the following proposals:[303]

- Take steps for more effective use and broadening of existing operative possibilities in the Bureau of the SI, in the headquarters of social democratic and socialist parties in West European countries;

- apply special efforts to reinforce the operative positions in SI parties that are in power or are participating in government coalitions in their countries, bearing in mind the aims that must be achieved in not just the framework of the SI, but in relation to other problems of international policy;

- increase work with youth organizations with a social democratic orientation, which occasionally take more radical positions than the parties themselves, especially among activists of similar organizations which may prove of interest in the future.

So alongside an external hardening of positions, there was a gradual preparation for a new turn toward détente, sweet dreams of which never died among European social democrats. This time all it

---

[303]9 April 1985* (473/PR/54), pp. 4–5.

took was to wave this carrot at the Menshevik donkey which, forgetting previous offences and lies, allowed itself to be hitched willingly to the Bolshevik wagon.

As for the Soviet leaders, their policy remained really "Leninist", unchanged since the 1970s at least. It is another matter that now, in view of the crisis, the proposal was to intensify it, in other words —gain their ends by any means.

6.2 "Reformers" and "Conservatives"

It must be admitted that the Soviet leaders were past masters at pulling the wool over people's eyes. Whispered rumors, obscure hints and at the best of times — the vague promises of the new General Secretary to "rebuild" something, were transformed immediately into already achieved "radical reforms." In reality, nothing happened: Soviet forces continued to destroy Afghan villages, political prisoners remained incarcerated, spies continued to steal Western technology, but now it appeared that the West was to blame for everything: it refused to meet the other side halfway, did not believe in benign intentions and refused to make concessions.

Even the Chernobyl disaster was not turned against Gorbachev and his regime, but against all other countries with nuclear power plants. He remained unaffected, although it was on his instructions that information about the meltdown was kept secret until the Finns and Swedes raised a hue and cry. For this alone many individual politicians would be cursed by public opinion, and in the West—imprisoned: but the result was that even more people were affected by radiation. Let us imagine that the President of the USA or the Prime Minister of the UK tried to conceal the fact of a radiation leak at a nuclear power plant—the cry that would have gone up is unimaginable. Yet in this case, the First of May demonstration in Kiev was not canceled—it was hoped that nobody would hear about what had happened. But the party bosses in Ukraine were getting their families out of harm's way by hurrying to send them to Moscow, as far as possible from Chernobyl.

All this was known to the Western press, but was served up in a totally different way: the poor Russians, what bad luck they had with Chernobyl—that is what having nuclear power plants leads to. Gorbachev's part in this story was not even discussed. The inflated Western "Gorbymania" was built on quicksand, on the "credit of trust" toward one person whom nobody really knew. It was just as absurd and irrational as the campaign for nuclear disarmament, and was implemented mainly by the same forces. The sole difference was that this time everyone else accepted this enforced game, concerned only with not "harming perestroika" and not telling people the truth. Doubts and skepticism almost amounted to sacrilege, which was risked by very few.

"Give him the benefit of the doubt" was the Western refrain, although nobody could actually explain the grounds for such doubt. Gorbachev was a man who had climbed the ladder of the customary party career, and beginning with 1978 as a secretary of the CC and later Politburo member, was complicit in all the crimes of the regime. All that was left to do was to endow the new General Secretary with certain attributes. For example, much was made of how his wife was "modern", "pro-Western", and a "philosopher" to boot (she taught Marxism-Leninism!). There were no bounds to the delight caused by the circumstance that she spent most of her time in Paris shopping and buying valuables from Cartier with an American Express credit card. At the same time, often on the same pages of the newspapers, there were denunciatory articles about Imelda, the wife of the Philippine dictator Ferdinand Marcos; just think, the country is suffering from hunger, and here she is buying designer clothes and thousands of pairs of shoes!

It was a disinformation campaign *par excellence*. As for the culmination of their efforts to overcome Western resistance—the meeting in Reykjavik—the Soviets performed, observing all the rules of high drama. The world held its breath: it seemed as though the very existence of the world was hanging by a thread. Entire religious communities prayed for the success of this meeting, as if on the brink of the Apocalypse. In fact, there was nothing special going on; top-level meetings had become quite commonplace by this time. The putative agenda of the meeting did not contain anything new—the same dreams of nuclear disarmament which the Soviet Union needed and the West did not. But it came to pass somehow that that it seemed that everything was about to be resolved. And if it was not, this would be solely Reagan's fault. Surprising, isn't it? The crisis was in the USSR, they were bankrupt, they had to save themselves, but for some reason it was the Americans who were expected to make concessions.

The astounding fact is that they almost pulled it off, fell just a little short of the target because they over-egged the pudding and became too greedy. Total nuclear disarmament, to which Reagan was almost ready to agree, was not enough for them: they latched on to the "Star Wars" (SDI) program. The result was that they went away empty-handed, and relations with America became more complicated (22 October 1986*, Pb).

GORBACHEV. We need to exchange opinions about measures regarding the new hostile action of the US administration. Developments after Reykjavik show that our "friends" in the USA have no constructive program and are doing all they can to inflame the situation. Moreover, their actions are crude and they behave like bandits.

[Mikhail] SOLOMENTSEV. Yes, they behave like highway robbers.

GORBACHEV. It is useless to expect any constructive actions or proposals from the US administration. In this situation we need to gather more propaganda aces, pursue clarifying endeavors addressed to the American and international community. This frightens the men in Washington. [US] Customs are withholding materials with my addresses to the press conference in Reykjavik and on Soviet television for three days.

[Alexander] YAKOVLEV. I had a phone call from comrade Bugayev who told me that American customs are still impounding these materials.

GORBACHEV. We need to apply more pressure on the American administration, making our positions known to the public and pointing out the responsibility of the American side for the failure to reach agreement on matters concerning the limitation and liquidation of nuclear arms.

Reagan and his entourage have found nothing better to do recently than undertake yet another hostile action—the expulsion of 55 Soviet diplomats. Five of our staffers have been declared *persona non grata* because, as Washington explains it, this was in retaliation to our expulsion of 5 American diplomats, and the 50 are added under the pretext of parity in levels of American and Soviet diplomatic representations.

This hostile anti-Soviet act cannot be ignored. We should not hesitate to take resolute steps. The Americans are making threats and state that if we resort to counter-measures, they will take further steps against our diplomatic personnel in the USA. Well, I think that in view of the limited nature of Soviet-American contacts, our embassy in the USA will be able to cope with its tasks.

We need to devise serious proposals. What can be done specifically? We should remove those of our people who are working in our American embassy as service staff. Furthermore, we should limit the number of visits to the US embassy in Moscow by American representatives on business trips. At present, some 500 American citizens arrive along this channel every year. Finally, there is the question of entry visas to guests of the American ambassador, up to 200 every year; this should be decided on the basis of parity. Our people rarely go on business and visit our ambassador as guests. In future, such trips should be on the grounds of strict parity.

Generally speaking, it looks as though my words to the President in Reykjavik are being confirmed; that the normalization of Soviet-American relations is a matter for future generations.

[...]

GORBACHEV. Do the comrades have any doubts regarding these proposals?

POLITBURO MEMBERS. No.

DOBRYNIN. It would also be feasible to determine the question of consulates in Kiev and New York.

GROMYKO. Under present circumstances, it would be better not to press this matter. There is no sense in it right now.

GORBACHEV. We should put a freeze on deciding this question. As for our general line of behavior, we need to act calmly, but decisively. This is important not only from the point of view of Soviet-American relations, but for international relations as a whole. If the Americans talk like this to the Soviet Union, just imagine what they will do to other countries.

I have spoken with Nikolai Ivanovich [Ryzhkov]. We should abstain from buying grain from the Americans.

GROMYKO. It is probably better not to mention this in our declaration, just carry it out *de facto*.

SOLOMENTSEV. Our document should include the figures mentioned by comrade Shevardnadze.

DOBRYNIN. The actions of the Americans against our military attaché's office are unprecedented.

GORBACHEV. We should also expel all the American military personnel.

CHEBRIKOV. We have another gambit in reserve that could be employed if necessary. As I have already informed the Politburo, we have found numerous bugging devices in our representations in the USA. This fact could be publicized in order to expose American espionage, hold a press conference demonstrating these devices.

GROMYKO. And how many of our bugging devices have they found in their representations?

CHEBRIKOV. Only one. The score is in our favor — 1:150.

GORBACHEV. This should be borne in mind.

SHEVARDNADZE. When should we publicize our declaration on the matter at hand?

GORBACHEV. As soon as the document is ready. We shall take a look at it and hand it over to the radio and television at once, as well as having it published in the press.

POLITBURO MEMBERS. Agreed.

GORBACHEV. I was thinking of holding a press conference today and show in which direction the Americans are pushing
after Reykjavik. Expose their lies and cheating. But it appears
that after the hostile action of the US administration, this is not
the right time. It would probably be better to forget the press
conference, but make a televised address to our people.

RYZHKOV. Yes, that would be right.

GORBACHEV. I shall not be making any proposals in the address. So there is really no need to have a special circulation
of the text. Within the framework of the position we have determined, it should be stressed that the US administration is fully
responsible for the breakdown of the Reykjavik agreements and
is undertaking deceptive maneuvers in order to distort facts and
confuse the public. It could also be mentioned that the development of events after Reykjavik shows that Reagan is unable
to manage his gang.

GROMYKO. That could be said, but in a form that would not
exonerate Reagan himself.

GORBACHEV. Yes, Reagan is acting like a liar. We need to find
the right formulation for this matter.

Do the comrades have any other proposals?

POLITBURO MEMBERS. No.

So who was finally blamed in the West? First of all, naturally,
that reactionary Reagan, who refused to "abandon the Cold War
mentality" and back down over the universally-hated "Star Wars"
program. And secondly, the "conservatives" and "reactionaries" in
the Politburo, whom the "reformer" Gorbachev still had to take into
account.

6.3   "New thinking"

However, the Kremlin leaders did not sulk for long: the crisis was
pressing. What could they do? — the attempt to get what they
wanted unceremoniously failed, so they had to carry on, and make
some concessions. Like it or not, the second phase of the plan had
to be launched under the name of glasnost and perestroika: human
rights, Afghanistan, "socialist pluralism", "socialist marketplace",
"a common European home".…

Now that the regime has collapsed, it is no longer a secret to
anyone in Russia that the so-called "new thinking" was devised by
various brain trusts of the CC long before Gorbachev's arrival on

the scene. This is now discussed and written about willingly by former party intellectuals—participants in this planning. Gorbachev confirmed this fact himself in 1988, when the failure of perestroika became obvious and there was a need to explain why the whole plan was so poorly thought through.

What do you mean, poorly thought through? It was properly thought through, and well before 1985: 110 research papers and drafts were submitted by then to the CC by different brain trusts.

We know today that supervision of the plans for "reform" of the Soviet regime was the responsibility of the International Department of the CC (and even under Yuri Andropov's control). Typically, the most daring ideas of these thinkers did not stray beyond the boundaries of Marxism: the concept was a certain revision of its "Leninist" version, bringing it closer to socialist democracy.

It is obvious what caused the search for such rapprochement. On one hand, by the end of the 1970s the imminent economic crisis was clearly evident, and it was imperative to find quick ways of averting it. First of all, it was vital to find ways of reviving détente which would grant access to Western aid in the form of loans and technology. On the other hand, the phenomenal success of détente at the beginning of the 1970s (and its unexpected collapse at the beginning of the 1980s) prompted the thought of the need for more substantial preparation, allowing for all the mistakes of the past. As we recall, originally détente was not the brainchild of Moscow, but Bonn (9 September 1969*, 2273-A); Moscow simply attempted to use it for its own ends, without changing anything on its domestic front. Combined with internal "reforms" of socialism and the relevant social democratic phraseology, détente became irresistible to the "northern" radicals and "Roman moderates" alike. Minimal alterations that posed no threat to the existence of the regime enabled achievement of the seemingly impossible: not only did they avert the crisis, but opened the way to "convergence" with the Menshevik West. Simply speaking, the reinforcement of Soviet influence in Europe.

What really hindered the full success of détente in the 1970s? Questions of human rights? The invasion of Afghanistan? The Polish crisis? Surely with a certain degree of flexibility, with the support of European social democracy and the leftist elite in the USA, this could be bypassed? As for the first issue, back in 1977 the current ambassador to the FRG, Valentin Falin, wrote to the CC about a possible solution (2 March 1977*, No. 74). Need it be said that the point at issue was not the introduction of democracy, but means for its successful imitation. Reporting that the partners in détente—the German social democrats–were not delighted by the campaign for human rights in socialist countries, he writes:

> The Social Democrats are already feeling the danger of anti-communist hysteria—the slogan of the CDS/CSU "freedom instead of socialism" shows that the SPD is not the last in line when the call goes out for a witch hunt. [...]
>
> They also note that the West was faster than the East to recognize that changes in the international climate shall not leave the internal climate in certain states unaffected. The NATO countries paid a considerable price for détente, but did not manage to cope with all the difficulties, including those of an ideological nature. But such difficulties are obvious in the West, as they have learned not to raise or accentuate the threshold of legality in the struggle of ideas in ordinary situations. Our social democratic friends say that socialist countries should have also taken into account the costs of restructuring international relations. [...]
>
> It must be said that discussions around the practice of work in socialist countries with dissidents and non-conformists are being conducted in circles that are loyal and friendly to the USSR and the CPSU. There are frequent questions that cannot be dismissed or passed off with general statements. For example, why are Picasso and Leger admired in the Soviet Union, while their own modernist painters are persecuted, and the works of many world-famous artists of the pre- and post-revolutionary period are not displayed or rarely displayed in exhibitions in our museums? Or—why is abstract and so-called experimental art recognized in Poland but persecuted in the USSR and some other socialist countries? Why do we accept certain compromises in music and ballet, but not in other cultural spheres? [...]
>
> Among other things, the legal and administrative practices of the FRG should be studied. The West German state enjoys a flexible and reliable means to avert and deal with undesirable activity, in which the emphasis is on prosecuting dissidents not for reasons of dissemination of information unwanted by the state, but for "anti-constitutional activity", breaches of public order, etc. The local system of court procedure is not uninteresting, as it allows an individual to be isolated for months or years before being sentenced, in fact to prosecute him long before the final examination of his case by a court at the highest level.
>
> This system functions successfully, as it is combined with a carefully thought-out glasnost and supplemented by other quasi-democratic attributes that allow the lid to be kept on the pot at an acceptable level. A considerable part of the work in

> suppressing opposition is still conducted under the overt and covert state supervision of the press, the Church, the school and bourgeois social organizations. For the latter, struggle against leftists in general and communism in particular was and is their main reason for existence. [...]

Let Falin's interpretation of the political system of the FRG remain on his conscience; the most important factor for us that his "political letter" was studied carefully by Gromyko, Andropov and the propaganda department of the CC, and the group of party intellectuals that developed the "alternative models" (I have no idea who made the above underlining in the text). Moreover, there is no doubt that the expressed ideas made a strong impression on the authorities, and Falin's career soared so that ten years later, when his dreams of the "creation of the appearance of self-cleansing and renewal of the system" began to surface, he was already head of the International Department.

However, Falin was not the only smart one in the ranks of the Soviet system. These ideas were already floating around, especially among that part of the Soviet elite which by virtue of its job was concerned with foreign policy—the KGB, the Ministry of Foreign Affairs, the International Department of the CC and their brain trusts. For instance, when Brezhnev's death was announced on 11 November 1982, the deputy of the head of the International Department of the CC, Anatoly Chernyaev, wrote in his diary about the program he expected Andropov to implement (Chernyaev's diary, 11 November 1982):

> The aim is to feed the people and restore their interest in work.
>
> Methods and main problems:
>
> 1. Liquidate Brezhnev's infrastructure—all those relatives, hangers-on, favorites and all those brought in from Moldavia and Dnepropetrovsk: the Trapeznikovs, Pavlovs [administrator of CC affairs at the time], Golikovs, Tyazhelnikovs, Schelkovs. ... Villas and out of town dachas, hunting reserves, excessive guards, hundreds if not thousands of menials. This is for the restoration of the moral authority of the leader.
>
> 2. Withdraw from Afghanistan.
>
> 3. Tell Jaruzelski to resolve his own problems and give everyone to understand that we shall not enter Poland under any circumstances.
>
> 4. Adopt a Khrushchev-style declaration of 1956 regarding socialist countries (the one that was violated immediately

in Hungary). Abandon the principle that what is not done our way must be jettisoned; this is not acceptable, and we shall not stand for it. Let them do whatever they want.

5. Remove the SS-20s from Europe.

6. Rein in the military-industrial complex. Openly dismiss American blackmail and reduce the army fourfold.

7. Place the Ministry of Foreign Affairs under the control of the CC. Appoint a duly authorized secretary of the CC on international matters. But whom? B.N. [Boris Ponomarev] is obviously unsuitable.

8. Release all dissidents to go abroad with [Andrei] Sakharov in the lead—those who are incarcerated and those whom Andropov has not yet managed to imprison.

9. Ditto regarding all Jews who wish to leave. But at the same time, declare anti-Semitism to be illegal. Equate Jews with at least the Armenians in the "system of friendship of the peoples."

10. Pension off 70%–80% of ministers.

11. Grant genuine independence to the republics, including the autonomous ones. Actual rights are to go to regional committees. Give all-round encouragement of horizontal contacts between the regions.

12. Supply cities and industrial centers—from regional and district resources. A minimized centralized fund: for capitals and certain others.

13. Release all wastelands to pensioners and to anyone who wishes to take them, for whatever purpose.

14. Reduce the CC apparatus, but raise the role of CC departments. Place them above ministries, so they will quake and fear penalties. Free departments of routine matters and administrative-regulating functions.

15. Propaganda. Put an end to cultism (that stands to reason), but maintain vigilance to ensure that it does not creep back through the cracks.

Allow more rights to the press—including criticism of party agencies. Freedom of expressing thoughts, ideas and manner of chastisement, to call, inspire, tell the people the truth, and generally engage in dialogue with the people, explain and give explanations—draw on literary journals and works returning to the greatness of Russian literature. In concentrated form, this is how *Pravda* should set an example.

This is the minimal program. It should be implemented and felt in Andropov's first year. Otherwise everything will wither once more.

However, why not give it a try? The bankrupt avant-garde of the proletariat had nothing more to lose apart from their chains, and they had the whole world to gain. In fact, they did not see this problem as particularly difficult: by virtue of their profession they could manipulate enormous masses of people in the West and third world countries, the free Western press and independent public movements without resorting to repressions and censorship. So why not try this on the domestic front, where the degree of control is much greater, where practically everything was in the hands of the party? The techniques of this sort of work had been cultivated to perfection, and the Soviet man in the street was much more dependent on their power than, say, a Western peacemaker.

Their version of détente really seemed to be a certain winner: it included all the more successful features of the old version—the use of social democracy, the leftist establishment of the USA, friendly businessmen and also the massive disinformation campaign (including the old chestnut of a struggle within the Soviet leadership between "hawks" and "doves", now renamed "conservatives" and "reformers"). The innovations were, firstly, the "executor" whose image, unlike that of Brezhnev, could be created easily as a "liberal reformer"; and secondly—the new internal "reforms" (in fact—an attempt to save socialism with minimal changes in the economy); and finally, the most important innovation was the imitation of a "human face" with full retention of control—a "carefully thought-out glasnost" to use Falin's expression. If even this proved insufficient for the revival of détente, there were other possible "quasi-democratic features" such as a fictional multi-party system, "free elections" to the "parliament", a withdrawal from Afghanistan and the "liberalization" of East European regimes....

A suitable crew had to be selected: from the beginning of Andropov's rise to power, and especially under Gorbachev, most of the candidates had foreign policy experience—from the KGB, the Ministry of Foreign Affairs, the International Department, research institutes and brain trusts. This is understandable: their task was not just to secure the revival of détente with the West, but also to transfer the system of harsh administrative-repressive control within the country to the more refined and manipulative one that in the past had only been employed in matters of foreign policy. Nobody else could have achieved this apart from professional manipulators.

However, serious implementation of this "domestic plan" was only set in motion after Reykjavik, when it became clear that nothing was to be gained by mere promises and surprise attacks. And the West? The West was ecstatic, unwilling to see the gigantic deception being played out before its eyes.

6.4   How to "leave" without leaving?

Despite being an accomplished liar, there was one thing in which
Gorbachev did not lie: his new policy was truly Leninist. His colleagues were fully aware of this: as faithful students of Lenin, the
Soviet leaders knew that they could get away with anything so long
as power remained in their hands. Like Lenin in 1921, Stalin in
1941 or Khrushchev after Stalin, they were not afraid of "shaking
the foundations" of their regime for the sake of its salvation. Only
one thing was necessary: retain the initiative and not allow reforms
to escape party control.

Meanwhile, none of their "reforms" that so shook the meagre
imagination of the West seemed to threaten party control at the
start. I have already gone into details of how "glasnost" was introduced, how political prisoners and Sakharov were "freed", how
simultaneously harsh was the suppression of any attempt to create
a genuine opposition in the country while a fictional "multi-party"
system was alleged, so-called "socialist pluralism." The result was
the achievement of something that eighteen years of Brezhnev repressions failed to do—an increase in the authority of the party
leadership. For the first time since the post-Stalin period, the public greeted the decisions of party congresses and conferences with
enthusiasm. And the more the former crimes of the regime were
exposed, the less responsibility for them was borne by the party.
Even the instituted public criticism of local party leaders only tight-
ened the control of the central leadership over the administrative
apparatus which, as we recall, threatened to break up into regional
mafias. In a certain sense, "glasnost" performed the function of
a party purge, something akin to the "cultural revolution" of Mao
Zedong.

Correspondingly, the new control system was implemented
throughout the empire, both the foreign and the domestic. Even
the republics of the USSR were offered a degree of cultural and
economic autonomy, and the satellites were forced to accept it. On
one hand, the bankrupt regime could not maintain them fully any
longer; on the other hand—its foreign policy aims required changing the image of the "Evil Empire." It was hard, for example, to
expect détente while Soviet forces were fighting in Afghanistan. Furthermore, the remaining "local conflicts" instigated by Soviet global
expansion had to be put on hold at the very least.

All this, however, did not mean a rejection of the empire or even global expansion. On the contrary, both only benefited from a similar appearance, and Soviet control did not weaken at all. The withdrawal of Soviet troops from Afghanistan is the best example of this. As we recall, the Soviet leadership had serious qualms about the occupation of Afghanistan, and never saw this decision as final. The question of withdrawal was already being discussed under Andropov (10 March 1983*, Pb).

> GROMYKO. In accordance with the resolution of the Politburo, a group of responsible party, soviet, military and economic officials visited Afghanistan. [...]
>
> As you know, the general situation in Afghanistan is complicated. In recent times there have been some signs of consolidation, but this process is slow. The number of [guerrilla] bands is not decreasing. Negotiations with Pakistan in Geneva are slow and difficult. Therefore we must do all we can to find mutually-acceptable versions of a political settlement. It can be said in advance that this will be a lengthy process. There are questions that require special discussion. It should be borne in mind that Pakistan cannot be given specific dates for the withdrawal of our forces from the country at this time. We need to be careful. Yes, the situation is stabilizing. It is good that the Afghan army has increased to 140 thousand men. The main problem is that the central authorities have not yet reached the countryside, communicate rarely with the masses, approximately one third of districts are not under the control of the central authorities and the state leadership is discernibly lax.
>
> In closing I wish to say that we shall probably have to take the steps set out in the recommendations submitted for your perusal. It will probably be necessary to have a meeting with [Babrak] Karmal and a group of leading workers of the People's Democratic Republic of Afghanistan at some point in April. It appears that it would be feasible to arrange a personal meeting between Yu.V. Andropov and Babrak Karmal. [...]
>
> ANDROPOV. You remember with what care and difficulty we decided the question of sending our forces into Afghanistan. L.I. Brezhnev insisted on an individual vote by Politburo members. The question was examined at the Plenum of the CC.
>
> In resolving the Afghan problem we must proceed on the basis of existing realities. What can you expect? It is a feudal country in which tribes have always reigned over their territories, and the central power did not always reach every village. The question is not Pakistan's position. We are engaged with American imperialism, which is fully aware that it has been defeated in this sector of international politics. So we cannot retreat.
>
> There are no miracles in the world. Occasionally we are an-

gry with the Afghans for their inconsistency, for their slowness
in conducting work. But let us recall our struggle with the
Basmachis. At that time, just about the entire Red Army was
concentrated in Central Asia, but the fight with the Basmachis
lasted until the mid-1930s. So in our relations with Afghanistan we need to be demanding, but understanding.

As for the recommendations drawn up by the Committee, are
they not too demanding in indicating what the Afghan side has
to do, and what we must do?

GROMYKO. We shall certainly do more work on the recommendations.

ANDROPOV. Yes, so that it will be a political document. It must
be expressed with greater flexibility.

This decision remained in force under Gorbachev. The need to
withdraw forces became increasingly acute, but nobody was prepared to yield to "American imperialism." The issue was how to
leave without leaving, i.e. how to preserve the regime and control
over it. The Politburo had already started to prepare for this decision in 1986, starting with deposing Karmal and replacing him with
the head of the Afghan KGB, Najibullah—a gambit very typical of all
Gorbachev's "reforms". The KGB reformer—just like his boss in the
Kremlin a little later—instituted "liberal reforms": he set up contacts with the opponents, introduced a new constitution, and even
changed the name of the country, omitting the word "democratic"
(presumably playing up to the Muslim opposition), and became the
President. It may be assumed that for the Kremlin "reformers" Afghanistan was a kind of test of the "new thinking", an experimental site. If the experiment proved successful, it could be launched
throughout the empire. This is why the Politburo was so on edge,
and preparations for the withdrawal of forces were done with all due
diligence. The Politburo committee on Afghanistan (Shevardnadze,
Chebrikov, Yakovlev; Yazov, Vladimir Kryuchkov) could not decide
until the last moment on the best way to carry out this task (24
January 1989*, Pb 146/VI).

In the complex situation in Afghanistan, there is a growing feeling of internal tension regarding the withdrawal of the remaining Soviet forces. The attention of the regime and the opposition
is focused fully on February 15, when pursuant to the Geneva
agreements the term of the presence of our military contingent
expires. For Kabul, this term is even narrower, as the last Soviet
military units must leave the Afghan capital at the beginning of
February, [...]

It must be stressed that our Afghan comrades are seriously concerned about the development of the situation. On the whole, they are increasingly resolute in their determination to stand up to the opponent, and for this purpose are undertaking a number of special measures and attempting a more rational placement of available forces. They have some reliance on the continuation of their contacts with a significant number of commanders of the armed units of the opponent, on the strong disagreements within the opposition and on the incompatibility of some of the leading political groupings such as the "Jamiat-e Islami" (Rabbani) and the "Islamic Party of Afghanistan" (Hekmatyar). [...]

Our Afghan comrades express and reaffirm their understanding of the withdrawal of Soviet forces, but at the same time, having a realistic view of the situation, admit they cannot manage fully without our military aid. This aid, in their opinion, could be rendered in other forms than at present, forms with a limited scope, but nonetheless a significant help at the practical and psychological level. The Afghan comrades consider that if the opposition does not manage to pounce on the main centers after the withdrawal of Soviet forces, then the Peshawar "Alliance of Seven" and the Teheran "Alliance of Eight" shall have to enter into negotiations with Kabul regarding the future state system of Afghanistan, something they are stubbornly refusing to do at the present time. [...]

There are some complicated moments for us in the given situation. On one hand, our retreat from accepted and publicized dates for the completion of the withdrawal on February 15 may result in highly undesirable repercussions at the international level. On the other hand, there is no certainty that soon after our withdrawal there will not be a very serious threat to a regime which is globally associated with us. Especially as the opposition may coordinate actions temporarily at that very decisive time, something it is being urged to do by American and Pakistani military circles. There are also certain doubts that there is no real unity in the NDPL, differences remain between wings, clans and other aspects. The arguments of some Afghan leaders are unduly impulsive; there are too many recollections of past "injustices." [...]

The most serious factors are that Islamabad's violations of the Geneva agreements are taking on not just an open, but demonstrative nature. Pakistani border guards are participating directly in military actions in Afghan territory. Shelling of Afghan border areas is conducted from Pakistan, arms are being smuggled in a steady stream, and armed bands are crossing the border into Afghanistan. Headquarters of Afghan opposition parties, their training centers and bases continue to operate unopposed in Peshawar and other cities. All this is proceeding from the inertia created under Zia-ul-Haq. It is not likely that B. Bhutto will be able to change this situation in the near future.

However, despite all this complexity, the question of the survival of the regime was reduced to the problem of the supply of foodstuffs and fuel to the main cities, especially Kabul.

> The obvious plan of the opposition is to organize an economic blockade of Kabul, to cut off deliveries of food and oil products, thus instigating discontent and even direct action by the population.

That meant creating significant emergency reserves, which could only be done overland. The only road from the USSR to Kabul, the Hairatan route, became vitally important.

> Comrade Najibullah claims that if the functioning of the route can be assured until around May, the survival of the regime can be guaranteed. It looks as though our Afghan comrades cannot ensure the normal functioning of this road without our help. We must proceed on the assumption that closure of the Hairatan-Kabul route is unacceptable. Special attention will have to be paid to the most vulnerable part of this route, the Salang Pass with its more than three-kilometer-long tunnel.

In connection with this, the Politburo discussed possible versions, each of which is noteworthy by itself, and very typical of the Kremlin "reformers":

> First version. Citing the difficult situation of the civilian population, leave one division *in situ*, i.e. approximately 12 thousand personnel along the Hairatan-Kabul route. This version is not really desirable, as it may lead to questions being raised in the UN about the non-withdrawal of all our troops. Irrespective of the fact that Pakistan is not observing its obligations under the Geneva agreements, it can be assumed that most of the countries in the UN will not support us, as the question of troops is at the center of the problem for most of them.

> Second version. Citing the threat of hunger in Kabul and other cities, call upon the UN to ensure immediate delivery of food and fuel to the cities and send in UN troops to keep the route operating. To leave our army units in these positions until the arrival of UN troops for purely humanitarian purposes—supplying the population with food and fuel. At the same time confirm that the withdrawal of the Soviet military contingent has been carried out. Declare that with the arrival of UN forces, our units shall return immediately to the Soviet Union. [...]

Third version. Withdraw all forces, as planned, by February 15 and confirm this on the international level by the declarations of the governments of the USSR and the Afghan Republic. Then, upon an appeal by the Afghan government to all countries of the world, begin sending columns with civilian goods, to be guarded by Soviet military units. The sending of such columns can be commenced approximately two weeks after the withdrawal of Soviet forces. By that time, broad public opinion should be formed to condemn the actions of the opposition, which is consigning the people in Afghan cities to death by starvation. With the background of such widespread public opinion, columns assisted by us will look like a natural humanitarian act. At the same time, this version would include some sections of this route and involve combat every time.

Fourth version. Withdraw almost all Soviet troops by February 15. Confirm this officially in the relevant declaration of the withdrawal of the Soviet military contingent. But under the pretext of transferring some posts along the Hairatan-Kabul route to the Afghan side, leave Soviet units at the more important points, including the Salang Pass. On our initiative, refrain from giving this action wide publicity, noting that the matter concerns only a small number of Soviet servicemen, who have been delayed for a short time because the Afghans have not yet taken over control of the indicated posts. Some time later, as in the third version, begin sending columns of aid to Kabul under the guard of our servicemen.

In all these versions, we can proceed on the assumption that our regular units will take part in these operations, but they shall be formed on a voluntary basis, primarily from the midst of servicemen performing military service in Afghanistan or those who have already finished their tour of duty and are back in the Soviet Union. Wages for common soldiers shall be set at 800–1000 rubles per month, part of them payable in Afghan currency, and officers' wages are to be increased substantially.

Grant international observers the right — and publicize this widely—to inspect that we are really convoying consignments of goods for the population. Talks should be conducted soon with Aga Khan, the Special Coordinator of UN programs on rendering humanitarian and economic aid to Afghanistan for the purpose of using these programs and the mechanism of the Special Coordinator to counter the plans of extremists to strangle Kabul and other large Afghan cities with an economic blockade. [...]

There is another plan that might be considered, a fifth version —Soviet troops withdraw fully by February 15, and we render the Afghan side additional aid, including financial, for organizing the guarding of the Hairatan-Kabul route by its own forces,

up to our taking these Afghan units on allowance for a certain
period of time, although this will be linked with undoubted difficulties, especially in ensuring the reliable accompaniment of
aid columns.

Basically, they approved the fifth version (with a bit taken from
the third), but there was no hunger in Kabul or other centers.

Of course, there was also massive aid in the form of military
equipment (31 July 1989*, No. 312/1/0297), including even missiles, as well as "the use of Soviet volunteer pilots drawing the relevant remuneration on aircraft of Afghan transport aviation or Soviet
transport aircraft that could be leased to the Afghan side." In 1989
alone, military technology was supplied to the price of 2.5 billion
rubles, and in the following year at least 1.4 billion, including military aircraft and helicopters (21 March 1990**, No. 318/2/0354).
This system continued until 1992 and collapsed only with the disintegration of the USSR.

Meanwhile, on the appointed date of 15 February 1989, Soviet
forces withdrew ceremoniously and in full order, marching in view
of television cameras from around the world and crossed the Amu
Darya River which separates the USSR from Afghanistan. That is
what "withdrawing forces" was meant by the Soviet leaders—unlike
the Americans from Vietnam.

6.5   The "Velvet Revolution"

The impressive changes of 1989 in the communist world remain a
puzzle to this day, which nobody seems to want to solve. It would
seem that a grandiose, almost incredible event had occurred before
our eyes: almost bloodless and without a particular struggle, the
mighty Soviet bloc in Eastern Europe fell apart. Yet not a single
Western government or international organization—NATO, the European Parliament or the UN—conducted a study of how and why
this happened. In any case, I do not know of any public report of
such a study, so if there was one, it must have been conducted in
strict secrecy. Mere mortals like us are supposed to rejoice quietly
at the result, without asking any leading questions.

Meanwhile the official or, rather, "generally accepted" version of
these events is so illogical if not to say laughable, that it is not repeated much nowadays, although it is not disputed. It is deemed
better forgotten, with no other explanations offered. In fact, reference works report[304] without a trace of irony that in Czechoslovakia,

---

[304]Brian Hunter (ed.), *The Statesman's Yearbook.* London: Macmillan, 1994,
p. 464, 591

for instance:

> "Mass demonstrations demanding political reform began in Nov. 1989. After the authorities' use of violence to break up a demonstration on 17 November, the Communist leader resigned. On 30 November the Federal Assembly abolished the Communist Party's sole right to govern, and a new Government was formed on 3 Dec."

And here is what is reported regarding the GDR:[305]

> "In the autumn of 1989 movements for political liberalization and re-unification with Federal Germany gathered strength. *Erich Honecker* and other long-serving Communist leaders were replaced in Oct.–Nov. The Berlin Wall was opened on 9 Nov."

The same year the BBC Nine O'clock News said this about Poland:[306]

> "Following strikes and demands for the reinstatement of Solidarity, the government resigned in Sept. 1988. After the parliamentary elections of June 1989 the Communists were unable to form a government against the opposition of Solidarity, and Tadeusz Mazowiecki, a Solidarity member, was elected Prime Minister by the Sejm on Aug. 24. Unconditionally free parliamentary elections were held in Oct. 1991."

Even with regard to Romania, where nothing had really changed except that communist Ceausescu had been replaced by communist Iliescu, it is stated:

> "An attempt by the authorities of 16 Dec. 1989 to evict a Protestant pastor, Laszlo Tokes, from his home in Timisoara provoked a popular protest which escalated into a mass demonstration against the government. Despite the use of armed force against the demonstrators, the uprising spread to other areas. On Dec. 21 the government called for an official rally in Bucharest, but this turned against the regime. A state of emergency was declared, but the army went over to the uprising, and Nicolae and Elena Ceausescu fled the capital. A dissident group which had been active before the uprising, the National Salvation Front (NSF), proclaimed itself the provisional government. Suggestions of Soviet involvement have been denied."

---

[305]Brian Hunter (ed.), *The Statesman's Yearbook*. London: Macmillan, 1994, p. 955, 1113.
[306]BBC Nine O'clock News, 18 November 1994.

All in all, just a chain of accidents and coincidences.

At the same time, nobody seems to doubt that these changes occurred due to a decision by Moscow and even under certain pressure from the Kremlin: as we recall, Gorbachev was awarded the Nobel Peace Prize for conducting this operation. As we were told then, he spread his policy of "glasnost and perestroika" to the "reactionary regimes" of Eastern Europe. Yet there is no answer to the obvious question: if that is the case, then what was the Velvet Revolution? A spectacle? A Kremlin conspiracy?

Where the circumstances of the revolution of 1989 were studied, this question was inevitable. It should be noted that out of all the new governments in Eastern Europe, such a study was conducted only by the Czechs,[307] but they established that all the early stages of unrest that brought about the fall of Milos Jakes' leadership were carried out by Czech security, and were organized under general Alojz Lorenc—the head of the intelligence administration of the CSSR—on orders from the head of the intelligence administration of the KGB, general Viktor Grushko. It emerged, for example, that the demonstration of November 17 and its exceedingly vicious suppression, as a result of which a student was allegedly killed, was part of their plan, and the "killed student" turned out to be a perfectly live employee of Czechoslovak state security. A documentary film based on these materials was shown by the BBC in the UK back in 1990.[308] Lorenc appeared on our screens and confirmed all this, however adding that they did not accomplish their task: following the "revolution" they were supposed to bring a "liberal" communist to power, not Havel.

More or less the same conclusions were drawn by journalists researching the events of 1989 in the GDR. For instance, in the documentary film "The Fall of the Wall"[309] all the former leaders of the GDR confirm that Gorbachev was practically open in demanding Honecker's deposition and encouraged the conspirators.

Of course, there is much that they do not say, but it is not hard to conclude that the first demonstrations calling for "liberalization" were organized by them with Moscow's blessing. It is inarguable that on their orders real force was not used in suppressing this un-

---

[307] Gerald Frost & Andrew McHallam, *In Search of Stability: Europe's Unfinished Revolution.* Westport, Conn.: Praeger, 1992. Pp. 79–80.

[308] See John Simpson, *The Darkness Crumbles: Dispatches from the Barricades.* London: Hutchinson, 1992. 1998.

[309] "A Hole in the Wall" (part 1), shown on 30 August 1994; "The Fatal Error" (part 2), shown on 6 November 1994, BBC2—two episodes of "Fall of the Wall," Television Documentary Archive, produced by David Ash and Stephen Clark, Brian Lapping Associates. See http://www.kingscollections.org/catalogues/lhcma/collection/f/xf10-001/.

rest. Now we have documentary evidence that Moscow kept its finger on the pulse of the conspiracy at all times, and Honecker's deposition several days after Gorbachev's visit to Berlin was no accident. On October 8 Gorbachev's aide Chernyaev noted in his diary[310] that among other impressions from the visit (8 October 1989):

> Krenz said to Falin: "It is our Erich who is leading everything, but does not want to admit anything." On the tenth the Socialist Unity Party of Germany holds a Plenum... maybe they will depose Erich. Otherwise it will soon come to a storming of the "Wall."

Three days later he writes in more detail:

> Recording of [talks] with Honecker.... M.S. called him an "asshole" (in a conversation with Schach). He could say to his own circle: I have had four surgical operations, I am 78 years old, a great deal of strength is needed... in such turbulent times, please "release" me; I have done what I had to do. Then maybe he would have had his place "in history." Even two or three years ago. Now he is in the same situation as Kadar. He's already been cursed by the people.

> The second day of the Plenum in Berlin. Krenz has told our ambassador to convey to M.S. that he will "raise the question" of changes. Honecker warned him: you will become my enemy! But it seems that [Krenz] has done so. How will this end?

Even the Romanian events, which nobody has studied, and the new leadership as we saw above "rejected Soviet intervention", are still rather suspicious. For instance, the key figures of this "revolution" were identified as Moscow agents by general Pacepa,[311] former head of the Romanian intelligence service who fled to the West in 1978. Calling them a "group of dissidents" can be done only with a certain degree of irony. The new Romanian president, Iliescu, was a fellow student of Gorbachev at university, and seemed to have maintained contact with him. Shorthand reports of their conversations, copied by Stroilov, demonstrate quite clearly that Iliescu was "Moscow's man" in Romania, and once in power coordinated all his actions closely with Gorbachev—including such sensitive questions as Moldavia. It is not by chance that in a conversation with a Bulgarian comrade who mentioned Iliescu, Gorbachev whispered (23 May 1990)[312]

---

[310]Chernyaev's diary can be seen online. In Russian: https://nsarchive2.gwu.edu/rus/Chernyaev.html

[311]Ion Pacepa, *Red Horizons: Chronicles of a Communist Spy Chief*. London: Hodder and Stoughton, 1989

[312]Gorbachev, 1990 (SA), p. 301.

Yes, he maintains measured, wise positions, shows readiness
for constructive cooperation. But I believe that the closeness of
our approaches should not be too widely known.

So there is no doubt that the "Velvet Revolution" of 1989 was
a Soviet operation. Why should the Kremlin directors stage such
a grandiose and dangerous show if they could simply replace the
leadership of any one of their satellites with any number of "liberals" at their own discretion? The mechanism of such "changes" was
honed to perfection over 40 years and never called for the organization of popular unrest: everything was done quietly, covertly, and
without risks. We have seen how Moscow decided whom to appoint
as ruler of Poland, and how easily this was accomplished. Actually, they did not bother to pretend between themselves: Moscow
appointed Jaruzelski, and he thanked Brezhnev for his trust (19
October 1981*, Pb 1942). So who in this instance was supposed to
be fooled by the staging of this "revolution"? The West? Their own
people? Or both?

It is hard to believe that the results of this operation fully corresponded with the plans of the Kremlin directors. We have just seen
how thoroughly the withdrawal of Soviet forces from Afghanistan
was planned, where the Soviet leaders were prepared to practice any
deception in order to preserve the regime "which is globally associated with us," as they wrote. But Eastern Europe was not simply
"associated" with them; it was an intrinsic part of them. It is hard to
believe that Afghanistan was more important to them than Poland,
Czechoslovakia, the GDR, Hungary, Romania and Bulgaria combined, the more so as the period between the withdrawal of forces
from Afghanistan and the "Velvet Revolution" was a mere couple of
months. With Poland, for instance, it was just two months: they
"left" Afghanistan in February, and the round table in Poland was
held in April–May.

Why bother mentioning Eastern Europe and Afghanistan if Moscow continued financing all the communist parties of the world
right up to 1990, difficulties with hard currency notwithstanding
(5 December 1989*)[313]? Could some Chilean communist party be
more important to them than the whole socialist camp? And it was
not merely a question of money—communist brethren all over the
world continued to be trained, supplied with arms and "technical
means." For instance, in February 1990, after the fall of the Berlin
Wall, this is how the CC planned to work with them (14 February
1990*, St 112/27):

---

[313] 17 December 1989*, pp. 3–4.

- Partially satisfy the requests of the leaderships of the communist parties of Argentina (CPA) and Chile (CPC) and invite 5 representatives of the CPA and *four* of the CPC to the USSR in 1990 for three months to receive *training in matters concerning ensuring the security of the party and its leaders, including the use of equipment.*

- Reception and rendering services to the indicated comrades will be handled by the International Department and the Administration of the Affairs of the CC CPSU, while their training, assistance in *documentation* and *special equipment* shall be provided by *the KGB of the USSR.*

- Expenses for the return travel of the representatives of the CPA and CPC between Moscow and their assigned places, including flights with foreign air companies, for their living expenses in the USSR up to three months, *special equipment*, training and other expenses related to fulfilling the requests of the leaders of these parties shall be charged to the reserve in the party budget.

There is a curious detail: just at the time the "liberation of Eastern Europe" was being worked out, my "fellow-criminal blood brother" Luis Corvalan who, as it emerges, lived illegally in Chile since 1983 with an altered face and led the underground fight of Chilean communists against Augusto Pinochet's regime, made a request to the CC to "legalize" him. There was no more need to hide out: the blood-stained Pinochet had held elections and retired even before the start of "perestroika" in the USSR. But—what a problem! —comrade Corvalan and his legalization meant that he had to return to the USSR, change his appearance again, and receive a legal passport (19 May 1989**).

They had time for schemes as complex as this: what you won't do for a global revolution. It wasn't just Chileans—Lebanese terrorists, and Turkish underground functionaries[314] as well as "the working people of Cyprus" (22 June 1989**, St 102/124) were not abandoned to their own devices. Their training, equipment and financing continued in spite of all the cataclysms within the Soviet empire. There was a plan to receive 20 Lebanese terrorists every year in 1989–1990 for "special military training by the Ministry of Defense of the USSR."[315] This was the rule, not an exception; moreover the money for these expenses came from the West—for the purpose of "saving perestroika."

I hear indignant cries: all these were schemes of the "conservatives" and "reactionaries" in the Politburo against the "liberals"

---

[314] 29 September 1989* (St 105/159).
[315] 18 January 1989 (St 95/62).

and "reformers"! No, they were not. I can show copies of documents with all their signatures: they were signed, for instance, by the main "architect of perestroika" Alexander Yakovlev, who was not rated as a conservative even in the West.

Furthermore it appears that "special services" of this kind were to be increased as perestroika progressed. Here is another document, also signed by Yakovlev (10 April 1989*, St 99/248), where this is stated quite plainly by Falin, Kruchina and Kryuchkov in April 1989:

> The leaders of a number of fraternal parties in non-socialist countries send annual requests to the CC CPSU to accept their activists for special training. Over the past ten years, more than 500 foreign party functionaries and 40 from communist and workers' parties (including Politburo and CC members) received special training. Pursuant to the instruction of the CC CPSU, their reception and maintenance is carried out by the International Department and the Administration of CC CPSU Affairs, and their training—by the Committee for State Security of the USSR. The special training of foreign party workers, and also the reception of the leaders of certain illegal parties who are in the USSR for consultations or special training is conducted in apartments belonging to the Administration of CC CPSU Affairs. Using these apartments for the indicated purposes requires the installation of special protective equipment in order to prevent possible breaches of secrecy and information leakage, and the installation of additional facilities required for the teaching process.
>
> In view of the above, we deem it feasible to implement additional measures to improve conditions for the special training of representatives of fraternal parties. It is suggested *inter alia* to assign a number of apartments at the disposal of the Administration of CC CPSU Affairs exclusively for the conduct of special training, equipping them with the required protective technical devices as well as everyday domestic appliances such as video equipment and radios with a broad band of short-wave reception.
>
> The KGB of the USSR could be charged with developing and coordinating a complex suite of measures with the International Department of the CC CPSU for ensuring the security and secrecy of the measures being conducted in the special apartments.

So the CC resolves to assign 12 such "special apartments" exclusively for the conduct of special training, and 5 for the housing of leaders of illegal parties.

This demonstrates that the Soviet leadership had no intention of relinquishing the empire or its expansion either in 1989 or at the beginning of 1990s. What, then, did they expect from the "Velvet Revolution"?

• • •

Many years later, I had the opportunity to pose these questions to Yakovlev in person, having encountered him at some conference: what was the purpose of the plan devised by the Politburo at that time? What was the approved decision? Alexander Nikolayevich pretended incomprehension, just kept reiterating that there was no such decision and that the subject of Eastern Europe was never discussed by the Politburo in that period.

"How can that be?"—I persisted—"you had all worked out five different versions for withdrawal from Afghanistan. Surely Eastern Europe was not less important for you? Never mind five, but you must have worked out and approved at least one plan, there must have been at least one decision on this matter?"

"There was no decision," he kept repeating in his characteristic Volga region accent.

However, Stroilov was to appear shortly with his documents, and the minutes of the Politburo meeting on 24 January 1989 contain this laconic notation (24 January 1989, SA):[316]

> On the institution of Politburo committees. It was resolved: regarding socialist countries—to be headed by Yakovlev, and the Baltics—[Vadim] Medvedev.

That is, there had been a committee on the socialist countries after all, it was headed by Yakovlev and developed the plan that was subsequently approved for implementation. Although we do not yet have the decision of the Politburo, there can be no doubt that it existed, and the course of its preparation can be traced now through documents.

It all began with Poland, where the direct threat of the collapse of the regime forced Jaruzelski to agree to a round table with the opposition. He was to tell Gorbachev later that if it had not been for the round table, the Polish regime would not have lasted another six months. The decision regarding the round table, naturally enough, was accepted with Moscow's approval: Gorbachev had a special meeting with Czyrek (23 September 1988, SA),[317] the Polish ambassador, on 23 September 1988, and after several searching questions, gave his approval:

---

[316] *Kak "delalas" politika perestroiki*, 1989 (SA), p. 43.
[317] *Kak "delalas" politika perestroiki*, 1988 (SA), p. 279.

"Our strategy"—explained the ambassador—"is aimed at reinforcing the social base of the party. The tactics are to divide
the opposition, draw it into a realistic constructive channel together with Walesa, into a process of national reconciliation and
renewal. This is noted by the Church, which wanted to move
toward meeting Walesa, but we acted first."

While approving this plan, Gorbachev understood full well that
the matter would not end with Poland. The problem was a common
one for the entire socialist world, and it was logical to conclude that
a repetition of the Polish scenario in Hungary, Czechoslovakia and
the GDR was just a question of time. But Jaruzelski was just as
much a born manipulator as Gorbachev, and if he was appointed
to his post specifically because he was capable of wriggling out of
critical situations, Moscow was not equally certain about the capabilities of Honecker, Zhivkov or Ceausescu. For this reason, Gorbachev ordered the development of a general strategy several days
after his meeting with Czyrek (6 October 1988, Pb, SA).

From the Politburo meeting of 6/X/88

At our meeting today we are discussing the results of talks with
the leaders or prominent figures of a number of socialist countries—K. Phomvihane, Vo Chi Cong, E. Honecker, N. Ceausescu
and Chi Khe Om.J. Batmonkh also requests [inclusion].

The situation in each country is unique, and we are acting correctly in not "lumping" them together, but are trying to determine the specifics of the situation in each one, and to formulate
our policy toward them on the basis of such concrete analysis.

At the same time, today's exchange of opinions and, looking further—all that we know, all the incoming information shows the
need for an overall assessment of the situation in the socialist community. Allowing for all the differences and nuances,
there are many indications that there are similar increasing and
acute problems in fraternal countries. The very coincidence of
the symptoms of this disease show that its catalyst is not some
pernicious germ that has infected the unwary, but specific factors rooted in the economic and political model of socialism, as
it formed with us and was transferred, with insignificant modi-
fications, to countries that entered the path of socialism in the
post-war period.

We have already discovered the weaknesses of this model and
are removing them consistently. In fact, this may be considered
the prime task of perestroika—to endow socialism with a new
quality. A number of countries have followed our example or
even preceded us on the way to in-depth reforms. Some, such
as the GDR, Romania and China have not yet acknowledged

the necessity of such reforms, either for political reasons or the unwillingness of the leadership to countenance any changes. Yet it is a fact that transformations are needed by all, although we do not speak of this publicly, so that we cannot be accused of attempting to enforce our perestroika on others.

But facts are facts: clear signs of a crisis call for radical reforms in the entire socialist world. Subjective factors play an enormous part in this. Even in thrice-backward Laos, Phomvihane is conducting matters wisely, and the results are quite good. But those who stubbornly reject the signs of the times simply drive the malaise deeper and complicate its future development even more.

This has a direct effect on us. We have shed the authority of the "big brother" in the socialist world, but we cannot refuse the leading role which the Soviet Union will always have, as the most powerful socialist country, the cradle of October. When a crisis occurs in one country or another, we have to render assistance at the cost of enormous material, political and even human sacrifices.

It should also be clear that the possibility of the future "quenching" of crisis situations by military means is categorically excluded. This appears to have been understood by at least the former leadership of such a country as Poland.

Now we have to stop and think of how shall we act if one or several countries become bankrupt simultaneously? The possibility is quite real, as some are already on the brink of currency insolvency (Poland, Hungary, Bulgaria, Vietnam, Cuba, Romania and the GDR). Even Czechoslovakia, which managed to keep its head above water until recently, is seeing its foreign debt soaring.

How shall we act if the social instability that is assuming a more threatening nature in Hungary coincides with the latest round of disorder in Poland, actions by the Chartists and so forth? In other words, do we have a plan to deal with a crisis that may engulf the whole or part of the socialist world at the same time?

This is a matter of concern for all of us. From time to time we receive alarming telegrams and try to enact what measures we can, but these are at best sticking plasters on injuries, and not a systematic, consistent treatment of an illness, to say nothing of after-care treatment.

[...]

Can socialist countries resolve the pre-crisis situation without Western aid?

What will be the price of such aid?

[...]

It is feasible to charge the newly-formed International Committee of the CC with preparing materials for such a discussion. The problem is immense both in scope and significance,
it demands constant attention, but the first exchange of views
should take place at the end of December–beginning of January
1989.

The International Committee of the CC was headed by that same
Yakovlev, and returning to the question in January 1989 the Politburo created a special committee to deal with socialist countries,
also headed by Yakovlev. Certain Soviet documents shedding light
on the course of the work of Yakovlev's committee in 1989 were
passed to me by Polish researcher Minewicz. By all accounts, the
committee followed the usual Soviet procedure in which various
agencies (CC, MID, KGB) and research centers submitted analytical
reports with their view of the situation. For instance the CC wrote
the following in a document entitled "On the strategy of relations
with European socialist countries" (24 January 1989, SA):

The complex, transitional nature of the present period lies in
that ruling parties can no longer rule the way they did in the
past, and the new "rules of the game", for reconciling emerged
group interests and reaching social consensus, remain to be
worked out. The more this process is drawn out and delayed,
the more parties may find themselves in an even more difficult
situation.

Against the background of general tendencies that can be observed in all socialist countries, there are the specifics of individual countries that require varied responses from us.

In Poland and Hungary, events are pointing toward a transfer
to political pluralism, the creation of coalitional, parliamentary
forms of government. Under existing conditions, the Hungarian and Polish parties can only count on retaining their positions within the framework of political alliances. A great deal
will depend on whether they will be able to attract part of the
opposition towards constructive cooperation. [...]

In the GDR with its external relative wellbeing, the situation
is becoming particularly complicated. Although compared to
other socialist countries the GDR enjoys a better economy and
standard of living, the economic situation of the country is deteriorating. Its debt is pressing and its dependence on the FRG
is increasing. The party leadership, driven significantly by personal ambitions, tries to avoid problems of renewal. While assessing the conservatism of the GDR leadership critically, it is
still necessary to see that it is based on certain objective factors.
The GDR arose not on a nationalist, but an ideological class ba-

sis, so a radical transfer to the rails of democratization, glasnost and openness could be accompanied by particular difficulties.

Romania is still suffering from the depressing atmosphere of the personality cult and authoritarian rule of Ceausescu. Attempting to isolate the country from our influence, he now tries to cloak himself in the garments of a "fighter for the purity of socialism" and enters into indirect polemics with us. Certain spontaneous outbursts may occur, but at present they are unlikely to become widespread. The situation will probably only change after the departure of Ceausescu, which could result in extremely painful consequences.

The leaderships of Czechoslovakia and Bulgaria are criticized in similar terms, after which the CC recommends spreading the model of the Polish round table to other East European countries.

There are several possible versions of the further development of socialist countries. One of them is a smooth progression of society toward democracy and the new form of socialism under the guidance of ruling parties. This does not exclude some concessions in the questions of power, a significant rise of self-government, the role of representative agencies in political life, attracting constructive opposition to public rule and its possible transformation into one of the forces competing for power. This course toward a parliamentary or presidential socialist republic that has taken place in a number of countries (Poland, Hungary, and Czechoslovakia) would be preferable from our point of view. If the initiative of democratic changes ensues from the ruling party, there is a great chance for the preservation of internal political stability and allied obligations.

[...]

Deeper consideration must be given to existing processes of the formation of structures of political pluralism in a number of countries, toward a coalitional, parliamentary form and the legalization of the opposition. Of course, this is an untried, risky path that requires the party to combine flexibility with loyalty to principles at a high level, and the ability to be at the head of this process and not allow it to be hijacked by opposing forces.

The lessons learned from a whole series of crises show that the main danger of an opposition is not the fact of its existence, but its ability to unite completely diverse forces and tendencies in society on the negative grounds of dissatisfaction with current conditions. Therefore attracting part of the opposition into the official structure, granting it responsibility for the constructive resolution of existing problems could play a stabilizing role.

The recommendations of the Ministry of Foreign Affairs and various academic institutions echo the same spirit. Although the final recommendations of Yakovlev's committee and the subsequent decision of the Politburo are unavailable to us, the logic of these and other assessments point directly at the "Velvet Revolution." They all accept the Polish-style round table to be the best of the available options, and recommend its implementation in other East European countries. In turn, this required the corresponding type of communist leaders, manipulators such as Gorbachev and Jaruzelski and not odious dictators like Honecker or Ceausescu.

At first, they really saw the round table as a very successful experiment, which virtually rescued the regime from the brink of the precipice, when the opposition, accepting a pure bluff, entered into an unnatural "coalition" with the communists and agreed to enormous and totally unjustified concessions. Despite the overwhelming electoral defeat of the communists in all districts without exception, they retained the post of President and two thirds of the Sejm. As Jaruzelski told Gorbachev, he "crawled on his belly to the post of President." The government, beginning with Prime Minister Mazowiecki, was composed of mostly compromise figures, five ministers were communists, and another six—former communists. Not by chance was Jaruzelski able to say to Gorbachev when they met in Berlin on 7 October 1989 that (7 October 1989, SA):[318]

> If we had not taken the risk of forming a government with Mazowiecki and participation in it, then half a year later, as they say, "our goose would have been cooked." [...] We retain a large base, from which we can influence the development of the situation. [...]
>
> It is indicative that those opposition forces that ended up in the government got caught in the same trap they had been preparing for us. After all, in the 1980s the opposition was inciting strike committees everywhere to obtain special privileges in practically all branches of industry. We had a fixed working week of 35 hours. It was established that the material situation could not be worsened by as much as one millimeter. The right to strike was proclaimed everywhere. And what do we have now? Walesa himself now says that strikes are a provocation. Solidarity calls for sacrifices, reducing consumption by 20–30 percent. There is growing conflict between the city and the village. In many ways this is also due to the past policies of Solidarity.
>
> There are increasing conflicts within Solidarity itself and growing competition between various groupings. Of these, 80 per-

---

[318]Gorbachev, 1989 (SA), pp. 380–381.

cent were factory workers. Solidarity membership is currently around 1,5 million. Workers are leaving Solidarity because its activists are engrossed in electoral struggles in the center and activity in representative agencies.

On one hand, the communists burdened the opposition with responsibility for their own policy, and on the other—they amassed political points by their privileged relations with Moscow, in which Gorbachev played along quite deliberately. Furthermore the round table provided excellent opportunities to split the opposition into all possible groups and factions, and then pervert them separately. Arriving in Moscow four days later, the First Secretary of the Polish United People's Party, Mieczyslaw Rakowski, told Gorbachev (11 October 1989, SA):[319]

The idea of round-table discussions was proposed by the PZPR in October 1988. We concluded that it was unacceptable to continue reducing party policy to mainly "imprisoning and releasing." All our attempts in recent years to employ methods of suppressing the opposition yielded no positive results, rather the reverse. The reasons for the existence of the opposition proved to be deeper than we had supposed.

Our attempts to organize a Movement of National Renaissance, putting pressure on the Church or flirting with it ended in failure. The only solution was to change our strategy.

Of course, one can say that we could have chosen and achieved better positions than the ones in which we are now. Undoubtedly, we made a series of tactical errors. But could they have all been avoided? I don't think so. We were like pupils in a school of democracy. Our imagination, or probably lack of it, let us down.

[. . .]

M.S.GORBACHEV. In your opinion, who qualifies as the opposition now?

M.RAKOWSKI. Its core is first and foremost the leadership of Solidarity headed by Lech Walesa and the civil deputies' club headed by Geremik. These two directions are in conflict. We could exploit this situation, but we have not yet learned how to do it. This also shows our insufficient experience of political struggle.

[. . .]

The main center of Solidarity was Gdansk. It was the center of the political thought of the opposition. It was the headquarters of the uncrowned king Walesa. Another center is forming now

---

[319]Gorbachev, 1989 (SA), pp. 386, 394–398.

in parliament. Moreover, there is the Mazowiecki government, and the lower classes realize that they were simply used in the course of the elections by those who became Solidarity deputies and senators.

Activists engage in big politics, leaving the voters by the wayside.

[...] Walesa is worried about losing control over the situation. He keeps projecting his ego, he wants to be somebody. The day before yesterday he gave an interview to a Dutch newspaper and stated that a number of trends have emerged within Solidarity: Christian democratic, social democratic, politological and Jewish.

The latter refers to Geremek, [Adam] Michnik, [Jacek] Kuron, Mazowiecki and others.

M.S.GORBACHEV. So the current situation does not suit him. How do matters stand with regard to his idea of becoming President?

M.RAKOWSKI. So far he is not aspiring to that post. But that is his dream. He said to Kiszczak: I'm 47 years old, there are youngsters up and coming, and I don't want to be sidelined. Walesa does not lack common sense, so he enjoys a certain authority among the workers. But he has become excessively proud, and that will be his downfall. It was he who spoke out in favor of a broad government coalition; to demonstrate his determining role in Solidarity he said that he will give them a Prime Minister. But the so-called Jewish leadership planned to come to power in four years, over which cadres capable of squeezing out the communists would be prepared.

Now the euphoria over the formation of Mazowiecki's government has passed. Walesa admits that consent to the formation of a government under Solidarity leadership was his mistake. I think that if we had retained full power, we would not have had even a janitor left six months later. Now time is on our side, not theirs.

M.S.GORBACHEV. We spoke with Jaruzelski that the fact that the opposition rushed into power is no bad thing. Let them know how hard it is to be in power. [...] We need to know about your relations with the opposition, so that we can take it into account when we start building relations with the new government.

In a recent conversation with E.A. Shevardnadze, Skubiszewski assured him of fidelity to the military union and said that we do not need to worry about the preservation of secrets and so on.

W.NATORF. That is exactly what we told him. It is good that he realized it.

[...]

M.RAKOWSKI. The new government is preparing a number of political demands (Katyn, rehabilitation, compensation). I would request, Mikhail Sergeyevich, that it should not turn out that all these issues that the PZPR government failed to resolve will be immediately settled by the Mazowiecki government.

M.S.GORBACHEV. These matters will be decided in accordance with the established procedure. There are not just Poles buried at Katyn, there are even Muscovites there. We have not found all the threads yet. A Politburo committee is working on the matter, conducting a diligent study of a mass of cases. This work is complicated, a whole number of cases can be found contained in one. Quite recently, three new cases were discovered in [Lavrentiy] Beria's file. At the political level, we want to report on this to the Twenty-Eighth Congress of the CPSU. We are treating this matter very seriously, without undue haste. If we discover something new, we shall inform you.

[...]

M.RAKOWSKI. [...] As for the financial situation of the PZPR, it is very serious. We have made the relevant requests and proposals to comrade A.N. Yakovlev. We would also ask the CC CPSU to extend a loan to the PZPR. We began to develop the economic activity of the party too late, so we will only have the first results in one or two years' time. The government can strangle us with financial limitations. Our request is of paramount importance to the survival of the party. We are constantly suspected of existing at Moscow's expense.

As for the Church: after the elections, the support of the Church was not so vital to Solidarity, especially the leftists. Michnik speaks dismissively of clerics as "the black ones." The left wing of the opposition fears the creation of a theocratic government. We do not exclude the possibility of temporary alliances with various parts of the opposition.

M.S.GORBACHEV. Michnik and Geremek visited here recently, contacted the most anti-Soviet groups and were delighted by the growth of their activity.

M.RAKOWSKI. We are now in a very delicate situation. We shall be playing all the keys of the Polish piano. The Church leadership dislikes the Jewish group in Solidarity, believing that it consists of "suspicious" people—those who are divorced, former PZPR members, Trotskyites and so forth. When we contact these groups within Solidarity, the Church is instantly on its guard against us. [Cardinal] Glemp is wary in his behavior, and is in conflict with the global Jewish community. He has not been forgiven for his comments about the monastery in Oswiecim [Auschwitz] claiming that all the mass media of the USA is in the hands of the Jews.

We do not refuse to cooperate and interact with the Church on the grounds that there is no need for quarrels where they need not exist. Yet we now have support in the army and security agencies, but the leading role shall be played by the intelligentsia, the intellectuals. That will be the deciding factor, not guns and prisons.

But if Jaruzelski could play these games no worse than Gorbachev, expecting such risky ventures from Stalinist dinosaurs like Zhivkov or Honecker was out of the question. Without doubt, according to the Gorbachev-Yakovlev plan, the "popular revolution" should have brought a new generation of manipulators to power in Eastern Europe, just like themselves. They needed a repeat performance of the "Prague Spring", a fictional "socialism with a human face" appearing at the alleged will of the people. They needed enthusiasm in the West and the East, one that would permit stabilization of the domestic situation and the receipt of vital Western support. But if this enterprise was successful in the West, it was a complete failure in the East. As a result, the only country in which their idea succeeded generally was Romania. In all the other countries, their stooges were unable to withstand the wave of popular rejection that spurned socialism with any kind of face.

The miscalculation of the Kremlin strategists was very symptomatic: like many other reformer-manipulators in history, they overestimated the power of their structures and underestimated the force of popular hatred of their regime. Maybe the result would have been entirely different if they had implemented their "reforms" in the 1970s. But the 1980s saw the decline of even the most elite party structures: decades of "natural" selection resulted in the rise of opportunists and conformists, incapable of improvisation, and their societies had lost any faith in the ability of the regime for renewal. While the manipulations of the Gorbachev leadership were accepted in the West at face value, the regime had discredited itself in the East to the extent that even the intelligentsia no longer believed in the sincerity of their leaders' intentions. Simpler people, having endured decades of constant lies were even more suspicious, almost paranoid.

In the end, the whole idea of socialism had worn itself out by the 1980s. This was particularly noticeable in Eastern Europe (Hungary, Poland, and Yugoslavia), where all sorts of reforms had been tried over 20 years, and practice showed that the system was not amenable to reform. Imre Pozsgay, the leader of the Hungarian communists, was probably the first among the East European leaders to admit this openly in May 1989, adding that the system "should be simply liquidated" (Radio Liberty interview, 25 May 1989).

I am willing to believe that many of these new realities were underestimated by the Kremlin, relying on its disingenuity and the trained passivity of the population which had no experience of political struggle. Furthermore, it is possible that skeptics who warned about the danger were ignored, deemed to be "enemies of perestroika", but in general the apparatus reported on the enthusiasm of the popular masses. However they could not have been entirely unaware of the dangers of the game they had put into motion.

Let us assume that they may have thought that a return of the "Prague Spring" to Prague would have satisfied the wildest dreams of the Czechs, and that "goulash socialism" in Hungary was sufficiently stable that changes in the leadership of this country would not set off a chain reaction of uncontrollable changes to the system. Yet there was still the GDR with an almost Stalinist regime. There was Poland, where the regime was hanging by a thread, practically on the bayonets of the Polish army. Certainly the opposition was tired, and the permanent instability and economic hardships would have exhausted the entire population. However it could hardly be expected that the agreements of the round table with the remnants of Solidarity, leaving roughly two-thirds of the power in the hands of the regime could stabilize the situation for long. In the other East European countries—Czechoslovakia, Hungary and especially the GDR—rejoicing at the unexpected arrival of the "Prague Spring" was replaced quickly by a desire to test the boundaries of their new freedom. In a word, even in the event of a fantastic success of their plans, Moscow should have anticipated the instability of the newly-created East European regimes. For one thing, their openness to Western influence would grow inexorably with the fall of the "Iron Curtain."

Let's really imagine that the operation was successful and liberal-communist power was firmly established in Eastern Europe. What does "firmly established" mean? Two Germanys side by side —the socialist and the capitalist, no longer divided by a wall. The Czechs and the Hungarians continuing to "reform" their socialism, and in Poland the remaining communists and remnants of Solidarity activists in a ratio of 2:1 are trying to cope with the country's disintegrated economy. This idyllic scenario is impossible, if only because it leaves no room for control by Moscow: in a year or two, when the original raptures have subsided, the economic crisis in the former socialist countries would force them to be drawn deeper into the orbit of the West. What could prevent them, despairing of any success with their "reforms", from going further and, in the event of any harsh objections from Moscow, asking to be admitted into NATO?

The problem of the GDR in the absence of the wall would be insoluble while the FRG remained a member of NATO: nobody could stop the entire population of the GDR from fleeing to the FRG or —as eventually happened—from reuniting with the FRG on Western terms. And one way or another, what would have happened with Poland? Could anyone seriously think that socialism in Poland could be preserved, especially in the hands of the unnatural coalition of communists and Solidarity, if the GDR vanished? Wouldn't the remaining socialist countries topple like ninepins? No matter how low we may rank the mental abilities of the Kremlin strategists, this was a plan they could not accept. It required some other missing element, allowing at least a little hope for the stabilization of the new regimes. When this book appeared in its first edition, I did not have any documents concerning these decisions at my disposal, I could only speculate about the unknown details of their plan. Now, twenty years later, I have documents from the Stroilov collection in my hands, which contain this plan in its entirety. Gorbachev's game was much more global, and his plans for expansion were much more ambitious than they seemed at first glance.

6.6   The "German Question"

When I was writing this book twenty years ago, I tried to recreate the Gorbachev plan for the union of Germany and Europe, using only indirect data and examples from earlier Soviet history. We know that a divided Germany was unacceptable to Stalin, who tried to "reunify" it in 1947–1948 to form a bloc of Eastern communists (who had renamed themselves the Socialist Unity Party of Germany) with Western social democrats. The idea of the Leader and Teacher was that a united Germany should remain neutral, demilitarized and. . . socialist, which would open the way to a peaceful seizure of Western Europe with the aid of a similar operation—a "union" of communists and socialists (the Anglo-American documentary "Messengers from Moscow", shown by the BBC in February 1995, told this story. See §6.11—Allies, fn. 372).

The project failed, mainly thanks to the Marshall Plan: massive American aid that defused public tension, cut the ground from under the feet of leftist forces and helped Europe to choose capitalism instead of socialism. The GDR and other countries of the socialist camp did not come into being because of a good life: the Iron Curtain was a certain admission of defeat by Stalin. Subsequent rulers of the USSR—each in his own way—tried to get rid of this problem. Beria tried to reunite Germany (see the book by Pavel and Anatoli Sudoplatov[320]) and even Khrushchev (for which he first had to achieve recognition of the GDR by the West). But Beria's plans ended with the 1953 uprising in the GDR, and Khrushchev's with the building of the Wall.

The policy of the USSR regarding Germany remained essentially the same in Brezhnev's time, when there was an attempt to achieve the same aims with the help of détente, which was more of the same —an alliance with the social democrats. As in Khrushchev's time, it started with the recognition of the GDR by the West pursuant to the Helsinki Accords, which legalized the Soviet gains and opened the way to the further "peaceful" seizure of Europe. And ended again with the Cold War.

As I have already written, the aim to make Europe socialist, make it serve the ends of socialism with its industrial potential, was the main direction of Soviet foreign policy from Lenin's time: this was vital to the survival of the USSR and the success of the entire socialist experiment. The key to the solution of this problem was always Germany. This became increasingly important in the post-war period: the reunification of Germany on Soviet terms—neutrality, demilitarization, etc.—meant the end of NATO, the withdrawal of the Americans from Europe and the almost total domination of the USSR from the Pacific to the Atlantic Ocean. From my point of view there was nothing surprising or even original in these plans being invoked again during the escalating crisis of the 1980s. The turn toward détente, which had been developed since the end of the 1970s, was not sufficient by itself to place the question of German reunification at the top of the list. What was the essence of détente if not the idea of "convergence" on the basis of an alliance of leftist forces in Europe? And how was this convergence to be accomplished without the removal of the Iron Curtain, in the first place—the Berlin Wall? The fact that both Germanys could not survive without the Wall was clear even in Khrushchev's time.

On the other hand, the reunification of Germany on Soviet terms, the subsequent collapse of NATO and the further integration of Europe on socialist principles was that very missing element in the plan without which the stabilization of the new regimes in Eastern Europe would be impossible, and the entire idea of the Velvet Revolution would have been suicidal for the USSR. Retaining con-

---

[320]Pavel Sudoplatov, Anatoli Sudoplatov, Jerrold L Schecter, Leona Schecter, Robert Conquest, *Special Tasks: The Memoirs of an Unwanted Witness—A Soviet Spymaster*. Boston: Little, Brown, © 1994, 1995. pp. 364–366.

trol over these regimes could only be achieved in the context of a
general European convergence, leaving them with no other clear alternative. Even intransigent Poland would have not escaped, with
the USSR on one side, and a united socialist Germany on the other,
with the addition of a strongly leftist Europe, striving for integration
under the leadership of a pro-socialist Eurocracy.

At that time this was just my guess; now I see in documents that
my guesswork on the basis of indirect data was quite correct. Back
in March 1986 Gorbachev's newly-appointed aide on international
affairs, Anatoly Chernyaev (former deputy head of the International
Department of the CC) prepared an extensive report for the Politburo on Soviet international strategy for the next couple of years
(10 March 1986, SA), which states among other things that:

> It appears feasible to pay more attention to the FRG, in the
> broadest possible sense. If we manage to draw it closer to us
> —and there would be more chances for this under the social
> democrats—it would be the greatest achievement of our Euro-
> pean and global policy. Everyone would start panicking again,
> from Washington to Paris and other capitals. The "Spirit of Rap-
> palo" is still alive and feared by some. Lenin's instructions re-
> garding the importance of the rapprochement of Germany and
> Russia should be remembered.

> Comrade Honecker's certain intractability in the so-called "Ger-
> man-German question" is well known. This calls for a degree
> of caution. Our position concerning his visit to the FRG a year
> and a half ago was quite correct. A repetition of that now is
> undesirable.

> It is worth considering whether we should tackle this entire
> "German-German question" in a way that would be to the ben-
> efit of the socialist community, socialism, and our policy. We
> hold the most important ace in our hands—settlement of the
> question of the "reunification of Germany." This could be the
> basis for our line of rapprochement with the Federal Republic.

The European Mensheviks, with their dreams of convergence in
a united socialist Europe, understood this as well. On 6 July 1989,
Francois Mitterrand and Gorbachev discussed Soviet-French relations which, it emerges, were strong, firm and close, and irreplace-
able for world peace. Among other matters they talked of history
and old Franco-Russian alliances. Suddenly, Mitterand said (6 July
1989, SA):[321]

> It is not just a question of history, but also of geography. Take,
> for example, the German question, which we shall probably

---

[321]Gorbachev, 1989 (SA), p. 256.

have to deal with together. At one time, this question was resolved by force. Now the issue is to find its resolution through harmony. [...] In our view, European borders should not be the border between two Germanys.

Documents show that their idea was to prolong the process of the reunification of Germany for some ten to twenty years, and combine it with the union of all Europe. In other words, convergence.

The fall of the Berlin Wall and the following reunification of Germany came as no surprise to Moscow and did not herald a catastrophe for their friends in the GDR. Immediately after Honecker was deposed, his successor Egon Krenz (formerly supervisor of the Stasi for the East German KGB), hurried to Moscow to report the details of the successful conspiracy to Gorbachev (1 November 1989, SA):[322]

> E.KRENZ. Thank you for your sincere and warm welcome. All the members of the Politburo send their regards. [...] We were able to proceed on a number of crucial questions after your visit on the fortieth anniversary of the GDR. [...]
>
> [...]
>
> I want to say that the path to the IX Plenum of the CC SED was very hard. Under an agreement with [Prime Minister Willi] Stoph, I prepared a draft statement about current political problems. The document was something of a compromise, based on the assumption that E. Honecker would remain party leader. [...] However, when Erich received the draft, he decided that it was a personal attack on him. [...]
>
> Despite these threats, I submitted the draft for consideration by the Politburo. At the meeting Honecker stressed this immediately, but everyone except one supported the draft. [...]
>
> M.S.GORBACHEV. The situation is clear from a political point of view, but it is dramatic from the human angle. I have been through this myself. I had reasonably good relations with E. Honecker, but he seems to have recently gone blind. If only he had accepted the necessary political changes on his own initiative 2-3 years ago, everything would be different now. [...][323]
>
> [...]
>
> E.KRENZ. [...] When you were in Berlin you must have felt how warmly all the young people greeted you, cries of "Gorby! Gorby!" echoed all over the city. Some people even scolded me:

---

[322] *Gorbachev and the German Question*, Gorbachev Foundation: Moscow, 2006, compiled by Alexander Galkin and Anatoly Chernyaev, http://www.rodon.org/other/mgigv/1989_2.htm#53; see also Gorbachev, 1989 (SA), pp. 441 and 442.

[323] Gorbachev, 1989 (SA), p. 452.

"What is this celebration you have prepared?" But a reception like that could not have been prepared artificially. It was just an indication that nobody had been able to ruin the attitude of the youth of the GDR toward the Soviet Union, toward perestroika.

M.S.GORBACHEV. Actually, it placed me in a rather awkward position, especially during the torchlit procession when I was standing next to E. Honecker.

In this same conversation they also raise the matter of relations with the FRG, the Berlin Wall and the outlook for the reunification of Germany—but only in the long run, within the context of the unification of all of Europe.

M.S.GORBACHEV. [...] I would also like to mention the need to pursue a principled and at the same time flexible line with regard to the FRG. They will probably pressure you. Effort must be made to ensure that decisions concerning the GDR are to be made in Berlin, not Bonn. But I repeat there is need for flexibility, as a strong blow could come from there.

E.KRENZ. I agree. I would be grateful for any advice on matters concerning relations with the FRG. I would like to have a clearer understanding of the place the Soviet Union is allocating to the FRG and the GDR in the common European home? This is very important for us. We are proceeding on the assumption that the GDR is a child of the Soviet Union, and decent people always acknowledge their children, at least allowing them to take on their father's name. (*Reaction from those present.*)

M.S.GORBACHEV. Yesterday A.N. Yakovlev had a meeting with [Zbigniew] Brzezinski and he, as you know, has a head "with global brains." So he said: if matters today were to take a turn that would enable the reunification of Germany, it would mean the collapse of a great deal. I believe that we have followed the right path until now: we have given firm support to the coexistence of the two German states. [...]

You must know: all serious political figures—Thatcher, Mitterand, Andreotti and Jaruzelski, as well as the Americans, although there are certain nuances apparent in the position of the latter—are not seeking the reunification of Germany. In the current situation it would be explosive. Most Western leaders do not want the dissolution of NATO and the Warsaw Pact. Serious politicians understand that these are all factors in an essential balance. Although let's say that Mitterand considers it necessary to mention his sympathy toward the idea of German reunification. The Americans are also talking about a similar sympathy toward the German wish for reunification. But I think they are doing this to please Bonn, and to a certain extent are apprehensive about too much rapprochement between the FRG and the USSR. [...]

I am certain that we should coordinate our ties with the FRG more successfully, which is something E. Honecker declines to some extent.[324] We are aware of your relations with the FRG, and you know ours. So there is no need for prevarication or concealment between us! It is worth considering a tripartite cooperation between the USSR, the GDR and the FRG, especially in the economic sphere. At one time there was a special Soviet-GDR committee on coordination. It still exists formally, although it has been inactive for a long time. I believe that Mittag is a member of it from the GDR side.

E.KRENZ. He may have had a hand in the termination of the work of this committee.

M.S.GORBACHEV. The work of this committee must be reactivated with allowances for ongoing changes. I think it would be profitable for us to use the potential of the FRG, try to tie it to us, especially as there is evidence of thinking along these lines by some. It is true that the FRG is prepared to go some way toward the USSR in exchange for our cooperation in the reunification of Germany. The Americans admit openly that the keys to this lie in Moscow. They would not mind a clash between us and the West Germans on this matter. I reiterate that they find the process of rapprochement between the USSR and the FRG most undesirable. Although frankly speaking, at the practical level, and primarily at the economic one, not much has changed in Bonn-Moscow relations.

Everything concerning relations with the FRG must be thought through very carefully. The more so that in your situation, the matter may take a turn that will leave you no room for ideology. Careful calculation should be the order of the day. You probably feel more secure with our participation in tripartite contacts. That would profit everyone and at the same time assist your relations with the FRG and enable the overall reinforcement of the political positions of the GDR. Furthermore, you ought to be able to be more forthcoming in establishing ties with other Western countries and not just the FRG. [...]

[...]

M.S.GORBACHEV. As for how the German question will be resolved in the end, we do not need to make any guesses at this stage. We should proceed from the situation "gifted" to us by history. Not taking this reality into account would be the worst political option. Maybe in several decades to come, the German question will be thrown into quite a different light if integration

---

[324]Gorbachev, 1989 (SA), p. 446 et seq.

processes develop normally. [. . .]

So today the question of reunifying Germany is not a priority. Please convey our firm stance on this to your Politburo and CC. I repeat, this stance is shared by our partners in the anti-Hitler coalition, which is not to be ignored. The top priority at this time is improving relations in Europe, otherwise everything could explode.

E.KRENZ. I agree with this framing of the question. It requires ideological reinforcement. E. Honecker issued five well-known demands to Bonn at the beginning of the 1980s—acknowledgement of GDR citizenship, and so forth. Since then, we have implemented a number of agreements with the FRG, not one of our demands has actually been satisfied. Moreover, this has created a false impression: people see E. Honecker, Mittag and Krenz going to the FRG and ask why they are forbidden to do so.

One difficult question for us. You often talk of common human values. I am all for them, too. But there are also common German problems. In this sense, the de-ideologizing of relations between the GDR and the FRG is overshadowed by great difficulties; it would entail refusing to protect socialism in the GDR. There are complicated problems connected with the Berlin Wall, with the regime across the border.

M.S.GORBACHEV. All this must be considered and a formula found that will enable people to enjoy their human needs. Otherwise we shall be faced with innumerable ultimatums. [. . .] Chancellor Kohl is still in contact with me and with you. We should influence him. Under pressure from the opposition, he has mounted the nationalist horse. The right-wingers have started to push their demands to the USSR for the reunification of Germany, and appeal to the USA as well. [. . .]

E.KRENZ. We have already taken a number of steps. Firstly, we have instructed the military to desist from using firearms at the border, with the exception of direct attacks on border guards. Secondly, the Politburo has approved a draft law on travel across the border. We shall offer it for public discussion and expect to see its adoption by the People's Chamber before Christmas. The draft law envisages that any citizen may, for a certain fee, acquire a foreign passport and exit visa. The only exceptions will be for security concerns. Other limitations will include a considerable shortfall of foreign currency for exchange into marks. It stands to reason that we will be criticized for this. But it will have to be said that we cannot ignore reality.

M.S.GORBACHEV. It should probably be mentioned that efforts are to be directed at acquiring the exchangeability of currency, and this will require all citizens to work better and produce competitive goods.

Nonetheless, even this conversation suggests certain concern that events could spiral out of control:

> E.KRENZ. [...] Mass demonstrations have created a difficult situation. They are formed of different groups, including our opponents, but the majority are simply those dissatisfied with the current state of affairs. Speaking in the People's Chamber, I stressed that political problems can only be settled by political means. As much as we can, we strive to avoid involving the police. The coming weekend will be a very serious one for us: on Saturday November 4 there is to be a large demonstration in Berlin. Seventeen creative associations intend to participate— artists, writers, etc. Up to half a million people may turn up.
>
> [...] We are assuming that not all the demonstrators are our opponents. At the same time, we are implementing measures against a mass approach to the Berlin Wall. The police will be there. If attempts are made to breach the Wall into West Berlin, the situation will be critical: a state of emergency will have to be declared. Hopefully this will not happen.
>
> M.S.GORBACHEV. Everything must be done to prevent this, although it is right to allow for the eventuality of the worst possible scenario.

Even though by November events had really gotten out of control, when the planned and very limited liberalization of the exit regime from the GDR resulted in the fall of the Berlin Wall, Gorbachev still thought that everything was going more or less to plan. Here, for example, is his conversation with the British ambassador (17 November 1989, SA):[325]

> The ambassador submitted a letter from M. Thatcher, which was a response to M.S. Gorbachev's appeal to her (and other Western leaders) regarding events in the GDR.
>
> Passing over the letter the ambassador, speaking on behalf of his Prime Minister, he stressed the importance of the current active exchange of opinions concerning "German problems" and the significance of the continuation of such contacts.
>
> "Mrs Thatcher", said Braithwaite, "has a high regard for your policy not just on the whole, but concerning the events in Germany. Everyone in the West was astounded by the speed and nature of these developments. At some moment there was a feeling of unclarity and instability... and unexpectedness."

---

[325]Gorbachev, 1989 (SA), pp. 468–469.

M.S.GORBACHEV. We experienced it to a lesser degree (stir in the room).

R. BRAITHWAITE. It was very unexpected for the West Germans. Now the ambiguity and instability have decreased. It is important that people in the GDR, having gained the option of freely visiting West Berlin and the FRG, are now beginning to return.

M.S.GORBACHEV. Yes, now the queues are in the other direction. And that is good.

R.BRAITHWAITE. Yes, it is good that people can live at home. It is good that the tension, if one can call it so, has relaxed. To a great extent, this is due to your policy. But the Germans— both Eastern and Western, must be given their due.

M.S.GORBACHEV. Yes, that is very true.

R.BRAITHWAITE. Recently Mrs Thatcher spoke to the press several times on this matter, and later in the Guildhall. She placed special emphasis on stability. In her opinion, the most important thing is that we cooperate with you, that everyone cooperates. Changes should be controllable. However, it is also important that the GDR leadership take the road of reform— along the path you have blazed.

There are international institutions (the ambassador meant the Warsaw Pact and NATO), that set the framework for the "management of events."

He went on to list forthcoming meetings at various levels between the leading figures of NATO countries, at which the situation in Central Europe would be discussed in collective and bilateral meetings.

M.S.GORBACHEV. As for the Paris meeting of 12 leaders of EU countries, Mitterand is probably collecting opinions prior to the meeting with me (stir in room). But—he added jokingly —if something untoward happens, I shall send the bill to Mrs Thatcher as the most experienced of them.

R.BRAITHWAITE. Mrs Thatcher has written in the letter and has said publicly something that I wish to stress here before you: we all—my government and our allies—have a good understanding that there should be no interference in GDR affairs, and not give any pretext for something that may be construed as interference or encroachment on the security of the GDR or indeed any Warsaw Pact countries and your security. This is most important—that there be no interference by any side.

M.S.GORBACHEV. It would be better to interfere in the affairs of the West Germans (laughter).

R. BRAITHWAITE. It would be interesting to learn what you think of that, too. As for the GDR, I think we should meet its people halfway, firstly that they should have free elections.

M.S.GORBACHEV. Now that is interference! We can evaluate, we have that right, but giving unsolicited advice as to what should be done, that is another matter. Let the Germans decide for themselves.

R.BRAITHWAITE. But this question is being decided in the People's Chamber today—about free elections....

In subsequent months, even though the GDR was rapidly slipping the leash of control, the Kremlin leaders remained convinced that Germany would remain theirs. Knowing the full situation in the GDR, they nonetheless experienced no doubts that it would be the West that kept it within the Soviet sphere of influence (26 January 1990, SA).[326]

Discussion of the German question at a limited meeting in the office of the General Secretary of the CC CPSU in the CC building on the Staraya [Old] Square on 26 January 1990 (recorded by Chernyaev):

Present: Gorbachev, [Nikolai] Ryzhkov, Shevardnadze, Kryuchkov, Akhromeyev, Chernyaev, [Georgy] Shakhnazarov, Yakovlev, Falin, Fedorov.

GORBACHEV: The situation with the GDR is the same as with Azerbaijan: there is nobody to lean on, nobody with whom to have confidential relations. And even when there is someone to reach an agreement with, it brings no decisive results. Even Modrow is distancing himself from the SED. It makes no difference that he is our sincere friend. There are no effective forces in the GDR.

Therefore the only way we can influence the process is through the FRG. Here, too, we are faced with the choice: Kohl or the SPD. The Social Democrats—despite all their comforting declarations and vows made by Brandt and his colleagues—have rushed to use the GDR in the pre-election battles.

Brandt is already the chairman of the united SDPG. Prominent members of this party are prepared to stand for the People's Chamber, reject membership of the Bundestag and return home—to East Germany, where most of them were born. They hope to steal a march on the CDU that way.

We can use this to our benefit. We need to invite Kohl and say to him: look at what is going on, but you are playing this game,

---

[326] *Gorbachev and the German Question* (2006), http://www.rodon.org/other/mgigv/1990_1.htm

too, and might lose. Social Democrats in the GDR have more chances than you. But we do not look at the German problem through your electoral spectacles; we look at it in the European and global context. That is also how your NATO allies regard it. You know full well the difference between what they say publicly and what they really think.

So there it is. We, dear Helmut, also offer to seriously adopt the European viewpoint on German matters—in deeds, and not just words.

This is what this means specifically: our troops are in the GDR, and NATO forces are in the FRG. This is a real fact, ensuing from the legal bottom line of the war, established by the victors. And it affirms the right of four powers to participate in the German process. You, and particularly Brandt, do not like it that France is among the victors ("honorary victor", as you say ironically). Fine. But today's reality is not the same as that of 1945. So let us convene not "4" but "5" and yes, Kohl, with your participation. Let us determine the rights of Germans, and the rights of the others.

CHERNYAEV: Mikhail Sergeyevich, I think we need to convene not "5" but "6"—four from the victors, and two from the German states.

GORBACHEV: Let us discuss this. Now to proceed. The main thing is that nobody should expect that a united Germany will join NATO. The presence of our troops will not allow it. We can withdraw them if the Americans withdraw their forces. They will not do this for a long time. Kohl will have to take this into account, and also that swallowing the GDR economically will also take several years. So these years are at our and your disposal. Let us use them wisely. And prepare for the 1990 top-level All-European Conference.

The action with "5" or "6" initiated by us returns us to the role of active and indispensable participant in the German settlement. This is a very profitable move.

SHEVARDNADZE: Mikhail Sergeyevich, the most important question for Kohl is now the "contractual community" which leads to the confederation FRG-GDR. We have no need to participate in the discussion on reunification. It is not our affair. Let the GDR display some initiative. Talks about the armed forces should be conducted only with the United States. I am against an "institution" consisting of four victors. That will give NATO the upper hand.

[Vladimir] KRYUCHKOV: The days of the SED are numbered. It is not a lever or a prop for us. Modrow is a transitional figure, he is hanging on at the cost of concessions, but soon there will be nothing left to concede. We should turn our attention to the

SPD in the GDR.

Our people fear that Germany will become a threat once more. They will never agree to the current borders.

We need to educate our people gradually regarding the reunification of Germany. The presence of our forces in the GDR is a factor in the all-European process. We must give active support to our friends—former personnel of the KGB and the Ministry of Internal Affairs in the GDR.

YAKOVLEV: Modrow needs to insinuate himself into the SPD and head its eastern part. America needs our troops in the GDR more than we do. It would be good if Modrow were to come forward with a program for reunification—without prejudices, on the basis of realities, and we would give him our active support. This will win us the sympathy of the German people. It should also be made clear that we have been championing the idea of a united Germany since 1946. And the conditions? Neutralization, demilitarization. There will be opposition from England, France and small European states. We put America into a position requiring deep reflection. In the meantime, we can sit on top of the hill and watch the skirmish at the bottom. With regard to the attitude of our people—Stalin himself advocated the preservation of a united Germany immediately after the war. In any case, we can no longer simply observe.

FEDOROV: This will be seized upon by revanchist forces. According to my data, they do not want reunification right now in West Germany. [...]

RYZHKOV: We have to evaluate the process realistically. It is unstoppable. The issue now is tactics, because we will not be able to keep the GDR. All the barriers have been swept aside. Preserving the GDR is a pipe dream. Confederation is a reality. But we need to put forward our conditions for a confederation. It is wrong to give everything to Kohl. If that comes to pass, then 20–30 years from now Germany will start a third world war.

GORBACHEV: The process we have and the process in Eastern Europe is an objective process. And it is too overheated. Where this process has come into contact with the stronger links in the chain—the GDR, Czechoslovakia and Romania—is where the rupture was greatest. It is a lesson for us: to keep up and not lag behind, and always have our eyes open to reality.

The people—even with all the extensive criticism it hears, do not attempt to encroach on perestroika. Rather, they do not favor the opponents of perestroika. Our society is the most rotten of all of its kind. Beyond salvation. We began to transform it ourselves. And we need to keep up our efforts, move forward and not lose the initiative. Marching on the spot is destructive.

There was the "Brest Treaty" № 1,[327] and now we are facing a possible "Brest Treaty" № 2. If we do not cope, we face the threat... that half the country will be seized again. It is very important to understand this. The public is overly ideologized, therefore real processes are overtaking us. And the party cannot simply renew itself.

Certainly, the GDR is a special case. It is not Romania. In the GDR, the communist party is a serious matter. Czechoslovakia, Bulgaria and Hungary have vested interests in us. They will be upset for a while, but will be unable to go very far. Poland is a special case. And the GDR is a very special case. [...] The main thing now is to prolong the process, whatever the end purpose (reunification). The Germans also need to get used to this aim, as well as the people of Europe and the USSR.

This is the strategy. All of West Germany is interested in retaining ties with us. They need us, and we need them. But not absolutely. Don't we need France and England? Thinking this way would be a grave error. The Germans need us. In turn, this makes us take this dependence into account. Business circles do not want freeloaders. There are 58 million people in the FRG and 16 million in the GDR. France is against the reunification. England is afraid of being left on the periphery. We must keep all these factors in mind. [...]

We do not refuse the position of victors. Put forward the "4+2" idea. But agree with France at first. Maybe I should go to Paris?

Channel the German question into the Vienna process. On the matter of troops in Europe, handle ourselves so that it will not seem that we are simply leaving on the fiftieth anniversary of the Victory. The presence of troops in Germany is closely connected with the Vienna process.

Kohl should be told—stay out of it. In this respect we can reach agreement with everyone. There is the potential of special relations with the FRG: with it and with the GDR. We should insist on this. There are mutual interests and there are grounds for mutual understanding.

The SED and us: there is currently "euphoria" there with regard to the SPDG. But it is forgotten that there are numerous problems—both European and German. After all, its membership is 2 million. Even if there are only 700 thousand now, writing them off would be stupid. A left-wing force will emerge in time. Let us hear what Gysi has to say.

Other socialist countries: we need to work with them. After all, they are allies. If we abandon them, they will be picked up by someone else.

---

[327]The Treaty of Brest-Litovsk (1918)

The idea of playing for time is the answer to the proposal of a "contractual community" with confederative features.

We should hold back those who are in too much of a hurry.

What are the next steps?

[...]

- propaganda support for the processes in Eastern Europe (Yakovlev, Falin, Fedorov),

- Gorbachev's interview regarding the reunification of Germany after meetings with Modrow and Kohl.

My one-day visits to London and Paris are not excluded.

Akhromeyev is to prepare the withdrawal of troops from Germany. Explain the "economic vulnerability" of the GDR to Kohl and Modrow.

Up to a certain time, at least prior to the spring-summer of 1990, everything seemed to be going to plan and none of them foresaw the looming collapse. Judging by everything, the panic only set in in March, on the eve of and after the elections in the GDR, in which the communists of the "renewed" and renamed "Party of Democratic Socialism" (PDS) suffered a crushing defeat.

It was only in October 1990 that the Politburo finally adopted a resolution "On measures regarding the persecution of the Party of Democratic Socialism (GDR)", which may be seen as an acknowledgement of defeat. The resolution prescribes (28 September 1990*, 06/2-439):

1. ... to organize the systematic publication in the party press and other media of materials regarding the persecution and hounding of former members of the SED, dismissed for political motives and qualify such actions as a breach of democratic principles and human rights.

   Special attention should be paid to cases of the institution of criminal proceedings against individuals who were state servants or engaged in political activity on charges of "national treason" or subversive activity against the FRG, especially when this concerns cooperation with the USSR.

2. In such materials reporting on the process of German reunification, due attention must be drawn to the activity of the PDS. React to attempts aimed at infringing the constitutional rights of the party and deprivation of its lawful property.

   The International Department of the CC CPSU is instructed to establish the regular receipt of information concerning the persecution of party members from the PDS, and also materials exposing the anti-socialist nature of the measures implemented by the West German side in the course of reunification.

3. Maintain a constant watch and react operatively to efforts aimed at building up pressure on the issue of the Western Group of Forces (ZGV) and sowing hostile attitudes toward the Soviet people.

4. Make provision for possible evacuation to the Soviet Union of persons who had cooperated actively with Soviet organizations and who are now subject to hounding and persecution by Bonn. Firstly, this may concern party workers, security agencies and members of the National People's Army of the GDR, figures in science and culture, qualified organizers of industry who have lost their jobs in the re-unified Germany due to political oppression. Implement active measures for finding them work and granting material assistance.

There is no doubt that up until October 1990, that is, up to the date of the reunification, Moscow was still hoping that it would take place on its terms. Yet from the very start, things did not go as planned: by sheer chance, the wall between the East and West was opened one day before schedule, which led to a loss of control over the migration of the population ("Fatal Error", broadcast by the BBC on 6 November 1994). Millions of people rushed through the breach, burying forever the myth of the GDR as a separate state.

Subsequently, despite all expectations, the election in the GDR on March 18 was a total catastrophe for the PDS, which predetermined the result of negotiations on the status of a united Germany between the Second World War allies and the two Germanys ("4+2") and the conclusion of the agreement of May 18 on the currency union of both Germanys. Finally, due to this election, the Christian Democratic majority in the GDR parliament (People's Chamber) simply voted on August 23 for the reunification of the Eastern lands with the FRG on the basis of a pre-war law, and it was all over. Moscow did not have the slightest opportunity to dictate its conditions for reunification, although up to the last moment Gorbachev tried to keep the GDR in the Warsaw bloc. Even in the summer of 1990 he continued to insist on the retention of the GDR army within the Warsaw Pact, which was absolutely ridiculous.

Naturally, something entirely different was envisaged: the collapse of the Wall was supposed to be their triumph, and not serendipity; the migration across the border was supposed to be strictly controlled, thereby lessening political penetration by the

West; moreover the election of 18 March was supposed to be won by their "renewed" placemen in the PDS. That would have been when Moscow could have dictated its terms for reunification, differing little from those of Stalin, Beria and Khrushchev: neutrality, demilitarization and socialism. It is unlikely that the West Germans would have rejected any conditions for achieving their dream—reunification with eastern brethren, especially as the social democrats would have been willing to support these conditions and even conduct an election campaign on that basis.

Achieving a "neutral" Germany, breaking up NATO and seeing off the Americans, it would not have been difficult to keep the remaining East European countries "within the framework of socialism." The "convergence" that had been the dream of West European Mensheviks for so long, would have finally come true.

6.7   The "Common European Home"

I am not exaggerating in the least: the plan for unification—not of Germany alone, but all Europe—had been devised by Moscow and its Western allies in full detail; so it was not by chance that from the end of 1988, and especially in 1989, the prevalent theme in all of Gorbachev's addresses became the creation of "a common European home." At the same time, there was a significant change in the attitude of the USSR to the process of European integration: if the Soviet Union had viewed this process with suspicion, not to say with extreme hostility in the 1970s and the first half of the 1980s, by 1989 this attitude had changed in the other direction. Until 1984 the head of the intelligence administration of the KGB, Kryuchkov, instructed his residents in Europe to increase efforts at penetrating all the structures of the EC and oppose its further integration because:

> "Obviously, progress in the integration of Western Europe, especially in the military-political field, runs counter to the interests of the Soviet Union."[328]

However from the second half of the 1980s, as integration progressed as well as the political orientation of the European Community as such, the attitude of the USSR toward it began to change: the more the socialists and social democrats gained the upper hand

---

[328]Christopher Andrew and Oleg Gordievsky, *Instructions from the Centre: Top Secret Files on KGB Foreign Operations 1975–1985*, Sceptre (pbk): London, (1993), Chapter 7, "The European Community", p. 237.

in the structures of the EC, the more benignly it was viewed by Moscow. By 1989 the creation of a "common European home" became their battle-cry, although naturally enough none of them admitted openly that this "home" was to be a socialist one.

The plan was approved at a meeting of the Politburo on 26 March 1987 (24 March 1987, Pb, SA):[329]

> (Recorded by Chernyaev)
>
> On the West European direction of foreign policy
>
> Report by KOVALEV on the concept of the "common European home":
>
> 1. Greater independence for Europe.
> 2. Distancing from the extremist policy of the USA.
> 3. Invite the Europeans and others not to look upon Europe through American spectacles.
> 4. Europe is particularly receptive to our perestroika and glasnost. Use this.
> 5. The problem of trust—through internal transformations in the USSR.
> 6. Removal of concerns, demonstration of the defensive nature of our military doctrine.
> 7. Develop a mandate for a humanitarian conference in Moscow.
> 8. Increase scientific work on European problems.
>
> . . .
>
> DOBRYNIN. . . . The idea of the "common European home" is gaining ground. . . .
>
> CHEBRIKOV. We will have a lot of work to do with respect to the humanitarian conference. We need to set terms—in six months, or in two years. This makes a big difference to us (i.e. the KGB).
>
> GORBACHEV. The Vienna conference is proceeding, not the longest one at this stage. How long did the Madrid Conference last? Three years. And there was no end in sight. Then the Korean airliner was shot down. Suddenly everything was decided! (Laughter). Sergey Leonidovich [Sokolov, Minister of Defense], maybe you can save the day: bring another army into Afghanistan, and everyone will scatter. It is our tendency to put forward an idea, invite famous people, and only then start to think it through!

---

[329] *Kak "delalas" politika perestroiki*, 1987 (SA), pp. 109–112.

SHEVARDNADZE. There is no serious analysis of the situation, our lapses, inadequacies and mistakes. There were plenty of them—our own defects. We did not follow through to the end. In drawing up such documents, there should be room for more self-criticism.

We also need to raise the question of military doctrine and review certain aspects of it thoroughly. We cannot leave questions such as control unanswered. Otherwise we will not overcome the psychological barrier of mistrust toward us. We are surrounded by military bases. And that is also our problem.

GORBACHEV (laughing). We have no "bases"! We have said so in Vienna! It is not acceptable for everyone to know that we have something, and we say we do not! These days everyone has government experts on all problems.

... We need contacts with opposition parties in Europe. They play an important role in many countries.

We need to develop the concept for relations with the Communist International. Communist parties turn away from confrontation with us, which is characteristic of the Italian Communist Party, the French Communist Party and the Communist Party of Spain.

... Let the institutes of the Academy of Sciences form at least a group of scientists to work for us on such fundamental issues such as "German-German" relations. There are many other problems.

I have understood from your statements that as far as we are concerned, "everything about Europe is clear." What is the actual progress of our perception? From a lesser ignorance to a greater one. There is a lot tied up in this, comrades. It is obvious that not a single question can be resolved without taking Europe into account. We need it even in our domestic affairs, for perestroika. As for foreign policy, nothing can replace Europe. It has the strongest bourgeoisie not just economically, but also politically. At one time it seemed that Japan had outpaced the whole world, when suddenly the FRG comes up with an enormous advance in the scientific-technological sphere. . . .

[. . .]

Western Europe does not have to be split off from the USA; the USA should be squeezed out of Europe. Will it work? I do not know. But we cannot pose such a question.

Europe is our business. We have immense interests there. There is no need to fear. "Strangle them in an embrace." [. . .] We need to strive for the withdrawal of American arms from Europe.

The Helsinki process offers us possibilities, and we must move into the next phase, step by step, set an example. An important task is to employ the scientific and technical potential of Western Europe, especially as our friends in the Comecon have become stuck in there. Our rapprochement with Western Europe will make their work easier.

See Europe as it is. For example, the reality of integration processes. What is profitable for us, and what is not? On the one hand, the power to influence the USA increases, on the other hand, military concentration increases.

Mitterand assured me that there is no need to fear this concentration. He claims it is in order to be free of American guardianship. But we can see the essence of the matter. We can oppose this only by cooperating in the disarmament of Europe. The stronger this process, the less they will be tempted to form a military grouping.

The second reality. See Europe in all its diversity. There are developed and less developed countries. There are England, France and the FRG. There are Finland and Austria. There are Holland, Sweden and others like them. There are Spain and Portugal. Small countries are our potential allies. Apart from that, there are opposition parties, communist parties, there are social circles. We have more active contacts with social circles in the USA than in Europe.

Many problems arise. We need to plan our work with Europe with great care. Create a regrouping of scientific forces. The forces are there, they just need to be regrouped.

Alexander Nikolayevich [Yakovlev]! Maybe we should set up a center for European studies?

And remember—Western Europe is our main partner.

As for the battle of ideas.... Wick [the director of USIA] said recently: "There is an ongoing war of ideas. To lose it is to lose everything!" So there it is.

I am coming to the main point: we need to do a lot of work to support propaganda—this is a very big question.

In a nutshell, our thoughts are moving in the right direction.

Europe is everywhere: in Kampuchea, in the Middle East, in Africa and, of course, among our eastern friends and even in Latin America. Without Europe, we will not really be able to move things forward.

This program was very close to the dreams of European leftists for convergence and the tactical plans of Western communists. It was particularly pleasing to the Italian comrades, who had preceded Moscow in devising complex concepts for saving socialism in the West. Now there was full mutual understanding between them and

Gorbachev. Their General Secretary, Alessandro Natta, was to say to Gorbachev in January 1986 (27 January 1986, SA):[330]

> ... Frankly, the present situation of communist parties in the West is critical. There was nothing like it 15–20 years ago. There is retreat, the loss of public influence, and not just in the elections. Schisms and deep crises within parties have affected the positions of the working class.
>
> We have managed to retain our positions in Italy, but we have the growing feeling that we are the black sheep, the exception in the general communist panorama. [...]
>
> We are in Europe, Western Europe; we were born here and are fighting the cause of socialism in Western Europe. The SDP, and the Labourites and the French Communist Party have encountered serious difficulties ensuing from the scientific-technical revolution, the collapse of the "social state" and unemployment. The socialist democrats have always conducted a traditional policy, but now they are also beginning to rethink things. The problems we are encountering are not entirely European. They occur in other parts of the world as well.
>
> The countries of Western Europe find it hard to support the alliance with the USA, to oppose the challenges of the USA within the framework of the alliance, to bear the position of subservience. This is why we are putting our cards on the European communities, the European choice. [...]
>
> Progressive decisions at the social level must fit into the European framework. In one country, even the most interesting decisions shall yield only partial results [...] the issue is not a new phase, but there are conditions for a new uplift of leftist forces.
>
> The policies of Reaganism or Thatcherism did not solve problems, just created new ones. Understanding this, we are coming to the conclusion that there must be a new impulse to the policy of the party. We need new efforts to broaden alliances not just in Italy, but in the European context, moreover this must extend to all leftist forces in the widest sense of the word. We need to ally not only with parties, the communist, socialist and social democratic ones, but the entire complex of movements, progressive forces with differing aims, including religious movements. In the struggle for peace there are some places where religious movements are well ahead of the communists if not in the field of ideas, then in organization. In Holland, for example. In Italy the situation varies: there are bishops promoting reactionary policies, but there are those who speak out in favor of social justice and equality.

---

[330]Gorbachev, 1986 (SA), pp. 10–12, 14.

However, in forming alliances the communist identity of the party must be preserved. Communist identity is a vital process, not set in stone once and forever. I repeat: conditions have become difficult, processes are moving forward and their laws are not established to be everlasting.

M.S.GORBACHEV. We are also discussing the question of succession: does it mean repeating the past, or moving on?

A.NATTA.   I was talking about the socialists and social democrats.

M.S.GORBACHEV. It is harder to invite some communists than social democrats.

A.NATTA. The attitude to leftists in Europe is complex. In Italy we see this in the example of our socialists. If leftist forces want to be more autonomous, they should have more ties with the Soviet Union....

[...]

M.S.GORBACHEV. [...] Here is a thought: making sense of one's work, it is important to think about the attraction of the socialist ideal, socialist perspectives. Others, even the social democrats, have other ideals, especially the conservatives. You are correct that on the left front there is no ready position but the problem of enriching the leftist movement, finding new allies. Maybe there will be transitional pauses on this path, which should be accepted without losing sight of our aims. In search of answers to the existing problems some may have strayed from the way, but this may result in a loss of positions altogether. I think it is not our problem to add anything to the social democrat experience. Looking for points of contact is essential, there may be temporary alliances. But the alternative to bourgeois parties is communism.

A.NATTA. We still lack a majority in Europe; neither we, nor the social democrats. Not even combined. There is a struggle for the minds of the people.

M.S.GORBACHEV. Let the conservatives take the responsibility for the reorganization of the European economy. The communists should proclaim more current slogans.

Gorbachev and Natta met again two years later. (28 March 1988, SA) [26]:[331]

M.S.GORBACHEV. How should the face of the future socialist alternative look? [...] You have already marked the circle of your efforts toward the uniting of leftist forces. I do not think this was easy. The Italian experience shows that this is so. And

---

[331]Gorbachev, 1988 (SA), pp. 150–151.

within the scope of Europe, even more. I see that leftist forces have the strength to ensure that the processes of integration serve the democratization of Western Europe, that social questions will be resolved.

[...]

What is occurring now in Western Europe will determine the course of events for many decades, or centuries to come. The PCI has realized the importance of a new approach to these manifestations, which unite numerous forces. But without the left, it is unlikely that the interests of workers shall be protected. That is why we welcome [...] your efforts.

Need it be said that the European Mensheviks seized the chance of the proposed union with the Bolsheviks yet again?

Let us look at another scenario: on 3 March 1989, Gorbachev received a visit from Francisco Fernandez Ordonez, the Minister of Foreign Affairs in the Spanish socialist government of Felipe Gonzalez (3 March 1989, SA):[332]

F.FERNANDEZ ORDONEZ. What you say is of great importance. In the perestroika process the main target is the result of ideological struggle. The success of socialist ideas in the contemporary world community depends on the success of perestroika.

M.S.GORBACHEV. Through our perestroika, through new ideas proposed by the socialists of Western Europe, we do not move further from one another, but draw closer. From our point of view we are now in the watershed period of the development of human history, and there are no reasons why two streams of the workers' movement should find themselves on opposite sides of the barricades again [...] We have a genuine comradely interest, sympathy and understanding of our problems and difficulties, an understanding of the importance of our task from the side of those countries in which socialist and social democratic governments are in power.

At that time there were not many such left in the West, but Gorbachev used them for all they were worth. Of the main Western countries, the socialists were in power only in France—so president Mitterrand was his main partner in the "common European home" program at first. Mitterrand entered history with the reputation of an anti-communist, but documents now show him in a completely different light. *Inter alia*, being one of the architects of the European Union, Mitterrand saw West European integration as just a step toward "convergence" with Moscow.

---

[332]Gorbachev, 1989 (SA), p. 56.

> A Europe united within the framework of the EEC [European
> Economic Community]—he said to Gorbachev in 1988—is only
> the first step toward the real goal, the achievement of which
> shall require much time—twenty-five, fifty years, and maybe a
> whole century. The real goal is all of Europe together.

As was to be expected, the West German social democrats were
not far behind, especially since Willy Brandt had become chairman
of the Socialist International at that time (17 October 1989, SA).[333]

> It is vital that perestroika should succeed, he said to Gorbachev
> back in October 1989. I would be grateful if you would say
> what you expect from the so-called West, and from us social
> democrats [...] in assisting perestroika. There is a great deal of
> talk that socialism "is ending", has outlived itself. But I believe
> that from a historical point of view we are dealing with a new
> beginning, a new quality of socialism in a very significant part
> of the world.

And when all was said and done, as the question concerned
their own survival, the Mensheviks were prepared to turn to any
villainy in order to pander to Gorbachev. For instance, by exploiting
his position in the Socialist International Brandt, acting through
his Scandinavian colleagues, organized restraining pressure on the
democratic opposition in Estonia, Latvia and Lithuania.

> W.BRANDT. [...] I am concerned by the situation in the Baltic
> republics. I am in contact with our northern friends [...]
>
> Our influence in this region is not great. But I assure you that
> if we exert it, it will only be in the interests of pacification. If
> necessary, we shall say to someone: questioning the federa-
> tion in the USSR is playing with fire. Preservation of the fed-
> eration opens broad opportunities for cooperation between the
> republics.

Actually, in Gorbachev's time, this matter was of concern not
only for the Mensheviks, and not only in Europe. Here is another
mysterious conversation that took place at the height of Moscow's
preparations for the "Velvet Revolutions" in Eastern Europe. On
18 January 1989 Gorbachev received a delegation of the Trilateral
Commission, a secretive and influential organization, uniting representatives of the political elite of the USA, Europe and Japan. The
delegation consisted of David Rockefeller, Henry Kissinger, Yasuhiro
Nakasone and Valery Giscard d'Estaing. Their purpose appeared
to be convincing Gorbachev to integrate into world economic and

---

[333]Gorbachev, 1989 (SA), pp. 404, 410–411.

financial organizations (GATT, IMF, etc.), convert the ruble and so on. Suddenly, Giscard asked to speak (18 January 1989, SA):[334]

> V.GISCARD D'ESTAING. Western Europe is currently undergoing restructuring, changing its structures. It is hard to say when this will come to fruition—in five, ten or twenty years. But a new, modern federated state will arise in Western Europe. We are moving in this direction, and the USSR should prepare to have dealings with a huge united West European state. This future state will be open and prepared for all types of cooperation.
>
> But at that time, possibly, the question will arise in one or another form—official or factual—of several states joining it. This will probably concern Austria, Switzerland, the Scandinavian countries, but also certain East European states. We have no intention of "poking around" in East European countries and disrupting the foundations of stability. We see the danger of destabilizing one country or another and have no interest in this. But we would like to know your reaction if several East European states, while preserving ties of security with the USSR, might wish to become associate members of the EEC?

Kissinger did not object, and was only keen for the USA to be part of this project:

> The second group of thoughts concerns the future of Europe, relations between its various countries. What is the outlook for the concept of "Europe from the Atlantic to the Urals"? What will be the place for that part of the Soviet Union that stretches east from the Urals? What will be the future relationship between the USA and this future Europe?
>
> I and my colleagues in the Trilateral Commission would like to make a constructive contribution to the building of such a Europe, in which the USSR and the USA would play an equally positive role.

Let us not forget that this conversation took place in January 1989, before there were any drafts of the Maastricht Treaty, let alone Amsterdam, Nice or the European Constitution. Nothing is said about these agreements requiring approval by referendums or at least the parliaments of European countries. How could these people know so precisely what would come to pass in European countries 15–20 years later?

As for the role of the USA, Gorbachev would be only too glad to play on American global visions on one hand, and on anti-American sentiment in Europe on the other. In either case, Moscow would be

---

[334]Gorbachev, 1989 (SA), p. 15 (Kissinger), 22 (Giscard d'Estaing).

the winner. For instance, here is how the deputy secretary of the International Department of the CC, Vadim Zagladin, reported on his conversation with the former French ambassador to the USSR, Henri Froment-Meurice (17 March 1989, SA):[335]

> Interlocutor [. . .] said that in recent times, our objections to the military alliance of EEC countries are causing concern in France. From the very first, Froment-Meurice continued, we have never intended to limit ourselves with just the "Common Market." We shall proceed further—I do not know in what form of political alliance, but we shall proceed. Maybe in the end it will be a federation or confederation, or an alliance, but there will be some kind of political unit. And such a union will, naturally, include defense.
>
> [I] reminded Froment-Meurice that two years ago M.S. Gorbachev said: we are prepared for contacts with the European Community in the political sphere also to the extent that that it will act as a political unit. And such contacts exist. With regard to defense, we are mainly concerned about its future development: that the unification of Europe in the military field might stimulate a new arms race. There has been a tendency toward decreasing the level of armaments on the continent.
>
> The interlocutor uttered assurances that nobody in the West is contemplating increasing armaments, on the contrary. Then, for some reason lowering his voice to a half-whisper, he said: "you must understand that this will not be an American union, but a European one, and not within the NATO framework." To my objection that most of the members of the EEC are participants in the military organization of NATO, the interlocutor winced, and replied: "Europe wants to have its own defense policy, and will discuss the issues involved with you later."
>
> The conversation on this subject ended with the interlocutor's expressed hope that we would not "overdo things" with the idea of the Common European Home, and not scare off the Europeans.

A mere couple of days after the Berlin Wall fell in November 1989, the French Minister of Foreign Affairs, Roland Dumas, hurried to Moscow—to make sure that the old plan was still in force (14 November 1989, SA):[336]

> How do you regard the move toward a new European order in the present situation from the point of view of ensuring stabil-

---

[335]Zagladin (SA), p. 298. Froment-Meurice was then adviser on foreign relations to a major private bank and had recently been appointed to head a commission on joint ventures with Soviet enterprises.

[336]Gorbachev, 1989 (SA), pp. 461, 467.

ity in the world? This echoes your words about the Common European Home.

After all, we in the West have already built the first floor of such a home—West European integration.

M.S. GORBACHEV. That is only an annex.

R. DUMAS. Yes, you could call it that. But if we are to build more floors on top, we need an extensive architectural plan, to try to make sure that these floors are compatible.

M.S. GORBACHEV. [...] Everyone is agreed that changes in Eastern Europe are proceeding apace. But is the West changing?

R. DUMAS. That's a good question.

M.S. GORBACHEV. It is important to not lag behind, to react in time to positive tendencies, and help them along. Incidentally, my conversation with you is made easier by the fact that we represent two tendencies of the socialist workers' movement. Have you not forgotten that?

R. DUMAS. If I look surprised, it is because I was just about to say the same thing.

Naturally, these plans were used to keep Eastern Europe under control, as well as the republics of the USSR. Even in 1991, several months before the collapse, the parties of the Socialist International continued their efforts to save the CPSU, discredit Yeltsin and support Gorbachev, as the International Department reported to the CC on 7 June 1991 (7 June 1991, 6-S-552^):

In turn, the processes of transformation in the Eastern and Central European states were proceeding under the banner of dismantling socialism, escalating elements of "rampant capitalism" and lowering the social security of workers. This caused anxiety in the leading European parties that were members of the Socialist International. They searched for methods to counteract undesirable tendencies in social development. In this, the Italian Communist Party (PCI), the Spanish Socialist Workers' Party (PSOE), the Austrian Socialist Party (SPO) and the Social Democratic Party of Germany (SPD) advocated the creation of a Common European Centre for the study of problems in relations between socialists and communists.

The most active advocates for discussing the problems that have arisen was the French Socialist Party (PSF), which is explained by its position as the ruling party and the position of its leadership, which is apparently alarmed by the prospects for survival of the socialist idea due to the crisis in Eastern Europe.

> Representatives of the French socialists have lately made fre-
> quent references to the need for discussion within the European
> leftist movement of a new concept for the actions of socialist and
> social democratic parties in a changing Europe. M. Maurois[337]
> has repeated his willingness to go to the USSR and discuss this
> complex of questions with the leadership of the CPSU.
>
> On the whole, there is an increasing understanding in the Euro-
> pean left that answers must be sought to the questions posed by
> the altered political situation in Europe, including countering
> political forces that actively promote ideas of "neo-liberalism"
> and are forming their own organizations and political structures
> in Eastern Europe.

I know nothing about "neo-liberal" forces, or about their attempts to create their own political structures in the East. However
the "forces of socialism" were working on it before the fall of the
Berlin Wall, including Poland, where due to their efforts the activists
of Solidarity continued to blindly follow the idiotic agreements of the
round table right up to the collapse of communism in the USSR.
Their influence was not negligible in other East European countries
either: it is said that Vaclav Havel received thousands of letters and
petitions from East European well-wishers, persuading him to "preserve the achievements of socialism" in Czechoslovakia.

The subject itself, advanced by them for rapid development,
sounds quite convincing: "The European Community and Eastern
Europe after the reunification of Germany: a challenge to the Left."
In which the International Department of the CC reported:

> Active discussion of this problem and its theoretical and prac-
> tical development, including the participation of European so-
> cialist and social democratic parties, and the search for joint
> approaches to the development of the socialist idea under new
> conditions would, in our opinion, promote the strengthening of
> the international contacts of the CPSU and its position as the
> leading force in the formation of new approaches to the global
> development of the socialist idea.
>
> Pursuant to this, it would be desirable to attract the attention of
> international political circles and the public to the unconstruc-
> tive position of Hungary, Poland and Czechoslovakia (which may
> be joined by Bulgaria) on the matter of new agreements between
> these countries and the Soviet Union. It is important to demon-
> strate that the objections of our former allies against obligations
> to refrain from participating in "any alliances, directed against

---

[337]Pierre Mauroy (1928–2013) French politician. From 1988–1992 first secretary
of the French Socialist Party. In 1992, succeeded Willy Brandt as the president of
the Socialist International.

one another" and the fact that this line is being followed in close contact with the Western bloc will introduce new elements into both the regional and European situation, ignoring the results of the Paris conference of the CSCE and threatening the balance of interests that opened the way to the building of a peaceful Europe.

As we see, the idea that Western Europe could force the Eastern one to remain in the Soviet bloc is not my invention. All these attempts are well documented now. Arriving in London for the G7 conference in 1991 (17 July 1991, SA),[338] Gorbachev complained that "there has been a breakdown of the economic ties between the Soviet Union and its neighbors." In reply the chairman of the European Commission Jacques Delors suggested "thinking about a mechanism for the restoration of your economic ties":

> .·. you have had to decrease your purchases in Eastern Europe, reserves have dwindled and private debt has grown. What is to be done? I think you should discuss this matter with the finance ministers [of the G7 countries], with the IMF, and provide information.

The theme was picked up by the Italian Prime Minister Giulio Andreotti:

> Today we are discussing how to assist in the improvement of relations between the Soviet Union and the counties of the former Warsaw Pact. I am happy that I have lived to see the day when we ask the Soviet Union not to leave this region.

The last nail was hammered in by the Prime Minister of the Netherlands, Lubbers (representing the European Communities with Delors). He melded the careful deliberations of Delors and the exuberant rejoicings of Andreotti into an ironclad decision. Additionally, Lubbers offered Gorbachev the services of the EEC in solving this problem:

> I would like to support G. Andreotti's thought regarding cooperation between the Soviet Union and the European Community in restoring ties with the countries of Central Europe. That is our common responsibility. You [Gorbachev] talked about a divorce after which former spouses realize just how much they needed each other [...] Mr Delors has suggested thinking about a mechanism that would enable the restoration of trade with these countries. I support this suggestion.

---

[338]Gorbachev, 1991 (SA), pp. 607, 612–613.

But the chairman (British Prime Minister Major, brought all these suggestions together and formulated them as the common decision of the G7":

> ... being aware, as President Gorbachev has noted, that there has been a breakdown of economic ties between the Soviet Union and its neighbors, we shall assist in the restoration of these ties....

Simply speaking—assist in the restoration of the Soviet empire, only an economic one this time, not a military one. They surely all understood that this was not a case of a voluntary return of the "former spouses" of the Soviet Union into the old harem. If the East European countries had wanted this, they would have restored trade without any external "mechanisms."

The point at issue was specifically the "survival of the socialist idea", and it was not by chance that at the same G7 meeting, an "alarmed" Mitterrand exhorted Gorbachev not to dismantle socialism:[339]

> I would advise you not to privatize everything. I am a socialist by temperament and will risk saying that most of those around this table are the same. The essence is in the synthesis of private enterprise, democratic struggle, competition and, at the same time, the role of the state. In all our countries the state acts, the differences are in degree. We cannot tell you to do this or that. One must respect the traditions of the Soviet Union.

Even at the end of 1991, when the Soviet Union continued to exist solely in Gorbachev's imagination, Mitterrand told him of his apprehensions (6 May 1991, SA)[340] that the disintegration of the Soviet empire shall lead to the "fragmentation of all Europe, its transformation into a chaos of states that could not be shaped into anything." He considered it essential to "at any price, devise the creation of structures that would enable reining in all these movements." His idea was that Moscow and Paris should become the two "poles" uniting Europe, and exercise joint control over everything that lies between them:

> ... they must be represented in every place where current problems are discussed, be it the German question, the evolution of the United States, separatist tendencies in Europe and so forth. I use the term "confederation." Obviously, something else could

---

[339]Gorbachev, 1991 (SA), p. 609.
[340]Gorbachev, 1991 (SA), p. 340 and 342.

be proposed. But there must be a common institution, an overall structure.

Like Gorbachev, the European Mensheviks tried to preserve the
Soviet Union until the last day. Mitterrand said (31 October 1991,
SA):[341]

> I reason quite coldly — it is in France's interests that there
> should be a central authority in the east of Europe. If there
> is disintegration, if we go back to what you had before Peter the
> Great, it would be a historic catastrophe, and that would be
> against France's interests.
>
> Centuries of history have taught us that France needs an ally
> in the South-East of Europe in order to ensure equilibrium.
> Any disintegration of integrity in the East causes instability.
> That is why we do not want and will not encourage separatist
> ambitions.
>
> [...] I am one of those who wish to see you as a strong partner
> —a new Union. Otherwise what are Russia, Ukraine, Belarus,
> Georgia, some other states? The result will be that the situa-
> tion in Poland will destabilize further. The same can be said of
> Czechoslovakia and Hungary.
>
> [...]
>
> If matters develop this way, my future successors will have to
> establish strong relations with Russia, as it will be the most
> powerful remnant of the old Union. But before that we may still
> find ourselves mired in anarchy. I am in favor of the outcome in
> which your country will be restored on a federative-democratic
> basis in 2-3 years. This would be the best outcome for the rest
> of Europe.
>
> You, Mr Gorbachev, are motivated by the reasoning of a patriot
> of your country. In this instance, I am relying on the affirmation
> of historical logic in the development of our continent.

6.8   The "Privatization" of power

In the context of the plan for the "survival of the socialist idea" the
sense of the persistent efforts of the Politburo mentioned at the beginning of this book becomes clear—transferring its aid to communist parties "into trade channels with firms controlled by fraternal
parties." As we recall, the first attempts to implement this plan began in 1987, then in 1988 and 1989 they were stepped up considerably: in the putative "common European (socialist) home", other

---

[341]Gorbachev, 1991.2 (SA), p. 250.

forms of the activity of communist parties and mutual interaction
of Moscow with them were required. Confrontation and the "class
struggle" would be changed to the "cooperation" of leftist forces, so
the future masters of the "home" from the Politburo hurried to affirm the situation of their spear carriers.

As of 1988, similar processes of "communist privatization" began
to be implemented in the USSR as well. On one hand, the structures
of the KGB and the International Department of the CC created numerous allegedly commercial "joint enterprises" with their Western
friends; on the other hand—acting under the cover of the new law
on cooperatives, the party-economic *nomenklatura* began to get its
hands on state property, becoming increasingly entangled with the
"black economy." By 1990 the process was active throughout the
country, mainly for the purpose of money laundering—funds stolen
from the party and the state—and their transfer into Western financial institutions.

Many documents about this process have already been published. Here, for example, is a memo from CC Secretary Shenin
dated 4 December 1989:

> On problems of party property.
>
> The development of the political process in the country and the
> formation of a multi-party system pose many new questions
> concerning the material support of the vital activity of the party,
> the creation of stable sources of financing in both Soviet and for-
> eign currency. The material base of the international connec-
> tions of the CPSU depends on this, as well as its capability to
> render at least minimal aid to foreign communist parties when
> the need arises.
>
> Meanwhile, according to the lessons learned from the commu-
> nist parties of Eastern Europe, the failure to take timely steps
> to adapt party property to the demands of commercial activity
> and include it in normal economic turnover, especially during
> the transfer to the market system, threatens the party with dire
> consequences.
>
> Symptoms alarming to the CPSU are already in evidence. This
> business must be started from scratch, and the party will have
> to work in unfamiliar circumstances, adapting to the demands
> of the market and competition. Party cadres that will be en-
> trusted with this activity must first tackle the difficult task of
> "learning how to trade." In certain cases this will involve the
> observance of reasonable confidentiality in using anonymous
> companies, masking direct access to the CPSU. The final aim
> shall probably be that alongside the "commercialization" of ex-
> isting party property, to create structures of an "invisible" party

economy, work with which shall be limited to a very narrow circle of individuals designated by the General Secretary of the CPSU or his deputy.

We now know the text of the agreement that the first Soviet oligarchs signed with the CPSU upon receiving the right to dispose of party property:

> Personal obligation to the CPSU
>
> I, _____, member of the CPSU from _____ year, Party card No. _____, hereby affirm my conscious and voluntary decision to become an authorized representative of the Party and execute the assignments entrusted to me by the Party at any post and in any situation, without exposing my inclusion in the institution of authorized representatives. I undertake to protect and make careful disposition of the financial and material means entrusted to me for Party interests, the return of which I guarantee upon first demand. I acknowledge that all my earnings ensuing from economic activity for the benefit of Party funds are Party property, and guarantee to surrender them at any time and in any place. I swear to observe strict confidentiality of the information entrusted to me and to perform all Party assignments forwarded to me through the relevant duly authorized individuals.
>
> Signature of the member of the CPSU _____
>
> Signature of the person undertaking obligation _____

Toward the end of 1990, even the *Pravda* newspaper was privatized, together with its publishing complex and polygraphic base, with Gorbachev's full approval (24 July 1990, No. 14724).[342]

However it is important to understand that the mass robbery of the country, which ended up looking like rats deserting a sinking ship, was not planned to be this way. They had no intention of leaving the stage: on the contrary, the intention of perestroika was to reinforce their power, to save socialism. But being Marxists, they chose the Marxist way of saving themselves: the key idea of perestroika ensued from Marx's well-known dictum regarding the three forms of the relations of the ruling class and property—ownership, use and management. And if during the last 60 years of its rule, practically since the end of Lenin's NEP, the party had in its hands all three forms of relationship to the means of production, perestroika would have been a return of sorts to the NEP. The Party proposed to keep property ownership in its hands, leasing disposition of the property to interested parties and thereby ensuring the

---

[342] 15 February 1991* (No 01499), p. 7.

use of all the country's means of production jointly with the producer. Although the Western press announced the "introduction of a market economy in the USSR" about ten times in Gorbachev's time (and some 15 times afterwards), in fact there was no suggestion of capitalism (and there is none even now). Gorbachev's economic "reforms" never went beyond encouraging cooperatives, family and brigade contracts, and finally—even joint-stock companies, by a simultaneous decrease in the party's role in the management of property at the cost of decreasing the role of Gosplan, central ministries and general party control over on-site production. In 1989, desperation drove the party to talk of "individual work activity" (amateur production), but legalizing *private property* was never contemplated. Gorbachev's favorite slogan, right up to his resignation was: "give socialism a second wind."

Is it any surprise that perestroika did not evoke any enthusiasm among ordinary workers? No matter how much the learned fraternity quibbled, they knew that until the enterprise was theirs, nothing would come of it. Joint "management of means of production" with the party clearly did not suit them: the "partnership" was too one-sided and the reputation of the "partner" was too pernicious. But the black economy that was already firmly linked with party structures flourished beautifully in these new forms. The cooperatives that appeared were mainly "intermediaries", i.e. "redistributors" of socialist production on to the private market. Consequently, corruption became the norm, the deficit of goods became even greater, queues to empty shop counters longer, and the party's tendency to fracture and form regional mafias only increased. This was facilitated by attempts at decentralizing management of the economy, which encouraged the growth of economic autonomy: instead of improvement, there was managerial chaos, and local authorities, speculating on the eternal nationalistic moods of their republics, strove for greater political independence.

But if these "reforms" clearly proved to be insufficiently radical to stimulate the economy, they were too radical for the political system. Even Lenin's NEP undermined the party significantly, resulting in a mass exodus from it, 60 years later the party had changed (much less idealistic and much more bureaucratic), at a time when the public retained no trust in it whatsoever. Moreover, during these decades a gigantic administrative apparatus had evolved, which had no desire to lose its "management" function, and most enterprises in the country were actually operating at a loss, existing by virtue of subsidies and grants from the center. They were beyond rebuilding, all that was left was to close them down, and throw millions of workers into the street. However the party cudgeled its brains, however it wriggled, it could not escape these problems by pushing the blame onto someone else and simply retaining the "controlling interest" of owners.

Steps to solve this problem were taken in the spring of 1989, the final phase of the "reforms", toward "sovietisation", that is— transfer of the center of power to the soviets [councils]. Once again, everything looked fine and quite Marxist on paper: if the "ruling class" decided to share its property rights to the means of production with others, it should also share power with them. Simply speaking, there could be no reliance on the stabilization of the situation without expanding the social base of power. It all sounded very Leninist, resurrecting the slogan "All power to the Soviets!" But what seemed reasonable in theory turned into a catastrophe in practice: elections to the Congress of People's Deputies of the USSR, just like the subsequent elections to soviets of other levels, despite all the cunning procedures of "nomination", "selection" and "registration" of candidates, despite the legally guaranteed third of places for the party *nomenklatura* and full control over the mass media, were a total party failure. Wherever "alternative" candidates managed to break through, the people voted for them, expressing their total lack of trust in the CPSU, if not to say their hatred of it. This first election campaign for 70 years stimulated the political activity of the population, stirred up people who had been intimidated for decades by terror, instead of a jubilant cry of: "All power to the Soviets!" they shouted: "Down with the communists!" To a certain degree this experiment was successful at the lowest level, at which the regional and district authorities simply swapped places into the chairs of local executive committees, and even so only in the provinces, not large cities.

In essence, party "perestroika" ended in 1989, showing beyond any doubt that socialist utopias had outlived their time. They had no supporters anywhere except in the West, and the attempt to introduce them everywhere led to a loss of control over the experiment. All that was needed was the removal of the barbed wire around the socialist camp for the prisoners to begin to escape. The first ones to slip away were the East European brethren, thereby burying the idea of the convergence of Europe in a common European home. They were followed by the republics of the USSR, where the republican Supreme Soviets, elected amidst much pomp and ceremony, immediately voted for the "sovereignty" of their republics. Even in Moscow, where by hook or by crook it proved possible to retain what Yuri Afanasyev called "the aggressive-obedient majority",[343] by some miracle 20 percent of "alternative deputies" genuinely elected by the voters attended the Congress of People's Deputies of the USSR. They were not backed by any party or financial structures, or all-Union organizations—their only support was the will of the people. It was they who were the main heroes of the drama that unfolded on television before the eyes of hundreds of millions of viewers, who watched the proceedings with bated breath. As the highest legislative body in the country, the Congress did nothing momentous, but it had a colossal enlightening significance, showing the public for the first time the nature of the regime in its true colors. Aroused by this hitherto-unseen spectacle, the strata of the nation began to stir—miners went on strike, nationalist movements in the republics gathered strength. And although it proved possible to pacify the miners to some extent with empty promises, the threat of the appearance of a Solidarity in the USSR continued to hang over the country. By the end of 1989–beginning of 1990, the country was already ungovernable, and the spontaneous popular movement threatened to unite in demanding the revocation of the CPSU's monopoly on political power. Gorbachev's "rebuilders" could do nothing but submit to this demand, revoking Article 6 of the Constitution which formally affirmed this monopoly.

So if what had occurred could be classed as a revolution, it was a revolution "from below" that came about not because of, but despite Gorbachev and his accessories. What was planned as quite moderate, inter-system changes got out of control and grew into a revolution, exposing the fundamental and incompatible difference between the intentions of the leaders and the hopes of the people. The leaders were too late in seeing this, but starting with 1990 and to their final collapse, all their efforts were aimed at stopping the chain reaction.

The first attempts to somehow put a brake on the process, especially the disintegration of the USSR into independent republics, began back in 1989 with the murderous suppression of peaceful demonstrations In Tbilisi, and the equally murderous pitting of national minorities against the indigenous population (in Abkhazia, Ossetia, Nagorno-Karabakh and Sumgait). This was followed by the military operation in Baku, and provocation of tensions in the Baltic states, where Russian settlers were used as a tool of imperialist policy. Nobody had any doubts now that the so-called "ethnic conflicts" were provoked by Moscow, acting in accordance with the

---

[343]A phrase coined by Yuri Afanasyev, Dean of the Historical Archives Institute. With Sakharov and others, he became a leader of the opposition within the Congress, the Inter-Regional Group made up of deputies from Russia and other Soviet republics.

old imperialistic formula of divide and rule. Yet although this blatantly criminal policy left the country with an inheritance of protracted and at times insoluble conflicts, the disintegration of the empire could not be halted. Provoking conflicts was easy, but controlling them was impossible.

In Russia itself, even the effort to control the process by means of fictional "parties" specially created by the KGB for that purpose and the infiltration of independent political organizations granted only a temporary success. This so-called "socialist pluralism", like its historical prototype the pre-revolutionary "Zubatovism", only aided further destabilization. Just as Zubatov's trade unionists ended up organizing the 1905 revolution, so the KGB-Gorbachev "pluralists", in the situation of an increasing polarization of society, found themselves facing the choice of falling by the wayside of the movement, or confronting the regime. Few wished to expose themselves and support the authorities. By the end of 1990–beginning of 1991, demands for the resignation of communist authorities became so unanimous that they were supported, it would seem, by the communists themselves.

However, by that time most party leaders were mainly occupied by the problem of personal survival, and the process of party "privatization" had acquired the nature of panicked flight. Establishing where these "party billions" ended up, together with a substantial part of Western aid to the USSR at that time, is practically impossible, just as it is impossible to trace all the tangled ties of the International Department of the CC and the KGB with Western organizations and individual politicians. The more so that after the failure of the August 1991 putsch, by some mysterious means the administrator of CC affairs N. Kruchina jumped out of the window of his apartment, as did his predecessor in that post, A. Pavlov— two men who were directly involved in the management of party property and finances during "perestroika." The other officials supervising the process of "party privatization" faded discreetly from the stage. The last head of the International Department of the CC, Falin, lives quietly as a pensioner, writing books about how he, Falin, devised the brilliant plan to save the Soviet empire which that fool Gorbachev was unable to put into effect properly. Just as peaceful is the existence of his former colleagues in different parts of the world. Nobody seeks them out or bothers to interrogate them: the world has decided generously that this is an acceptable price for their "voluntary retreat from the stage."

It is quite amazing: these people had been wrecking the country for more than 70 years, exterminated entire nations, sowed bloody unrest over the whole world, suppressed the smallest sign of human spirit, and spent the last seven years in desperate attempts to save their regime, not stopping at bloodshed or the most blatant deceit. Finally, when they lost control and robbed the country, they took to cowardly flight and hide behind the backs of their Western cronies. And we are now supposed to be grateful to them!

6.9   Chronicle of the collapse

As I have already mentioned, the most important documents of this period, especially the period of the so-called "putsch" were destroyed, but there is no doubt that from the end of 1990 the Politburo began to make active preparations for turning things around. The plan for this seems to be little different from the plan for the declaration of martial law in Poland in 1981, and it is particularly significant that Gorbachev was at the center of its preparation. All the legends about a "conspiracy" against him by "conservatives" and "reactionaries" are nothing more than a continuation of disinformation about the "struggle between reformers and conservatives" in the leadership which, as we see, never existed. Right up to 1989 there were no signs of so much as disagreements in the Politburo, and those who began to voice perfectly justified fears of losing control over events were removed from power immediately. It could not be otherwise—that was how the communist system of power worked; differences within the leadership were acceptable only in discussions of a problem, but not after a decision was reached. The word of the General Secretary was final and not subject to discussion.

Now it sounds almost laughable to hear talk that Gorbachev allegedly knew nothing about this or that decision of his colleagues. The General Secretary was informed of everything, even the most trivial details regarding all measures and events. For example, here is the "List of certain documents on which instructions were received from comrade M.S. Gorbachev in 1990" (15 February 1991, No. 01499). This list, naturally, is not exhaustive, there are missing pages, but even what is left leaves no doubts as to the thoroughness with which the General Secretary was kept informed. Virtually everything landed on his desk: from economic problems in the regions, the state of affairs in individual party organizations to international events. Every document bears his instruction, "assignment", the performance of which is recorded a bit lower. The machine of the CC apparatus could not work any other way: it was created to work without stopping. He had all the information, even more than necessary at times, but in the process of loss of control over events it reflects the beginning of panic. He receives information in February on "some thoughts on resolution of the German question", and writes:

> To comrade V.M. Falin. Please read. Yes, we need a plan of action for the near future. M. Gorbachev.

And on his order, the material is sent to all the members of the Politburo (26 February 1990, No. 03997).[344]

At the same time, Falin sends "additional information on the Katyn tragedy." The matter is a brainteaser: to admit or not that imprisoned Polish officers were executed on Stalin's orders? It is a bad thing to admit, but denying it is now impossible. Gorbachev writes (23 February 1990, No. 03900):[345]

> Comrades Yakovlev, Shevardnadze, Kryuchkov and Boldin. Please submit your thoughts.

Or in another case, people's deputy of the USSR comrade Yulin "expresses critical remarks about the CC CPSU, the Politburo of the CC for adopting political and economic decisions that he considers erroneous." Gorbachev writes (25 April 1990, No. 08597):[346]

> Comrades Stroyev, Monyakin. Talk to comrade Yulin.

However as of April 1990, the loss of control becomes increasingly obvious. Even the Central Television starts showing signs of disobedience. Gorbachev writes in desperation (23 April 1990, No. 08400):[347]

> Comrade [Vadim] Medvedev. Work must continue on regrouping forces within CTV (while there is still time!)

But the problems continued to grow: the economy was falling apart, energy outages became more frequent, an "uncontrolled spread of radioactive nuclides" caused by the Chernobyl disaster, the "breakdown of the state program on liquidation of the consequences of the earthquake in the Spitak district" in Armenia. . . . By autumn the panic is loose: emergency measures are invoked for "the acquisition of real estate abroad and the creation of joint ventures" (18 May 1990, No. 70460 and 9 August 1990, No. 71404).[348]

---

[344] 15 February 1991* (No 01499), p. 2.
[345] 15 February 1991* (No 01499), p. 2.
[346] 15 February 1991* (No 01499), p. 5.
[347] 15 February 1991* (No 01499), p. 3.
[348] 15 February 1991* (No 01499), p. 12.

Suddenly another signature, that of Leopold Rothschild, appears on a document dated 18.09.90 (Great Britain N16383), that "Confirms Great Britain's interest in creating a bank syndicate for granting loans under guarantee of placement of gold."[349]

Whether this is directly related or not I do not know, but after the August "putsch" it suddenly became known that the gold reserve of the USSR had "vanished" without a trace. . . .

As for mass killings—in Tbilisi in 1989, in Baku in 1990 or Vilnius in 1991—indeed, any military actions could not be decided by anyone other than the General Secretary. Of course, Gorbachev tried to avoid such methods insofar as his game was built on his reputation as a "democrat." But as documents show, in principle he never ruled out the possibility of a situation in which he would have to give such an order, just as the Chinese comrades did in Tiananmen Square (4 October 1989).[350]

> Politburo, 4 October 1989 (recorded by Chernyaev)
>
> [. . .]
>
> LUKYANOV reports that in fact 3,000 people perished on Tiananmen Square.
>
> GORBACHEV. You have to be realists. They also have to hang on, just as we do. Three thousand. . . . So what? Sometimes you have to retreat. For that you have strategy and tactics. If a line is adopted, there can be various maneuvers within its framework.

And in fact, documents completely refute claims that orders resulting in mass murders in Tbilisi, Baku or Vilnius were issued over Gorbachev's head. Two days after the killings in Tbilisi, in a shorthand report of Gorbachev's conversation with SPD leader Vogel, we find a passage that cannot be evaluated as anything other than an admission (11 April 1989):[351]

> There are destructive elements, extremists and even anti-Soviet groups that try to exploit glasnost, democratization for their anti-Soviet purposes. But we shall not allow any encroachment on our interests, the interests of socialism and the people. We shall protect ourselves. You have heard about the events in Georgia. There was an organized outing of committed anti-Soviets led by one [Zviad] Gamsakhurdia. They speculate on democratic processes, inflame passions, and flaunt provocative

---

[349] 15 February 1991* (No 01499), p. 8.

[350] *Kak "delalas" politika perestroiki*, 1989 (SA), p. 324.

[351] Gorbachev, 1989 (SA), p. 115.

slogans up to demanding the entry of NATO forces on the republic's territory. You have to put people in their place, actively counter these political adventurers, protect perestroika—our revolution.

The following year saw the mass murders in Baku and the proclamation of a state of emergency in Azerbaijan. Politburo member Vadim Medvedev wrote this in his diary (19 January 1990):[352]

> 19 January 1990
>
> On the morning prior to the meeting in the Great Kremlin Palace, Gorbachev gathered the leadership. There was consultation on the situation in Azerbaijan, which is deteriorating. The authority there has practically disintegrated; the buildings of the CC, the republican Council of Ministers and the Presidium of the Supreme Soviet are virtually empty. Emergency measures are needed.
>
> Meeting with the press group for the Trans-Caucasus. The usual TASS [news agency] information this time is more detailed and dramatic, allowing for the forthcoming declaration of a state of emergency and sending in troops. The Order of the Presidium of the Supreme Soviet on the declaration of the state of emergency has been sent to TASS under embargo. Lines for its transmission to Azerbaijan are ready.
>
> It was agreed at the Politburo meeting that CC secretaries must be at their posts all night. Everyone except Yakovlev carried out this agreement.

Meanwhile, moods throughout the country continued to radicalize. Even hitherto controllable and scattered opposition organizations were beginning to unite, as Gorbachev was informed (24 October 1990*, Pb 1193).[353]

> 20–21 October 1990 in Moscow, in the cinema theater "Rossiya" there was a constitutive congress of the "Democratic Russia" movement. It was attended by 1270 delegates from 73 regions, districts and autonomous republics—representatives of parties opposing the CPSU, public organizations and movements. 23 People's Deputies of the USSR, 104 People's Deputies of the RSFSR, deputies from the Moscow City Council, the Leningrad City Council and other local councils took part in the congress. More than 200 guests from the union republics were invited to the congress, also from the USA, Great Britain, the FRG, France, Japan, Poland and Czechoslovakia. The work of the

---

[352] *Kak "delalas" politika perestroiki*, 1991 (SA), p. 21–22.
[353] 20 October 1990 p. 1.

congress was covered by around 300 Soviet and foreign correspondents. [...] The main attention of the congress was
directed toward the organizational strengthening of the democratic movement in the struggle against "the monopoly of the
CPSU on power", creation of an information network of democratic forces and their political infrastructure, "activation of the
masses" and the conduct of joint actions with other opposition
movements. [...] The distinctive feature of the congress was
rampant anti-communism. Strategy and tactics were devised
for ousting the CPSU from the political arena, dismantling of
the existing state and social system. [...] Unbridled insults
were flung at the President of the USSR M.S. Gorbachev, the
chairman of the Supreme Soviet of the USSR A.I. Lukyanov, the
chairman of the Council of Ministers of the USSR N.I. Ryzhkov,
the chairman of the KGB USSR V.A. Kryuchkov and the Minister for Defense D.T. Yazov....

The harsh, uncompromising tonality of the documents adopted
by the congress is obvious. Essentially, they all call for confrontation, civil disobedience and further destabilization of the
situation in the country. An analysis of the documents adopted by the founders of the congress, the nature of addresses,
the entire atmosphere of the congress and the campaign that
led up to it point unerringly to the formation of a united bloc of
anti-socialist, anti-communist forces, whose aim includes dissolution of the social and political foundations of the country,
seizure of power and the removal of the CPSU from the political
arena.

However the Politburo members regarded this attempt, the very
appearance of a certain unifying center of opposition was a deadly
danger to them. They had to act, and act fast. I think it was then
that they decided on a change of course and the proclamation of
martial law. By the end of the year Gorbachev had changed practically his entire crew: playing at "reform" was over, new tasks needed
new people—blind followers, who would not be frightened by the
sight of blood. Some, like Shevardnadze, left of their own accord,
knowing well in which direction the wind was blowing. Others like
Ryzhkov and Bakatin were dismissed by Gorbachev personally. It
is really humorous to assume that there was something he did not
know—he was the main organizer of the turnaround.

From January 1991 he and his new team began implementing
the plan, starting with Lithuania as usual, and Gorbachev was informed the same day (11 January 1991*, No. 00766):

According to reports from responsible personnel of the CC CPSU
[...], located in Lithuania, on January 11 this year paratroopers took control over the building of the House of Print and

the DOSAAF [Voluntary Society for Assistance to the Army, Air Force and Navy] in Vilnius (where the department for regional security was quartered) and in Kaunas—the building for officers' courses. On the whole, this operation passed without strong clashes. At the same time, the unobjective information regarding this action broadcast by the "Mayak" radio station should be noted. *Inter alia* this information mentioned the excesses of the military and alleged victims and wounded. At 17:00 hours local time the CC of the Lithuanian Communist Party held a press conference at which the head of the ideological department of the CC, comrade Yu.Yu. Jermolavicus stated that a Committee for the Salvation of Lithuania had been formed in the republic. This Committee assumed full power. [...] the Committee approved an appeal to the people of Lithuania, and also sent an ultimatum to the Supreme Soviet of the Lithuanian SSR, demanding an immediate response to the appeal of the President of the USSR.

The Supreme Soviet of the Lithuanian SSR declined the ultimatum, calling the convened Committee "self-proclaimed" and lacking any legal grounds to speak on behalf of the Lithuanian people.

We should note that the putsch in Moscow seven months later repeated the same scenario: troops were stationed at key points, a press conference, and the formation of a Committee claiming "full power". This was just the dress rehearsal. It is also indicative that Gorbachev's more intelligent assistants, who worked directly with him in those days, must have been aware that all this took place on their patron's orders. This is how Chernyaev describes the torments his intelligent soul suffered in his diary:[354]

13 January 1991, Sunday.

[...]

I never thought that this would be the inglorious end of Gorbachev's inspiring beginning. I am weary with perplexity and, alas, disorder in work, some kind of "spontaneity" in affairs, and mainly—the tendency to believe one's own and seek their support (the CPSU!).

All this led to "spontaneous" actions of paratroopers and tanks in the Baltics and ended with bloodshed. It is said that there were 180 wounded and 14 dead in one night in Vilnius!

[...]

---

[354]The Diary of Anatoly Chernyaev, 1991 (https://nsarchive2.gwu.edu/NSAEBB/NSAEBB345/)

On Friday I insisted that Gorbachev telephone Bush regarding the Persian Gulf on the eve of day "X". The conversation was "friendly." But on the topic of Lithuania, Gorbachev lied like a trooper and promised to avoid the use of force. [...]

The Lithuanian affair destroyed Gorbachev's reputation completely and probably cost him his post. Yes... that is so, even though he claims to detest "panic merchants." [...]

So once again I am facing the situation of 1968—Czechoslovakia. But at that time the problem was to break away from Brezhnev, with whom I was barely acquainted. And now it is Gorbachev, with whom a great historical endeavor is associated, even if he is ruining it with his own hands. In the press, on the radio at home and in the West there are guesses: was the Vilnius action undertaken with Gorbachev's knowledge, or has he lost total control over everything in the country? Or was it an independent action by the Lithuanian communists and the military? I am also riven by doubts. But I suspect that Gorbachev, maybe even subconsciously, wanted something like this to happen. The provocation was the workers' demonstration in front of the Supreme Soviet in Vilnius that brought about the resignation of Prunskiene. Yet if this had not happened, something else "would have had to be imagined." I find it unthinkable that M.S. would betray Burokevicius and Schwetz (secretaries of the CC CP of Lithuania). It seems that from the very beginning they were nurtured as a fifth column in Brazauskas' communist party.

[...]

I foresee that there will be enough lies to sink a ship in the Supreme Soviet tomorrow. Lukyanov will make sure. [...]

14 January 1991.

[...]

This morning Igantenko talked to me about resigning. Andrey Grachev came along from the meeting of the Supreme Soviet and asked not to be confirmed as head of the International Department under the President. "1968 and 1979 were enough for me. It's unbearable." And what about me?

[...]

15 January 1991.

I did not go to Gorbachev's meeting with Velikhov's Fund for the Survival of Humanity. Meeting him was repulsive. I feel ashamed to look people in the face. I thought that under the circumstances he would refuse to attend the meeting. I had prepared all the materials and his speech before the events in Lithuania. But I "underestimated" him again. He went. Took Yakovlev and Boldin with him, as well as Bessmertnykh, newly-confirmed at the meeting of the Supreme Soviet. And just as if nothing has happened, he spent almost two hours playing up to the Americans and other acolytes of the new thinking. As was to be expected, they asked no awkward questions. . . .

Igantenko arrived. He said that last night he, Yakovlev and [Yevgeny] Primakov tried to persuade Gorbachev to go to Vilnius, lay a wreath, speak in the Supreme Soviet, visit collectives, the military, etc. It seemed as though Gorbachev was in favor of the idea. He said: have the texts for appearances there ready by morning. They composed the texts and put them on his desk. Ignatenko spent the whole day running around to catch Gorbachev and ask him for his decision. Gorbachev acted as though nothing had happened, and that there had been no conversation with those three. From this Igantenko concluded that M.S. is not "misinformed" as many think. He is carrying out his plan for intimidating the Balts. [. . .]

16 January 1991.

Today is the last session of the Supreme Soviet. Gorbachev had a last chance to cope with the Lithuanian business, meaning his own image as the leader of perestroika. He even asked Primakov this morning to rough out a text. Zhenya and Ignatenko did as he requested, naturally condemning what had occurred. But M.S. did not use it. After the report by Demetey, who headed the delegation of the Supreme Soviet (Oleynik and Ter-Petrosyan) to Lithuania—(the report is useless, a mere formality) and after the "unfolded discussion" suggested. . . suspending the law on the press and introducing a censor into every entity from the membership of the Supreme Soviet. This caused an uproar. M.S. did not persist. But he showed his face, and his idea. It appears that he is on the side of those who killed in Vilnius—this is something to conceal, not display. [. . .]

Primakov tendered his resignation today. M.S. replied: "It is I, not you, who will decide about you."

[. . .]

There was no reply to our proposal to meet with assistants. My daughter Anna is clearly in favor of my "leaving." I saw her for the first time today after returning from Copenhagen. Gave her a brief outline of how I see Gorbachev, whose logic is directed only at remaining in power at any price. His new attack on Landsbergis and about Yeltsin's press conference, like his last address in the Supreme Soviet, was muddled, deprived of any real meaning, off the point, petty and "personal." Totally unsuited to the moment.

17 January 1991.

[...]

After Gorbachev let everyone go at around nine in the morning, he suddenly motioned me into his study. He talked about Lithuania. [...] Gorbachev spoke as if with regret, that things had happened that way. Such opposition, such a split, such enmity in society, wall to wall fighting. I said to him: "Well, they should have been left to fight it out among themselves, even to the death. But why bring in the tanks? It means the demise of your mission. Surely Lithuania is not worth that?!" "You don't understand," he said. "The army. I could not simply dissociate myself and condemn them after all the insults the military has had to bear in Lithuania, as well as their families in the garrisons."

[...]

It is a fact that the events in Lithuania evoked an incredibly violent reaction throughout the country, not just in the republics, which identified themselves readily with the Lithuanians, but in Russia as well. People understood instinctively that the authorities had launched an offensive against them. In Moscow, where anti-communist demonstrations had been building up all autumn, hundreds of thousands took to the streets, as Gorbachev was informed (23 January 1991*, Pb 223):

> On 20 January this year, a manifestation sanctioned by the Moscow City Council took place from 11:00 to 14:30 hours, organized on the initiative of a number of People's Deputies of the USSR and the coordinating committee of the "Democratic Russia" movement, The column of demonstrators proceeded from Mayakovsky Square along the Garden Ring and the Kalinin Prospect to the fiftieth Anniversary of October Square, in which a 1.5-hour meeting took place.
>
> Up to 150 thousand people participated in the demonstration. The composition of organizations and politicized movements was traditional. Experts estimate that the majority of the participants were representatives of the scientific and creative intelligentsia, persons belonging to nationalities not consistent with the indigenous population of Moscow, and also out-of-town

individuals. [...] The nature of the meeting was markedly anti-presidential and anti-communist. Typical slogans were such as: "Mikhail the Bloody—Nobel Laureate", "Bring Gorbachev and his gang to justice", "Put the President of the USSR in the Dock", "Bloodshed in Lithuania—the latest crime of the CPSU", "Red Fascists of the CPSU—hands off Russia and the Baltics."

The structure of the slogans and addresses, of the 33 main themes the anti-presidential issue ranked first, followed by the anti-communist and in support of the current Lithuanian leadership, the third being support for Yeltsin—the fourth [...] A significant place went to demands for putting Committees of National Salvation on trial and rebuttal of the "reactionary course of Gorbachev and the CPSU", up to an All-Russian strike (this was among the resolutions of the meeting) and armed resistance in the event of use of force....

The resolution adopted contained demands for the "withdrawal of punitive forces from the Baltics", dismissal of M.S. Gorbachev and G.I. Yanayev, dissolution of the Congress of People's Deputies of the USSR and the Supreme Soviet of the USSR, the creation of a Russian army, calls for the formation of a political organization with cells in workers' collectives and residential localities on the basis of the "Democratic Russia" movement.

In our opinion, this action should be interpreted as confirmation of the course adopted by opposition forces aimed at the alteration of the state and social system, and the removal of the current leadership of the country from the political arena.

The quality of the tactics of forces opposed to the center and the CPSU are changing. The core of consolidation of democratic and national-democratic movements in the republics is the Supreme Soviet of the RSFSR headed by B.N. Yeltsin....

It is true that Yeltsin and the Supreme Soviet of the RSFSR took center stage as the only functioning political structure: in February Yeltsin took advantage of a direct transmission on Central Television to call the country to "declare war on the government." The situation was provoked further by a sharp increase in prices in January. This was followed by a wave of demonstrations and strikes, which culminated in a half-million strong demonstration in Moscow in March, conducted despite Gorbachev's official prohibition and the entry of armed forces into the capital. At the end of March, all of Belorussia went on strike, and it was not the most rebellious of the republics, as Gorbachev was informed (15 April 1991, No. 03182):

If a month ago the attitude of most workers' collectives toward miners' strikes was restrained, in recent days support for their actions had increased significantly. Looking at the example of

Belorussia, it is clear that the economic demands advanced by
workers influenced by opposition forces are becoming political
and inter-linked, expressed primarily by distrust of central bodies of power and the CPSU.

The official Soviet trade unions were also thrown into confusion,
as "the workers are increasingly failing to support the trade unions,
but spontaneously formed strike committees." In order to reassert
their authority by some means, even the official trade unions decided to hold a one-day strike, in which 50 million people took part!

In order to somehow dissipate the wave, plans for the proclamation of martial law were shelved temporarily, and "negotiations" were
begun with the Baltic republics. At the same time, Yeltsin agreed to
talks with Gorbachev, which ended with the "Novo-Ogarevo Agreement." This was followed by a lull, akin to a truce, which couldn't
last long: not a single problem was really resolved, and the republics
refused stubbornly to sign any new "union agreement." Control over
the country was not reinstated, and there was no end to the crisis
in sight. A return to the scenario of martial law was inevitable,
and it is ludicrous to assume that Gorbachev's subordinates hid
anything from him. The more so that implementation of such a
wide-sweeping "conspiracy" as the "putsch" of 19 August could have
taken place without his knowledge. Without his sanction, not one
agency of power, or military unit, or KGB subdivision could act.
Incidentally, that killed off his plan, his spectacle of a "putsch" in
August, when his subordinates had to implement the scenario of
proclaiming martial law allegedly without his sanction: not a single
commander agreed to act without a direct order from Gorbachev.
Everyone was perfectly aware that without such an order, their actions would qualify as treason, for which they would be executed on
the spot, accused of responsibility for the "putsch."

In the absence of documentation, we can only guess at Gorbachev's reasoning in thinking up such an incredible trick as a
"conspiracy" against him. All the details of that strange "conspiracy" convince me that it was copied thoroughly from the scenario
of the ousting of Khrushchev in 1964, and built on disinformation regarding the "struggle between reformers and conservatives"
in the Politburo. Let us recall that this disinformation, disseminated so painstakingly during the period of Gorbachev's rule, was
the foundation of his success in the West. Even the most committed anti-communists (Reagan, Thatcher) bought this claim, constantly saving Gorbachev from mythical "conservatives", and pro-
Soviet forces turned it into a lawful basis for transferring millions of
dollars into the Kremlin's coffers. What could be more logical than

using the same gambit for proclaiming martial law? Finding itself on the brink of a precipice, the Kremlin reprised the same scenario that had been used for seven years to scare both the West and the East: a "conservative conspiracy" and the ousting of Gorbachev, at the same time "pacifying" the country with the aid of the harshest methods. Then Gorbachev would return triumphantly some three months later, and mercifully "mitigate" some of the drastic measures of his subordinates and resume a moderate "perestroika" to the full exaltation of the West. Under such circumstances, I bet he would have been able to entice the West into parting with another 30 billion dollars....

However just as with the Velvet Revolution the Kremlin strategists, despite all their cunning, failed to take one factor into account—the reaction of their own people. They were so accustomed to ignoring it, that the role it might play in the planned spectacle did not enter their heads. They did not realize to what extent their own power structures were disintegrating. The party was already scattering into "commercial structures", the military command had no desire to be made the scapegoat, and even the KGB personnel had no idea of what would happen to them in the closing act of the show. None of them wanted to lay down their lives in attempts to rescue the putrefied regime, and nobody believed Gorbachev, who was tangled in his own lies, except the West.

It is curious that encountering the mass disobedience of the country, the so-called putschists lost their nerve and... rushed off to Gorbachev in the Crimea, probably to beg him to come out of the shadows and head a return toward military law. Some conspiracy, wasn't it, in which conspirators flee to their "victim" for advice and protection? You can just imagine them trying to persuade Gorbachev:

—Mikhail Sergeyevich, nothing is working out without you. The army refuses to budge without an order from the commander-in-chief, the people are crowding around the White House, and there is no way of dispersing them without bloodshed. You are the only hope....

Of course, he rejects this now and so do the "putschists"—simply speaking, the entire leadership of the country confirm that they acted on his orders. One can only guess at who is right or wrong. Getting to the truth is impossible without an independent, objective and impartial court, which did not exist. One thing is inarguable: the whole preparation for the proclamation of martial law was conducted under his direct leadership. Whether he had last-minute doubts like Jaruzelski in his time, or whether he really devised this diabolical game in order to look good in the eyes of the world after returning from the Crimea in the guise of a peacemaker into a country already controlled by his subordinates is not known to this day.

In the end, it is not that important: three days and nights of overall disobedience was enough for the regime to collapse. With the failure of the "putsch" the CPSU was proscribed, the building of the CC sealed, and crowds drunk with freedom roamed Moscow, pulling down leaders' statues. Yet no matter how intoxicating this moment of freedom was, it was not a revolution. Deprived of a pivot, the country simply disintegrated into separate parts, controlled by their party mafias. The "new" political elite that had floated to the surface turned out to be the old *nomenklatura* which had had time to adapt itself to new conditions. This new elite did not want any radical changes, nor did it need the old ideology, because it held on to the "commercial structures", and property, and fictional parties, and the mass media as well as former international ties with old friends. This heralded the start of the era of "shadow power", where it is no longer possible to distinguish who is serving whom. An era of kleptocracy which I fear Russia will never be able to shed.

Only Gorbachev, returning to Moscow, kept talking about the renewal of socialism, the new role of the already vanished CPSU, and a new "union agreement" with non-existent republics....

6.10   "I am not naive, you know..."

It is easy to understand the rejoicing of the left over "perestroika" as well as the revolution which never came about—for them, from the very beginning, there was never any alternative to détente but the preservation of the party elite under the guise of a democracy consonant with their wishes. Only this version could cover up their complicity in the crimes of the regime, in which the regime would not appear criminal or, at least, would seem "reformed." In this sense, Gorbachev was a find for them—if he had not existed, he should have been made up.

Actually, that is how it was: the "reformer", "liberal" and "democrat" Gorbachev was an invention of the Western leftist elite, buttressed by Soviet disinformation. Remember, there were efforts to credit Yuri Andropov with the same image of a "liberal" and "reformer" when he came to power in 1983; but Andropov's health let him down and he died without being awarded the Nobel Peace Prize. Gorbachev was younger and healthier than his mentor and patron —that is the only difference. Had Andropov's kidneys been in better shape, he would have become the idol of progressive humanity, and the whole world would have watched his "courageous struggle with the conservatives" in the Politburo with bated breath. He, and not Gorbachev, would have been named man of the decade by "Time" magazine (1 January 1990), the "Copernicus, Darwin and Freud in one person" of communism, and flocks of Western sheep would have bleated ecstatically: "Yuri!", "Yuri!" instead of "Gorby! Gorby!"

Strictly speaking, what is the difference—Gorbachev or Yegor Ligachev, Andropov or Konstantin Chernenko? The issue lies not in the abilities of Soviet leaders, but in the presence of powerful forces of "peace, progress and socialism" in the West, to whom the survival of the idea of socialism was a question of their own survival. Thanks to them, the world sank into post-totalitarian absurdity instead of recovery from the communist plague. While they united in saving their idol from his own people, there could be no formation of any "uncontrolled" opposition that would be able to depose the *nomenklatura* and stabilize the situation. Nor could the decapitated, glasnost-bedazzled people go against the opinion of the whole world. "The opinion of the West" became the absolute and sole criterion of truth in that troubled time of fantastic lies. How could the people know that this opinion was also a manipulation by the ideological brothers of their jailers? In the absence of political experience, how could the people know that delay was akin to death: either the country, or an alien idea had to be saved, and the protracted death throes of the regime would render the recovery of the country practically impossible. The seven years wasted on the party perestroika and "support of Gorbachev" would rebound with a vengeance.

But the success of "glasnost and perestroika" would not have been as great and their effect so catastrophic for the world if the overall euphoria had not also paralyzed the conservative circles of the West. It is much harder to comprehend the reasons for this paralysis, especially as the word "paralysis" is hardly one would apply to a number of leading conservative politicians of that time. For instance, we all recall that one of the first and consistent supporters of Gorbachev was Margaret Thatcher, who declared him to be a man with whom she could "do business" even before his accession to power.[355] How could a politician of her class, moreover one who devoted her life to the struggle against socialism in her country, fail to see the bald truth that her new friend was doing the exact opposite? Or at least that the General Secretary of the CPSU is not

---

[355]TV interview, 17 December 1984, quoted in Jonathan Haslam, *Russia's Cold War: From the October Revolution to the Fall of the Wall*, Yale University Press: New Haven & London, 2011, pp. 348–349.

a tsar, and that the communist regime is not a monarchy; whatever his personal inclinations, "business" would have to be done not with him, but with the entire communist regime.

Mrs Thatcher's words were not a slip of the tongue. Her personal loyalty to Gorbachev made her say and do some amazing things. I remember being unable to believe my ears when I heard what she said in 1988 on a BBC live transmission to the USSR.[356] Jamming of Western radios had just ended, and here the Soviet people, already dazed by "glasnost", heard the "most popular woman in the USSR" state that "I think it remarkable that after 70 years of what I might call the old-fashioned form of communism, that is, the one that you're trying to get away from. . . . I think they [the changes]. . . are historic." And what was the "historical change" perceived by the legendary "Iron Lady"? Apparently that the recent party conference in Moscow [28 June 1988] was "a milestone in freedom for discussion" because "people came up to the platform to speak. . . they didn't always speak from fixed notes, but sometimes they spoke just as they felt"

Furthermore, as if forgetting the existence of the Soviet "Evil Empire", she practically called for the various peoples of the USSR to stay "loyal to the Soviet Union as a commonwealth of nations", to be content with a certain degree of cultural and religious autonomy, like the various tribes in Nigeria. And this was said at the time of the offensive against the sovereignty of the Baltic republics, whose absorption into the USSR was never acknowledged by Britain or the USA.

Alas, Thatcher was no exception. Even Ronald Reagan, President of the USA, a man for whom the very name Lenin was always anathema, did not fail to praise Gorbachev for his "return to the paths of Lenin." This was also said in a radio address transmitted to the USSR. As for his successor, George Bush and his Secretary of State Jim Baker, they outdid everyone, opposing the inevitable disintegration of the USSR until the very last day.

"Yes, I think I can trust Gorbachev,"—said George Bush to *Time* magazine[357] just when Gorbachev was beginning to lose control and was tangled hopelessly in his own lies—"I looked him in the eye, I appraised him. He was very determined. Yet there was a twinkle. He is a guy quite sure of what he is doing. He has got a political feel."

---

[356]BBC World Service, tape No 90R41-AO85G, Phone-in with Soviet residents, 11 July 1988, Archived 3 June 1990. First quote—Min. 13:22; Second quote—Min. 00:40. (https://www.bbc.co.uk/programmes/p033k7t4)

[357]"The Presidency A Game of One-on-One," Sidey, Hugh, *Time*, 18 December 1989, Vol. 134, Issue 25.

It is notable that this phrase is illogical: if your opponent "believes deeply in what he is doing" does not necessarily mean that he is trustworthy. After all, Hitler also "believed deeply in what he was doing." But the thought that their aims were diametrically opposed did not enter George Bush's head. It is not surprising that with such presidential perspicacity, their top-level meeting in Malta (2-3 December 1989) was strongly reminiscent of a second Yalta: in any case, after this the US Department of State invariably maintained that the growing Soviet pressure on the Baltics was "an internal USSR matter." Even two months prior to the collapse of the Soviet Union Bush, on a visit to Kiev, exhorted Ukraine not to break away.

The extent to which Bush's administration did not understand the Soviet games in Europe is clear from its position on the reunification of Germany. Secretary of State Baker, who hurried to Berlin immediately after the fall of the Wall, evaluated this event as a demonstration of Gorbachev's "remarkable realism. To give President Gorbachev his due, he was the first Soviet leader to have the daring and foresight to allow the revocation of the policy of repressions in Eastern Europe."[358]

And possibly in gratitude for this, Baker's main interest was to respect the "lawful concern" of his eastern partner by slowing down the process of reunification by all means.[359]

"... in the interest of overall stability in Europe, the move toward reunification must be of a peaceful nature, it must be gradual, and part of a step-by-step process."

The plan he proposed was a total disaster, for it corresponded completely to the Soviet scheme of the creation of a "common European home": it was envisaged at first to reinforce the European Community, the Helsinki process and promote the further integration of Europe. All this, naturally, without undue haste but "step by step"[360] over the passage of years.

"As these changes proceed, as they overcome the division of Europe, so too will the divisions of Germany and Berlin be overcome

---

[358]James Baker, US Secretary of State, "A New Europe, a New Atlanticism. Architecture for a New Era" (Speech delivered to the Berlin Press Club on 13 December 1989): *Vital Speeches of the Day*. 1/15/90, Vol. 56 Issue 7, p195-199. 5p. (https://www.cambridge.org/core/journals/foreign-policy-bulletin/article/euroatlantic-architecture-from-west-to-east/52C89037A07F88A54B258D2859EC3592)

[359]James Baker, *Berlin Speeches*, p. 12.

[360]Official State Department (James Baker) statement, Joseph Fitchell, "Europeans Laud Baker Vision of U.S. Role on the Continent," *International Herald Tribune*, 14 December 1989, France, English, p. 1. (https://archive.org/stream/InternationalHeraldTribune1989FranceEnglish/Dec%2014%201989%2C%20International%20Herald%20Tribune%2C%20%2333220%2C%20France%20%28en%29#page/n0/mode/2up)

in peace and freedom."

Furthermore, even without consulting Bonn, he rushed to embrace the Kremlin's new puppets in Eastern Germany in order to signal "US intentions to try to improve the credibility of the East German political leadership and to forestall a power vacuum that could trigger a rush to unification."[361] And this was in January 1990, i.e. shortly before the elections in the GDR that actually solved the key question: would Germany reunite on Soviet conditions, or Western ones? Luckily the East Germans were less "patient" and smarter: knowing well what they were dealing with, they voted for immediate reunification, ignoring Baker and the pressure of the whole world.

Why, then, did the West and the USA with its seemingly conservative, even anti-communist administration, yearn for this "stabilization" or, to put it more simply, salvation of the Soviet regime?

Let us allow that Baker was ignorant, pompous and big-headed, dreaming of some kind of global structures "from Vancouver to Vladivostok", of which he would be the architect[362] ("the Baker doctrine"). I remember at one press-conference I even suggested introducing a unit of measurement for political brainlessness—one baker (the average man in the street would be measured in millibakers). At the very height of the bloody Soviet show in Bucharest at Christmas in 1989, he stated that "They are attempting to pull off the yoke of a very oppressive and repressive dictatorship. So I think that we would be inclined probably to follow the example of France, who today has said that if the Warsaw Pact felt it necessary to intervene on behalf of the opposition, that it would support that action."[363] The new pro-Soviet policy of the USA after the top-level meeting in Malta he explained by saying that "the Soviet Union has switched sides, from that of oppression and dictatorships to democracy and change."[364] This was said at the moment when the Soviet army was smashing the democratic opposition in Baku, killing several hundred people (which Baker also "treated with understanding"). But Baker was not alone, and this cannot be explained away

---

[361]Official State Department clarification, *International Herald Tribune*, 14 December 1990.

[362]James A. Baker, "Aspen Institute Address: 18 June 1991", *Berlin Speeches*, p. 15. (https://www.cambridge.org/core/journals/foreign-policy-bulletin/article/euroatlantic-architecture-from-west-to-east/52C89037A07F88A54B258D2859EC3592)

[363]NBC Meet the Press, Sunday, December 24, 1989. (https://search.alexanderstreet.com/preview/work/bibliographic_entity%7Cvideo_work%7C2405992)

[364]Don Oberdorfer, "A U.S.-Soviet Meeting of Minds," International Herald Tribune, 2 January 1990, France, English, p. 1. (https://archive.org/details/InternationalHeraldTribune1990FranceEnglish)

by sheer stupidity. That is the tragedy, that such an idiotic position was shared by practically all Western governments, including the conservative ones.

Even Ronald Reagan, who started out with such a successful economic war against the USSR, virtually folded it up in his second presidential term, especially in 1987. As if unbelieving their own success, both Reagan and Thatcher began to play uncharacteristic games of "support for the reformers" in the Kremlin, not even wondering where these had come from. The limitations on the drain of technology fell away, as did those on loans and credits. Toward the end of 1987 the OECD noted: "at present, the monthly debt of the USSR has reached 700 million dollars," and the total debt of the Soviet bloc rose by 55 percent since 1984.[365]

> "Remarkably, as the debt rises, terms decline. From 1983 to 1986, the Soviet Union saw the average interest rate it pays drop from one to 0.15 point above the Libor bench mark. Brazil pays at least 0.75 of a point above Libor."

President Bush and his administration simply continued this tendency of sliding into détente, reducing it to the point of logical absurdity when Gorbachev was being "saved" from his people: from miners, from demonstrations of the democratic opposition, and from nations enslaved by communism demanding independence. Just as with the Persian Gulf War, the "Cold War" was terminated just a little too soon than was required for victory, leaving us all with the worst possible version: the vile regime had not been destroyed, the country was wrecked, and the demoralized public no longer had the strength to complete what had been left unfinished. Indeed, it was even worse in a way—at least the Kurds were not forced to listen to fairy tales about that savior of humanity, Saddam Hussein, who for some reason was not awarded the Nobel Peace Prize....

So what happened with our former allies in the struggle against détente, seemingly convinced anti-communists? The novelty of the "glasnost and perestroika" campaign lay in that the party, which had built up its power over 70 years on the basis of communist dogma, was now saving that power by demonstrating "anti-communism." This was directed at anti-communists, whom the Kremlin appeared to grant any changes made to order. The West was racking its brains: what should we ask from them now?

"Let them first release Andrei Sakharov, free political prisoners, then we can talk."

---

[365]Editorial, "Going into the Red," *Wall Street Journal*, Eastern edition; New York, N.Y., 7 December 1987. 1.

They released. They freed.

"Now let them leave Afghanistan."

They left.

"Well, if they publish Alexander Solzhenitsyn, then really...."

They published him.

You could feel the effort, the strain with which the brains of Western thinkers worked, trying to find criteria for distinguishing a normal country from a totalitarian regime. It emerged suddenly that nobody had given this much thought in the past, and all of them now invented their criterion which, when satisfied, gave Moscow another ally. Finally, President Reagan's crew, which was regarded as the most "unbridled" at that time, had its say:

"Let them bring down the Berlin Wall."

So the Wall came down.

This was the tragedy of our time, that if one part of humanity had a perfect understanding of the essence of the communist idea (but sympathized with it), the other part, seemingly hostile to it, did not understand it, believing the symptoms of the disease to be the disease itself. People who understood that it was the communist idea that was the root of all evil, that the regime is not inhuman because it persecutes people for their convictions, occupies neighboring countries and threatens the whole world but, on the contrary, does everything because it is inhuman—were few and far between. But they, because of this circumstance, did not belong to the establishment. They were seen as the same kind of renegades, "extremists" like us, and our common influence in the perestroika years was negligible. What could we do? Write an article which might be published alongside dozens lauding perestroika? The conditions of life here equate you to a charlatan and an obvious Soviet agent: he has an opinion, and you have an opinion. They see no difference between an opinion and knowledge.

However, the establishments—both left and right—lived by their own rules, not permitting too much deviation from the consensus, from the need to be re-elected (in the case of politicians) or mutually respectful (in the case of public activists, academicians and journalists). That long-putrefied, banal world lives in accordance with "golden rules" instead of brains: here the attitude toward communism was determined not as to whether it is right or wrong, but by how "moderate" it happens to be. Hordes of charlatan-Sovietologists and so-called Kremlinologists made their careers on contrived reasoning as to who was a "hawk" and who was a "dove" in the Kremlin, who was a "reformer" and who was a "conservative." And similar hordes of similar charlatans lived at the cost of the bastard "process of control over armaments", even though it was clear to all that it was not a matter of armaments, and nobody really knew how much of them the Soviet Union had. Not to mention the army of professional diplomats, for whom the highest value on earth is stability at any cost (even at the cost of freedom), and their main task in life is the improvement of relations (even with the devil).

Anyway, being of the establishment themselves, the elite could not but feel a certain kinship with the Soviet elite, the Soviet establishment. To them it was comprehensible, closer, and more convenient than uncontrolled crowds of people, especially those like us, the "extremists."

"Better the devil you know than the devil you don't." That was their entire wisdom. But even the most honest politician has to exist alongside this horde of bootlickers and time-servers, and take it into account: it is impossible to rule without it. So it came to pass that the left establishment knew what it was doing, and the right did not find a response. Even Ronald Reagan, with his instinctive hatred of communism, did not know what to say when he was asked:

"What will happen if Gorbachev is ousted tomorrow, just like Khrushchev, and everything goes back to Brezhnev's times? The whole world will curse us for not supporting him."

Alas, upon closer scrutiny, real anti-communists, who understood fully what we had to deal with, were fewer in the West than in the Soviet Union. In its heart of hearts, the West capitulated. The best that could be envisaged was the hope for a relaxation of the regime, its liberalization, i.e. the miraculous appearance of a "reformist tsar" in the Kremlin. So they took the bait proffered by the wise CC. It is not surprising that humanity refuses stubbornly to work out exactly what happened. It does not want investigations or documents from Kremlin archives, or the penitent memoirs of former executioners: everyone knows that they will not find much that flatters them. Even now, despite all the facts, it is preferable to repeat blatant lies about the courageous reformer Gorbachev, who rescued humanity from the horrors of communism. It is more peaceful, more convenient that way....

But, I will be told, not everyone is like that. The "Iron lady", for example—isn't she better? It cannot be that she also came to terms with communism, capitulated to it: that would be totally incompatible with her image. True, it is incompatible. This question bothered me for all the seven years of perestroika and even later. Attempts to argue with her, explain something, were useless: she simply refused to listen. At the mention of Gorbachev's name she would only say with a proud toss of her head, as a mother would about her child:

"Isn't he marvelous?"

That ended the discussion. But I persisted, and at every new meeting returned to the painful question. For me, it became a sort of fixed idea. Finally, in 1992, when I was digging in the CC archives in Moscow, I came across a document dated 1984 regarding Soviet aid to striking British miners.[366] There was little in it that was new—it was no secret that at a critical moment in the strike, the USSR transferred a million dollars to them. To be more precise, the fact was known, but it was thought that the aid was sent by Soviet trade unions to their class brothers. Looking at that document now I realized that the decision to send aid was, naturally, made by the CC, and among the signatories was Gorbachev—the Second Secretary of the CC at that time, without whose signature not a single decision could be approved.

Naturally, upon returning to London I hurried to see Thatcher, anticipating the effect. Knowing how crucial the 1984 miners' strike was to her, a strike that could have brought down her government, I did not doubt that I had finally hit the bullseye. Yes, when she saw her friend's signature, she paled:

"When was this signed?" she demanded. I pointed at the date.

"This is even worse," she said quietly. "I asked him about this at that very time, and he said he knew nothing about it."

This was my long-awaited moment of triumph:

"The difficulty of 'doing business' with communists is that they have the disgusting habit of lying while looking you in the face," I said slowly and clearly, enjoying every word.

There was a long pause. Possibly, too long.

"I am not naive, you know. . . ."

In the book of her memoirs, which was being prepared for print, a mysterious footnote appeared on the relevant page:[367]

> In fact, I have since seen documentary evidence suggesting that he knew full well and was among those who authorized payment.

6.11 Allies

I fear that the perestroika years only exposed the ever-present difference in the evaluation of communism by conservatives here and us—former citizens of communist countries who have experienced real socialism on our own skins. If for me communism was and is

---

[366]See 20 November 1984, for Scargill request to Soviet ambassador in London for funds for the National Union of Mineworkers (in Russian).

[367]Margaret Thatcher, *The Downing Street Years*. London: Harper Collins, 1993, p. 369, footnote.

an absolute evil, worse than anything imaginable, for them it is just another problem among many, and not necessarily the most pressing. Moreover, I think they have never understood the universality of this evil, its international nature and, consequently, its general danger. Deep down, most of them have been inclined to think that this disease poses no threat to "civilized" people, and that those who have become infected by it have somehow earned it, just as in the distant past an epidemic of the plague was deemed to be God's punishment for people's sins. For example, a myth believed widely among [Western] conservatives is that communism in Russia is a consequence (or a variety) of specifically Russian despotism.

"The answer to many puzzles of Soviet behavior lies not in the stars, but in the tsars. Their bodies lie buried in Kremlin vaults, and their spirits live on in the Kremlin halls," writes Richard Nixon, former President of the USA.[368] If this is so, why start détente? Russia cannot be changed; it is as it is by the will of history, so all that is left to hope for is the appearance of an enlightened monarch on the Moscow throne.

Or here is the opinion of our favorite conservative thinker, worth about one "baker", addressing the feather-headed Europeans in 1991:[369]

> "Ironically, perhaps, the narrow nineteenth-Century European nationalism gave way to another, and a very different rationalism and universalist ideology that would also transcend national borders — Marxism. In the Soviet Union, Bolsheviks blended this ideology with a Slavophile movement that was itself a reaction against allegedly alien Western values."

Where he found Slavophilism among the Bolsheviks is a mystery, but he is firmly convinced that he knows the antidote:

> "To me, the transatlantic relationship stands for certain Enlightenment ideals of universal applicability."

Let us put aside these illiterate excursions into history—what can one do if this is how our thinker and his friend George Bush were "enlightened" in some place such as Yale University, the fraternity to which they belonged in their student years.[370] What is important is since they do not understand that Marxism emanated from the "ideals of the Enlightenment", they do not see where its

---

[368]Richard Nixon, *The Real War*, New York: Simon & Schuster (1990), p. 49.

[369]James Baker, *Berlin Speeches*, p. 16.

[370]Claire Messud, "Bones of a Conspiracy," *The Observer*, 31 July 1994, pp. 21–23.

true danger lies. In their eyes, Marxism without the "Slavophile" distortion becomes acceptable for the "new world order", so why fight it?

Curiously enough, in this they are at one with the European Mensheviks, for whom the myth of a good socialism and a bad Russia, which allegedly distorted it, always served as self-justification. (It is not clear, though, why they insisted so obdurately on supporting this distortion in all the seventy-four years of its existence?) If this was only a convenient lie for them, conservatives proceed to repeat it, not even seeing that in that case they will have to legalize the socialist experiment in their own country. In this sense, European conservatives were no better than Nixon and Baker: as far as they were concerned, communism was never a national evil and our fight against it never became a common fight. Just look at the eternal confusion of "Russian" and "Soviet", which is the intermixture of the regime and the people, the hangman and the victim. This could evolve into utter absurdity: it would be said in one breath that "the Russians invaded Afghanistan" which was denounced by "the Soviet academician Sakharov." Is this simply a linguistic mistake, illiteracy? I do not know. Real friends were more careful in their choice of words, bearing in mind the difference between fighting against your people, or against the regime that enslaved them. The more so as they were in no hurry to fight the regime. I recall that the former Prime Minister Harold Macmillan once said to me:

"It is not our business to try to change the Soviet system. That is something for the Russians to do. Our task is to agree with them on supporting balance in the world."

The same received wisdom was repeated by Margaret Thatcher in her interview, when she told the world that she could "do business" with Gorbachev. "We shall not try to change them, and they will not change us" she said then. I remember answering her in the "Survey" magazine:[371]

> "What a wonderful basis for "constructive mutual relations"! Ordinary business—you give them credits and technology, and they will give you hard currency in exchange [...] at the cost of undermining the economy. You build them factories manufacturing trucks, and they will send those trucks full of their soldiers to Afghanistan. Do not try to change them—one way or another, they will change you. That is the essence of the economic reforms for which your friend Gorbachev is striving: the West is building the Soviet economy; meanwhile they are building communism throughout the world."

---

[371]Vladimir Bukovsky, *Survey*, Spring 1985, Vol. 29, No 1 (124), pp. 79–87.

The reader can understand my *Schadenfreude* when seven years later I found the aforesaid document concerning Soviet aid to striking British miners.

Our alliance with Western anti-communists was never equal, we united in their difficult times of the Cold War or the détente of the 1970s, but in our difficult times of perestroika they did not spare us a thought. Yet even in the time of the alliance there was never any full mutual understanding: their interpretation of the Soviet threat was too narrow, focusing mainly on its military aspect. But the fact that in the war of ideas armaments have a merely psychological significance, and that same war has no front or rear, remained beyond the boundaries of their understanding. It is hardly surprising that having achieved the bankruptcy of the USSR by 1986, they settled down, not taking the matter through to the end: as soon as the USSR ceased to be a military threat to the world, they lost interest in it. The further fate of millions did not concern them, possibly because of the abovementioned arrogance (if not chauvinism), assuming the mystical fate of peoples punished by communism.

Therefore our differences, albeit dampened by the existence of a common enemy, began to manifest themselves almost immediately: by the end of the 1970s, when the world realized that the USSR had no intention of abiding by the demands of the Helsinki Accords on human rights, our positions diverged. We believed that the only adequate response to the arrests of members of the Helsinki Groups should be a denunciation of the Helsinki Accords or at least the threat of denunciation—and an ultimatum for the release of those arrested. The West was inclined to pretend that nothing serious had occurred, and "continue the Helsinki process." This position could be understood while leftist parties remained in power in most Western countries, but it did not change by the beginning of the 1980s either, when there was a rapid shift to the right. Even Reagan's administration did not dare to touch this question, although many influential Republicans, being in opposition, shared our point of view openly.

Meanwhile this was the key problem in the entire policy of relations between the East and the West. The Helsinki Accords, their shortcomings aside, contained the fundamental principle of these relations—equality and the unbreakable bond between their three baskets: security, cooperation and human rights. They contained the extremely important acknowledgement of the fact that the external Soviet aggression is unbreakably linked with the anti-democratic, repressive nature of the regime, and without changing that it was senseless to speak of security, and any form of cooperation became capitulation. Economic relations became aid to the enemy, cultural ties an instrument of Soviet propaganda, and even diplomatic contacts simply served to affirm the false image of the Soviet Union as a normal state.

Furthermore, the Helsinki Accords enshrined another very important concession on the part of the West: "acknowledgement of the inviolability of the post-war borders of Europe", which was *de facto* acknowledgement of the Soviet occupation of East and Central Europe, its legalization. It stands to reason that Brezhnev considered these Accords to be the major achievement of his rule and even remarked to one of his assistants[372]

"If we manage to complete Helsinki, I can die satisfied."

This is not surprising: he wanted to "go down in history as the continuator of the line toward victory, as the one who affirmed victory in the war on the political plane." Only an acceptance of Soviet achievements in Europe could enable moving forward—to the expansion of influence over all Europe, the "struggle for peace" and disarmament. For the USSR, these Accords were the *palliative of post-war peaceful agreement in Europe*, affirming their empire.

This affected the entire strategy of the West over the subsequent decades: a denunciation of the Helsinki Accords would equal a revision of the Yalta agreements and would raise the question of the legitimacy of the Soviet occupation of East European countries (including the Baltic states and even Ukraine and Belorussia). It was characteristic that even a hint of the possibility of such a turnabout in relations, when a number of US senators and congressmen suggested putting these questions to the 1980 Madrid Conference, threw Moscow into a panic—as a horrified CC reported (25 October 1979, St 182/27):

> The initiative of the abovementioned congressmen was supported by the majority of the House. So far this does not obligate the administration to take concrete steps, but these dogmatic proposals may give Carter cause to launch another hostile campaign against the USSR.

In other words, the Helsinki Accords could have been an excellent instrument of foreign policy, if the West had ventured to use them. However not only Carter, but also Reagan, Thatcher and Kohl, who were practically in control of Western policy in the 1980s, did not take up the issue, and the Helsinki Accords simply became an instrument of Soviet policy for suppressing dissidence and the

---

[372]Interview with Anatoly Kovalev, head of Soviet delegation at Helsinki negotiations in 1975. Quoted in "The Centre", part 4 of the documentary *Messengers from Moscow*, Barraclough Carey productions, Los Angeles.

development of further advances on Europe. Instead of forcing Moscow to defend itself, moreover on its own territory (Eastern Europe, the republics of the USSR), the West allowed it to pass on to "peaceful" advance, which almost cost Western Europe its freedom.

Incidentally, it was not too late to take this position even at the height of the peace-making hysteria inspired by Moscow at the beginning of the 1980s. Instead of accepting the Soviet rules of the game and talking about an abstract "peace" outside the historical context of East-West relations, instead of endless bickering over the numbers of missiles and warheads, which frightened the unenlightened population even more (meaning that this was to the advantage of the USSR), there should have been a return to the context of the Helsinki Accords that would allow linking issues of security with the nature of the Soviet regime. This position would have been a winning hand for the West, bringing debates back on the right track, where the guilty party was obvious, and the political settlement of the East-West conflict was already proposed, and the presence of the Soviet signature under the Helsinki Accords would block talk of any conditions "unacceptable" to Moscow.

And really, what could be Moscow's response to an ultimatum demanding its observance of the Helsinki Accords at that time? Nothing but demagogy. Yet their denunciation by the West offered the latter an excellent game: to propose convening an international conference for executing a *post-war peace agreement*, which would lead to inevitable questions concerning the self-determination of European countries occupied by the USSR under the pact with Hitler. Who could oppose a peace agreement at that tense time? Even frankly pro-Soviet forces would be hard put, and unprejudiced public opinion would certainly be on our side. This is not just my presupposition: in 1984, just when the anti-nuclear hysteria reached its peak in the USA, we staged a convincing experiment in two of the most liberal states of the USA—California and Massachusetts. Los Angeles voters were posed the following question at a referendum:[373]

> Shall the Los Angeles County Board of Supervisors transmit to the leaders of the United States and the Soviet Union a communication stating that the risk of nuclear war between the United States and the Soviet Union can be reduced if all people have the ability to express their opinions freely and without fear on world issues, including a nation's arms policies; therefore the

---

[373]Ted Vollmer, "Human Rights Measure Okd for County Ballot," *Los Angeles Times*, June 4, 1984. Editorial Pages, CC/Part II (http://www.newspapers.com/image/401342424/)

people of Los Angeles county urge all nations that signed the International Helsinki Accords on Human Rights to observe the Accords' provisions of freedom of speech, religion, press, assembly and emigration for all their citizens?

Despite the desperate resistance of professional peacemakers, the proposal was approved by two thirds of the vote! The same resolution was approved in Massachusetts in October:[374]

... Urging the Soviet Union to abide by the Universal Declaration of Human Rights of the United Nations and the Helsinki Agreements as a Means towards Reducing the Threat of Nuclear War.

Without doubt, the US government could have extended this experiment over the whole country and completely neutralized the movement of pro-Moscow peacemakers. But despite clear popular support, Reagan's administration could not bring itself to take this step. Nor did they try to make it their international stance, as for denouncing the Accords or the idea of convening a "peace conference" in Europe—these were not open for discussion.

Alas, the conservatives proved totally incapable of grasping the principles of ideological warfare. Even the aid to anti-communist movements, the so-called Reagan doctrine, was limited by the purely financial aspect, more frequently in the form of money or military aid. But the enormous propaganda effort required to ensure public sympathy was beyond their comprehension. This and much more fell to us, who were without means or political opportunities. How much could be achieved by purely public groups with donations from public and private funds? The "International Resistance" set up by us in 1983 was pulled in all directions in attempts to counteract all that was performed in the USSR by enormous, well-financed and powerful structures. At times our Western friends did not understand what we were hoping to achieve. They could understand working with the press, conferences and press-conferences, but anything more complex would encounter unconquerable obstacles of bureaucratic misunderstanding.

The more illustrative example was our proposal to encourage mass desertion from Soviet units in Afghanistan. It was plain to see that no matter how much the mujahideen received in the form of arms, they had no hope of a military victory. That meant exploring other options that would make the Soviet occupation too expensive. The most obvious solution would be to enable the defection of Soviet

---

[374]Massachusetts Archives, The Commonwealth of Massachusetts, H.R. October 25, 1984.

servicemen abroad. Imagine how it would be if on a weekly basis, the Politburo was informed that several hundred more Soviet soldiers from the "limited contingent" had deserted, and the preceding several hundred, having reached the West, gave press-conferences. How much information of this kind could the Politburo take before beginning a rapid plan for withdrawing their forces? The direct participation of Soviet units in combat operations would be reduced to zero, to prevent further possibilities for desertion. Even this reaction would have been a great relief for the Afghans—they would be able to cope with the demoralized government army.

The fact that Soviet soldiers were deserting even without the faintest hope of coming through alive, let alone reaching the West, was known to us through our Afghan mujahideen friends. I never doubted it, realizing how unpopular this war for communist interests was among young Russians (to say nothing of those from the republics). Several dozen of them were already held prisoner by the Afghans, which created difficulties for mobile partisan groups. Moreover Soviet commanders, receiving intelligence about the villages in which these prisoners were held, bombed them unmercifully in order to teach the Afghans the price for such hospitality.

This problem needed attention in any case. The simplest part was to reach agreement with the mujahideen: they were fully aware of the value of the project. It was also understood by Zia-ul-Haq, the Prime Minister of Pakistan, who closed his eyes willingly to the conduct of the escapees through his territory. It was only Western governments that refused to comprehend the crux of the matter, insisting stubbornly on the humanitarian nature of the operation, which was its smallest scope. All of us, various public groups tackling this problem, had enormous difficulties in bringing out a total of some 15 men, not more. There could be no talk of hundreds or thousands of escapees: not one single Western country would agree to accept them....

This is just one example, but it is very indicative of the main reasons for our differences: despite all our efforts, even the more conservative Western circles did not want to understand *that dozens and hundreds of millions behind the Iron Curtain were their natural and most powerful allies and not a "humanitarian problem." Communism could only really be defeated together with them.*

6.12   I did all I could...

Yet this was still the blessed time when the presence of a common foe made us allies to some degree, and ensured the support if not of governments, then at least of some forces within society. Then the mindless euphoria over glasnost and perestroika in those days deprived us of this last vestige of support, our last allies. The temptation to conquer without a fight, to win with no effort proved too great for them to resist. Just at a time when we could have set about building legitimate opposition structures with no fear of serious repressions—the means and sympathies of the West were on the other side. Just at the time when political prisoners in Soviet prisons and camps were being subjected to the most refined pressure for the purpose of their ideological neutralization, the West applauded Gorbachev's humanity. When Spetsnaz forces were killing Georgian democrats in the city square in Tbilisi, the National Front of Azerbaijan was being crushed by tanks in Baku, when government buildings were being stormed in Vilnius and Riga, there was only one thing worrying the West: that all this might "harm Gorbachev." As for financial aid to the Kremlin reformers, it was measured in astronomical figures: over the seven years of the party's perestroika, the Soviet foreign debt rose by around 45 billion dollars! That was the price paid by the West to ensure that no genuine democracy could arise in the former USSR, and no market economy. They would have paid even more had the August "putsch" been more successful: there was a new Marshall Plan in the offing, discussed in all seriousness at the meetings of the G7.

It would seem that the very mention of the Marshall Plan, which saved Europe from communism, would require a pause for thought: there would have been no idea of offering it 50 years ago to a Germany *that had not yet been beaten!* Could it have been offered to Petain's France, Mussolini's Italy or Quisling's Norway? At least out fathers had more sense than to defeat the enemy first, force it to *capitulate unconditionally*—and only then talk about economic aid. Had they acted differently, Europe would not have seen democracy, but lived for decades in a "post-totalitarian" absurdity.

Naturally, we attempted to counter this lunacy right to the last, doing our best to support independent forces and publications inside the USSR. The New York-based "Centre for Democracy in the USSR", created for that purpose, even began to translate and publish these editions in the USA in an attempt to bring them to the notice of the public until its funds ran out. In order to make the most rational use possible of our meagre resources, it became necessary to pool everything into one "organization uniting democrats from all republics" under the general slogan-title "Democracy and Independence." But even the conservative *Daily Telegraph* found us too right-wing.[375]

> "To many dissidents, the West is gobbling up sophisticated dis-information, to the effect that Gorbachev is a genuine democrat, and that he is under threat from conservative opponents.... Yet the more these lone voices decry glasnost, the more the suspicion grows that they are standing still, shifting the goalposts that mark reform in order to ensure their past bravery was not in vain. ... They see conspiracy everywhere[...]."

Of course! Even Margaret Thatcher... and even Ronald Reagan.... Only a tiny handful of journalists (Abe Rosenthal of the "New York Times", the editorial columns of the "Wall Street Journal") were brave enough to support us in those times. Luckily, the increasing crisis in the country elicited a sharp radicalization of society, and by 1990 even the Moscow intelligentsia began to understand the nature of the matter. New opportunities arose; new forces emerged from under the control of the authorities, shedding the magic spell of perestroika. In the summer of 1990 we made a final serious attempt to somehow unite the opposition—we organized a conference in Prague, inviting all the old dissidents and the new members of the opposition from all the republics of the USSR, and those Western conservative circles that still appreciated our efforts.

Prague was an ideal venue for this purpose not just because of its proximity to the USSR or eased entry conditions, but first of all because of the obvious symbolism, which Vaclav Havel pointed out in his welcoming address. As the only head of state among others in the world who had come to power as the result of an anti-communist revolution, he was not afraid to declare solidarity with our position, did not betray his party, but spoke about our common principle—that freedom and justice are indivisible.[376] "If they are under threat anywhere, they are under threat everywhere."

Alas, he really proved to be the only one. In order to become a genuinely functioning center of opposition we required considerable means, printing equipment, computers, and communications—all that a large-scale organization needs for its normal operation. But despite all our frantic searching, we found nobody who would equip us with all of the above—no foundation, no government, not a sympathetic patron. It looked as if the future fate of the world was of no interest to anyone. Some replied quite frankly: "If you are right and the USSR will disintegrate soon, why should we spend money

---

[375]John Kampfner, "Gulag survivors bitter as appeals go unheard", *The Daily Telegraph*, 13 May 1989, p. 14.

[376]Robert L. Bartley, "An Independence Day for Europe," *Wall Street Journal*, Eastern edition; New York, N.Y.: 6 July 1990, p. A6.

on this?" The possibility that it might disintegrate in very different ways was not something anyone wanted to think about.

It was a curious state of affairs: the regime was still alive and it could drag hundreds of thousands of people with it into the grave. Furthermore, it became obvious in 1990 that Gorbachev and his adherents were preparing for something. But this did not worry anyone. Scraping up some money we established (in Poland, another newly liberated country) a training and coordination center called "Warsaw-90." The Poles, former activists of Fighting Solidarity, undertook the rapid preparation of groups of activists from various parts of the USSR to work under martial law conditions. At our request they even restored their clandestine workshop for manufacturing radio transmitters and tried to supply them to every group returning to the USSR. We all remembered how under the conditions of the mass repressions of martial law, reliable and timely information is worth its weight in gold. The lives of thousands and thousands of people would rely on it.

In full confirmation of our forecasts, the regime launched its attack on the Baltic states in 1991 by raising prices and generally clamping down. There was no doubt: the proclamation of martial law could be expected at any time over the next few weeks. If there was something that restrained them, it was the growing resistance of the population that threatened to spill over into a general strike. By spring, confrontation seemed inevitable, and from my point of view—desirable. This was a unique moment in our history, one of those rare moments that determine the life of a country for generations to come. For the first time in 70 years of pitiless oppression, people issued an open challenge to the regime. Such an entirely popular outburst, uniting all the ethnic and social groups in the country with a desire to defend their honor and freedom, was invaluable. It meant that in these seemingly cowed people there lay the seeds of true democracy. But suppositions were not enough. Weak and inexperienced opposition forces needed forging in the process of fighting the old regime in order to develop into a proper political structure, capable of sweeping the *nomenklatura* from all levels of state rule. Only a struggle like this could produce real leaders, popular organizers in every district, in every industrial plant, thereby creating a genuine political *alternative*. Without this struggle there could be no *system changes*, and the new putative system would not have the necessary support.

The country was ripe for revolution. And the stupidest thing that could be done under the circumstances would be allowing the authorities to keep the initiative, letting them choose their own moment to attack. The regime had to be confronted when it was least prepared for it and wanted it least. But influencing the attitudes in an enormous country from abroad, without an organization, without a nationwide means of communication, was impossible. We were unable to achieve anything like that, having been abandoned without support and resources all over the world. There was one last chance—attempt to go there.

Getting to Moscow with enormous difficulty in April 1991, armed with a five-day visa, I threw myself into a maelstrom of meetings, interviews and conferences. The hope that something could still be corrected, saved, gave me strength, even though I was well aware that all I could offer people was advice, not money, technology or organizational structures, or even the sympathy of the Western world from which I had come. This was a desperate attempt to convince, a hope that one loudly said word may be sufficient. After all, had we not been using words to fight this regime for thirty years? Were we not accustomed to doing all that was in our power in even more hopeless times?

"Confrontation is inevitable"—I said at a press conference immediately upon arrival.[377]—"The only thing that needs to be thought about is avoiding bloodshed. I have said a thousand times and say again: what is needed is a general strike. This is the only way to avoid blood and famine. [...] Don't you understand: there will be famine before the winter? Gorbachev will not retire voluntarily. The KGB will not retire voluntarily. That means they will shoot.

"I believe that you cannot remain passive today. If our country does not arise as one and not tell the communist regime to leave, the alternative will be famine in Ethiopian proportions and a Lebanese-style civil war."[378]

"I do not understand how you can morally support striking miners and continue to go to work,"—I challenged people in subsequent interviews.[379]—"How can that be: miners are striking not for themselves, but for their common cause, while you go to work.... I went through the camps. If one prisoner went on hunger strike, the entire camp went on hunger strike. The country must go on strike. [...] If this regime remains in power, your children will be fighting somewhere in Poland or Moldavia. They shall crush a rebellion by the Azeris. Do you really want that?"

"Democratic structures need to be organized as soon as possible. Your deputies sit in your Russian parliament and lose time.

---

[377]*Ogonyok*, April 1991, No 18, pp. 26–27.

[378]Vitaliy Buzuev, "Exiles: When I return: Observations from the Press Conference of Vladimir Bukovsky," *Rossiyskaya Gazeta*, Saturday, 20 April, 1991, p. 4.

[379]David Gai, "Vladimir Bukovsky: The People's Passivity Surprises Me," *Vechernyaya Moskva*, No 76, 18 April, 1991, p. 3.

Surely they understand that there is nothing backing them, no power? Take away their microphones tomorrow and they are no longer there! People must unite. Call it a forum, or a party.... You must realize that the country will collapse, and there will be nobody there."[380]

In fact, this was the core of the problem: the country was ready to throw the regime out, but it was the new elite that was not ready, the new "democrats" that grew up under perestroika. On the whole, they were incidental people, who had come to the fore in pseudo-elections, when any new face looked better than the old; they were closer to the regime than to the people. They were not at all anxious for radical changes which could move them aside, too, depriving them of the unexpectedly acquired position of "leaders." Attending a session of the Supreme Soviet of the RSFSR, I was astounded by their inadequacy: they spent half a day in useless bickering regarding which group of deputies would use which microphone. At the end of stormy debates on this very important subject they even put the matter to a vote and, delighted with their own democracy, called a recess. At that time the country was so inflamed that several days later even communist trade unions were forced, as I have mentioned earlier, to hold a one-day strike in order to retain at least some of their influence. More than 50 million workers downed tools, moreover in the face of an official prohibition.[381]

Making use of the parliamentary recess, I mounted the stand and tried to bring them back to reality. Fat chance! Just like other Russian leaders they dreamed of a civil peace and negotiations at a round table with the communist regime. No matter how hard I tried to explain that even in Poland (where the leaders of Solidarity had at least millions of people backing this organization and who had already experienced martial law) the round table had proved to be a mistake: it only slowed down the movement of the Polish public toward democracy, but the Russian "democrats" did not want to understand that in their situation such a round table would be anything but round. In the conflict between the people and the regime, their instinct was to choose the side of the regime that fathered them. Yeltsin, their undisputed leader at that time, even abandoned the striking miners to their own devices in order to agree a temporary truce with Gorbachev. Furthermore, out of all the currently existing political groups, he selected the "liberal communists" as his allies—his future deadly foes: he appointed Alexander Rut-

---

[380]Ogonyok, April 1991, No 18, pp. 26–27.

[381]"Fifty million Russians strike for an hour in defiance of ban" (Reuters) *International Herald Tribune*, 27–28 April 1991, p. 5.

skoy as his Vice-president, and Ruslan Khazbulatov as Chairman of the Supreme Soviet of Russia. Just four months later this choice became fatal to the entire subsequent development of events, to the whole country, making dismantling the old system impossible. Tangled in conspiracies, drowning in putsches, the regime was to fall like an overripe fruit. But all the structures of the new authority were blocked by the old *nomenklatura*, paralyzed by the egotism of the new elite from the ranks of the "liberal communists" so dear to the heart of Boris Yeltsin. With no mass structures to lean on, the new democracy was suspended in midair, and power was seized by the greedy and soulless bureaucracy. . . .

Still, why blame only the permanently drunk former party *apparatchik*? It would be hard to expect anything else from him. But the entire "flower of the nation", the intellectual elite of the country was no better, taking fright at their compatriots at the critical moment, more than a *chekist* retribution. They started moaning and sniveling:

"Oh, God forbid, a Russian uprising. . . . Oh, there will be tanks under our windows. . . ."

> *"From the comfort of Cambridge it may seem that if the factories stop working, loaves shall start falling from heaven," I would be preached at daringly by some lady[382] from the intelligentsia, who had never seen anything more frightening in her life than a party rebuke. "But we are from here, and can see perfectly well that this is no jump into the 'realm of freedom', but a step toward destruction and chaos, epidemics and famine. With the aid of a general strike, it will be impossible to avert civil war—just hasten it. . . numerous wise heads realized long ago that if there is one thing we have to fear, it is 'blazing revolutionaries', displaying fearlessness in front of advancing tanks."*

Well, that is why you are given "wise heads" to "see perfectly". . . . Several weeks later there were tanks under windows that required displaying fearlessness, but it was too late to save the country from destruction and chaos. That incandescent April, when everything was simply black or white and everything was achievable will be remembered by more than one generation of impoverished, devastated people, huddling in their homes in fear of marauding bands. As for me, just like thirty years ago, I have nothing to say to them but:

I did all I could. . . .

---

[382]Alla Latynina, "When the Iron Curtain rises," *Literaturnaya gazeta,* No 29, 24 July 1991, p. 9.

Afterword

By David Satter, author of
Age of Delirium: the Decline and Fall of the Soviet Union
and
Darkness at Dawn: the Rise of the Russian Criminal State

In *Judgment in Moscow*, Vladimir Bukovsky exposed the crimes of the Soviet regime, using relevant documents from the Communist Party's own archives. But there were certain things that Bukovsky could not do, perhaps because they were beyond the capabilities of any one man. He could not convince the West that the crimes of the Soviet Union were the inevitable fruits of the Soviet ideology, and that the only way to free Russia of the legacy of communism was to use the truth about the past to discredit the ideas on which communism was based.

As Bukovsky wrote, what Russia needed was "moral cleansing" and for this, "the entire system and the crimes it perpetrated needed to be put on trial." Despite Bukovsky's efforts, reflected in this book, such a trial never took place. In the new, post-Soviet Russia, the ideology was rejected, but only formally. Its roots, in particular the conviction that the individual is raw material for the purposes of the state, were left in place. They spawned a new system that was not diametrically opposed to the old system but organically related to it. That new system almost immediately began to commit new crimes.

Viewed from the perspective of 2018, the entire 27-year history of post-Soviet Russia is a tribute to the failure to eradicate the influence of communism. The "young reformers" identified themselves as free-market radicals, but the attitude toward their fellow citizens was a communist one. "Above everyone," wrote Solzhenitsyn, "stands a power that is endlessly indifferent to the fate of the people... and even whether they survive or not". The reformers were determined to introduce radical measures while society was dominated by an atmosphere of confusion. Their concern was to reach a "point of no return" beyond which the economic changes they were introducing would be irreversible (in this way, they repeated the behavior of the Bolsheviks in 1917). Putting property into private hands was a goal in itself.

As the privatization process got underway, many of the beneficiaries were criminals, but the reformers believed the market would separate out the efficient owners from the inefficient owners and the efficient owners would prevail. In fact, in Russia, the reforms led to a competition to carve up the remains of the Soviet economy with the help of criminal methods, and once property was put in criminal hands, efficiency was no longer an issue. The criminals had no intention of giving it up.

The pillaging of the country, however, led to economic collapse. In the period 1992–98, Russia's gross domestic product was cut in half. In 1999, as Yeltsin's second term in office was coming to an end, opinion polls showed that he was supported by only 2 per cent of the population. The same level of support was recorded for Yeltsin's hand-picked successor, Vladimir Putin, the prime minister and former head of the Federal Security Service (FSB).

In September 1999, however, four apartment buildings were blown up in Moscow and in two other cities, killing 300 people. The bombings were blamed on Chechen terrorists. Putin was put in charge of a new enterprise—a second war in Chechnya under circumstances in which he could pose as the defender of the Russian people. The second Chechen war was even more brutal and indiscriminate than the first (1994–96). However as a result of initial success, Putin's popularity rose and he was elected President of Russia.

As it happened, however, a fifth bomb was discovered in the basement of an apartment building in the city of Ryazan, and the people who placed it there were captured and found to be not Chechen terrorists, but agents of the FSB. Since then, a mass of overwhelming and incontrovertible evidence has accumulated showing that not only the failed attempt to blow up a building in Ryazan, but also all four of the successful apartment bombings were the work of the FSB. The murder of hundreds of randomly chosen innocent Russian civilians who died in the blasts was the means by which the new "democratic" leadership preserved its hold on power.

Once he became President, Putin showed that he had no use even for the remnants of democracy that had been tolerated under Yeltsin. First, the press was subjected to control, especially the national television stations. Next, the business community, which grew out of massive 1990s corruption, was subordinated with the help of the imprisonment of Mikhail Khodorkovsky, the head of the Yukos Oil Company, who had tried to act independently politically. In 2004, Putin eliminated the direct election of governors. Meanwhile, the place of gangsters and corrupt businessmen was increasingly taken by state officials and the appropriation of resources by officials reached epic proportions.

To a degree which is extreme even by the standards of kleptocracies, the Russian "elite" today behave like occupiers in their own country. Vladislav Inozemtsev, a prominent economist, said "There is not a single country in the world where officials... became wealthy so quickly and on such a scale, [and] people showing such a lack of professionalism achieved such success." These people, in turn, are oriented toward the West. Insofar as corrupt wealth in Russia is a product of patronage and the political constellation is always susceptible to change, Russian oligarchs and major businessmen establish a second life for themselves in the West where they keep their bank accounts, property and families. Many of them spend as little time as possible in Russia. An American lawyer familiar with Russia's new rich said, "The lack of patriotism is astounding."

The situation that Bukovsky foresaw in 1995 has come to pass. His most important point, that without a proper reckoning with the past, Russia will never have a decent future, was confirmed repeatedly under Yeltsin and Putin, and particularly in the 1999 bombings which saved the corrupt Yeltsin entourage and brought Putin and the FSB to power. Now, just as after the Soviet Union's collapse, the need for a historical reckoning has to be faced, with the sole difference being that it is not only necessary to face the truth about the communist period, but also about the post-communist period. This is the only way to achieve the moral cleansing that Bukovsky called for when *Judgment in Moscow* first appeared, and for Russia to establish a system based on law that attaches value to human life. Only such a reckoning can expunge the legacy of the events of November 1917, and by reaffirming the value of individual human life, create the conditions for Russia's moral and political resurrection.

Also by Vladimir Bukovsky

To Build a Castle: My Life as a Dissenter

A major document in the literature of human rights, this now-legendary memoir was a worldwide bestseller when first published in 1978.

At the age of 20, as punishment for his political protests, Bukovsky was falsely declared insane and committed to a psychiatric hospital—standard practice for communism's critics in 1963. But the quack doctors and brutal guards who kept him captive didn't realize: Bukovsky wasn't locked up with them. They were locked up with him.

In this compelling, beautifully-crafted memoir, Bukovsky details with equal parts burning outrage and bitter humor the cruel theater of life for Soviet prisoners of conscience. But he also recounts how he found his inner truth and strength.

Bukovsky offers powerful firsthand testimony to the importance of personal integrity and perseverance under seemingly boundless, endless oppression and abuse.

"Vladimir Bukovsky has written an extraordinary account of his life in the Soviet Union. . . . Listen closely."
—*New York Times*

"This book is important."
—Former US President Ronald Reagan

"This is a landmark book and a human document that remains vital."
—Sir Tom Stoppard, Oscar-winning screenwriter of *Shakespeare in Love*

"If human bravery were a book, it would be *To Build a Castle*."
—Garry Kasparov, Chairman of the Human Rights Foundation

"A huge story we must not forget. Even inside prison, a revolt of the mind is possible."
— Masha Alyokhina, co-founder of the anti-Putinist punk rock group Pussy Riot

Available for Kindle from Amazon: https://amzn.com/B06XDSCM3B

Appendices

Appendix A

Only a Trial Will Do This Time

The Author's Argument for a Trial of Communist Leaders[383]

On Sunday, 18 March 2018, Vladimir Putin ran for the Russian presidency for a fourth time and won easily in the first round, claiming 77 percent of votes cast (by 68 percent of the electorate), in a contest that was neither free nor fair.

Following the murder of Boris Nemtsov, early in 2015, his most prominent opponent was Alexei Navalny, who was not allowed to register as a presidential candidate and take part in the 2018 elections.

In a set of 15 theses, drawn up and published in 2013, Vladimir Bukovsky argued that the popular campaign against corruption (Navalny famously denounced the United Russia as the party of "conmen and crooks") did not address the main problem posed by the Putin regime. That had its roots in the issues not tackled in the early 1990s, after the demise of the USSR.

As a consequence, an unreconstructed KGB lieutenant colonel became President of Russia in 2000 and has led the country since the beginning of the twenty-first century.

• • •

1. The situation in Russia can no longer be resolved by round-table negotiations, only a trial will do.

Present Russian arguments about whether it is possible to negotiate with the regime of "conmen and crooks" misses the very heart of the problem, in my view. We all know we are facing not just thieves or embezzlers, but murderers. As yet, only a few have had the audacity to say this out loud.

2. This regime began its existence with crimes against humanity, blowing up apartment blocs in 1999 (in Buinaksk, Moscow and Volgodonsk), and committing genocide in Chechnya (1999–2005).

For as long as it has existed, Putin's regime has murdered people: Galina Starovoitova in 1998; Yuri Shchekochikhin and Sergei Yushenkov in 2003; Anna Politkovskaya and Alexander Litvinenko in 2006; Yury Chervochkin in 2007; while Stanislav Markelov, Anastasia Baburova, Natalya Estemirova, Maksharip Aushev and

---

[383]Notes and translation by John Crowfoot. Also available at the online Bukovsky Archive (https://bukovsky-archive.com/2018/05/05/only-a-trial-will-do-this-time/).

Sergei Magnitsky were all killed in 2009.[384] And they are only its best-known victims.

Until such crimes have been investigated and those responsible have been brought to justice we cannot say that we have put an end to the Kremlin gang.

3. Why do many of those who so eagerly (and rightly) accuse the regime of corruption, deceit, falsification, provocation and even the usurpation of power, hesitate to speak of its most heinous crimes?

Undoubtedly, it is a heavy responsibility to bring such accusations. With conmen and crooks, it is possible, perhaps, to reach a peaceful agreement. If they will give back what they stole and leave the scene, that is enough.

When we talk about murder, however, a stolen life cannot be restored: as a result, there can be no compromise with the killers. When companies like Gazprom and Lukoil were stolen from the people and the votes they cast at elections were taken from them, the nation might forgive the thieves. No one can forgive a murderer: the living have no right to do so.

4. Dealing with the assassinations committed by the State is not an abstract moral issue—it is a matter of pressing political

---

[384]Murdered opponents in chronological order of death:

Galina Starovoitova—shot 20 November 1998, aged 52, in St Petersburg. Ethnographer, veteran politician and likely 2000 presidential election candidate.

Sergei Yushenkov—shot April 2003, aged 52, in Moscow. Ex-army, veteran politician, State Duma deputy, apartment explosions committee.

Yuri Shchekochikhin—poisoned and died in July 2003, aged 53, in Moscow: veteran journalist (*Novaya gazeta*) and State Duma deputy (1993–2003). On the Apartment Explosions committee.

Anna Politkovskaya — shot 7 October 2006, aged 48, in Moscow. Journalist (*Novaya gazeta*) writing about Chechnya and Putin's Russia.

Alexander Litvinenko—poisoned 23 November 2006, aged 44, in London. Former FSB investigator, covering links between organized crime in Russia and Spain.

Yury Chervochkin—died on 10 December 2007, aged 22, as a consequence of a severe beating on 22 November. Opposition activist.

Stanislav Markelov—shot 19 January 2009, aged 34, in central Moscow. Lawyer (e.g. Budanov case) and Antifa activist; and **Anastasia Baburova**, shot 19 January 2009, aged 25, in Moscow. Journalist (*Novaya gazeta* intern) and Antifa activist.

Natalya Estemirova — shot 15 July 2009, aged 51, in Ingushetia. Journalist (*Novaya gazeta*) based in Chechnya, close colleague of Politkovskaya.

Maksharip Aushev—shot in October 2009, aged 53, in Kabardino-Balkaria. Ingushetia activist and journalist, succeeded Magomed Yevloyev (shot 2008) as owner of opposition news website.

Sergei Magnitsky—died, aged 37, in Moscow pre-trial detention on 16 November 2009. Company lawyer exposing corruption.

Boris Nemtsov — shot 27 February 2015, aged 55, next to Moscow Kremlin. Deputy prime minister for a while under Yeltsin; opposition activist and leader since 1988.

importance.

The main slogans of public protest have today been formulated in terms of criminal justice. The country has risen not against a policy or an ideology, but quite specifically against the rule of lawless behavior throughout Russia.

Such a revolution cannot end with a round-table discussion. That would be like a deal between the judicial system and the criminals. This uprising can only end with a trial and, in the worst scenario, with a lynch mob.

5. Attempts to "engage in dialogue" with the regime are not merely harmful—they are suicidal.

Tens and hundreds of thousands of people have been coming out on the street to demand justice, not round-table negotiations with the punks in the Kremlin. The protestors will see negotiations in such a situation as a criminal conspiracy. Whoever agrees to such talks will be regarded as an accomplice of the mafia.

After living for an extended historical period under a mafia regime, the Russian nation has a quite subtle understanding of how such criminals settle their scores. It is natural, and entirely justified, to apply this understanding to the present confrontation with the Kremlin.

On his deathbed, Don Corleone advised his young successor, "There's no way to avoid a war: the first person who suggests holding talks with the enemy is a traitor." Our people have watched *The Godfather*. Furthermore, they have lived in Russia. Society has little faith in politicians today. Talk of a "dialogue with the regime" will destroy what little confidence remains.

6. Such a firm attitude to our self-appointed negotiators is justified, among other things by our own historical experience.

Twenty-five years ago, the democratic opposition in the USSR wasted a decisive moment on "dialogue" with a Soviet regime that was on its last legs. The conmen and crooks of the old *nomenklatura*, as a result, were able to calmly redefine themselves as "democrats" and remain in power.

Supposedly, dialogue was then necessary for a peaceful and bloodless change of regime. Within a few years it became clear that there had been no change of regime, merely an alteration in its outward appearance. The same gangsters in a different uniform started killing people in Moscow, in Chechnya and in police stations all over the country. . . .

Instead of a bloodless revolution there were rivers of blood; freedom and democracy remained as remote as ever.

7. The 1989 round-table discussions in Poland were hardly a positive historical example.

Among other things, during the transition period the Communist regime in Poland managed to negotiate for itself two-thirds of the seats in the Sejm and a continued tenure of the presidency. Naturally, the Polish *nomenklatura* used this breathing space to fortify its own position, and survive, well-funded, in the new Poland with control of the regime and of the media. For a generation, the round table held back the healing of Poland as a country and rendered the process more difficult.

As the archives would reveal, there was no need for the opposition to make concessions. Within his own circle, Jaruzelski acknowledged, if it had not been for the round table his regime would have only kept going for a few months. Eventually, the Poles were obliged to put the general's accomplices on trial. It was twenty years too late.

8. Post-war West Germany is the classic example of a country that rapidly rid itself of the totalitarian plague.

The healing of West Germany after the war became possible thanks to the Nuremburg Tribunal. Only by uncovering and condemning all the crimes of the Nazi regime could the country move forward. Poland needed almost 20 years before its own experience made it realize the same. Kampuchea required more than 30 years, but, in the end, it had to put the leaders of the Khmer Rouge on trial.

By not deciding, at the right moment, to put the Soviet regime on trial, Russia has paid more heavily than any other "post-Communist" country. I would like to believe, this time, that we shall not repeat that mistake. It is beyond doubt that the Kremlin mafia will strive, at any cost, to avoid such a trial.

9. The present Russian leadership are no longer the kind to fight heroically until the last bullet.

They will make full use of their trump card—the real or illusory threat of bloodshed.

Most likely they will deploy this threat to push us towards round-table negotiations. At the very least, this will provide immunity from prosecution for a whole range of Kremlin thugs and punks. Immunity is not just a civilized rejection of vengeance: it means that any investigation of their crimes is being rejected.

They may toss a couple of the most hated courtiers (men like Vladimir Churov[385], say, and Putin himself) onto the halberds of

---

[385]**Vladimir Churov** (b. 1953) is a close colleague of the President from his Leningrad days. In the 1990s, he worked with Putin in the external affairs department of the Petersburg city administration.

From 2007 to 2016, Churov headed the Central Electoral Commission, although he lacked the legal training previously required of anyone holding the post. Today he is an Ambassador at Large for the Ministry of Foreign Affairs. Bukovsky's reference the rebellious guards. It would be dangerous to let Putin live, in any case, because he knows too much and, if a trial was ever held, he might betray his accomplices. Yet it is not stamped on the foreheads of Russia's myriad conmen and crooks that that is what they are.

A dispassionate investigation and a fair trial are necessary. Granting such figures immunity will be to leave them forever with a presumption of innocence. There will be a change of leaders, certain cosmetic reforms, but no change of regime. Once again, the criminal gang from the Lubyanka will evade responsibility and remain in power, stealing this new revolution from under our noses —they are conmen and crooks, when all is said and done.

10. In short, if the round-table solution is adopted we shall be the fools who allowed a hard-won victory to slip through our fingers.

When, like the Civil War partisans in the Far East, the whole country rebels and takes the justice it has been denied into its own hands, who will condemn it? The people will not be to blame. The responsibility will then lie with the self-styled leaders of the revolution who betrayed their just demands, crying with them "We shall not forget or forgive!"—only to offer official amnesia and clemency in return for seats in the government.

11. We should not be thinking of a round table now, but of our own debt to history and to our country. We must ensure that justice prevails, and that it takes a civilized form.

Fortunately, while Moscow's intellectual politicians still nurture such illusions, more responsible people have been found in Russia.

Beyond the capital a movement has begun, setting up public tribunals to investigate and deliver a legal assessment of the crimes of the present regime. Even if they are not endowed with punitive functions these tribunals can, on the one hand, help to avoid lynch mobs and, on the other, prevent impunity.

Of course, there must be a national tribunal, to complement these regional tribunals and to investigate the most extensive of the regime's crimes. Doubtless, it will begin with the "original sin" of Putin's regime: the September 1999 blowing up of four apartment buildings in Dagestan, Moscow and southern Russia. If there is insufficient evidence and testimony, the release of documents and the calling of witnesses and suspects are entirely lawful demands for such an investigation. Moreover, the work must begin today. Tomorrow it may be too late.

---

to courtiers and rebellious guards is an allusion to the Revolt of the Palace Guard in 1698, when unpopular courtiers were put to death in Red Square.

12. Of course, the regime will defend itself. It would be naive and irresponsible to expect an easy victory after holding a couple of rallies.

The regime already finds itself cornered, like the rat Putin once chased as a boy. As it turned to fight him, Putin gazed into its eyes and saw his future. If he did not then understand that prophetic encounter, he undoubtedly realized what it meant in December 2011.

Will we give the rat a chance to attack us, or will we strike first? That is the only question today. And if we are going to strike, then we must aim where the creature is most vulnerable. The sooner we finish off this rat, the less painful it will be for Russia.

13. We must not delude ourselves. A showdown with the regime cannot be avoided and we must prepare for it. If we draw on the experience of the Poles, we should look to their post-1981 resistance to the State of Emergency, not to the roundtable talks of 1989.

The regime will try to seize opposition leaders in Moscow and across the country. We must be prepared for that. We must set aside apartments, telephones, Internet access and simple printing devices against that day.

Communication via the Internet and mobile phones may be blocked for some time: we must be ready with alternative means of communication. Opposition media will not be able to function, and we should reach agreements in good time about emergency forms of communication and organization.

14. A confrontation is inevitable: we should be thinking how to avoid bloodshed.

Negotiations are of no help in such a situation—just as it makes no sense trying to do a deal with a cornered rat. You might get the regime's agreement not to use force, but will that save anyone? Who can trust them at their word? So long as those serial killers remain in the Kremlin the danger of bloodshed will not go away. We must save the country, and innocent lives, from their clutches—not by reaching an agreement with them.

If the regime is strong enough to put down a revolution, it will not agree to significant concessions. It will use any talks to divide and compromise the opposition. If the regime is so weak it is ready to hold serious negotiations, then we must not make concessions. In that case, we must demand unconditional surrender. We cannot permit the revolution to spill blood or to be false to itself. Experience shows that a phony revolution also ends in great bloodshed.

15. Of course, it is impossible to foresee all potential scenarios.

Remember, we are dealing with liars and criminals. We cannot trust them and no compromise with them is possible. The investigation of the crimes of the regime cannot be subject to negotiation, neither can the release of political prisoners or the holding of fair and free elections.

That is the indisputable and clearly expressed will of the people. Any concessions on these issues will rightly be regarded as treachery. And so long as the regime is not ready to surrender, there is nothing to discuss with the country's present rulers.

First published on 19 January 2013,
Echo of Russia online journal
(http://ehorussia.com/new/node/7082)

• • •

Written early in 2013, after two years of rallies and protests in Moscow and elsewhere, this publication refers to the period before renewed external aggression — Russia's March 2014 annexation of Crimea and subsequent invasion of eastern Ukraine — was added to the mounting internal repression.

Appendix B

Interview with Vladimir Bukovsky

Excerpts from the Interview with Radio NVC, April 2018,
Host: Leon Weinstein.

Original interview in Russian: https://youtu.be/rjTAfSEWkFU
Translated by Lubov Yudovich

Leon Weinstein: We are discussing Vladimir Bukovsky's book *Judgment in Moscow*, which was originally written in 1996. I learned of the story of its publication just recently, when I received proofs of the English translation. The story is mind-boggling, so I wanted to talk about it with Vladimir Konstantinovich. The thing that makes this so incredible is that it happened here in America, not in Russia where it was first published.

Vladimir Konstantinovich, if I am not mistaken, there was a publishing house that had contracted with you to publish the book here in the US in English. By that time the book had already been published in other languages, and was selling quite well. However, the US publisher canceled the contract because you refused to 'make changes' they had asked for. Here we're not talking about minor edits. They were asking for the kind of changes that you could never agree to make; and as a result they would sever their relationship with you, and not publish the book. Could you tell us exactly what happened, what sort of changes they required, and why you wouldn't agree to make them?

Vladimir Bukovsky: Part of my correspondence with the publishing house editor can be found in the first chapter of the final version of *Judgment in Moscow*, so those who are curious can read the correspondence and judge for themselves what happened. In essence, they demanded that I re-wrote the entire book from the point of view of a liberal of the left. For example, I write [*in my book*] that a specific publisher [*George Bobolas, Greek construction magnate who ventured into media*] entered into a contract with the Soviets to publish articles about the Soviet Union under the direct editorial control of the Soviets. . . .

Leon Weinstein: You've got to be kidding me?

Vladimir Bukovsky: No kidding. Everything is documented: all the agreements with all the archival data—you can see for yourself. Another example is of several companies who agreed to do business with them [*the SU*], again under their ideological control; and so on. So, the publisher demanded that I threw all of that out. We corresponded by fax, back and forth, for quite some time. In the end I just replied that *"Due to certain peculiarities of my biography, I am allergic to political censorship, so I can't do what you are asking me to do."* So, they canceled the contract; it was a large contract as well.

Leon Weinstein: I get that.

Vladimir Bukovsky: It slowed me down enormously. I spent a very long time looking for a new publisher. As you understand, publishing is a small world—if one publisher drops you, the others grow cautious too. But finally, I did find a publisher—an old small publishing house in the UK—John Murray. They don't exist anymore, but at the time they did. They were a very proud family publishing house. The point of pride was the fact that at they had originally published Byron. They bought the rights to my book; and the next thing we knew—a team of lawyers is paying them a visit and telling them, "You try to publish this book, and we will bankrupt you. You will be sued non-stop. Non-stop! You are a family publishing house, you don't have the resources to fight us." And they didn't fight. They gave up. They dropped the contract. They didn't try to keep it a secret from me, I later received all this information.

This is why I couldn't get the book published in English for such a long time. It had been already published in French, Italian, German, Polish, Romanian, not to mention in Russian—that version had been published instantly. Nobody anywhere thought of stopping its publication. Nobody had tried to sue; it should be obvious that there were no grounds. But the English-language publishers kept silent, and didn't dare publish the book.

Finally, a group of supporters in America, who are not professionals in this field, decided to publish the book in English using their own resources and investing their own labor. Everything is being done by the efforts of volunteers. The translator who translated this book from Russian, people who worked on footnotes and searched for references, the editors—all these people worked for free. This is pure enthusiasm. They understand that this book must exist, and that people want to read it, so they put in the effort. Let's praise and thank them.

Leon Weinstein: Absolutely! But your other books were published in English, is that right?

Vladimir Bukovsky: Yes, of course. My first book even became a bestseller in several countries.

Leon Weinstein: So then, just this one specific work containing accurate, undisputable facts, and supported by documentation— that book for some reason was not. The only thing, I am assuming, they could have contrived was to allege that you had manufactured all these documents yourself; or had obtained them from some completely different source. But it's such an unlikely allegation, that I doubt anyone would have tried to make it.

Vladimir Bukovsky: But you see, it would have been completely useless to try to do that. There was a hearing of the Constitutional Court in Moscow, where I insisted on most of these documents being admitted into evidence in the court records. These documents are exhibits in the court case. You can go to the Constitutional Court, check out the case file, and read through them.

Leon Weinstein: Oh, that's great. And it sounds like it would also nullify any future attempts to sue.

Vladimir Bukovsky: Of course.

Leon Weinstein: But still, why? Were some famous public figures mentioned who had worked with the KGB, or the Political Bureau, or the Central Committee of the CPSU? I mean, those are all the same really, all of them worked toward the same goal.

Vladimir Bukovsky: Sure....

Leon Weinstein: Were there Americans who would have wanted to keep their names out of such a damaging book?

Vladimir Bukovsky: Of course. The establishment left, including artistic circles, had been open and willing to have contacts with the Soviets. They [*the left*] thought that was a way to secure peace on earth. Take a certain Cyrus Vance, who later became a member of the Palme Commission in Sweden. That Commission was basically engaged in the justification of Soviet foreign policy. I have a lot of material in my book on this. At one time, Cyrus Vance together with a group of other left-wing actors approached Arbatov—the Soviet representative on the Commission, and told him, "Look, could you not use such blatant Soviet language for the declarations on the Commission's decisions? It's very difficult for us to have our decisions announced in such an obvious Soviet style. At least rephrase them." This is shown in one of the documents that I have.

Leon Weinstein: Cyrus Vance is very well known here. And what about modern-day Hollywood personalities?

Vladimir Bukovsky: Well, I have a document which shows that in 1979 Francis Ford Coppola, at the request of President Carter approached the Soviet Cinematography Committee with a proposal for a documentary on disarmament. The Soviets agreed, but only on condition that the Soviets would have total control of the production. And the Americans accepted. They were ready to roll, but in the end this film was never made, because the invasion of Afghanistan interfered, and relations went to hell, but the Americans were ready to do it.

Leon Weinstein: That's just incredible. To agree to make a film about disarmament under Soviet control! I always thought that Carter saw the world through rose-tinted glasses, but I clung to the belief that at least he held anti-Soviet views, mostly because of his stance toward Iran and that whole border region. But now you are dispelling my illusions. My goodness: to do a film about disarmament and to surrender control over the final cut to the other side! My background is in film, so I know exactly what that means.

Vladimir Bukovsky: Yes.

Leon Weinstein: Tell me this: we say that the Cold War was over with the collapse of the Soviet Union. But is it really over? I get the feeling that we have moved from the Cold War into some sort of a new phase. And also, who exactly won when the USSR collapsed?

Vladimir Bukovsky: Those were the exact questions I was asking in *Judgment in Moscow*, writing 25 years ago: is the Cold War over? And if so, who won? Show me how it's over, explain it to me. Because I didn't see it as being over. I didn't think it could be over until communism was put on trial in Moscow. This is the central message of the book *Judgment in Moscow*.

Leon Weinstein: In liberal, or as they call themselves 'progressive', circles here in the United States and Europe, the established opinion is that Moscow supports the American right wing; the "fascists", the nationalists and the like. I however have the feeling, that in fact Moscow is left-wing-oriented. What is your view on this?

Vladimir Bukovsky: You see this is an old, old trick; the so-called false dichotomy. It was conceived by the Communist International (Comintern) in the 1930s, and it works like this: if you are for Stalin, then you are against Hitler; and if you are for Hitler, then you are against Stalin. This trick has been used to brainwash the world's population until very recently. Even today many still don't see through it. For example: either you are for the gays, or you are for Putin. If you are against Putin, then you are for the "sodomites". [*Laughs.*] It's a marvelous trick—false dichotomy; you just can't lose. Anything beyond it is "tertium non datur" [*"no third possibility is given"*], as the ancient Romans would say; a third option does not enter into people's minds.

Leon Weinstein: Some people in Moscow and in Russia took to calling us who live in the US, "Americosi" to rhyme with the gay slur and term of abuse "pendosi". . . . It's the same trick.

Vladimir Bukovsky: Yes, yes.

Leon Weinstein: In my view, national socialism/fascism and international socialism are not even two sides of the same coin, they are one and the same side of the same coin. . . .

Vladimir Bukovsky: You know, the only person in my memory who grasped this was Margaret Thatcher. She said that fascism was not a right-wing movement, but a left-wing one, the same as bolshevism.

Leon Weinstein: Precisely. And another thing: we are constantly being told that Moscow doesn't want to see a united Europe (EU). But you write that it was Moscow who came up with the very idea of the EU in the first place. Why did they do it?

Vladimir Bukovsky: Well, you see, at that time the Soviets were still hoping to save their system. Gorbachev—contrary to current opinion—was very much trying to save the Soviet system. He went about it in a very sophisticated way, and put extraordinary effort into it. One of the means for saving the Soviet Union was to set up a sort of quasi-Soviet structure in Europe. Gorbachev did not come up with this idea himself, but when he was approached with it he gave it his support. If you look at the documents, at the end of the 1980s this idea was proposed as "Our Shared European Home". This is how they articulated it.

Gorbachev was hoping that it would stabilize him and prevent the dissolution of the Soviet Union and the Eastern bloc. Because where would all these Eastern European countries run to get away from the Soviet Union? They would run to the European Union— which would be a good thing, because he was going to come to an agreement with the EU leaders on this. It was all going to be done within the framework of socialism—that was the original plan for the European Home, and that was the original agreement with the leaders of the future EU. But what happened was that the need for such a 'European Home' disappeared. Russia fell by the wayside; Eastern European countries went each on their own way; some of them joined the European Union, some didn't. But generally speaking, the main reason for creating such a bipolar system, to keep the Eastern European countries and Russia latched on to each other, disappeared.

Leon Weinstein: So what you are saying is that originally the concept of a "European Home" included [*was conceived in collaboration with*] Russia, who wanted to get a foothold inside the European Union, and then, with the assistance of their socialist 'brothers', proceed to suck the lifeblood out of this very large European entity?

Vladimir Bukovsky: You know, they state it quite clearly. There are minutes of the negotiations between Mitterrand and Gorbachev where Mitterrand says plainly "We need a strong Soviet Union to control everything between Paris and Moscow." A simple idea, isn't it? [*Laughs.*]

Leon Weinstein: It's a shocking idea, really.
Vladimir Bukovsky: Yes, and we have it in black and white.

Appendix C

Additional Online Resources

Judgment in Moscow in the original Russian – *Московский Процесс*:
https://readli.net/moskovskiy-protsess-chast-1
https://readli.net/moskovskiy-protsess-chast-2
http://e-reading.club/book.php?book=8941
http://e-reading.club/book.php?book=8942

Bukovsky Center's curated list of Bukovsky's
writings, video appearances, biography and news:
https://vladimirbukovsky.com/

Twitter feed with news about the author:
https://twitter.com/BukovskyCenter

Facebook group about the author and his work:
https://facebook.com/groups/219843491748776

Mailing list for discussion of the Bukovsky and Stroilov archives:
https://groups.google.com/forum/#!forum/bukovskyarchives

Essays referenced in Judgment in Moscow:

"The Peace Movement and the Soviet Union" (Chapter 1)
https://commentarymagazine.com/articles/
the-peace-movement-the-soviet-union/

"Is Glasnost a Game of Mirrors?" – a letter by ten writers, artists
and dissidents known as the "The Letter of the Ten" (Chapter 3.4)
https://nytimes.com/1987/03/22/opinion/
is-glasnost-a-game-of-mirrors.html

An epilogue by Bukovsky for
an earlier version of this book can be read here:
https://vladimirbukovsky.com/epilogue

Bukovsky and Stroilov's two essays
about Diana West's book *American Betrayal*,
which explores the theme of western collusion with the USSR:
https://breitbart.com/big-government/2013/09/28/
its-worse-than-a-conspiracy-it%20-s-consensus
https://breitbart.com/national-security/2013/11/27/
bukovsky-american-betrayal

Glossary

A

Active measures—Actions of political warfare conducted by the Soviet and Russian security services (Cheka, OGPU, NKVD, KGB, FSB) ranging from media manipulation to outright violence.

Agitprop—From *otdel agitatsii i propagandy*, the Department of Agitation and Propaganda. Political propaganda, originally plays but later any art or entertainment with an explicit political message.

Apparatchik—Derogatory term for a person in a professional capacity of the Communist Party of the Soviet Union or the Soviet government apparatus.

B

Bay of Pigs invasion—Failed 1961 counter-revolutionary invasion of Cuba by a group of Cuban exiles and US military personnel, trained and funded by the CIA.

Belgrade Conference—1961 meeting of heads of state of nations not formally aligned with or against either Communist or Western blocs, led by Yugoslavia, Egypt and India.

Berlin Wall—Guarded concrete barrier dividing Berlin from 1961–1989, built to prevent unhindered crossing into West Berlin from the surrounding communist-controlled German Democratic Republic.

Bolshevik—Faction of the Marxist Russian Social Democratic Labor Party (RSDLP) that split in 1903 to become the dominant group which led the Russian Revolution and established the USSR.

Bundestag—German federal parliament.

C

CC CPSU—Central Committee of the Communist Party of the Soviet Union. The highest body of the CPSU, by official rules, directing all Party and government activities between Party Congresses. By Stalin's death, it was primarily symbolic, and the Politburo was the *de facto* governing force.

Cheka—Secret police (1917–1922), founded and headed by Felix Dzerzhinsky. Succeeded by GPU, OGPU and NKVD.

Chekist—Agent of ChK or Cheka, the Bolshevik security force or secret police formed by Lenin 1917. Later a derogatory term for an agent of any of the Cheka's many descendants—NKVD, KGB and FSB.

Comintern—The Communist International, an international organization from 1919–1943) dedicated to advancing world communism by all means, including military force.

Containment—Cold War geopolitical strategy of the United States and its allies to stop the expansion of international communism through multiple strategies in Eastern Europe, China, Korea, Africa, Vietnam, and Latin America.

Cossacks—Group of tribal communities in southern Russia and Ukraine with strong military and self-government traditions until the 17th century. Later integrated into the Tsars' Army. After declaring independence from the emerging USSR, they were subject to purges. Today, millions who identify as Cossacks or their descendants inhabit Russia, Kazakhstan, Ukraine and Belarus.

CPSU—Communist Party of the Soviet Union (cf. CPSU Central Committee). The single political party during the USSR.

D

Dekulakization—Campaign of arrests, deportations, and executions of millions of prosperous peasants ("*kulaki*") and their families from 1929–1932, in which the USSR expropriated farmlands by declaring the landowners to be class enemies.

Détente—French for "loosening" or "relaxation". Foreign policy of easing relations between hostile nations. During the Cold War, usually referring to easing relations between East (communist countries) and West (democratic countries).

Dialectics—Philosophy of science and nature based largely on writings of Marx and Engels. Communism was viewed as the natural and necessary end goal of human society.

Duma—The lower legislative body of the Russian Federation (1993–).

E

EEC—The European Economic Community, a regional organization created in 1957 by Belgium, France, Italy, Luxembourg, the Netherlands and West Germany. It was expanded and renamed the European Union in 1993.

Eurocommunism—a revisionist trend in the 1970s and 1980s within some Western European communist parties who sought to undermine Soviet influence.

F

Finlandization—The process whereby a country is induced to favor, or refrain from opposing, the interests of a more powerful country with which it is not aligned, as Finland was during the Cold War.

Ford Foundation—American private foundation with the mission of advancing human welfare. Created in 1936 by automobile magnates Edsel Ford and Henry Ford.

FRG—Federal Republic of Germany, the official name of West Germany.

FSB—*Federal'naya sluzhba bezopasnosti*, the Russian Federal security agency, one of the successor agencies to the KGB.

FSLN—Spanish *Frente Sandinista de Liberación Nacional*, the Sandinista National Liberation Front of Nicaragua.

G

Gauleiter—Political official governing a district under Nazi rule.

Gdansk agreement—1980 accord between the Polish government and striking workers, whose primary demand was the right to create a trade union independent of the Communist Party.

GDR — German Democratic Republic, the English name for the *Deutsche Demokratische Republik* or East Germany.

Glasnost—Literally meaning "openness" or "transparency", used as a slogan by Mikhail Gorbachev and his government to project an image of reform of the Soviet system.

Gosplan—Abbreviation of *Gosudarstvennaya Planovaya Komissiya*, "State Planning Committee." The central economic planning committee for the USSR.

H

Helsinki Accords—Non-binding agreements between 35 Western and Communist nations in 1975 in an attempt to improve relations by renouncing violence and supporting human rights.

Helsinki Groups—Social groups for monitoring observance of the Helsinki Accords

Hungarian revolution—1956 uprising against Soviet-imposed policies suppressed by a military invasion in which at least 2,500 Hungarians and 700 Soviet troops were killed.

I

Izvestia—Soviet newspaper founded in 1917, which expressed the official views of the Soviet government. Post-USSR, continued to have close ties to the Russian government.

K

Katyn massacre—Mass execution of an estimated 22,000 Polish officers and intelligentsia carried out by the NKVD in April–May 1940, which Soviet authorities claimed was done by German soldiers.

Kerenskyism—From Alexander Kerensky, a leading figure in the Russian Revolution. Derogatory term for policies of appeasement to Communist influence, enabling their rise to power.

KGB—*Komitet gosudarstvennoy bezopasnosti*, "Committee of State Security," the main USSR security agency for the USSR from 1954 until its dissolution in 1991.

Komsomol—Abbreviated from *Kommunisticheskiy Soyuz Molodyozhi*, "Communist Youth League." Political youth organization established after the Russian Revolution.

Kosygin reforms—1965 set of economic policy changes under Premier Alexei Kosygin that introduced sales and profitability as key indicators of business success.

Kronstadt rebellion—1921 uprising in the Kronstadt Bay area against the Bolsheviks by Russian sailors, soldiers and workers. Several thousand are estimated to have been killed in combat or executed.

Kulak—From Russian kulak, "fist," a tight-fisted person. Originally a term for affluent independent farmers, later applied to any peasant who resisted collectivization of their land or crops.

L

Lenin Peace Prize—Award instituted by the Soviet government to recognize prominent communists and supporters of the Soviet Union outside the USSR. Usually awarded to several people each year on an *ad hoc* schedule.

M

Menshevik—Member of the moderate non-Leninist wing of the Russian Social Democratic Workers' Party, defeated by the Bolsheviks.

MGB — *Ministerstvo Gosudarstvennoy Bezopasnosti*, "Ministry of State Security." The intelligence and secret police apparatus founded in 1946, succeeded by the KGB in 1954.

MP—Member of parliament.

N

Nagorno-Karabakh conflict—Fighting between Armenia and Azerbaijan over disputed territory which began in 1988. Despite a 1994 cease-fire, sporadic hostilities continue.

NATO—North Atlantic Treaty Organization, an intergovernmental security and military alliance of North American and European countries created for mutual protection against the Soviet Union. Created in 1949 by 12 countries, in 2019 it consists of 29 member nations.

Neutron bomb—Nuclear bomb designed to maximize lethal neutron radiation while minimizing physical blast and heat. Its aim is to kill people while leaving buildings and grounds intact and habitable.

New Economic Policy — Economic policy proposed by Lenin in 1921 to authorize limited free-market and private entrepreneurship to rebuild the Soviet economy, which had collapsed after the attempt to implement a communist economy in 1918–1920. The policy was revoked by Stalin in 1928.

Newspeak—Fictional "politically correct" language in George Orwell's novel *1984*. The term is used derogatorily to describe language crafted to promote propaganda or exert social control by creating or banning specific words.

NKVD—*Narodnyy Komissariat Vnutrennikh Del*, the People's Commissariat for Internal Affairs. Primarily operated as the secret police. Headed, successively, by Yagoda (1934–1936), Yezhov (1936–1938), Beria (1938–1945), and Kruglov (1945–1946). Succeeded by the MVD USSR, *Ministerstvo Vnutrennikh Del*, the Ministry of Internal Affairs of the USSR.

Nomenklatura—Literally "list of names," the key circle of people in the USSR; the Soviet Communist Party leadership as well as key positions in the government.

O

OGPU—*Obyedinyonnoye gosudarstvennoye politicheskoye upravleniye*, Unified State Political Directorate, the secret police of the USSR

(1923–1934). Preceded by the Cheka, succeeded by the NKVD.

OSCE—Organization for Security and Cooperation in Europe, set up after the signing of the Helsinki Accords in August 1976.

Ostpolitik—German abbreviation for "new Eastern policy." A set of strategies meant to improve relations between West Germany and communist Eastern Europe beginning in 1969.

P

PEN—Acronym for "poets, playwrights, editors, essayists, and novelists." A writers' association founded in 1921 to promote freedom of expression among writers worldwide.

Perestroika—Literally meaning "restructuring", a general policy during Mikhail Gorbachev's government intending economic improvement of the Soviet Union via some loosening of central control, though not fully transitioning to a market economy.

Politburo—The most powerful body within the Communist Party and the USSR.

Prague Spring—Brief period of liberalization in Czechoslovakia in early 1968, which ended with a Soviet invasion that August and the installation of communist hardliners.

Pravda—Literally "Truth," a Soviet newspaper, founded in 1912 and active official press of the Russian Communist party from 1912–1991. Post-USSR, it was first sold to private concerns, and then later split up into multiple owners, including the Communist Party of the Russian Federation, which acquired the newspaper.

Procuracy—From Russian *Prokuratura*, a Soviet watchdog organization whose goal was to ensure the enforcement of laws and dictates by individual officials and citizens.

Putsch—August Coup of 1991, an attempt by hard-line members of the KGB to retake control of the country from President Gorbachev. It collapsed after two days, hastening the dissolution of the party and the USSR.

Q

Quisling—A traitor, a collaborating leader. From Vidkun Quisling, Norwegian politician who led a Nazi-inspired political party in the 1930's and became head of Norway's government during its occupation by Germany in World War II.

R

Realpolitik—foreign policy based on specific conditions, not broad philosophy/ideals. Its main underlying thrust is that world politics is always a field of conflict with various parties seeking power.

Refuseniks—people who were denied permission to emigrate from the USSR and other Eastern bloc countries; primarily referring to Soviet Jews wanting to emigrate to Israel. Other religious groups and ethnicities were also targeted.

RF—Russian Federation, 1991 to present, the successor State to the USSR.

S

SALT II—The second round of Strategic Arms Limitation Talks, through which the United States and USSR agreed to reduce their nuclear missile arsenals in 1979, following seven years of negotiations.

Samizdat — Dissident literature, spread through clandestine means. Vladimir Bukovsky summarized it as follows: "Samizdat: I write it myself, edit it myself, censor it myself, publish it myself, distribute it myself, and spend jail time for it myself."

SDI—Strategic Defense Initiative, an ambitious U.S. defense system against Soviet long-range nuclear missiles proposed by President Reagan in 1983.

SDP—Social Democratic Party, a centrist UK party founded in 1981. Merged with the Liberal Party in 1988 to form the Social and Liberal Democrats.

Sinyavsky-Daniel trial—Infamous trial held in Moscow in February 1966. The first Soviet trial where writers were tried based on their literary work.

Socialism with a human face—A program announced by the Communist Party of Czechoslovakia in April 1968 to allow moderate liberalization and democratization.

Socialist International—Worldwide association of political parties seeking to establish democratic socialism. Founded in 1951, it has 153 member parties from more than 100 countries in 2019.

Solidarity—Polish *Solidarność*, trade union founded in 1980 whose demands included the right to union independence from the Communist Party.

SPD—SPD—Sozialdemokratische Partei Deutschlands, The Social Democratic Party of Germany. Changed its name in 1890 from the Socialist Workers' Party of Germany (Sozialistische Arbeiterpartei Deutschlands, SAPD), which had been founded in 1875 in the merger of two German Marxist parties. One of the major political parties in post-war West Germany and then re-unified Germany.

Spetsnaz — Abbreviation for *Voyska spetsialnovo naznacheniya*, "special purpose forces." Soviet SAS, special forces of USSR and later Russia, involved in many counter-insurrection and anti-terrorism operations.

Stasi — Short for *Staatssicherheitsdienst*, State Security Service. The East German secret service, established in 1950 and ended with the reunification of Germany in 1990.

SVR—*Sluzhba vneshney razvedki*, the Foreign intelligence service of the Russian Federation. One of the successor agencies to the KGB.

T

Tbilisi massacre—Also known as the April 9 Tragedy. Violent suppression of a massive anti-Soviet demonstration in 1989 in Tbilisi, capital of Georgia.

Trilateral Commission—Non-governmental, non-partisan discussion group founded by American banker David Rockefeller in July 1973 to foster closer cooperation among Western Europe, North America and Japan.

Troika—A triumvirate—a three-person or three-entity power structure, usually *de facto* and not officially.

U

USSR—Union of Soviet Socialist Republics, established in 1922 and dissolved in December 1991.

W

Warsaw Pact—Collective defense treaty originally signed in 1955, covering the Soviet Union and seven Soviet satellite nations. Original signatories: Albania, Bulgaria, Czechoslovakia, East Germany, Hungary, Poland, Romania, and the USSR. Dissolved in 1991.

Biographical Information

A

Akhmatova, Anna (1889–1966). Born Anna Gorenko. Russian poet. In the poem cycle *Requiem* (1935–1940), she condemned Stalin's purges. Short-listed for the Nobel Prize in Literature in 1965 and 1966. Most of her work was suppressed in her lifetime. Her first husband, poet Nikolay Gumilyov, was shot in 1921 by the Cheka (Soviet secret police); her son Lev Gumilyov and common-law husband Nikolay Punin spent many years in the Gulag from 1938 to 1953.

Alliluyeva, Svetlana (1926–2011). Born Svetlana Stalina. Also known as Lana Peters. Daughter of Joseph Stalin. Left the USSR in 1966, became a naturalized U.S. citizen in 1978, returned to the USSR briefly (1984–1986) and reclaimed Soviet citizenship, and finally settled in the United Kingdom, becoming a British citizen in 1992. Published several books of memoirs.

Amalrik, Andrei (1938–1980). Russian historian. One of the first human rights activists in the post-Stalin USSR. Expelled from Moscow University in 1963, imprisoned and persecuted as a political dissident, left the USSR in 1976. Killed in a car accident in Spain on the way to the Madrid gathering of the Organization for Security and Cooperation in Europe.

Amin, Hafizullah (1929–1979, assassinated). Afghan communist politician. Leader in the Saur Revolution in Afghanistan (1978), in which President Mohammed Daoud Khan was murdered, leading to the seizure of power by communist President Nur Muhammed Taraki. Amin overthrew Taraki (1979) and ordered his death. Amin himself was assassinated by Soviets three months into his own rule in response to Taraki's death.

Andropov, Yuri (1914–1984). Soviet politician. Head of state of USSR (1982–1984), head of KGB (1967–1982), Soviet ambassador to Hungary (1954–1957). Key figure in the suppression of the Hungarian Uprising (1956) and crushing of the Prague Spring (1968). A strong proponent of the suppression of dissidents, he proposed and implemented the abuse of psychiatry to confine and discredit them.

Arafat, Yasser (1929–2004). Palestinian political leader. Chairman of the Palestine Liberation Organization (1969–2004). President of the Palestinian National Authority (1994–2004). Founding member of the Fatah political party, which he led from 1959 to 2004.

Born in Egypt, he became an Arab nationalist during his university years in Cairo. Fought with the Muslim Brotherhood in the 1948 Arab-Israeli War. Was ejected from Egypt, along with other guerrilla forces, after the 1956 Suez Crisis. Arafat founded the Palestinian group Fatah while in Kuwait, which was dedicated to founding a Palestinian nation through armed struggle by Palestinians, as opposed to other anti-Israel groups that took pan-Arabic approaches. Came to prominence after the Six Day War in 1967, as pan-Arab forces were defeated by Israel, and the 1968 Battle of Karameh, in which Palestinians first used suicide bombers. Involved in various campaigns to defeat Israel and/or found a Palestinian state, many sponsored by the KGB. Received a Nobel Peace Prize with Israel Prime Minister Yitzhak Rabin and Israel President Shimon Peres in 1994 for the 1993 Oslo Accords, which called for the establishment of Palestinian self-rule in areas of the West Bank and Gaza Strip.

Arbatov, Georgy (1923–2010). Soviet political scientist. Adviser to Central Committee of the CPSU (1964–1967), adviser to five General Secretaries of the Communist Party. Following the dissolution of the USSR, he was an adviser to the Russian legislature and a member of the foreign policy council of the RF foreign Ministry (1991–1996).

Aron, Raymond (1905–1983). French philosopher and writer. Prodigious writer on political science and philosophy, taking a strong anti-totalitarian position. His best-known book was *The Opium of the Intellectuals* (1955), which looked at the behavior of the French intellectual elite in its defense of Marxist oppression and atrocities and its attack on democracy and capitalism. Aron's 1973 book, *The Imperial Republic: The United States and the World, 1945–1973*, influenced many notable American political players, such as Henry Kissinger and Zbigniew Brzezinski.

B

Babayan, Eduard (1920–2009). Russian medical doctor. One of the senior heads of the Serbsky State Scientific Center for Social and Forensic Psychiatry, and defender of the political use of psychiatry in the USSR.

Bahr, Egon (1922–2015). West German SPD member. MP in the Bundestag of West Germany (1972–1990). Minister in the West German government (1972–1976) under Willy Brandt and Helmut Schmidt. Creator of Ostpolitik. Key figure in negotiations between East and West Germany, as well as those between Germany and the

USSR.

Bakatin, Vadim (1937–). Soviet politician. Last director of the KGB (1991). Oversaw dismantling of the KGB into separate organizations during the dissolution of the USSR, though the same people staffed the successor organizations FSB and SVR.

Beria, Lavrentiy (1899–1953, executed). Soviet politician. Chief of the Soviet security and secret police (NKVD) under Joseph Stalin. Oversaw vast expansion of Gulag labor camps, and the Soviet atomic bomb program. Supervised the execution of Polish prisoners of war on Stalin's orders—the Katyn Massacre (1940). Widely known for both effectiveness and gleeful cruelty, he both served and challenged Stalin, conducting purges but intervening in the persecution of Jews. In the struggle for power following Stalin's death, he became First Deputy Premier and Minister of Internal Affairs with plans for liberalizing some of Stalin's policies. Three months later, ousted by Khrushchev's coup, Beria was tried for treason and terrorism—including actions ordered by Stalin. Found guilty, he was personally executed by military hero Pavel Batitsky.

Bogoraz-Brukhman, Larisa (1926–2004). Russian linguist, writer, and human rights activist. Married to fellow dissident Yuli Daniel, and later married to Anatoly Marchenko. Organized the Red Square protest in 1968 against the Soviet invasion of Czechoslovakia and was exiled to Siberia as a result. Co-wrote *Memory*, a book on Stalin's terrors. An active writer in the Soviet dissident movement, she continued her human rights activism post-Soviet Union.

Borovik, Genrikh (1929–). Russian writer. According to a senior archivist of the USSR's foreign intelligence service, Borovik was a KGB agent in the United States, one of whose successful projects was the propagation of false theories regarding John F. Kennedy's assassination. Wrote a book on Soviet spy Kim Philby.

Brandt, Willy (1913–1992). Born Herbert Ernst Karl Frahm. West German politician. Leader of the SPD (1964–1987), West German Chancellor (1969–1974). Proponent of Ostpolitik, received Nobel Peace Prize in 1971 as result of this policy. Resigned as Chancellor when a close aide was exposed as an agent of the Stasi.

Brezhnev, Leonid (1906–1982). Soviet politician. Leader of the USSR (1964–1982). Reversed Khrushchev's liberalization of Soviet cultural policy. His reversion to prior Soviet policies led to economic stagnation. Major proponent of the foreign policy of détente, however he oversaw aggressive actions such as invasions of Czechoslovakia (1968) and Afghanistan (1979).

Brodsky, Joseph (1940–1996). Russian and American poet and writer. Beginning in 1955, he wrote and published poetry in samizdat literature. His work was denounced as anti-Soviet in 1962, and he was subsequently sentenced to five years' hard labor for "social parasitism". His sentence was cut short due to international protests by prominent figures including Jean-Paul Sartre. Expelled from the USSR in 1972 and emigrated to the US, where he taught at prominent universities. Won the 1987 Nobel Prize in Literature.

Brzezinski, Zbigniew (1928–2017). Polish-American diplomat and political scientist. Counselor to President Lyndon Johnson (1966–1968), National Security Adviser to President Jimmy Carter (1977–1981). Critical of policy emphasis on détente in the Nixon and Ford administrations, and part of formally ending that policy early in Carter's presidency. Involved in the US's encouraging of human rights activists to reduce Soviet influence, he ordered a boosting of the broadcast power of Radio Free Europe.

Bukharin, Nikolai (1888–1938, executed). Bolshevik revolutionary and Soviet politician. Exiled in 1911 for his political activity with the Bolsheviks, met with Lenin in 1912. Met with and worked with Trotsky and Stalin during his own exile. Returned to Moscow in May 1917 and was a prominent leader in Moscow during the October Revolution. In the power struggle following Lenin's death in 1924, Bukharin allied himself with Stalin, but later opposed Stalin's policies in 1928 when Stalin reversed the New Economic Policy. Was expelled from the Politburo in 1929 and lost his position in the Comintern and editorship of *Pravda*. Was rehabilitated in 1934, becoming editor of *Izvestia*. During Stalin's Great Purge, Bukharin and other Old Bolsheviks were arrested in 1937 and subjected to show trials. The crimes to which Bukharin confessed were so obviously untrue or absurd that many prominent communists broke with communism due to his trial. Bukharin was sentenced to death and shot.

Bulgakov, Mikhail (1891–1940). Russian writer and medical doctor. Best known for his novel *The Master and Margarita*, a satire against the atheistic USSR, published in the late 1960s and considered a masterpiece. The book was written over a period from 1928–1940, with Bulgakov needing to rewrite the novel from memory due to his burning of the manuscript during political repression in 1930.

C

Carter, James Earl (Jimmy) (1924–). American politician. Thirty-ninth president of the US (1977–1981). In foreign affairs, his administration ended the policy of détente toward the USSR and pursued the second round of Strategic Arms Limitation Talks (SALT II).

Awarded the Nobel Peace Prize in 2002 for co-founding the Carter Center, a nonprofit organization supporting human rights and public health.

Chamberlain, Neville (1869–1940). British politician. Prime Minister of the United Kingdom (1937–1940). From Birmingham, had been a businessman who became prominent in local politics, as both his father and uncle had been mayors of Birmingham. Entered Parliament in 1918 as a member of the Unionist Party, which later merged with the Conservative Party. Served in various positions in the Conservative Party and became the Chancellor of the Exchecquer in 1931 under Prime Minister Ramsay Macdonald and the next Prime Minister, Stanley Baldwin. When Baldwin resigned in 1937, Chamberlain became PM as next in line. Known for the policy of "appeasement," in which escalating demands from Hitler were acceded to in the interest of preventing another Great War. His best-known quote referred to the ultimately futile Munich Agreement as "peace for our time." Resigned as PM in May 1940 after members of the Labour Party refused to join in a coalition government under him. Served as Lord President of the Council under succeeding PM Winston Churchill until his death from cancer in November 1940.

Chebrikov, Viktor (1923–1999). Soviet politician. Head of the KGB (1982–1988). Joined the Communist Party in 1950 and rose through multiple party offices in Ukraine. Brought to Moscow in 1967, was deputy chairman of the KGB under Yuri Andropov (1968–1982). Was appointed head of internal security under Gorbachev. During his stint as KGB head, he was able to dismantle CIA operations using information from double agent Aldrich Ames.

Chekhov, Anton (1860–1904). Russian writer and medical doctor. Known for his plays and short stories, considered one of the greatest for short fiction. Considered one of the key playwrights in the development of early modernistic theater. One of his major plays, *The Cherry Orchard*, highlights class and economic changes at the turn of the twentieth century in Russia, and the results of the abolition of serfdom and modernization of Russia.

Chernenko, Konstantin (1911–1985). Soviet politician. Had risen in Politburo under Brezhnev. Soviet head of state (1984–1985). Represented a return to the policies of the late Brezhnev era after Andropov's death. Oversaw an increase in hostility to the US, and led the boycott against the 1984 Summer Olympics held in the US.

Chichikov, Pavel (fictional). Main character in Gogol's novel *Dead Souls*. The character travels rural Russia to buy the names of dead serfs as part of a financial fraud. References to Chichikov in contemporary Russian culture allude to people who are outwardly pleasant and respectable in manners, but inwardly untrustworthy and exploitative in their ultimate behavior.

Ceausescu, Nicolae (1918–1989, shot by firing squad). Romanian politician. Communist head of state of Romania (1967–1989). Condemned 1968 Warsaw Pact invasion of Czechoslovakia, but soon after, he oversaw what was considered the most brutal and oppressive of the Eastern European governments. His policies led to a deteriorating state and civil unrest, culminating in the Romanian Revolution of 1989. After trying to flee the revolution, he was caught, summarily tried, and executed by the Romanian armed forces.

Corvalan, Luis (1916–2010). Chilean politician. Head of Chilean Community Party (1958–1990). Arrested after military coup led by Augusto Pinochet in 1973, awarded the Lenin Peace Prize(1973–1974). Exchanged for Vladimir Bukovsky in 1976, and received asylum in the USSR. Returned to Chile in 1988.

D

Daniel, Yuli (1925–1988). Russian writer, poet, and translator. Wrote under the name Nikolay Arzhak. Was married to fellow dissident Larisa Bogoraz-Brukhman. Wrote topical stories critical of Soviet leadership which were smuggled out of the country for publication. In 1965, Daniel was arrested and tried in the infamous Sinyavsky-Daniel trial. He was sentenced to 5 years hard labor for "anti-Soviet activity." After imprisonment, he refused to emigrate and settled in Kaluga.

D'Estaing, Valery Giscard (1926–). French politician. President of France (1974–1981). Member of the French Resistance during World War II who participated in the Liberation of Paris. Entered French government service in 1951, in the area of finance. Entered elective office in 1956 as a member of Parliament, served as Secretary of State for Finance (1959–1962) and Minister of Finance (1962–1966; 1969–1974). After the death of French President Georges Pompidou in 1974, he ran against Socialist candidate Francois Mitterand and won in the closest Presidential election in French History. Lost 1981 election against Mitterand. Retired from politics in 2004.

Dzerzhinsky, Felix (1877–1926). Soviet leader. Led the first two Soviet state security organizations, the Cheka (1917–1922) and the OGPU (1922–1926). During his leadership, the Cheka was known for mass summary executions, targeting counter-revolutionaries and other political opponents. In the post-revolutionary USSR, he ran the secret police OGPU after the Cheka was dissolved.

E

Eaton, Cyrus Stephen (1883–1979). Canadian-American businessman. Provided financing for the original Pugwash Conferences on Science and World Affairs (1957–), a conference for scientists with an aim of eliminating all weapons of mass destruction. Outspoken critic of US Cold War policy, leading to the awarding of a 1960 Lenin Peace Prize to him.

Esenin-Volpin, Alexander (1924–2016). Russian-American poet and mathematician. First imprisoned in 1949 for "anti-Soviet poetry", shuttled around prisons, psychiatric prison hospitals, and exile. Was released in 1953, in the general amnesty following Stalin's death, but was imprisoned two more times in 1959 and 1968. One of the first dissidents to adopt a "legalist" strategy, by demanding strict adherence to the letter of the law. Emigrated to the US in 1972 and continued his mathematical career at Boston University.

F

Fainberg, Viktor (1931–). Prominent dissident and philologist. One of the seven people who participated in the 1968 Red Square demonstration against the invasion of Czechoslovakia. In the aftermath, he did not receive a trial, but was instead examined by a Serbsky State Scientific Center for Social and Forensic Psychiatry commission, and committed to a psychiatric hospital, where he was confined from 1969 to 1973. Emigrated in 1973 to the UK, later received French citizenship. After emigrating, he initiated CAPA (Campaign Against Psychiatric Abuses) to fight the political abusive use of psychiatry in the USSR.

Falin, Valentin (1926–2018). Soviet politician and diplomat. Held a variety of positions related to the Soviet government from 1951 to 1991. Soviet Ambassador to West Germany (1971–1978). Political observer, editor, and then chief editor of *Izvestia* (1982–1986). Left government service after a failed 1991 coup against Mikhail Gorbachev.

Fermi, Enrico (1901–1954). Italian and naturalized American physicist. Creator of the first nuclear reactor, as part of the Manhattan Project. Received his doctoral degree at the young age of 20, based on his thesis on X-ray diffraction images. Developed Fermi-Dirac statistics in 1926, a method used in statistical mechanics. Became a professor of theoretical physics at the Sapienza University of Rome in 1926 and further developed particle physics, before switching to experimental physics in the 1930s. Received the Nobel Prize in Physics in 1938. Left Italy for the U.S. with his wife after the Nobel ceremony, as anti-Jewish laws in Italy affected her. Created the first nuclear chain reaction with the Chicago Pile-1 in 1942, a key event in the U.S. development of nuclear bombs. After World War II, was on the Atomic Energy Commission General Advisory Committee, where he advocated against the development of the hydrogen bomb, though he also did research that led to its development.

Frenkel, Naftaly (1883–1960). Member of the Cheka. Arrested in 1923 for "illegally crossing borders," he was sentenced to 10 years' hard labor in the Solovki prison camp, which came to be known as the first Gulag. Rapidly rose from prisoner to camp commander, in an unclear way. Requested early release from his sentence in November 1924, with request granted in 1927. Some have claimed his rise was due to his proposal to camp administration to tie the amount of food given to prisoners based on their productivity, and other ideas to make the prisons maximally productive. Frenkel's methods of boosting prison labor spread to other labor camps throughout the Soviet Union.

G

Gabay, Ilya (1935–1973, suicide). Russian teacher and writer. Assisted in editing the *Chronicle of Current Events*, in particular issue 3 on the 1968 Red Square demonstration against the invasion of Czechoslovakia. Involved in the struggle of Crimean Tatars for autonomy and in samizdat publication. In 1970, he was tried and sentenced for producing and circulating samizdat. After his release in 1972, was harassed by the KGB and barred from employment. Died by suicide in 1973.

Galanskov, Yuri (1939–1972, died in camps). Russian poet and historian. Founding editor of samizdat *Phoenix* (1961–1966), an almanac of criticism of the Soviet government, including works by Boris Pasternak and Natalya Gorbanevskaya. Subjected to psychiatric punishment and later sentenced to seven years in a labor camp in Mordovia. Wrote about conditions in the camp, and died of an ulcer after being denied medical care.

Galich, Alexander (1918–1977). Soviet poet, writer, and dissident. Created the genre of "bard song" in the Soviet Union, writing songs about WWII and concentration camp prisoners. As time went on, his writings became more anti-Soviet. Expelled from the Union of Writers of the USSR in 1971; Galich had been a member since 1955. Expelled from the USSR in 1974, and lived in various European countries afterwards. His 1977 death by supposedly accidental electrocution was considered suspicious.

Gamsakhurdia, Zviad (1939–1993). Georgian politician, writer, and dissident. Was active in samizdat, contributed to the *Chronicle of Current Events*, and was active in the Helsinki Groups during the 1970s. Arrested in 1977, tried in 1978 for "anti-Soviet activities", sentenced to labor camps for three years and exile for three additional years; his sentence was commuted to two years exile in Dagestan. First democratically elected president of Georgia in 1990. In December 1991, a coup d'état targeted his administration, and replaced him in March 1992 with Eduard Shevardnadze. Died in 1993 under unclear circumstances.

Ginzburg, Alexander (1936–2002). Russian poet, writer, and dissident. Co-founder of samizdat almanac Sintaksis (1959–1960), produced first issue of samizdat magazine *Phoenix* (1959). During the 1960s, was arrested and sentenced three times to Soviet labor camps. A founding member of the Moscow Helsinki Group in 1976. Expelled from the USSR in 1979 along with others as part of a prisoner exchange.

Glazunov, Ilya (1930–2017). Russian artist. Was known for Russian patriotism, and anti-democratic/pro-monarchical views. His paintings were known for religious or historic themes; also painted portraits of many prominent people, including actors and politicians. One of the co-founders of the All-Russian Society for the Protection of Historical and Cultural Monuments in 1965. Founder of the Russian Academy of Painting, Sculpture and Architecture in 1987.

Goebbels, Joseph (1897–1945, suicide). German Nazi politician. Minister of Propaganda of Nazi Germany (1933–1945). Joined the Nazi party in the 1920s, known for publications and speeches denouncing Marxism and promoting Nazism in that decade, and provoked violent attacks against the Communist Party of Germany. Greatly involved in Nazi propaganda production starting in 1926, and key figure in Hitler's inner circle. Once Hitler became chancellor of Germany in 1933, became head of the newly created Propaganda Ministry. Was named successor to chancellorship in Hitler's will; one day after Hitler's suicide, committed suicide himself with his wife after they had poisoned their 6 children.

Gogol, Nikolay (1809–1852). Born Nikolay Yanovski. Russian writer of Ukrainian descent. Wrote plays, essays, short stories, and the novel *Dead Souls*. Large influence on later writers, and explicitly mentioned in works by Dostoevsky and Chekhov; his works have been adapted in film and opera. Considered by his contemporaries as a preeminent figure in the Russian literary realism school, though later critics noted his use of the grotesque and surrealism. Some later works satirized Russian political corruption.

Gorbachev, Mikhail (1931–). Soviet and Russian politician. Last head of state of the USSR (1985–1991). Best known for his programs of perestroika and glasnost, in addition to being in power during the fall of the Berlin Wall, the Eastern Bloc, and the Soviet Union. Received the Nobel Peace Prize in 1990 for abandoning the Brezhnev Doctrine, which led to the Eastern Bloc countries democratizing in 1989–1990.

Gorbanevskaya, Natalya (1936–2013). Russian poet, translator, and civil-rights activist. Co-founder and first editor of the *Chronicle of Current Events*. Took part in the 1968 Red Square demonstration against the invasion of Czechoslovakia. Sentenced to psychiatric prison in 1970 for "sluggish schizophrenia" (a common diagnosis imposed on dissidents). Released from prison in 1972, emigrated to France in 1975 and found to be mentally normal by French psychiatrists. Was stateless from 1975 until 2005, when Poland granted her citizenship.

Grigorenko, Pyotr (Petro) (1907–1987). Soviet Army commander of Ukrainian descent, later a dissident and writer. Commanded Soviet troops in WWII, continued his military career after the war by teaching at a military academy, and reached the rank of Major-General. In 1961, started criticizing the Soviet government on the grounds that Lenin wasn't being followed, and formed The Group for the Struggle to Revive Leninism. Was sent to psychiatric prisons for a total of six years (1964–1965, 1969–1974), and stripped of military rank. Helped found two Helsinki groups in the USSR in the 1970s. While in the US in 1977 for medical treatment, was stripped of Soviet citizenship, and never returned to the USSR.

Gromyko, Andrei (1909–1989). Soviet politician. Minister of Foreign Affairs (1957–1985). Played a direct role in Cuban Missile Crisis, negotiator on multiple arms limitation treaties with the US and other parties. As Brezhnev's health failed in 1975, formed a troika with Yuri Andropov and Dmitry Ustinov, driving Soviet policymaking. Was replaced when Mikhail Gorbachev became head of state, being sent to a largely honorary role of Chairman of the Presidium of the Supreme Soviet.

H

Hall, Gus (1910–2000). American politician. General Secretary of the Communist Party USA (1959–2000). Grew up in a Communist household in Minnesota, where his parents were early members of the Communist Party USA (CPUSA). Joined the CPUSA as a teenager and became an organizer for the Young Communist League in the upper Midwest. Studied for two years at the International Lenin School in Moscow (1931–1933). Was a leader in a strike against steel companies in 1937 which failed, after which Hall focused on political activities. Became leader of CPUSA in Youngstown, Ohio (1937), and rose to further prominent CPUSA positions. Was convicted under the Smith Act in 1948 for "Conspiring and Teaching Overthrow of the U.S. Government by Force or Violence" and imprisoned for five and a half years. Was elected CPUSA General Secretary in 1959 and spent decades attempting to rebuild the party. Hall made frequent appearances on Soviet television programs in the 60s and 70s. Ran for U.S. President four times from 1972 to 1984.

Hammer, Armand (1898–1990). American businessman who ran Occidental Petroleum from 1957 until his death. Also known for his art collection, his philanthropy, and his close ties to the Soviet Union. In 1921 he traveled to Soviet Russia to give aid to the country's famine victims. Was persuaded by Lenin to turn his business talents to account there instead. In 1925 obtained a concession from the Bolsheviks to manufacture pencils for the Soviet Union. His business ventures were bought out by the Soviets in the late 1920s. Returned to the United States in 1930, bringing with him innumerable paintings, jewelry pieces, and other art objects formerly owned by the Romanov imperial family and sold to him by the Soviets.

Handal, Schafik Jorge (1930–2006). Salvadoran politician. Leader of the Communist Party of El Salvador (1973–1994). Guerrilla leader in the late 1970s and early 1980s, part of the groups that formed the guerrilla group Farabundo Martí National Liberation Front (FMNL). When FMNL became a political party after the peace accords in 1992, Handal was its general coordinator. Deputy in the Legislative Assembly of El Salvador (1997–2006).

Havel, Vaclav (1936–2011). Czech politician, playwright, and former dissident. President of Czechoslovakia (1989–1992). President of the Czech Republic (1993–2003). Was a prominent participant in the liberal reforms of 1968 (the Prague Spring). After the Soviet clampdown on Czechoslovakia, he was repeatedly arrested and served four years in prison (1979–83) for his activities on behalf of human rights in Czechoslovakia. During antigovernment demonstrations in Prague in November 1989, Havel became the leading figure in the Civic Forum, a new coalition of noncommunist opposition groups pressing for democratic reforms. After the Czech communist party capitulated in December 1989, he was elected to the post of interim president of Czechoslovakia. Known for his plays *The Garden Party, Leaving,* and *The Memorandum.*

Hegel, Georg Wilhelm Friedrich (1770–1831). German philosopher widely viewed as a leading influence on Western philosophy. Developed a view that emphasized the progress of history as a necessary and inevitable development of human society, a central component of communist philosophy as espoused by Marx.

Honecker, Erich (1912–1994). German politician. East German head of state (1971–1989). Joined the Communist Party of Germany in 1930, was detained and imprisoned by the Nazis (1935–1945) for communist party activities. Was the chief organizer of the construction of the Berlin Wall in 1961 and supported the "order to fire" along the West-East German border. Pushed back against Gorbachev's glasnost and perestroika policies. After the fall of the Berlin Wall, was forced to resign, was detained more than once, and fled to the Soviet Union. Sought asylum at the Chilean embassy in Moscow, was expelled in 1992, and was sent back to Germany and detained. Put on trial with other ex-East German officials for the death of people killed in attempting to escape East Germany. Was released due to ill health, flew to Chile to reunite with his family, and died of liver cancer.

I

Ilyin, Viktor (1947–). Soviet soldier. Attempted to assassinate Brezhnev in 1969, in response to the invasion of Czechoslovakia and inspired by the assassination of John F. Kennedy. After investigation, he was considered insane and placed in solitary confinement in Kazan Psychiatric Hospital until released in 1990.

J

Jaruzelski, Wojciech (1923–2014). Polish military officer and politician. Last head of the communist government of Poland (1981–1989). Imposed martial law in Poland in 1981 to try to crush pro-democracy movements like Lech Walesa's Solidarity under the pretext that the Soviet Union would invade Poland. In the following years, the Polish government censored, persecuted, and jailed thousands of political activists and journalists without charge. Jaruzelski resigned after the Polish Round Table Agreement in 1989, which led to democratic elections in the country.

K

Kafka, Franz (1883–1924). German-speaking Czech writer. Life-long resident of Prague, born to middle-class Ashkenazi Jews in that city. Influential writer of novels and short stories. Some of his best-known works are the novella *The Metamorphosis* (in which a man wakes up to find himself turned into a giant insect), the novel *The Trial* (in which a man is put on trial, but neither he nor the reader ever determine the nature of the supposed crimes), and the short story "A Hunger Artist" (about a man who fasted as a public performance).

Kahane, Meir (1932–1990, murdered). Born Martin David Kahane. American-born Israeli political activist and rabbi. In the mid-1960s wrote books and a weekly column for the Jewish Press and rallied support for U.S. involvement in Vietnam. In 1968 formed the militant Jewish Defense League (JDL) which sent armed patrols of young Jews into black neighborhoods in the U.S. After being imprisoned for conspiring to make bombs, he moved to Israel in 1971. There he formed the Kach Party and stirred nationalist fervor against Arabs, whom he campaigned to remove from Israel. Won a seat in the Israeli Knesset in 1984, but his term ended when Israel banned the Kach Party. Shot dead in New York by a naturalized American of Egyptian descent in 1990.

Kalinin, Mikhail (1875–1946). Bolshevik revolutionary and Soviet politician. In official Community Party posts from 1919 until his death in 1946, but held little real power, especially starting in the 1930s. Factional ally of Stalin in the struggle for power after Lenin's death in 1924. One of the few of Stalin's inner circle from a peasant background, this fact was often touted in the Soviet press when covering him. Kept a low profile during Stalin's purges and repressions in the 1930s, even as his own wife was arrested, tortured, and imprisoned for criticizing Stalin.

Kalugin, Oleg (1934–). KGB operative (1952–1990). Often posted to the U.S. to pose as a journalist or press officer of the Soviet Union, but in reality working for the KGB. Ultimately promoted to KGB general in 1974, and was head of the Soviet Embassy in Washington, D.C. In the 1980s, was suspected of being an American spy as part of an intrigue involving internal Soviet politics. Was a supporter of Boris Yeltsin in the post-Soviet era, and was fired from his position in 1991. Accepted a teaching position at the Catholic University of America in 1995, and remained a U.S. resident thereafter; became a U.S. citizen in 2003. Identified George Trofimoff as a Soviet spy in the U.S. military in a 2001 espionage trial.

Kapitonov, Ivan (1915–2002). Soviet politician. Secretary of the

CPSU (1965–1986), having held multiple posts in the Soviet Union since 1941.

Karmal, Babrak (1929–1996). Afghan politician. Leader of Afghanistan (1979–1986), installed by the USSR when they invaded. Leading figure in Afghan Marxist party People's Democratic Party of Afghanistan (PDPA) since its founding in 1965. Was ousted from this position by the Soviet Union following a series of policy failures, after which he was exiled to Moscow (1986–1996) with a brief return to Afghanistan in 1991–1992.

Kerensky, Alexander (1881–1970). Russian lawyer and politician. Head of the Russian Provisional Government (July 1917–November 1917), leader of the moderate-socialist faction of the Socialist Revolutionary Party. His government was overthrown by Lenin's Bolsheviks. Escaped to France, where he lived until the German invasion in 1940, and then emigrated to the U.S. Taught at the Hoover Institution at Stanford University, and contributed to its Russian history archive.

Khrushchev, Nikita (1894–1971). Soviet politician. Leader of Soviet Union (1953–1964) following Stalin's death in 1953. Pronounced a policy of de-Stalinization of the USSR, though changed persecution of dissidents from sending to prison camps to threat of job loss or forced institutionalization for being "socially dangerous" people. Held summits with U.S. Presidents Eisenhower and Kennedy. Key figure in the Cuban Missile Crisis (1962), crushed revolt in Hungary (1956), and approved the building of the Berlin Wall (1961). Ousted by Brezhnev in 1964 after losing the confidence of party members over the missile crisis, bitter relations with Chairman Mao in China, and outright failure of his plans to bolster the Soviet economy as proof of communism's superiority to capitalism.

Kiesinger, Kurt (1904–1988). German politician. West German head of state (1966–1969). Joined the Nazi Party in 1933, worked as a lawyer in Berlin (1935–1940), worked in the German Foreign Office (1940–1945). Post-war, he joined the Christian Democratic Union, was elected member of the Bundestag (1949–1958, 1969–1980), and became Chancellor after forming a coalition with Willy Brandt's Social Democratic Party. Willy Brandt succeeded him in the chancellorship.

Kissinger, Henry (1923–). Born Heinz Alfred Kissinger. German-born American political scientist. Served as National Security Adviser for Presidents Richard Nixon and Gerald Ford (1969–1975) as well as Secretary of State (1973–1977). Pioneered foreign policy of détente in the U.S. with respect to the Soviet Union, supported improvement of China-U.S. relations, and won the 1973 Nobel Peace Prize for cease-fire talks to end the war in Vietnam (though those talks ultimately failed.) A controversial figure for his practice of Realpolitik, supporting some authoritarian governments if they were considered anti-communist, or at least pro-U.S.

Lord Killanin (1914–1999). Born Michael Morris. Irish journalist, writer, and sports official. Succeeded to his title in 1927, upon the death of his uncle, the second Baron Killanin. President of the International Olympic Committee (1972–1980). The 1976 Games saw the entry of the People's Republic of China. After boycotts of the Games in Moscow were planned in 1980 by 62 of 142 member countries, he resigned his presidency of the IOC. Soon after he was elected Honorary Life President of the IOC (1980–1999).

Korobochka, Nastasya (fictional). Character in Nikolai Gogol's novel *Dead Souls*. The first of the landowners who sells a list of names of dead serfs from her estate to the con artist Pavel Chichikov. Initially hesitant, and trying to sell other items to him, she eventually relents, and then spreads gossip in town about what Chichikov did, playing up her widowhood and inexperience.

Kosygin, Alexei (1904–1980). Soviet politician. Held multiple positions in the Politburo, Chairman of the Council of Ministers under Brezhnev (1964–1980). Initiated the 1965 failed economic reform, also known as the Kosygin reform. Was the chief negotiator with the West in the 1960s and signed the 1970 Moscow Treaty with West Germany which officially recognized the border between East and West Germany. Retired due to ill health and died soon after.

Kravchuk, Leonid (1934–). Ukrainian politician. First president of Ukraine (1991–1994) in the post-Soviet era. Joined the Communist Party of Ukraine in 1958 and rose through the ranks. Became nominal head of state of the Ukrainian Soviet Socialist Republic (1990–1991) and resigned after the August 1991 Soviet coup attempt. People's Deputy of Ukraine (1994–2006).

Kreisky, Bruno (1911–1990). Austrian politician. Austrian Foreign Minister (1959–1966). Austrian Chancellor (1970–1983). Joined the Socialist Party of Austria in 1925, fled to Sweden (1938–1945) to escape Nazi persecution of Jews after the annexation of Austria. In post-war socialist Austria, rose to central leadership of the Socialist Party. Promoted the policy of détente alongside Willy Brandt and Olof Palme. In 1983, sent a letter to Soviet premier Yuri Andropov to support the release of dissident Yuri Orlov; the letter was ignored.

Krenz, Egon (1937–). East German politician. Succeeded Erich Honecker as head of East Germany in 1989 but was ousted less than three months later amidst the collapse of the communist regime. After the reunification of Germany in 1990, he was sentenced to six and a half years in prison for manslaughter for his role in crimes of the East German regime. Released from prison in

December 2003. As of 2019, he resides in Germany and is viewed as one of the last surviving leaders of an Eastern Bloc nation, alongside the Soviet Union's Mikhail Gorbachev and Poland's Wojciech Jaruzelski.

Kryuchkov, Vladimir (1924–2007). Soviet lawyer, diplomat, and the last head of the KGB before the collapse of the Soviet Union. Head of the Soviet Foreign Intelligence Branch of the KGB (1978–1988). Head of the KGB (1988–1991). Leader of the abortive August coup in August 1991 that attempted to arrest the President of the USSR, Mikhail Gorbachev. Arrested and imprisoned for his participation in the coup (1991–1994). Freed by the State Duma in an amnesty in 1994. Published books of memoirs during his retirement years: *Personal File: Three Days and a Lifetime* and *On the Edge of the Abyss*.

L

Landau, Lev (1908–1968). Soviet physicist. Nobel Laureate (1962) for his development of a theory of superfluidity and noted for other key developments in physics. Arrested in 1938 for comparing Stalin's regime to Hitler's. Released from prison in 1939 due to personal appeal by prominent Russian physicist Pyotr Kapitsa, who threatened to resign if Stalin would not release him. Was investigated by the KGB in the 1950s due to his views on the Hungarian Uprising. Also co-wrote a letter to the New York Times in 1965, opposing U.S. intervention represented by the Student Struggle for Soviet Jewry.

Ligachev, Yegor (1920–). Soviet politician. First Secretary of the Party in Tomsk, Siberia (1965–1983), during which he led a cover-up of Stalin-era mass graves in Tomsk. Was viewed as one of Mikhail Gorbachev's closest allies when he became General Secretary in 1985, was member of the Secretariat (1983–1990). Notable for criticism of Gorbachev's actions in 1990 at the Twenty-Eighth Congress of the CPSU.

Litvinov, Pavel (1940–). Russian physicist, writer, and human rights activist. Editor of the *Chronicle of Current Events* samizdat publication. Participated in 1968 Red Square demonstration against the invasion of Czechoslovakia. Sentenced to five years of exile in Siberia. Emigrated to the U.S. after his return from exile (1974). In the U.S., taught physics and math at a New York prep school (1976–2006) until his retirement.

Lyubimov, Yuri (1917–2014). Russian stage actor and director. Founded the Taganka Theatre in Moscow (1964). Produced an adaptation of Mikhail Bulgakov's novel *The Master and the Margarita* in 1977. All of Lyubimov's productions were banned in 1980 by Soviet authorities. Was stripped of Soviet citizenship in 1984 and worked in the West until 1989. Returned to the Taganka Theatre in 1989, when his citizenship was restored.

M

Mandela, Nelson (1918–2013). South African anti-apartheid revolutionary leader, political leader, and philanthropist. President of South Africa (1994–1999). Was the country's first black head of state and the first elected in a fully representative democratic election. His government focused on dismantling the legacy of apartheid by tackling institutionalized racism and fostering racial reconciliation. Ideologically an African nationalist and socialist, he served as President of the African National Congress (ANC) party from 1991–1997. In 1961 he co-founded the militant Umkhonto we Sizwe in 1961 and led a sabotage campaign against the government of South Africa. Arrested and imprisoned in 1962. As a result of the Rivona Trial, he was sentenced to life imprisonment for conspiring to overthrow the state. Released in 1990 amid growing domestic and international pressure.

Mandelstam, Osip (1891–1938, died in camps). Born Joseph Mandelstam. Russian poet and writer. Arrested and exiled for writing an anti-Stalin poem in 1934. After a suicide attempt while in exile, he was allowed to serve his exile in the nicer locale of Voronezh. In 1937, there was a concerted media campaign against him due to his supposed anti-Soviet views. In 1938, he was lured to Moscow and arrested for "counter-revolutionary activities". Sentenced to five years in a labor camp and died due to cold and hunger in a transit camp in Vladivostok.

Marchenko, Anatoly (1938–1986, died on hunger strike). Soviet dissident, author, and human rights activist. One of the first two recipients of the Sakharov Prize for Freedom of Thought (1988) alongside Nelson Mandela. Started his professional career as an oil driller and was arbitrarily sent to labor camps after a disruption alongside others (1958); escaped from the camp in 1960, and was tried and sentenced for treason in 1961 when recaptured. Author of *My Testimony* (1967), which recounted his experience in the labor camps. Continued to write about the labor camps through 16 years of imprisonment after multiple convictions by Soviet authorities. One of the effects of his death by hunger strike was Gorbachev authorizing a broad amnesty for political prisoners in 1987.

Maximov, Vladimir (1930–1995). Born Lev Samsonov. Russian writer, publicist, and dissident. Adopted his ultimate pen name of Maximov in young adulthood, while traveling around as a construction worker and being in and out of jails and labor camps following a similarly itinerant childhood. Published written works via samizdat with pieces advocating Christian ideals. Expelled from the Union of Writers of the USSR in 1973 and spent several months in a psychiatric ward. Left the Soviet Union in 1974, was stripped of Soviet citizenship in 1975, and settled in Paris. Launched the literary magazine *Kontinent* in 1975, in the tradition of supporting Russian literature in exile. Head of the executive committee of the anti-communist organization Resistance International.

Maxwell, Robert (1923–1991). Born Jan Ludvik Hyman Binyamin Hoch. British media proprietor and Member of Parliament. Originally from Czechoslovakia, he rose from poverty to build an extensive publishing empire. After six years as an MP during the 1960s, he turned to business by buying the British Printing Corporation, Mirror Group Newspapers and Macmillan Publishers, among other publishing companies. Lived in Oxford and was conspicuous for his flamboyant lifestyle. He was notably litigious and often embroiled in controversy, including about his support for Israel at the time of the 1948 Arab-Israeli war.

Mayakovsky, Vladimir (1893–1930). The leading poet of the Russian Revolution of 1917 and the early Soviet period. At age 15 joined the Russian Social-Democratic Workers' Party and was repeatedly jailed for his activity. He began to write poetry during solitary confinement in 1909. After his release, attended the Moscow Art School and joined the Russian Futurist group, where he became its leading spokesman. From 1919 to 1921 worked in the Russian Telegraph Agency as a painter of posters and cartoons. In 1924 composed a 3,000-line eulogy on the death of Lenin. After 1925 traveled to the United States, Mexico, and Cuba, recording his impressions in poems. He began to have misunderstandings with the dogmatic Russian Association of Proletarian Writers, and with Soviet authorities. Facing increasing disappointments in his personal life, alienation from Soviet reality, and denied a visa to travel abroad, he committed suicide in April 1930. Mayakovsky is considered the most dynamic figure of the Soviet literary scene. His notable works include "The Bedbug," "Mystery Bouffe," "Cloud in Trousers," and "The Backbone Flute."

Meany, George (1894–1980). U.S. labor leader. President of the American Federation of Labor Congress of Industrial Organizations (AFL-CIO) (1955–1979). After joining the United Association of

Plumbers and Steam Fitters of the United States and Canada in 1915, was elected a business agent of a Plumbers and Steam Fitters local in 1922. In 1932 was elected a vice president of the New York State Federation of Labor and served as its president from 1934 to 1939. In 1939 was elected a secretary-treasurer of the American Federation of Labor (AFL) and later in 1952, became the AFL's president. His greatest accomplishment was the merger of two competitive and dissimilar labor organizations: AFL, which was organized by craft, and the Congress of Industrial Organizations (CIO), which was organized by industry. In 1963 Meany was awarded the Presidential Medal of Freedom. In 1977 helped to lead the United States out of the International Labour Organization when it refused to criticize repressive communist policies.

Medvedev, Roy (1925–). Twin brother of Zhores Medvedev. Russian political writer. Criticized Stalinism from a Marxist perspective in his book *Let History Judge* (1969) and subsequently expelled from the Communist Party. Engaged in samizdat publications, sought a reformist version of socialism. Co-authored *A Question of Madness* with his twin brother Zhores, in which they described Zhores' punitive commitment to a psychiatric hospital. Re-joined the CPSU in 1989, and has been a supporter of Putin as of 2018.

Medvedev, Zhores (1925–2018). Twin brother of Roy Medvedev. Russian biologist and dissident. Received his doctorate for research into the sexual processes of plants. Wrote a history of Soviet genetics, later published in the U.S. as *The Rise and Fall of T.D. Lysenko* (1969). Had several prominent positions in Soviet research labs and fell into disrepute in the USSR in 1969. Due to his subsequent dissident publications, was forcibly detained in a psychiatric hospital in 1970. Many prominent international scientists protested his imprisonment, leading to his relatively quick release. He co-wrote *A Question of Madness* with his twin brother Roy, published in 1971. Returned to prominent scientific positions in the USSR, leading to a position in London where he remained until his retirement in 1991.

Mikoyan, Anastas (1895–1978). Armenian Soviet revolutionary and politician. Able to remain at the highest levels within the CPSU, even as the leadership shifted; maintained his relatively high political positions through the leaderships of Lenin, Stalin, Khrushchev, and Brezhnev. Key figure in Nikita Khrushchev's de-Stalinization project, delivering the first anti-Stalinist speech at the Twentieth Party Congress (1956) following Stalin's death. Often deployed by Khrushchev for foreign diplomatic missions in the 1950s. There has been some suspicion that Mikoyan was involved in ousting Khrushchev in 1964. Retired in December 1965.

Molotov, Vyacheslav (1890–1986). Born Vyacheslav Skryabin. Soviet politician. As a protégé of Stalin, Molotov came to prominence in the Soviet government in the 1920s, holding multiple successive important positions, such as Minister of Foreign Affairs during WWII and the post-War period (1939–1949). Ultimately dismissed from power by Khrushchev in 1957, and officially retired in 1961. Best known as signatory of the Molotov-Ribbentrop Pact, the Nazi-Soviet non-aggression treaty (1939). Throughout his life, defended Stalinism, and harshly criticized Stalin's successors. Finnish soldiers during the Winter War of 1939 coined the sarcastic term "Molotov cocktail" for a homemade firebomb after Molotov claimed on Soviet state radio that bombing missions over Finland were actually airborne food deliveries to starving Finns.

N

Nakasone, Yasuhiro (1918–). Japanese politician. Prime Minister of Japan (1982–1987). Leader of the Liberal Democratic Party (1982–1989). After graduating from Tokyo Imperial University in 1941, served as a lieutenant in the Imperial Navy during World War II. In 1947, was elected to the lower house of the Diet (Japan's parliament), becoming one of the youngest to hold a seat in that body. Held several successive cabinet posts, including that of transport (1967–68), defense (1970–71), and international trade and industry (1972–74). Elected prime minister in 1982. As prime minster, Nakasone sought to strengthen Japan's ties with the United States by increasing Japan's contribution to its own defense and by lowering Japanese trade barriers to American goods. The Japanese economy continued its sustained growth under his administration, and by the end of his second term Japan had become the world's largest creditor nation and had begun to rival the power of the United States in the world economy.

Natta, Alessandro (1918–2001). Italian politician. Secretary of the Italian Communist Party (1948–1988). Took part in the opposition to Benito Mussolini's Fascist regime. During World War II was sent to Greece, where he was captured by German troops. In 1945 Natta returned to Italy and joined the Italian Communist Party, dedicating himself to the party full-time. A strong supporter of the "Italian road to Socialism," he gained a position in the party Secretariat. Elected party secretary in 1984. Natta tried to improve the party's tense relations with the Communist Party of the Soviet Union. His organized trip to the Soviet Union generated controversy within the party. Nevertheless, he was later confirmed as party leader during the Florence Congress in 1986, but in 1988 was forced to resign following a heart attack.

Navalny, Alexei (1976–). Russian lawyer and self-described nationalist democrat, Russian Opposition Coordination Council member and leader of the Progress Party. Came to prominence through his blog hosted by LiveJournal, which he used to publish documents about corruption by Russian state officials, organize political demonstrations, and promote his campaigns for office. Arrested multiple times. The Memorial Human Rights Center considered him a political prisoner. In March 2017, Navalny and his Anti-Corruption Foundation created a documentary accusing Dmitry Medvedev, former president of Russia, of corruption. In 2016 began a campaign to run for President of Russia, but was barred by Russia's Central Electoral Commission in December 2017. In May 2018, was sentenced to 30 days in prison after being arrested for attending an unsanctioned protest against Putin in Moscow.

Neizvestny, Ernst (1925–2016). Russian-American artist and philosopher. Much of his artwork was destroyed in the USSR before he was forced to emigrate to the U.S. in 1976. Known for his expressionistic monumental sculptures, such as *The Mask of Sorrow* (1996), which commemorates the prisoners who suffered and died in the prison camps of the Kolyma region (1930s–1950s).

Nemtsov, Boris (1959–2015, murdered). Russian physicist and liberal politician. One of the most important figures in the introduction of capitalism into the Russian post-Soviet economy. Had a successful political career in the 1990s under Yeltsin. His conflict with Putin's government centered on widespread embezzlement and profiteering ahead of the Sochi Olympics, as well as Russian political interference and military involvement in Ukraine. Published in-depth reports detailing corruption under Putin, which he connected directly with the President. Nemtsov was also an active organizer of and participant in numerous marches, civil actions and rallies directed against abuses by Russia's ruling elite. Prior to his assassination, he was in Moscow helping to organize a rally against military intervention in Ukraine and the Russian financial crisis. Was also working on a report demonstrating that Russian troops were fighting alongside pro-Russian rebels in eastern Ukraine. On 27 February 2015, he was shot several times from behind while crossing the Moskvoretsky Bridge in Moscow. His last report on the war waged by Russia against Ukraine, *Putin.War*, was published posthumously in 2015.

Nixon, Richard Milhous (1913–1994). American politician. Thirty-seventh president of the United States (1969–1974). Vice President to Dwight D. Eisenhower (1953–1961). Very involved in foreign policy during Eisenhower's administration; met with Khrushchev during his tour of the U.S. in 1959, leading to the famous "Kitchen Debate" over the merits of capitalism vs. communism. During his Presidency, visited communist China (1972), leading to better relations between the countries. Nixon oversaw détente policy with the Soviet Union, including the 1972 summit in Moscow with Brezhnev, and the agreement for two arms control treaties: SALT I and the Anti-Ballistic Missile Treaty. Resigned presidency due to Watergate scandal (1974).

O

Oppenheimer, J. Robert (1904–1967). American physicist and science administrator. Director of the Los Alamos Laboratory (1943–1945) during the development of the atomic bomb. Director of the Institute for Advanced Study, Princeton (1947–66). In the early stages of World War II, Oppenheimer began to seek a process for the separation of uranium-235 from natural uranium and to determine the critical mass of uranium required to make an atomic bomb. He was instructed to establish and administer a laboratory that would search for a way to harness nuclear energy for military purposes, an effort that became known as the Manhattan Project. Served as chairman of the General Advisory Committee of the Atomic Energy Commission, which in 1949 opposed development of the hydrogen bomb. In 1953 was notified of a military security report unfavorable to him and was accused of having associated with Communists in the past. In 1954, accusations of disloyalty led to a government hearing that resulted in the loss of his security clearance and of his position as advisor to the highest echelons of the U.S. government. In 1963 U.S. President Johnson presented him with the Enrico Fermi Award of the Atomic Energy Commission.

Orlov, Yuri (1924–). Russian-American physicist, Soviet dissident, and human rights activist. Expelled from the CPSU due to a pro-democracy, anti-Stalin speech (1956), and fired from his job. Received his doctorate (1963), becoming an expert in particle physics. Supported Sakharov in 1973, and wrote articles published in samizdat. Organized the Moscow Helsinki Group (1976) and became its chairman. Arrested in 1977 after ignoring KGB demands to disband the Helsinki Group. Sentenced to 7 years in a labor camp, and five years of internal exile (1978). Stripped of Soviet citizenship and expelled from the Soviet Union (1986). Became a U.S. citizen (1993). Professor of Physics and Government, Cornell University, has worked at Cornell since 1987.

Orwell, George (1903–1950). English novelist, essayist, and critic famous for his novels *Animal Farm* (1945) and *1984* (1949). Born Eric Arthur Blair, he changed his name to Orwell, which is derived from the river Orwell in East Anglia. In the 1930s he traveled to Spain to report on the Civil War there, and eventually joined the Republican militia. In May 1937, after fighting in Barcelona against communists trying to suppress their political opponents, Orwell fled Spain in fear for his life. The experience left him with a life-long dread of communism, first expressed in his vivid account of his Spanish experiences in *Homage to Catalonia* (1938). During World War II Orwell headed the Indian service of the British Broadcasting Corporation (BBC). Left the BBC in 1943 to become the literary editor of the Tribune, a left-wing socialist paper. In 1944 he published *Animal Farm*, a political fable based on the story of the Russian Revolution and its betrayal by Stalin. In 1949 he wrote his last book, *1984*, a warning on the twin menaces of Nazism and Stalinism.

Owen, David (1938–). British politician and physician. British Foreign Secretary (1977–1979) under Labour Prime Minister James Callaghan. Split from the Labour Party in 1981, forming the Social Democratic Party with three other politicians, and led the SDP from 1983–1987. Wrote the book *Human Rights* (1978) on issues in Africa and the Soviet Union. Was chairman of Yukos International UK BV (2002–2005), a division of the former Russian oil company Yukos. Was consultant to Epion Holdings, owned by Russian oligarch Alisher Usmanov until 2015.

P

Palme, Olof Sven Joachim (1927–1986, assassinated). Swedish politician. Led the Swedish Social Democratic Party (1969–1986). Prime Minister of Sweden (1969–1976, 1982–1986). Special mediator of the United Nations in the Iran-Iraq War. Supported third world liberation movements after decolonization, first Western head of state to visit Cuba after its revolution. Murdered on a Stockholm street in February 1986; his assassination is still unsolved.

Pasternak, Boris (1890–1960). Soviet poet and author. One of the most influential Russian poets of the twentieth century. His best-known work is the novel *Doctor Zhivago* (1957), its action spanning the failed Russian Revolution of 1905 to WWII. The novel was banned in the Soviet Union and was smuggled to Italy for publication. Awarded the Nobel Prize for Literature in 1958 but was forced by the CPSU to decline the award.

Pavlinchuk, Valery (1937–1968). Soviet physicist and writer. Expelled from the CPSU in 1968 for circulating and reproducing the samizdat periodical *Chronicle of Current Events*.

Pelse, Arvids (1899–1983). Latvian Soviet politician and historian. Active in the October Revolution of 1917. Joined the Cheka in 1918. First Secretary of the Latvian Socialist Republic (1959–1966). Chairman of the Party Control Committee of the CC CPSU (1966–1983), a body which oversaw the discipline of party members.

Petain, Philippe (1856–1951). French military leader and politician. Considered a national hero after WWI and given the nickname *The Lion of Verdun*. Chief of state of the Vichy government of France (1940–1944) after the Nazis invaded and occupied the country. After WWII, was tried and convicted of treason. Original sentence was death, but due to national appreciation of his WWI service, his sentence was commuted to life imprisonment. Died in prison.

Pinochet, Augusto (1915–2006). Chilean politician. President of Chile (1974–1990). Commander-In-Chief of Chile (1973–1998). Was a leader of the military junta that overthrew the socialist government of President Salvador Allende in 1973. During his dictatorial reign, tens of thousands of opponents of his regime were tortured as he tried to exterminate leftism in Chile and reassert free-market policies in the country's economy. The reversal of the Allende government's socialist policies resulted in a lower rate of inflation and an economic boom between 1976 and 1979. In 1976, Pinochet approved the release of prisoner Luis Corvalan (1916–2010), the leader of the Chilean Communist Party, in exchange for the release of Vladimir Bukovsky by the USSR. During the 1980s, his free-market policies were credited with maintaining a low inflation rate and an acceptable rate of economic growth. Pinochet remained in office until free elections chose a new president in March 1990. In 2000, he was ordered to stand trial on charges of human rights abuses, which were dropped in 2002. In 2005 the Chilean Supreme Court voted to order Pinochet to stand trial on charges of illegal financial dealings, as well as a case involving the disappearance and execution of at least 119 political dissidents. He died prior to trial the following year.

Platonov, Andrei (1899–1951). Born Andrei Klimentov. Soviet Russian poet and writer. His works were banned during his lifetime, due to his experimental style (a forerunner to existentialism) and his implicit criticism of Stalin and collectivization. His teenage son was sent to a labor camp during the Great Purge, contracted tuberculosis in the camp, and then was released back home as his disease was terminal. Platonov contracted the disease himself while nursing his son.

Plissonnier, Gaston (1913–1995). French politician. Joined the

French Communist Party in 1935 and rose through the ranks. Assisted illegal communist parties in Europe at the behest of the Soviet Union. Credited with limiting the French Communist Party's disavowal of the Soviet invasion of Czechoslovakia.

Plyushch, Leonid (1928–2015). Soviet and Ukrainian mathematician, writer, dissident, and human rights activist. In 1968, protested against the misconduct of the Galanskov-Ginzburg trial; protested the Soviet invasion of Czechoslovakia. Joined the Initiative Group for the Defense of Human Rights in the USSR, which requested the UN Human Rights Commission to investigate human rights violations in the Soviet Union. Arrested in 1972 for anti-Soviet activity, jailed for a year before the trial began, was declared insane, and sent to a psychiatric prison hospital. Wrote letters from the hospital, compiled and published into a book *The Case of Leonid Plyushch* (1974), published in Russian and then English. His imprisonment was protested internationally, by mathematicians and many others. Released and left the Soviet Union in 1976 and settled in France. Retained his communist beliefs but supported anti-totalitarian publications in communist countries.

Podgorny, Nikolai (1903–1983). Ukrainian Soviet politician. First Secretary of the Central Committee of the Communist Party of Ukraine (1957–1963). Chairman of the Presidium of the Supreme Soviet (1965–1977). As a protégé of Nikita Khrushchev, became a member of the Politburo and traveled with Khrushchev to the UN headquarters in 1960. Acted as Soviet ambassador to several nations. Was opposed by Brezhnev, who saw Podgorny as a threat to his power. Brezhnev was finally successful in removing him from the Politburo in 1977. He kept a low profile after his ousting.

Ponomarev, Boris (1905–1995). Soviet politician and historian. Chief of the International Department of the CC CPSU (1955–1986), controlling the policy of the World Communist Movement. A key participant in the development of Soviet foreign policy.

Pozner, Vladimir (1934–). French-born Russian-American journalist. Known for defending Soviet policies on television and radio during the Cold War, speaking fluent English, Russian, and French. Worked on various Soviet publications and programs: the English-language magazine *Soviet Life* (1961–1967), multilanguage Soviet magazine *Sputnik Monthly Digest* (1967–1970), program *Voice of Moscow*, Chief commentator on the North American service of Radio Moscow. From the 1970s to 1990s, often appeared on American radio and TV talk shows. Co-hosted the Donahue/Pozner weekly show with television journalist Phil Donahue on CNBC (1991–1994). Returned to Russia in 1996. Since 2010, hosts an interview show on Russia's Channel One.

Primakov, Evgeny (1929–2015). Russian politician. Prime Minister of Russia (1998–1999). Also served as Foreign Minister, Speaker of the Supreme Council of the Soviet Union, and chief of the intelligence service. He became involved in politics in 1989, as Chairman of the Council of the Soviet Union. From 1990 to 1991 was a member of Soviet leader Mikhail Gorbachev's Presidential Council. After the failed August 1991 coup, was appointed First Deputy Chairman of the KGB. After the formation of the Russian Federation, he shepherded the transition of the KGB First Chief Directorate to the control of the Russian Federation government, under the new name Foreign Intelligence Service. Served as Minister of Foreign Affairs from 1996 to 1998. In 1999 was fired by Yeltsin over the ostensibly sluggish pace of the Russian economy.

Putin, Vladimir (1952–). Russian politician and intelligence officer. President of Russia (1999–2008, 2012–current). Prime Minister of Russia (1999–2000, 2008–2012).Was a KGB intelligence officer for 16 years, rising to the rank of Lieutenant Colonel before resigning in 1991 to enter politics in Saint Petersburg. Moved to Moscow in 1996 and joined Boris Yeltsin's administration, rising quickly through the ranks to become Acting President on 31 December 1999. His first presidency was marked by economic growth and an increase in GDP. Won a third term in the 2012 presidential election with 64% of the vote, and gained 76% in the March 2018 election. Despite high approval for Putin, confidence in the Russian economy is low, dropping to levels in 2016 that rivaled the recent lows in 2009. In July 2018, his approval rating fell to 63% and only 49% said they would vote for Putin if presidential elections were held again. Russia under his leadership has scored poorly in Transparency International's Corruption Perceptions Index. Human rights organizations and activists have accused him of persecuting political critics and activists, including ordering them tortured and assassinated.

R

Reagan, Ronald (1911–2004). American actor and politician. 40th president of the United States (1981–1989). Governor of California (1967–1975). During his presidency, escalated the Cold War. Well-known for calling the USSR the "evil empire" and also for the line "Mr. Gorbachev, tear down this wall!" (Brandenburg Gate speech, 1987). Reagan's policies were to build up the U.S. military in terms of both manpower and missiles. The arms and military race led to an economic undermining of the Soviet system. Reagan's policies have been credited with spurring the largely nonviolent dismantling of communist states years later.

Rockefeller, David (1915–2017). American banker and philanthropist, the youngest of the five sons of John D. Rockefeller, Jr. Graduated from Harvard University, London School of Economics and the University of Chicago. After service in the U.S. Army during World War II, joined the staff of the Chase National Bank of New York in 1946. Rose steadily to become senior vice president in 1952 and was instrumental in the 1955 merger of Chase National and the Bank of the Manhattan Company to create Chase Manhattan Bank. His specialty became international banking, and he was a familiar figure to ministers and heads of states of various countries around the world. In 1973 founded the Trilateral Commission, a private international organization (North America, Europe and Japan) designed to confront the challenges posed by globalization and encourage greater cooperation between the United States and its principal allies. Attended and contributed financially to the Bilderberg Conference, an annual three-day meeting attended by approximately 100 of Europe's and North America's most influential bankers, economists, politicians, and government officials.

Rostropovich, Mstislav (1927–2007). Soviet and Russian musician. Considered one of the greatest cellists of the 20th century, known for commissioning new pieces for cello and premiering over 100 pieces to expand the cello repertoire. Had close working relationships with Soviet composers, including Prokofiev. In the early 1970s, supported Alexander Solzhenitsyn; as a result, he was banned from touring abroad. Left the Soviet Union in 1974 and settled in the U.S. Awarded the 1974 Award of the International League of Human Rights. Musical director and conductor of the National Symphony Orchestra in Washington, D.C. (1977–1994). Supported Boris Yeltsin and was on friendly terms with Vladimir Putin. Celebrated his 80th birthday in the Kremlin, where he was praised in a speech by Putin and awarded the Order for Services to the Fatherland.

Rousseau, Jean-Jacques (1712–1778). Swiss-born philosopher, writer, and political theorist. His writings inspired the leaders of the French Revolution and the Romantic generation. His books "Discourse on Inequality" and "The Social Contract" are considered cornerstones of modern political thought, espousing the theories that private property is the source of social inequality, and that a government's authority comes from the consent of the people rather than a divine right or the use of force. Believed that morality came not from societal norms but was innate, based on the natural human aversion to witnessing the suffering of others. The concept of the "noble savage," widely attributed to Rousseau, does not appear in his writings. Rather, he advocated that civil society creates new negative impulses in its members. Nonetheless he is widely cited as the inspiration for "back to nature" trends in society and child-centered approaches to parenting and education.

Rudenko, Roman (1907–1981). Ukrainian Soviet lawyer. Procurator General of the Ukrainian Soviet Socialist Republic (1944–1953). Procurator General of the USSR (1953–1981). Chief prosecutor for the USSR during the Nuremberg Trials (1946), chief prosecutor for the trial of Polish Underground leaders (1945). One of the chief commandants of an NKVD prison camp (an ex-Nazi concentration camp) that closed in 1950; about 12,000 prisoners had died at the camp of malnutrition and disease during its operation. Served as judge at the closed trial of Lavrentiy Beria following Stalin's death (1953). Elected to the CC CPSU in 1961. Devised multiple measures to suppress the Soviet dissident movement without stirring international reaction, such as declaring dissidents mentally ill and confining them in psychiatric hospitals.

Rutskoy, Alexander (1947–). Russian politician and former Soviet military officer. Commander of a Soviet air assault regiment in Afghanistan, shot down twice, and once captured and held as a prisoner of war in Pakistan. Awarded title Hero of the Soviet Union (1988). Vice President of Russia (1991–1993). During Russian constitutional crisis of 1993, was proclaimed acting President in place of Boris Yeltsin, though not recognized as such outside Russia. When two-week standoff ended, was arrested, dismissed as Vice President, fired from the military forces, and imprisoned until 1994. Governor of Kursk Oblast (1996–2000), elected as joint candidate for communist and "patriotic forces". Was still active in Russian politics after his governorship.

Ryzhkov, Nikolai (1929–). Soviet and Russian politician. Head of the Economic Department of the Central Committee (1982–1985). Last Chairman of the Council of Ministers before the dissolution of the Soviet Union. Responsible for the cultural and economic administration of the Soviet Union during the late Gorbachev era, until he lost the position in 1991. The same year, he also lost his seat on the Presidential Council and went on to become Boris Yeltsin's leading opponent in the 1991 Russian Presidential election. In 1996, was one of the founders of the CPRF-led alliance of leftists and nationalists known as the People's Patriotic Union of Russia. Currently serves as Chairman of the Federation Council Commission on Natural Monopolies, as a member of the Committee on Local Self-Governance.

S

Sakharov, Andrei (1921–1989). Russian physicist, dissident, and human rights activist. Designer of the Soviet Union's first two-stage hydrogen bomb (tested 1955). After 1965, turned to particle physics research. Became active in anti-nuclear proliferation activism in the 1960s, playing a role in the 1963 Partial Test Ban Treaty. Wrote essay "Reflections on Progress, Peaceful Coexistence, and Intellectual Freedom" (1968), which was spread via samizdat and published in the West; as a result, Sakharov was banned from military-related research. One of the three founding members of the Committee on Human Rights in the USSR (1970). Awarded the Nobel Peace Prize (1975); Sakharov was barred from leaving the USSR to receive it. Protested the Soviet intervention in Afghanistan (1979), was arrested, and sent to internal exile in Gorky (1980), a city off-limits to foreigners. Went on hunger strike twice to protest the Soviet treatment of his wife Yelena Bonner (1984, 1985). Allowed to return to Moscow in 1988, when Gorbachev was promoting the ideas of glasnost and perestroika.

Sartre, Jean-Paul (1905–1980). French novelist and playwright. Exponent of Existentialism—a philosophy acclaiming the freedom of the individual human being. Was awarded the Nobel Prize for Literature in 1964, but declined it on grounds he wished to remain independent from institutional associations. After World War II took an active interest in French political movements, gradually moving further left. Became an outspoken admirer of the Soviet Union, which he visited in 1954. However, after the Budapest uprising in 1956, he condemned both the Soviet intervention and the submission of the French Communist Party to the dictates of Moscow.

Schmidt, Helmut (1918–2015). German politician. Chancellor of West Germany (1974–1982). Co-publisher of the influential weekly Die Zeit (1983–1989), acting director of Die Zeit (1985–1989). Served in Wehrmacht (German Army) during World War II and was awarded an Iron Cross. After the war. joined the Social Democratic Party and was elected to the Bundestag (1953–1961), returned to service in Hamburg (1961–65), and was reelected to the Bundestag in 1965. Became vice-chairman of the Social Democratic Party in 1968 and served as minister of defense (1969–72) and minister of finance (1972–74) in the government of Chancellor Willy Brandt. Was elected to the chancellorship of West Germany in 1974, after his predecessor Willy Brandt's chief of staff was exposed as an East German spy. He served there from 1974 to 1982. Resigned in 1982 upon a vote of no confidence in the Bundestag. Was the author of numerous books on German political affairs and

European international relations.

Semichastny, Vladimir (1924–2001). Soviet politician. Chairman of the KGB (1961–1967). Emphasized developing security and intelligence services in Eastern bloc states and recruiting top college graduates to the KGB. Supported communist "liberation" movements worldwide. Suppressed dissidents and nationalist movements within the Soviet Union and Eastern Bloc. Participated in the successful coup against Khrushchev (1964). Replaced by Yuri Andropov (1967).

Sharansky, Natan (1948–). One of the most famous former Soviet refuseniks. Israeli politician, author and human rights activist. Born Anatoly Sharansky in Donetsk, Ukraine, he became involved with the refusenik movement and one of the foremost dissidents and spokesmen for the Soviet Jews. In 1978 was convicted of treason and spying on behalf of the United States and sentenced to thirteen years' imprisonment in a Siberian forced labor camp. He was released by Gorbachev in 1986 as part of an East-West prisoner exchange. Emigrated to Israel in 1986. In 1988 elected President of the newly created Zionist Forum, an umbrella organization of former Soviet activists. Served as Minister of Industry and Trade from 1996–1999, and Minister of Housing and Construction and Deputy Prime Minister from 2001–2003. Resigned from government in 2005. In 1988 published the memoir *Fear No Evil* in the United States.

Shevardnadze, Eduard (1928–2014). Soviet and Georgian politician. Leader of Soviet Georgia (1972–1985). Soviet Minister of Foreign Affairs (1985–1990, 1991). As Minister of Foreign Affairs was a key player in foreign policy, involved in ending the war in Afghanistan, negotiating arms treaties with the U.S., approving the reunification of Germany, and withdrawing the Soviet army from Eastern Europe and the USSR's border with China. Resigned his position in 1990, in protest against communist hardliners coming to the fore in government, and briefly re-held the position in the last month of the USSR's existence. Leader of post-Soviet Georgia (1992–1995). President of Georgia (1995–2003).

Sholokhov, Mikhail (1905–1984). Soviet writer. Primarily known for his 4-volume epic novel *And Quiet Flows the Don* (1940), depicting the struggles of Cossacks during WWI, the Russian Revolution, and the Russian Civil War. Won the Stalin Prize (1941) and Nobel Prize in Literature (1965) for this novel. On relatively good terms with Stalin, and wrote letters to Stalin about the poor conditions at the collective farms along the Don River in the 1930s. Joined the CPSU (1932), elected to the Supreme Soviet (1937), joined the CC CPSU (1961), and held membership in many other Soviet organizations.

Sinyavsky, Andrei (1925–1997). Russian writer and dissident. Published his works in the West under the pseudonym Abram Tertz. Depicted realities of Soviet life in short fiction. Was arrested and tried with fellow writer Yuli Daniel (1965) in the infamous Sinyavsky-Daniel trial. Sentenced to 7 years hard labor due to "anti-Soviet activity". Released from prison (1971) and emigrated to France (1973). Co-founded the Russian language almanac *Sintaksis* (1978).

Snezhnevsky, Andrey (1904–1987). Soviet psychologist. Fabricated the concept of "sluggish schizophrenia", which spread through the USSR and Eastern Bloc in the 1960s as a means to suppress dissidents; this concept was not accepted in international professional psychiatry organizations outside communist groups. Diagnosed multiple dissidents with this condition, some even in absentia. In 1980, as a Corresponding Fellow of the Royal College of Psychiatry, was asked to respond to charges by the Special Committee on the Political Abuse of Psychiatry that he engaged in such abuse. He refused to answer these charges and resigned his fellowship. Director of the Institute of Psychiatry of the USSR Academy of Medical Sciences (1962—1987). Director of the All-Union Mental Health Research Center of the Soviet Academy of Medical Sciences (1982–1987).

Solomentsev, Mikhail (1913–2008). Soviet politician. A secretary of the CC CPSU (1966–1971). Chairman of the Council of Ministers of the RSFR (1971–1983). Chairman of the Party Control Committee of the Central Committee (1983–1988), which oversaw the discipline of party members. Accused of aiding corruption in Uzbekistan during a series of criminal trials in the late 1980s and fired from his position by Mikhail Gorbachev.

Solzhenitsyn, Alexander (1918–2008). Russian writer. Served as Soviet Army commander during World War II. Arrested in 1945 for anti-Stalin remarks in private letters, sent to Lubyanka prison for interrogation, sentenced in absentia to 7 years in a labor camp. Completed his sentence at multiple locations, ending at a special camp for political prisoners in Ekibastuz. Sent to internal exile in 1953 when his prison camp sentence ended. Freed from exile in 1956 and exonerated. Was allowed to publish only one novel *One Day in the Life of Ivan Denisovich* within the Soviet Union, based on his experiences in the Ekibastuz camp. Other books, *Cancer Ward* (1968), *August 1914* (1971), and *The Gulag Archipelago* (1973), had to be published in the West via smuggling out manuscripts, given the KGB had seized some of his materials in 1965. Won the Nobel Prize in Literature (1970), which he could not receive until after his expulsion from the Soviet Union in 1974. Returned to Russia in 1994.

Sorsa, Taisto Kalevi (1930–2004). Finnish politician. Began political career in 1969 in the Social Democratic Party of Finland. A 2008 book by historian Jukka Seppinen suggests Sorsa was at that time already receiving support from the KGB. Prime Minister of Finland (1972–1975, 1977–1979, 1982–1987). Leader of the Social Democratic Party of Finland (1975–1987). Minister for Foreign Affairs (1972, 1975–1976, 1987–1989). Vice president of the Socialist International in the mid–1970s. At the time, the Socialist International supported détente, and Sorsa had extensive contacts with U.S. and Soviet officials with regards to East-West relations and arms treaty talks. In 1994, he withdrew from Finnish presidential primaries as SDPF's candidate, due to Vladimir Bukovsky's revelations of Sorsa's covert relationships with the Soviets for decades.

Stalin, Joseph (1878–1953). Soviet revolutionary and politician. Born Joseph Vissarionovich Dzhugashvili in the Republic of Georgia, then part of the Russian Empire. Ruled the Soviet Union from the mid-1920s until his death in 1953. Initially presiding over an oligarchic one-party system that governed by plurality, he became the *de facto* dictator of the Soviet state by the 1930s, holding the posts of General Secretary of the Communist Party of the Soviet Union (1922–1952) and Premier (1941–1953). Instituted the "Great Purge," in which over a million were imprisoned and at least 700,000 executed between 1934 and 1939. Widely considered one of the 20th century's most significant figures, he transformed the Soviet Union into a major industrial and military world power over three decades. Center of a pervasive personality cult within the international Marxist-Leninist movement, Stalin today is the focus of a nostalgic trend in Russia that attempts to minimize the brutal aspects of his regime.

Steen, Reiulf (1933–2014). Norwegian writer and politician. Active in the Norwegian Labor Party (1958–1990), Vice chairman of the party (1965–1975), Chairman of the party (1975–1981). Norwegian ambassador to Chile (1992–1996). Vice president of the Socialist International (1978–1983). Chaired Norwegian branch of Helsinki Committee for Human Rights (1986–1992).

Stroilov, Pavel (1983–). Russian historian living in London after being granted asylum by British judges in 2006. Fled Russia in 2003 after stealing 50,000 unpublished top-secret Kremlin documents from the archive of the Gorbachev Foundation. Wrote *Behind the Desert Storm*, a book that discusses what the stolen documents reveal about the First Gulf War. Translated Alexander Litvinenko's book *Allegations* into English and co-authored several works about the European Union with Bukovsky including *EUSSR*, which drew parallels between the EU and Soviet government.

Sudoplatov, Pavel (1907–1996). Member of the intelligence services of the Soviet Union and rose to the rank of lieutenant general. Was involved in several famous episodes including the assassination of Leon Trotsky, the espionage program which obtained information about the atomic bomb from the Manhattan Project, and Operation Scherhorn, a deception operation against the Germans in 1944. In 1953 was arrested as Lavrentiy Beria's collaborator and sentenced to 15 years in prison. Served full term and was released in 1968. His autobiography *Special Tasks* made him well known outside the USSR, and provided a detailed look at Soviet intelligence and Soviet internal politics during his years at the top.

Suslov, Mikhail (1902–1982). Soviet politician. Second secretary of the CPSU (1965–1982). Head of Propaganda Department of the CC CPSU (1949–1952). Abandoned teaching in 1931 to become a full-time politician. Took part in repressions and purges during Stalin's rule. Suffered a political reversal upon Stalin's death, but soon returned to some power in 1955, being re-elected to the Politburo. Opposed Khrushchev's policy of de-Stalinization and played a key role in Khrushchev's ousting in 1964. One of the most influential Soviet politicians in the 1960s.

Sverdlov, Yakov (1885–1919). Soviet revolutionary and politician. Joined the Russian Social Democratic Labor Party (1902) and soon after joined Lenin's Bolshevik faction. Was involved in the failed 1905 Russian Revolution, while living in the Urals. Spent most of 1906–1917 either imprisoned or in exile. Was exiled in Siberia (1914–1916), along with Joseph Stalin. Elected to the CC CPSU (1917) and played an important planning role in the October Revolution. Chairman of the Central Committee Secretariat (1917–1919). Key planner and participant in repressions and mass killings in the Russian Civil War. Probably died of the Spanish flu pandemic.

Szilard, Leo (1898–1964). Hungarian-German-American physicist and inventor. Conceived the nuclear chain reaction in 1933, presented the idea of a nuclear reactor with Enrico Fermi in 1934, and in 1939 wrote a letter for Albert Einstein's signature that resulted in the Manhattan Project which built the atomic bomb. Received the Atoms for Peace Award in 1959 and Albert Einstein Award in 1960.

T

Taraki, Nur Muhammad (1917–1979, assassinated). Afghan politician. President of Afghanistan (1978–1979). One of the founding members of the People's Democratic Party of Afghanistan in 1965. Initiated the Saur Revolution (1978), along with Hafizullah Amin and Babrak Karmal, establishing the communist Democratic Republic of Afghanistan. Taraki initiated a very unpopular land reform in January 1979, locked up dissidents, and oversaw massacres of villagers; this led to popular uprisings. Tried but was unable to get the Soviet government to intercede and restore order. Overthrown in September 1979 and murdered in October 1979 upon the orders of Amin.

Tarkovsky, Andrei (1932–1986). Russian filmmaker and writer. Directed the first five of his seven feature films in the Soviet Union, switching to Western production after defecting in 1982. During his Soviet years, he was censored heavily, having productions stopped by authorities and his films strictly controlled in distribution within the USSR. In 1983, his film *Nostalghia* was presented at the Cannes Film Festival, and Soviet authorities managed to block the film from receiving the coveted Palme d'Or prize; this interference hardened Tarkovsky against returning to the Soviet Union. In 1984, he publicly announced he would never return to the USSR. Died of lung cancer.

Tarsis, Valery (1906–1983). Ukrainian writer. Joined the CPSU as a young man, became disillusioned in the 1930s, and officially broke with the party in 1960. Had his works smuggled outside the Soviet Union for publication. The overseas publication of his novel *The Bluebottle* (1962), led to a punitive psychiatric imprisonment. He wrote about his 8-month stay in the autobiographical novel *Ward 7* (1965), one of the first published works on the abuse of psychiatry in the Soviet Union. Emigrated to the West in 1966 and was stripped of Soviet citizenship soon after. Lectured at various universities and colleges in the West after emigration, ultimately settling in Switzerland.

Thatcher, Margaret (1925–2013). Born Margaret Roberts. British politician. Prime Minister of the UK (1979–1990). Leader of the Conservative Party (1975–1990). Dubbed the "Iron Lady" by a Soviet journalist, she was closely aligned with Ronald Reagan's Cold War policies once he assumed the American presidency. Condemned the invasion of Afghanistan (1979), saying it exposed the bankruptcy of the policy of détente. The first British PM to visit China (1982). Went on a state visit to the USSR in 1984, meeting with Mikhail Gorbachev.

U

Ustinov, Dmitry (1908–1984). Soviet military leader. Minister of Defense of the Soviet Union (1976–1984). In the aftermath of WWII, played a crucial role in requisitioning German military resources, leading to the development of the Soviet missile and space programs. Under Brezhnev, Ustinov was in charge of developing the Soviet Union's ICBM system and strategic bomber force. Strong proponent of the invasion of Afghanistan (1979). He made the development of a Soviet space shuttle top priority, worried that the U.S. shuttle would be used to deploy nuclear weapons over Soviet territory. Advised Andropov not to disclose possession of the black box from downed Korean airliner KAL 007 in 1992, as its tapes did not support the claim that the plane was on an American spy mission.

V

Vance, Cyrus (1917–2002). American lawyer and politician. Secretary of State under Jimmy Carter (1977–1980). Deputy Secretary of Defense under Lyndon Johnson (1964–1967). Secretary of the Army under John F. Kennedy and Johnson (1962–1964). Originally supported the Vietnam War, but by the late 1960s opposed administration policy and resigned his position in 1967. During the Carter administration, pushed for closer relations with the Soviet Union, often opposing National Security Adviser Zbigniew Brzezinski's harder stance against the USSR. Negotiated SALT II agreement with Soviet ambassador Anatoly Dobrynin (1978), which was signed by Carter but not ratified by the U.S. Senate, so never went into effect. After the Soviet invasion of Afghanistan (1979), Vance's softer stance on the USSR lost him influence. Resigned in 1980 in protest against Brzezinski's push for a military solution to the Iranian hostage crisis.

Vishnevskaya, Galina (1926–2012). Russian soprano opera singer and recitalist named a People's Artist of the USSR in 1966. Wife of cellist Mstislav Rostropovich. They performed together regularly and were friends of composer Dmitri Shostakovich. In 1974 she and her husband left the Soviet Union and initially settled in the United States, then later in Paris. After the dissolution of the Soviet Union, she and her husband returned to Russia, where in 2002 she opened her own opera theater in Moscow. She died in Moscow in 2012.

Voroshilov, Kliment (1881–1965). Soviet military officer. One of the original five Marshals of the Soviet Union (1917–1953). Member of the Politburo (1926–1960). Joined the Bolshevik faction of the Russian Social Democratic Labor Party in 1905 and became closely associated with Stalin during the Russian Civil War (1918). Played a key role in Stalin's purges of the 1930s, denouncing many military colleagues at Stalin's request. Incompetently commanded Soviet troops in the Winter War with Finland (1939–1940), leading to the death of about 185,000 troops; was shunted aside by Stalin to less critical military roles. Supervised the establishment of a communist regime in Hungary (1945–1947). After Stalin's death, was part of the troika responsible for Lavrentiy Beria's arrest, conviction, and execution. Pushed to less important roles and retired during Khrushchev's reign. After Brezhnev toppled Khrushchev, Voroshilov was pulled out of retirement for a figurehead position.

Voslensky, Mikhail (1920–1997). Soviet writer, scientist, and dissident. Was an interpreter for the Soviet Union during the Nuremberg Trials. In 1953–1955 he worked with the World Peace Council. Later he worked at the Soviet Academy of Sciences. Between 1954 and 1968 published four books on Germany's international relations and taught history at Lumumba University in Moscow. In 1972 defected from the Soviet Union and later took on Austrian citizenship. In 1977 was stripped of Soviet citizenship, a decision revoked by Mikhail Gorbachev in 1990. Authored the book *Nomenklatura: The Soviet Ruling Class* (1980), which was translated into 14 languages.

Vyshinsky, Andrey (1883–1954). Soviet official. Known as a state prosecutor of Stalin's Moscow trials and the Nuremberg trials. During 1935 he became Chief Prosecutor of the USSR, and legal mastermind of Stalin's Great Purge. During 1936, achieved international infamy as the prosecutor of the Zinoviev-Kamenev trial, the first of the Moscow trials during the Great Purge. In 1939, he introduced a motion to the Supreme Council to bring the Western Ukraine into the USSR. In 1940 was sent to Latvia to supervise the incorporation of that country into the USSR. Minister of Foreign Affairs from 1949–1953, after serving as Deputy Minister of Foreign Affairs for Vyacheslav Molotov since 1940. He also managed the Institute of State and Law of the Academy of Sciences.

Vysotsky, Vladimir (1938–1980). Soviet actor and singer-songwriter. Iconic Russian and Soviet cultural figure. Generally ignored by Soviet officials, wrote hundreds of songs and poems about Word War II, Soviet labor camps, the criminal underworld, and anti-Soviet material, disguised through allegory, parable, and buffoonery. Associated with the Taganka Theatre since 1965. Some controversy over his death, though his alcohol and drug use were likely the causes.

W

Walesa, Lech (1943–). Polish politician and labor activist. Co-founded Solidarity in 1980, the first independent labor union in the Soviet bloc. As a result of Solidarity's activities, the communist Polish government declared martial law (1981–1983). Won the Nobel Peace Prize (1983). Continued Solidarity activities underground through the 1980s, leading to the Round Table Agreement with the Polish government, resulting in free elections in 1989. President of Poland (1990–1995).

Y

Yakir, Iona (1896–1937, executed). Soviet military leader. Joined the Bolshevik Party in 1917 and participated in the Russian Civil War on the Bolshevik side. Following the Civil War, Yakir was an army commander in Ukraine, and started military reforms in training, strategy, tactics, and logistics. One of his major military reforms was allowing officers to act on their own initiative, a policy disliked by Stalin. In the Great Purge of 1936, several of Yakir's associates were arrested by the NKVD; Yakir tried appealing to Stalin, which made Stalin even more distrustful. Yakir was arrested in 1937, along with 7 other military leaders; they were accused of being Nazi agents and Trotskyites. Was tortured into a confession and executed the day after the trial. Father of Pyotr Yakir.

Yakir, Pyotr (1923–1982). Soviet historian and human rights activist. Wrote *Childhood in Prison* (1972), about his time in the prison camps after the death of his father, Iona Yakir. Pyotr and his mother spent almost 20 years in the prison camps. Pyotr being 14 years old when he was first imprisoned, with an initial sentence of 5 years, his crime being the son of "an enemy of the people", with his sentence repeatedly renewed. Released and rehabilitated in 1957, thereafter studied at the Moscow State Historical and Archival Institute, after which he worked at the Institute of History of the USSR Academy of Sciences. Took part in human rights activism in the USSR starting in the mid-1960s, co-founder of the Initiative Group for the Defense of Human Rights in the USSR and protested the 1968 Invasion of Czechoslovakia. Arrested in 1972 after he published his memoirs, tried in 1973, and sentenced to internal exile.

Yakovlev, Alexander (1923–2005). Soviet politician and historian. Member of the Politburo (1987–1990) and Secretariat (1986–1990) of the CPSU. Soviet Ambassador to Canada (1973–1983). Joined the CPSU (1944). Called the "godfather of glasnost", considered to be the intellectual force behind the policies of glasnost and perestroika during Mikhail Gorbachev's leadership. Founded and led the Russian Party of Social Democracy (1995) until its merger with other similar parties into the Democratic Choice of Russia – United Democrats bloc. After the dissolution of the Soviet Union, wrote and lectured on history, politics, and economics.

Yakovlev, Yegor (1930–2005). Soviet journalist. Named editor-in-chief of *Sovietskaya Pechat* journal in 1966, became a special correspondent for the *Izvestia* newspaper in 1968. Named editor-in-chief of the English-language newspaper *Moscow News* in 1986, transforming the paper in line with Mikhail Gorbachev's policies of glasnost and perestroika. Chairman of VGTRK (All-Soviet Television Company). Publisher of *Obschaya gazeta* (1993–2002).

Yakunin, Gleb (1934–2014). Russian priest and human rights activist. Member of the Russian Parliament (1990–1995). Ordained a Russian Orthodox priest (1962), and appointed to a parish in a town near Moscow. Wrote an open letter with fellow priest Nikolai Eschliman (1965), arguing that the Russian Orthodox Church must be liberated from Soviet control; the letter was distributed by samizdat. In retaliation, he was not allowed to continue his parish ministry (1966). Created the Christian Committee for the Defense of Believers' Rights in the USSR (1976) and was arrested and convicted for anti-Soviet agitation (1980). He served his sentence in a KGB prison, then a labor camp, and then internal exile; was granted amnesty in 1987 by Mikhail Gorbachev. Returned to his ministry as a priest, working until 1992. In 1992 published materials about the cooperation between the Moscow Patriarchate and the KGB. Published code names of several KGB agents who held high-ranking positions in the Russian Orthodox Church. Was defrocked by the Russian Orthodox Church in 1993.

Yeltsin, Boris (1931–2007). Soviet and Russian politician. First President of the Russian Federation (1991–1999). Member of the CPSU (1961–1990). Joined the Secretariat of the CC CPSU under Mikhail Gorbachev (1985) and became a member of the Politburo (1986), though he resigned soon afterward due to the slow pace of reforms. Won presidency of the Russian Republic in 1991 in its first democratic elections, after which a coup against Gorbachev was launched by communist hardliners, and in the aftermath the Soviet Union was dissolved. Yeltsin then became President of the Russian Federation, during which he attempted radical reforms, bringing a market economy to Russia. Favored friendly relations with the West. Widely accused of allowing corruption in the new systems, setting up economic oligarchs. Resigned in 1999, choosing Vladimir Putin as his successor.

Yevtushenko, Yevgeny (1932–2017). Born Yevgeny Gangnus. Soviet and Russian poet. Politically active during the Khrushchev Thaw (1950s-early 1960s), and wrote the poem *Babi Yar* (1961), a chilling dedication to the persecution of Jews by both the Nazis and Soviet Union. This poem and others by Yevtushenko were set to music by Dmitri Shostakovich in his Symphony No. 13 (1962). Despite his criticisms of the Soviet regime in this and other poems, he was able to travel extensively abroad when there generally were restrictions on foreign travel by Soviet citizens. Many contemporaries accused him of duplicity and collaborating with the Soviet regime. Since 2007, he divided his time between the U.S. and Russia, teaching at the University of Tulsa (Oklahoma) and City University of New York. Died of heart failure in Oklahoma.

Yezhov, Nikolai (1895–1940, executed). Soviet official. Head of NKVD (1936–1938). Joined the Bolsheviks in 1917 and fought in the Red Army during the Russian Civil War. Rose through various political positions in the 1920s. Appointed head of various departments in 1930, elected to the Central Committee of the Communist Party in 1934, and became a secretary of the Central Committee in 1935. Became favored by Stalin during the Great Purge, as Yezhov was tasked with interrogating those who had fallen out of favor and getting them to confess in show trials via the use of torture. In 1938, was replaced as head of NKVD by Lavrentiy Beria, as it became clear he had fallen from Stalin's favor as the purges were subsiding. Arrested in 1939, he was tortured and forced to confess to multiple political and other crimes in a manner similar to those he had overseen in the Great Purge. Sentenced to death and shot. Best remembered for a photograph with Stalin from which Soviet censors removed his presence.

Z

Zagladin, Vadim (1927–2006). Soviet politician. One of the leading theoreticians of perestroika. From 1964–1988, First Deputy Secretary of the International Department of the Central Committee of the Communist Party of the Soviet Union. From 1988–1991, a close advisor to Gorbachev on perestroika and glasnost. Continued his advisory role within the Gorbachev Foundation until his death. Vice-President of the Association for Euro-Atlantic Cooperation (AEAC), which promoted links between Russia and NATO. A personal friend of Francois Mitterrand, Willy Brandt and Giorgio Napolitano, Zagladin was the theorist of a reformed communism that would be very close to European social democracy. He authored many books on international relations.

Zedong, Mao (1893–1976).   Chinese communist revolutionary. Founding father of the People's Republic of China, which he ruled as Chairman of the Communist Party of China from its establishment in 1949 until his death in 1976. His theories, military strategies, and political policies are collectively known as Maoism. Following the foundation of the People's Republic, he solidified his control through land reforms and a psychological victory in the Korean War. In 1957 launched a campaign known as the Great Leap Forward that aimed to rapidly transform China's economy from agrarian to industrial. The campaign led to the deadliest famine in history and the deaths of 20–45 million people between 1958 and 1962. In 1966, Mao initiated the Cultural Revolution, a program to remove so-called "counterrevolutionary" elements in Chinese society, which was marked by a violent class struggle. In 1972, he welcomed American President Nixon in Beijing, signaling the start of a policy of opening China to the world.

Zhirinovsky, Vladimir (1946–). Born Vladimir Eidelstein. Russian politician. Leader of the Liberal Democratic Party (1992–); Leader of the LDP in the Duma (2011–). Ultranationalist populist in ideology, known for his confrontational style and anti-Western rhetoric. Co-founder of the Liberal Democratic Party (1991), which, according to former Politburo member Alexander Yakovlev, was a joint project of the CPSU and the KGB. The LDP plays a nominal role as opposition to Putin's regime.

Zhivago, Yuri (fictional).   Titular character of Boris Pasternak's most famous novel, *Doctor Zhivago.*   This character, a doctor, is portrayed as a poet, idealistic, sensitive and indecisive through the revolutionary changes in Russia from 1905 to World War II.

Zhivkov, Todor (1911–1998).   Bulgarian politician.   Communist leader of Bulgaria (1954–1989). Completely submitted to Soviet directives for Bulgaria, and even requested Bulgaria to be incorporated into the USSR twice (1963, 1973), though it is not clear how sincere those requests were.   In the 1980s, following Soviet policy, Bulgaria became more economically stagnant and the Bulgarian Communist Party's increasing corruption undermined Zhikov's rule. He ultimately resigned in 1989 after out-of-control public riots, leading to multiple deaths. Placed under house arrest in 1990, tried for embezzlement in 1991, and convicted and sentenced to seven years' imprisonment in 1992. Allowed to serve his sentence under house arrest due to age and ill health. Later acquitted (1996), and died of pneumonia in 1998.

Zia-ul-Haq, Muhammad (1924–1988). Pakistani four-star general who served as the 6th President of Pakistan for almost ten years.

The country's longest-serving *de facto* head of state. Educated in Delhi University, Zia saw action in World War II as a British Indian Army officer in Burma and Malaya. Fought as a tank commander in the Indo-Pakistani war of 1965. In 1970 led a military mission to Jordan, instrumental in defeating the Black September insurgency against King Hussein. Assuming the presidency in 1978, Zia played a major role in the Soviet-Afghan War. He was killed in a mysterious plane crash near Bahawalpur in 1988.

Zinoviev, Alexander (1922–2006). Russian logician and writer. Criticized the Soviet political system in the 1970s through his novels *Yawning Heights* (published in Sweden in 1976) and *The Radiant Future* (1978), losing his academic post in the Logic Department at Moscow State University as a result. Emigrated to West Germany (1978), and continued writing books criticizing the Soviet system. Ceased to criticize communism at the start of perestroika, and began defending some aspects of Soviet communism. Returned to Russia in 1999.

Zorkin, Valery (1943–). Russian judge. Chairman of the Constitutional Court of Russia (1991–1993, 2003–). Disputed the legality of Boris Yeltsin's decision to dissolve the Supreme Soviet of Russia (1993). As a result, was forced to resign as Chairman of the Constitutional Court but remained a judge. Briefly forced off the court at the end of 1993, reinstituted in 1994. Elected Chairman again in 2003.

Zubatov, Sergei (1864–1917). Russian official during the Tsarist era. Director of the Moscow security (Okhrana) Bureau between 1896 and 1902, and Director of the Special Section of the Interior Ministry's Department of Police in 1902–1903. Known for his establishment of a system of surveillance to monitor the activities of revolutionary organizations. Between 1901–1903, created legal pro-government trade unions to divert workers from social agitation into organizations that demanded purely economic reforms and operated under the secret surveillance of police. After a series of strikes, the unions were disbanded and Zubatov expelled from office. He committed suicide during the February Revolution in 1917 after hearing the news of the Tsar's abdication.

Acknowledgments

From the Author

I wish to thank the Margaret Thatcher Foundation for valuable assistance in my work and, despite our various differences, Baroness Margaret Thatcher personally for her unwavering support of my efforts to finish writing this book.

I am also grateful to Oleg Gordievsky, Eugene Novikov, Mikhail Voslensky, Victor Suvorov, Leonid Finkelstein, Inna Rogachy and Vladimir Pimonov for valuable help and advice. Heartfelt thanks to many helpers and well-wishers in Moscow (whom I cannot name for their own safety), and numerous friends in the West for their support and assistance.

I am particularly obliged to my old friend and publisher Charles Ronzac, whose unfailing faith in my ability to finish this work supported me through all these difficult years.

—Vladimir Bukovsky

From the Publisher

This book could never have been published without the generous help of many volunteers. Our deepest gratitude goes out to them all.

We cannot overstate the great scholarly work that John Crowfoot has done on this book and on the archival documents. He created a new website for the Bukovsky Archive documents, organized the documents, and translated dozens of them. For this book he restored, as footnotes and in-text notes, the many references in the French edition. He permitted us the use of his own translation and notes for "Only a Trial Will Do", and allowed us to adapt his essay about Yulia Zaks. The scholarly value of the book has been greatly increased due to his efforts. We are grateful for his time, expertise, and patient friendship in helping us bring this edition to the level of accurate sourcing and context that it deserves.

Mary Pat Campbell wrote most of the biographical notes and glossary, organized information, and contributed her software skills to the project.

John Conner led the effort to locate the original English-language text for every English language source quoted in the book. He surprised us by locating every one. He also served as second editor to review the book as a whole.

Gregory Glazov, Maya Topadze Griggs and Carol Patricia Malczynski performed extensive checking of citations and other error checking.

Alexandra Sellers took charge of the cover.

Leon Weinstein gave us his interview with the author, which Lubov Yudovich translated.

Many other tasks were made possible only through the help of these volunteers:

Additional citation research and checking: Sergey Bondarchuk, Philip Boobbyer, Alissa Ordabai.

Biographical note and glossary advisors: Philip Boobbyer, Phillipe de Lara, Alyona Kojevnikov.

Other help with the biographical notes and glossary: Philip Averbuck, John Conner, Michael Del Rosso and Robin Snyder, with special thanks to Vitaly Sherbina.

General advice and support: Philip Boobbyer, Karl Gallagher, Alyona Kojevnikov, L. Jagi Lamplighter, Alexandra Sellers.

Miscellaneous translation: Sergey Bondarchuk, Jeremy Bornstein, Maya Topadze Griggs.

Marketing plan: Mary Pat Campbell, John Conner, Maya Topadze Griggs, Carol Patricia Malczynski.

Additional information organization: Jeremy Bornstein.

Thanks to Alissa Ordabai, for advice about copyright, and for transferring the notes and footnotes into the manuscript.

We are grateful for the many contributions of those who prefer to remain unnamed.

Our awe and gratitude go to the library professionals who located documents that no amount of Googling would ever find: Amber J. D'Ambrosio at Willamette University Archives and Special Collections, Kaitlin Connolly at the State Library of Massachusetts, Julie Grob and Alexandra Simons at the University of Houston Libraries, Caitlin Jones at Massachusetts Archives, and the Fondren Library of Rice University.

Thanks to journalist Claire Berlinski for bringing *Judgment in Moscow* to our attention in the first place.

Finally, special thanks to Alyona Kojevnikov, who tended to this book throughout its preparation as if it were her own.

Yulia Zaks (1937–2014)

The online archive of Central Committee documents surreptitiously photocopied by Vladimir Bukovsky was created and made accessible and usable largely through the work of Yulia Zaks, a Moscow native who, alongside an accomplished professional career, devoted much of her life to assisting dissidents in her homeland, and later from the United States.

Born in Moscow in 1937, Zaks received a doctorate in chemistry and became a senior researcher at the Research Institute of Plastics in that city. In 1968, when Yury Galanskov, Alexander Ginzburg and two co-defendants were put on trial, she was one of those who signed petitions protesting against their prosecution and the closed-door conditions in which the trial was held.

In 1976 she was a witness for the defense at the trial of her stepbrother Andrei Tverdokhlebov, who had participated in setting up a Russian branch of Amnesty International. In 1977 she signed a petition in defense of political prisoners in the USSR. The following year she put her name to the Moscow Helsinki Group's document (No 58) "Ten Years Ago", concerning the events of the Prague Spring. Fined for "sheltering" her brother, she was subjected to searches of her apartment and other forms of harassment.

In 1979 she became one of the administrators of the Solzhenitsyn Fund, providing vital assistance to Soviet political prisoners. This charitable enterprise was seen by communist authorities as a criminal organization. Many of her predecessors had landed in prison. Zaks, harassed by the KGB, was on the edge of arrest when she emigrated with her two sons and parents to the United States in the summer of 1979.

Zaks settled in Indianapolis. There she worked as a polymer research fellow for AT&T Bell Labs (now Lucent). She also continued working with the Solzhenitsyn Fund, organizing and managing a group of Soviet immigrants who sent parcels to political exiles in the USSR.

In 1999 Zaks created the website bukovsky-archives.net, formatting and organizing Bukovsky's 4,500 pages of scanned documents into a researchable archive organized by topic, including English translations of selected documents that others had translated.

She was diagnosed with cancer in 2011, and died on 11 July 2014. Her site, still online, provided the core materials for the current bukovsky-archive.com site to which this book's source references link.

Index

D

II

Z

About the Author

The most widely-known prisoner of conscience in the Soviet Union, whom *The New York Times* called "a hero of almost legendary proportions", Vladimir Bukovsky was expelled from Moscow University at age 19 for publishing criticism of a state youth program. By the time he was 35, he had spent a total of twelve years in Soviet prisons, labor camps and ersatz psychiatric hospitals for a series of protests and leaked documents.

After his expulsion to the West in 1976, he accepted an invitation to continue his interrupted studies at Cambridge University, where he earned a master's degree in biology. His status as a leading irritant to the Soviet government was ensured by the publication in 1978 of his powerful bestselling prison memoir *To Build a Castle*, recently re-released in digital format.

Bukovsky continued for decades to write and speak about the dangerous abuses of state power. Having survived torture himself, he warned post-9/11 America in a *Washington Post* essay that torture also traumatizes its perpetrators: "Our rich experience in Russia has shown that many will become alcoholics or drug addicts, violent criminals or, at the very least, despotic and abusive fathers and mothers."

Even into his seventies and despite failing health, he has continued to be a burr under the saddle of Russian leaders. In 2014 his testimony helped the British inquiry into the murder by radiation poisoning of his friend, Alexander Litvinenko, conclude that President Putin had likely sanctioned the killing.

Bukovsky sees Russian leadership not as a series of changing regimes, but as an unbroken chain of murderous meddling at home and abroad. After the 2018 radiation poisoning of military intelligence defector Sergei Skripal and his daughter in England, he quipped: "If two cruise missiles were to be launched at the Lubyanka, the level of terrorism worldwide would drop by approximately 80 percent."

Vladimir Bukovsky lives in Cambridge, England.

Made in the USA
Middletown, DE
11 November 2019